To

Jack and Helen Graham

RELIGION ON TRIAL

With 800 Material Witnesses

Chester Dolan

RELIGION ON TRIAL

With 800 Material Witnesses

Chester Dolan

Mopah Publications

P.O. Box 8544
Long Beach CA 90808

Published by Mopah Publications

Library of Congress Cataloging-in-Publication Data

Dolan, Chester
    Religion on Trial: "With 800 Material Witnesses" / by Chester Dolan.
    Includes bibliographical references and index.
    1. Religion – Controversial literature. I. Title

Library of Congress Card Number: 99-95668

ISBN: 0-9631042-9-2

Printed in the United States of America

Religion on Trial

Contents

Preface

This book aims at being easy to read. As controversial as it is, the subject matter needs to be approached directly, without complicated or pointless verbiage. It hopes to be congenial to our new sound-bite societies, impatient with circumlocutions or drawn-out discourses. It will appeal to those of us who like to save time, even if sometimes that means only saving time for leisure. We prefer to get our messages in précis packages. Single-page–size essays suit us admirably.

When dealing with controversial issues involving religions, readers commonly dismiss opinions they disagree with by assuring themselves that they were expressed by incompetents. Such dismissal is difficult when the disputed ideas are introduced, as they are in *Religion on Trial*, by some eight hundred different authors, most of them well known for their remarkable achievements and intellectual acumen. Among them are Abraham Lincoln, George Washington, Susan B. Anthony, Albert Einstein, Voltaire, Steve Allen, Nehru, Albert Schweitzer, Mark Twain, Ralph Waldo Emerson, Robert Frost, H.L. Mencken, Elizabeth Cady Stanton, Jean Paul Sartre, Albert Camus, Sigmund Freud, Aldous Huxley, Carl Sagan, and Alfred North Whitehead.

Most religious people acquired their particular brand of piety by happenstance, not by circumstances over which they can be said to have had control. Many believe because their neighbors believe and they for the same reason. Others believe because they were born into, married into, or "fell victim to" religion for one or another of a wide variety of circumstances. If in other facets of their lives they learn to plan and program their activities using logic and reason, it may occur to them to wonder why they have not done the same in regard to religion. Even those who are sure they belong to the one true religion may begin to see that adherents of other religions feel the same. They understand that two opinions flatly opposing one another cannot both be right. They also see that the chances of any given religion having all the right answers is remote. Reason takes over and introduces a new mode of thinking. Proposed new ideas are for the first time subjected to authentic verification. Nothing is taken

for granted or simply   assumed   to be true. Nor are convictions ever
seen   as   immutable.   All   may   be changed if additional evidence
overrides that which   at   the   time prevails. Strident   arguing
is   seen   as   settling nothing. Calmly citing verifiable facts and
furnishing credible reasons is the rational way to change minds.

Having traveled that far along the road to rationalism, many begin
to see flaws in the fundamentals of their religions. They understand
that in every other field of endeavor symbols have clear referents that
anyone can point to. If words such as houses, trees, and cows require
ostensive   referents,   then so too do   souls, angels, and gods.

Science, religions, (all disciplines) claim existence for their
entities only when the claims made for them are verified. We must
admit to living in dream worlds as long as our symbols cannot be
shown to stand for something more than other symbols or for ideas
fashioned out of whole cloth in our minds.

In the creed-bound atmosphere in which we live today, effective
dialectic is suppressed. Very few people dare relate the salient truths
about religion. Such neglect gives religion the stranglehold it has
over malleable, unreflective minds everywhere. The few that do
understand the nature of religion, also see what gives religion the
stranglehold it has over malleable, unreflective minds everywhere.

Religion's premises have gathered to themselves a large variety
of postulates and presumptions   that   need verification.   Doubt
invades every facet of our lives. Analysis of the credibility of our
beliefs must give us firm bases for our convictions. Either that or we
must suspend judgment.

The existence of a supreme deity overseeing this universe must be
fairly examined. That there are angels, devils, jinn, or half-god go-
betweens intervening in our lives must, for the sake of our
equanimity, be demonstrated. That there is an afterlife will be
considered creditable when someone produces evidence that there is.
The heaven and hell that some religions postulate will be taken
seriously only when someone presents good reasons for believing.

When   religious   leaders   become   inured   to   the   pervading
uncertainties of our societies and ignore the prophylaxis of doubt,
these leaders interfere with progress. Progress occurs when in the
evolution of our ethical codes we learn to face problems honestly,
with determination, and with worthy goals. We seek practical
solutions, discriminating carefully between those missions that are
truly impossible and those that are well within the bounds of human

potential.

Whatever ethical instincts man is born with seem to be annulled by the skewed morality that pervades religion. Religion and nationalism (a close cousin) instill in us a hatred and hubris that becomes so deeply imbedded that we cannot look upon the citizens of neighboring countries without revealing our own smug, overweening conceit. When there are glaring economic differences between us and our less fortunate neighbors, a callous disregard for the evident appalling disparity is a shameful response.

Thomas Edison may not have been overstating the case when he said that religion is all bunk. We continue to allow fraudulent, carefully calculated, artfully planned deception to control our lives. Religion will remain a burden to our societies as long as its leaders do not understand that their only legitimate purpose is to teach us to live amicably, usefully, morally, and as happy at all times as circumstances allow.

Many of us are searching for something meaningful in religion. So it is that we seek answers: Please explain what "dying for our sins" means? Why do bad people prosper and good people suffer? Why do messages from God seem designed always to help fill church coffers and excuse the preacher's extravagances. Why does God wait to be asked before He will do good? Why are prayers more often than not – not answered. What makes certain real estate sacred? Why do we fight wars over religious differences? Why is "reason" religion's enemy? What is the merit of confession, celibacy, pageantry, speaking in tongues, icons, a three-part deity, gilded crosses, stained glass, etc. There is much for religion to explain.

Questions about the pronouncements we hear from the pulpit and on radio and television programs demand attention. When we get evasion instead of answers, we have reasons to suspect that deception not elucidation is the principal raison d'etre of religion. We see that much of what religious leaders teach us about gods and morality is contradictory, evasive, self-serving, and amounts to thinly veiled coercion. The exhortation, garrulity, bombast, and drivel that is increasingly replacing calm, reasoned, and meaningful dissertation disturb us. In a world that insists on rational explanations, religions seem less sure of the fantasy and fustian they pass off as fact and perspicacity. The desperation in the harangues of pulpiteers is becoming more and more evident as they lose the battle for credibility.

Sir Arthur Conan Doyle, when writing his book "proving" that fairies exist, was well aware that he would have to produce evidence verifying his remarkable affirmation. "Truth," he knew, if it is to have any significant meaning, must be talking about how reliable any statement said to be true actually is. Truth that is, implies a correspondence between "what we say" and "what we say it about."

George Adamsky, when writing his book *Flying Saucers Are Real*, also knew that the burden of producing evidence was his. The evidence available to him when he completed the book, it seems, was not enough to make him a "true believer." But "evidence" forthcoming since that time has been more than enough.

Ruth Montgomery. When writing *Strangers Among Us*, and Shirley MacLaine, when writing *Out on a Limb* also knew that to prove their theses about "walk-ins" and "reincarnation," respectively, they must give us reason to believe that what they say is "true." How did Doyle, Adamsky, Montgomery, and MacLaine do in convincing us of their remarkable theses?

Whether the fairy tales of religions deal with angels or devils or any of the other denizens of Tara (the angels' residence above), they are solely the product of human brain activity. Until someone can demonstrate that they have an external reality, they must not be considered true. Ultimately, religion's fairy tales are seen as a vast network of deliberately contrived fabrications cleverly designed by religious leaders to give them control over their people. Their congregations become deluded subjects, not enlightened citizens of a democratic society.

The word truth can be very useful if we use it consistently, always to refer to language (and other symbol systems), and always to mean that whenever positive declarations are made about whatever subject, these declarations must be founded upon evidence reliable enough to be accepted with complete confidence. Unfortunately for the sake of sanity in this world, the word truth has no legitimacy when speaking of religion. It cannot apply to *negative* statements about the existence of the cast of characters in religious narration because such statements cannot be proved. How would anyone go about proving that fairies do not exist? Any suppositions that deny the existence of gods, angels, devils, or jinn, that is, can never be said to be true. Such statements cannot even be said to be reliable unless it can be shown that those taking the positive side of the proposition cannot produce authentic evidence for saying what they say. Also the word truth cannot apply to *positive* statements about the existence of celestial entities, for such statements have never in history been shown to have the slightest truth value.

Most of the more than eight hundred thinker-writers from all periods of history whose quotations appear in *Religion on Trial* have chosen to defend the negative side of propositions about religion. Although they cannot prove what they say, neither can the religionists. The essence of wisdom for both is to be skeptical and never to accept propositions as true until there is conclusive evidence showing that they are true.

The 800 essays of *Religion on Trial* make up a comprehensive critique of religion. Just about every question the reader may have in mind about religion is discussed. Books by authors of the boxed quotations constitute a veritable library of additional information for those who desire to know still more.

The reader will notice that the brief essays that comprise this book have not been arrayed according to subject matter. Instead, the intent has been to arrange the essays in a manner to accommodate certain principles of learning efficiency, and to provide gradual, step-by-step reorientation.

Of course, for special research projects, the need will be to examine the book subject-by-subject. The book's detailed index will facilitate that purpose. No index of any book can be said to be complete. Because those using the book for research may find themselves returning repeatedly to items not indexed, extra margin is provided on each index page for notes and to amplify the index to serve specific purposes.

The reader will find in *Religion on Trial* repetitions of certain quoted words beyond what may seem appropriate. Stendhal, Whitehead, and other authors given to pithy epigram are heard from repeatedly. It is the custom of readers of books partitioned as is this one to excerpt and mail passages of particular interest to special friends and acquaintances. For that reason, an effort has been made to write each essay in a manner that it will stand alone, giving it independent and effectual coverage of its particular topic.

Some of the most intriguing and informative of the essays of this book appear in the last pages, among the last hundred or so essays. They are last only because ideas they entertain were judged as somewhat dependent upon ideas that precede them.

Chapter I

Amiable Altercations

1

A brief introduction written first for Holy Daze, which was not widely distributed, may earn its credits here: Even before you begin reading this book can we agree at the outset with a rather magisterial opinion?: There are no good reasons for any human being to make a firm and final decision that he will read only that with which he agrees. To make such a decision, it seems evident, is to commit intellectual suicide.

As long as we read only that with which we agree, we learn nothing. The next time you read a controversial book ask yourself when you finish which parts most stimulated your thinking. Almost certainly your mind will return to points that most infuriated you. Franz Kafka is quoted in a *New York Times* book review as saying: "I think we ought to read only the kind of books that wound and stab us." He too must have been thinking that it is from such books that we learn. We might enjoy other books more, but we read them and forget them.

Since the author of *Religion on Trial* is not reticent about expressing opinions on every conceivable subject, it is a good bet that no reader will agree with everything. It is unfortunate that two people who find themselves at odds often do not recognize what a rare opportunity they have to find-tune their rhetoric. If they can argue amicably, remarkable benefits may accrue.

If you are the kind of person who is not afraid of ideas, even those with which you disagree, you may see in the fulminations of these essays an acceptable challenge. Like any thinking person, you have many firm convictions, some of which have served you well as defense against the agglomeration of nonsense that is thrown at you from all quarters. Your attitude is: "Dear author, you say you are going to change me. Good! It will be interesting to see you try! Even if you make me angry, you may at the same time make me think. Let's have your polemic, and we will see how we come out."

2

It is useless to attempt to reason a man out of what he was never reasoned into.

Jonathan Swift (1667-1746)

"Almost useless," is better. If useless, those of us still with hopes of instilling good sense into societies would be sad indeed. What man has done can be undone – even if it means unraveling point by point every absurdity that has ever been infused into his unsuspecting brain.

For a fanatical religionist to renounce his religion, something like the following would have to occur, which is known to happen, rare though it may be: First he begins to suspect that adherence to dogmatic principles is not the only way to attain the needs, such as self-extension and security that he instinctively feels. Second, he seems to be noticing that some of his needs are being satisfied without the intervention of his church or his religion. Third, some of the delusions he has been living with in regard to his church are disclosed in discrepancies between actions of the church and events taking place in his community and in the world at large. Fourth he sees his church changing in ways he does not approve of – even though the change may be really only in himself, an intellectual growth that permits discernment where he was previously blind. He becomes disillusioned with the church, takes a sabbatical from his religiosity, which then is extended to include the rest of a long and productive life.

3

It is so much easier to assume than to prove; it is so much less painful to believe than to doubt; there is such a charm in the repose of prejudice, when no discordant voice jars the harmony of belief.

W.E.H. Lecky (1838-1903)

Dolce far niente: It is pleasant to do nothing, the Italians say. Most of us have a streak of laziness in our being. Particularly, Intellectual laziness afflicts us all. Confronted with a problem that we see is going to require deep concentration, we are likely to set it aside for awhile – perhaps never to get back to it.

Assuming rather than proving, believing rather than doubting, prejudging rather than analyzing to get a true perspective, are common. Most of us choose to let others do our thinking for us, knowing how painful thinking can be. This might be a perfectly sane way of behaving if we could trust those who are glad to relieve us of the duty to think.

It is sad to report that we cannot always trust those who become our mentors. Too often they take advantage of our trust and contrive ways to manipulate us into catering to their own insatiable drive for power. For them, not money, not love, nothing gives them the satisfaction that does controlling large numbers of their fellow human beings.

4

So many gods, so many creeds, / So many paths that wind and wind,/
While just the art of being kind / Is all the sad world needs.

Ella Wheeler Wilcox (1850-1919)

Those four lines were so popular that in the years that followed, another person claimed to have written them. It is, however pretty well agreed today that Ella is the author of this *abba rima*. She has more than twenty volumes of verse to her credit.

Near the end of the same century that Ella helped begin, a leader of one of the two great superpowers dared to use "kindness" as an expressed principle of national policy. The leader of the other superpower showed not only in words but also in deeds that he was willing to reverse in small but very encouraging measures the unkindness that in his country had long been the rule, especially in national policies.

Any idea that power can achieve peace and harmony for any community is manifest absurdity. Only kindness can do that. Not until a deep-rooted kindness prevails in the corridors of government and in daily exchanges among peoples everywhere, can we attain unity, discipline, and mutual respect in our societies. The era of Stalin is over, and the era of distrust here at home may be over too. When we see a small glimmer of light in the long pervading darkness, we may be excused for a resurging optimism that may or may not be warranted.

5

> Religion does not necessarily make better citizens, whether of their neighborhoods or of the world; on the contrary, it tends to engender a smugness which is essentially antisocial.
>
> H.L. Mencken (1880-1956)
> *Treatise on the Gods*

Religion augments and perpetuates factionalism. Making better citizens is the exact opposite of what occurs. Whenever populations are broken up into more and more labeled groups, it is certain that hatred, bigotry, and snobbery will increase. The prime purpose of such groups is to separate "us" from "those others."

Religions are all saying: "We have thought through to the very core the community's problems. We deserve to make the decisions as we are the successful people, the elite, the winners."

Even in their charities, religions demonstrate hubris. "See how we have reached such a degree of success that we are able to help others." The strings attached to their giving often reveals the basic insincerity of their generosity: "We will help put you back on your feet, and in exchange we expect you to become one of us, to help in fund raising, proselytizing, and political wrangling."

It is fair to say that no matter how much religion a person professes, he is not religious in any real sense when he is blind to the needs of the hungry and deprived. But he is a saint regardless of religious affiliation who selflessly gives his mind, his heart, his hands in service to his fellowman.

6

It is folly for a man to pray to the gods for that which he has the power to obtain for himself.

Epicurus (341-270 BC)

Meditation, which in essence all any sensible prayer is about, is useful, and I would venture to guess that many of the useful ideas and inventions of history were conceived during periods of meditations. It is often what one is planning to do for himself that he is meditating about. During meditations, a person can consolidate his plans, and picture solutions to sticky problems that physical activity may have been preventing him from seeing. Kekulé tells us that he saw the solutions of the benzene ring in a dream. I have found that if I have constructions to do, I almost always find the best way to proceed is to meditate about them before I pick up hammer or saw.

When those mediating believe a deity is listening and will grant the favors asked for, they are likely to be disappointed. The needed advice is usually not forthcoming and even with repeated supplications never does come. There is little doubt that if a credible scientific investigation of prayers could be made, answers to them would be seen as no more frequent than if attended to by a rededicated individual doing his own search for the needed advice, knowledge, or information. Most prayerful supplications would be like my meditations about household problems. The person praying answers his own prayers, and gains respect for and confidence in himself by so doing.

7

Nothing is so unbelievable that oratory cannot make it acceptable.

Cicero (106-43 BC)

(Paradoxa Stoicorum)

Hitler knew that well, as do almost all tyrants who reach positions of power. By convincing their subjects that the rigid discipline and self-sacrificing loyalty called for is for their own good, for a time at least, tyrants keep things running smoothly.

Now in the year 2000, preachers continue to see in Cicero's observation an essential guiding principle for their Sunday morning sermons. Oratory, honed to perfection, continues to beguile unsuspecting audiences into accepting fictitious supernatural entities as well as their celestial abodes.

Seminary instructors begin the procedure when they reshape callow students into ordained ministers. Those new ministers with skills in oratory well developed are able to revamp the deceptions taught them in the seminary to suit their own congregations. Unless somewhere along the line sanity intervenes, the whole megalomaniac delirium will continue ad infinitum.

Ordination, mostly, is a license to lie. The processing that goes on during their years in the seminary, conditions our promising young citizens automatically to confuse myth with reality, to describe events flatly and unquestioningly in contradiction to the way they really are. They learn to accept imposture as a perfectly natural way for a person to practice his profession.

For such a system of fraud to continue aeon after aeon, a continuous supply of credulous recruits is necessary. If high-school and university education in the United States were it make a point of teaching young people the nature of the myth and legend upon which most religions are based, the entire masquerade would collapse and sanity would return. Effective oratory, designed to appeal both to the intellect and to the emotions, would separate statesmen from tyrants as well as from the ordinary run of politicians. We would have a very different world.

8

The mind resorts to reason for want of training.

Henry Adams (1838-1911)
The Education of Henry Adams

If Adams means, "want of training in conformity," I can agree with him. Picture a human nervous system developing in an environment without fairytales to distort it, no Santa Claus imposed upon it, and no talk of mythological celestial beings interpolated among the stimuli bombarding its receptors.

That nervous system would be unique. It could be said to have had no training for living in a world filled with fables, fantasies, prejudices, and superstitions. There would be nothing to obstruct its functioning in accordance with what reason decides is right, wise, or sensible. Such a mind would have the power to make inferences from whatever reliabe information it may have and to draw from such inferences conclusions that enable it to understand the world and to relate such knowledge to the attainment of useful consequences. It would not operate as do most minds today, restricting themselves only to responses on the level of the lower animals. It would quite naturally resort to reason. It could no longer find excuses for not making full use of its powers of judgment and conception.

If the reader has felt that there is some common characteristic in the minds of the authors of most of the quotations introducing the brief essays of this book – that is it! They reason. They have the ability to form sound judgments and reach valid conclusions. They have the power to comprehend, to infer, and to plan in an orderly, rational way.

Reason is contrasted with another indispensable faculty of mind, imagination, which allows us to form mental images of that which is not actually present and move these images around in different combinations in our minds as we like. Reason ultimately takes over and makes sense of these images, if sense there is to be made.

9

Our own theological church, as we know, has scorned and vilified the body till it has seemed almost a reproach and a shame to have one, yet at the same time has credited it with the power to drag the soul to perdition.

Eliza Farnham (1815-1864)
Woman and Her Era

It must be difficult for religionists to reconcile their contention that God made us in His own image (Genesis 1:26), and the tendency today in all "civilized" religions to revile the human body. We can watch bullets, swords, knives, even chain saws and torture chambers tearing human bodies into shreds, but we must not look upon God's handiwork. "Mother's milk is best," one wag declared. "You have only to look at the container." But looking at the container is one thing, according to our twisted taboos, we must not do. We are encouraged to witness man's inhumanity to man on the small and large screens in all of its gory detail, but we must not see two human beings making love to each other. We abandon good sense in fabricating our taboos, and then go on to defend them frenetically against any hint of ridicule.

Shame must be the most grotesquely distracting of man's emotions. Self-styled arbiters of decency and propriety seem to delight in heaping it upon others. Sometimes the others seem to enjoy heaping it upon themselves. The cases of uglified shame are legion, and shame becomes subplots in many books and movies. Yet no one seems ever to have dealt adequately with shame as a guide or goad, often a burden, in our societies. What a shame!

10

She was trying to get rid of a religious hangover.

Simone de Beauvoir (1908-1986)

All Men Are Mortal

That is the worst kind! No thought of sleeping it off – or "hair" of the dog that bit you. It may take an entire lifetime of unraveling, point by point, to get rid of a religious hangover.

Many religionists prefer not to try. They prefer to give in to the addiction. It was mostly addicts of this kind who called in on Sunday nights to a KABC program called "Religion on the Line."

A priest, a minister, and a rabbi, discreetly selected by their respective clerical boards for the program, became skillful apologists for their unsustainable doctrines of faith, trying desperately to defend the indefensible, to support the inscrutable sacraments and arbitrarily imposed dogma of Catholicism and Protestantism, as well as the no less incomprehensible rules and rites of Judaism. Those in the audience expecting something more than rehashed inanities felt betrayed.

Rather than put religion on the line, the total effect was to perpetuate, not to eliminate the holy hogwash and pietistic tripe that has accumulated within religion through aeons of time. The program, instead of a challenge was nothing more than a platform to expound Biblical texts and personal and pontifical theses that are suitably inoffensive and devoid of any concrete sense or meaning. Justifications for the existence of religion or discussions of how to avoid religious wars and the universal hatred that religion engenders were avoided. Any semblance of challenge was the last thing to expect from the weekly programs.

11

A heretic is one with a penetrating and a courageous heart, unwilling to accept a ready-made creed that seems unreasonable, unrighteous, or inconsistent with his conception of divinity and the good life for man.

Robert O. Ballou – *The Nature of Religion*

Ballou is using the word heretic according to its primary acceptation in the Greek, where the word originated. It is still used that way today when not under control of self-appointed authoritarians protecting the orthodoxies from those who refuse to accept their "one-and-only truth." For these authoritarians, the word "heretic" means "enemy."

Were it not for heresy, the entire world today might be under the control of one universal religion whose leaders may long ago have decided to eliminate all who did not subscribe to that "God-ordained" religion. Certainly, all of the 350 sects of Christianity were founded by heretics. Joseph Smith, Mary Baker Eddy, Martin Luther, John Wesley, George Fox, and Charles T. Russell were some of them. Heresy in any religion is an indication that it lives. In dead religions, there are no more heresies. Frederick Neff said: "To deprive history of its heretics and radicals would be to deprive it of that rare quality known as independence of mind."

The heretic may be the conservative insisting on returning to the ancient religion of the founders, repudiating all the changes that comprise that religion today. The heretic may be the die-hard monotheist who refuses to accept half-gods such as saints, or virgins, all of which then get equal billing with God. The heretic may be one who denies icons, shrines - all of the "sacred" trinkets and talismans of religion. The heretic may insist on a pure, religion without the pageantry, rituals, rites, and sacraments that he finds has polluted his precious system of beliefs. The heretic may also be one who, after leaving his church, finds none to replace it. Finally, he leaves his religion as well. Ballou, in his book, names many other heretics: Arius, Pelagius, Abelard, Origen, Waldus, Ekhart, Wycliffe, Hus, Servetus, Joan of Arc, Savonarola, and Gandhi. Some were excommunicated, some executed, but all have an influence on religion far greater than those who condemned them as heretics.

If people generally began to listen to the voices of the best of our heretics, the flimsy structure of the orthodoxies would tumble like a tower of playing cards in a storm. Accompanying this collapse would be the shedding of guilt complexes with which many people are burdened. Also, it would mean the disintegration of the meaningless taboos that keep people skipping from specious decorum to spurious propriety in hope of avoiding condemnation by the hypocritical society in which they live.

12

Believe nothing, O monks, merely because you have been told it... but whatsoever, after due examination and analysis, you find to be conducive to the good, the benefit, the welfare of all beings – that doctrine believe and cling to, and take it as your guide.

Guatama Buddha (563-483 BC)

Henry Thoreau, more than two millennia later, expressed the same idea in terms of "proof": "No way of thinking, however ancient, can be trusted without proof." Anatol Rapoport, after another century had passed, found Buddha's "due examination and analysis" and Thoreau's "proof" vague. He chose to describe the procedure involved in establishing grounds for belief in terms of the predictive content of questioned propositions.

Rapoport's "criterion of predictability," set forth in his book *Operational Philosophy*, describes the only kind of proof man has ever devised that does not involve him in an infinite regress. The procedure is simple to describe and applies equally whether it is a scientist in his laboratory or you and I trying to determine the authenticity of anyone's proclamations.

We begin by making predictions of what would be the consequences if our statement were shown to be true. Then we use every possible means to try to verify the predicted consequences. The scientist in his laboratory can do better than we can in most instances, but you and I often have the means to examine and to analyze (as the Buddha suggests) to see if that which is predicted does in fact occur. If it does not, and expert help is not available to us, of course we must for the time being give up. It is better not to believe than to believe without evidence.

But suppose we are able to verify what we predict. Now can we believe?: No, just one verified prediction is usually not enough. We must verify other predictions until reasonable doubt come so close to vanishing that we decide we can live with the little doubt that remains.

The number of significant predictions that turn out as we say they will is a measure of the validity of our proof. But never is truth absolute. Always additional predictions can be made and verified, giving the statement even more truth-value. "That doctrine," as the Buddha says, "we can believe and cling to and take as our guide."

We must keep in mind, however, that the criterion of predictability can be misused. Among us are many people, even organizations of people, trying to convince us that completely unfounded assertions are worthy of belief. The members of one such organization, by way of example, tell us that *Flying Saucers Are Real*, and then they compose expedient anecdotes to convince us that what they say is true. Predictions they make deal with photographs of flying saucers, pieces of crash-landed flying saucers, extra-terrestrials explaining how they managed to travel the long distances from their home, even crew members of flying saucers giving guest rides in their spacecraft.

Members of "Understanding Incorporated" insist that all of these predictions have been verified, but they give us no real evidence. It turns out that no one has ever convincingly shown that flying saucers do in fact exist.

13

The church attacked the habit of the bath on the ground that everything which makes the body more attractive tends toward sin. Dirt was praised, and the odor of sanctity became more and more penetrating.... Lice were called the pearls of God, and to be covered with them was an indispensable mark of a holy man.

Bertrand Russell (1872-1970)
Marriage and Morals

How did the church at that time reconcile the ugliness they prefer in human beings with the beauty that has always been preferred in other aspects of nature. We love a sky spotted with billowy clouds. They arouse in us emotions of serenity and comfort. We love all species of deer. They are so beautifully proportioned and so lithe. We love crystals and even pay high prices for them. Should we then admire all the more our holy men if they stink, are covered with lice, and look as if they had just come out of a hog wallow?

Religion can be whatever we want it to be. Then why has it always been full of black-and-white, polarized inconsistencies? It accepts virgin birth, is against test-tube babies. A son shall not be made to suffer for his father's sins (Ezekiel 18:20); I will punish children and grandchildren to the third and fourth generations for the sins of their fathers (Exodus 34:7). God is not a man who changes His mind (1 Samuel 15:29); The Lord had compassion and changed his mind (Amos 7:3). A man shall not marry his brother's wife (Leviticus 20:21); Her husband's brother shall take her as his wife (Deuteronomy 25:5) The Bible is full of examples.

14

I had never been as resigned to ready-made ideas as I was to ready-made clothes, perhaps, although I couldn't sew, I could think.

Jane Rule – *Lesbian Images* (Introduction)

Thinking is a pretty handy activity. More people ought to try it. As an antidote to blind acceptance of other people's ideas, it has no substitute. As a formula to give zest to life, there is nothing like it. As a device for helping us learn to live meaningfully it has no equal. If all people would learn to think, thereby rejecting all the nonsense rampant in the world, we could live in an ambience free of the slavery other people are trying to foist upon us. Superstitions, prejudice, baseless gossip, zealotry, bigotry, jingoism, falsehood, hate, xenophobia, and cupidity, would die aborning. Even jealousy and envy could not withstand close analysis, genuine thinking.

We must learn to use our brains for something more than its marvelous capacity as a sponge, as a device for nourishing reflex actions, as a storage for facts, or as a recall mechanism for stereotyped responses. To make conscious mental efforts to formulate plans, to frame purposes, to design projects, to conceive programs, to sort out the significant from the trivial, to weigh and evaluate alternatives, to consider problems from all angles, to scrutinize the obscure, to ponder relationships, and to make order out of chaos would be for all a revolution. On the seventh day, we could rest in our new utopia.

15

> He who does not bellow the truth when he knows the truth makes himself the accomplice of liars and forgers.
>
> Charles Péguy (1873-1914)

Society disintegrates when lying becomes normally acceptable behavior. Once no one can depend upon anyone else to say what he really knows, believes, or thinks about any subject or situation, progress stops. Truth is a cohesive factor in all human relations. Whenever one fails to tell the truth when it needs to be told, the result is the same: chaos and alienation.

Truth is a measure of the relation between what we say and what we say it about. When father tells his daughter Marie: "Mother is visiting with Aunt Claire," and the child later finds that mother is very sick and in the hospital, communication between father and daughter is never again quite the same. Marie sees the father as contributing to an atmosphere of deceit.

We must learn to recognize the deceit that threatens to overwhelm us. When nothing the salesman says about the product he is trying to sell us makes sense, we must reject what he says. When nothing the preacher says has any meaningful relation to the world in which we live, we must reject what he says. So that others may avoid the treachery of both salesman and preacher, we warn others of their duplicity.

16

> In heaven all the interesting people are missing.
>
> Nietzsche (1844-1900)

Elbert Hubbard doesn't inspire Nietzsche to hope for more. In *The Note Book,* Hubbard says: "Christianity supplies a Hell for the people who disagree with [Christians] and a Heaven for [their] friends." "Enemies of Christians" and "interesting people" to Nietzsche are one and the same. Both Hubbard and Nietzsche are phantasizing, or course. Neither knows any more about heaven than do Beulah's beagels. On that score, all people are equal. Even the Judeo-Christian scriptures have little to say about what to expect in Heaven.

If heaven and hell really exist, it should not be impossible to find them. Astronomers can see galaxies up to fifteen billion light years away, and particle physicists can detect neutrinos smaller than the mind can imagine. But neither can find a trace of heaven. Geologists can examine earth composition miles deep, and ocean bottoms in the deepest trenches, but find no signs of hell. Why we pretend these abodes are anything more than fanciful fabrications is worthy of investigation.

TV evangelist Robert Schuller suggests that heaven may be in galaxy M-31, the galaxy we see when we look through Andromeda. It is a mere two-and-a-half million light years away, some 80 billion years away traveling at the speed of Pioneer. Even traveling at the speed of light, souls might get a little bored before they finish the journey.

17

The civilized man has a moral obligation to be skeptical, to demand the credentials of all statements that claim to be facts.

Bergen Evans
The Natural History of Nonsense

The man who by nature or rational education is skeptical and demands evidence to substantiate alleged facts is by virtue of such behavior demonstrably civilized and exhibits an important ingredient of morality. Certainly no one who lives totally oriented by myth and mumbo jumbo can consider himself a contributing member of a truly civilized society. If he is moral, he is moral as a result of his indifference. He does no harm to others because he does little else but vegetate. Only when he strives to instill in others his own farcical fantasies does he become publicly and significantly immoral.

The important thing is that we do not accept pretentious pronouncements that offer no scintilla of certification. The human species cannot live in an ocean of lies. Before it is too late, we must extricate ourselves from the sham that is disrupting our lives. We must exorcise our illusory gods and demons and begin to live in a world of reality. If we do not, we may find ourselves having forfeited the intellectual power and maturity required for developing a world in which we can survive – and perhaps even live in pleasantly and peacefully.

18

An agnostic is one who withholds belief because he does not know and is unwilling to accept as proof the evidence of revelation and spiritual experience.

Definition – a *Merriam-Webster* dictionary

But that is precisely the definition of an atheist! Perfectly aware of the impossibility of proving a negative, the atheist knows he can go no further. It follows that both the definition and idea of agnosticism is superfluous. The term atheism covers the concept.

We cannot "know" anything about anything, except the fact of our own existence. Of course, if we are to live sanely, we must go through life as if we *do* know. We must behave as if we do know that fairies, flying saucers, gods, ghosts, mermaids, devils, abominable snowmen, sprites, trolls, werewolves, elves, angels, incubi, unicorns, souls, chimeras, or haploid (parthenogenic) human beings *do not* exist – and almost certainly never have existed in any part of the universe with which we have had immediate contact.

Agnosticism may be useful as a euphemism, but is not by any means a description of how individuals do in fact behave. We at times speak of ghosts and phantoms, souls and saints, angels and demons, and it becomes difficult not to assume that such entities are in fact traipsing around within our skins, houses, skies, and cosmos. But we can never in actual fact believe in them. We must keep ourselves attuned to a practical world of objective ideas and tangible things, the macroscopic world manufactured by our own nervous systems.

19

There may be other ways of detecting error and discovering truth than that of free discussion, but so far we have not found them.

Henry Commager (1902-   )

Commager may have put his finger on the reason why religion has always been a taboo topic for everyday conversation: Religionists know that free discussion would mean the death of religion. Sooner or later the participants would understand that religion is nothing more than a conglomeration of legend, poetic fancy, mysticism, and carefully contrived lies - nothing more than a vast and deliberately planned complex of dissimulation imposed on mankind to keep us in line.

Duplicity, double-dealing, guile, chicanery, imposture, mendacity, and bad faith become so much the rule for theologians that they can weave all their fraud and falsifications into their sermons without a murmur of conscience. Devious, evasive, furtive phrasing becomes second nature to them. It does not matter to them that they have no scintilla of evidence for what they say. Theologians wax lyrical about the leviathan, dramatic about demons, rhapsodic about resurrections, devout about deities, impassioned about immortality, infatuated with iniquity, delirious about divinity, maudlin about misery, fanatic about faith, without ever touching on truth. If we become infatuated with our preacher, it is often because of his declamatory style or the musical tone of his voice, not because there is anything sensible in what he says.

20

The belief that we someday shall be able to prevent war is one with the belief in the possibility of making humanity really human.

Ellen Key (1849-1926)

War, Peace, and the Future (Preface)

In Chapter one, Key tells us that "The natural forces which are the causes of war are human passions which lie in our power to change." In Chapter six, she tells us that war "forces men collectively to commit acts against which as individuals they would recoil against with their whole being." "We do not have to be savages," she says in Chapter one.

That strikes me as a pretty good regimen: All of us can learn to act human, then be human, making humanity human. Can anyone think of a better one? When enough people believe as Ellen Key does, we will "make humanity really human."

Unless it is in putting undue trust in the meaning of "humanness," we seem here to be on the right track. No one has said anything in favor of yielding to mythologies, of entertaining hope for an afterlife, or asking for divine guidance. We are on our own, and we will progress when we decide to progress, with everyone working together. There are no magic solutions, and although utopia will remain an ideal, a chimera, it still serves well as a goal. With unattainable goals, we need never stop striving. It would be disastrous for us ever to think that "now we are there" and can relax and make no more plans for making this a still better world than the one we have.

21

> No priesthood can longer make man content with misery here in the hope of compensation in the hereafter.
>
> G. Stanley Hall (1846-1924)
> *Senescence*

Parents try this trick with their children. It seldom works there and probably does no better in religion. Just as the threat of delayed punishment often does little to discourage wrongdoing; the promise of future rewards does not guarantee submissive behavior or acceptance of an out-of-this-world hierarchy of worship-worthy figments. Parishioners are no longer as credulous as they may once have been.

"A congregation convinced against its will is of the same opinion still," to widen the purview of a well-known aphorism. To be convinced against one's better judgment and against every law of logic also may not accomplish what pulpiteers imagine themselves to be achieving. A preacher preaching his heart out to an affirmatively nodding congregation just might find that heart broken if he learns how little of what he expresses in his impassioned eloquence is accepted by that congregation. In sober moments beyond the mesmerizing spell of his bible-thumping entreaties, they rethink.

Beginning to analyze more closely what they really believe about the things their preacher has been saying to them for years, they may find that they not only reject most of what he says, but they have never really accepted the stated doctrines of their church, nor do they wholeheartedly embrace the fanciful sacraments they have been asked to accept.

If the priesthood is to salvage anything from the patchwork persuasions that pass for religion, they must learn to concentrate their efforts on improving the lives of their parishioners, eliminating histrionic diatribes about heaven, hell, and their dubious denizens.

22

> Great Yahweh fingered through the Bible / Thought on it, and filed suit for libel.
>
> X. J. Kennedy

If you or I were to read a book that made of us the shabby character that the Bible makes of God, we, too, would sue for libel. Alfred North Whitehead in *Adventures of Ideas concurs:* "As for Christian theology, can you imagine anything more appallingly idiotic than the Christian idea of heaven? What kind of deity is it that would be capable of creating angels and men to sing his praises day and night through all eternity? It is, of course, the figure of an Oriental despot with his inane and barbaric vanity. Such a conception is an insult to God."

The thing that makes it all so disturbing is that the church leaders who call the Bible "God's Word," read those same words and somehow in their perverted minds find a God worthy of worship. Pulpiteers do not help things a bit. Their call for "fear of God" must make God want to up the premium in His libel suit to the maximum.

The Bible makes of God the worst murderer in history, killing babies, destroying entire towns, sending plagues, floods, famines, and storms. If God is both omnipotent and omniscient as He is made out to be, then He is guilty of every murder that has ever taken place. Prescient and Omniscient, he knows about all the atrocities of history even before they happen. Omnipotent, he could have prevented them, but chose not to.

If the Bible's stories about God's atrocities are pure fiction, we should expect to see God's libel suit in the courts at any time now. On the other hand, if the Bible'' stories are true, we should have the right to sue God for damages for all the injuries and deaths caused by (His) "natural" disasters such as plagues, earthquakes, hurricanes, droughts, floods, and fires. Since religions claim to do God's bidding on Earth, they should be responsible for God's actions and the actions of their leaders. A disaster fund should be established, with all religions in The United States required to contribute enough to pay for all such disasters.

23

> Man is nothing else but what he purposes, he exists only insofar as he realizes himself, he is therefore nothing else but the sum of his actions, nothing but what his life is.
>
> Jean-Paul Sartre (1905-1980)

This, Sartre's definition of existentialism, is not as simple as it may at first seem. We must keep in mind that what we "purpose" points to the future and had its genesis in the past. "Realizing oneself" presumes that there are visions, ours and those that others have for us. Everything melds into an all-embracing and overriding present, squeezed between the before-now and the after-now until it seems not to exist, but nevertheless is the only substance, the true reality of our existence.

All the worlds a man fashions, including mythology (with its gods and demons) exist only within himself - as described in essay 503. With his intentions, purposes, goals, and actions, man is in charge, and as Sartre says, "responsible all the way. Man is responsible not only for himself, but for all men."

The existentialism of Sartre and Camus is not a depressing discipline. Both were happy men, confident not only of themselves, but also that the world will progress, especially if the world's citizens become wise in the ways they should be wise. Reading the books that Sartre and Camus leave to us is a pleasant experience, instilling freedom and mitigating anxieties. Their books are very practical guides for living. Unfortunately, Camus' life was interrupted by an existential mishap. It is my opinion that by that car accident in Algeria, the world was incalculably and grievously bereaved.

24

> Some keep the Sabbath going to Church. / I keep it staying at home / With a bob'link for a Chorister / And an Orchard for a Dome.
>
> Emily Dickinson (1830-1866)

More and more people are finding reasons for not going to church, some because they find that God is not there, others finding that God is not there or anywhere else.

Adlai Stevenson said in *American Chronicle* (1957): "Some of us worship in churches, some in synagogues, some on the golf course." There is a question about in which of the three milieus would we find the name "God" invoked most frequently.

My friend Raphael as well as Lenny Bruce (essay 67) seemed to think that in the church was the last place to find God. Jesus certainly would not find God in any modern church – possibly not even in a synagogue. He founded no church, and except for his belief in hell and demons, did not believe in creeds and dogmas, nor had anything to do with sects or denominations. He would find the racism, hatred of homosexuals, discrimination against women, advocacy of violence, biased nationalism, war mongering, and the tremendous wealth found in many churches very distasteful.

25

Fear of God is not the beginning of wisdom. The fear of God is the death of wisdom.

Clarence Darrow (1857-1930)

Fear is a debilitating and a regimenting emotion. If those fabricating a religion want its members to be strong and free, surely the last thing they will want to do is instill in them fear.

To say that fear of God is the beginning of wisdom is to speak arrant absurdity. A young person conditioned for years by fear, whatever may be the cause of that fear, will never be able to operate as a loving, wise, sympathetic, and caring human being. Fear of God is not the ordinary kind of fear (the fear of insult, injury, or death), but the awful, abject, disabling kind of fear of something unseen, unknown, threatening in ways beyond imagination.

When fear reaches the proportions of excessive, irrational suspiciousness and mistrustfulness of everyone, all is lost. Systematized delusions of persecution (overmastering, unreasoning, and perpetual) take over. The victim of such fear becomes useless and unreliable, a danger even to himself.

Fear of hell is a hell of a burden to put on mankind. It was invented by sadists and is perpetuated by psychopaths. From those who believe in God and believe that there is purpose in what he does, we need an answer: What possible purpose does burning in brimstone forever serve? Hell brandished before children during their formative years is almost sure to instill neuroses difficult to eradicate. The stifling straitjacket of rules imposed upon many children, and the guilt for not adhering to them, help form distorted mentalities. Only a few very fortunate children will ever learn to operate adequately in today's societies.

26

Doesn't all petitionary prayer treat God as a kind of divine vending machine? What does the simple act of begging for this or that, presuppose about our understanding of God, the world of nature and ourselves?

Kenneth L. Woodward
"Is God Listening"
Newsweek, March 31, 1997

The two sentences in the quotation above ask important questions. Woodward understands, as he goes on to say, that "There is... no way to prove empirically that an event, even if it cannot be explained, is an act of God." It is well, if we are to accept any religion, to admit that we do so not because there are rational reasons for doing so, but simply because we "want" to do so. "Why we do" may never be explained, even to ourselves.

In the *Newsweek* article, Woodward speaks of answered and unanswered prayers. But it easy to argue that all prayers are answered. Even "no" or silence is an answer. It is even easier to argue that no prayers are answered. Just as it is true that one event following another does not always mean that the first causes the second, so it is true that because one gets what one asks for does not mean that one gets it because one asks for it. Statistical coincidence is enough to account for many so-called answered prayers. If Woodward is right in saying that 80% of America prays regularly, that means a lot of people are asking God for things. Those who get what they ask for are more likely to advertise that "fact." Many millions of unanswered prayers every day are never brought to anyone's attention.

In Zoroaster's sacred writings (Avesta) we read: "He who sows the ground with care and diligence, acquires a greater stock of religious merit, than he could gain by the repetition of ten thousand prayers."

27

> May a renewed belief in ourselves and others, firmly bonded in love, expand to envelop the entire universe!
>
> Phyllis Diller
>
> *My Prayer*

Now *there* is a prayer for all time! If there is a God to answer prayers, please dear God, pick that one. You may well reject the myriad of prayers sent Your way that are selfish petitions designed only for personal gain. For Your own reasons, whatever they are, You may even reject prayers seeking alleviation for sick friends. But please, dear God pick Phyllis Diller's magnanimous prayer. By so doing, You might just save the lot of Your sixth-day creations that populate this globe. Now wouldn't that be a project worthy of Your Divine Highness? Just one quick wave of your omnipotent wand and You could rest on Your laurels forever. From then on, pay us no more heed if You choose. Just imbue us with a sustaining love that nothing or no one can ever annul.

Prayer, if it is to be of any use to us, must not exacerbate the violent emotions that evolution seems to have left seething just below the surface of our genetic inclinations. It must seek to assuage those emotions. Prayer must not favor intellectual capitulation with every addlepated opinion expressed by self-styled gurus. It must prompt us to evaluate carefully all opinions. Prayer must not foment hatred by suggesting that we isolate ourselves from those others whom we consider hopelessly in error. It must inspire love by emphasizing the brotherhood of all mankind. That is precisely what Phillis Diller asks of God in the prayer from which the above is an excerpt.

28

> Government and religion can be friends, neighbors, but they must not share the same house and never, never should they get married.
>
> Robert L. Maddox
>
> *Separation of Church and State*

The first amendment to the Constitution is no less adamant: "Congress shall make no law respecting an establishment of religions, or prohibiting the free exercise thereof." Anne Nicol Gaylor said in *Free Inquiry*: "To be free from religion is an advantage for individuals; it is a necessity for government." As Jefferson and all signers of the Constitution believed: The first amendment meant building a wall of separation between Church and State. Nothing is left for doubt. Clearly outlawed is public funding of religious schools, decorating the halls and walls of government buildings with religious symbols.

If they can contrive borderline cases that seem to have merit, various religious groups will try to insinuate them into public school systems. Some of their schemes have surfaced: broadcasting student prayers on the public address system, using school property as after-school religious retreats, wearing yarmulkes, chadors, crosses, ashes on the forehead, etc. The courts will be settling cases for years to come.

Politicians in India and Pakistan called their recent nuclear acquisitions the "Hindu bomb" and the "Islamic bomb." respectively. The mass-pride reaction in these two adversaries is revealing. It never occurred to the first countries similarly armed to call their artifacts the Protestant, Catholic, Jewish, Anglican, Or Eastern-Orthodox bombs.

The line between Church and State in most countries is becoming more and more obscure. The fatwas of Islam, the Hindu bans on American TV programs and CD music covers, and the "conversion manuals" of various sects of Christianity are designed to increase their influence even beyond their borders. Despite professed tolerance, each of the major religions would prefer that all the others disappear from the face of the earth.

Devotion to deity and devotion to country are melding into a kind of sacred succotash that is awesome. If ever a dominant, monopolistic, worldwide religion becomes established as the ruling power, the search will no longer be for truth. The search will be only for ways to establish this religion as the guiding principle of all institutions. Citizens will become subjects, and politicians and even the military will tremble before religion's awesome power. The world theocracy that some religious leaders aspire to impose on the third rock from the sun would mean the end of anything resembling a sanely operating society.

29

> The Jews are a frightened people. Nineteen centuries of Christian love has broken down their nerves.
>
> Israel Zangwill (1864-1926)

The English language is full of phrases that reveal Christian attitudes toward Jews. Alexander Pope may have said it best: "Damn with faint praise, assent with civil leer. / And without sneering teach the rest to sneer."

Christians are quite capable of lip homage, feigned affection, artful admiration, hollow harmony, canting moralism, oblique obeisance, and guileful goodwill when dealing with Jews. Israel Zangwill, Nobel prizewinner, states this sad truth poignantly, satirically. The thought he expresses is typical of religion-versus-religion attitudes all over the world.

The Jews, of course, have another reason to be frightened. A third of their numbers were murdered by the "good Christians" of Nazi Germany, and assassinations continue even after the war. As I write these words, the radio announced that Prime Minister Yitzhak Rabin was assassinated by one of his own people because of his dream of eliminating the hatred in his country. Some Arabs still talk of pushing the Jews into the sea, and Kahane Jews still plot ways to drive the seventeen percent of Palestine (Israeli) populations who are Arabs from their homes and from their country.

When will the citizens of the world learn that to take seriously any of the so-called religious scriptures can seriously disrupt our ability to make intellectual choices or decisions or come to intelligent conclusions. They twist human minds into morbid patterns of prejudice and hate.

Among the absurdities constantly repeated by religious leaders, whichever of the organized superstitions they adhere to, is that without the unifying presence of religion, our loosely integrated humanity would break down thoroughly. They are sure that we human beings need a Divine Disciplinarian to convince us to behave ourselves. Without His fearful hand (Deuteronomy 28:58), His dreadful day (Malachi 4:5) His terrible acts (Psalms 145:6), and His threatened Hell, we would go astray.

Of course, none of His strategies work. Our overloaded prisons attest to that dismal failure. Even insofar as human beings are convinced to treat one another civilly, it is not religion that is to be credited for that summum bonum. There are at least two other reasons for the prevailing conviviality we enjoy. First, it is our nature to be civil. Instances of dishonesty, disrespect, and abuse are the exception, not the rule. Most of us go through life amicably associated with our fellowman. Second, it is our systems of rules, regulations, and laws that help keep things in order. Sadly, those trained to prevent or detect and then to prosecute people guilty of misdoings find that members of religions do more than their share of serious infractions or transgressions of our laws and customs. P.R. Hightower (essay 206) and Steve Allen (essay 51) make that clear.

The quotation introducing this essay reveals a double-faceted insight on the part of it author. Zangwill reminds us of the irrational hatreds we exhibit in our treatment of others who differ from ourselves. And he makes it clear also that many of us are hypocrites with respect to these entrenched hatreds. We use words in talking to (and about) "those others" that ordinarily would mean the opposite. "Love" in what Zangwill is saying, of course, is our word, not his, and it substitutes for its antonym, which we would be using were we to be honest in our communications. Hypocrites often become experts in dissembling their true feelings.

It must seem obvious to all of us that this hatred and this hypocrisy are totally unnecessary. It is definitely not difficult to teach children in our homes and in our schools to regard one another as equals, deserving of equal respect and consideration in all situations. It is so easy, in fact, to teach democracy to children, that it will develop automatically if in the attitudes of parents and teachers no slight hint of antipathy or favoritism appears in their teaching.

30

> It is wrong always, everywhere, and for everyone to believe anything on insufficient evidence.
>
> W.K. Clifford (1845-1879)
> *Lectures and Essays*

Jacob Bronowski, in his book *Science and Human Values,* first introduced me to this quotation, now well over a hundred years old. How that much wisdom could have been expressed that long ago and ignored ever since is beyond comprehension. If everyone would read and understand what Clifford says, the world would immediately undergo revolutionary change.

If anyone doubts that Clifford's consummate good sense has been disregarded, he need only look about him. Some eleven thousand different religions that are said to exist would disappear overnight if their adherents were somehow convinced to heed and comply with the implications of these fourteen words. The world would begin to operate on the basis of reason instead of the irrationality that now prevails. All institutions, whether government, commercial or military, would immediately begin to operate efficiently and in good faith. Simple, isn't it? To make this a much better world, we need do only one thing: Stop believing when there is insufficient evidence for believing!

31

> Our church picnic was a gas. Why not do that every Sunday? The freedom from Christianity at the picnic, that keeps intruding in church activities on other Sundays, was a bang-up godsend.
>
> Teen talk (overheard)

A brief article in the June 1999 *Freethinker* suggests that there is a growing concern about what we would put in its place if we did manage to get rid of Christianity. But why would we need a replacement? What is there about Christianity that we would miss?

I suppose if we were constrained to do so we could find substitutes for the most prominent features of Christianity. Let us see: In the place of crusades, holocausts, inquisitions, and witch hunts, we could print carte blanche licenses for all of our violent prisoners and set them loose on our societies. For its dreary sermons, we might substitute drip torture, or recordings of Prabhupada reciting the name Krishna. To replace its collection plates, tithing, and coerced donations, we could impose a tax on coughing and yawning in churches. For its seminaries, we could substitute lessons in insider trading, palm reading, and professional wrestling. For its prejudices, superstitions, and bigotry, we could substitute frontal lobotomies. For its mythologies, we could substitute *Aesop's Fables*. Have I neglected any of the highlights of Christianity? For its entirety, we might substitute a hominoid version of *Animal Farm*.

32

Pure religion... is this, to visit the fatherless and widows in their affliction....

James 1:27

There are those who would limit the range of authority or competence of religion in our societies. But if religion is to be worthy of its expressed intent to improve the lot of the masses, tremendous tasks face it, and wide is its domain. What will it do in a world in which:

Politicians seek personal power, not social progress.

Lawyers see prestige and wealth, not justice.

Policemen look for bribes and confiscated loot, not prevention of crime.

Soldiers want just to get by, not protect democracy.

Clergymen plan for sainthood and ignore poverty and prejudice.

CEOs seek to rank in Fortune's five hundred, not to run civic-minded corporations that give interesting jobs and living wages to its employees.

"Good citizens" conform to the popular will rather than set out new paths to follow.

Pacifists at all costs avoid strife rather than struggle for an egalitarian society.

Students seek to pass examinations and not necessarily to acquire expertise in their chosen professions.

Conservatives fight to preserve the status quo, blind to changes so desperately needed.

Religion, if nothing else, should be the savior of mankind. But its doctrines and canons offer little to eliminate man's inhumanity to man. Religion may have a place, but rarely does it seem to find it.

33

> If religion cannot restrain evil, it cannot claim effective power for good.
>
> Morris Raphael Cohen (1880-1947)
> *The Faith of a Liberal*

Of course, it can do neither. Religion can do nothing beyond that which it is programed to do. The programers have made the firm decision that all it will require of religion is that it instill in those who are sufficiently gullible the same hierarchy of organized superstitions that were formulated millennia ago. It has never mattered to formulators, programers or programees that nothing subsumed under the name religion can be shown to have substance. Little that is called religion can be proven to be other than figments of imaginations run wild. Unrestricted phantasizing has been going on in human minds since recorded time and will probably continue long into the future.

Education in morality, not religion, will restrain evil if ever evil is appreciably restrained. Religion rather than restraining evil has become one of the greatest evils that exists and itself needs restraining. Religion teaches hatred and xenophobia, and is the cause of most of our wars. Religions divide mankind into opposing factions, each bent on becoming the ruling theocracy that would, if it attained the position it seeks, repress all other religions in the world.

To read Cohen's important contributions is to understand that he knows very well that religion cannot claim effective power for good. Cohen, probably more than any other philosopher that this country has produced, points out the horrors of religion and the need to revise religions from the ground up if they are ever to be of benefit to mankind. If religion cannot restrain prejudice and superstition, Cohen might have said, it cannot claim effective power for good. Organized superstition is a synonym for religion, and prejudice is religion's most obvious product.

Leo Pfeffer, a Hungarian-born (1910) American Lawyer, tells us: "Religion has been leading man toward a nobler vision, a better day, a higher hope, and a fuller life. The church, on the other hand, has been worldly, obscurantist, arrogant and predatory."

Pfeffer has it right in his assessment of attitudes in the church, but religion does not by any measure satisfy the imperative suggested by Cohen in the quotation above. Pfeffer is talking about what religion could be, not about what religion is. We need only look about us to know that religion does not restrain evil and therefore is not an effective power for good. Religion forfeits its claim to be a benefit to man when it directs most of its efforts toward foisting on us its mythology. Religion well deserves Pfeffer's encomiums "nobler, better, higher, and fuller" when it concentrates on teaching us to behave in a manner that is generally accepted as good or right. Morality, that is, should be the goal of every sermon and of all other activities of the church. When the result of religion is a human species that is happy, useful, truthful, and free from guilt or blame, then we will all applaud its efforts, regardless of the names by which it is called.

The taxes we pay in every country in the world are used mostly to restrain evil. Ninety percent of government activities is dedicated to that end. There are, and probably always will be people bent on mischief, and are often very clever in doing it. We are forever seeking ways to redirect a tendency toward malevolent behavior to a sincere desire to treat other people benevolently.

It becomes habitual for some people to act covertly, insidiously, or obliquitously, while others by nature are disposed to be thoughtful and empathetic. The very presence of known delinquents in any community bodes evil and often ends in disaster, while a society of genial people expects only kindness and charity. Freedom in any society denotes as much as anything else the right of its citizens to feel safe, while all are slaves who must be constantly afraid of their neighbors. C.K. Streit, American writer, speaks of nationalism as changing from a beneficent to a maleficent force. Cold, hostile, spiteful, merciless behavior cost societies billions of dollars. If all savage malcontents, could be convinced that brotherly love is the only rational behavior, what a wonderful society we might have. If our religious leaders could understand, as does Edmund Wilson , the baleful consequences of fanaticism and superstitions, we might put an end to our religious wars.

34

Is the heaven the ecclesiastics so ardently commend really something to look forward to?   Chester Dolan – Blind Faith

Most people would be miserable in the heaven of the religionists. Can we imagine our western cowboy heroes choosing an eternity of cavorting with lambs, the devoted couple after fifty years of "playtime at bedtime" looking forward to everlasting harp playing, the corporation president choosing an eternity of idle sterility, the staid old college professor hoping to end up eternally traipsing with angles, our Olympic-caliber athletes encumbered with halos, flowing robes, or inoperative wings, the dying laboratory scientist enjoying endless hymn-singing?

If we think this earth overpopulated, what must we think of heaven? With immortality assured, without birth control, and with one hundred percent eligibility the goal of religionists, heaven will never lack for tenants. But is heaven equipped eternally to provide space for all? Or will heaven, too, inevitably become one hell of a place in which to live? As for hell itself, brimstone logistics must by now be driving Stygian bargemasters bonkers!

35

Of all the animosities which have existed among mankind, those which are caused by a difference of sentiments in religion appear to be the most inveterate and distressing, and ought most to be deprecated.

George Washington (1732-1799)
Letter to Edward Newenham – October 20, 1792

Am I the only one reading words like these of our esteemed first president who wants them screamed from the housetops so that everyone will hear? Until we understand that fanatical religionists are the world's worst and most intransigent enemies, we are not safe. The very persons who should be our mentors in all aspects of friendship and social stability are those who foment the invidious devisiveness that keeps us hating one another.

If wars are analyzed carefully they are all seen to be of one genre. Nation, like religion, is seen as a package of passions capable of turning their adherents into unthinking automatons, ready to lay down their lives to keep themselves separate from other nations, other religions. The deities of each, the State (with its symbol the flag) and God (with his Holy Ghost and Divine son), inspire fanatical worship. If one were to make a list of the various traits that nation and religion have in common, the parallels would be seen as extensive and basic. Both are in effect modified tyrannies that have sets of laws (canons) that their members must adhere to. Both demand loyalty, and in times of conflict both teach that dying for *the* cause is the supreme sacrifice. Treason (heresy) for both is an abominable crime for which they may be deported or excommunicated. The laws (canons) for both are regarded as sacrosanct. Both turn their citizens (adherents) into unthinking automatons. Both are in their own way trying to gratify the basic needs of their members, and both are committed to a coming ideal society.

When demagogues rule nations and mystagogues rule religions, they declare as ideal citizens only those members who slavishly submit to their dominion. When the jealous god of nationalism must share the scene with the jealous god of religion, there will always be problems of separation of Church and State.

36

I see that sensible men and conscientious men all over the world were of one religion – the religion of well-doing and daring.
Ralph Waldo Emerson (1803-1882)
Lectures and Biographical Sketches

The religion Emerson speaks of in the quotation above needs no name. If we must refer to it in some kind of succinct manner, why not simply call it the good-sense religion? This religion needs no special denizens to populate dreamed-up celestial abodes, no archfiend to serve as scapegoat for our defects and failures, and no superbeing to explain all that baffles and perplexes us about the universe.

Emerson's religion of well-doing and daring is the cement that holds society together. The so-called truths of orthodox religions tear us apart. With the religions that are guiding us today, frictions are increasing, and wars are the result. There is undoubtedly in the world about us a substantial core of rational thinking, capable of fashioning the religion Emerson describes. These good-sense religionists ignore the horoscopes in newspapers, news of spectral visitations, proclamations of miracles, and talk of haunted houses. They do not join pilgrimages to holy shrines, apotheosize self-styled prophets, or crave the opiates of orthodoxy. They are willing to stand up and be counted and declare themselves as on the side of sanity: for brotherhood, against sectarianism; for unbiased perceptions, against bigotry; for love, against hate. If there is ever to be a heaven on earth, they will be the ones to build it.

37

A believer is a bird in a cage; a freethinker is an eagle parting the clouds with tireless wing.

Robert Ingersoll (1833-1899)

Episcopal Bishop John Shelby Spong tells us: "...religion provides a security shell around people." Whether with cage or shell, religion limits the stimuli that can help educate us to the ways of the world. In its most confining rubric, religion denigrates "science," a word coined to encompass all objective investigation of the universe and its countless entities. Any confining discipline limits our chance for freedom of operation and does us untold harm. Until we become the eagle, uninhibited by irrationally imposed restraints, we will not be fully functioning beings.

I am reminded of the country-song lament: "How can I soar like an eagle when I'm stuck with a turkey like you"? For our purposes, "turkey like you" becomes whichever of the debilitating religions people find themselves saddled with.

As Sartre says, man is condemned to be free. He has no choice. No one is putting restraints on him except the laws he agrees to and he himself. Being free, he alone is responsible. He cannot blame gods or devils for his difficulties. Nor can he expect gods to bail him out when he gets himself in trouble. Religion has been a scapegoat for him. But once he understands that he is fully in charge, he will stop passing the buck. He will take things into his own hands and as best he can fight his way through to whatever goals he finds worthwhile. Being responsible is being mature, being a full citizen of the world.

With goodwill and a judicious use of his native insight, he will accomplish amazing things.

38

> Justice is love distributed.
>
> Joseph Fletcher
> *Situation Ethics*
> *Moral Responsibility*

The principal theme of both of the books named above is the same: "Justice is love distributed." These four words become more than an aphorism. As Fletcher proceeds in his dissertations, we see them as axiomatic. Love, surely, is the basic principle of any genuine religion. With that there cannot logically be any dispute. It follows that in genuine religions church leaders will dispense with their monstrous mythologies and strive only to instill brotherhood in the minds of those they seek to indoctrinate. When love replaces the hate, prejudice, bigotry, and intolerance that now govern so many lives, we will have a world worthy of being called home. Our neighbors will be a happy people that a truly moral God would look down upon with supreme satisfaction.

An unreserved and genuine devotion of all human beings for all other people of good will: That is the love Joseph Fletcher seeks. We must incorporate in the curricula of our schools a carefully and methodically designed ethical system. The best minds of our societies must be dedicated to this important task.

39

> My father was an educational missionary padre in India. He always said he'd be wrong to try to convert Bengales to Christianity when they had a perfectly satisfactory religion of their own.
>
> E.P. Thompson
> Quoted by John Mortimer – *In Character*

Almost every missionary that has ever gone abroad does exactly what E.P. Thompson's father says would be wrong. If the air space within the missionary's skull has even the slightest hint of gray matter lurking about, he knows that in his proselytizing and conversions he does more harm than good. If the candlepower of the missionary's insight equals that of an ailing glowworm, he knows that a religion that has served native peoples for thousands of years cannot be improved by the intrusion of Christianity or any other modern orthodox religion. The Jewish policy against proselytism, if adapted universally, might by itself end most of the world's conflicts caused by extremism.

Most primitive religions are highly structured and are no more illogical than are our modern orthodox religions. We see that in the circumstances in which they function, they serve their adherents in a manner that is on the whole distinctly positive. The native's religion may be older than that of the missionary and may have served him better than the missionary's religion ever will, but fanaticism is blind to such "inconsequentials."

Anthropologists assure us that the chances of becoming psychotic in most primitive societies is less than it is for those who live in modern cities with all their obvious benefits such as psychiatrists, group therapy, and books to deal with every kind of emotional instability. Like the Bengales, most primitive societies have "perfectly satisfactory religions of their own."

40

A nun, at best, is only half a woman, just as a priest is only half a man.

H.L. Mencken (1880-1956)
Minority Report

A resident nun in a southern Colombia town (ca 1980) appeared on television to "inform" her people that the earthquake that morning was God's punishment for the wickedness of the people living in that town. I would imagine that she had had a conversation with God earlier that day, giving her authority to make that statement on His behalf. Before that (ca 1962), the roof of a church in Bolivia collapsed, killing three nuns and some 200 children.

The God that (after the fact) asks a nun in Colombia to pass on His message could not (before the fact) warn three nuns in Bolivia that they had fifteen minutes to clear the church in order to save their lives? The message in the first case and the lack of message in the second seem to tell us two things. First, our God of love was perfectly willing to see many people die through no fault of their own. The other thing He seems to be saying is that He does not much care for nuns, the one in Colombia whom He charged with passing on that vindictive message and the other three whom He let, along with their 200 students, die in his own house of worship.

41

There is the story of Cain and Abel, in which the question is raised, "Am I my brother's keeper? I have turned that around into an affirmation. I say, "I am my brother's keeper." When all human beings will make that affirmation, then maybe, just maybe, they will put an end to the horrors of this world.

Ralph Shapey
Quoted in *The Search for Meaning* by Phillip L. Berman

Ralph Shapey, in the quotation above, describes a world in which human beings become truly human, sincerely concerned with the welfare of others. To the poor we will be generous and to the sick sympathetic. As enlightened and sensitive human beings, we will do our best to help eliminate adversity in whatever form and wherever it may occur. We will do what we do, not because of a celestial decree threatening us with punishment if we do not. We will behave morally because of a predilection that is inherent in all of us to behave morally. It will not be tradition, conventions, laws, or some kind of celestial ethical principle that motivates us. It will be because we accept the responsibility we have as members of the "human" race.

42

So act as to elicit the best in others, and by so doing elicit the best in thyself.   Felix Adler (1851-1937)
An Ethical Philosophy of Life

Felix Adler's "Golden Rule" is not the Christian bargain or the Kantian egotism. Nor is it exactly what James David Corrothers of the Black Cat Club had in mind when he said, "Do de other feller before he do you." In whatever interchange we have with another member of our species, most important is that we leave that member feeling good about himself. Expressions of the golden rule are found in our oldest religious literature. In whatever form it is said, its concept is basic. We should do our best to observe it.

Chapter II

An Open Mind

43

The first chapter of *Religion on Trial* has offered suggestions for surviving the proselytizing propensities of our compatriots unscathed. The following eighteen chapters will continue to encourage vigilance, and explain how important it is that we preserve our individual identities. We must maintain our immunity to the pietistic persuasions that threaten to enslave us.

Keeping an open mind means we carefully weigh all sides of all issues. But we remain determined to accept nothing we read because it claims to be self-evident or the product of revelation. We want facts, empirical evidence, and accept only words that lead to something more than just other words. Knowing how difficult it is to prove a negative, we will not expect proof when statements are nothing more than reasonable doubt, but we will not permit anyone to make outlandish pronouncements without challenge,

Reason is essential for both sides in any debate, not just the side that happens to be burdened with proof. Fairies may or may not exist. Who can say for sure? I may quietly insist that my reasonable doubt is indeed very reasonable, but that is as far as I can go. I may even decide to conduct myself as I would if fairies were *not* a fact of this universe. But proof for me will never be even two points in the law, and I must admit it.

The most important part of this book is the boxed quotations. They are tone setters, triggers, and often pithy précis of the total. As Israel Zangwill would say, the rest is commentary. A great deal of effort has been made to gather together current and past opinions that express the rational approach to the process of living. With such an anthology of informed opinions, *Religion on Trial* becomes a history of reason, tracing the ascendancy of rational thought through the words of writers who base intellectual assent on the weight of empirical evidence and not on blind acceptance of present authority. The state of mind of those who pursue truth through the evidence of their senses is honest doubt and not misguided trust, always leaving as little to speculation and chance as possible.

44

A major obstacle to cooperation between the religions of mankind has been the inhospitable attitudes of Christianity toward other religions.

Lowell D. Streiker
The Gospel of Irreligious Religion

Which religion presumes to be superior to all other religions on earth and is aiming to supplant them? It is Christianity, which more than any other religion is opposed to science; Christianity, which Alfred North Whitehead considered to be one of the great disasters of the human race; Christianity, the enemy of reason; Christianity, whose pageantry is more important than moral discipline; Christianity, which has surpassed all other religions by far in the money spent on ostentation; Christianity, more proficient than any other religion in meddling in other peoples' religions; Christianity, the only religion which binds its own scriptures between the same covers as that of another religion in order to increase its own prestige; Christianity, the religion that has plagiarized more of the ideas of older religions than any other religion in history; Christianity, which in its history has supported anti-Semitism, slavery, and racism; Christianity, whose principal strength comes from brainwashing children before they have reached the age of reason.

That Christianity is the "major obstacle to cooperation between the religions of mankind."

45

I think there are innumerable gods. What we on earth call God is a little tribal God who has made an awful mess.

William S. Burroughs
Paris Review – Fall 1955

I do not believe in gods of any kind, but if we do crave a big-P Patsy upon Whom to shift our responsibilities, let us have a cadre of them. After all, just one solitary god is a frightful contemplation. Certainly we need at least one more, one higher on the pecking order, to deal with the bloodthirsty God the Christians have fashioned for us. With many gods, if one overweening Wonder Worker gets outlandish ideas about how to run the cosmos, the others can chasten Him and set Him straight.

Allah in the Koran repeats ad nauseam that He is "one" God and has no offspring or partners (a slap at the divine Jesus myth). We get so disgusted with Allah's airs that we are sure that what He needs most is an Allah-ita to sooth the feverish brow. Allah is so biased against women that the surest way for any of His subjects to earn a ticket to hell is to suggest that He has a wife and that the angels are his daughters. According to Allah, Angels are not his daughters; they are not even females!

A single ayah will give the reader an idea of what Allah thinks of women:

4/34: Men have authority over women because Allah made the one superior to the other, and because they spend their wealth to maintain them. Righteous women are devoutly obedient.

As for those [of your wives] from whom you fear disobedience, admonish them and send them to beds apart and beat them. Then if they obey you, take no further action against them.

46

> We are loath to believe that which hurts when believed.
> Publius Ovidius Naso (ca year zero)

The heaven our religion describes to us would be an excruciatingly boring place to live. Yet many of us would be grievously hurt to find out that no such place exists or that there is no hope we will end up there.

Joy is the word for our anticipation of heaven. Hurt is the word for no such prospect. Which do we choose? We are certainly loath to believe that which hurts when believed, so we choose the former, however chimerical it may be. Unfortunately, there is no cosmic law that says that truth must be something we like.

It hurts to believe that there are no guardian angels to watch over us. It hurts to believe that there is no satan to blame for our misdoings. It hurts to believe that there is no God to advise us on matters of morality. We are not about to believe anything that hurts when believed, so we accept only fables and fairy tales that promise roseate endings. We want no stories of persons, events, or situations that do not turn out favorably for people like ourselves. Life must be beautiful, assuring, giving us confidence that everything is purple and fine linen. Plays or novels that have unhappy endings are avoided. We frolic in rose gardens and wear blinkers in caves of despair.

47

> It is, I think, an error to believe that there is any need of religion to make life seem worth living.
>
> Sinclair Lewis (1885-1951)
> Quoted by Will Durant
> *On The Meaning of Life*

I think so too, and so do many others. But there are billions who do not, perhaps most of the human inhabitants of this globe. It is they who keep this world wallowing in religious infamies. Religious crusades, wars, and genocides are the obvious examples, but individual crimes perpetrated in the name of religion are the examples most conspicuous in our daily news. The efforts to reduce human conflicts could find no single remedy more effective than to rid the world of its dependence on mythologies.

What was clear to the Durants, the Sagans, and most of the authors who wrote the quotations that introduce the essays of this book, should be clear to every human being who can weigh the pros and cons of the controversy fairly and cogently. It is not clear to those who base decisions on anecdotal evidence: I know God answers prayers because the Martins prayed that God would cure the terminal cancer suffered by their nine-year-old son, and he went immediately into miraculous remission. I know that God intervenes in human affairs because He saved Leonardo de Vinci's painting of *The Last Supper* when all buildings around it were bombed to smithereens. I know my guardian angels were looking after me when a big wave turned my boat over, and the next wave turned it upright, and it stayed that way until I reached shore. We all need a clear idea of the nature of statistical evidence and what it means to prove that a statement is true or false. By reading Anatol Rapport's *Operational Philosophy,* we may answer any questions we still have about this aspect of our education. Essay 12 provides a brief summary.

48

> The fear of the LORD is the beginning of knowledge, says the proverb *17.* Yet this is an odd saying, if it be true that "God is Love."
> Alfred North Whitehead *(1861-1947) – Religion in the Making*

To Christians, and to a lesser extent to Jews and Muslims, the world is ruled by mysterious and unpredictable forces to which the only reasonable response is fear. As a result, children, as well as adults with children's minds, live in abject terror of hellfire and damnation.

Once liberated from the pretense that is theistic religion, the unbeliever no longer lives in a milieu of fear: fear of God, fear of hell, fear of excommunication, fear of ideas that do not agree with his own. Free of the oppressive sham and nonsense that once overwhelmed him, he can get on with making sense of the world in which we human beings do in fact live.

49

> Man's plight would, indeed, be sad if he had to be kept in order through fear of punishment and hope of rewards after death.
> Albeit Einstein (1879-1955)
> "Religion and Science"

Without hell, according to the opinions of most religious leaders, religion would undergo immediate dissolution. Without Satan, preachers would have little to say. Fear is the cementing ingredient of all the major religions. The congregations that face preachers and their weekly diatribes could not be trusted to behave morally if they were not scared half out of their wits by threats and ominous admonitions.

When a human discipline expects fear to be an effective means to assure moral behavior, it expects what any reasonably competent mind knows is absurd. The fear of God and the fear of hell that Christianity preaches do nothing but harm. Fear generates a disordering agitation that often leaves us neurotic and withdrawn. Fear makes cowards of us, incapable of intimacy and love. Organized religions, with their awesome doctrines and enervating precepts, deprive us of the strength of mind and firmness of purpose that we need in order to live full and meaningful lives. Prolonged and pervasive fear stultifies the mind.

Einstein contradicts the opinion of a writer who made his debut more than two thousand years ago. Polybius, in *Histories VI* said in 125 BC: "The masses ... must be filled with fears to keep them in order. The ancients did well, therefore, to invent gods." Today's church leaders keep telling us that not unless we learn to observe and respect "ancient wisdom" will we, too, become wise.

50

Religion, in conquering old terrors, brought [man] new terrors of its own. It introduced him, in other words, to the conception of hell, and of all imaginings that have ever beset the human mind, I know of none which have worked such a havoc of dismay as this dreadful dogma.

J.H. Holmes
The Sensible Man's View of Religion

The Reverend DuSean Berkich in his book *How to Keep on Living* says that if ever we have a worthwhile religion, it will have no hell in its liturgies. He believes, with Mencken, that no truly civilized man could believe in hell. For Berkich, an ideal religion must be strictly a religion of love. In his two books, Joseph Fletcher develops this same theme.

For most Christian fundamentalists, hell is the *sine qua non* of their religion. From the harangues of our electronic-church preachers, we know that nothing offers them greater pleasure than imagining their enemies as consumed in the fires of hell. They could not get along without hell or without Satan. It is Satan who keeps them in business. He is their savior, the principal topic of their sermons. Without hell and without Satan, Christian fundamentalists are sure that their religion would fall apart. They are probably right. We should be so lucky!

51

Most of the embezzlers, swindlers, con men and thieves - God help us - are card-carrying members of one religious denomination or another that formally pays respect to the Old and/or New Testaments.

Steve Allen
Ripoff

Barnes and Teeters in their book *New Horizons in* Criminology document this assumption to a point that leaves little doubt about its verity. Both Walter Kaufmann's *The Faith of a Heretic* and my book *Blind Faith* summarize their findings. Without further analysis of the tremendous harm that religions do to our societies, these statistics given by Barnes and Teeters should by themselves be enough to discount religious affiliation as a benefit to human lives.

Prisons are filled with what Steve Allen calls card-carrying members of our orthodoxies. No study ever made shows that attendance at Sunday school decreases the chance that a child will lie, steal, or end up in reform school. No study shows that adherence to orthodox religions reduces the chances that adults will spend part of their lives in jail.

To read the Bible is to understand why. Its deceit, contradictions, inconsistencies, violence, and lessons in immorality teach those who take it seriously that it is perfectly normal for us to behave as depraved human beings. My book *Blind Faith* and all the books listed in its bibliography are for the most part documents of the failure of our modem theistic religions to instill morality in the members of the human species.

52

Religion without humanity is a poor human stuff.

Sojourner Truth (1797-1883)
Interview: Battle Creek, Michigan

If religion ever serves a purpose in human societies, it will be when it is seen as of service in the welfare of all mankind. As long as human societies are seen only as a kind of adventure that a Supreme Eminence has established for His own amusement, we will fare badly. Of course we have only ourselves to blame. Religion is an attitude, a mental matrix that we have contrived. Religion will improve when we decide that it must improve.

When we understand thoroughly that we are in full control, we will begin to do what must be done. Sojourner Truth seems to Have understood that truism a hundred years ago. Others we quote in this book did also. How can we continue to ignore what they say? Let us take matters in our own hands and build societies made up of thoughtful and caring people who are not burdened by superstitions, prejudice, and mysticism.

Let us learn to take care of this earth, our only hope of ever having anything approaching a utopian place to live. Let us learn to avoid desecrating nature, learn to live in harmony with it, and learn to disseminate the requisite information to everyone else so that they might do the same. We must learn how to keep what is left of pristine nature from slipping away from us.

53

I want nothing to do with any religion concerned with keeping the masses satisfied to live in hunger, filth, and ignorance.
            Jawaharlal Nehru (1889-1964) quoted in Edgar Snow's
                                    Journey to the Beginning

It has long been the policy of religion everywhere to keep potential members ignorant. Education, in the view of many religious leaders, is an appalling prospect. Not only do well-informed people see through the flimsy pretenses of religious dogma, but in some cases they go on to explain to those not so well informed that what they are accepting is obviously a travesty of moral and intellectual behavior. As time goes on, well-informed people become less and less easily convinced to become blind, sequacious adherents to nonsense.

The large well-financed "universities" maintained by some of our affluent religions would seem to be a contradiction of the view expressed above. First of all, it must be said that the term university usurped by these institutions is a glaring misuse of language. These schools were formed precisely in order to avoid universality in their teaching. Universities are precisely what they are not. They do not teach anything remotely resembling rigorous, dynamic science. These schools must be very selective. Only those ideas that will not contradict their own parochial points of view will be accepted.

Thinking people, even those not facing the benighted India that Nehru had to contend with, want nothing to do with any religion concerned with keeping people ignorant. They will not allow themselves to be a party to depriving the masses of an unimpeded access to education.

54

The dogmas of the quiet past are inadequate to the stormy present.
Abraham Lincoln (1809-1865)
Second-Annual Address

No discipline other than religion arrogates to itself the right to make its case on the basis of dogma. "Dogma" is sorcery, a desperate expedient like "faith." "A dogma is not advanced as reasonable and worthy of acceptance but laid down as true and beyond dispute," according to a Merriam-Webster dictionary. "This is so," dogma is saying. "It is an apodictic absolute. Accept it!" The idea of refutation is ridiculous. It would be like denying that the moon is too far away for an afternoon walk. "Some things are so simply by the nature of things" we are told, "and dogma is one of those things."

Really, to say that dogma is set in stone, immutable, is quite preposterous, you know! Dogma is man-made, and anything made by man can be changed by man. To worship dogma is to worship goblins. One has as much sensory authority as the other.

The arbitrarily imposed dogmas of Christianity (see essay 319) are a denial of natural law, of a natural code of ethics, of man's naturally endowed responsibility. For religionists to declare that dogma is absolutely indispensable, of course, is understandable. It is indispensable for the existence of their religion. A religion is its dogma. If its dogma were to cease to exist, so would the religion.

55

I ought to feel free, yet I cannot keep my hat on in a church, even when no one is looking.
E.M. Forster *(1879-1970)*
Quoted by Raymond Mortimer
Try Anything Once

Why is it that completely nonsensical conventions, even more than Federal laws, will sometimes determine how we behave? I assume that England has no law that says a man must remove his hat in church or that a woman must have her head covered. The forms of worship and rituals in any church seem designed more to make visiting strangers uncomfortable than to have any practical value.

The only time in my life I ever participated in the ritual of a Catholic Church was when I was called on to give away in marriage the oldest daughter in a three-generation family of indigenes in Ecuador. They have been a part of my life now for twenty-four years. I walked down the aisle with the beautiful bride, holding hands as a pair of ice skaters do and had no idea where I was to go when I handed her over to the groom. Things got straightened out, but I was agonizingly uncomfortable throughout the proceedings. No one in the church had much doubt that I was not the biological father.

E.M. Forster gives us one more example of the stranglehold religion has over people everywhere. Its superstitions keep us hopping like puppets on strings even when we know exactly how idiotic they are. We ought to be free, as Forster says, but we never will be as long as we have that ring in our nose.

56

> The truth is that no profession of faith or lack of faith has anything to do with a man's morals.... [It is not true] that to be good we must be pious.
>
> Lester Ward (1841-1911)
> *Iconoclast*

Faithful and reverent worship of mythological entities is in no sense a manifestation of moral behavior. A man's morality and his religious piety are more often than not inversely proportional. Dealing with nonsense as if it were worthy of serious consideration is on a low level of human integrity. If such behavior becomes habitual, it cannot help corrupting a man's sense of ethical responsibility.

Morality means conforming to an accepted standard of what is right and good. Morality means not lying, not stealing, and not treating other people shabbily. It means being charitable, kind, generous, honest - observant of the golden rule.

Religious leaders spend their entire lives immersed in a vast tissue of lies where almost everything they say is about nothing that observation can verify. This practice for them is indeed habitual, so much so that until it is pointed out to them, they do not know, or pretend they do not know, they are doing it They may consider themselves paragons of piety, but their morality is sorely compromised by their deceitful behavior.

57

The child who must be rewarded for being honest and truthful is under such emotional strain that he tends to be such only by stealth or fraud.

H.E. Barnes
N. Teeters
New Horizons in Criminology

The minute you reward a child for being honest that minute you have planted in his mind that there is something abnormal about being honest. No longer can it be the everyday, commonplace, usual way to behave. He soon learns, as well, that being honest is not the really important thing. Important it is to *seem* to be honest. He cannot be honest even about his honesty.

One can imagine that bank embezzlers, real estate swindlers, and inside traders like Ivan Boesky and Michael Milken, when children, were rewarded for their honesty. They were taught, in effect, that when not being rewarded, it was perfectly all right to be dishonest. Later in life, when in positions of financial power, they learned that they could make vast sums of money by being dishonest. Fraud soon came easy to them. Also, as when deceiving a parent, it may be assumed that their cleverness in perpetrating their deceptions gave them an adrenaline rush, a fillip, a satisfaction that behaving like everyone else did not give them. Aldrich Ames, spy extraordinary, who sold himself to the Russians, must have felt the same way. Honoré de Balzac in 1845 said that "behind every great fortune there is a crime." What the case against Boesky and Milken tell us more than anything else is how few such white-collar criminals are ever duly prosecuted for their crimes.

58

> A religious awakening which does not awaken the sleeper to love has aroused him in vain.
>
> Jessamyn West
> *The Quaker Reader* (Introduction)

Religious awakenings are fine as long as they are spontaneous awakenings, not affected or effected by an external or internal compulsion of the will, instead coming about so naturally that they are manifestly unpremeditated and definitely unprompted. Any "awakening" planned beforehand is more correctly identified as carefully contrived indoctrination. If the so-called awakening is subsequently called confirmation, communion, invocation, circumcision, baptism, transubstantiation (any new category that sets a man apart even more from his fellow human beings than he was before), it is not an awakening, but a usurpation of personal freedom that is akin to slavery.

If the newly awakened person then finds himself to be "born-again," he is not simply awakened but transmogrified into a new being, now belonging to a strictly minority elite who is "nearer my God than thee," barely tolerating the ordinary run of religious man.

We are reminded of Rudolf Otto's "numinous" (see essay 261), which seems to describe mind function whenever it fails to track properly. Numinous can apply to all manner of weird, manic, convulsive, sublime, or grotesque moods, attitudes, excitements, and hallucinations. Otto offers "intuition of the holy" as the equal of his numinous. I wonder if "*non compos mentis*" does not describe the mental equivalent more accurately.

59

> If I am so quickly done for / What on earth was I begun for?
> Words on a gravestone of a little child

To answer the child's question in the boxed couplet is to deny deity. If there were a God, He would be hard put to explain away such wanton cruelty. Letting innocent children die may be the saddest event we adults ever have to face.

It is interesting to note how much of our pulpiteers' time is spent trying to explain the behavior of their putative Deity. They fail constantly, but are adept at pretending that they never do. Those of us who are emancipated from the thrall of theology, free to ask the embarrassing questions, want to know: Why does God suffer the existence of Satan? Why does God hate us so much, killing us right and left without plausible reasons? Why does God start mankind out as inevitable sinners? Why does God allow so much injustice to plague our lives? What about those "acts of God"? Are they, really? Why does God call David (guilty of adultery and murder) one of his favorites? Why did God torture Abraham and Job, asking Abraham to sacrifice his son Isaac, and killing all of Job's family and livestock? Felix Adler says, "What fiend so fiendish as such a God!"

60

> It is fear that first brought gods into the world.
> Petronius Satyricon (First century AD)

The environment that primitive man grew up in was hostile, and fear was essential for survival. Even today fear can be useful in keeping us out of trouble. But like all emotions to which the nervous system is subject, fear must be tempered by reason. Paranoia, anxiety neurosis, or pathological withdrawal may result if fear is not controlled. To create gods to explain the fearful phenomena of nature and then to petition these gods to protect us from the special evil they control is seriously disordered thinking. Edward Anhalt, Freud, and Whitehead (see essays 48 and 255) are others who believe that our gods have been conjured up mainly to help us overcome our fears. We could have saved ourselves years of torment had we listened to what they tell us and to what Petronius Satyricon said two thousand years ago.

Each member of the Judeo-Christian-Muslim religions has his own personal God, each one different from all the rest. With one all-encompassing infusion of sanity into religious minds, we could eliminate all of these gods and establish a sane interface between ourselves and the world. Once we learn that careful, concerted planning is a better way to confront fears than turning to gods to help us, we will exorcise the few gods that still have evaded the deicides of the centuries. Once we eliminate the irrational fears that plague us, we will begin to live liberated and exciting lives. We will then see before us a world that is irresistibly fascinating, compellingly enchanting, so full of opportunities in which we may become usefully involved that we wish we could be several persons so we could take advantage of all of them.

61

As a journalist in active practice I have spent most of my life among scoundrels but I can recall very few, even in high office, who deserved to be put alongside the Heavenly Father described in 2 Kings 2:24; Exodus 12:29; 2 Samuel 12:15; Deuteronomy 20:17; and Matthew 27:46. No wonder Thomas Jefferson pronounced Him "A Being of terrific character - cruel, vindictive, capricious, and unjust!"
     H. L. Mencken (1880-1956) - *Treatise on the Gods*

If you or I were to fashion a religion, giving it the usual appurtenances, a heaven and hell populated with a supreme deity and some lesser beings to fill out the bill, we would do better. One thing for sure, we would see to it that all the parts were to our taste. We would be foolish to make a religion we didn't like.

We ask, then, why have Christians, Jews, and Muslims done so poorly; especially why is the Deity they chose to run things such a blatant tyrant? He seems always angry about something, and repeatedly behaves in a way to make us deathly afraid of Him, constantly threatening us with mayhem, and setting up rules that take much of the fun out of life. He kills indiscriminately - even first-born babies.

Since our God is omnipotent, can do anything He wants to do, we wonder why He solves problems with so much violence. His hell is a nightmare right out of the torture chambers of medieval Europe. You and I will probably have no chance to fashion a popular Deity, but we certainly need not dote on the one Mencken describes.

62

I look forward with great anticipation to the death of the church. The sooner it dies, the sooner we can be about the business of living the gospel.   *Sally* Gearhart - *The Lesbian and God-the-Father* or *All the Church Needs is a Good Lay - On Its Side*

"A Good Lay" can mean one thing for a golf ball, another for a poem, and still another for a young lady (never used by herself). But lay in religion is an adjective that anticipates a noun such as member or brother. We assume that used as does Gearhart, it reverts to being a noun, but we are not sure whether in sense of poem, golf ball, or young lady. We finally give preference to the golf ball type of acceptation.

Unfortunately the church will survive as long as anything exists that can be called gospel in the sense of the four books (mostly fiction) that begin the New Testament. Sally Gearhart has the cart before the horse. Gospels must first be replaced by the efforts of intelligent people of goodwill, planning smoothly operating societies that serve everyone. Then, not churches, but social organizations should be formed to help in making the new plans as applicable as possible. I hope, then, that Sally Gearhart gathers a large following, as she will continue to be a tremendous voice in the making of a better world.

63

Everybody has got to die, but I have always believed that an exception would be made in my case.

William Saroyan (1908-1981)

Each person knows that in one respect, at least, he is radically different from every other human being on earth. It may be this difference that convinces young people that they are immortal. If they can be that different in this one respect, phenomenal as it is, can they not be different in this other respect as well?

Of all the six billion or so persons on this earth with all their differences, Saroyan, too, knows that he is, always has been, different: He is the only person who can observe the world using the very special nervous system (his own) that observes what so far as he knows is the only world that exists.

"With our thoughts," the Buddha said, "we make the world." When we die, it is logical for any of us to surmise that the entire world will cease to exist as well. We each have our own individual world, but we do not find it apparent that the people who populate our world have their own individual worlds, similar to ours and not dependent on ours.

Samuel Butler said: "To himself everyone is immortal; he may know that he is going to die, but he can never know that he is dead." Almost all theologians teach that there is continuity between the person before and after death. Without postulating this continuity, all this folderol about souls and heavenly rewards, etc., is not just nonsense, but "obvious" nonsense. If the soul in heaven cannot relate to a human being once on earth, then words like rewards and deserved punishment are patently ridiculous. Heaven and hell would cease to be meaningful concepts. All religions would be manifest nonsense - which there is little doubt they truly are.

I have a sneaking hunch that most people believe as did Saroyan about their own immortality. It is simply an aspect of solipsism, which quite logically may lurk, barely out of focus, in the back of every individual brain.

64

Do we, holding that gods exist, deceive ourselves with insubstantial dreams and lies, while random careless chance and chance alone controls the world?

Euripedes (484-405 BC)
Hecuba

Euripedes, you are right about our self-deception concerning the existence of gods. But you are wrong about the world being controlled by random chance. Since your time, scientists such as Copernicus, Galileo, Newton, Plank, Einstein, Bohr, Heisenberg, and many, many others have shown that the universe and its constituent parts behave in response to definite cosmic laws.

Fairy tales are fun. Most of us can remember back when parents or teachers read to us the various popular fairy tales and how enamored we were of them. We wanted no one the likes of Euripedes telling us that the stories were not true, that nothing like that ever happened. Now we are adults. We still love those fairy tales and even read them to our children. But we now know that they are not true. Dr. Richard Gardner of Columbia University tells us that those fairy tales were not even good for us. The fantasy and violence of fairy tales give the child a shaky foundation for beginning a life of peace and integrity.

Our religions are worse. From the day we are born till the day we take our last breath, they teach us the fantasy of heaven and the violence of hell, as well as other fraudulent fables, all certified as incontrovertible in some "sacred" book or another. Any human being brought up on these amorphous myths and goblin-will-getcha legends will almost certainly be tormented with neuroses and deprived of discriminating judgment for the rest of his life.

65

> To live anywhere in the world today and be against equality of race or color is like living in Alaska and being against snow.
>
> William Faulkner (1897-1962)
> *Essays, Speeches & Public Letters*

Not quite! Snow in some circumstances can be extremely harmful. It can cause snow blindness, chilblains, frostbite, even death. It can camouflage treacherous crevasses, and in the form of avalanches, destroy entire towns. Even in Alaska, being against snow is not entirely illogical.

Race or color, on the other hand, has no inherent power to do harm. Differences in race or color, for reasons difficult to explain, can give rise to prejudices. It is these prejudices that stir up irrational hatreds in ignorant minds - with nefarious consequences of every kind - even wars that kill millions of people.

C. Lenon Ramond points with shame to the cant and cacophony of those who can teach virtue, preach righteousness, and pray blessings only for those with skin colored like their own. William James is quoted as saying, "A great many people think they are thinking when they are rearranging their prejudices."

Human beings are not truly civilized until all members of all societies have equal voice. We are not civilized until we get rid of all prejudices, especially those that are constantly interfering with our well-intentioned efforts to make this a better world. Alexander Meiklejohn tells us that "civilization is reasonableness." It is never prejudice. Insofar as we harbor sinister prejudices we are uncivilized.

66

> All progress has resulted from people who took unpopular positions.
> Adlai E. Stevenson (1900-1965)
> Speech at Princeton, March 22, 1954

It would be discouraging to believe that all progress depends on fighting a battle against people who oppose progress. But anyone can find instances when he will concur with what Adlai Stevenson says.

For most practical purposes, we know what constitutes immorality, and we condemn it. But unfortunately any attempt to convert religions into organizations designed to instill morality as the primary guiding principle in all human endeavors is opposed. Myth gets in the way. Myth, in religions, is so deeply entrenched and given such overwhelming prominence that it eclipses every other purpose religion can have.

The hell God fashioned, it seems, has been immensely successful. In Proverbs 5:14 we read: "Hell has enlarged itself and opens its mouth beyond measure." It is far more important that we believe in heaven and hell and all the presumed inhabitants of those imagined places than that we be moral human beings.

Most of us do not put murder in the same category as failing to worship a deity. But both the Bible and the Koran do. To suggest that Allah has partners or offspring is a sure ticket to hell. Wife beating is condoned. The worst sin in the Judeo-Christian-Muslim religions is blasphemy. Adlai Stevenson finds views such as these outrageous. When all of us do, the world will see moral progress the likes of which have never been seen before.

Another unpopular position that needs consideration looms in our legal systems. Juries and court judges are giving longer prison sentences for selling drugs than for armed robbery. This by any measure of justice is preposterous. Selling drugs may someday be like selling booze in Pennsylvania. What is unmoral depends on circumstances and who does it. If an enterprising grocer does it, it is criminal. If the State does it, it is all right. Both prison and hell have enlarged themselves, have "opened their mouths beyond measure."

67

> Ah doan go to none o' them; moas o' da sinnun is in da churches.
>
> Raphael

So spoke a delightful and obviously very religious native of tiny Harbour Island in the Bahamas, an island entirely without cars. The island has seven churches and a total population of six hundred "souls." Raphael was a lobster fisherman and at finding traps in a sea without signposts he was uncanny. I never figured out how he did it. He simply had a sense I do not have.

His judgment of churches in general, too, was probably right on the mark. Pierre Berton in *The Comfortable Pew* and Vance Packard in *The Status Seekers* agree. As Herbert Spencer said: "Volumes might be written on the impiety of the pious."

Brotherhood often has an uphill battle in the churches, where members are often looked upon as if divided into castes. The faithful see themselves as petitioners for a suitable and secure place in heaven, which they imagine the church has a divine right to grant. As petitioners, they demean themselves and assume an attitude of abject servility. Fear of being unworthy of the favor they ask degrades even more the low opinion they have of themselves. The Church's sacraments of confession and atonement of sins humiliates them even further and deprives them of all incentive to improve their position in the church and in life. In the book *The Essential Lenny Bruce,* we read: "Every day people are staying away from the church and going back to God." Raphael was obviously one of those people.

68

> Men never do evil so completely and cheerfully as when they do it from religious conviction.
>
> Blaise Pascal (1623-1621)
> *Pencées*

Seldom has there been an understatement more obvious than this. "Anti-religion" books surreptitiously disappear from library collections more than any others. Reputations are destroyed by those who disapprove of the sexual orientations of their neighbors. Good Christians "know" that their ends justify whatever means.

Nearly all of the thirty or more wars going on in the world right now are religious wars. In fact, if understood in their subtle implications, all wars are religious wars. God is declared by all camps as being on *their* side in the conflict. Also, the god of nationalism has so much in common with the god of religion that at times they are indistinguishable. Soldiers follow the dictates of one god or the other in all of our wars.

Muslims blew up one of the World Trade Center buildings to avenge imagined offenses against their religion. Religionists will sin whenever they are convinced that sin will win. Since martyrs always go to heaven, according to those who urge them into martyrdom, they take to arms cheerfully and die willingly.

69

When, and how, and at what stage of our development did spirituality and our strange notions of religion arise? [From where came] the need for worship which is nothing more than our frightened refuge into propitiation of a Creator we do not understand?

Vita Sackville-West (1892-1962)
No Signposts in the Sea

It is the nature of the human being to want explanations for things. The need to worship also seems to be among man's instinctive propensities. The gods man has invented to explain natural phenomena, and our worship of "athletes" in sports and "stars" in the movies, I would think, make that obvious. To seek the answers as to how and why such instincts evolved is to delve into physiology, psychology, and perhaps philosophy at depths far beyond the scope of these brief essays. Surely, somewhere there are answers, or at least partial answers, and many will be seeking the answers still to be found.

Even the Talmud admits to an inability to answer fundamental religious questions: "It is beyond our power to explain either the prosperity of the wicked or the affliction of the righteous." And I might ask if there is purpose in God's creations, why fifty billion galaxies and unimagined trillions of solar systems that by all that is logic do exist?

70

> If God exists, and if he is in the least interested in the human beings He has created, is it unreasonable to suppose He should give men some evidence of His existence?
>
> Arnold Lunn
> *Science and the Supernatural*

One is led to wonder why if God wanted us to know that He exists, why not give us some practical evidence: Why miracles?

No one seems disposed to expand upon the obvious reason for believing that there is no God taking care of the universe He reputedly created. If a caring, loving, omnific, omnipresent, omniscient, omnipotent, omnibenevolent God were around overseeing this spinning spheroid, that fact would be so evident that every living human being would know it beyond any shadow of a doubt. His presence would be manifest at every troubled moment of every human life. He would shake a monitory finger at us to divert untoward intentions whenever He sees us going astray. He would cleanse our hearts of hate, prejudice, bigotry, and xenophobia. He would instill in us instead an all-encompassing love that would turn us into saints. If He did nothing more than dump all our weapons, from cap pistols to hydrogen bombs on some deserted planet in galaxy M-31, we would all know that He is here and cares.

All the excuses we make for God not doing these things are nothing more than doubts that there is such a God with the attributes we assign to Him. The real question for us to ponder is: "Why are we so stupid as to believe what is so obviously false, and why do we not take our destinies in our own hands and build a world where we can all live in peace?

71

> When religion fails, cults appear.
>
> Daniel Bell
> *Religion in the Sixties*

All religions will fail eventually and the cults right along with them. There will be a day when we are free of all superstitions.

The ranks of people who understand and contribute to the

failure of religions increase as the members of societies become educated into the techniques of sound, rational thinking. If President Clinton is successful in assuring that "all" young people are educated at least through two years of college, there may eventually be few simpletons left for religious leaders to recruit into their institutionalized inanity. Without simpletons to recruit, organized obscurantism could then be replaced by assemblages of luminaries, and world progress would accelerate prodigiously. We Homo sapiens will earn our appellation, and the world will become one grand think tank in which the people are peaceful world citizens. The resulting new edifying methodology will help us develop a stable global community without terrorism, wars, bigotry, xenophobia, prejudices, and enervating superstitions. Educational systems will be motivated to teach morality, nonviolence, social consciousness, and an all-embracing love. Lifelong learning in an exciting new world will keep us alert to changes and help us adapt to them.

72

> What is science? It is only another name for the careful and scrupulous use of the human mind.
>
> Arnold J.Toynbee (1889-1975)
> Reply to a criticism by Pieter Geyl

When the church declares itself as opposed to science, it is setting itself against knowledge, good sense, reason, rational thinking and, therefore, against progress.

When those living in the United States speak of the incompatibility of science and religion, it is almost invariably the Christian religion that has claimed their attention. No other religion in history has marshaled its forces so energetically to oppose and suppress astronomy, physics, and the biological sciences. For many, psychology, anthropology, and the sects of Christianity have been added as religion's principal adversaries. Psychology, especially, invites censure for its "insidious intrusions" upon what was once the exclusive province of religion. There are, however, some churches that, in recent years, have incorporated among their activities departments of psychotherapy, which hopefully alleviate some of the mental and emotional disorders that fanatical religious attitudes cause.

73

> Even if God exists, I think it would be better for men not to know of his existence and not to believe in Him, because to believe in a Supreme Power is an ultimate denial of personal responsibility in life.
>
> Rex Beaber
> quoted in *The Search for Meaning* by Phillip L. Berman

He goes on: "Certainly if I am wrong and God exists, it's difficult to believe God would dislike me and punish me for reasonably concluding... that he did not exist. I mean that would be a most extraordinary form of God. So I certainly have no concern that my disbelief in the existence of God would wreak havoc on me. If God wanted me to believe in Him, He can arrange it."

Compare this speculation with that of Blaise Pascal when he announced his "wager" (essay 102). Which God would you rather have around: (1) Pascal's, unable to distinguish between reasonable doubt and unreasonable belief and Who, regardless, would avenge anyone who chooses to doubt, or (2) Beaber's, Who could understand and forgive someone coming to a reasonable but incorrect conclusion?

Pascal, of course, had reasons for his demeaning opinion of the God of the Bible, depicted (as He is) as jealous, arbitrary, despotic, cruel, and vindictive. Beaber is more in agreement with X.J. Kennedy, who describes God as perfectly justified in suing for libel those who sully his reputation by describing Him in the Bible as some kind of barbaric monster.

74

> Faith has no merit where human reason supplies the truth.
> St. Gregory, the Great (590-604 AD)
> *Homilies*

Faith, when it becomes a substitute term for religion, has no merit, period. It is ersatz reasoning, the opposite of sound, rational thinking. Faith is the word religionists use when, as is so often the case, they have no real answers to the questions that are bound to come up when trying to make sense of nonsense: "Will my eight-month-old baby brother who died last night go to heaven?" "He will if your have faith!" "Will the Pope die of the cancer he has?" "He won't if we all have faith."

"The just shall live by faith," we read in Galatians 3:11. Then in the next verse "the law," not faith, becomes the factor essential to living. Today, many people find that disobeying the law can indeed be detrimental to life, but disregarding the mawkish myths that ecclesiastics ask us to live by can do nothing but improve our situation,

Jesus said, "If you had faith as a grain of mustard seed, you might say unto this mulberry tree, 'Be thou plucked up by the root, and be thou planted in the sea,' and it will obey you." (Luke 17:6). Want to make a believer of me? Call upon the man who possesses the faith you describe, and ask him to perform. Over and over the Bible indicates that those living at that time had not learned a simple axiom that most people today are abundantly aware of: "Saying a thing is so does not make it so." If you cannot or will not demonstrate that which you say is true, you may as well save your breath.

75

It matters not how strait the gate. / How charged with punishments the scroll. / I am the master of my fate. I am the captain of my soul.
William Ernest Henley (1849-1903)
Invictus

William Ernest Henley in the boxed quotation above shows that he is willing to accept responsibility for his own destiny. The rest of us should do so too. If we are not victims of wars, disease, dictators, criminals, or the like, we are in charge. When we drop out of school, take only the easy subjects, are habitually late for work or appointments, drink or eat too much, use drugs, chain smoke, commit robbery, etc., etc., we have abandoned responsibility and give ourselves little chance for a long, useful, and peaceful life.

Elizabeth Cady Stanton wrote in *Home Life* in 1875, "It is something to know that life's ills are not showered upon us by the Good Father from a kind of Pandora's box but are the results of causes that we have the power to control."

Henley was ill most of his life and had a hard row to hoe. If he could come through it all unbowed, most of the rest of us should be able to do so also. With a strong will, a determination to succeed at some profession that pleases us, we usually need not succumb to adversities. Some, for whom the struggle is beset with more obstacles than usual, do have a serious challenge. But some fight through to victory despite the odds.

76

> Christianity has ever been the Enemy of human love.... Christianity has made of death a term which was unknown to the gay calmness of the Pagan.
>
> Marie Louise de la Rancée (1839-1908)
> pseudonym: Ouida
> *The Failure of Christianity*

As Ouida tells us in the quotation above, hate, not love, is the ruling passion of Christianity. First it teaches hatred of all other religions. Then it fashions a God, Himself so full of hatred, that hate to his subjects seems the norm.

The sectarianism, bigotry, and parochialism of Christianity are synonyms of hate. Disputes over what is authentic baptism have upset Christianity for years. Racial and sexual prejudice is still rampant in some churches. Agreeing with how to deal with mixed marriages, homosexuals, and married priests keep factions at loggerheads. Satan, the personification of hate, is the most popular figure in Christian literature. Jesus seemed to delight in his references to the denizens of nether-nether land. Christianity is the enemy of much that is worthwhile in our lives: love, compassion, empathy, candor, and education.

The world has become too dangerous a place for us to let it wallow in hate. We must dethrone all gods, take our destinies in our own hands, eliminate contrived differences, and cooperate to reach our common goals. We must convince ourselves that the problems that face us are not beyond human comprehension and solution. When the world becomes divided into irreconcilably armed camps bent on mutual destruction, it will be too late. Something must be done now. The battle against the forces of irrationality must be won. To lose is unthinkable.

77

> And almost every one when age, / Disease or sorrows strike him,
> Inclines to think there is a God / Or something very like Him.
>
> Arthur Hugh Clough (1819-1861)
Dipsychus

This "in extremis" conversion pattern has been a refrain of religionists throughout history. There is only one thing wrong with it. It does not square with the facts. They cannot cite statistics to prove their contention for the simple reason that such statistics do not exist. Most nonbelievers at the time of their death behave like Tolstoy, who threw the priest who came to administer extreme unction out of the room in the train station where he died.

Another of their commonly cited fictions is that there are no atheists in foxholes. This, too, is not borne out by any kind of investigation. Believers have all kinds of fictitious aphorisms to persuade others that their flimsy allegations have wide acceptance. They do their cause more harm than good by reciting them.

Dr. Mark Geier, quoted in *The Search for Meaning* by Phillip L. Berman, speaks plainly: "Those who believe in God... as a single entity that reflects the shape of mankind... to me they belong in The Flat Earth Society." Those who make good members of The Flat Earth Society are those who accept unreflectively all of whatever baseless system of organized superstitions that are offered to them.

78

> It is necessary to assail the towering superstitions of the day, painfully necessary, not only because they are absurd, but because they are immoral, because they tend to degrade mankind and to brutalize him.
>
> Felix Adler (1851-1937)
"The Chosen People"

To be superstitious is to believe certain relationships for which there is no evidence. Anecdotal confirmations are not evidence, unless, of course, the anecdotes are verified in numbers that far surpass other anecdotes that refute them. If in nearly every instance where a black cat is seen to cross a person's path, a horrible accident happens to that person, immediately we become believers: Black cats are bad luck! Of course no such overwhelming anecdotal evidence is forthcoming. Path-crossing black cats, sneezing without an immediate "bless you," *salud*, or *gezundheit*, walking under ladders, having an office on the thirteenth floor, accepting a third light on a match, etc., etc., are equally free of dire consequences.

In the pages of this book the reader has come across the epithet organized superstitions" as identical to "orthodox religions." The expression is unfair only if those who object to it can point out verified confirmations for the many proclamations of religion. If, after many years of observing religions and their practitioners, one has never seen the slightest proof for any of religion's basic presumptions, he has every right to express his opinion of religion in such manner.

79

One may no more live in the world without picking up the moral prejudices of the world than one will be able to go to hell without perspiring.

H.L. Mencken (1880-1956)

Only one year remained before my graduation from the University of Minnesota when F.D.R. permitted students to spend three summer months in the CCCs to help earn their way through. In a camp near Two Harbors, Minnesota, I spent a delightful three months, but found myself among seasoned CCC boys who turned the King's English into Satan's sacrilege. Never before or never since have I heard so few respectable words squeezed in among so many vulgarities. And I guarantee you, dear reader, you cannot begin to imagine the tenor of those words. I have always prided myself on my gift for invention, but they outdid me - every one.

I was in training to be a teacher and could not afford to pick up anomalous language habits, so I was on guard every minute. But before my three months were up, my own spoken sentences were interspersed with many of those same forbidden words. Mencken has it right. A person cannot help picking up the indiscretions of the environment in which he lives, be they moral prejudices or whatever.

80

> Let us start a new religion with one commandment "Enjoy thyself."
> Israel Zangwill (1864-1926) - *Children of the Ghetto*

Jules Renard said in his *Journal*: "We are in the world to laugh. In purgatory or hell we shall no longer be able to do so and in heaven it would not be proper."

The hedonist says that pleasure (or happiness) is the chief good in life. The altruist speaks of "the greatest good for the greatest numbers." There is no reason the altruist and the hedonist cannot be one and the same person. Happy indeed is the man who enjoys his work and becomes in it a reasonably temperate workaholic.

People are most likely to be unhappy when they find that for protracted periods of time they have had no chance to be useful. Especially, they want to think of themselves as serving in ways that not many others can. I doubt that Thomas Edison was ever unhappy when in his laboratories inventing things to increase the well being of present and future generations.

For reasons hard to explain, there evolves a class of religious fanatics who believe that to enjoy life is inherently sinful. The formula for a sin-free populace is simple: Find out what it is in the lives people live that makes them cheerful, and then deny them access to that particular ecstasy stimulant forever. The "burdensome sin" that our clergy instills in the minds of their congregations penetrates them throughout, from their most profound thoughts to their idle reflections. God's elite are those with narrow minds - with horizons limited just enough to preclude doubt in His "sacred" words.

81

> The day will come, when the mystical generation of Jesus, by the Supreme Being as his father, in the womb of a virgin, will be classed with the fable of the generation of Minerva in the brain of Jupiter.
> Thomas Jefferson (1743-1826)
> Letter to Adams, April 17, 1823

J.E. Renan and H.E. Taine took a close look at the holy mess religion had become some hundred years ago and predicted it would all collapse within fifty years. It is even a bigger mess today.

By chance did any of you readers, too, notice some other-worldly voices arguing: "And also, Tom old boy, if I were you I'd be a little more careful about who is calling whose sacred postulations 'fable.' We ancient Romans are as sensitive about Minerva origins as you Christians seem to be about Jesus."

82

To begin with clear and self-evident principles, to advance by timorous and sure steps, to review frequently our conclusions and examine accurately all their consequences ... are the only methods by which we can ever hope to reach truth and attain a proper stability and certainty in our determinations.

David Hume (1711-1776)

Science is not all that new, is it? The basic method of science was first stated clearly more than two hundred years ago. If everyone had behaved according to this simple description of what constitutes sane behavior during all of these two hundred years since Hume wrote these words, the world today would not be filled with superstitions, whether individual or institutionally organized.

We would not be wearing or carrying amulets, talismans, yarmulkes, praying shawls, rosaries, or phylacteries. We would not have homes cluttered with censers, crucifixes, crèches, mezuzahs, menorahs, or relics of saints. We would not have churches bedecked with prayer rails, altars, sacring bells, prayer wheels, ciboriums, thuribles, pyxes, and talliths. We would not have our great orthodox religions scaring us, subjugating us, filling us with lies, and teaching us innumerable things that are not so. We would not have faith healing, possession exorcism, penitential flagellations, ritual dancing, animal sacrifices, devil worship, or witch covens. Such religious concepts as The Fall, Resurrection, transubstantiation, afflatus, heaven, hell, baptism, catechisms, confession, atonement eternal damnation, communion, reification, Immaculate Conception, papal infallibility, faith, reincarnation, and souls would long ago have disappeared.

Chapter III

Morals and Morale

83

Our morale (the state of our animation as a group, from dour to vivacious) and our morals (the state of our probity as individuals, from good to bad behavior) seem very different ideas. Spanish, however, gets along with one word for both. In this book we talk mostly about morality, without which the morale of most groups would be low.

When doubly endowed individuals, both moral and intelligent, accomplish something that advances human well being they are usually showered with rewards for their momentous contributions. They are rewarded, that is, if at the same time they do not threaten vested interests of local power-hungry mystagogues.

The quotations that introduce the brief essays in each of the nineteen chapters of *Religion on Trial* are, for the most part, the words of authors who recognize the baleful power of the fanaticism and superstitions of religion. They show their concern. The consequences of that concern is one of the themes of this book.

The truly moral person knows, of course, that he must not be left out of the equation. Unlike Simone Weil, he will not destroy himself in his zeal to help others. He understands, however, that in doing good for himself the concomitant good he does for others is the only good that outlives him. Whatever of the good he does that is not also of benefit to posterity is, in the long run, of little avail.

84

> Man is a credulous animal and must believe in something. In the absence of good grounds for belief, he will be satisfied with bad ones.
>
> Bertrand Russell (1872-1970)
> *Unpopular Essays*

To Russell, "credulous" is more than simply an adjective meaning "excessively willing to believe." To Russell, the credulous person is one who is not only willing to believe, but has an instinct or at least an innate proclivity to believe.

Instinct in the "lower" animals is quite obviously a strong force leading them to behave in predictable ways in many circumstances. Without such instinct, the Plaza de Toros would become obsolete overnight. What a bull does when confronted with a waving cape is almost as predictable as what a steel ball does when released on a smooth incline. But instinct, clearly operative in a child's first years, steadily loses its hold, according to behaviorists, and whether or not man has any real instinct for religion is by no means settled.

It is true that almost all primitive societies ever studied do seem to have formulated something resembling religion in their communities. But that may be because in the ancient past, not more than 200,000 years ago when Homo sapiens first roamed the earth, there was no developed science to explain the causes for many of the significant events that were occurring. With cause and effect so commonly the sequence in his experience, primitive man assumed quite logically that all events must have causes. When he could not see the causes, he invented them, and gods and the concomitant religions followed. Good sense, using the knowledge base he had, was enough. He needed no instinct to help him formulate religions. For him to believe as he did was quite logical, the only thing he could do.

Modern man, too, has no need of instincts to help him believe. Still ignorant of the methods of scientific thinking, most people resort to the same kind of mental processes primitive man found comforting. Many of the components of modern man's religions were handed down to him from these same primitive human beings.

The commonly repeated enigma about the jungle primitive, completely ignorant of modern civilization, finding a functioning pocket watch in his jungle area, fails to teach its most obvious lesson.

To infer a watchmaker is quite logical, of course, but certainly not one like *our* putative Divine Creator. If God created us, he certainly worked from a different brand of blueprint than that which guides a watchmaker.

We, the product of God's creation, are an assembly of redundancies (two lungs, two kidneys, two eyes, two brains) each so inadequately constructed that duplication is needed. We contain parts so susceptible to malfunction (gall bladders, uteruses, prostate glands) that at times we are found to be better off without them. We include in our construction completely useless parts (tonsils, adenoids, vestigial gills, tails, etc.). Because God is (as our religionists insist) perfect, we wonder about the creation story they try to impose upon us. The product of a perfect Creator would be perfect, never in need of alteration. The watchmaker will, as time passes, make better watches, with arm-movement winding, crystal timing, and with several alarm reminders. God, making only perfect beings, will not (could not) improve them with a more-adequate brain, more-efficient muscles, more-trouble-free knee joints.

The biological evolution that many religionists denounce is entirely compatible with the anomalies of today's plant and animal formation, but an omnipotent Superconstructor is not. The only logical explanation is that such a God does not exist. A watch presupposes a watchmaker. Nature, with its many contradictions, presupposes nothing of the kind. The only conceivable God is one who set evolution on its course as a fundamental principle of the universe and then left it to its own devices. So why, then, are "creation scientists" so adamantly determined to discredit biological evolution?

85

God has come only to make sure you fear him, so you will keep from sinning.

Moses (Exodus 20:20)

Job in 31:23 said: "The fear I have of God's punishment keeps me from doing bad things." Fear was the stratagem of slave masters to keep slaves in line. Fear is the motive that keeps employees working at jobs and for bosses they do not like. Fear is the deterrent that keeps may people from learning to fly, to ride a bicycle, to snorkel in coral reefs, to speak before audiences, to approach people openly, even to marry, to adopt children, or to love.

It is because preachers are completely aware of how effective is fear in directing people's behavior that they incorporate it into their sermons. Members of the congregation will not become sovereign, fully functioning, independent individuals unless they understand the consequences of the religious education that is being foisted upon them.

Any discipline that depends on fear to keep proponents in line is an abomination. Fear of hellfire and damnation warps children's minds. Fear of being unworthy of God's grace destroys self-esteem. The fear of change that religions instill in us stultifies our minds. Fear of ideas makes us functionally illiterate. We dare not read for fear of encountering ideas that contradict our own. While fear (according to Freud) is the principal formative factor of religion, we must reject fear and the religions it generates and look to a constant and all-encompassing brotherhood as the bonding interest that can save us.

86

The primary theoretical expression of the religious experience is myth.

Joachim Wach (1898-1955)
The Comparative Study of Religions

Today, many of us have become too sophisticated to allow the anecdotage of the doddering Methuselahs of history to influence us. Biography rather than mythology has become our religion. Movie stars, sports figures, authors, gang leaders, and scientists are our gods. As long as we are not led to imbue them with fairy lore, to caparison them with religious regalia, or to pay homage to them with holy rites and ceremonies in order to express our admiration, it all remains a delightful game. Modeling our lives on systems of innocuous myths does no harm unless we begin to take the myths seriously.

When we become so enamored of our new mythologies that we insist that others follow our example, we begin to do harm. We apotheosize our modern "heroes" and fawn over and flatter them excessively. It is often said that there is something innate in human beings that require us to create religions. The way we turn bigwigs and big wheels into gods, movie premiers into pageantry, and *People* magazines into Bibles gives credence to this contention. If human beings are to that extent slaves to inborn proclivities, our best hope is that we choose the most innocuous of such persuasions to serve us. Movie stars, etc. may be best.

But there are still a few of us for whom life without gods of any kind is a fascinating journey. We end our three score and ten certain that is has all been worthwhile. If we can count on some one of our endeavors as having contributed to making this a better world, we are satisfied. If we know that generations to come will find the world more enjoyable because of us, we are content.

87

> The first effect of existentialism is that it puts every man in possession of himself as he is, and places the entire responsibility for his existence on his own shoulders.
>
> Jean-Paul Sartre (1905-1980)
> *Choice in a World without God*

The world is as it is, not as freewheeling daydreamers or bleary-eyed mythmongers describe it as being. We must assume responsibility for ourselves and for all our fellow human beings as well. With a free will to act as we ourselves decide is best, we make our lives as pleasant and fruitful as possible, refusing to see virtue in immolation, suffering, or in dull, tedious, onerous occupations.

Not by ancient, effete, irrelevant rules, but by the consequences of what others and we ourselves do, we decide what is indecent and what is decent, what is wise and what is foolish, what is good and what is bad. We know that morality is not imposed from "out there" in some empyrean realm, but is here now, manifest in how we behave toward ourselves and toward others. What we do is best when it keeps people free, happy, satisfied with their lives, enjoying the company of others and generally finding each day meaningful. We are doing well when we keep superstitions, prejudice, bigotry, fanaticism, zealotry, jingoism, and hate at a minimum. Sympathy, empathy, love, kindness, and sincere concern will characterized our attitudes toward others, however different they may be from us. We will ask of those immersed in mysticism, spiritualism, astrology, alchemy, mythology, pseudosciences, and all other varieties of hokum only that they demonstrate honestly the base and consequences of their beliefs. We will confront ignorance calmly and do our best to eliminate it.

88

> Those who cannot remember the past are condemned to repeat it.
>
> Santayana (1863-1952)

Santayana, in his famous statement, was making a judgment about the past not commonly made. Past history, for him, was largely a record of man's folly. What we can gain from remembering it, therefore, is a future that is better. If we maintain an awareness of past misconceptions, miscalculations, and botched performances, we will not mindlessly repeat them. There is hope for the future only if we remember – and then forge ahead with new plans that lead to less ominous consequences, hopefully to a new and better world.

The past for many people, however, are those good old days that they would like to repeat. Nostalgia is a deceptive emotion. It filters out bad memories and retains only the good. We would not want to repeat days with washing machines we pump, kitchen stoves we cut wood for, lamp chimneys that blacken, Oleomargarine that must be stirred to give it color, outhouses that must be walked to at 30-below temperatures, libraries that six months of reading would exhaust almost everything worthwhile, five cents on Saturdays a child's allowance, a bank going bankrupt that took thirty-two dollars, all of a child's years of savings, and a university education earned at working for thirty-five cents an hour – all part of my own past.

89

> If Christ were here now, there is one thing he would not be – a Christian.
>
> Mark Twain (1835-1910)

Nor would Muhammad be a Muslim, nor Buddha a Buddhist, and maybe the same should be said of Confucius, Calvin, Luther, Wesley, Lao-tzu, Zoroaster, Joseph Smith, and Chuang-tzu. The religion of one millennium may be a very different religion in the next. Those with religious or political power, that is, often remake the religions in their countries to such an extent that the founders would not recognize them. They may improve the religions, but it is more than likely that they revamp them in ways to give power-hungry mystagogues and demagogues even more power.

Religious demagogues that seem on the verge of establishing a theocracy in many countries of the world have a stake in using religion to help them gain power. Many of the aspects of their religion are "refurbished" to serve their purposes. Children are brainwashed in new ways. Television testimonial programs, Bible hours, and religious pamphlets are all newly attuned to demagogic rule. Thinking is discouraged. Textbooks are rewritten. Knowledge is given new meaning. Editorialists are advised to give their newspaper columns a new slant. People are cleverly turned into subjects, slaves, and pawns.

90

> The surest way to lose the truth is to pretend that one already possesses it. The blind man who knows what he knows is almost sure to know very little.
>
> Gordon W. Allport
> *Becoming*

Knowing how little we know is the beginning of wisdom. The person who understands well that he knows very little of what might be useful to him will listen when his teachers and others speak. He will pay attention to what he reads, and will be a student all of his life.

I have never met an atheist who was not an avid reader of religious materials and glad to read all sides of the every religious subject. He does not have the fear that religious people have of facing the ideas of those who disagree with them. Since logic is on the side of the atheist, defense of his own convictions is no problem. Rather than denounce reason, he makes an ally of it and calls on it to help him explain whatever obscurity.

The gargantuan ignorance of many religionists can be accounted for only by the habit they acquired in their religious education to shut out all information that does not agree with what they already know. Their religious teachers make a point of listing for them which books they must not read. They will get no chance to read books written by the hundreds of authors quoted at the beginnings of the essays of *Religion on Trial*.

The education of many religionists will remain parochial, circumscribed, lacking in depth and comprehensiveness, totally inadequate for facing the modern world. Their companions must be others as simpleminded as themselves, for they would be lost in a milieu of erudition.

91

> What's past is prologue.
>
> Shakespeare (1564-1616)

Is it prologue to privation or prosperity, to regression or to reform? That which is past includes Spanish Inquisitions, Christian Crusades, Thirty-Year Wars, and unremitting enmity between Protestants and Catholics, Christians and Muslims, Sinhalese and Tamils, Jews and Arabs, Hindus and Sikhs, Shia and Sunni, Turks and Armenians, etc. If that which is past does not become prime mover of what becomes future, it is because perceptive human beings decide that it should not and must not do so.

Nietzsche tells us that it is often the events in our past that keep us in chains. An undue fixation on that which has already happened often keeps us immobile or reacting to false values. We must learn to recognize those elements of history that stultify our minds and instill in us prejudice and limit our sense of responsibility and deprive us of a will to direct our own destinies.

Nietzsche believed that taking history too seriously will disfigure, emasculate or betray us. Decadent cultural forms borrowed from the past turn us into fools. We become lazy, dishonest, cowardly, and easily swayed by false beliefs, both political and religious. We should embrace only those historical accounts that are plausible and that enable men to live and act freely and creatively and that serve to strengthen the foundations of the truly vital aspects of our culture.

92

> Prejudices, it is well known are most difficult to eradicate from the heart whose soil has never been loosened or fertilized by education; they grow there, firm as weeds among stones.
>
> Charlotte Brontë (1816-1855)
>
> *Jane Eyre*

We are disposed to label as "elitist" those who take it upon themselves to speak thus of others who have not had the good fortune of receiving formal education. But the sentiment continues in vogue and should be analyzed. Does prejudice array itself in the way that Brontë says it does?

Education, if worthy of the name, certainly teaches us that all people deserve equal consideration regardless of their ethnic origin, skin color, religion, or sexual orientation. If we can keep an open mind during such education, we probably learn also that most traits evaluated in statements of prejudice apply as much to one such group as they do to another; to the Asian as to the European, to the white as to the black, to the Hindu as to the Sikh, to the straight as to the gay. If our formal education in schools and our informal education in the home, in gangs, in clubs, etc., do not combine to assure enlightenment, Charlotte Brontë expresses a profound truth. She gives us an incentive to revise and expand our educational system so that it will teach, above all, the brotherhood of all members of the human species.

93

Most people make the mistake of thinking that religion is necessarily a good thing and fail to realize that many, if not most, religions are thoroughly bad.

W.R. Inge (1861-1954)
Dean of St. Pauls

Inge seems to imply that he could make the choice between "good" religions and "bad" ones. Let me guess, his religion belongs on the good side of the ledger. Since when is any kind of belief system good if it means living entirely according to someone else's cleverly formulated and patently unfounded persuasions?

Any body of organized superstitions that has nothing to do with the welfare of mankind is bad, period. The methodized nonsense taught in our churches serves only to turn man against man and disrupt the social cohesion necessary for a viable society. Not until we get rid of all religions can we hope to live in peace and harmony, with love the principal determinant of human felicity.

"How many evils have flowed from religions?" Lucretius the Roman poet asked before the Christian era began. And we might ask,

"How many more have been added in the two thousand years since Lucretius posed that question? Crusades, inquisitions, genocide, and wars are only the most conspicuous of the atrocities perpetrated in the name of religion. We hardly pick up a paper without reading news of a murder or mayhem defended because "God's plan for us" was thereby being served. In the name of religion, first humanity then language falls victim to wanton savagery.

According to Salman Rushdie, "André-Georges Malraux believed that the third millennium must be the age of religion." Rushdie demurred, "I would say rather that it must be the age of which we finally grow out of our need for religion." "Ojalá!" as they say in Spanish

94

> That life only is free which rules and suffices for itself.
> Edward George Bulwer-Lytton (1803-1873)
> English Novelist

A life that rules itself is not an adherent of any confining discipline. The free human being is not a member of any white supremacy society, black power group, secretly organized militia, or denominational church. He belongs to no organization that establishes rules proscribing moral, recreational, or occupational activities beneficial only to the members. Governmental, military, religious, and social organizations encourage freedoms only when they offer reasonably unfettered thinking and doing.

A life suffices for itself when it needs no guarantees of celestial rewards or afterlife to be satisfying. The self-sufficient human being lives unencumbered by the ascription of some kind of cosmic meaning to his life, satisfied to enjoy himself and to know he is contributing to the efforts to make the world a better place to live for all of its present and future inhabitants.

Freedom in a country like the United States is something we allow to slip away from us more often than it is something forcibly taken from us. We are completely at liberty to join or reject membership in any totalitarian organization. If we belong to religious organizations that dictate how we will spend our money, what books we will read, what movies and television programs we will watch, and what doctrines we will adhere to, we have only ourselves to blame. We are born free, as Joy Adamson says, and with any attention at all to what is happening to us we can stay that way. *Religion on Trial* may have given us all the advice we need to remain free. We need only understand it and take advantage of it.

95

> Orthodoxy means not thinking—not needing to think. Orthodoxy is unconsciousness.
>
> George Orwell (1903-1950)

The act of establishing an orthodoxy is that of putting together a complete program of rules, rites, and dogma, with nothing left out. There is no need for serious meditation or reflection on the part of anyone. Those persuaded to adhere to such an orthodoxy can relax, vegetate, slide through life plump, dumb, and delirious, to dress up slightly a common saying. Though they may need Sunday morning reinforcement, for the most part they can turn their heads to more pressing problems such as who hosts the bridge club this week, or where to go for their next vacation. Religion ceases to be a topic of conversation. As long as he gets paid enough to live comfortably, the preacher is content to perpetuate this state of affairs. He will take care of the God business. No need for his congregation to worry their pretty little heads about it. Life for everyone goes along in prescribed routines, with nothing disturbing the tranquillity.

One Christian sect has distributed eight million copies of a ninety-page booklet that elevates hate to pure psychopathic ecstasy. Its portrait is an enigmatic triptych: (1) *The Beast*, which is the papacy; (2) *The Mark of the Beast*, which is designating Sunday as the Sabbath; (3) *Armageddon*, which is horrific, selective, and imminent. We are asked to assign significance to that which has none and to conform to their elaborate superstitions by letting them scare the hell out of us. Ninety pages of unadulterated hogwash demonstrate what minds distorted by fanaticism are capable of.

96

> Theobold's parishioners would have been equally horrified at hearing the Christian religion doubted, as at seeing it practiced.
>
> Samuel Butler (1835-1902)
> *The Way of All Flesh*

Knowing which Christian religion we are talking about makes a difference. There are Christians for whom a Christian life means unremitting drudgery. Dancing, card games, drinking, smoking, and public petting are all forbidden. Even laughing is suspect. Other Christians permit all of these things in moderation and live fairly sensible lives. Almost no Christian sect, however, permits doubt about the Divinity of Jesus, the Trinity, and the Resurrection. The Unitarian-Universalists are exceptions, relaxed about even these inflexible dogmas.

Many Christians would not miss a Sunday at Church for anything in the world. They listen Sunday after Sunday to all the taboos they are supposed to be avoiding, then leave the church and forget everything. They swear like troopers, tell racial jokes, hate homosexuals, do not say grace at meals, and perpetrate all manner of shady business deals. Church for them serves a very different purpose than it does for the seriously devout. From appearances alone, it is not easy to distinguish the genuinely from the speciously pious.

97

> The Jesus of Nazareth who came forward publicly as the Messiah, who preached the epic of the kingdom of God, who founded the kingdom of Heaven on earth, and died to give his work its final consecration, never had any existence.
>
> Albert Schweitzer (1875-1965)
> *The Quest of the Historical Jesus*

The Jesus who was not long on patience, no great shakes as a prophet, not a great intellect (nothing compared to Socrates, Plato, or Aristotle), the Jesus who demands of his followers mindless obedience and conformity, who asks them to suppress feelings, desires and emotions, to forgo questions and critical examination, to become like children (who will believe almost anything), *that* man *did* exist.

Jesus believed, as did almost everyone else at the time, that David was the author of all of the Psalms. Today's psychologists would say that he burdened his followers with a sure-fire formula for producing all manner of neurotic disturbances. It is this down-to-earth human being who could believe in hell and demons, condemn "the goats" to everlasting fire, send innocent Gadarine swine to drown in the sea, curse a perfectly harmless fig tree, talk in riddles, approve improvidence, abhor knowledge, predict imminent world disaster, and express contempt for familial unity. With at least as much satisfaction as those in heaven have when looking down upon their neighbors frying in hell, Jesus asks that his enemies be brought and slain before him (Luke 19:27).

Jesus was also a man who had a message for mankind. We would do well to heed it.

Then what should we do about Christmas? We have already done it. If we have a Washington day, a Lincoln day, a Martin Luther King day, why not a Jesus day as well?

If we define canonization as simply acknowledging that certain persons of history were preeminent, perhaps a step above all the other outstanding men of recorded times, we do well to reserve a day to pay them special homage. All four (Washington, Lincoln, King, Jr., and Jesus) were worthy of being remembered. But there is no excuse for us to become dotty in our encomiums. These four prodigiously gifted men will serve far better as examples to strive to equal if we agree all were mortal, fallible, human beings - all with egos, exalted self-esteem, and foibles. That is to say, all were human and understandably at times less than perfect. We will recognize their extraordinary character, but still consider them within reach of emulation by anyone who would like to be similarly respected.

98

> Souls may be placed in the same category as unicorns and mermaids, Cyclops and Cerberus, the whangdoodle and the whifflebird.
>
> Chester Dolan
> *Blind Faith*

In the *Search for the Soul*, the editors of Time-Life Books tell us how the soul fared in various philosophies: "Plato declares that the soul, not the body, forms the real or true person." Socrates phrases it, "Either man is nothing at all, or if something, he turns out to be nothing else than the soul." Plato argues for a three-part soul (the parts rarely harmonious): a rational element (reason) and two irrational elements (the spirited part and the bodily appetites). Both Plato and Socrates opted for an immortal and immaterial soul. Both believed in reincarnation.

The mature Aristotle abandoned most of Plato's metaphysics and considered the soul not to be a separate entity. It was "the animating form of a living body," like "the captain of a ship." He assured his followers that "there is no eternal life... and no reincarnation." The Buddha claimed the soul as no more than the totality of human desire. He, too, did not believe in reincarnation.

Descartes in his *Discourse on Method* (1637) spells out his Cartesian dualism: "Reality consists of two kinds of substances, mental (the soul) and physical. The mental has no spatial extension and is not measurable. The physical is extended in space and is measurable by geometry."

George Santayana, in recent times (circa 1948) asks: "If we are born of nothingness, should not death only mark our return to the void?"

Morris R. Cohen described the soul as metaphor, "a fruitful source of confusion if taken literally."

For further elucidation of the concept soul, see essay 388.

99

Every time in history that man has tried to turn crucified truth into coercive truth, he has betrayed the fundamental principle of Christianity.

Nicolas Berdyaer
Dostoevski

When religions try to implant their mythologies by force, we might interpret Berdyaer as saying in the boxed quotation, "they fail as religions." If ever we have a religion that really serves mankind, it will be a natural religion without supernatural entities. It will be a kind of natural morality with doctrines that do nothing more than try to bind people together with love, human decency, and respect for life. It will have little need for pageantry. Its hymns of praise will be praise for ourselves when we live in peace, serenely, with no thought of coercion of any kind. Its sermons will be practical lessons in how to eliminate frictions in human behavior. Its prayers will be quiet meditations taking stock of ourselves and how we are doing as fathers, mothers, offspring, co-workers, and friends. Its pledges of allegiance will be pledges to all citizens of the world, saying that all are deserving of shelter and food and the right to live without fear. Its Bible will be a kind of expurgated Koran, without the Koran's overweening deity, its suppression of women, and its indulgence of slavery and xenophobia, but with its effort to be a detailed guide covering every aspect of cordial human relations.

Maybe if the Bible of this new natural religion were written clearly enough and inclusive enough, and with benign forethought, this religion would need no meeting houses, pageantry, or demands on our time. The Bible, constantly updated, would be the religion's only formality, an emblem for a global community, with all of its citizens kings.

100

We Americans must now throw off our childishness and parochialism and create a new idea of man acceptable to thinking people the world over.

Agnes Meyer (1887-1970)
Education for a New Morality

Jesus asks us to be like children. Agnes Meyer asks us to throw off our childishness. Which gives us the best advice? The answer seems obvious. With a world population that no longer matures beyond unfledged naïve childhood, societies would degenerate into human masses of hopeless mediocrity.

Some church leaders divide their administrations into smaller and smaller units, into autonomous parishes where the people all begin to think alike. Agnes Meyer deplores this regression to parochialism. Again, she is the one who gives us the most enlightening message: We will progress only insofar as we become independently thinking individuals, all contributing to a viable global community.

With people the world over thinking, really thinking, we may "create a new idea of man." That man, we hope, will end our submission to mysticism. He will plan a new world in which each human being gets the education he needs to help the world advance toward sanity. He will learn to think like a mature adult with a view broad enough to encompass the entire world. Kant's "categorical imperative" will be his guide: "The behavior of the individual should be governed only by principles that can be applied across-the-board, to govern the behavior of all people."

101

> If I wake up on a fine summer morning, feeling exceptionally well and high spirited, it does not follow [as Robert Browning said] that God's in his heaven and all's right with the world. But it is precisely on such rationalizations that reason leads men, by inexorable logic, into...quagmires of error...
>
> Aldous Huxley (1894-1963)
> *Texts and Pretexts*

Robert Browning is not unique in this respect. We today revere with the same religious fervor our sports heroes and movie stars. We make saints of persons of exalted character, and we worship them exactly as we do gods. We deify Socrates, Einstein, a Jewish prophet, his mother, and even venerate relics supposedly associated with such persons, regarding them as holy, sacred, or sacrosanct. Throughout history, for reasons of fear, desire, or cause-effect persuasions, with what may seem almost an instinct for doing so, man has invented gods.

It lightnings, and we invent a god of lightning. The prairie or forest bursts into flame; a disgruntled god of fire is to blame. Rain, rain gods; volcanic eruption, a god of volcanoes; the earth quakes, and of course a god of earthquakes must be appeased.

Even today, the truth is that each believer fashions his own personal God, and there are as many gods as there are believers. And why not? There is no reason we cannot live with any gods anyone might want to throw into the hopper. If we do not take our apotheosizing seriously, all of us, dream-gods and people, can live together in peace.

102

> It is prudent to believe in God's existence, since little can be lost if there is no God, and eternal happiness can be gained if there is one.
>
> Blaise Pascal (1623-1662)

"Pascal's Wager," which he lifted from Islamic speculations, is expressed in capsule form in the above boxed quotation. We see, especially, Pascal's muffed opportunity to point out the difference between what *only seems to be* and what *is* truth and reality. Pascal, it seems, would have us believe in a god so stupid that He is unable to weigh the relative merits of reasonable doubt and unreasonable belief. As is so often the case, the gods we create seem to have less intelligence than we the creators.

Why must we limit our betting options? If I were to bet on the existence of God, it certainly would not be Pascal's eternal-pleasure / eternal-pain God, a God that fabricates a hell in which all who do not show Him servile obeisance will burn in brimstone forever.

As more and more people accept Pascal's "prudent" as a guide for conduct, the stranglehold of religion over mankind becomes tighter, and the citizens of the world accede to becoming subjects in an inflexible theocracy. Religion leaders become dictators over a populace willing to waive all logic or rationality, willing to relinquish its right to think.

The very fact that Pascal could consider making his wager is disheartening, showing as it does that "religion" maintains its hold over minds of people everywhere - even over minds otherwise accustomed to avoiding the kind of fallacy and superficiality that permits belief where there is no evidence for belief.

103

> Most people seek in life occasions for persisting in their opinions rather than for educating themselves... It seems as if the mind enjoys nothing more than sinking deeper into error.
>
> André Gide (1869-1951)
> *Pretexts*

The explanation for people's resistance to change may begin with a bit of Jesuit hubris: "Give me the child till he is seven, and I will give you the man." Those seven-year-olds, the implication is, will forever be seeking in life "occasions for persisting in their opinions."

Any orthodox religion would be proud to find that theirs is the kind of education that can lead to a Charles Robinson, 13-year-old ordained preacher in Chattanooga, Tennessee. He watches no TV, is home-schooled, and reads only "Christian" books. His congregation obviously has immature minds equal to that of their preacher. They go to church on Sunday mornings asking a childish, cramped mentality that knows nothing of the ways of the world to guide them.

A liberal education for them would be futile. They already know everything important that they will ever need to know. They do not understand Gide's "sinking deeper into error," for they do not realize that their childhood whimsies are yearly becoming more and more deeply ingrained.

We understand, too, why Paul Kurtz is so adamantly opposed to children being indoctrinated into set forms and procedures, traditional rituals, before they reach the age of reason. Study the lives of great thinkers and writers, and you will find people that the Jesuits never got hold of. They enjoyed latitude in their own childhood behavior and saw to it that their children, too, were not dispossessed of self-esteem and therefore became confident that they had the abilities to become whatever it turned out they wanted to become. They set their sights firmly, and with patience and perseverance moved toward their goals, enjoying the journey every step of the way.

104

> Religions tend to disappear with man's good fortunes.
>
> Raymond Queneau (1903-1976)
> *Une Histoire Modele*

The more wealth a man has accumulated, the more he finds religion an impediment in his struggle to acquire power. Religion, after all, denies that it was developed to help the rich man. If it ever has a worthy raison d'être, it must be to encourage an egalitarian society, with the poor man equally capacitated to make his contribution to human progress. Each and every person wants and deserves his place generally in the scheme of life's many low- and high-ranking dramas. If democracy has a meaning, it surely means a society with everyone governing.

For religion to disappear is commendable. But we want it to go for valid reasons. Religion, which has turned out to be mostly a system of mythology and deceit, cannot be a part of honorable societies. The human being must be making decisions on the basis of honest, well-founded data, not pie-in-the-sky wishful thinking that exists only in capricious imaginations. Life is not a game without rules.

Even the cosmos puts limits on our activities. We cannot build a house on the sun or stand naked on the moon. We cannot travel faster than the speed of light and return on the previous night (as the Limerick goes). We cannot communicate with entities that do not exist, nor is saying a thing is so enough for making it so. Words have power, but not that much power.

No one who has ever thought the matter through will choose to live his life governed by nonsense - by the dictates of people who cannot tell the difference between real events and a world of unalleviated sham. Easy it is to say but difficult it is to do: Man must learn to reject all nonsense!

105

No man's religion ever survives his morals.

Robert South (1634-1716)
English Clergyman

The Elmer Gantrys, Jimmy Swaggarts, Jim Bakkers, Oral Roberts, Priest pedophiles, and hate-filled Jerry Falwells and Pat Robertsons all lose their clout. Preachers who restrict membership of their church only to those who share their own particular prejudices usually cause the church to lose members. A patronizing attitude on the part of preachers may also cause some members to leave when the prestige of the preachers wanes. When whisky priests cannot stay out of the communion wine and become hopelessly addicted, they are quietly asked to leave. When the Catholic Church keeps its priesthood celibate and finds priests scarce, their bigoted prejudice against ordaining half the eligible members of the world population, is a form of moronic self-destructioin.

When a church loses its vision of a peaceful and joyful future for mankind, and forgets that unity, morality, equality, freedom, and decent living conditions for all people are its legitimate goals, that church may fade away. When the accumulation of wealth, the imposition of fairy tales, and hatred of enemies becomes the essence of religions, members loose interest and leave. If membership in a church falls off markedly for any of these reasons, the elders of the church may discharge the preacher or vote to close down. The last thing it occurs to them to do is to rethink their position.

106

Religion is the venereal disease of mankind.

Henri de Montherlant (1896-1972)

When religion is not being described variously as mother's milk, moral rectitude, or the illuminated path, other terms are found to define it more realistically - as an obstacle to human welfare or an impediment to human fulfillment. Mao Tse-tung called it an opiate. Oscar Wilde called it a substitute for belief. Schopenhauer thought of it as carefully planned animal training (man the animal). William James called it a treatise on human egotism.

We think of the hate religion engenders, the fanaticism it breeds, the debilitating fear, dependency, sense of insignificance, and stultification it instills. We see the witch hunting, crusades, inquisitions, human sacrifices, satanic cults, ritualistic stupidities, superstitions, dogma, prejudice, massacres, genocide, and wars perpetuated in its name. We also see the part it plays in obstructing reason, science, and sane behavior. The list could go on and on.

When Montherlant called religion "the venereal disease of mankind," he is not exaggerating. We will not return to sanity, peace, and fruitful lives until we rid ourselves of those aspects of religion that are pure inventions of human minds.

107

In the beginning there was no word. The beginning was Matter and Motion.

Philip Wylie (1902-1971)
The Magic Animal

Later, much later it was, a new epoch arrived when there was an animal that could use words. "The first word was not 'God' but 'Fraud'," Wylie said. "The first word became the saints and demons, the angels and fiends, the endless phantom-gods men cling to with intense, high-wrought emotion."

New assumptions converted into doctrines "included a soul, an afterlife, and mysteries beyond human understanding." The new religion that was the result, Wylie said, was "more important than honesty, realism, logic, truth, plain common sense, or even sanity." It all evolved in a manner to defend the essential lie about immortality in a realm beyond death.

Some parents refuse to observe the tradition of Santa Claus, believing that lying to them is a deplorable way to bring up children. Then these children are taken to Sunday Schools where the lies they are taught destroy any hope that they might someday live in a tranquil world of truth and reality. They mistrust the adults who never fully explain to them the demons, devils, fall of man, hell, and Armageddon that are talked about. No one explains why they are the sinners they are said to be. If they are alert, they sense the expurgations and evasions that occur when Sunday School teachers read to them from and talk to them about the Bible. The prevailing atmosphere of deceit seeps into their consciousness and can do a great deal of harm.

108

It's funny the way most people love the dead. Once you are dead, you are made for life.

Jimi Hendrix
Rolling Stone

We read constantly of some new comical epitaph someone discovered at a cemetery. "See, I told you I was sick," and so on. Using Hendrix' words, we have another possibility:

Ah, how peaceful!
I've got it made for life.

I would use it for my own epitaph, but: "Anyone who thinks he will put me in a grave with a carved stone on top of it, wasting land that could be put to good use, has another think coming. He will do it over my dead body."

To speak glowingly of a dead man who is deserving only of recriminations is like turning him into a saint without canonization. But to speak ill of anyone who cannot talk back is also reprehensible. Condemning with faint praise is the commonly accepted happy medium.

If love of the dead sometimes seems hypocritical, what are we to think about love of a God who does not exist? He may be our own tyrannical God who carries on in the malevolent manner described in the Bible.

Let us have just one more Manhattan Project. We will get together all the best minds from all over the world and together they will fashion a Deity who is really worth worshiping. They will make a God concordant with what Karl Popper considered inexorably essential to any philosophy concerned with the health and serenity of all the earth's creatures. "To minimize avoidable suffering" was

Popper's categorical imperative. With a new God so inclined, there will be an end to all the premeditated cruelty described in essays 61, 268, and 291. How much fun we will have with a God who truly wishes us well and teaches us to live together in harmony.

109

Life is an end in itself, and the only question as to whether it is worth living is whether you have enough of it.

> Oliver Wendell Holmes, Jr. (1841-1935)
> Speech to Bar Association: Boston, Mass

For those of us who never seem to get done all we schedule for ourselves each day, obviously we do not get enough of it. For those of us who are concerned that we may not live long enough to finish the projects we have in mind yet to do, obviously we do not get enough of it

Bergen Evans, when he was still a young man said publicly that he could not imagine anyone wanting to repeat their sojourn on this planet. He personally had had enough. At least when he died, he would accept the event gracefully, even with a sense of relief. A man with *his* intellect and *his* constant and many valuable contributions to society would not choose more of the same? Then why do so many of the rest of us find life enjoyable and would not mind if it ran on a few centuries more - other things (health, etc.), remaining the same.

The choice is a function of many factors, no doubt, and Holmes' "whether we feel we have had enough of it" sums them up. I can remember many unhappy moments in my life, but none that I could not say, "this too will pass" and know that soon again I would figure out how to solve my problems and resume an enjoyable life.

Suicide has never for a moment entered my mind, and until I am in great pain, a vegetable, and a burden to others, it never will. At the end, I would like to anchor myself at the bottom of a beautiful coral reef to give the carnivorous coral fishes a spell when they would not have to go far to seek food. It would be payment for when I was living on fifty cents a day, depending on them as my main source of food. Now there is a pleasant thought I am sure everyone will enjoy! No doubt I will have to settle for some second or third choice, or maybe I will have no choice at all.

110

> Nobody has ever ventured to describe a whole day in heaven, though
> plenty of people have described a day at the seaside.
>
> George Bernard Shaw (1856-1950)

The Koran comes close to describing a day in heaven, a day without strife or cares - but the Bible makes no such attempt. Catering slaves and subjugated women in the Koran's heaven are probably the luckiest ones. They at least have something left to fight for. It would be well if the NAACP, ACLU, and NOW could earmark some of their reform literature for Heaven. Hell will require more radical measures, I suppose.

No one has ever described adequately the various persons mentioned in the scriptures. Such descriptions are a case mostly of repeating traditional legends and fiction. If we cannot describe persons that probably had true historical existence, how silly it is to imagine that we could describe heaven, hell, angels, God, or Satan. Does Satan really have horns; angels, wings; heaven, a stream of milk and honey; hell, brimstone and fire? Does God have the form the Mormons and Church of God say He has? Anything we say is just words, no closer to truth than non-words—or what a chimpanzee might type out at random on a typewriter.

111

> Clinging to worthy standards, rather than chasing illusive goals, will
> serve to enhance our prospect of more fully enjoying the game we
> call life.
>
> James Day Hodgson
> Ambassador to Japan (1974-1977)

Illusive goals are legion. Whenever we indulge ourselves with formulations that make no use of our sense receptors, they appear. Their only "substance" is a structure that originates within and among the neurons, axons, synapses, and electro-chemical impulses that comprise autogenous brain activity. Our marvelous imaginations, the conscious part of this brain activity, give life much of its joy. But "enjoying the game" may elude us if imagination is not restrained. The mythology component of our theistic religions is one of the results of unrestrained imaginations. We postulate "mansions in the sky" populated with phantasms as varied as we like and fashion styles of reverence for these phantasms to suit our whims.

Our search for worthy standards in life's game is not difficult and does not evoke serious strife. We know, almost instinctively, what these standards are. We know, for example, that we must be honest in our dealings with fellow human beings. We praise others for their good deeds, and with kindness help them change course when we see them going astray. With our enlightened morality, punishment ceases to be a motive, and protecting society the only reason for keeping people in jail. We will not kill anyone without overwhelming reasons. Abortion and capital punishment will disappear. The golden rule will be our unwavering guide – and leaving people feel good about themselves our hope in every transaction.

112

We have stained more glass and hung more drapes and gilded more crosses and plated more chalices than any era of Christendom.

David Poling
The Last Years of the Church

Poling speaks of air conditioning and closed circuit television and imported bell towers and carved pulpits and authentic handcrafted pipe organs at $75,000 per. For a religion accustomed to such extravagance, the bank passbook becomes more important than the prayer book. They are as ready to fleece as feed the hungry, more prone to hoax than house the poor.

It seems hardly necessary to say that the extravagantly sumptuous basilicas and cathedrals of the world are symbols of material ostentation, not of spirituality. Tacked up on a closed side-street door of one such grand and glittering cathedral in Barcelona, Spain, I saw a professionally prepared poster condemning the United States for its extravagant moon-landing program. The poster had the imprimatur of a religious order, presumably one affiliated with the cathedral where the notice appeared. Those religions that can operate amidst one of the most lavish and fatuous examples of squandering human resources that man has ever contrived hardly have the right to find fault with some else's extravagance.

113

> God is the immemorial refuge of the incompetent... He will set them above their betters.
>
> H.L. Mencken (1880-1956)

It is easier to pray for it than work for it. And if prayers are really answered, those who pray will come out way ahead of those who work. In monasteries and convents, the day starts out with an hour of prayer. In some monasteries, four hours of each day are spent in communicating with God. Isn't there some kind of scientific experiment that could prove whether or not passing those hours in productive work would be better for all concerned? Has anyone ever tried to figure out how much monks and nuns add to the gross national product of the countries in which they reside?

Gregor Mendel is an example of what happens to a monk who really tries to do something worthwhile. Scientists who were successful in submitting their achievements to posterity despite suppression by their religions are Pasteur, Ampère, Galvani, Volta, Newton, and Galileo. The Bishop of Occam and Pierre Teilhard de Chardin also had their problems with religious authorities. Only the incompetent, it seems, can expect to live serenely. They are really God's chosen people.

114

> I believe in Spinoza's God, who revealed himself in the harmony of all being, not in the God who concerns himself with the fate and actions of men.
>
> Albert Einstein (1879-1955)
> Telegram in answer to a Bishop's question:
> Do you believe in God?

Because of the coercive atmosphere under which they were uttered, Einstein's words may need some interpreting. To me they say: "I am a dyed-in-the-wool atheist, but I would find it inconvenient to say so under the present circumstances." Joseph McCarthy seemed on the verge of succeeding in getting Einstein deported, and the answer to the Bishop was critical.

Spinoza's God is no God at all, as Charles Dibble explains in his book *When Half-Gods Go*: "Unless there is an effective relationship between God and the intelligible world, the idea of God is meaningless." A standoffish God (one who does not concern Himself with the fate and actions of man) is a contradiction.

The phrase "harmony of all being" in Einstein's telegram, I suppose, must include, among other things, the annihilation of our solar system in some five billion years that scientists predict, and even quasar explosions and the large stars that become supernovas, which probably obliterate a million worlds and destroy countless forms of life, some of them intelligent. Even if we consider only our own little corner of the universe with its earthquakes, hurricanes, volcanic eruptions, droughts, and floods, "harmony of all being" seems to be a strange choice of words to describe it.

115

Going to church doesn't make you a Christian any more than going to the garage makes you a car.

Laurence J. Peter

What will happen to a person who goes to church is impossible to predict. Each churchgoer responds differently to the stimuli he receives. One sees hypocrisy where another sees sincerity. One interprets as hatred and smugness what another sees as love and humility. One person seems to absorb Christianity by osmosis without reacting one way or another. One person may see faults in the church, and as an elder suggests improvements. Because of him, the church may become more responsive to the community of which it is a part.

The car analogy, of course, is a bit bizarre - unless you are a part of the television program *My Mother the Car*. What happened to Jerry Van Dyke's mother (Ann Southern), I suppose, eventually could happen to him, as well. Do talking cars run in the family? Some souls, it seems, seeking abodes for metempsychosis, will stoop to almost anything.

116

All the words of Jesus' sermons, so far as they are known, would not fill a sixty-page pamphlet, yet more than sixty thousand "Lives of Jesus" have been written. It is obvious that much of what has been written about Jesus can be classified as opinions or educated (and not-so-educated) guesses.

If all of us decide to follow the religion of Jesus, of course, we would all be Jews, for the religion of Jesus was Judaism. Just as some Muslims (the Sunni) accept four caliphs as rightful successors of Muhammad, and others (the Shia) only one (plus the Imam), so in Judaism some preach a coming messiah and others preach that he has already come (one of their own) and will come again. Sunni and Shia are all Muslims. "Has-come" and "will-come" theorists among the Jews could as well remain all Jews, with no need whatsoever for the name Christianity ever to have intervened.

Although Christianity began with St. Paul, Paul never used the word "Christianity." It was first used in the New Testament account of the Acts of the Apostles by the author of the Gospel According to Luke. Without Paul, there would almost certainly be no such thing as Christianity, but Luke gave it its name.

At another point in history, three centuries after Paul, Christianity again stood at the brink of threatened nonexistence. This time it was Constantine who gave it life. Mistakenly, he confused Jesus worship with sun worship, which was his own choice. Mithraism, an equally meritorious contender, was shut out.

117

Small fragments? The number of things about the universe that are still unexplained far exceeds the amount we do know about.

We do not know what is dark matter, which, it seems, makes up form 90 to 99 percent of the mass of the universe. We cannot explain much about the form in which our submicroscopic world really exists. String theory, which would unite quantum mechanics and general relativity, is one answer to what is the basic "matter" of the universe, but for most particle physicists string theory is still only rhapsodical speculation. We are also speculating, more than describing, when we talk about black holes and supernovas. The formation and disintegration of galaxies and stars are only vaguely understood.

We learn all the time, but in small increments compared to what is still left to be learned. When I was young we spoke of our nearest star, alpha Centauri. Then for years it was said to be a double star. Now it is "known" to be a triple star.

Reik is certainly right about the "supernatural," less a word than it is a subterfuge. Theologians nonchalantly toss such words around as if they were really saying something. What they do tell us is how gullible we are when we subscribe to their inexhaustible supply of senselessness.

118

Divine wisdom...has done well to cover with a veil the prospect of the life to come; for if our sight could clearly distinguish the opposite bank, who would remain on this tempestuous coast of time?

Madame de Staël (1766-1817)

French author

There are none of God's antics, as one person may describe them, for which someone else will not make excuses. Also, there are several explanations other than the one de Staël gives us for not rushing off to that "opposite bank."

First of all, a veil is not needed to keep us ignorant of what lies between ourselves and that which does not exist. What evidence is there that there is a "life to come" that we would see with all veils lifted? Second, what evidence do we have that there is such a thing as divine wisdom? Third, how can we be sure that "heaven" would be an improvement over our present abode? From what the Bible or Koran tell us about it, it sounds as if it would be an insufferably boring place to live. Madame de Staël seems to think otherwise. So she, too, has a pipeline to God? Fourth, why rush off? If, as some religionists have it, we will not make that trip to heaven until the day of last judgment, whether that be years or a millennium or two from now. We might as well wait it out here until a natural death ends our sojourn on earth as to wait in the cold, cold ground.

Evidently, Madame de Staël was having a bad time of it at the turn of the eighteenth-nineteenth century. I am not having a bad time, and would gladly prolong my stay here, even making the rounds a couple of more times if that were possible. Keep your heaven, to answer de Staël's question. I will remain here - gladly.

119

I have no objections to churches so long as they do not interfere with God's work.

Brooke Atkinson
Once Around the Sun

Meant to be satire, for those who never have taken it for granted that what churches do is God's work, Atkinson's quotation fails in its intended purpose. To be meaningful as straightforward talk, simple and direct, first we must determine whether there is such a thing as God's work, what it is if so, and whether there is a God doing work.

Atkinson seems to think he knows what God's work is but does not find it done in many of the churches. He is saying that churches, even if and when they try to do God's work, often do the exact opposite. They interfere.

Lenny Bruce, and many others, considers churches the last place to find God, and even many theologians deny that churches which preach bigotry, racism, hatred of homosexuals, etc., have meaningful rapport with God.

Emerson in his *Journals* also does not indicate much chance of finding God-talk in churches when he says, "If I should go out of the church each time I hear a false sentiment, I could never stay there five minutes." Annie Dillard in *Teaching a Stone to Talk* in an essay titled *An Expedition to the Pole* also shows little love for the churches. Her question: "Why do people in churches seem like cheerful, brainless tourists on a packaged tour of the absolute?" expresses her opinion of churches.

It is not surprising that churches, synagogues, mosques, temples, whatever they are called, do not acquire much favor among thinking people, who can see through their subterfuges. As long as religions continue to base their philosophies on myth, legends, and folklore that have never known real, honest worlds of sense perception, they must continue to be content to preach Emerson's "false sentiments" to Dillard's "brainless tourists." Religions, it seems, will never occupy the firm place in intelligent minds that theologians want them to.

120

Christianity preaches only servitude and dependence. Its spirit is so favorable to tyranny that it always profits by such a regime.

Jean-Jacques Rousseau (1712-1778)

Christianity owes its very existence to a tyrant who died at the age of thirty-one. The "great" Roman emperor, before he died in 337, had a vision in which the sun, which he worshipped, and Christ were identical. At that time in history, Christianity was in dire disfavor with the Roman Empire. Had not Constantine given it his blessing, it would in all likelihood have disappeared. It was Constantine who convened the council at which the Nicene Creed was born. As a king who murdered his way to power, Constantine was not exactly an ideal exemplar of goodness, probity, and pure life for Christians to follow.

It is obvious that Christians do not mind being subjects. At the time when they still called themselves Jews, they chose to give up their personal independence to one of their prophets and in increasing numbers embraced his teaching and obeyed his bidding. For reasons that are not clear, they began to ascribe divinity to this new leader, which later was interpreted as a father-son relationship, God being the father. Finally, they demoted themselves to the status of pawns, puppets on strings, manipulated by a mythical God. They seemed happy to unload their burdens and personal responsibilities and leave their problems for this God-Son duo to solve. Today, if their pastors can convince them that God is talking to them, they will do anything, including give up their lives, to obey God's commands.

121

> What a superstition it is which forbids people who really think to talk to one another on religious matters.
>
> Mark Rutherford (1831-1913)
> *Last Pages from a Journal*

Those who are content to live according to a hierarchy of superstitions differ mainly in one simply defined manner from those who are not: They are willing to believe other people's proclamations even when there is no evidence for believing them. Rutherford's word "superstition" is of the second-order variety, superstition about superstition. Religious mythology, too, is superstition. Rutherford might better have said, "What stupidity it is that prevents us from comparing our respective superstitions! Believing in either leprechauns or God is equally superstition because there is no more proof for the existence of one than for the other.

"Is"-"is not" arguing about religious matters is always frustrating. But talking about religions in the way we now are can be useful. The reluctance to talk about religion is not new. It was at one time taboo even to write the name Yahweh (Jahway; Jehovah) and include the vowels. Substitutes such as "Lord," "Providence," "the Deity," "the Almighty," "the Everlasting," and "the Creator" arose just to avoid saying the word God.

122

> We may safely say that the attempt to make the facts of history prove the truth or validity of Christian ethics is convincing only to those who are determined to be convinced beforehand.
>
> Morris R. Cohen (1880-1947)
> *Reason and Nature*

If Old and New Testament stories of Jesus, Noah, Jonah, Moses, and small and large arks, etc., were anything more than fiction, we would repeatedly be finding genuine archeological or paleontological specimens to substantiate their claims. Some who reflect upon such things say it must have been a large wooden ship and not a cross that Jesus dragged to Golgotha, judging by the number of relics it has produced.

The shroud of Turin was carbon-dated some thirteen hundred years too late to have been worn by Jesus. Traces of Noah's ark have never been authenticated. The covenant box and its stone contents left no traces. The behemoth, leviathan, giants, a rodent that chews its cud, or a fish that could serve as human habitation for three days are unknown among fossil remains. Talking animals, transubstantiation, planets stopping in their orbits, ladies turning into salt or having babies at 90 years of age are scientific impossibilities.

Scientists, too, must be wary of having preconceived ideas of what their various experiments and investigations will disclose. Double-blind studies were devised precisely to eliminate this tendency even of scientists to find what they are looking for. Whether scientists or religionists, we are all human and human beings often see what they want or expect to see. More than a thousand "authentic" visions of the Virgin Mary attest to that.

123

This bacon was cured at Lourdes.
                    Sign in a butcher shop window in Ireland.

When at Lourdes, General Max Weigand looked over the crutches piled up at the entrance and mused, "Not one wooden leg!" A faith healer who cannot convince his God to make a truncated leg whole, cannot convince Him of anything else either. The crutches discarded at Lourdes are not evidence that anything or anyone is cured at Lourdes. The best that can be expected of faith healers and faith healing spas is that they cure a few people of their credulity. Surely there are a few who will at last see through the obvious sham that bilks the public of billions of dollars every year.

Supermarkets in the United States dedicate one entire isle to "kosher" foods. A company I once worked for gave away a free turkey to every employee at Thanksgiving. Everyone, it seems, suddenly became a Jew. It was noticed that turkeys in the kosher pile were larger than those for gentiles. The rabbi had done more than just bless the turkeys he chose for his people. At last a logical reason for selecting kosher foods!

The rabbi, I assume, believes that whatever he does to food really does make it a better product for whoever eats it. He does not count on a placebo effect. It is fair to assume also that he does not believe that the consumer needs to know that what was done was actually done. Whether he knows or not, it is a better food for him to eat. Then why on earth doesn't the rabbi, without fanfare, just do it to all the food? Is it that he hates gentiles and would be glad to see them suffer the consequences of eating "unclean" food?

Harold Glicken, in an editorial on the Sunday Forum of the Long Beach Press Telegram (Sept 14, 1997), adds his confirmation: "The accredited rabbi would examine chickens for signs that they were kosher... If one was *treif* (unfit) it would be given to a gentile neighbor."

124

Even today one may come upon scenes in the streets of Mogador or Marrakesh which have the strangest outward resemblance to those recorded by the Synoptic Gospels.

Rudolf Otto (1869-1937)
The Idea of the Holy

Otto continues: "Holy Men...now and then make their appearance, each the center of a group of disciples, and about them the people come and go, listening to their sayings, looking at their miracles, observing how they live and what they do."

I have not the slightest doubt that with similar planning, similar chance concatenations of circumstances, similar luck in being followed in less than eighty years by "gospel" recorders and the extraordinary one-man phenomenon "Paul," and with some manner restricting today's communication media to their role two thousand years ago, another anointed one could arise from among them, as is said to have happened so long ago. In time, another "Christianity" could develop with all the hate, fanaticism, hypocrisy, bigotry, and intolerance of the splintered Christianity we already have.

Untold numbers of other religions have come into existence with even fewer legitimate motives than is the case with Christianity. As Aldous Huxley is quoted as saying in essay 101, exuberant emotion alone is enough to launch religions. The legalities and financial risks involved in starting a new religion are less by far than are those involved in starting a new business. Also, if things do not pan out, and failure is the outcome, the substantial consequences are less devastating for those who found religions. If the would-be preacher has not allowed himself to become too emotionally involved, he can "pick himself up, wipe himself off, and start all over again."

Chapter IV

Christian Credulity

125

Christianity is not treated gingerly in the quotations that comprise much of *Religion on Trial*. Most of the authors of the quotations that introduce the essays consider Christianity a complete negation of common sense and sound reason. It would be fine if Christianity were only that. We can live with nonsense. The world is full of it. But Christianity is different, especially when its adherents consider its operating procedures absolutely imperative for running the universe.

When a particular religion decides that it has all the answers and merits the favor of every human being on earth, it has begun its journey to world dominance. The second important phase is for it to become a monstrous moneymaking machine able to finance whatever undertaking might be a step toward success. Third and most crucial is that it have exceedingly prescient and capable leaders able to keep their gargantuan egos under control and with patience enough to see each project through to completion before starting the next.

Perhaps the best guess as to how Christianity will turn out is that, sooner or later the leaders, not as wise and patient as they need be, will overreach. Misjudging an audience different from their accustomed TV and church memberships, they will give their hand away before it is defensible - before people generally have become sufficiently brainwashed to accept their paths to paradise. For a long time yet, many people will not exchange their freedom for slavery no matter how alluringly the slavery is packaged.

126

It is no cynical joke, it is literally true, that the Christian churches would not recognize Christianity if they saw it.
Lincoln Stephens (1866-1936) – American Journalist

Christianity today is a far cry from the Christianity that emanated from the lips of Jesus. One need only read what are considered to be his words to know that that is true. Modern Christians have added folklore and hypocrisy that Jesus would not accept as his own. Of course, Jesus, too, did not always make sense and could be downright disappointing—as in Luke 19:27. The real Jesus was a man somewhat impatient, devious, credulous, and imperious. He was a poor prophet and capable of misguiding his followers, setting them up for neuroses or worse.

What the churches teach today and that becomes the Christianity of evangelical tirades from the television screen, is a kind of exaggerated mystical, devil-dependent, and thoroughly commercial religion. It is designed more to separate viewers and congregations from their money than to teach social cohesion and human probity.

There is another kind of idealized Christianity that for the most part does not reach the level of printed words. It in the value system we talk about in phrases such as, "Christian attitude" or "Christian behavior." This idealized Christianity we understand is as likely to be found in Judaism, Buddhism, Shintoism, Confucianism, Islam, or even in Atheism as it is in the religion that supposedly descended from the teaching of the Jew of Nazareth. It is this Christianity which "Christian churches would not recognize...if they saw it."

127

Theology is an attempt to explain a subject by men who do not understand it. The intent is not to tell the truth, but to satisfy the questioner.

Elbert Hubbard (1856-1915)
The Philistine

The sad part of the truth of what Hubbard says, is how easy it is to satisfy the questioner. The teachers in their respective theological schools cannot explain the subject because the subject is unexplainable. They teach their students not to try to explain it. They know, and their students learn, that there is no such thing as explaining mythology. The mythology serving as a basis for their theology must be taken on faith. The important lesson the students learn, therefore, is how to interpolate the word faith into any pretended explanation as unobtrusively and effectively as possible to make it appear to make sense.

The phrase "attempt to explain a subject" in Hubbard's quotation, we see, is an evasion. No attempt is being made to explain the subject, because such efforts as they well know, would be futile. The attempt on the part of the theological-school teacher, at best, is to make it seem as if he is seriously trying to explain a subject. He is in truth surreptitiously avoiding doing so.

To read the mythologies of Christian theological opinion is to be swayed this way and that by conflicting beliefs, faiths, dogmas, and creeds. Whether the authors are Graham, Barth, Niebuhr, Tillich, Pike, or any of the innumerable lesser-known gurus of history, each frantically searches for ways to be convincing, and all seem to search also for one or two other theologians with whom they can fully agree. None are successful in either search. Resolute Christian laymen reading such anthologies and eager to find answers to nagging questions are disappointed – especially if they hoped to be reborn in a promised land of Christian certainties. The same is true of books written for Jews, Hindus, Muslims, or members of any of the other theocentric belief systems. Although their books, too, presume to be guides for virtuous living, what they really teach is dissension and hate.

Even in those rare instances where the questioner suspects he is not being dealt with honestly, usually he does not object. He may feel that his revered prelate is in fact explaining the subject, but that he, the questioner, simply does not understand. More likely, he is aware that no explaining is being done because the best teacher in the world cannot explain the unexplainable. Either way, he sees that to push the interrogation further is to embarrass someone, himself or the "explainer," so he gives up. The truth, as well as sanity, suffers.

The "do not understand it" in Hubbard's quotation is another evasion, this time on the part of Elbert Hubbard. One cannot understand that which contains nothing to be understood, which is true of all mythology. The game is played out day after day, year after year, actually millennium after millennium. Now we start another, a thousand years more of attempting to explain the unexplainable.

128

The eleven o'clock hour on Sunday is the most segregated hour in American life.

James A. Pike
Obituary: September 19, 1969

The truth must be faced. There are a certain percentage of our churches that are sanctuaries for bigots of various points of view. Even when not explicitly designed as such, there are all-white churches, all-black churches, all-gay churches, all-straight-people churches, all-educated-people churches, all-underprivileged-people churches, all-rich-people churches, all-male churches, and all-female churches (sometimes within the same church). James A. Pike was one of those preachers who at a certain point in his life renounced them all. Later he came crawling back, probably for the same reason as Pierre Berton's one-of-the-boys pulpiteer: "I got into this God-racket boys because I found it the easiest way to make money." Better to be a hypocrite than a skeleton.

It is not piety that motivates most people to go to church as much as it is "the need to belong." Anatol Rapoport in his book *Operational Philosophy* says this is one of man's four invariant needs. In satisfying it we make ourselves human. Because most people will not extend the effort necessary to understand and associate with people different from themselves, they choose churches in which they find people like themselves. The "birds of a feather" adage operates among human beings as well. Very few preachers discourage the segregation that results, and what James A. Pike says becomes the rule.

129

Religion: a daughter of Hope and Fear, explaining to ignorance the nature of the unknowable.

Ambrose Bierce (1842-1914)
The Devil's Dictionary

To try to explain to ignorance is to preach continence to rabbits. It really doesn't matter much whether what we care trying to explain is knowable or unknowable. To Ignorance it is all the same. The ignorance manifests itself as much in the act of trying to explain as in the hope on the part of the listeners that they will understand. How can they be expected to understand that which is unknowable, indeed is devoid of substance to be known?

In place of "hope" Freud said "wishful thinking," but for both Freud and Bierce "fear" is the espousing companion in the origin of religion. Be careful of what you hope for (wish for), someone wisely said, you might get it. That is exactly what happened. As a breeding couple, hope and fear are an unhappy pair. The daughter (religion) that resulted from the mating is a continuing travesty that has captivated man's attention for millennia. We got what we wished for; we got a grotesque imitation of an edifying discipline. We did not get a philosophy to serve as a guide for sane human behavior. We wonder why we did not wish for something better.

130

In the very idea of miracles there is a contradiction which logic must either outlaw or be outlawed by. No event can be a miracle unless it is an event that is impossible, and in an effort to show that the impossible can happen logic must either destroy the notion or destroy itself. If we undertake to save logic, then the definition of miracles slides away from the strictly impossible toward the unusual and rare.

Barrows Dunham
Heroes and Heretics

"Miracle," except as hyperbole, is a nonsense word. An event is called a miracle, as the term is commonly understood, only if it has all three of the following characteristics: It is unusual, good, and "impossible." No one speaks of a miracle, no matter how inexplicable and desirable if it is an event that is occurring daily or at least fairly frequently. No one speaks of a miracle when the event is something undesirable, the unexpected death of a friend, for example in an accident that simply "could not" and "will never" happen again. And no one speaks of a miracle when an event, however desirable and rare it may be, is easily explained; its occurrence violates none of the known "laws" of nature.

"Supernatural happenings" (miracles) can be accepted as a legitimate concept only if "supernatural" is accepted. Miracle, that is, like all that is supernatural, is the name for an act of brain functioning related to nothing in the world outside of the brain itself. Is it not strange that many religionists, who tell us that God created the entire universe, find only in the interruptions in its laws, evidence of the existence of God?

131

Doesn't suicide seem a little like going where you haven't been invited?   Richard Eberhart
How It Is

That is not the only horror of suicide. The greatest horror resides in what you do to those you leave behind. G.K. Chesterton, with the humor that frequently emerged, said: "There are many who dare not kill themselves for fear of what the neighbors might say." Even that fear, if of consequence, relates to those the neighbors say it to, those who know and love you.

There is no doubt that there are times when suicide solves problems. One, certainly, is to end unbearable pain. Another might be that the cost to maintain you during a terminal illness is going to leave your spouse and children penniless. There are dozens of other imaginable reasons for suicide, but probably more often than not suicide is a despicable act of cowardice. For many people whose every whim has been indulged through years of immaturity, the prospect of fighting their way out of financial difficulties or the like is overwhelming. It is so much easier to pull a trigger, pop a few pills, or tie a plastic bag over the head.

But once done, there you are, your body that is, waiting for others to remove, weep over, and sometimes to feel guilty about. A funeral interrupts many lives, and is a sad remembrance for some. It usually means that a plot of ground is taken out of production, doing no good to anyone. If you are like many who kill themselves, you make no arrangements such as cremation, being dropped off at sea, or other means where the bother you cause is minimal and soon ends once and for all.

132

So, oft in theologic wars the disputants, I ween, / Rail on in utter ignorance of what each other mean / And prate about an Elephant not one of them has seen!

John Godfrey Saxe – *A Hindoo Fable*

Does the above verse sound familiar? If not, there is a good reason. It is the ninth and last verse of the famous poem about *The*

Blind Men and the Elephant. Almost invariably this verse is omitted in reproductions of the poem in books where the poem has appeared.

This is one more example of what religionists are capable of doing. Book burning, book banning, character assassination, lying, are not enough. They must also, where possible, eliminate every reference to good sense concerning the mythology of religion. They quote Mark Twain, Thomas Jefferson, Albert Einstein, Robert Frost, and others with artful selectivity in order to disguise the real opinions of these authors concerning the deceitfulness of religion.

Especially in those publications most likely to be read by people in general, good-sense about religion will not appear. Robert Cirino says in the extraordinary chapter "A Consumer's Viewpoint" of his *Power to Persuade*, "Counterbalance must exist in mass media in order to be effective both in influencing the performance of journalists and in giving people a real choice."

133

If the human race is to survive, it will have to change its ways of thinking in the next twenty-five years more than it has in the last twenty-five thousand.

Kenneth Boulding

But can we hope to solve our problems if we continue to depend on the same myopic mentalities that created the problems? There must be a drastic alteration of mind-set among those upon whom leadership devolves.

Unfortunately, change is as unpopular in many minds as is the epithet liberal in today's politics. The prevailing consensus seems to be that we are living in the best of all possible worlds and that preserving the status quo should be our passion.

To be labeled a liberal, one who sponsors change, now seems to be political suicide for those engaged in political campaigns. The disproportionate success of incumbents is one reflection of the conservatism in vogue. The reluctance of voters to accept term limits for all politicians is another. Our failure in reforming campaign financing is still another.

I doubt that anyone has assessed whether or not the improvements Kenneth Boulding suggests to save the human race were forthcoming. I do not doubt, however, that change has been considerable. Whether or not we are making exactly the changes necessary to save Homo sapiens is not at all apparent.

It is my own opinion that the human species will survive only if the changes envisaged include removing the stranglehold orthodox religions and nationalism have over our lives. If we do not do something to rid our societies of the prevailing hate and bigotry that keep us fighting wars all over the world, prospects are not good. At any moment, things could get out of hand. With possessions of weapons of mass destruction spreading, things get more and more critical. There will almost inevitably come a day when even terrorists will be able to get their hands on these weapons - especially in view of the fact that many terrorist individuals are sponsored by terrorist nations.

134

The ignorant are always prejudiced and the prejudiced are always ignorant.

Charles Victor Roman (1864-1934)
Science and Christian Ethics

Since ignorance means lacking knowledge, it seems obvious that the ignorant will be prejudgment prone. It follows also that prejudgment types (those who make judgments before they have adequate knowledge on which to base judgments) are ignorant. Though we usually distrust any pronouncements containing superlatives such as "always," in this case Roman is expressing a self-defined or apodictic statement, an axiom.

Roman is on the same wavelength as Charlotte Brontë who says in her inimitable style elsewhere in this book that uneducated people are much more likely to be prejudiced than those who are educated. Laurence J. Peter expresses doubt, wondering if education doesn't simply engender a *higher grade* of prejudice, exacerbating a problem that is already pandemic.

When Jacob Bronowski suggested that a man who has no education in science is certain to be in some measure a slave, he said exactly what Roman said years earlier. Science is knowledge. Without knowledge we are ignorant. And if we are ignorant all manner of prejudices may obtrude, making rational thinking impossible. We are likely to become a slave to the distorted "mind functioning" that colors whatever thought we may have. Both Roman and Bronowski are saying something very important. They ask those who are now making plans to improve our schools to listen to what they say.

135

> The urge to save humanity is almost always a falseface for the urge to rule it. Power is what all messiahs really seek, not the chance to serve.
>
> H.L. Mencken (1880-1956)
> *Minority Report*

Human ego has its place in the scheme of things. It sometimes impels us to undertake worthy projects. Form then on a balanced interest between self and others may take over and good works ensue. Speaking of ego, Alexander Pope says:

> [It] serves the virtuous mind to wake,
> As the small pebble stirs the peaceful lake.
> Friend, parent, neighbor, first it will embrace:
> His country next, and next all human race.

Mencken is concerned that the path may be very different. Ego translates to ambition, to the lust for power, the urge to dominate others, not to serve them. The egos of Albert Schweitzer and David Livingstone certainly led them to do good, but for many young missionaries today it does not. They do more harm than good, introducing into native societies abrasive customs and religions and an emotional discontent that few of them survive unscarred.

Insofar as man is gaining power over the external world, it is through science and not through religion. Science liberates the potential of nature. Religion too often suppresses the potential of men. The power that many ecclesiastics arrogate to themselves means the opposite for each of the individual members of the religious populations of the world. It is loss of power. It is dependence, helplessness, slavery for anyone who takes these ecclesiastics and their authoritarian pretenses seriously.

136

> Anyone who does not hate his father and mother, wife and children, brothers and sisters, yes and even his own life, cannot be My disciple.
>
> Jesus (Luke 14:26)

We find these words of Jesus so preposterous that we hope upon hope they are a mistranslation. But however may translations we look to, though a few words will be different, they all say essentially the same thing. If Jesus had had the opportunity to speak off the record (as modern politicians sometimes do) to a group of applicants for discipleship, we can imagine he might have spoken in that manner - but surely not for public consumption.

Jim Jones, David Koresh, and others of their ilk are recorded as having spoken words much worse than these to their flocks, but this, our Jesus, our paragon of the perfect man, how could it be? We sincerely believe that in our society family harmony is the firmest rock in its foundation. If all our families would stay together, play together, and love one another, we are sure most of the violence of this world would disappear. Was Jesus carried away by some contretemps of the moment or did he really have this kind of disdain for family unity?

137

> Verily I say unto you, there be some standing here shall not taste of death till they see the Son of man coming in his kingdom.
>
> Jesus (Matthew 16:28)

Robert G. Ballou in his book *The Nature of Religion* tells us of Smohalla, who founded the "Cult of Dreamers" among the Indian tribes living on the Columbia River in Washington and Oregon. Smohalla assured his tribesmen that the white men would be expelled by the Great Spirit whose spokesman he was.

Since the Christian Son-God and the "Dreamers" Founder made their unprophetic statements, there have been many self-styled prophets who have set new dates and gathered followers on a hilltop to await the hour.

Allah in the Koran assures the Muslims that they need not be concerned with the strength of their own military forces or that of their enemies because He would see to it that they would always be victorious in battle. After their many defeats at the hands of the Jews in Israel, some Muslims keep up their hopes by rewriting "would always be" to "would eventually be" and await the day. Allah even promised them He would send angels dressed in military uniforms to make sure they won. Defeats in Turkey, Egypt, and Algeria must be severely testing their credulity.

138

> The First Crusade [1096]...began with a massacre. "The men who took the cross," wrote [Lord John] Acton, "after receiving communion, heartily devoted the day to the extermination of the Jews..." They killed about ten thousand of them.
>
> Malcolm Hay
> *The Foot of Pride*

Some Christians berate the Jews for killing one Jew. Here the Christians killed ten thousand Jews and all in one day. Hitler, a "good Christian" (he seemed to think) killed six million more. The brutality of Christians throughout history is nothing they can be proud of. In the Spanish Inquisition and European and American witch-hunts, they account for more than 230,000 additional deaths. In early North America, heresy, among some Christians, was a capital crime.

For almost all religions, violence becomes official policy. Reciprocal killing is common among Hindus and Sikhs, Tamils and Sinhalese, Shia and Sunni, Jews and Muslims. In Ireland, there are still skirmishes between Catholics and Protestants. In the Sudan the killing is between Muslims and Christians. In Iran it is between Muslims and anyone else.

Can anyone read paragraph after paragraph describing how two great peoples, both Semites with similar nomadic origins, both espousing monotheistic religions, but both plotting and perpetrating the most horrible crimes man has ever devised to inflict on fellow human beings; can anyone, I ask, read the six hundred and more pages of *Oh, Jerusalem* by Dominique LaPierre and Larry Collins and not end up "knowing" that we must get rid of all the invidious elements of our "great religions" if we are to have peace? Reading Malcolm Hay's book should eliminate every vestige of doubt.

139

Democracy, if I understand it at all, is a society in which the unbeliever feels undisturbed and at home. If there were only half a dozen unbelievers in America, their well being would be a test of our democracy, their tranquility would be a proof.

E.B. White (1899-1985)
The New Yorker Feb 18, 1956

The bigoted efforts of those who would deny rights to atheists need moderating for their own good. Even if they were to accomplish their goals of silencing all those who do not think and believe as they do, not only those they silence but also they themselves would suffer. Fortunately, this will never happen. For every lie they tell, for every book they burn, for every man they silence a new truth, another book, and another undaunted Friedrich Nietzsche or Clarence Darrow will arise. Truth cannot forever be suppressed, and fanatical religions cannot forever enslave the minds of humankind.

If the day should come when we no longer insist upon freedom *from*, as well as *for*, religions, that day democracy will have failed. The bigoted religious leaders of the world will lead us into an all-encompassing, invincible theocracy from which there will be no escape

Those who "hate" make up a large fraction of our population. Those who hate irrationally make up exactly the same fraction. All hatred, whether of women, Negroes, homosexuals, or the members of any religion or easily identified nationals, is irrational.

Love, the sentiment that means affection, tenderness, warmth, and an unswerving loyalty to friends is everywhere in evidence. The preeminence of love assures us that hate will never shape us into predominantly hostile societies.

140

There is something indeed criminal in the lightheartedness with which people seek their pleasures amid the mounting injustices and abominations of modern life.

J.H. Holmes
The Sensible Man's View of Religion

Guayasamín, the world-famous Ecuadorian painter, was asked in a television interview if he was happy. "As happy, I suppose, as anyone has a right to be in a world with so much injustice," was more or less his reply. Siddhartha Gautama, the Buddha, set out in search of enlightenment by just this sober contemplation of the amount of misery and injustice in the world that would not permit him to live in peace. Guayasamín, Holmes, and the Buddha show the kind of compassion that makes the human being truly human.

"Moral indifference is the malady of the cultivated classes," said Henri-Frédéric Amiel more than a hundred years ago. I wonder what Amiel would think of drive-by shooting, car-jacking, and crimes against children today. Could he have even imagined a Hitler, Stalin, and Pol Pot? He must have been sure that before another hundred years had passed, the world would have solved the problem of war. Now we say that before the end of the next century such problems will surely be solved. Have we any more reason to be optimistic today?

141

The memory of my own suffering has prevented me from ever shadowing one young soul with the superstitions of the Christian Religion.

    Elizabeth Cady Stanton (1815-1902) – *Eighty Years and More*

To encumber any young person with Christianity is to do that person no favor. If he carries the burden for as much as four of five years, he may never be able to shake it off. For the rest of his life he is doomed to share the bigotry, prejudice, hubris, and hostility that a disproportionate number of Christians have in common. He may soon adhere to a system of organized superstitions that include the trinity, bodily resurrection, demon possession, transubstantiation, virgin birth, extreme unction, reification, sacred ground, holy water, faith healing, exorcism, etc., etc. Once he is a fully-fledged Christian, his mind will be so warped and wizened that he very likely will never again be able to think clearly about anything.

Elizabeth Cady Stanton, co-staring with Susan B. Anthony in the Woman Suffrage movement, was one of the greatest women in American history. She lived 87 years, every year actively fighting for women's rights. Every women on this continent owes her a great debt of gratitude. Her only serious misstep was a brief, misguided opposition to black suffrage three years after the civil war, which she felt would do harm to women's struggle for equality. She had fought hard every inch of the way for an end to slavery, and up to her lecture tour in Kansas in 1867, spoke equally for black and woman suffrage. Upon ratification of the fifteenth amendment in 1869, her brief disfavor with black suffrage was forgotten.

142

> The United States is not a Christian nation any more than it is a Jewish or a Muslim nation.
>
> George Washington (1732-1799)

On the two-hundredth anniversary of the Declaration of Independence, Jerry Falwell said in a sermon: "The idea [that] religion and politics don't mix was invented by the Devil to keep Christians from running their own country."

Washington, our first and always president, said the United States is not a Christian country. Jerry Falwell said it is. Since Jerry Falwell would not contradict our universally esteemed first president, then between the dates 1787 and 1976, it follows that "is not" transmogrified to become "is." Can Jerry Falwell tell us precisely what year the United State became a Christian nation?

Many of the citizens of the new United States when Washington made his statement were people who had fled religious persecution. They would not look favorably upon turning the country over to power-hungry fanatics of any one religion. The founding fathers knew this well and fashioned a constitution that recognized no favorites among religions. They could not be bought by the religious orthodoxy that had power even then.

There are several one-religion or largely one-religion countries in the world today, and they are all disasters. Muslim countries in the Middle East and North Africa, Catholic countries in Central and South America, Hindu India, Muslim Pakistan, communist Cuba are examples. Whenever one religion has ascendancy in a country, religious freedom disappears. Turkey has won freedom and is improving. Egypt, still officially secular, nevertheless makes no pretense of separation of mosque and state. Egypt is in no sense a democracy, and the Coptic Christians are discriminated against in all official matters. Anyone can build a mosque in Egypt, but to obtain the right to build a church is almost impossible. The United States gives Egypt 3.1 billion dollars a year, but that seems in no way to be moving the country in the direction of becoming a free society. Religious freedom in the world as a whole is long ways away.

143

> If reason be a gift of Heaven, and we can say as much of faith, heaven has certainly made us two gifts not only incompatible but in direct contradiction to each other. In order to solve the difficulty, we are compelled to say either that faith is a chimera or that reason is useless.
>
> Denis Diderot (1713-1784)
> French encyclopedist

Chimera is not exactly the right word. Fraud comes closer. "Faith" when used to cover up religion's impostures is deliberate. Chimera is an after-the-fact label that applies to that which appears wildly or fantastically visionary or unreal. It does not include the idea if deliberately deceiving others in order to camouflage the failures of a large group of people. "Faith" (in the mystical sense that religionists use the term) and "reason" are incompatible, the one denying the existence of the other.

Reason is indeed a gift, a highly prized gift, but unfortunately a gift that some people do not appreciate and therefore do not often use. If there is such a thing as a gene for reason, it functions adequately only in the presence of other genes that enhance its actions. It needs genes for aspiration, altruism, and goal-orientation to encourage it. In the presence of other genes for ill will, lethargy, and hostility that would inhibit its operation, it will be inoperable. Reason is not only useful, it is the indispensable faculty of mind for all human progress.

144

> If an angel appears to me, what is the proof that it is an angel; or, if I hear voices, who can prove that they proceed from heaven and not from hell, or from my own subconscious or some pathological condition? Who can prove that the voices are really addressed to me?
>
> Jean-Paul Sartre (1905-1980)

In his book *The Logic of the Sciences and the Humanities*, F.S.C. Northrop says of two such visions, "Nor does the former image come with a tag on it saying I am illusory, or the latter image come with a tag reading I am the image of a real, public, external animal. Both images are equally factual, the one as real, so far as pure empiricism can tell, as the other."

Man has no innate sense of compass direction as do pigeons, whales, elvers, salmon, turtles, and many other creatures. Neither does he have a sense of what is and what is not reality.

Few are aware, as were Sartre and Northrop, of how easy it is at times to get lost in worlds of fancy, to confuse visions whose origins are entirely within their own minds and those that have external reality.

145

> A large portion of the noblest and most valuable teaching has been the work of men...who knew and rejected the Christian faith.
>
> John Stuart Mill (1806-1873)

Eliminate the words "the Christian faith" and replace them with the word "religion" and you include most of the great scientists of all time in all parts of the world. Despite the drivel heard in contradiction in past years, science and religion are incompatible. They cannot exist together in a single, honest human mind. Science is knowledge. Religion is anti-knowledge. The scientist functions on the basis of facts and truth. The religionist functions in a world of myth and error.

Not only scientists, but all men with a passion for truth contribute to "the noblest and most valuable teaching" that Stuart Mill talks about. Our "great" religious universities make of truth a travesty. If the religionists have their way, we will become a nation awash in overwhelming absurdity, a nation of fools.

146

> Let any clergyman try to preach the truth from its very stronghold, the pulpit, and they would ride him out of his church on his own pulpit banister.
>
> Herman Melville (1819-1891)
> Letter to Nathaniel Hawthorne, 1851

To preach the truth, Melville knew more than a hundred years ago, would be to deny most of what clergymen have been saying in their sermons since churches were invented. It would destroy religion, because it would destroy mythology, the very foundation of all religion.

An unprovable statement is as much a lie as is one that tells the opposite of what is known to be true. To say, "God exists," is as much a lie as to say, "God told me to bet on Orange Blossom in the 4th at Santa Anita."

Even for a preacher to explain what he is doing when he uses the word faith would be enough to turn his entire congregation against him. With his newly discovered delight in speaking only the truth, he might become a new, changed human being, ready to fight for truth wherever it might take him.

A theologian, after the brainwashing of the seminary and a few years of presiding over a denominational religion, is more often than not destined for obscurity. Fortunately, there are exceptions.

A redeemable ex-preacher, while negotiating the convolutions of his own brain, may finally see himself as escaping the abode of the effete. He sees "reason," and braces himself for a radical change. He will never return to his days as a pawn, a robot content to defer to the dictates of self-styled spiritual guides or to a "sacred" compendium of "absolute truth."

147

> Though the only road to freedom be through the gates of death, those
> gates must be passed, for freedom is indispensable.
>
> Charlotte Brontë (1816-1855)

Joan of Arc, John Brown, Joseph Smith, Servetus, Jesus, Giordano Bruno, Jan Hus, and Mohandas Gandhi risked and lost their lives in their quest for freedom, and we admire them for doing so. But we find it difficult to compare human beings who value freedom that highly with other members of the same species who relinquish their precious freedoms so readily to the persuasions of religious demagogues.

The church begins its process of relieving us of our freedom at a tender age. The hatred engendered by sectarianism may be firmly implanted in children even before they begin to learn their ABCs. Religious instruction becomes carefully formulated method, designed to take advantage of children's still undeveloped intellectual discrimination in order to trap them as adherents of whatever nonsense. Sunday schools seek more and more effective ways to enslave the child's brain and condition him to be forever dependent.

But Charlotte Brontë goes too far. Deliberately including self-immolation in one's plans for attaining justice is usually self-defeating. Those who set themselves aflame in front of the capitol steps or starve themselves to death in the plaza, are more often than not written off as extreme fanatics or hopeless psychotics, and are soon forgotten. It is left to the living to fight their way through to success in attaining the reforms desired. Most people who kill themselves for a cause in the full bloom of a healthy life are incapable of imagining what a lifetime of speaking out, writing letters, or working for that cause could do. Suicide is too easy; it is cowardly, and it is thoughtless disrespect for friends and relatives who are left to grieve over a member of the group or family.

There is a place for suicide. One cannot help admiring Sarah Churchill in her own planned demise. For her, "attempted" suicide would be a farce and unacceptable. She planned well, left no doubts about the conclusion, and died painlessly and peacefully, improving the life of those who might have been left with years of onerous duties caring for her.

148

The true tests of the value of any man or woman (whatever their colour) are those who can serve best..., help most..., and sacrifice most.... They are the people who will be loved in life and honoured in death. All questions of colour [will be] swept away, [and]...free citizens shall meet on equal grounds.

Anne Wood Besant (1847-1933) – Wake Up India
Jawaharlal Nehru

Nehru, when he became the first Prime Minister of independent India in 1947, made it clear that he disapproved of the caste system in India. But that kind of reform does not happen by fiat. It happens, if at all, in the hearts of people. Of course, hearts sometimes need prodding.

It was not until the Untouchability Act of 1955 that effective steps were taken to get rid of the caste system. The act provided penalties to enforce provisions of the constitution that outlawed the practice of untouchability. Anne Besant helped establish a receptive atmosphere for reform when she made her plea for an egalitarian India years before. Her sincerity is clearly seen in the quotation above. Yet even today it is mainly the "untouchables" that are the downtrodden of India.

149

Truth in matters of religion is simply the opinion that has survived.

Oscar Wilde (1854-1900)

W.R. Inge, Dean of St. Pauls, said: "A religion succeeds not because it is true, but because it suits the worshipers." If opinion survives because it suits the worshipers, these two contemporaries (though Inge lived more than twice as long) say pretty much the same thing: Truth is what we want it to be. When we use the word truth to mean simply conformance between one set of symbols and another, it is an obscure term, not to be trusted.

Religionists would make of truth a vague something out there in metaphysical space that they particularly like to contemplate. They would be hard put to define it. Truth in religion becomes really "that which is comfortable." It is comfortable when they are sure it helps to preserve their comforting religion. The truth of religion will survive as long as the comforts of that religion are important enough to be defended.

"Truth," as the Preface of this book makes clear, cannot in its conventional acceptation be applied to religion. It cannot be applied to negative statements about existences whether in religion or any other field. It cannot be applied to positive statements about existences when such statements have no application except as might pertain to the realm of myth. To establish the truth of any statement is always to determine its predictive content - how many significant predictions made on the basis of the statement turn out to be true. This, Anatol Rapoport called the "criterion of predictability," a fundamental and paramount ingredient of all rational thinking. Truth as religionists use the term is something quite different. F.S.C. Northrop suggested that the truths of religion be called "comforts."

150

During the last century, man cast off the fetters of religion.
                                        Albert Camus (1913-1960)

Mencken in *Treatise on the Gods* says pretty much the same thing. But it is so obviously not true that we wonder why they say so. Religion is alive and well and not about to disappear. You can be sure that all the Christian sects in this country consider themselves the enlightened future of religion, in no way vanishing.

A hundred years ago, Renan and Taine analyzed the religion of their time and "knew" it could not last another fifty years. Throughout history intelligent men have observed the religion they grew up with and become embarrassed to think they had been so gullible. They and those trained in rational thinking (that is, our scientists) almost all reject organized religions.

Religion will not disappear. As long as there are people who enjoy being deceived and prefer to live in a make-believe world, religion will survive. As long as religion has at its disposal the vast sums of money now flowing into the coffers of the TV evangelists, religion will flourish. As long as there are the subjugated peoples of third world countries living in squalor and ignorance, any respite from their dreary lives is welcome. They will not give up religion. There will always be a certain proportion of childlike minds who believe the fairy tales of the mystagogues and see the prospect of rewards greater than those any seculaar regime can offer them.

151

In this case [medicine], it becomes literally true that no imposition is too great for the credulity of men.

Henry David Thoreau (1817-1862)
A Week on the Concord and Merrimack Rivers

Wait until he checks in on religion. The quackery there makes that of medicine or any other profession pale by comparison. The majority of our doctors are competent, and they do amazing things, giving me back vision in one eye, for example, with as much grace as serving afternoon tea. If someone were to devise a system of fair payment for all competent workers at all levels, most of the inequities and quackery in our professions and trades would disappear.

The exception is religion. Being competent in religion means ability to impose irrational beliefs on gullible people. Religious leaders become experts at destroying some people's capacity for sound evaluation of other people's ideas. Every year the hierarchy of absurdity increases and is more intricately woven into the fabric of human behavior.

Theologians talk nonsense as matter-of-factly as others discuss the weather or the opera, or any other fact of daily life. All religionists become so inured to lies, duplicity, deceit, and fakery that they deal with them as if they were normal behavior. It no longer occurs to people steeped in religions that pronouncements should be tested before they are believed, or that words should have meaningful referents if they are to be taken seriously.

At least subconsciously, most religionists understand that they live in a world of sham and that to avoid discord, religion, as a topic of conversation must be considered taboo. The diversified religions in which world populations are so deeply immersed no doubt seems to most people more important than daily changes in the weather. Then why does the weather evoke conversation while religion does not? Religion's mythological mystique, tendentiously maintained, increases our reluctance to bring it up as a topic of conversation.

152

So long as the natural man increases and multiplies without restraint, so long will peace and industry not only permit, but they will necessitate, a struggle for existence as sharp as any that ever went on under the regime of war. If Istar [the Goddess of Nature] is to reign on the one hand, she will demand her human sacrifices on the other.

T.H. Huxley (1825-1895) – Evolution and Ethics and Other Essays

Darwin's contemporary spokesman, grandfather of Aldous and Julian Huxley, continues: "So long as unlimited multiplication goes on, no social organization which has ever been devised...will deliver society from the tendency to be destroyed by the reproduction within itself." Arnold Toynbee in the *National Observer* for June 10, 1963 says: "We have been God-like in our planned breeding of our plants and animals, but we have become rabbit-like in our unplanned breeding of ourselves."

Two alleviating factors are in operation: Agriculture today, a hundred years later, is more productive than it was in Huxley's time, and birth rates are decreasing in some parts of the world. But each year millions still die of starvation. There are limits to the amount of food the earth can produce, and 80 million people are at present added to the world's population every year.

There are several "ifs" that would probably eliminate this explosive situation: If every human being on earth had more education, if our most effective contraceptives and day-after pills were cheap and available to everyone, if all religions were to promote any and all contraceptive means: rhythm, pills, condoms, etc., if all men in the world who do not want children were given vasectomies, paid for out of a world fund, if all women in the world who do not want children were to have their fallopian tubes tied. Which solution do you prefer? It is not as if we do not have means to stop the population explosion. If we do nothing, starvation, or perhaps an atomic world war, will do it for us.

153

A British physician, when asked what during his long life had done the most to relieve human suffering, replied: anesthesia and the decay of Christian Theology.

Lucien Price, editor - *Dialogues of Alfred North Whitehead*

I can imagine these two ideas have never been juxtaposed elsewhere in the history of conversation. I wonder which he considered the most important: the decrease of human sensitivity to pain or the decay of Christian theology. If the latter were possible, I would choose it. Humanity would by now have found substitutes for what is now called anesthesia, but Christian theology, if it extends its influence as the far-right Christian Coalition plans, could well be the end of all of us. Encouraged with each glimmer of success, the Christian Coalition will never give up. In their efforts to control the world, they may well involve us all in the final conflagration, which Samuel Pisar says will be the end of the human species.

If the reader would like to witness an unusual mind operating in a manner that is little short of miraculous, by all means read this book. Alfred North Whitehead's mind, of course, but I am thinking of the mind of Lucien Price. Tape recorders were not yet invented when these dialogues took place, and Lucien Price took no notes. Yet he would go home after long sessions with Mr. and Mrs. Whitehead and a few students and friends and transfer into writing everything he had heard - almost verbatim. We are greatly indebted to him and wonder if there was another person on earth who could have taken his place.

154

Today no really civilized man or woman believes in the cosmology of Genesis nor in the reality of Hell, nor in any of the other imbecilities that still entertain the mob.   H.L. Mencken (1880-1956)

Were it only so, but sadly it is not. We find on radio and television an ever-increasing saturation of these imbecilities. Good sense, instead of increasing, is increasingly rare. Ranting fanatics on the broadcasting media and in the pulpit are a daily fare. Listening to their harangues, no rational person can have much doubt that all is not well with religion. Ecclesiastics are leading us toward a bedlam of sectarianism and strife. They teach us fear and hatred rather than the love and noble aspirations that could help us further the brotherhood of mankind.

One sees in the audiences of TV evangelists men and women all eyes and ears, agog, doting on every hate-filled word. They become alienated more and more from their less-gullible neighbors who refuse to be taken in by the bombast of power-hungry religious mystagogues. The behavior of such viewers is not far removed from the organized hysteria or complete loss of control found in dervish whirling and voodoo dancing.

There will always be a certain proportion of childlike minds that demand greater security than any kind of secular regime can offer. The promise of eternal life and perpetual bliss is especially attractive for those who have never learned to cope with the world as it is. They prefer to vegetate until they can live in another, a perfect world, which they will not have to lift a finger to prepare.

155

We are not essential to planet earth...but newly arrived interlopers.
Steven M. Stanley
Children of the Ice Age

Do we human beings have a special purpose here on earth? Are we essential in the total domain of living things? Not in the least, says Professor Stanley, paleobiologist at Johns Hopkins University.

Stanley's story begins with the subtitle of his book: *How a Global Catastrophe Allowed Humans to Evolve*. His theses have to do with precarious environmental crises, and man's adaptation to them, and why a large brain resulted in the process of this adaptation. He agrees with the concepts of purpose and chance that are developed elsewhere in *Religion on Trial*, but in a new and interesting way that is well worth considering.

If and when the time comes that we become extinct, if we bow out in a way that does no harm to other species, they will not miss us. Isolated instances can be cited where creatures will suffer without us, of course, but with good will, we could mitigate that suffering by preparing captive and dependent species for surviving on their own. *Born Free* by Joy Adamson, tells of preparing a pet lion for release. The California condor programs talk of the pains taken to prepare these birds for living in the wild. The same could be done for many dependent species in many parts of the world.

156

> If you talk to God you are praying; if God talks to you, you have schizophrenia.
>
> Thomas Szasz – *The Second Sin*

Talking to God every night of one's life without getting any kind of answer is sane behavior? That may also be schizophrenia. Imagine calling your boss at that hour, that often, and that regularly in order to tell him how to run his business! If your boss never gave you any slight hint in reply, but you continued to call anyway, somebody ought to carry you off to the booby hatch.

As for getting answers from God is concerned, just listen to radio and television evangelists for a few sessions, and you will know that all of them have a two-way pipeline to God. They are constantly relaying the messages to us they received and that God wanted us in particular, for some special reason, to know. In conversations they will say: "In answer to your question, God told me that..." In sermons they often give us information they receive that flatly contradicts that which the next preacher receives. But such discomfiture does not faze them. As the Bible clearly shows, consistency is not one of God's foremost attributes. The essays listed under "Contradictions" in the index will give you some idea of how frequently God's word contradicts itself.

"If you talk to God you are praying," Szasz says. If you think God is there listening to you, the world would be interested in knowing what authentic evidence you have for thinking so. If you believe, as most people do, that saying a thing is so does not make it so, then what *does* make your contention so? If you believe all the long lists of adjectives ecclesiastics give us averring that God is not knowable, never has been and never will be, then where do you find your evidence? If your answer is "One must have faith!" please tell us why have faith in that one unlikely assumption about the way things are.

157

> Only that aspect of religion serves us that intensifies our love for our neighbors, and strengthens our self-esteem.
>
> George Christian Anderson –*Man's Right to Be Human*

If this be true, religion has little to say for itself; for hate, not love, is the principal legacy of religion. By dividing the world's religious peoples into Jews, Buddhists, Christians, Muslims, etc., and with these further divided into sects, religions shape the members of humanity as enemies of one another, making religious differences the cause of most of the wars of history.

When Sinhalese kill Tamils in Sri Lanka, when Catholics kill Protestants in Ireland, when Turks kill Armenians in Anatolia, when Muslims kill Christians in Sudan and fight a bloody war in Palestine, love is a stranger. Nearly every time new sects or new religions are formed it is because heated altercations arise in established flocks, where rebellious cliques storm out in anger, forming a "new and better" group.

The love existing between different religions is the love between rival street gangs, between competitive football teams, between the Cosa Nostra and the Cosa Vostra.

Love may be the world's greatest need, yet we spend little time actively trying to cultivate it. If half our university courses were designed to teach all peoples to love one another, it would be time well spent. It's either love or perish; love our only rational choice.

158

Man must humbly but with courage accept responsibility for the destiny of mankind. Any other postulate is a frightened retreat, which leads to the blank wall or precipice of chaos unthinkable.
Clyde Kluckhohn (1905-1960) – *Mirror for Man*

Here is expressed one of the great dangers of religion. It leaves people content to languish, to let God do it, to abandon the struggle to make this a better world. If we "know" that everything will come out all right with no special effort on our part, we will allow our leaders repeatedly to take us to the brink of total disaster without the sense of panic required to persuade us personally to get involved. We know there is a *deus ex machina* who has his arms around us to pull us back from the brink in the nick of time. Even the total destruction of this world does not alarm some religionists. We always have heaven to fall back on - and heaven is a better place anyway. The fact that we are destroying our environment and exhausting our natural reources does not concern us. The God looking out for us us is omniscient, omnipotent, caring. That is enough for me. I will not worry about it. See you tomorrow, God willing!

159

> Such is the irresistible nature of truth, that all it asks, and all it wants, is the liberty of appearing.
>
> Thomas Paine (1737-1809) – *The Rights of Man*

Once it knows a new truth, Paine says in effect elsewhere in the same book, the mind is never again the same. It cannot be put back to its former, less-enlightened, state.

Religion is the enemy of truth and the friend of myth. As religion uses the word truth, it seems to have no definable meaning. It is sometimes of value presumably, but exactly what it is, is anybody's guess. If in some religious contexts, it means vision or insight these words should be used. If it implies some indefinable "good" out there in cloud cuckooland, it should be avoided.

Of course, if religion wants to use the word truth as an antonym of lies and errors, as Paine is doing, it has every right to do so and then will be communicating to us. If religion uses the word truth to say that the words being considered have a real-world relationship, it uses the word in a way we can understand. If Mormonism says that it is building seven new churches in Quito, Ecuador, and we count them and find the statement is true, the word is used in its common acceptation. If Catholicism can say it has no women priests, a statement that can be verified, their statement is true in the sense that you and I use the term in our everyday affairs. If Christian Scientists tell us that their religion was founded by Mary Baker Eddy, and we check the history books to see that what they say is true, they use the word well and wisely. If when the Bible says, "The truth will make you free," and it refers to statements like God exists, Jesus died for our sins, heaven is in Galaxy M-31, Satan is evil incarnate, wicked people burn in hell forever, the word truth is an obstructive emission that is much worse than being simply useless; it does a great deal of harm. Only when statements can be verified by observation, experiment, or reliable history do they make sense and can be said to be true.

160

> We first crush people to the earth, and then claim the right of trampling on them forever, because they are prostrate.
>
> Lydia Maria Child (1802-1880)

Lydia Child was appealing for justice for African-Americans, and in that brief statement she tells the whole story. We have denied blacks fair salaries and then complained because they do not live up to our standards. We have denied blacks education, and then complained because they are ignorant. We have forced them to live in ghettos and then complained because they do not fit into high society.

Lydia Child goes on to say, "Slaves have stabbed themselves for freedom – jumped in the waves for freedom - starved for freedom - fought like very tigers for freedom! But they have been hung, and burned, and shot - and their tyrants have been their historians!" What Child said back in 1838, applies as much to downtrodden people today, whatever their color or country of origin. Even when their misfortune is the result of nothing but bad luck, and the affluent circumstances of their oppressors has been the result of good luck, sometimes inheriting a fortune, this oppressor-oppressed relationship obtains.

Once a person has fallen into bad times, it is extremely difficult for him to get back on his feet. Just as success breeds success, adversity breeds more of the same. It is easier to find a job when one already has one. Prospective employers are suspicious of someone who is not working at an age when he should be working. Without recommendations, the person who has been unfortunate enough to find himself drifting, cannot easily get back in the swim. It is a Catch-22, no-win situation in an economic system that is definitely not always fair.

161

> The fundamental fact about the Greek was that he had to use his mind. The ancient priests had said, "This and no farther. We set the limits of thought." The Greeks said, "All things are to be examined and called into question. There are no limits set on thought."
>
> Edith Hamilton (1867-1963) – The Greek Way

The difference between the attitude of the priests and the Greeks has ever been the difference between religion and science. The priests, knowing that nothing they say can stand scrutiny, depend on the ignorance of their parishioners for their very survival. Scientists, advocating an open system, know that everything capable of being known must be known, and that theirs is an eternal quest to know it. They want ignorance eliminated so far as possible in all human minds. Nothing must be held back.

If the populace learns theories that later prove to be false, these theories must be revised. Each error corrected is another step toward universal truth. In science the ideal is to make our interacting systems out of all the elements of knowledge in a manner that eventually they all fit together without contradictions. Although scientists know that they will never attain full realization of that ideal, they will continually try - and will find the process of trying fascinating.

Edith Hamilton said nearly thirty years later in the Bryn Mawr School Bulletin, "It is not hard work that is dreary. It is superficial work." Scientists enjoy their work. Priests live in perpetual fear of being found out. On September 19, 1918, Kathe Kollwitz wrote in her *Diaries and Letters*, "Men without joy seem like corpses." Men who are unhappy with the work they do function like zombies.

162

It is not the nature of man to consider truth of any great value.
Stanislav Andreski
Social Science as Sorcery

It seems that we like to be deceived. How else do we account for ghosts, witches, elves, fairies, leprechauns, chupacabras, devils, souls, angels, gods, incubi, and unicorns? Why else do we put credence in tarot cards, Ouija boards, phylacteries, horoscopes, seances, palmistry, fortune telling, phrenology, amulets, and talismans?

Andreski's word "truth" refers to the use of the word in everyday affairs. When mother asks little Johnny if he is telling the truth, she wants to know if what he is saying conforms to the facts. "I did (did not) slap Mary," if a clear statement of actual fact, should be saying that there was (was not) violent and ill-intentioned contact between Johnny's hand and Mary's face. We are assuming, of course, that the "liar" is aware of what he is doing. Lying and being mistaken are poles apart. Truth always implies a correspondence between map and territory, between what we say and what we say it about.

Religionists fail to value this correspondence between symbols and symbolized. All the things they say about heaven and hell and the supernal entities that populate those abodes have no verifiable referents. The "what they say it about" in the equation is missing - except in their own imaginations. No one has ever had or ever will have any proof that the territory exists. The "truth" of conventional acceptation, that is, does not apply in discussing the premises of theistic religions.

163

In my religion, there would be no exclusive doctrine; all would be love, poetry, and doubt.

Cyril Vernon Connolly (1903-1974)
The Unquiet Grave

Many of those who recognize today's religions for the organized ignorance they are have their own aphoristic ways of saying so. The beautifully utopian religion of Cyril Connolly may never be achieved, but his is the goal we should be striving for. First must be the doubt that gives us room for fostering love and poetry. Then our proposed religion must be universal, catholic, and ecumenical, intended to include everyone. It cannot be Jewish, Muslim, Christian, Buddhist, Hindu, etc. Nor can it be any of the sects of these religions.

A religion of love would be a revelation. The religions we know well teach sectarianism, which is hate. The God of the Jews, Christians, and Muslims murders human beings by the thousands and designs a hell where the majority of them will fry for eternity when they "leave this world." He tolerates a Satan, who leads us all into temptations - hardly a God of love. He is a God who made us in his own image, the story goes - then despises us, as He repeatedly shows - which doesn't say much even for His own self-esteem. He overlooks slavery in many countries and even in His own Koran and Bible has much more to say in favor of slavery than against it. A careful reading of Genesis 24:35 and Exodus 21:1-11 gives us a sense of the attitude toward slavery in the Bible. Surah 16, ayah 75 does the same for the Koran. Neither augurs well for what we can expect of religion.

164

> The trouble with born-again Christians is that they are an even bigger pain the second time around.
>
> Herb Caen
> *San Francisco Chronicle*: July 20, 1981

Born-again Christians are like a successful graduate of *Alcoholics Anonymous* that I met in Key West, Florida in the 1960s. AA procedures seem successful, especially if they can substitute for booze addiction a childlike addiction to a simplified, idealized Christianity that seemingly was founded by a Jewish prophet who lived two thousand years ago. The born-again concept had not been invented at that time, but what AA offered was something closely akin to it. Everyone subject to a few minutes of this AA member's proselytizing agreed that he could not have been half as obnoxious as an active alcoholic as he now was as a reformed alcoholic bent on "saving" everyone he met.

Any family that has one member (whether aunt, uncle, cousin, offspring, or in-law) who is fanatically religious and who by manner or constant innuendo puts all other members beyond the pale will understand what it was that irritated everyone forced to deal with this AA alumnus. Gratuitous, incessant, abrasive preaching will alienate the most patient of friends.

In or out of the orthodox religions, an inevitable consequence of fanaticism is the breakdown of rational communication. Fanaticism suppresses insight, that inner vision which, as William Henry Hudson says, "sees further than the eyes." Whenever one knows that *his* truth is *the* truth, communication with the rest of the world suffers. No one is going to accept error (that which others believe) or forfeit truth (that which we believe) when both are "obvious."

Our pulpiteers set the stage for permanent, unrelenting, no-holds barred, better-dead-than-infidel conflict. Their inviolable concepts of absolute truth, religious faith, and a single, narrow, "Christian" path to perfect after-life bliss leave no room for the possibility of permanent peace.

Chapter V

Hip, Hip, Hypocrisy

165

Those schooled in orthodox religions are shocked to find their religions variously described as organized superstitions, methodized nonsense, structured madness, assembled ignorance, collective insanity, and bureaucratic religiosity. As long as religionists pretend they "know" what they in fact do not know and cannot know, derogatory phrases will inevitably be used to describe this pretense.

The Orthodox Church is by its very nature authoritarian. The dogma, doctrines, and tenets become principles outlining for the faithful how they are to believe and behave. The church is not content with having members who are devout and undefiled, but it demands that they be subjects and imposes upon them behavioral patterns and prohibitions that have little or nothing to do with morality. The orthodox church, for example, decides what its subjects can read, how they may think and behave, what movies they may see, what university courses they may take, what candidates they may vote for, etc. Disobedience will be dealt with severely - even possible excommunication.

In the deep recesses of the mind, where firm convictions are stored, those of religionists are well protected from rational intrusions. Like ova that sperm are never allowed to approach, their convictions remain untouched, uncontaminated, unthreatened and sterile. There is no hope that these convictions will ever become general participants in viable earthly intercourse. If ever they are discussed, it will be only within the coterie habitually sharing their own cozy and comfortable pew.

166

I believe that it is impossible for a person who does not live an ethical life to be happy.

Raymond Smullyan
Professor of Philosophy
Herbert H. Lehman College

A person who must always be looking over his shoulder is not happy. A person who puts a small value on all human life, including his own, is not happy. A person who finds himself despised in news items and editorials is not happy. A person who everyone, even his friends, knows cannot be trusted is not happy A person whose behavior has consequences harmful to hundreds, even thousands of members of society is not happy. A person who is dead is not happy or unhappy. He is, as Ecclesiastes says in the book bearing his name, nothing. "There is no work, no planning, no knowledge, no wisdom in the world of the dead...."

In rehabilitation classes, important lessons must be taught. Films showing moral people leading truly happy lives should be one part of the program. The point Smullyan makes, if poignantly, penetratingly, and clearly presented, will be another.

167

Question with boldness even the existence of God, because if there is one, he must more approve of a homage of reason, than that of blindfold fear.

Thomas Jefferson (1743-1826)
Letter to Peter Carr, August 10, 1787

Yes, by all means question with boldness, and be ready to find out that there is no God. If God did exist, we would have known that fact beyond any shadow of a doubt long before now. Despite the excuses the clergy give us for God's indifference, there are no excuses. If there really were a God, two-way Sunday morning fireside chats with our divine deity would long have been the norm. Answers to cosmic questions that have mystified our scientists would be answered. What about that big-bang theory? What about gravity waves? What is dark matter? Is the universe finite? Is there intelligent life elsewhere in the universe? Our lives are filled with practical problems that also need answers.

If there were a Supreme Being listening to us, we would ask real favors that would solve real problems. Teach us to rehabilitate criminals, to cure, or better yet, to prevent cancer, AIDS, Alzheimer's disease, multiple sclerosis, all the diseases that plague us. Write us a real Bible, in clear language, without fear, hate, anger, killing, fairy tales, maybe with a bit of humor thrown in to make it interesting.

Above all, teach us to love one another, to be always kind, to cast away selfishness, to live in peace. Why not, God? Why do you abide a world full of injustice and suffering when you could as easily give us a utopia without serious problems?

Any human being who is truly honest with himself knows there is no God. If there were, all of these things would have been done from the beginning. Either that or the God we have is worse than none, and we should ask him to find some other galaxy to annoy. Leave the Milky Way for us to run.

168

It is the maturest fruit of Christian understanding to understand that Christianity, as such, is of no avail.

Paul Tillich (1886-1965)
The NewBeing

Maturity is indeed a worthy goal. To be mature is to be able to weigh evidence on both sides of any proposition. For the mature individual, the body of evidence that wins the battle is that which is based on reality, on the empirical world exposed to the scrutiny of our proverbial five senses.

In a letter to Voltaire dated July 7, 1737, Frederick the Great said, "Religion is the idol of the mob; it adores everything it does not understand." We do ourselves a great disservice when we pretend to see sense in that which makes no sense - and then to dote on it. We are lost if we give credence to a body of organized superstitions that is the product of unrestrained human imaginations. We cannot run a world on conjecture, suppositions, and dreams that have never stood any kind of test of authenticity. Mature minds outline for us commendable ways to behave. The childishness that is preached from pulpits and through the microphones of television's "religious" programs must be relegated to the category of make-believe, not to be taken seriously. The Reverend Paul Tillich tells us that Christianity, behaving in the way it usually does, is of no avail.

169

"It is a curious thing," he thought, "that every creed promises a paradise which will be absolutely uninhabitable for anyone of civilized taste."

Evelyn Waugh (1903-1966)
Put Out More Flags

If we are to believe either the Bible or the Koran, God is of the opinion that in heaven man will want his every whim satisfied without himself expending the slightest effort. Can the God or Allah we are asked to believe in be that ignorant of the nature of the creatures he spent his sixth day creating? Human beings would be bored to death in the heaven described to us. Betrand Russell, in his *The Conquest of Happiness*, too, without mentioning heaven, gives us an idea of how we would fare in such a place: "To be without some of the things you want it is an indispensable part of happiness."

Even in the life we live here on earth, we are given hints of how dull and tedious would be God's heaven. If we are fortunate enough to reach one of our cherished goals, we almost certainly remember that the struggle along the way was the best part. We are let down to find it finished—no more challenges; no more obstacles to overcome. It becomes imperative to set up another even more ambitious project. If the ultimate goal this time turns out to be completely unattainable, perhaps all the better.

170

The only religion is conscience in action.

Henry Demarest Lloyd (1847-1903)
Wealth Against Commonwealth

To suggest that an active conscience is the only religion, it seems to me, is to put a heavy burden on conscience. I wonder if it is warranted. Is the proverbial elf on my shoulder capable at any moment of offering reliable guidance on moral matters? I have ample cause for doubt, you know! When I look around me and see how many of these shoulder-riding elves are failing their trust, I may wonder if we might not be overestimating their prowess.

The caliber of anyone's conscience depends on what was the accumulated morality in its owner's past that fashioned that conscience. Serial killers may be obeying their conscience, but what kind of conscience? It is not the kind of conscience I would like to see proliferated. The greatest value of what Henry Demarest Lloyd says accrues from the many, many things it is saying about what religion is not: An effective religion is not mythology, and it is not discrimination, prejudice, superstition, or hate. It is not the genocide of the Christian Crusades, nor of Hitler, Stalin, or Pol Pot. It is not sectarianism, asceticism, dogma, sacraments, penitential flagellation, faith healing, human sacrifice, mesmeric incantations, or sacred literature.

Religion does not necessarily imply piety, divine revelation, or the existence of deity. Rabbi S. Guthman of Long Beach, California, probably gives us an acceptable account of what religion is when he describes an interchange between a self-appointed school inspector and the school principal: "Where in your timetable do you teach religion?"

"We teach [religion] all day long. We teach it in arithmetic by accuracy. We teach it in language by learning to say what we mean. We teach it in history, by emphasizing good human relations. We teach it in geography by enlarging horizons and breadth of mind. We teach it in astronomy by instilling the spirit of reverence. We teach it in the playground by fair play. We teach it by kindness to animals, by courtesy, good manners and by helpfulness in all things. We teach it by showing the young that we, their elders, are their friends." The religion that that school teaches serves us well. The *Long Beach Press-Telegram* favors us by passing the Rabbi's message on to us in its July 6, 1999 issue.

171

If I were convinced that immortality is a fiction, I would seal my lips about it.

Henry Ward Beecher (1813-1887)

The deceit that is religion is everywhere the same. Religionists prefer to live in a world of make-believe rather than to face what is truth about the cosmos. Fantasy is in religion the only "substance." Facts do not count.

Immortality, heaven, hell, devils, angels, prophets, trinity, virginity, and divinity are all woven together into to one monstrous fabric of deceit and delusion. Although there is not a shred of evidence for the gigantic fairy tale "religion," most people prefer, like Beecher, to seal their lips about it. They are so absolutely certain that deceit is more desirable than truth that they will perpetrate deceit regardless. If everyone were to adopt this attitude, the world would devolve into an abyss of imposture. The world cannot run on sham and deceit.

Knowing that religious leaders are capable of that kind of deceit, we are no longer surprised to read that Henry of Navarre in 1593 became a Roman Catholic in order to seat himself on the throne of France, or that Charles II returning to England in 1660 discreetly renounced Catholicism. They are like the fellow whose friend answered for him when he was asked what was his religion. "Oh, he's an Anythingarian; his mind keeps open-house." His friend, having known him for a long time, was aware that he was capable of being whatever at any given moment it was convenient for him to be.

172

The greatest and most immediate danger of white culture ... is its fear of truth, its childish belief in the efficacy of lies as a method of human uplift.

William Du Bois (1868-1963)
Dusk of Dawn

Du Bois had his agendum, of course, but his quotation is surely not restricted to one particular culture. It is a universal truth, valid for all. It is the thesis of this book that if the vast majority of our religious leaders could not lie they would be mute. Every time they open their mouths they talk of things they know nothing about, while all the time pretending that they do. They must lie—and hope that we will listen to them. If we take them seriously, we, too, are soon enveloped in their grand latticework of lies, never again able to talk intelligently about anything.

It is obvious that humanity cannot survive immersed in competing systems of lies. Until truth is considered as fundamental and essential to all believing, we will not progress in human affairs. To sanctify deceit is to ordain human deprivation. With each sect insisting that its fabrications are the only truth, the eventual result is sure to be more and ever-more-bitter religious wars. We must recognize the value of truth and do everything we can to promote it. Only then can we live sane and meaningful lives, leaving us the energies to pursue the love and universal brotherhood so urgently needed in all societies everywhere.

173

No African antelope is clever enough, when there is a drought and he watches his precious grasslands dry up, to imagine that the rain is being withheld by evil spirits, or as punishment for sins.

Aldous Huxley (1894-1963)
Texts and Pretexts

He goes on: "The lions, watching their food supply migrate to greener pastures, do not ritually urinate in hopes of persuading the gods to do the same and send down rain. The zebras do not bray incantations to the blazing sun in cloudless skies."

Climbing the evolutionary scale, it seems, there is in some respects such a thing as reaching a level of too much intelligence - not too much ability to reason, but too vivid an imagination and not enough ability to discriminate sense from nonsense, fact from fiction, and visions fabricated internally without outside stimuli from visions that have a counterpart beyond our own skins.

The words above are a slight paraphrase of Huxley's precise ruminations in order to give them a measure more of coherence. Both versions imply censure of man with his overly exuberant fantasizing - fabricating fables and then worshiping his own fabrications. It may all have started with early kings losing control over their subjects and improvising means to restore that control. Mythologies that instilled both fear and awe in their subjects proved to be just what the situation required.

174

Better build schoolrooms for "the boy," / Than cells and gibbets for "the man."

Eliza Cook
"A Song for the Ragged Schools"

How many ways this has been said, how true it is, and how foolish we are to disregard it! Today we spend billions on churches, synagogues, mosques, and prisons, while far lesser monies are needed to keep children out of gangs, off the streets, and engaged in activities that they would enjoy and that would train them for useful and prosperous lives.

Our governments seem to have some kind of perverted proclivity for wasting our money. If the billions of dollars fighting drug wars were spent on teaching young people the folly of using drugs, we would surely have fewer drug users and a welcome feeling that we are not living in a military society. If we were to put some of our best advertising writers to work writing and filming ads against drug use, they would surely do much more good than do laws against drugs. People react sanely to well-presented education for their own good, but they react stubbornly against the increasing number of laws restricting their behavior.

Our religious organizations are worse than our governments. They spend trillions on church property and use it to teach us mythologies that do not serve us in any way - but instead warp and befuddle our minds until we cannot think clearly or act intelligently. Morality well taught in our schools would serve us far better and would leave us living in sane societies capable of building a better world.

175

Men despise religion, they hate it, and they fear it is true.

Blaise Pascal (1623-1662)

Pensées

If religion has any meaningful part to play in our lives, fear would certainly be the operative word. In fact, whether people are or are not religious, fear has been a sensible response to religion throughout recorded history. The number of people who have been murdered in the name of religion is reason enough for fear. To recall the Christian Crusades, the Spanish Inquisition, and witch-hunting is only a beginning. Most of our wars have been religious wars, even those going on today. Most of our prejudice is prejudice against religions that are different from our own.

Pascal has little idea of what the word true means as he uses it. No one does. I have never heard or read a meaningful definition of religion's word truth - unless the interpretation F.S.C. Northrop gives us is adequate. He suggests that it is the equivalent of "comfort." Whatever religionists mean by truth is a far cry from its meaning in everyday contexts: a correspondence between symbols and what they symbolize.

If, as Pascal says, men despise and hate religion, they have good reasons for doing so. It has been the reason for more "ill will" among the members of the human species than all other reasons combined. We will not have peace in the world until we get rid of our religions. The solution that the Christian Coalition strives to foist on us would be the worst solution imaginable. We need only look at what religion does in countries with an official state religion to know what a single, universal, worldwide religion would mean.

176

Nuns don't like priests.... Because we've treated them like cheap help in the church for ages - they kept the schools and hospitals going on minimal salaries.... It's hopelessly unfair.

Andrew Greeley
Quoted in *Modern Maturity* May-June, 1996

Churches do not pay taxes on property worth many billions of dollars. All of us, therefore, subsidize these institutions, whether or not we approve of them. Churches pay their help less than minimum wages. Any other employer would be fined or spend long terms in jail for doing the same thing. In return for billions of dollars of donations, churches promise their members that in return they will receive salvation and other benefits - when they cannot in any way demonstrate that the donors will receive the benefits promised.

Not only nuns, but women in general are given short shrift by the patriarchal clergy of most of the churches. Women are not equally represented as deacons and elders and especially are not to be the ordained *Primus inter pares* of the church. We have a while to wait for a female pope.

The Bible teaches that sin, death, and the fall of man are all to be blamed on that first woman, the mother of all humanity. As Elizabeth Cady Stanton said in the *Freethought Magazine* for September 1896: "The Bible and Church have been the greatest stumbling blocks in the way of woman's emancipation." Two months later she said in the same magazine: "The whole tone of church teaching is, to the last degree, contemptuous and degrading."

177

> Faith in a holy cause is to a considerable extent a substitute for the
> lost faith in ourselves.
>
> Eric Hoffer
> *The True Believer*

We seem confident enough in our abilities to reach our own goals, but for holy causes we must be more than just confident. Holy causes accept nothing less than fanatical adherents, and nothing can be allowed to stand in their way. Especially when both religions and nations become involved, crusades can grow into genocides. For fundamentalists, there are no limits. Even if unspoken, world conquest is the goal, and even if progress is slow and there are setbacks, they keep edging toward that goal, gradually gaining ground. The Taliban in Afghanistan, and other Muslim movements in Algiers, Egypt, and Turkey are going to be difficult to deter.

The word faith, used twice in Hoffer's statement is simply our word "confidence," important if we are to succeed at any endeavor. But faith as preachers commonly use the word is quite a different thing. It is the preacher's equivalent of "Believe what I say, not because I give you evidence for believing, but simply because I say it." The preacher cannot know everything; in fact he knows very little. Worse yet, he knows a great deal less than he pretends to know. That which serves as structure for his religion, he does not know at all. "Faith," then, serves as his magical mantra to cover up his ignorance of what he is talking about. "What I say is so *is so*. Please do not ask questions. Do not ask why I make such an outlandish statement; just believe it - please. Have faith!"

If the method the preacher uses to come to his conclusions were used by scientists, they would all still be alchemists. We would still be living in the dark ages.

178

> Lord, I know that no man is the master of himself; no man has
> control over his own destiny.
>
> Jeremiah 10:23

Where was Jeremiah when the word was passed out? Almost all of the Bible is a contradiction of that contention. The constant talk of man's sins and God's punishment of them posits man's free will and responsibility for what he does. Could we ever hold anyone responsible if we did not believe in freedom? But this is a way of saying that in our deep, innermost convictions we are atheists. To postulate an intervening God is to say that we are not free, that we are controlled by Him; we are his pawns. To speak of the "sin" or "crime" of human beings then is a contradiction, as God would be the only sinner and the only criminal.

As individuals, we "know" we make decisions as surely as we know the green of grass, the bouquet of wine, or the harmony of music. We cannot imagine what the determinist is talking about when he denies this "inner vision"—as obvious as color or sound. Why do a Skinner, Calvin, *et al.*, find it difficult to posit free will when they, like all of us, accept "consciousness-of-self" as obvious. A nervous system that can look upon itself is no easier to explain than one that is able to make choices. The latter, it seems to me, is subordinate to, and implied by, the former. If consciousness-of-self is beyond the scope of rational analysis so also is free will. But this is not to deny that both are realities - as we all intuitively know.

179

Force is not a remedy.

John Bright (1811-1889)

"You can't get a man with a gun," Betty Hutton sang with wistful resignation. Nor can we get justice, obedience, respect, submission, sympathy, allegiance, or affection by force. Coercion is seldom a wise course of action, whatever the objective. Physical force, moral pressure, or arbitrary constraints seldom prove effective for getting our way, whatever that way may be.

Recalcitrant, intractable, and refractory are terms coined specifically to describe any of us who oppose those who would force us to surrender to their will. We react angrily to autocrats who contrive to run our lives. We love nonviolent, peacefully inclined organizations and people.

In this regard, science is an ideal field of study. It has no need for force to achieve its supremacy. Its logical processes stated clearly and honestly, win respect without coercion. Its appeal penetrates the most obtuse of mentalities. The dogmas and doctrines of entrenched mythologies will eventually disappear, nullified by the supreme dominion of our constantly progressing rational disciplines.

Science rejects absolutism, despotism, oppression, or inter-science dissent. Science is the consummation of good sense. It is knowledge, acquired through effective use of the mental faculties. Science accepts for belief only that which gives good reason for belief. It does not divide itself into irreconcilable sects or warring factions. It deplores the fact that other disciplines take advantage of its achievements in order to make wars more deadly. The world of science is a peaceful world whose sole objective is human progress.

180

We need a religion... that permits every mind to change its beliefs every time a new truth [emerges].

Philip Wylie (1902-1971)
The Magic Animal

We can expect human progress only when there occurs an explosion of new truths and an implosion of the old truths that have too long held us in thrall. Man's condition improves directly as his ability to envision, conceive, invent, and to create new truth improves. His condition worsens insofar as he continues to allow himself to be suffocated by false beliefs, allowing other people to exercise sovereignty over his right to think.

We must learn to defend new theses that seem worthwhile, and make every effort to remove abuses, correct corrupt practices, and to make changes when needed. We must reject fear of the unknown and not allow ourselves to be fooled by pious words about sanctification, or about mythical beings or life after death. We must avoid all the pseudo-explanations that pseudo evangelists use to inspire us to accept their spurious arguments and false claims. Those "truths" that cannot stand any kind of "test of truth" must be discarded. Those that can be confirmed repeatedly by the simple methods scientists' use in their laboratories are retained. We begin with a supposed new truth, make predictions based on that "truth," then test these predictions. Only if all predictions we can think of to make and that seem logical are confirmed do we accept the truth of whatever it is we set out to prove.

181

I cannot imagine a God who rewards and punishes the objects of his creation, whose purposes are modeled after our own - a God, in short, who is but a reflection of human frailty. Neither can I believe that the individual survives the death of his body, although feeble souls harbor such thoughts through fear or ridiculous egotisms.

Albert Einstein (1879-1955)

Even if Einstein could imagine any other kind of God, he would not have a language to describe Him. To expect mere mortal men, even if all had the extraordinary brain that Einstein had, suddenly to be expatiating in some kind of transcendental phrasing about a God that is beyond the extrapolating potential of any man is to let imagination run wild.

Obviously Einstein does not envisage the presently contrived God—nor any other. He is, in short, an atheist. Why not say so rather than string words one after another in the form of trivial circumlocutions that explain nothing. No theologian would agree that Einstein describes a believable God, certainly not Einstein's god that created a being who cannot survive the death of the body. It may seem picky to ask, but I will: If not men, what possibly are the "souls" (feeble souls) Einstein speaks of? And while I am at it, which God is it that does not play dice?

182

For seventeen hundred years the Christian sect has done nothing but harm.

Voltaire (1694-1778)
Letter to Frederick the Great

Generalizations containing words like never, always, absolutely, nothing, everyone, in their minute details, are often wrong. Voltaire might better have said, "on balance do more harm than good." But however it is said, it is important to say it. Voltaire said "seventeen hundred years." No doubt along the way, there were writers who said one hundred years, two hundred years, three hundred years, and so on.

But Christianity should not be singled out. The same could be said of any religion that for some period of history held large numbers of people in thrall. The conclusion we should reach is that all religions do harm. Even though they also do good, on balance they do far more harm than good. If anyone doubts that, please let him tell me the good religion does to compensate for: (1) The many innocent people killed every day in religious wars in many parts of the world? (2) The awful superstitions that breed in the voodoo atmosphere of all sects of all the major religions? (3) The hatred that is constantly being rekindled between the faithful flocks ("us") and the pharisaical droves ("those others")? (4) The countless millions of dollars that TV evangelists are bilking from their credulous and trusting viewers and members? (5) The dreary sermons and antiquated rituals that waste our time and increase the disharmony in our societies? (6) The general ambience of sham and deceit, the holy daze in which nearly every child in this "religious" world is raised? The ultimate legacy of religion may well be the annihilation of the human species. Where are the benefits that religion offers us to compensate for our possible extinction?

183

My heart, once captured [by religion], I deliberately and, with a sort of frantic joy, showed reason the door. I accepted everything, I believed everything without regret, and without false shame. How could I blush for what I had learned to adore?

George Sand (1804-1896)
Story of My Life, Vol. I

That George Sand enjoyed her life beyond her years of religion seems clear. She also enjoyed her various indulgences: smoking, drinking, Chopin, and writing.

Her word "captured" gives us an idea of what religion was doing to her before she got religion. Sorry, I mean, "got rid of religion." When she learned to live without religions, with her new freedom she must have understood Ingersoll, a contemporary, when he said, "... a freethinker is an eagle parting the clouds with tireless wing."

George Sand, like Martin Luther, understood that reason is the enemy of religion. She found it necessary to show reason the door before she could hope wholeheartedly to embrace religion's unreasonable precepts.

When George Sand tells us about the years when she was joyously, easily, painlessly, unregretfully, shamelessly, and unblushingly religious, she tells us why many religious peoples' lives are simple and serene. Their lives are nothing like those of Jane Goodall, June Goodfield, Sally Ride, Elizabeth Stanton, Robyn Davidson, or Susan Anthony. Those satisfied with serenity, anyway, will never lose their lives in the pursuit of a dream as did Dian Fossey and Amelia Earhart.

184

Why is it that even in times of peace every nation and all individuals within a nation should disdain, hate, and abhor one another is indeed a mystery.

Sigmund Freud (1856-1939)

Perhaps the mystery can be resolved if we examine the propensity of human beings to seek solutions to their problems by turning to mythologies. Rather than look to the world as it is and devise solutions to our problems based on reason and reality, we invent gods to explain the existence of volcanoes, storms, earthquakes, avalanches, plagues, and forest fires. We invent demons to explain the evil in men's hearts and the presence of human suffering. We invent psyches, souls, and dream worlds to assure us of immortality, eternal bliss, and other ethereal fictions. We evoke class, race, gender, as well as geographical and religious distinctions to give us bases for our hate, bigotry, prejudice, intolerance, and superstitions. Since each person does the explaining differently, all kinds of frictions arise as to what are the correct explanations.

When we cast aside all such inventions and realize that we are one people living in one world and dedicate our efforts toward educating that people and improving that world, Freud's concerns will begin to disappear.

185

Example moves the world more than doctrine.

Henry Miller (1891-1980)
The Cosmological Eye

The person who declares, "Do as I say, not as I do," seeking to vindicate his own bad behavior, is barking up the wrong tree - and consciously. He knows as well as does Miller that "Actions speak louder than words." The truth of what Miller says is so well known that any expression of it becomes a cliché - and that is too bad. The advice is so profound that it could indeed move the world if imbedded in our consciousness in a way that it would direct thought and action every working moment of every day. Wordsworth speaks of "little, nameless, unremembered, acts of kindness and love."

We all are aware that politicians are generous with words and niggardly with deeds that hypostatize those words. Preachers are schooled in otherworldly words that have no counterpart in actions, whether by themselves or anyone else, "on earth as it is in heaven." Lawyers judge words by their money value - and often get paid more per word than the butcher gets per packaged pound of hamburger.

Words are important, but the people who deserve our encomiums are those who day after day go quietly about observing the afflictions of their fellow human beings and do everything they can to alleviate them. "Quiet diplomacy," "silence is golden," "words are cheap," "the springs of action," and other such expressions creep into our language to remind us of the merit of doing. Shakespeare said: "Words pay no debts," "Action is eloquent," "Deeds most win the prize," and gives us hope when he says, "I'll endeavor deeds to match those words."

186

The world is now too small, and man's stake in sanity too great for any more of those old games of Chosen Folks (whether of Jehovah, Allah, Wotan, Manu, or the Devil) by which tribesmen were sustained against their enemies in the days when the serpent could still talk.

Joseph Campbell (1904-1987)
The Masks of God

Joseph Campbell is best known for his long radio and television dissertations dealing with the world's mythologies. My objection was that too often he did not explain to gullible minds that he was simply talking about mythologies and was not in the least saying there was any substance in them. For him to unburden himself as he does in the above quotation is refreshing. Campbell knew well that the mythologies of the Judeo-Christian-Muslim religions, as well as those of any other of the "great" religions, are in no way better than the mythologies of the ancient Romans, Greeks, Norsemen, Hindus, Egyptians, etc.

There is certainly merit in being aware of the extent of the folly of our ancestors, but we should be reminded constantly that we are at least as gullible as they. We accept that which is false as true, that which is counterfeit as genuine, that which is ignorance as wisdom, that which is mundane as sacred, and that which is an expression of manifestly sane, objective, realistic insight as blasphemy.

Bertrand Russell in *Why I Am Not a Christian*, when contemplating the idea that everything must have a cause, asks, "Then why not God? If we can make exceptions, it is just as logical to single out the world as an exception as to fabricate a God and declare Him as the one entity without a cause."

Bertrand Russell says about Christianity and Judaism what Joseph Campbell says about all of mythology. Both men do us a tremendous service. If we accept their advice and stop allowing ourselves to be duped by Biblical folklore and the vast literature of mythologies from all countries in the world, we will augment prodigiously our hope of living sane, productive lives.

187

"Is the good Lord deaf," a priest in Belgium expostulated, recalling all the prayers said for two missing girls allowed to starve to death when held by a pornography ringleader.

Newsweek (page 51) September 2, 1996

Not deaf, nonexistent, as any scientifically conducted analysis of prayer would effectively show. Prayer (like music) is good for those doing the praying (playing). but cannot serve the intended beneficiaries if they are out of earshot.

It is a sad truth, difficult for all the dittoheads of the world to accept, but the world functions quite well without the help of mystical prayer or any other kind of magic. Causes are not always easy to trace, but for pseudo-causes like prayer (and we may as well add extreme unction, blessings, mortification, penance, confession, conversion, and sanctification) there is nothing to trace. The cause of nothing is nothing, and effect is not affected. Those who pray waste their time as much as do sorcerers and astrologers. Crystal-ball gazers, tarot card dealers, channelers, palm readers, and faith healers are enemies of sanity. Nonsense will always be nonsense, and there is no use pretending we will ever be able to make great inroads into eliminating it. Those who choose to spend their lives immersed in myth and magic or indulge themselves with trivia or find identity only in distractions have little in common with those whose nature demands that they be creative and productive. The future belongs to people who use their minds constructively, seeking ways to make this a better world.

Violence such as that which so horrified the Belgium priest is one of the world's greatest enemies. Another is the expectation that prayer is a remedy for violence. Much of the effort of all caring people must be directed toward trying to rid our societies of physical and metaphysical barbarity.

188

No historian would deny that the part played by crimes committed for personal motives is very small compared to the vast populations slaughtered in unselfish loyalty to a jealous god, king, country, or political system.

Arthur Koestler (1905-1983) - *Janus*

Once people define themselves as belonging to groups, they function in a manner very different from when acting alone. Members of neighborhood gangs commit crimes they would not consider when simply free-spirited scamps unaffected by the pressure of unscrupulous peers or the example of worthy role models. Members of established religions unite to perpetrate atrocities they could not and would not do as unaffiliated individuals.

The barbarities committed by groups are often done with complete conviction that their murders and ravages are for the long-term benefit of mankind. Christian Crusaders kill Jews, Muslims, or Turks, "knowing" that their God approves. Nazis kill eleven million of their countrymen and those of neighboring countries to make this " a better world." What Pol Pot, Pinochet, Stroessner, Stalin, Castro, Perón, Idi Amin, and their henchmen do to their own people, only a psychopath, utterly devoid of social or moral conscience would think of doing.

Die-hard members of orthodox religions have only contempt for any but their own beliefs. Their group mentality is a curse, not a beneficence. Even members of the so-called liberal religions are often found quarreling (essay 253). Speaking of Unitarianism, Alfred

North Whitehead said: "It is the belief that there is at most one god: Unitarianism, that is, leaves room for some differences of opinion."

Anyone who believes passionately in the value of all human life (essay 316), in the equality of all people of good will (essay 63), and in an unrestricted love for all moral human beings, however and wherever they live (essay 38), will find a measure of compatibility with many members of the Unitartian-Universalists, and with both unorganized and organized atheists, atheists who do and do not do their own individual thinking.

Those who become emancipated from the yoke of orthodox religions and "orthodox" atheism usually find themselves rejecting all authoritarianism. For them to become a member of (or especially a member of the governing clique of) whatever religions, think tanks, political parties, fraternities, or secret societies would mean forfeiting individuality. They defend their freedom to choose from among all views, opinions, and convictions - ultimately shaping a consistent personal philosophy they can live with peacefully. My own experience with atheist organizations is to find only two who could tolerate me and my foibles—one in Canada and one in Scotland.

189

Religion is only in the service of the people; it is not in the rosary and the prayer-carpet.

Mosleh od-Din Saʻdi (1213-1292)
Persian Poet

When we ascribe supernatural spirits to inanimate objects, giving them powers to bring luck, repel evil, or guarantee success, we reach the extreme limit of superstition and stupidity. Holy water, prayer wheels, sacred vessels, divine light, and hallowed ground are moronic coinages. Thuribles, rosaries, crucifixes, crèches, mezuzahs, and menorahs are fanciful fetishes with the efficacy of a gelatin hammer. Repelling evil, working spells, speaking in tongues, and laying on of hands might be called asinine behavior were that not so unfairly depreciatory of the nimble, noble ass. Religion, if anything, is "brotherhood," which does not require gimmicks and gimcracks or even deities—as Buddhism, Confucianism, and Taoism make clear.

Phillip L. Berman in *The Search for Meaning* tells us that Maria

Cheng repudiated not only the gimcracks, but the whole shebang. She seemed to believe that religion is no place to look for meaning of any kind.

190

> Heresy is only another word for freedom of thought.
>
> Graham Greene (1904-1991)

Those who overcome provincial ways of thinking are bound to become heretics, for there is so much to be heretical about. Most orthodoxies eventually become outlandish in their declarations and, sooner or later, members, once obsequious and content, become educated and alarmed. They begin to see how they are being deceived. Things come to such a pass that the most enlightened among them cannot stand it any longer, and they rebel. They become what mother orthodoxy calls heretics, those who no longer can believe what "the church" believes.

Heresy is not a pollution, but a benediction, an illuminating hope for mankind. *The Faith of a Heretic*, Walter Kaufmann called his book, and talks movingly of the delights of breaking out of the prison of religious zealotry. Once accustomed to the fresh air and sunshine that envelops those at last free to use their minds untrammeled by the restraints of convention and tradition, most will never return to intellectual slavery.

Some, it is true, do fall back again into subjugation. It seems they miss the security of absolutism and the comfort of dogmatism and slip back into their old ways of thinking and doing. Others suffer an even worse fate; they found new religions of their own, no better than the old. They have their explanations, but to disinterested observers the difference makes no difference. It is like the choice in rotten apples, or the difference between six and a half dozen. They have wasted their time, but worse still, they have failed when opportunity knocked. They could have become free.

191

> Religion *per se* seems to me a barbaric superstition.... The clergymen who do any good don't pay much attention to religion. They teach people the conduct of life, and on the whole in a high and noble way.
>
> Charles S. Peirce (1839-1914) – Letter to William James

To teach people how to behave sanely with any degree of efficiency is to cite examples of moral conduct among one's compatriots. These examples will not be found among the clergy of any denomination. The clergy have been schooled in deceit to the point that they are hardly aware of when they are being deceitful. There are exceptions, of course, and Peirce seems to think he has found a few of them who do really talk primarily of moral behavior. They leave religion out of their discourse, knowing that it interferes rather than helps in their objective of teaching morality.

The Bible does not help, and reading it may be worse than hearing it recited by preachers. The reader includes its violence, pornography, bigotry, prejudice, sexual discrimination, xenophobia, and its many contradictions and inconsistencies. The preacher will leave these out. The only hope for the churchgoer is to seek a preacher who does teach morality. He (the churchgoer) will not find a preacher whose principal theme is morality among the evangelists who sermonize on television. Their main concern is neither "religion" nor "the conduct of life"; it is how to coax viewers to part with more of their savings.

192

The forging of myths is an intrinsic necessity of the thought process, to such a degree that even the arts unveil only a fragment of the human capacity in that direction.

Ezequiel Martínez
X-ray of the Pampas

Joseph Campbell, in a long lifetime as a student of mythology, documents well what Martínez says. Campbell's books are the best possible source for anyone who would like to know more about the world's mythologies.

An interesting example of the forging of myths occurred in our own country shortly before and after the year 1800. It revived from ancient persuasions and probably dates in its modern renewal from 1624, the year Lord Herbert of Cherbury published his *De Veritate*. It finally came to be called deism. The God of Leibnitz, Voltaire, Franklin, Paine, Jefferson, and John Adams, to name a few of the deists, was said to have begun this rat race and will be around to choose the winners, but has had nothing to do with the race itself. In 1970, William Paley, who in his *Horae Paulinae* declared it improbable that the New Testament was "a cunningly devised fable," four years later, in his *View of the Evidences of Christianity* (1794) argued in refutation of deism.

One cannot become very excited about a God who started the universe going and then dropped it like a hot potato never to bother with it again. Certainly, prayers to such a God would be the most egregious kind of nonsense. Deism, like Pantheism, was little more than an evasion. And to be to that extent liberated from the debasing and repressive theology of Judeo-Christian-Muslim religions and not to have achieved the final emancipation, for me is beyond comprehension. It is hard to believe that either deists or pantheists were ever serious about their nonsensical speculations.

193

The thought which the word God suggests to the human mind is susceptible of as many varieties as human minds themselves ... and not only has every sect distinct conceptions of the application of this name, but scarcely two individuals of the same sect... find perfect coincidence of opinion to exist between them.

Percy Bysshe Shelley (1792-1822)

Every human brain has imbedded in its cellular structure some physical analogue of all the experiences the owner of that brain has had in all his previous years. Whenever he forms a new concept, the manner of its formation depends to a large degree on the concepts already there. Since no two persons have had identical experiences, no two brains are the same and gods and whatever else he adds to the cellular structure will be different from those of another individual. What Shelley says about varieties of gods is obviously true.

Does it seem a little strange that with all the communication lines our many preachers have to God, they know almost nothing about Him that agrees with what anyone else knows? If they ask questions and get answers that disagree with those others get, they must be asking some strange questions. Or is it possible that the answers they get with their pipelines to God are indecipherable or, as Robert Frost decided, that God simply isn't there. The answers, then, are either hallucinations or tendentious fabrications.

194

Prejudices ... are like rats, and men's minds are like traps; prejudices get in easily, but it is doubtful if they ever get out.

Lord Francis Jeffrey (1773-1850)
Scottish critic and jurist

Prejudice is indeed not easily eradicated. Race riots and absurd jury decisions in the United States in recent years indicate that we are not making nearly as much progress as we may have thought. Charlotte Brontë, Laurence J. Peter, and Charles Victor Roman (elsewhere in this book) speak of the relation between education and prejudice. Gordon W. Allport wrote a book on prejudice, and Jean-Paul Sartre wrote an excellent essay dealing with the subject. Religion, unfortunately, continues to increase rather than decrease the amount of prejudice in the world.

Every high school and college curriculum should have a credit course on prejudice. Radio and small- and large-screen programs should deal with the subject more efficaciously than they do. Not until every human being understands how prejudice comes into being and how it can be eliminated can we learn to live with one another without the rancor and hatred now so disruptive of our societies.

We must learn that differences are the very essence of progress. No species and no societies can evolve into improved forms unless they are made up of members that are different one from another. Selection is not possible if there are no differences from which to select. Only if we learn to treasure and even encourage differences will we become a world population that can survive the social and political upheavals that threaten us. The problem is urgent. The effort to find solutions cannot be postponed.

195

We might as well give up the fiction / That we can argue any view, For what in me is pure Conviction / Is simple Prejudice in you.

Phyllis McGinley
"Note to My Neighbor" – *Times Three*

The way we view things often depends on whether or not we accept unfounded assumptions as gospel truth. Our personal convictions depend on the myriad of personal experiences we have had in our past life—and on how gullible or skeptical we are in interpreting those experiences. No two people have had the same experiences, and therefore we will all think differently, and live with different convictions. Religion has solved the problem by proclaiming dogma, which by definition must be accepted as true. The rest of us solve the problem by being amenable or pigheaded, and if the latter, for the sake of peace, agreeing to disagree.

Usually in a conversation with anyone, we perceive the McGinley attitude if it is there and know that meaningful interchange will be impossible. We may discuss the weather, but little else.

Those who believe their convictions have a basis in reason often love to argue because they are sure their beliefs will not suffer when confronting convictions that cannot withstand logical analysis. If they find they have been wrong, that it is they who have been making false assumptions, they may lose face, but they must admit their error and retreat in good grace.

Those who are aware that their beliefs are founded on faith, on the other hand, are reluctant to engage in lively discussion, and do not expect to change their beliefs ever. Both they and those with whom they have argued in the past have learned that there is no answer to their it-is-so-because-it-is-so kind of argument, so why go through it all over again. They will discuss religion only with those who believe exactly as they do. Discussion for them must be a mutual-admiration exchange in which no one learns anything. If the slightest hint of contention arises, they will terminate the dialogue.

196

The only reconstruction worthwhile is a reconstruction of thought.

Kelly Miller (1863-1939)
Reconstruction of Thought

The ten years of reconstruction after the Civil War helped return us to being a viable nation. If, beginning right now, we could have a Manhattan project of ten years of reconstruction of thought, this country could be turned into a veritable paradise. It would mean a revolution - with bold thinking and bold action and with everyone involved. We would stop flirting with metaphysical nonsense, rid the big and small screens of violence, and reward writers in proportion to the inspiration for good in their words.

Our churches would be converted into schools for teaching morality; our schools would turn out students competent in all subjects needed in our new world. Carefully planned software for helping teachers in every subject would be available. Computers would correct exams in seconds, giving teachers time for other important tasks.

Prevention would be emphasized in medicine, cutting Medicare costs to much less than they now are. New electronic prostheses for the disabled would help many more of them become productive citizens.

197

> The civilized man has a moral obligation to be skeptical, to demand the credentials of all statements that claim to be facts.
>
> Bergen Evans – *The Natural History of Nonsense*

How could it be otherwise? If we fail in what Evans asks of us, the world will soon be overrun with senseless beliefs and opinions. We will live in a jumble of debilitating absurdities that could well be our undoing. We have already allowed the mystagogues, who have a vested interest in deceiving us, to convince us to accept an entire hierarchy of mythologies that have no basis in fact that anyone has ever been able to discern.

Bergen Evans, professor at Northwestern and for years host of the program *The Quiz Kids*, in his statement above tells us something that should be obvious to any six-year-old child.

Religionists profess to be interested in morality, but failure in their "moral obligation to be skeptical" demonstrates that morality is the last of their concerns. If they were all to become diehard skeptics, all religions would disappear immediately. To "demand the credentials of all statements that claim to be facts" would be to find that in most aspects of religion no such credentials exist. "Hypocrisy" is the word that comes to mind when trying to follow the sophistry of the religious mind.

Bergen Evan's book does not deal with religions, but it does deal with the kind of human minds that will believe the myths that afflict human beings and disturb their relations with the world in which they live.

198

The time must come inevitably when mankind shall surmount the imbecility of religion, as it has surmounted the imbecility of religion's ally, magic.

H.L. Mencken (1880-1956)
Minority Report

Mencken continues: "It is impossible to imagine this world being really civilized so long as so much nonsense survives. In even its highest forms, religion embraces concepts that run counter to all common sense. It can be defended only be making assumptions and adopting rules of logic that are never heard of in any other field of human thinking."

Only with respect to the time interval that Mencken might be thinking of can I disagree with him. It will happen eventually, but almost certainly not within the next hundred years, possibly, yes, within the next thousand. It may never happen, for mankind may eliminate his own species from the face of the earth before it can.

The auguries are not good. The God religionists have invented seems to favor war. This means that all believers have imbedded in their nervous systems the concept that war is an acceptable solution to the world's problems. If a third world war threatens, they will urge it on. "The next world war will be a war to end all wars, because it will end all warriors," said F.S.C. Northrop. Samuel Pisar, quoted in *God in America* by Furio Colombo, adds: "To me, we are facing quite possibly the thermonuclear gas chamber of the future—a kind of global Auschwitz."

199

This is a depressing country, we have no slums, no poverty. We all have a good standard of living, good jobs, pay, medical care, education, unemployment insurance, social security, and retirement plans. But there is no challenge in life. There is nothing to struggle for.

A young Swedish social worker
Quoted by Roderic Gorney, M.D., Ph.D.
The Human Agenda

The best advice any psychiatrist can give to those suffering from depression or a sense of the utter futility of their existence, often is that they lose themselves in an absorbing hobby, social service, or in any other activity in which they can judge themselves as creative. If they are accomplishing something that not just anyone else can do, or is likely to do, all the better.

Unfortunately, too many respond to the psychiatrist's counsel with efforts that are of no earthly use to anyone. They accumulate personal wealth with unbounded rapacity. Their efforts to dominate over others becomes a passion. They find it monstrously satisfying when they succeed in imposing their groundless religions on others. They do nothing to ameliorate the miseries that oppress fellow human beings: poverty, hunger, ill health, ignorance, or lack of shelter.

Many participate in what is going on in the world only vicariously. Spectator sports, movie-star worship, TV game shows, Cinderella stories, and beauty pageants become for them the substance of their lives. For others, make-believe becomes a dominating diversion. With the help of mind-altering drugs, endless reveries, or meaningless palaver, they while away life's precious hours. They would welcome the Swede's stifling overabundance.

200

Concerning the gods, I am unable to discover whether they exist or not, or what they are like in form.

Protagoras (485-410 BC)

Plato in *Cratylus* quotes Herogenes as saying: "When we respond to the dictates of our own good sense we confess that we know nothing about the existence of gods, nor of their personalities, nor of their names."

In the more than two thousand years since Herogenes and Protagoras, we know nothing more, but we pretend that we do. We talk to God, and supposedly He answers. Quite recently Gunter Grass said: "I don't know about God.... The only things I know about are what I see, hear, feel, taste, and smell." We know nothing about gods, but still we write millions of words about them. How much better off the world would be if we restricted ourselves to writing about things we know something about.

In the Judeo-Christian-Muslim religions, we invent a single all-powerful Deity and then we have *Him* writing scriptures. These scriptures are repetitious, monstrous, contradictory, and full of redundancies and inconsistencies, hardly the work of an omniscient illuminatus. He would not win any Nobel or Pulitzer prizes for literature. Reading the scriptures will assure any moderately intelligent person that they were written by mortal men and on the whole are shallow and morally untenable accounts. They certainly are not worthy of being read and reread, as some do, limiting their education to this one gloomy, demeaning and, pretentious book. Nowhere in the Bible are there book-length narratives, except in the case of Joseph and His Brothers. Even there, Thomas Mann did and infinitely better job.

201

What can we do to prevent human rights abuse before it happens. The most obvious answer must be to assure that the guilty parties don't get away with it.

Caroll Bogert, Communications Director
Human Rights Watch

Nearly all despots of past history did get away with it. Most died natural deaths, some at the pinnacle of their reign of terror. Their example is precisely the wrong message to give to acting and would-be dictators today. All tyrants bent on despotic rule of their country must be made aware that they will be deposed for their first flagrant atrocity and spend the rest of their lives in jail.

Just previous to the time of this writing, there seemed to be some possibility that Augusto Pinochet might stand trial for his crimes. If so, it would be the first ray of hope that world attitudes with regard to the immunity of ruling despots are changing. England had Pinochet under arrest. Spain and other countries petitioned his extradition for purposes of standing trial in their countries. Now that he has returned to Chile, there is a possibility that his arrest in England has roused passions enough to give the families of his 3000 victims incentive and cause to demand his prosecution.

Haiti's Baby Doc, now in Southern France, may suffer a similar fate, with Patriots there planning to try him for his crimes. His successor, Raul Cedras in Panama City, Uganda's Idi Amin in Saudi Arabia, Paraguay's Alfredo Stroessner in Brazil, and even lesser criminals such as Mexico's Carlos Salinas in Dublin, Ireland, may also be resting less easily in light of the Pinochet arrest in England and his disfavor at home.

Some still in power: Fidel Castro of Cuba, Efrain Rios Montt of Guatemala, Slobodan Milosevic of Yugoslavia, and Saddam Hussein of Iraq also have murdered hundreds, thousands, even hundreds of thousands of their own people in order to keep themselves in power. The fiction that ruling despots must be considered immune from prosecution is a moral anachronism. Even God, though a figment of human imagination, should be held accountable. Millions of murders have been committed in His name in the past, and the future looks no better.

202

No one with any sense of humor ever founded a religion.
                                   Robert G. Ingersoll (1833-1899)
                                   Prose-Poems and Selections

Perhaps not, but humor does crop up at times: Luis Brnuel says, "I am an atheist still, thank God." G.K. Chesterton said, "Angels can fly because they take themselves lightly." P.B. Medawar talks of those who are bunkrapt. Christopher Fry said: "What, after all, is a halo. It is only one more thing to keep clean." Oscar Wilde intrigues us partly because of his constant and uncanny wordplay and witticisms. Almost no author can be perpetually serious. Occasional wordplay, irony, repartee, or good-natured banter will do wonders to keep a reader reading and alert.

An anthologist determined to keep his literary specimens completely serious would find his task difficult. It is human nature to enjoy humor. Then why do we find one of the greatest anthologies ever written—made up of some 39 books—completely devoid of humor? The authors are opinionated, imperious, dour, and dull as ditchwater. Those whose only reading is the Bible become as insular and dull as the book they read. They are poor company, and would be irksome, even in heaven.

If, as is claimed, we are made in God's image, where did we get our sense of humor? God, obviously, has none. A deity, who can kill a man for innocently touching a covenant box, and 250 others for bringing Him incense, is past redemption. We would find Him a poor companion at the swimming hole or at a charivari (shivaree, where I grew up). Any time we wanted to have fun, we would slip off without Him.

203

> Observe how the greatest minds yield in some degree to the superstitions of their age.
>
> Henry David Thoreau (1817-1862)
> *Journal*

Father Dominic Devas urges motorists "to have the medal of St. Christopher honorably and firmly affixed to their cars."

Ruth Montgomery tells us that there are thousands of "walk-ins" among us.

Shirley MacLaine spent many pages of print as well as hours of television time trying to convince us that reincarnation is a fact of the cosmos.

Baptists and other Christian sects believe that sprinkling water on a baby's head or dunking the entire baby will wash away sin and admit the baby to Christianity.

Newspapers in the United States would lose subscribers it they did not print horoscopes daily for people to read.

Thirty-nine adult men and women killed themselves in Rancho Santa Fe in southern California, expecting a celestial vehicle to pick them up and carry them to a higher level.

Catholics, Buddhists, and Muslims thumb their way through strings of beads while saying prayers to keep themselves eligible for heaven.

In a lecture titled "The Chosen People," given on December 15, 1878, Felix Adler said, "It is necessary to assail the towering superstitions of the day, painfully necessary, not only because they are absurd, but because they tend to degrade mankind and to brutalize him."

204

> There is a Christian hypochondria, from which those singular, religiously agitated people suffer who place always before their eyes the suffering and death of Christ.
>
> Friedrich Wilhelm Nietzsche (1844-1900) – *Human, All Too Human*

Upon leaving our hotel room in Panama City, I noticed I had cut my finger while laying down my razor, so I returned to put iodine on the cut. Partly to reassure my wife, who would recognize my voice, and partly to get myself on my way again, I shouted into the bathroom where she had secluded herself, "Would you please hand out the iodine to me." Just as I finished treating myself, I saw the bathroom doorknob turning so I quickly positioned myself to apply iodine to a profusely bleeding stab wound in a statue of a crucified Jesus the hotel had placed on a radiator mantel near the entrance to the room. What has forced me to remember the incident, was probably not my wife's ready-to-kill reaction, but thoughts somewhat akin to what Nietzsche expresses. The statue was nothing pleasant to confront, so the fact that is was a bulk-fabrication item and had sales potential must surely be accounted for by Christian delight in observing it constantly in their homes and places of business.

The pleasure some people get from being made miserable is evident in another religious event that has long begged explanation. How else do we account for confession. Today we find the practice losing favor; even many who consider themselves good Catholics no longer go to confession. They see that to recount in agonizing detail every imagined transgression of "holy law" is a kind of masochistic folly. To submit to schoolteacher grading on a scale of good and evil each such transgression is to compound absurdity. To believe that a Father Confessor has a right to toss you to an angry God who callously sentences men and women to perpetual torture is to live in a chamber of horrors.

205

Where true religion has prevented a crime, false religions have provided a pretext for a thousand.

Charles Caleb Colton

The Christian Crusades, Thirty Years War, Spanish Inquisition, and witch burnings we have talked about are obvious examples. But the pages of our newspapers day after day give us additional examples of crimes committed by fanatical religionists who tell us they are acting in the name of God.

Bombs are going off almost daily in many parts of the world planted by fanatical religionists who tell us they have the right to take innocent people's lives in order to do God's will. We see them hating members of other sects, of other races, of other sexual orientations— all strangely assuming that thereby they are furthering the cause of religion.

We find religionists constantly depreciating science, seemingly denying that truth will emerge only if all human disciplines with integrity and respect are allowed to have their say. They seem unaware that only the "truth" that legitimately wins its place in the sun without chicanery or coercion will survive.

Too often in our societies the antics of preachers *is* the crime: extortion, lechery, pedophilia, adultery, alcoholism, as well as all the political shenanigans of the Christian Coalition and the ersatz science of creation scientists. Crimes committed by ecclesiastics are doubly repugnant because it is they who pretend to be exemplary models for us to follow. At least they should not be models of iniquity.

206

"The Good Book"—one of the most remarkable euphemisms ever coined.

Ashley Montagu

But for some people it *is* the good book, Mr. Montagu. It is good for tyrants who want people divided into warring factions, ever at each other's throats. It is good for amassing wealth, helping the Jerry Falwells and Pat Robertsons of the world to bilk millions of dollars from naïve television viewers. It is good for teaching us to worship fantasies: divine deities, wingéd angles, virgin mothers, immortal souls, and haploid demigods. It is good for teaching prejudices: Devotees can read it as favoring slavery, despising homosexuals, scoring family unity, abhorring contraception, and depreciating women. The Bible is a good book for those whose intentions are bad, a large percentage of the people of this world.

Included among that large percentage is one preacher in particular. He finds the Bible good for teaching hate, sure that hatred is an essential ingredient of piety. Fred W. Phelps, pastor at the Westboro Baptist church in Topeka, Kansas said on the World Wide Web, speaking of the Bible: "For every one verse of God's mercy, love, compassion, etc., there are two verses about his vengeance, hatred, wrath, etc. Phelps accuses the preachers of today's societies of being maudlin, failing to explain that the Bible preaches hate."

In *that* the Reverend Phelps is right. The Bible does indeed preach hate. But Phelps is not "lamenting the fact." He is rejoicing in it. He sees the Bible's (and God's) hatred as man's salvation. Most of the people of Topeka are appalled. They bemoan the fact that there are not legal means to eject him from their city. They are fed up with his outrageous behavior (picketing funerals) and his offensive language (God hates fags).

Even those pillars of the church who are sure the Bible is divinely inspired scripture are unable to document positive consequences that result form veneration of the Bible. As studies made by George Rex Mursall in the Ohio Reform School and by P.R. Hightower, testing three thousand children, show, the tendency of children to lie and cheat was in direct proportion - and not in reverse ratio - to their knowledge of the Bible and scriptural precepts. Children exposed to progressive educative methods, based on secular premises and modern psychology appear to have a far better record as to honesty and dependability. Religious indoctrination does not improve the moral behavior of either children or adults.

Chapter VI

Myth and Mysticism

207

Myths arise from the effort to give meaning and form and to inject purpose into meaningless, formless, and purposeless reality. Myths are not like fairy tales and fables, meant only to entertain or to teach a moral lesson. Myths are intended to relate factual aspects of reality, absolutely necessary if people are to live meaningfully. Success for fabulists and fairy chroniclers depends only on finding readers who enjoy and feel uplifted by their delightful fictions. Success for the mythmongers depends on finding an audience gullible enough to believe them.

Judaic, Christian, and Muslim religions in closed societies, having made their choices among gods, demons, demigods, intercessors, prophets, angels, jinn, messiahs, and saints, seek to teach an absolute supremacy. Buddhism, with *The Tibetan Book of the Dead*, is seen as full partner of all religions based on myth and make-believe. Their goals never vary. None will be satisfied until they rule the world.

The children of progressive societies usually surpass the maturation of their parents. Their children, too, continue to progress. Somewhere among future generations there will be those who understand what their behavior is leading to. They will refuse to reify supernal coinages and then worship these reifications. When this happens among large percentages of the population, we can expect the citizens of the world to form a viable global community, with enough influence to disregard the ambitions and pretensions of the mythmongers. Sanity will return, and the world will become a much better place in which to live.

208

> The universe is a spectacle which the Good God gives for his own amusement.
>
> Ernest Renan (1823-1892)

Trying to ascertain just what the Good God is up to, we do finally come to the conclusion that Renan is truly the wise old bird. Unfortunately, God's amusement seems to include a lot of murder and mayhem that His victims could well do without. The Bible talks about how much God relishes the smell of burning fat. That may explain hell and possibly His delight in burnt offerings and fires. But there is much else that needs explaining.

Of course if God is as sadistic as He is made out to be, most of the Bible could be an account of God amusing Himself. He does seem to enjoy ladling out blood (Hebrews 9:18-22). Also, God sheds the blood of His sixth-day creations freely. The number people He kills with famines, plagues, storms, fire, war, and personal intervention could number in the millions. The number of additional millions of murders that God is guilty of by not restraining a Stalin, Hitler, and Pol Pot lead us to wonder if Stendhal may not be the one who really has it right: "God's only excuse is that He does not exist."

Assuming that Stendhal does have it right, we see that by falsely postulating the existence of God many Biblical personages have gotten away with murder. Reconsidering, we would have to decide that it was David who killed Uzzah (2 Samuel 6:7), that Moses killed his brother Aaron (Numbers 20:28). Who was it really that killed Job's family (Job 1:13-19)? Who destroyed Sodom and Gemorrah? Who killed 14,700 Israelites (Numbers 16:49), then 70,000 more (2 Samuel 24:15), then 70 others (one translation says 50,070) (1 Samuel 6:19), and later 250 others (Numbers 16:35). Without a God to blame, there is no end to crimes described in the Bible that need reexamination.

209

There is no Heaven, there is no Hell; These are the dreams of baby minds; Tools of the wily Fetisheer, To fright the fools his cunning blinds.

Sir Richard Francis Burton (1821-1890)
The Kasidah VIII

Burton is saying in verse what Seneca says in prose elsewhere in this book: "Religion is regarded by the common people as true, by the wise as false, and by the rulers as useful." Burton's Fetisheer is clever enough to take advantage of the naïveté of the common people in order to further his own ends. Heaven (rewards) and Hell (prison), he has found, are effective tools for altering behavior. Fear is God's favorite device for turning his subjects into sequacious followers.

There are no atheists among the unthinking masses. It requires a habit of analyzing the things one is asked to believe, in order to become an atheist. One must understand how one is being manipulated by rulers before one can rebel against that manipulation. Those wise enough to realize that religion is false will take over, and they will educate the common people and find among themselves new enlightened rulers.

The atheist believes in no supernal entities or infernal machinations. He is Ingersoll's eagle, parting the clouds with tireless wing. Without the encumbrances the mystagogues would heap upon him, he is free to do some real good for his fellowman, to explain to them the authority of good sense and the reach of human potential. Especially, he can give them insight into what is really needed to make this a better world.

210

The only points in which I differ from all ecclesiastical teaching is that I do not believe that any man ever saw or talked with God. I do not believe that God inspired the Mosaic code....

Elizabeth Cady Stanton (1815-1902) – *The Woman's Bible*

Two questions for Mrs. Stanton: Has any man ever seen or talked with Hamlet? Do you believe that God inspired the *Book of Mormon*?

If the answers, again, are "no" in both cases, could the reasons be that God and Hamlet do not exist? It is very difficult, we know, to see or talk with fictional characters. Could the reasons that God did not inspire the Mosaic code be that He did not inspire, or have anything whatsoever to do with any scripture?

Perhaps Stendhal gave the simplest and most definitive answer to all such questions when he reminded us that we have no reason whatsoever to believe that God exists and many reasons for believing that He does not. Now we can get on to considering problems that really do have significance in our lives.

Elizabeth Cady Stanton, surely one of the greatest women in American history, was far ahead of most people of her time. In her references to religions she probably went about as far as she could go and still hope to reach her goal of attaining woman suffrage. She and Susan B. Anthony (1820-1906), life-long confederates in the struggle of equality for women, must still today be tremendously inspiring models for all women.

211

Every man who has been drugged by the opiate of the orthodox theologies must fight his way through to reason by the path of revulsion, agony, and repudiation....

J.H. Holmes
The Sensible Man's View of Religion

To hear these words from a preacher is what surprises and amazes us. But who would have better opportunity to see what orthodox religions do to people? Holmes goes on to say: "We must not blame those men who shock us, perhaps, with the fury of their hostility to religion. Rather we must praise them for their acuteness in discovering that the religion which they have known is a dangerous drug, for their willingness to meet the agony and endure the pain which must accompany the fight against it, and for their heroism in winning at last deliverance for themselves, and thus for other people. These men are champions of truth and servants of life."

The complete lack of evidence for the existence of gods, ghosts, and gremlins will not discourage true believers. As Neil Postman once said, "If a man wants to believe something badly enough he will find "evidence." False testimony can always be "authenticated" to serve the purpose. Illusions and hallucinations can easily be metamorphosed into gospel truth. Evidence can be fabricated out of whole cloth in exactly the form needed to substantiate whatever is considered important to believe. Those who strive to debunk such evidence will indeed face anger and vengeance. All the powers of piety will combine to destroy anyone who would reveal the truth about religion.

212

> God ... could not make Antonio Stradivari violins without Antonio.
> George Eliot (1819-1880)
> *The George Eliot Letters*

And *with* Antonio, He would not need to. We can choose to believe George Eliot, or we can choose not to. Many enlightened people today choose to believe her. They might say that God's excuse for not being able to do so (to recall the prescience of Stendhal) is that He does not exist. We are safe to face saber-toothed tigers, mastodons, and tyrannosaurus; to play leapfrog with unicorns, leviathans, and Cerberus for the same reason: the first three because they do not exist, the last three because they never have. For God, we must select from one of three categories: "does," "does not," and "never has." If we bet on the basis of what is really evidence, we will choose the last.

After the first few pages of the Bible, we find God so frequently asking some human being or angel to do his bidding that we wonder if He can ever do anything by Himself. But of course, we forget. He made the entire universe with no help from anyone that we know of. And He did it in four days—no mean feat. Counting some hundred billion galaxies, each perhaps with some 400 billion stars, and no doubt many trillions of planets and a few quintillion rocks floating around here and there, he must have had a busy four days. We do not know if in the last two days, which He spent populating one tiny speck of the universe, He populated any of the other trillions of possible habitable planets as well.

213

I don't believe in God because I don't believe in Mother Goose.

Clarence Darrow (1857-1938)

The implication being, of course, that the existence of a theomorphic daddy in the clouds is as unlikely as is an anthropomorphic mama in the goose down. The evidence for believing in God is the same as that for believing in leprechauns, wood nymphs, abominable snowmen chupacabras, goblins, and gremlins.

It is strange to see how church leaders who are constantly intent on burdening their flocks with all the absurdities of religion will at the same time and with equal fervor warn the members of their congregations against the sham of fortune tellers, soothsayers, psychics, palmists, crystal-gazers, and witches.

"I don't believe in God because I don't believe in anything for which there is no shred of evidence," would be more to the point. I *do* believe in ring-tailed lemurs in Madagascar. I do believe that black-footed ferrets are not extinct. I do believe in a certain species of Darwin finch that will use a tool to dig a grub worm out of a hole in a tree because I have witnessed the performance with my own eyes. Recently, in a television documentary, I saw a crow do the same thing. I do believe in that for which there is ample, incontrovertible evidence. Until such incontrovertible evidence presents itself for gods and goblins, truth for me will await confirmation.

214

Baptism is not valid if it is done by pouring, sprinkling, daubing with a damp cloth or cavorting under a fire hose.

Herbert W. Armstrong
What Do You Mean—Salvation?

Only complete dunking in a polluted river or lake, or in a chlorine-laced backyard swimming pool makes baptism valid. This is no doubt spelled out clearly in the Bible - or is it possible that some mere mortal has taken upon himself the right to decide when baptism is or is not valid? Surely, Herbert W. Armstrong would not have thought of doing such a thing.

The same mere mortals who wrote the Bible, built and consecrated the churches, anointed saviors, and invented the gods, also fashioned the various sacraments prescribed in man-made religions. To imagine that any or all of the constructions of man cannot be altered or repudiated also by man as he sees fit is remarkably presumptuous. The Herbert W. Armstrongs of the world never say, "as I see it," "according to my best guess," or the like. They all say flatly, "this is the case" [now and forever].

215

I wonder when Christianity will have decayed sufficiently for the fact to be driven into men's heads that pleasure is not hurtful nor pain beneficial.

W. Somerset Maugham (1874-1965)

More and more people are waiting for the decay, not the development, of Christianity to give them hope for a rational future. Alfred North Whitehead considered Christianity to be one of the greatest disasters that has ever befallen the human race.

Those among Christians who abjure pleasure and welcome pain in order to atone for imagined sins are the worst enemies Christianity has. The churches of such religionists are drab, unadorned, without candles, incense, bells, icons, or ritual. Sermons are devoid of eloquence, humor, metaphor, or melody. Everything they say and do observes the doctrines of a dreary religion and its doleful deity. The remedy is not to revise such religions, but to get rid of them.

To be "Christian" in the sense that many of us commonly accept that term is commendable. But we wonder that when we do find a candidate especially deserving of that appellation, he is as likely to be a Hindu, Buddhist, Muslim, Jew, Sikh, or an unaffiliated atheist - at least as likely as to be a member of the religion named after the protagonist of the New Testament. Camus was right in finding little relation between the words of that Nazarene and the preaching today that arrogates to itself exclusive succession from the practical moral counsels of Jesus. As a matter of common experience, in fact, to be a devoutly desired Christian (moral, kind, and generous), it has come to seem almost essential that the individual so considered not be the Christian of day-by-day observation. Certainly he will not be lecher

Jimmy Swaggart, swindler Jim Bakker, faith healer Oral Roberts, passionate avenger Jerry Falwell, or any of the other hypocrites that preach at us from the television screen. Christians may be the most convincing argument there is against Christianity! Lowell D. Streiker in *The Gospel of Irreligious Religion* says: "A major obstacle to cooperation between the religions of mankind has been the inhospitable attitudes of Christianity toward other religions."

216

Nature is honest; we aren't. We embalm our dead.

Ugo Betti (1892-1953)
Goat Island

It makes no difference to those who are dead if they are buried with all the pomp and grandeur of wealth, or tossed into a potter's field.

A gringo decorating a grave in a cemetery on November 2 in San Patricio, Jalisco, Mexico asked a fellow similarly engaged nearby: "When do you expect your wife to come up to eat the food you are providing for her?" "When your wife comes up to smell the flowers you are putting on her grave."

The vast amounts of money spent on burying people could be put to many uses far better than that. The best monuments are the good deeds performed by people before they die. The Taj Mahal could have been a beautiful public school dedicated to Shah Jahan's favorite wife.

Nature is not honest by design. It is honest because that is just the way thing are. Nature is not *for* us or *against* us; it offers no rewards or punishments. From its processes, we can expect only consequences. Then, if we do not like the way things turn out, they can be changed. That is what culture is all about—changing nature in order to make things proceed in a way that more adequately suits our whims and purposes.

"Nature in the raw is seldom mild," is an ad most readers are not old enough to remember. Nature can be raw indeed. Nature, at times means suffering beyond imagination. Few of nature's creatures live to a ripe old age. Most die in excruciating agony long before they would die in an environment made ideally for them. Thousands, often millions of animal and vegetable "seeds" are produced for one that survives. That is true of the Chinese elm tree that grows some thirty feet from where I am sitting. Bushel baskets are needed to carry away its tiny seeds. That is true of sperm. Each man produces billions during a lifetime, lucky to produce two, three, or four children. That is true of spores produced by ferns and mushrooms. Nature is profligate, but again not by design. That is just the way things have evolved to be.

217

It does me no injury for my neighbor to say there are twenty gods or no god.

Thomas Jefferson (1743-1825)
Notes on the State of Virginia

The key word in Jefferson's statement is "say." As long as neighbors talk nonsense and do not try to impose that nonsense on me, they do me no harm. As long as they do not get the anomalous notion that their nonsense is an edict of God that must be obeyed worldwide, they can still be friends. It is when saying is not enough, when worship becomes a passion and proselytizing an addiction, that danger looms.

In addition to witch-hunts, inquisitions, and wars, there are day-by-day consequences of religion: One of the significant reasons both before and after marriage young couples break up is that religious differences intrude. Children in two-religion families sometimes suffer from quarrels between father and mother concerning religion. Religions often turn the days of human lives into long, tedious, successive hours of drudgery, taking all the fun out of living.

Religion makes hypocrites of people, of those unable to adhere to unrealistic moral precepts preached at Sunday services, while they live as skeptical, normal human beings the rest of the week. Religion becomes a taboo topic for conversations. They can discuss with neighbors and colleagues family life, business tactics, and political matters, but not religion—without arousing unresolvable animosities.

Religion alters the level of sanity at which people live. Taught to accept myth as gospel in their religion, why not accept what the crystal-ball gazers tell them? Why not believe in palmistry, phrenology, fortune-telling, horoscopes, tarot cards, reincarnation, channeling, amulets, talismans, patent medicines, good luck, bad luck - whatever fraud or fantasy anyone comes up with? Why not indeed! Most religionists do.

218

> What one Christian does is his own responsibility. What one Jew
> does is thrown back at all Jews.
>
> Anne Frank (1929-1945)
> *Diary of a Young Girl*

It occurs to me that Christianity, with a little luck, might have become a perfectly acceptable discipline - not like any religion that anyone has imagined. Had he not died so young, Jesus, unhappy with the way Jews at the time were running things, might have thought of many ways to improve things. Jesus seems to have been perfectly capable of founding a religion, and with a little advice about myth and superstition, and especially about that God-son or son-God concept, might have become the moral leader of all the world today. His heart seemed to be in the right place, and he was not overly infatuated with ritual, ostentation, and pageantry.

Of course, without the anointing, consecration to leadership, the religion could not have been called Christianity. So what could this radically revised religion be called? If no other name could be found for it, why not call it Judaism?

If the Shia, accepting Ali as the only rightful successor to Muhammad, and the Sunni, accepting four caliphs as rightful successors to Muhammad, and their new testament (the Summa) as additional scripture - if they both can still agree to call themselves Muslims, why cannot Jew and Christians, with one name, do it as well? Why split up Judaism? Taking part of it and calling it Christianity was a foolish thing to do. The Holocaust and many other problems would never have occurred had no one dreamed up that stupidity.

Just toss out the mythology and the silly superstitions about food, circumcision, messiahs, phylacteries, mezuzahs, menorahs, the folklore about resurrection, walking on water, feeding thousands with few fishes, and all other mumbo jumbo about miracles. What would be left is Judaism's concept of charity, nonviolence, the golden rule, and love of all people. Rabbis would be strictly teachers and synagogues strictly institutions of learning and nothing else. Without that "old-time religion" that even Anne Frank could see through, what a religion the world would have!

219

> The Bible tells us to love our neighbours, and also to love our enemies; probably because they are generally the same people.
>
> G.K. Chesterton (1874-1936)

What Chesterton said agrees in part with what Jesus said: "A prophet is not without honor except in his own country and in his own house." The answer as to why it is that we expect less fame and fewer heroic deeds among our neighbors than we do from people who live far away may require analysis by competent psychologists. Simply on the basis of numbers, however, a certain degree of logic obtains. Our neighbors probably include some few thousand people. Beyond the area in which they live, we can find some six billion people. It is logical that we will find more people agreeing with us among the billions than among the thousands.

Another explanation is the propensity of all of us to apotheosize celebrities. Give anyone the title of prophet and we "know" that we are dealing with a palpably extraordinary individual. We probably imagine a visible aura, a halo, an angelic countenance, or the like. We look at our neighbors and see none of these telling signs. We laugh to find any of them arrogating to themselves divine prescience. If a coming Messiah were growing up in our community, none of us would know it.

220

> Our admiration is so given to dead martyrs that we have little time for living heroes.
>
> Elbert Hubbard (1856-1915)
> *The Note Book*

T.S. Eliot in *Murder in the Cathedral* tells us that the true martyr is he who has lost his will in the will of God. He is talking about all the religious pawns, puppets, robots, and automatons of history. Anyone who forfeits his own will for any reason whatsoever is lost to the world insofar as anyone can expect meaningful contributions from him.

The biggest lie preachers ever tell is when they assure others that when they give up their lives in defense of their religions they are martyrs and will go straight to heaven. Preachers know no such thing. No person on this earth could prove that statement, and it seems never will be able to do so. They are talking "nonsense" in the literal acceptation of that term.

If we want to praise heroes, we should do it while they are alive. We should write letters to them, praising them, and speaking of their good deeds. We must let them know that their efforts have not been in vain. We might go on to write public tributes, encomiums, panegyrics, and biographies in their honor. We can encourage others to do the same.

The statues we erect in the memory of heroes do them no good, and the epitaphs we inscribe at the foot of these statues are equally useless to those so honored. A very large percentage of the statues we erect praise reprobates. As examples, name every despot that has ever lived.

221

It is difficult to imagine anyone having any real hopes for the human race in face of the fact that the great majority of men still believe that the universe is run by a gaseous vertebrate of astronomical heft and girth, who is nevertheless interested in the minutest details of the private conduct of even the meanest man.

H.L. Mencken (1880-1956)
Minority Report

When societies describe the gods they believe in, they say more about themselves than they do about deities. Those that anthropomorphize most are those who work and live in a world principally of things. They want a god they can feel, describe, walk along side of, sit at the right hand of. To talk of an omnipresent god to them would be meaningless. Their god, like they themselves, can move from place to place. He has eyes to see with, arms to lift with, fingers to point with. These down-to-earth people are not at home in a world of the immaterial, imagined, impalpable, unintelligible, formless, disembodied, fanciful or spiritual.

The truth is that their more realistic gods may survive the test of time better than the gods who have non-empirical referents. We do better with gods that are man-beings, described in terms that relate to our own lives. When we attempt to sell ordinary people on the idea of a transcendent god exalted above the world beyond experience by our known senses, we fail utterly. We are talking gibberish – pure unadulterated gibberish that fails all standards of communication practicability.

222

In the Prophets and in parts of the New Testament—though only in parts - love, justice, and humility appear to be all that is asked of men, and questions of belief entirely peripheral, while precise formulations about God, "his attributes and his relation to the universe," are altogether out of the picture.

Walter Kaufmann
The Faith of a Heretic

Religious leaders are not about to encourage questions concerning the mythology upon which their religion is based. To do so would be to destroy what has taken aeons of artifice to construct. To replace present congregations of submissive automatons with inquisitive human beings would be to destroy all religions at once. The foundations of religion cannot stand scrutiny. "Dogma" and "faith," indispensable to religion, would be immediately recognized as subterfuge terms coined to prevent investigation. All the vague, evasive, equivocating language of religion arose quite naturally to discourage the members of congregations from becoming curious about the real nature of their systems of belief. The dreaded entrant to membership in any congregation is the intelligent mind that can see through religious flimflam and dares to seek answers to the "religious mysteries" that clamor for attention.

223

If [I] believe in an all-powerful God [I] would cease curing the sick and leave that to him.

Albert Camus (1913-1960)
The Plague

Dr. Rieux was asked why he showed such devotion to the afflicted people of Oran, considering the fact that he did not believe in God. His answer is the quotation above.

Devout Christians ask themselves why they should be concerned with nutrition when it is God that is responsible for one's good or bad health. Christian Scientists carry this idea to its most ridiculous extreme. In 1950, I drove three Christian Science ladies in a Studebaker Land Rover from New York City to Los Angeles. They were the most delightful travel companions I have ever had, for they would never admit to malaise or discomfort. One of them, who weighed a little less than a small pony, practically lived on ice cream.

Being a caring Deity and being omnipotent are the only two attributes commonly assigned to the Christian God that would be necessary for Dr. Rieux logically to abandon his medical practice. The fact that doctors continue their dedication to curing our maladies, that factories continue enforcing their safety regulations, and that we all take reasonable precautions to keep ourselves healthy and alive, says a great deal about how seriously we take our dogmatic theologies. In no other field do we behave so irrationally as we do in religion.

224

A bishop keeps on saying at eighty what he was told to say when he was a boy of eighteen.

Oscar Wilde (1854-1900)

Most intelligent people go on learning forever. However many graduate-school degrees they earn, each year that follows finds them wiser and with significant increase in their accumulation of knowledge. The graduates of seminaries seem to do the opposite. Instead of having added to their store of knowledge, they seem more and more burdened with an accumulation of information that is misinformation. Their learning becomes an ever more bulging *vade mecum* of mythology. They become better and better equipped to delude their congregations.

In *The Plumed Serpent* by D.H. Lawrence, we read: "I am the poor old Bishop of this diocese, faithful servant of the Holy Church, humble child of the Holy Father in Rome.... I live by my sacred office." Like most members of his church, the bishop can have no opinions of his own and can see nothing from any point of view other than that authorized by the ruling clergy. He has learned nothing since the day he was ordained. He will die as simple-minded as he was at eighteen: completely immersed in fairy lore, incapable of operating humanly in a sane society. Most religious leaders lead an increasingly precarious existence in the modern world, where science persists in pointing out their specious arguments and circular reasoning. Bishops and their confreres make themselves more and more at home in their comfortable metaphysics. There they find a refuge protected by its absolute truth and credal certainties.

Others compose outlandish orations furnished as they like with all manner of mythical monsters and dreamed-up heavenly entities. They can create their own versions of heaven and hell and populate them as they will. No celestial roster is too absurd, as the hundreds of deities in countries world-wide well show. Some prefer to remain aloof, safe, cloistered. They can then live contented in their community playhouses, shut off from the rest of the world.

225

Cruel persecution and intolerance are not accidents, but grow out of the very essence of religion, namely its absolute claims.

Morris Raphael Cohen (1880-1947)
The Faith of a Liberal

Absolutely certainty does not permit forbearance or discretion. It leaves no room for feelings or emotion. Testimony or demonstrations are superfluous. Invalidation, refutation, rebuttal, or argument is out of the picture. Qualifications, reservations, skepticism, limitations, or concessions are out of the question. When the religionist says "absolute certainty," and he uses it to apply to all the mythology that comprises his religion, all debate is off. Thinking is ridiculous. Everything has been decided "absolutely." There are no ifs, ands, or buts.

"Take it or leave it" is not the cry once Orthodoxy is in power. The cry then is: "Take it or else." History is replete with examples of what "or else" implies. Murders in the name of orthodoxy run into the millions. All the scriptures give example after example. If we learn only one thing in the Bible, it is that life has little value, and taking human life needs little or no provocation. Wars favored by God take countless lives, and famines, plagues, floods, and storms sent by God kill many millions more.

226

Life is a jest, and all things show it. I thought so once, and now I know it.

John Gay (1685-1732)
Inscription on a monument of John Gay

"Life has no transcendental meaning," Gay in essence is saying. What we can expect is the existential "what we see."

A life without purpose would of course be vacuous, but we must not expect myth to provide that purpose. To depend on our hierarchy of traditional legends to give meaning to life is to live precariously. When it is finally understood how flimsy is the structure of our dream lives, we are left with nothing. We may well end up as the psychiatrists' most pitiable patients. Suicide is often the result of people expecting life to emerge into a kind of perpetually blissful romance. They cannot appreciate or accept a life that remains an exciting, unending quest, with hopes never fully realized and goals never totally attained. They see all struggle and uncertainty as onerous, when in fact it is precisely this struggle, this uncertainty, which provides the fillip, the incentive, and the joy of fully functioning being.

In almost every novel, every biography, and especially in every autobiography we read, we find this constant search on the part of the protagonists for a vague, transcendental something that they expect will magically put all the pieces together and solve the cosmic riddle. The struggle that goes on in the life of each individual person from the day he first assumes responsibility for his own being until the day he dies has at least as a backdrop this quest. Each man or woman assumes there is something beyond reality waiting for him, even though no one in history has ever described in comprehensible language what this transcendental something is. Nor has anyone said that he himself has achieved it. Or if anyone does finally insist that he has indeed arrived at the end of his quest and tells us about the search and what he searched for, we see that what he has achieved is a kind of resignation. *The Quest for Being*, Sidney Hook says in a book so titled, is a futile quest.

If their search is not to be in vain, those searching for meaning must not search too far afield. They must not expect magic or abstruse revelation. Tranquility comes to those whose search is for ways to make life easier and more pleasant for all their fellow human beings. They most adequately reach goals and can teach us about meaning. They have no need to invent nirvana or heaven or any other kind of mythical celestial bliss to come. They have made of this world their idyllic abode. They have learned that the only meaning of the human species is the same meaning that exists for every species -

that of its own survival - in man, of course, elaborated with the infinite and complicated and utterly fascinating ramifications called living.

227

Religion, it seems to me, can survive only as a consciously accepted system of make-believe.

Aldous Huxley (1894-1963)
Texts and Pretexts

Huxley surely cannot be serious about large groups of people agreeing to play make-believe with their religions. Believers in any of the systems of organized superstitions on this planet today will not tolerate the slightest desecration of their "sacred" doctrines and dogmas. Nonbelievers, too, would balk at the slightest perception of being restrained, repressed, or hampered in their freedom to think and do as they themselves judge wise. Neither believers nor nonbelievers would consider for a moment agreeing to meet in some consciously contrived intermediate realm of make-believe.

If ever we lift the burden of religion from our societies it will be through carefully planned and persistent education. That education must first of all eliminate the tremendous profits that today accrue from perpetuating religions. Then it must eliminate the completely irrational notion that man can shift the responsibility for his own destiny onto some incomprehensible deity that he himself has invented. It will not be easy, but it can be done.

228

If the liberties of the American people are ever destroyed they will fall by the hands of the clergy.

Marquis de Lafayette (1757-1834)
French statesman; intimate associate of George Washington

This has already happened in many of the theocracies of the world, and that trend is not over. If the Taliban Muslim fundamentalists ever take over Afghanistan, it will happen there. If the Dorje Shugden god of the Geluk sect of Tibetan Buddhism ever rules Tibet, it will happen there. If the Christian Coalition ever takes over the United States, it will happen here. Religious bigotry in India divided that country into what are now three countries: India, Pakistan, and Bangladesh.

To live in any of the countries of South America where Catholicism is the official religion is to begin to see what happens to liberties in a theocracy. Few people there ever have an opportunity even to consider another religion. In Ecuador, where I lived for eleven years, every rite, ritual, ceremony, nearly every event in people's lives, almost every thought people dare to express publicly is the *de facto* property of the church. It is officially stated that other religions have rights to existence in the country, but no "alien" religion has ever made great inroads, and all other religions together have a small fraction of the influence of the Roman Catholic Church. Catholicism, especially in rural areas, may get infused with traces of indigenous religions as long as the infusion is insignificant. If any were to make important changes in Catholicism, they would be suppressed. When the M-19 guerrilla group of Colombia murdered the leader of *the Instituto Lingüístico de Verano*, Ecuadorians used the incident as an excuse for banning the Institute from their country. Hospitals and schools that functioned for 30 years are now disappearing into the maw of the insatiable jungle.

229

When people talk of freedom of writing, speaking, or thinking, I cannot choose but laugh. No such thing ever existed.

John Adams (1735-1826)
Letter to Thomas Jefferson, July, 1818

Now, some hundred and eighty years later, Edgar Watson Howe in *The Indignations of E.W. Howe* agrees: "You often hear that this is a free country, and that a man is at liberty to express his opinions. It is not true."

Amendments to the Constitution about freedom of speech are like the laws against crime. They express goals but give us no guarantee that the goals will be realized. Nor do they list all the exceptions or limitations that turn up in court. We would like to think that we enjoy the freedoms Adams lists above to a greater degree than would be the case had there been no Constitution. But where is the evidence?

The evidence is that freedom of the press in the United States is no more real today than it was when Adams wrote his letter to Jefferson in 1818. If any reader thinks I exaggerate, let him imagine a large city newspaper including in its pages a daily editorial column made up of brief essays like these that make up this book. When will we see in such a newspaper even a simple review of what this book is about.

Our local *Press-Telegram* will as readily carry in its pages the syrupy submissions to mysticism of a Joy Thompson and a Rabbi Eli Hecht as it will their excellent orations against immorality. But for the *Press-Telegram* or any of the 500 largest newspapers in the United States to allot any space to tell the truth about religion is at present beyond the realm of realistic possibility.

230

> Charlie Church was a preacher who praught. Though his enemies called him a screecher who scraught.
>
> Phoebe Cory (1824-1871)

A pun is fun, and if Phoebe is the teacher who taught that one we we will not fault her. But more important than the pun is the lesson she points out – that there is for many of us a clear line between preachers who preach and those who merely screech.

Preachers who preach *can be* all-right guys. We need a little "preaching to" now and then. Mothers know that, and play their part well, proving that one does not need eight years of higher education to learn how to preach. A dozen mothers can do far more good with their preaching than all the preachers who ever praught.

Unfortunately, the kind of preaching mothers do so well is seldom heard from pulpits. Mothers stick to moral lessons that stick with us. They do not preach fairy tales, and they make it clear that when they read fairy tales to us, they are just that and not facts of the cosmos. Too much of the preaching from pulpits are fairy tales that preachers take seriously, believing, or pretending to believe, that imaginary beings and their abodes are real, honest-to-god "people and places."

We need preaching mothers, but we might well dispense with preaching preachers. On the whole, they probably do far more harm than good. They scare the pants off us with their gory stories of hell and the likelihood that that is where we will end up. They promise us a bliss they cannot define with their vague stories of heaven and then make it quite clear that most of us will never get there. The result is that we do not have even the peace of a definitive death to look forward to. No wonder more and more people are rejecting the religions of the mythmongers and are choosing the freedom of a world without religions that deal in mysticism.

231

Happiness lies not in the mere possession of money; it lies in the joy
of achievement, in the thrill of creative achievement.

Franklin D. Roosevelt (1882-1945)
First Inaugural Address: March 4, 1933

Elbert Hubbard in *The Note Book*, published just four years before
Roosevelt gave his first inaugural address, emphasizes what FDR
said: "Life without absorbing occupation is hell - joy consists in
forgetting life."

These last five words need some explanation. Joy consists in
being so busy at a pleasant occupation, usually one in which one is
being creative, that time ceases to exist. One may begin immediately
upon awakening at 5 a.m., returning to an interesting project, and the
next thing one knows, it is two or three in the afternoon. Eating
breakfast, lunch, or making an important telephone call are forgotten.
One cannot imagine that so much time has passed. Work on the
project may have continued hours more had nature not demanded a
long overdue trip to the bathroom.

Roosevelt and Hubbard give us the best reason imaginable for
getting an education. Life is hell for anyone who has not acquired
sufficient aptitude to pursue an occupation that offers the "thrill of
creative achievement." The more native intelligence a person has, the
higher must be that education in order to give him assurance that the
work engaged in demands the maximum of one's abilities.

Studs Terkel, doing research for his book *Working* saw that people
who were happy in their work found that work important and
fulfilling. Those who were unhappy found their work an excruciating
bore – and of no consequence.

232

Now I'm a believer, and I try to live a Christian life, but I'd as soon
hear a surveyor's book read out, figgers an' all, as try to get any
simple truth out o' most sermons.

Sara Orne Jewett (1849-1909)
"The Courting of Sister Wisby"
Atlantic Monthly

In the name of simple human compassion, perhaps we should not
wish upon preachers that they become aware of the little significance

most listeners ascribe to their Sunday-morning diatribes. Truth in most sermons, as Sister Wisby discovered, is nowhere to be found. By uncritical acceptance of divine existences, the preacher assumes himself to be the essential and only possible intercessor between man and God.

In theological school, the student is burdened first with a bizarre mythology and then with an unwarranted assumption of the total depravity and helplessness of human beings. As preacher, he teaches his followers that they cannot on their own protect themselves from the machinations of the ever-vigilant devil. To support his posture as preacher-redeemer, the preacher postulates "salvation" as a prospect that can be vouchsafed only by supernatural divinity, with him essential in its implementation.

Salvation, that is, is by no means automatic. To be saved, petitioners must grovel and beg in incessant prayers. Abject obeisance and slavish church attendance are essential. A single misstep and one goes straight to hell.

233

Sermons remain one of the last forms of public discourse where it is culturally forbidden to talk back.

Harvey Cox
Secular City

And there is so much need to. Cultural correctness saves the preacher. He need not be concerned that what he says cannot really stand the glare of public scrutiny, for he knows there will be no rebuttal. Even when the sermon consists almost entirely of mythological mumbo jumbo, no one talks back.

There is no dearth of newspeople who will agree with almost everything that is said in this book, but they nevertheless avoid the subject like the plague. To rebut a sermon given in a local church, despite our constitutionally guaranteed free speech, would be to sign one's death warrant as far as continuing a normal life in that community. All the forces of Christendom would descend upon anyone with courage enough to describe the true nature of orthodox religions. The good Christians of the community would mock his words and conspire to get him fired and unable to get another job. There is no fury like a fanatic scorned, and to him any means are justified to attain his ends.

"The half-baked sermon causes spiritual indigestion," says Austin O'Malley. "The glow of a good sermon always makes me regret that religion is not true," says Augustine Birrell in his *Essays and Addresses*. Here we have more indications of what sermons do to those who listen to them. Rabbi Lionel Blue, a sermonizer himself, offers another in *Kitchen Blues*: "It seems to me easier to give sermons than to sit through them." Of course, we have long known that most people prefer "talking" to "listening," sermon or not. Time passes pleasantly and fast when we are doing the talking, drearily and slow when someone else has the floor.

234

Indiscrimination: "that damning, near universal delusion" whereby "most of the public think of science as technology."

Philip Wylie (1902-1971)
The Magic Animal

Stephen Jay Gould finds no such distinction. To him science and technology are one. Since the beginnings of science, scientists have found it useful to assign some measure of demarcation between the tinkerer and those who tell him when his pursuits accord with the basic order and harmony of the cosmos. We distinguish between the medical technician and the medical researcher, between the design engineer and the particle physicist.

Technology sometimes precedes science by developing tools that subsequently are found to be necessary to science. But scientists as often become involved in designing the equipment that their objectives indicate they will need. Technology and science work hand in hand.

In our dictionaries, science is defined as the establishment of verifiable general laws or truths dealing with facts and systemized knowledge derived by the drawing of correct inferences from such facts. Technology, on the other hand, is defined as applied science, the practical applications of science - or, "the use of technical processes."

Which of the contrasting views between Wylie and Gould should we favor? Gould is undoubtedly right (who can argue with him?). The intimidating giggle that accompanies all of Gould's recitations of his convictions make it clear that it is ridiculous that anyone could think to disagree with whatever he says. And *he* says that technology and science are just two sides of the same coin. The subject, obviously, is closed.

235

> The question of whether or not there is a God... can never be answered by books, by parents, philosophers, or saviors.
>
> Jiddo Krishnamurti (1895-1986)
> *Freedom from the Known*

When Gilbert Ryle said, "The only light that comes from the East is the sun," he certainly had not read the several small books written by Krishnamurti.

In a biography written in 1951, we are told that there are two Krishnas, the one represented by the above quotation and those in essays 334,380,520,602, and 778 of this book. The other Krishna was a vain, self-centered man, dishonest, gullible, and ignorant of science. Be that as it may, from reading his books we find a man who was an important teacher of good sense and rational exposition.

Krishnamurti in his books says most of the things that need be said to convince receptive and discriminating young minds to avoid oppressive torpor and to welcome enlightened vivacity. If Krishnamurti's books and not the Bible were used in our Sunday Schools, soon we would have a nation of minds able to think their way through the maze of trumpery that is the world today.

The question of whether or not there is a God can never be answered, period. Many of the authors of the quotations in this book corroborate Krishnamurti's contention. Even Bob Dylan, setting aside his characteristic lyrical style for the moment, agrees (quoted in *Newsweek*, The Arts, page 64, October 6, 1997): "I don't adhere to rabbis, preachers, evangelists, all of that. I've learned more from the songs than I've learned from any of this kind of entity."

236

> All real progress in the world is in the last analysis produced by rationalism.
>
> Albert Schweitzer (1875-1965)

As obviously as is Schweitzer's declaration, it needs constant repetition. The forces in our societies that would have us believe that irrationalism is the better way seem about to overwhelm us.

Whenever we consent to believe when there is no evidence for believing, we are being irrational. Despite our good intentions, irrationalism persists in most of our lives.

Much of our ill health results form frivolous selection and ingestion of food and drugs. Superstitions, prejudices, and propensities to violence become instilled in us, despite our vigilance. Our natural kindness, generosity, and sympathy toward others become effectively suppressed by the malign counsels that beguile us.

If sanity is to survive, we must learn that "piety" is not "morality," "scripture" is not "history," "heresy" is not "error," "dogma" is not "authority," "doctrine" is not "truth," and "from remote antiquity" is not a synonym for "oracular."

The motives, means, and objectives that determine our behavior increasingly stalk us from metaphysical ambush—even when we imagine ourselves alert and reacting only to the observable universe about us.

237

The day this country ceases to be free for irreligion it will cease to be free for religion—except for the sect that can win political power.
Robert H. Jackson (1892-1954)
U.S. Supreme Court Justice
Zorach vs. Clauson

The conservative Christian far right in this country knows this very well. Since only if they can have their own way will they be able to get rid of all atheists and opposing religions, they must contrive to be the favored sect that wins political power. The campaign they have launched in order to do just that accelerates.

No more than three or four years ago, a few journalists with hidden cameras managed to film parts of an in-house meeting where Pat Robertson was describing to initiates some of the steps in a process that would assure success in their campaign. Any constitutionalist watching that film would be appalled.

The film was aired on PBS one time and never repeated. Since during summer months all significant films get a second and third showing on PBS, we wonder what steps the ever-more-powerful conservative right took to get that film squelched. Some significant films do not get even the first chance to be seen. The Australian film describing Barbara Thiering's work on the Dead Sea Scrolls, so far as I know, has never been shown in the Los Angeles area.

238

Man is kind enough when he is not excited by religion.
Mark Twain (1835-1910)

Since the arguments of religionists from the beginning of time have been fashioned from whole cloth, arguing against them is futile. It is indeed difficult to reason a man out of what he was never reasoned into. Religionists start with assumed premises, "God exists and the Bible is His infallible word." From there on they fabricate inferences as they like that have no more substance than their premises. If pressed for explanations, they will counter with, "God has His reasons," and that must be that. If you insist that their arguments are not valid because their premises are not valid, watch out!

Pope Innocent, The Third, told his adherents: "Use against heretics the spiritual sword of excommunication, and if that doesn't prove effective, us the material sword." One way or the other the religionist must win. If you value your life and your cause, choose not to start arguments. If you are tempted to argue, know when to stop. There are other ways to infuse sanity into irrational minds. It is hoped that reason will begin to take over when with patience and concern we explain any perplexities and questions posed by the authors of the quotations introducing the brief essays of this book.

239

Theology is the art of befuddling oneself methodically.
Jules Michelet (1798-1874)
French historian

What is needed in our societies is a morality not blighted by religion. Dogmas, creeds, autocratic persuasions, all the organized superstitions that comprise our modern religions, must be abandoned. The tremendous efforts of Buddha, Confucius, Lao-tzu, and Jesus to introduce a modicum of sense into the morass of prejudices and bigotry that prevailed in their time failed. Things are no better today. We will not have peace in the world as long as the intense ill will among our major authoritarian religions continues. The atheism of John Mackie, Sidney Hook, Paul Kurtz, Pierre Berton, Bertand

Russell, George H. Smith, Richard Robinson, and Friedrich Nietzsche must be seen as an intellectual course worthy of our attention.

The obsessive urge to depend on theology to guide human behavior has many unintended repercussions: Fear, self-depreciation, diffidence, obsequious servility, and vacillation all result from not being our own indomitable stewards. If we do not learn to trust our own ingenuities, things will not get done. We have only to look around us to see that that is so. There are no brownies to make shoes, no fairies with magical powers, no cupids to inflame couples with love, no leprechauns to reveal hidden treasures, no nymphs to adorn our rivers, no banshees to warn of death, and no gremlins to thwart our plans. Just as certainly, there are no gods to answer prayers. So far as we know at present, we are the only thinking beings in the universe, and we had better get on with making a more secure place for ourselves if we are to survive.

240

Connoisseurs in irony are well aware of the fact that the only editor in England who denounces punishment as radically wrong, also repudiates Christianity....

George Bernard Shaw (1856-1950)
Preface to *Major Barbara*

If a criminal's manifest immorality is not the result of an intrusive chromosomal code, then presumably it is acquired and is a legitimate target for rehabilitation. Punishment would only interfere. If the criminal's immorality is genetically caused, then the criminal is not to blame. Punishment would be absurd. Either way punishment does not seem to be an appropriate response to crime. Even if it can be defended as a way to discourage crime, it does not follow that punishment is essential or wise. Imprisonment may be enough - and needs no overtones of punishment to help it deter crime. Imprisonment is the way a sane society protects itself from criminals who prove unresponsive to rehabilitation.

If prisons could become efficient rehabilitation institutions that really work, the benefit to society could be enormous. If there are certain criminals who, after every conceivable effort has been made, show that they cannot be rehabilitated, imprisonment should be effected solely in response to the need for society to protect itself, and in no sense on the basis of the desire of society for revenge. Seeking revenge, we cater only to the brute in ourselves. We are not thinking about our only legitimate goal, that of doing what we can to reduce crime.

241

Not one man in a thousand has the strength of mind or the goodness of heart to be an atheist.

Samuel Taylor Coleridge (1772-1824)
Letter to Thomas Allsop

To suffer the slings and arrows of outraged ecclesiastics requires strength of mind. Clergymen are fighting for an untenable system of beliefs that cannot stand the light of reason. A liberal education into the realities of the cosmos and the myth upon which theistic religions are based is gradually dissipating the superstitions that have long undermined civilization. Ecclesiastics understand very well how vulnerable is their intellectual position, and they see their sinecures slipping away. Atheists, of course, especially those whose voice is heard, are the brunt of religionists' fears and anxiety. The frantic efforts to muffle the words of atheists are understandable.

Caring about others is the essence of goodness. To care is to want everyone to live free: free of being deceived by power-hungry charlatans of all kinds; free to denounce, without repercussions, that which is false; free to express one's opinions about all things; free to choose friends, regardless of whether or not they conform to conventions; free to ignore peer pressure when it is detrimental to one's well-being - in sum, free to be oneself. The poetry of Samuel Taylor Coleridge eulogized the man who dares to be free, the man who cannot be subdued by the forces of obscurantism. Visions of every human being as a dignified, sovereign individual motivated many of his poetic compositions.

242

Sect and error are synonymous.

Voltaire (1694-1778)

The thing that amazes me most about Voltaire is to find anyone having that much insight about current affairs, writing more than two hundred years ago. Often when reading Voltaire I forget that I am not reading an editorial in the day's newspapers.

When established religions splinter, it is usually the result of some buddy-buddy group within the religion taking hold of an idiotic doctrine of the religion and reformulating it into another equally idiotic doctrine. They attach such importance to their new brainchild and raise such a furor about it that there is nothing left for them to do but break off and form a new sect. Christianity is now divided into more than three hundred and fifty sects. All of the "great" religions are splintered.

Rosemary Harthill in her book *In Perspective* says, "Sects tend to have doctrines that resemble some of the beliefs of mainstream religions, but skew them in certain directions. A colleague of mine once received three leaflets in the same week, one from Christadelphians, one from Christian Scientists, and one from Jehovah's Witnesses. All three began with 'Christendom is astray.' All three thought they had the only solution."

Of course "error" did not begin with sectarianism, and would not end if sects were entirely eliminated. The word "faith" as religion uses the term was coined to cover up errors that have existed since the beginning of religious time. The proclamations of religions, because they are unfounded, must be accepted on faith. Without them religion could not exist. The concept "theistic religion" itself is error, based as it is on myth and unsubstantiated legend. Voltaire should have been more inclusive: "Religious faith and error are synonymous."

243

> Santa Claus, we know, can scare or wheedle children into being good, but no one suggests that this is proof that Santa Claus exists.
>
> H.L. Mencken (1880-1956)
> *Minority Report*

Leslie A. White, Professor of Anthropology at the University of Michigan, wrote in *The Scientific Monthly* for February, 1939: "So far as the present writer knows, there is no convincing proof to the nonexistence of Santa Claus. Man progresses, often, not by disproving propositions but by outgrowing them." It can be assumed that Virginia finally outgrew her belief in Santa Claus. When will humanity outgrow its belief in gods?

The difficulty in proving a negative is proverbial. If anyone thinks he can prove that Santa Claus does not exist, let him list the steps he will take in doing so. The burden of proof is always on those taking the positive side of any proposition. Only when believers in Santa Claus cannot prove what they contend does the nonbeliever have a basis for his doubts.

Both those who express the positive as well as those who express the negative side of a proposition, we understand, cannot be absolutely sure of their opinions. A high degree of predictive content for those who affirm, and reasonable doubt for those who deny is the best that either can hope to attain. Unfortunately, the history of religion shows that predictive content has little or nothing to do with what religionists accept as gospel. Conclusions are based on vague fancy and in no way upon empirical or rational demonstration. Religious leaders construct hierarchies of folly that nothing can oppose.

244

I have only a small flickering light to guide me in the darkness of a dark forest: Up comes a theologian and blows it out.

Denis Diderot (1713-1784)

Denis Diderot, the redoubtable encyclopedist, had a unique way of expressing himself—and a vast knowledge of how things work to back him up. The harm done to the collective mentality by theologians is so all encompassing and invincible that it is impossible to exaggerate. It is hard enough for us to keep our feet firmly planted on solid ground without a phalanx of theologians continually undermining our foothold.

Our pulpiteers can make consummate good sense when they strive to improve our moral principles and convince us to behave in accordance with these principles. But when they start to compose their mawkish mythologies, they are reduced to spewing out floods of lies. When they tell us about their constant communications with God, angels, Jesus, saints, and ancient prophets, they trifle with truth. They cannot demonstrate that in the history of man any such communications have ever taken place.

In a desert campground, several other people and I had gathered around a man holding a diving rod with which he said he could find gold. He had a small bag of gold dust to prove it. With everyone else seemingly willing to accept his story, I felt obliged to challenge him. "I will dig 15 shallow holes in the flat piece of ground in front of us and with all backs turned, let me put your bag of gold in one of them, cover each with a sheet of paper and then you find your gold with your diving rod." But of course he had a perfect evasion. He would not trust his bag of gold out of his sight for a minute. When I produced a solid gold watch to substitute, he made other feeble excuses. We would just have to have faith in his story about the effectiveness of his diving rod. Theologians, too, tell us: "You must have faith!"

245

The people have a right to the truth as they have a right to life, liberty, and the pursuit of happiness. It is not right that they be exploited and deceived with false views of life, false character, false sentiment, false morality, false history, false philosophy, false emotions, false heroism, false notions of self-sacrifice, false views of religion, of duty, of conduct, and manners.

Frank Norris (1870-1902)
The Responsibilities of the Novelist

Although in novels we expect a certain latitude of fabrication, we see a difference between outlandish sophistries and good story telling, and we expect authors to recognize that difference too. Anachronisms, geographical mislocations, historical distortions, and mistranslations are anathema and must be condemned.

It is even more important in nonfiction that words relate to facts. Without all the human rights Frank Norris speaks of, societies would fall apart. We cannot exist in a milieu of deceit where no one can trust anyone else to tell the truth. Fortunately, people are generally honest, fair, and competent in their contributions to society. We trust department stores, contractors, servicemen, and salesmen not to cheat us, and usually our trust is not misplaced. We walk in traffic, cross bridges, buy homes, sign contracts, etc., with faith that at least ninety-nine percent of the time people will honor their obligations. Of course, all of us have been cheated in business transactions, but on the whole, the world operates honestly and smoothly.

That is why, I believe, some of us are so disappointed in finding that an exalted discipline affecting our lives more than any other is one vast breeding ground of dissimulation and exploitation. Many religions are growing rich taking advantage of the gullibility of people who do not see through their guile and duplicity. Religion, as it is practiced, is fakery and not much else. It scares us out of our wits in order to keep us in line. It constructs a vast hierarchy of mythomania, which it asks us to accept without question. Something must change. We must have competent leaders who have the courage to expose the sham and help us become thinking beings, immune to the increasingly corrupting effects of religious deception.

246

The existence of God as a separate entity can be dismissed as superfluous; for the world may be explained just as adequately without positing such a being.

Julian Huxley (1887-1975)
The Observer July 17, 1960

Not only can the world be explained just as adequately, but it would continue to function just as adequately without the fiction of an intervening supreme being. For an adequately functioning world, morality is necessary, reason is necessary, education is necessary, but mythology is in actual fact much worse than unnecessary, it is disruptive of all our attempts to make this a better world. Flat-earth defenders do nothing but waste our time. With reason in ascendance, souls, devils, idols, angels, both immanent and transcendent gods, and all other such invented entities would cease to exist, and we would begin to live as free individuals for the first time.

If it were convincingly established today that God is dead or never has existed, we would wake up to the same world tomorrow. Reason, returning to replace nonsense, would occasion an acceleration of human progress in days to follow, and no repercussions would ensue. False starts and failures would be more easily corrected, and leaps of intuition and serendipities would be more easily used to advantage. Wars would become obsolete, and pseudo-problems would disappear. Without the superfluous God that Huxley speaks of, all of us would know that we must depend on our own ingenuities. We would find potentials in ourselves that we never knew we had, and life would become more enjoyable. Watching ourselves putting things together in more decipherable order would increase our self-esteem, and the world would evolve as never before.

247

> Locality, nationality, race, sex, or social manners may differ, but the accord of desire for civil liberty ... is ever the same.
>
> Mifflin Wistar Gibbs (born 1823)
> *Shadow and Light*

Born Free was written about a lion. At rodeos, we see with what reluctance a horse gives up its freedom. Even the beetle we hold in our hand struggles to get free. In the processes of evolution, the snapping beetle acquired an amazing mechanism specifically for that purpose. In all of the animal species, freedom is high on the list of priorities.

Patrick Henry said, "Give me liberty or give me death." Throughout history, men and women have given up their lives in preference to being under someone else's control. Mifflin Gibbs is certainly right about how highly we prize freedom.

That is why I am constantly amazed at how readily people will give up their individual sovereignty to the control of religious and political demagogues. They will swallow the line of a David Koresh or a Jim Jones and behave toward them like slaves. They will accept the gibberish of a Jerry Falwell or Pat Robertson and turn them into gods. In the spell of faith healers and Christian Science practitioners, people cede completely their right to think. They behave as automatons or like Charlie McCarthy under the control of Edgar Bergen. Psychiatrists still have a lot to explain.

248

> The religion that is afraid of science dishonors God and commits suicide.
>
> Ralph Waldo Emerson (1803-1882)
> *Journals*

Religion's fear of science is understandable. Emerson's implication that there is a possibility of reconciling science and religion is not. A human discipline based on myth and faith cannot face up to another human discipline that effectively dispels myth and exposes bogus schemes for acquiring positions of power.

Science is knowledge. Religion is anti-knowledge. Any religion that is honest about its vision of the future agrees that every advance in knowledge about the way this cosmos really functions is a step toward the demise of religion.

Anyone who does not believe that religion is pathologically afraid of science need only watch the comic efforts of creation scientists trying to explain away the discoveries of science that contradict the fables of Genesis.

One thing that is not funny is the use of the word science as a description of some religions. Mary Baker Eddy, L. Ron Hubbard, and the creation scientists do science a great disserve when they take a word referring to the advancement of knowledge and apply it to their puerile ruminations. They know well that science is their enemy. But their admiration for the successes of science in advancing our communities persuades them nevertheless to use the word in the titles of their mystic symbolisms. Reconciliation of science and religion by twisting language is no reconciliation at all. The incompatibility remains, even though cleverly camouflaged. There are no words sufficiently persuasive to convince true men of science that they can concede anything to organized systems of superstition and prejudice.

Chapter VII

Insanity Institutionalized

249

Astute laymen understand that what every preacher in orthodox religions is in effect saying to his congregation is: "We know that most of what we say to you cannot be defended by any of the rules of good sense and logic, but we want you to believe our declarations anyway, without proof, without verifications of any kind. You understand our predicament do you not? Without belief in our patently unbelievable pronouncements, all that is important in the world would become suspect."

The preacher knows that without belief in his unsupportable pronouncements the people who face him every Sunday would learn to think for themselves. They would learn to live without the abject fear instilled by his brimstone-and-hellfire tirades. They would even learn to live without the rhapsodic joy infused by his divine-grace sermons. Thinking for themselves could lead to understanding how all-encompassing is the fraud underlying theistic religions.

The preacher is desperate. What can he do? His solution at first blush seems so obvious and shallow that we wonder how it could possibly work. He coined the word "faith" to cover all of his muddled mentation. The word faith becomes imbued with such an aura of mystery and mysticism that his audience hears it not as just a word but a magic formula to camouflage all the pretense and posturing of the church. "Faith," Mark Twain said, "is believing what you know ain't so," all of the senseless and absurd pretensions of religion.

250

> We find that the lack of religion and moral training has been repeated *ad nauseam* as the cause of delinquency and criminal behavior.
>
> H.E. Barnes
> N. Teeters
> *New Horizons in Criminology*

Religious education is notoriously ineffective for decreasing criminal behavior. The book *New Horizons in Criminology* does its job well in showing the nullity or even harm of religious education. The reason seems obvious. Religious education consists of words – perhaps in the form of sermons or reading from the Bible. The student soon becomes aware that many of these words are lies, half-truths, or sinister evasions. The lesson to the student really is that this kind of behavior is normal, even desirable. Once he is convinced of that, it is easy for him to turn to criminal behavior.

Moral training, Barnes and Teeters should have pointed out, is very different from religious training. If parents and teachers did not teach morality, we would have a sad world today. Morality is at most only partly instinctive. It must be reinforced by well-planned education.

Charles Murray, the living author of *The Bell Curve*, scoffed at the efforts of Mava Collins, a Chicago teacher in an inner-city school, whose pupils seemed to be doing extraordinarily well. Now sixteen years later, a follow-up investigation shows he was just plain wrong. None of her students are now dead, in jail, or on welfare. On the contrary, all are in, or well on their way to, good positions. All are useful citizens to the communities in which they live. When we learn to clone human beings, let us add to our supply of Marva Collinses.

251

> No considerate God would destroy the human mind by making it so rigid and unadaptable as to depend upon one book, the Bible, for all the answers....
>
> Alan Watts (1915-1973)
> *The Book*

Several times in my lifetime have I heard people declare that the

Bible is the only book they read. What self-immolation more clearly destructive than that!

There are important questions for which no book has answers. If ever we do find answers to these questions, they will not come from the Bible. What is worse, much of what people point out in the Bible as valuable information is more accurately described as misinformation. The Bible tells us that the rabbit chews its cud (Leviticus 11:6) Lot's wife turned into salt (Genesis 19:26) snakes (Genesis 3:1-5) and asses (Numbers 22:30) talk. The sun and moon can stop in their orbits (Joshua 10:13). Bread and wine can turn into flesh and blood (Mark 14:22-25). Sticks can change into snakes (Exodus 4:3). Dust can change into lice (Exodus 8:17). Sarah, at ninety, gave birth to a child (Genesis 17:17). Giants on the earth were sons of human women and supernatural beings (Genesis 6:4). Jonah could live in the belly of a fish for three days (Johah 1:17). We could go on and on. The Bible is the last place to go to find reliable answers for anything.

252

Did universal charity prevail, earth would be a heaven and hell a fable.

Charles Caleb Colton
Lacon

Alexander Pope in his famous *Essay on Man* wrote: "In faith and hope the world will disagree / But all mankind's concern is charity."

The need of poor people is so great that many of us despair of doing anything to alleviate it. Others will do anything to alleviate it. We cannot help admiring preachers for their uncanny cunning and cleverly contrived ingenuity in coaxing members to part with their money. If the money they collect is used for good purposes, we do not fault them.

Charity is like sweeping in front of one's own door. Opportunity presents itself to everyone. If each person does what he can in his own immediate vicinity, much of the world's suffering would disappear.

World charity organizations, of course, need our help, and the fact that they usually get it is the best argument we have for the concern people generally have for the welfare of others. We are not such a bad lot after all. Our news media concentrate to such an extent on crime and other examples of man's inhumanity to man that we tend to overlook what is undoubtedly our dominant characteristic. Although our charity does not make news, it must be by far man's overriding disposition. The world could not survive without it. If we analyze our own experiences, we find most people we meet are cheerful, helpful, and worthy of praise for the concern they have for their fellowman.

253

How angry we get with people who disagree with us depends in part on what we expect of them. People who are like us we expect to think like us, and get especially unhappy when we find they do not.

Chester Dolan
From a discarded page of this book

Petty fracases in a church can escalate into civil war when egos are injured. Church members, overly infatuated with their own self-righteousness, bridle at innocent or not-so-innocent insults. Marquis of Queensbury and Golden Rules are abandoned, while an adrenaline rush assumes command. We are reminded of school children flailing at each other in fury, with reciprocal jeers, taunts, and mockery.

In adults, animosities can last a few minutes or a lifetime. In the case of Ireland's "troubles" the agony has continued for many generations. The Bosnian orgy of hate and destruction, of similar ethnic and religious origins, has roots in antiquity. We begin to understand why there are so many kinds of Baptists, Presbyterians, Catholics, and Methodists. Splintered religions are the rule, not the exception.

I [Helen Graham] have seen this rancor close at hand in my own church, the Unitarian-Universalist denomination. Like other religions, we take tremendous pride in our "intellectual superiority." Factions arise and threaten dissolution. We discharge worthy ministers caught in the crossfire, spew venom in legal battles, and violate every tenet of our "gentle, liberal" faith. A staff of skilled psychological counselors is required to deal with irrational, destructive anger in our own as well as in other denominations.

When will evolution free us of our iniquitous genetic inclinations?

254

> That fear first created the gods is perhaps as true as anything so brief could be on so great a subject.
>
> George Santayana (1863-1952)
> *The Life of* Reason

Man has made no end of gods. As Montaigne expressed it, "Man who cannot possibly make a worm and yet will make gods by the dozens."

When ancient man faced threatening mysteries of nature, the fears engendered were allayed by the invention of gods capable of creating and controlling the phenomena that needed explanation. The inclination to incorporate some kind of deity into every tribal fantasy, fear, or ego-projection seems to be deeply woven into the fabric of all primitive societies. Most religions today are relics of these same primitive needs. Amplified, attuned, and adapted for changing societies, primitive gods remain today's deities.

This is not to say that the gods today are better than the gods from which they evolved. The new gods, in fact, do not even have the merit of serving as explanations, but have degenerated into obscurantism, an opposition to genuine explanations. Superstition remains superstition and bigotry has not lessened. The hope is not to improve our gods, but to get rid of them.

If human brings did not exist and had never existed in this part of the universe, there would be in our vicinity no gods and no religions. Other animals are incapable of such fabrications. The fact that there evolved a rare offshoot in evolutionary progression, an animal capable of looking upon itself and furnished with imagination and the ability to reason did not change the fundamental facts of the cosmos. Only within the exceptional cellular activity of that rare animal did this new, significant element appear. The last appearing, intricately convoluted tissue in the human brain may have made it all possible. It is the most remarkable organ evolution has produced.

255

> I count religion but a childish toy. / And hold there is no sin but ignorance.
>
> Christopher Marlowe (1564-1593)
> *The Jew of Malta*

Edward Anhalt, too, has nothing good to say about religion. "God ... an infantile fantasy, which was necessary when men did not understand lightning."

Wishful thinking and fear were Freud's explanation for the origin of God. A transfer of affection from a real live mother to an imaginary superbeing was Mencken's explanation. But ancient religious history seems to indicate that gods evolved to explain various phenomena of nature and of evolving human culture: Earth gods, hearth gods, moon gods, sun gods, sea gods, rain gods, wind gods, thunder gods, agriculture gods, war gods, and even gods of love and lightning were common. The names of gods in various religions run into the hundreds. I am reminded of a cartoon showing a satyr (half horse, half man) walking into a clearing in a Greek forest where he saw a beautiful blond riding a black stallion. The caption has him saying: "Hello mother; hello father!"

256

> The idea of a disembodied psyche or soul is as meaningless a concept as that of ... the grin of the Cheshire cat without the cat.
>
> Hudson Hoagland
> *Reflections on the Purpose of Life*

For an entity that cannot now exhibit or has not in the past ever exhibited the slightest evidence of existence, the soul must rank first in literary and cliché use. We hear the word in everyday conversations so commonly that it is hard not to believe that lurking somewhere in some small corner of the universe is a soul that will someday come forward and announce itself.

If it is not human bodies, but souls that are cavorting in heaven and frying in hell, we must revise in our minds just what this thing called soul is like. There must be something material to cavort in heaven and certainly something combustible to burn in hell to feed those everlasting fires. Then why, here on earth, can we not see, catch in a net, or observe the mode of transportation of souls leaving the body? The Bible explains nothing, but Allah in the Koran talks of supplying new skins for whatever (whoever) is frying in hell so that they suffer more for their misdeeds. For additional information on souls, see essays 98 and 388 and others listed in the index.

257

> Today, there is indisputable evidence that religion can make us very sick, especially when it is misused.... The way some people practice their religion is clearly linked up with masochism, sadism; with psychotic and neurotic emotional disorders.
>
> George Christian Anderson
> *Man's Right to Be Human*

Bertrand Russell said: "My own view of religion is that of Lucretius. I regard it as a disease born of fear and as a source of untold misery."

For some Christians the delicious "agony" they suffer upon seeing other people enjoying themselves is a kind of perverted pleasure. It becomes their most prized topic of conversation. The legacy of religion in their hands is a dreary world in which human life becomes a kind of perpetually bequeathed banality. A Catholic friend of mine in 1953 in New York City told me that at confession when 15 years old she admitted to "sins" that included what, to me, seemed quite innocent petting. The Father confessor exploded, calling her a liar, saying he knew what was going on among teenage girls in that neighborhood. She never in her life went to confession again. She died in May 1996 in Hamden, Connecticut in her 78th year of life, keeping all her lifetime of "sins" to herself.

Psychiatrists, trying to amend the kind of harm religion does to people like my friend, speak of religion as the "enemy." Religion in its protean forms operates to deform the mind, inhibit inborn tendencies to do good, and stifle mental growth. The lament of psychotherapists, according to M. Scott Peck, is the excessive amount of time that must be spent to free young minds from the clutches of religion.

258

> There is only one step from fanaticism to barbarism.
> Denis Diderot (1713-1784)

The ease with which fanaticism leads to barbarism is one of the saddest pages in history. The number of people killed reaches many, many millions. The Holocaust, Stalin's farm collectivization program, Pol Pot's Khmer Rouge, the genocide of Armenians by Turks in Anatolia, the Christian Crusades, the Spanish Inquisition, the witch trials, the Balkan Wars, the genocide in Rwanda and Cambodia, the Rape of Nanking, the Thirty Years War, the genocide in East Timor and Tibet, all affirm what Diderot said.

The list of famous leaders killed by fanatics grows longer every year: Joan of Arc, Jan Hus, Giordano Bruno, Jesus, Gandhi, Socrates, Joseph Smith, Michael Servetus, Jacob Hutter, Jack Kennedy, McKinley, Lincoln, Martin Luther King, Jr., Indira Gandhi, Bobby Kennedy, Yitzhak Rabin, and many, many more. Terrorist activities all over the world kill hundreds. There seems to be no end of man's inhumanity to man. Many wars begin with incidents perpetrated by terrorists. Strange it is to find that many terrorists claim that their orders to kill came from God.

259

> Irrevocable commitment to any religion is not only intellectual suicide; it is positive unfaith because it closes the mind to any new vision of the world.
>
> Alan Watts (1915-1973)
> *The Book*

Before considering Alan's quotation, let me mention that *The Book* was not *The* Book. It was only a device for mentioning a book he might write. Too bad he did not write it.

A religion corrals the god-worshiping proclivities of its adherents within one walled microcosm that blinds them to all other possibilities. It leaves them no room for thinking for themselves – no room for rummaging through the world of ideas that might sharpen their wits and open their eyes. It makes them comfortable and contented like a clam is; for the clam knows no other world then that of the rocks among which it feeds – in fact "assumes" it to be the only world.

The irrevocable commitment Watts speaks of is often not deliberate or even conscious, but simply comes about through constant hammering – like a pile driver building a dock. The pile may not be much impressed with each jolt it receives, but before it knows what has happened, it is so deep in the ocean floor that nothing can remove it.

For some of us the attraction of "religion" is that it protects us from contact with the suffering and injustice of the world in which we live. We become so encapsulated in our own religious microcosm that we become blind to the adversities that beset our fellowman. Serenity, not morality, is our goal, and we reject everything that disturbs that serenity.

260

Man is condemned to be free, responsible all the way.

Jean-Paul Sartre (1905-1980)

This statement by Sartre, the essence of existentialism, is both supported and contradicted in the Bible. Jeremiah (10:23) said the opposite: "Lord, I know that no man is master of himself; no man has control over his own destiny." Yet almost all of the Bible is a contradiction of what Jeremiah says. The constant talk of man's sins and God's punishments of them assumes man's free will and responsibility for what he does. Without this postulate we would have to assume that God is the only sinner.

Of course we are free. If we were not: (1) Authoritarian ecclesiastics would lead us around like a judas goat leads sheep to slaughter. (2) There would be only one religion. God would speak, and everyone would obey. (3) We would be automatons, moved around like a child moves his toy soldiers.

To pretend that we do not have a free, will as Calvin, B.F. Skinner, Jeremiah, or as Gerhard Szczesny in his book *The Future of Unbelief* says, would be to end everything important on earth as we know it. Nothing would have meaning, and human life would be less even then that described by Shakespeare: "A tale told by an idiot, full of sound and fury, signifying nothing."

261

The image of a supernatural being "out there" who is in some sense (metaphysical and moral if not spatial) outside his universe, has become a serious liability to Christianity.

J.A.T. Robinson
Bishop of Woolwich – *Honest to God*

Both Kant and Schopenhauer deny the possibility of our having any knowledge or understanding of "God" or any knowledge that we have souls and still less that they or we survive death. Yet Kant could not accept for himself the epithet atheist, and Schopenhauer, although he could (and did), is found contriving spectral anomalies totally preposterous and inane.

If theologians can be as successful as they are by constantly talking about what they know nothing about, Kant, Otto, Robinson, and Schopenhauer seem to have said to themselves, maybe we can do the same. All ventured off into vague and obscure fantasies that have no more intelligibility then do the sophistries of the theologians.

Schopenhauer was the quintessential atheist. No beating about the bush for him. He was outspokenly out of the closet and proud of it. That, it seems, gave him license to elaborate his own nebulous symbolisms which we see as little better than those he was rejecting. Schopenhauer's mysticism was "noumenal" like Rudolph Otto's mysticism was "numinous." Both entail "cosmic sources of energy renewal" which mystics keep telling us we can tap into whenever we like.

J.A.T. Robinson, Rudolph Otto, and Kant have no hesitation in affirming God's existence, but the God they affirm, as well as Schopenhauer's speculations, are described as incomprehensible, ineffable, inconceivable, indefinable, boundless, formless, and unapproachable – confirming that what they talk about are figments of human imagination and nothing more.

J.A.T. Robinson helpfully agrees that "heaven is not over our heads," nor is God "above the bright blue sky," "out there," "beyond outer space" or in any named geographical location. All obscurantism, whoever may be its proponents, clears the way for our own descent into a world of empty utterances and moronic drivel. If we go along, we, too, will soon be living in a quagmire of insensibility.

262

If the Bible teaches the equality of women, why does the church refuse to ordain women to preach the Gospel, to fill the office of deacons and elders, and to administer the Sacraments.

Elizabeth Cady Stanton (1815-1902) – *The Woman's Bible*

But the Bible does not teach the equality of women, and Mrs. Stanton says so herself many times in her lectures and writings. The Bible is a bigoted document which repeatedly depreciates women and accords them a position only as servants to the human male. If God really is accountable for what is said in the Bible, He is a thoroughgoing misogynist, and not particularly loath to admit it. Deuteronomy 24:4, Numbers 18:10, 1 Corinthians 14:35, 1 Timothy 2:11-12, make that quite plain. Proverbs 6:24 and 9:13 do not stress the role of the man, only the women, as if the fault is entirely hers. More often than is called for, women in the Bible are not given names, but are simply designated as the property of some male: Lot's wife, Jephthah's daughter, etc.

It is the Bible that gives the Catholic Church its excuse for the subjection of women, and favors human males in all parts of the world where it presides. Robin Morgan in the Introduction to her book *Sisterhood is Powerful* tells us that the Catholic Church is to blame for much of the prejudice against women. The church, to Robin Morgan, is an obscenity – an all-male hierarchy that skillfully lobbies to prevent legislative change, arrogating to itself the right to control the lives of all the women who call themselves Catholic. Where Catholicism is the predominant religion of a country, even those who are not Catholics must abide by its rules if they are to get along.

263

Creeds grow so thick along the way, / Their boughs hide God.
L.W. Reese (1856-1935)

Louise Driscoll in Stanza five of her "Spring Market" says, "There you will find what every man needs. / Wild religion without any creeds." A religion without creeds would be a religion without religion. Its creeds are its essence. The Apostles' creed, "I believe in God the Father Almighty...", the Nicene Creed, "I believe in one God... etc.", and the Athanasian Creed, "I believe in the Trinity," are prime ingredients of Christianity. The proliferation of creeds can be good as well as bad. For some, there is hope that the creeds of one religion may annul those of another, keeping all of them from spawning a dictatorial mystagogue.

In South America where Catholicism comes close to having the field all to itself, the disadvantages of a monopolizing religion is clear. Pancho Villa blamed the church for most of Mexico's problems, and in Quito, Ecuador, where I lived for eleven years, I found certain members of the one-house congress very concerned with the dominion of Catholicism in that country.

In our own country, the Christian Coalition, with Pat Robertson at the helm, envies the Catholicism of Mexico and South America and probes the reasons for its success. They make it clear that Onward Christian Soldiers, Marching as to War. To Win the World for Christ, precisely defines their goals. Unless, people become alert to the Coalition's sinister insinuations into all facets of their lives, they may wake up one day in the metaphorical chains that Pinsker and Marx (contemporaries) deplored.

264

The focus on heaven can be a lifetime pursuit, and there is no way to test whether the goal was worth the effort.

Alice Rossi
"The Blackwell Clan"
The Feminist Papers

Even whether or not the goal was achieved that, too, will never be known. Can there be wisdom in a lifetime of pursuing a chimera? If there is a God observing us, wouldn't He think us foolish walking blindly toward oblivion? Certainly, He would not condemn us for not engaging in such a pursuit.

If we can keep the pursuit of heaven in perspective and do not become overly zealous in the pursuit, however, it may do no harm. If it is a waste of time, certainly it is better than a pursuit of revenge or a life of crime. Getting there is half the fun, a travel ad says, and that may be true even when the destination does not exist.

José Ingenieros, in his book *The Mediocre Man* says that unattainable goals are the best kind. Korczak Ziolkowski gives us an excellent example. He started his work on carving a mountain into Chief Crazy Horse, knowing full well that he could not finish it. Seven of his ten children are continuing the work, knowing that they, too, will not see its completion.

Those who reach attainable goals, after long years of arduous struggle, sometimes experience horrifying letdowns. Sometimes the experience is so traumatic that they commit suicide.

Of course, even in unsuccessful pursuits, there may be ancillary benefits along the way that make the trip worthwhile. That is often true in science. Also, even though the goal is not reached, it may amount to steps on the way to a worthwhile goal. After the death of the pursuer, another may take over, continue the quest, and reach the goal – of tremendous benefit to all of present and future humankind.

265

Skepticism ... is socially very valuable, immensely more valuable, in fact than any sort of faith.

H.L. Mencken (1880-1956)
Treatise on the Gods

In a world permeated with so much fraud, skepticism has become the only sane attitude possible. Skepticism does not mean rejection, it means only maintaining a healthy doubt about the integrity of individuals or institutions when something has led us to wonder about their honesty.

Our survival may depend on how well we learn to discriminate between the widespread sham that unfortunately in some quarters is in superabundant supply and the unreserved honesty with which other enlightened members of the human species conduct their affairs. It behooves men of reason, in straightforward language, without circumlocutions or fustian, to teach us how to recognize that for which logic wavers and to believe only after carefully scrutinizing all suspicious assertions. So long as we continue with our present gullible readiness to permit religious charlatans to deceive us, there is little hope that we will survive our present dismal plight unscathed.

Whether or not we accept the flimsy assertions of our religious leaders has to do with a common human trait called credulousness. The credulous person accepts without evidence. The skeptical person does not. The credulous person's acceptance is called faith.

Skepticism is required not only in examining religion, but in analyzing all the pretentious nescience subsumed under the rubric "paranormal."

Determining whether the correlation between "religious belief" and "belief in the paranormal" is positive or negative had been the subject of various inquiries. The results of elaborate tests done by Erich Goode in 1996 are in marked contrast with tests performed by Rodney Stark and Williams Sims Bainbridge in 1980. (Skeptical Inquirer, January/February 2000, pages 29-35). If some degree of consistency in the operation of individual human minds is a reasonable premise, simple logic as well as the polled statistics favors the results Erich Goode obtained. Minds which readily accept UFOs as extraterrestrial vehicles, the existence of good and bad luck, psychic powers, and astrology, are the same minds that accept the verity of gods, angels, jinn, devils, heaven, hell, miracles, creation science, and a ten-thousand-year-old universe.

266

> If men believe as I do that this present earth is the only heaven, they would strive all the more to make heaven of it.
>
> Sir Arthur Keith (1866-1955)
> Scottish anthropologist in England

If Khomeine knew what Sir Arthur Keith knew, many innocent children would be alive today who were senselessly killed. Khomeine could convince unarmed children to face bullets as the front ranks of an army division because he had first convinced them that martyrdom assured them a future in heaven, better than anything they could expect on earth.

If ecclesiastics know what Sir Arthur Keith knew, they will not preach a prefabricated celestial heaven and hell ready for use before there was any sign of sinning. We will be vying with one another in our efforts to design and fabricate our own heaven here on earth.

If star-crossed lovers know what Sir Arthur Keith knew, they will not plan a suicide pact, hoping to have a better life together in the heaven to come. Instead they would make every effort to solve their problems here on earth, and might just find themselves doing so and having long and interesting lives together in the only heaven they will ever know.

267

> There is not much practical Christianity in the man who lives on better terms with angels and seraphs than with his children, servants, and neighbors.
>
> Henry Ward Beecher (1813-1887)

Dagobert D. Runes ventures to ask a question that probably you and certainly I would never have thought to ask: "If God could make angels, why did he bother with men?"

Angels and seraphs never talk back. Life in their company is simple. They do only what you want them to do. If they misbehave, you need only rearrange things in your mind to change their behavior to suit you. They dare not disrupt your beautiful reveries and utopian dreams.

An irritating friction often arises between people and the routine, dreary world in which they live. Mythology is so much more comfortable, acceptable, and manageable. Religion in its purest form is the way to go. Let the children, servants, and neighbors do their thing if they like, and be victims of their own brand of complacent self-sufficiency. You will interact with them only as each situation demands – and live *your* life among the angels.

Not many people, of course, let religion take over their lives to that extent. They can call themselves Christians (or whatever) and still carry on their daily affairs. However, they still believe that the only thing that can keep them behaving morally is belief in a celestial pseudo-world of flying saints and frying sinners.

268

> They are always saying God loves us. If that's love I'd rather have a bit of kindness.
>
> Graham Greene (1904-1991)
> *The Captain and the Enemy*

Preceding the quotation above could be an account of any of the numerous murders God commits as described in the Bible. Greene could react the way he did to any of many others of God's atrocities: when He turned Miriam into a leper for murmuring against Moses (Numbers 12:10) when Elisha, the man of God, turned Gehazi and all his descendants into lepers forever because of greed (Numbers 15:35-36), when He ordered a man stoned to death for picking up

sticks on the Sabbath (Numbers 15:32-36), when He orders 42 boys
to be mauled by two bears because the boys called Elisha "baldhead"
(Kings 2:24); when God killed 70,000 men (a Hobson's choice He
gave to David, 2 Samuel 24:15); when God said to the children of
Israel: "You shall destroy every nation that the Lord your God places
in your hands and show them no mercy (Deuteronomy 7:16).

The God of love that pulpiteers preach about invariably turns out,
on examination, to be a God of harsh and arbitrary penalties and
brutalities. The God of Jews, Christians, and Muslims is not a just
God, but rather a God equally capable of doing evil as doing good.
He is to many, as he was to Moses, a partisan God, a champion of
their conflicts with other peoples or nations. In this role He is the
foremost instigator of international and internecine wars. "How odd
of God to choose the Jews," said W.N. Ewer, a foreign
correspondent.

269

It is immoral to baptize infants, confirm adolescents, or impose a
religious creed on young people before they are able to consent.

Paul Kurtz
A Secular Humanist Declaration

Driving, drinking, getting married, signing contracts, etc., waits
until a young person has reached an age where it is fair to say that he
has acquired the acumen to know what he is doing and what are the
consequences. Then why are religions allowed to impose upon
children various sacraments long before they have reached such an
age? How can anyone, even a parent, look at a child and know that
he would, when mature, prefer becoming a Christian rather than a
Buddhist, Jew, or Muslim?

With its infant baptism, children become full-fledged members of
the Catholic Church at what is indeed a tender age. Not only is the
choice not theirs, but it will be many years before they can possibly
know what it means to be a member of the church. Life's edifications
may provoke some of them to resent the fact that affiliation was
arbitrarily imposed upon them before they were old enough to make
the decision for themselves. The Jew may remember how little he
knew about what was going on when he was bar mitzvahed at
thirteen years of age. He, too, may wonder why all the hurry.

Learning as adults what was done to them as children, some may demand explanations. If reasonable explanations are not forthcoming, rebellion is not unlikely. The destinies of some of the greatest leaders as well as some of the most despicable tyrants of history were motivated by deceitful childhood indoctrination.

270

In the religious attitude of the adult toward God, we find a repetition of the infantile attitude of the child toward the father.

Sigmund Freud (1856-1939)

Ontogeny recapitulates phylogeny, is a phrase thrown at first-year zoology students. Now we find something akin operating in religion. Religious imprinting awaits birth before it begins its sinister history but may continue throughout life. Ontogeny, not at all a sinister history, begins at conception and is sometimes defined as having definite cut-off point at puberty.

Mencken repeats what Freud contends, but gives mother, not father, the credit. Like in most other considerations, I assume, every family is different. Among aunts, uncles, and grandparents may well be found the apotheosized precursor to God.

For the child, the worship may be vital. It keeps the child within nurturing distance of its sustenance and keeps it from leaving home before it has been provided the education it will need to survive the jungle out there. For the adult who does not outgrow its childhood dependencies, the adulation may be pathological. Some "adults" remain as children all their lives, attached to their mother's apron strings as long as she may live. If finally they marry, the spouse becomes a substitute mother or father as the case may be.

If society did not keep furnishing us with new theological-school graduates bent on continuing our adulthood dependence, things might not be so bad. With a normal education we might outgrow our undue reliance on forces outside ourselves and become independent, fully functioning members of a sane society. As it is, there is little hope for us. Taught that we need a salvation that only some supernal entity can provide, we never realize our own potential and never accomplish what we might in our brief sojourn on this planet.

271

Enlighten the people generally, and tyranny and oppressions of body and mind will vanish like evil spirits at the dawn of day.

Thomas Jefferson (1743-1826)

"Enlighten the people," Jefferson said in his letter to Pierre Du Pont de Nemours. Enlightenment, we know, is in part the result of a good education. But miseducation, can be oppressive and tyrannical, leaving people less able to accommodate themselves to the social conduct, mores, and demands of modern societies.

An education at Liberty and Regent and many other religious universities leaves students unable to express ideas in a systematic manner and come to rational conclusions. Without an unimpeded study of science and mathematics the student will, in later life, leave himself vulnerable to all manner of chicanery and deceptions.

An authentic "university" educates in all aspects of authentic knowledge. Regent and Liberty are not universities – if we choose not to distort that word into meanings it was never intended to have. They are parochial schools, intent on reducing us to pawns.

It is amazing to see how just a smattering of education in mathematics and science save us from errors of many kinds. In Quito, Ecuador, where I lived for eleven years, soup begins almost every large meal. I never walked into a home where dinner was in preparation that the housewife was not boiling the soup furiously to make it cook faster. Propane is bottled, must be carried from distant stations, and is expensive – a tremendous waste for poor people in Ecuador. To use so much of it just to turn water into vapor is a shame. In a pressure cooker, too, it is well to learn that with the rocker slowly moving, the contents are as hot as they will ever get.

Facts one learns in a beginning high-school science class helps. A friend I fished with on a lake in Minnesota put 20 psi extra of air pressure in the tires on his boat launcher so they would give more lift when half submerged in the lake. One of our past presidents was appalled when told that half the people in the country were below average in intelligence.

Science, well learned and accepted, would end all mystical religions immediately. A belief in miracles, holy shrines, or supernal beings, would be impossible. No religion could hope to challenge the discernment and foresight that a broad education provides.

272

> Whatever crushes individuality is despotism, by whatever name it is called.
>
> John Stuart Mill (1806-1873)

Not infrequently it is called orthodox religion, which shapes its faithful with procrustean zeal, eliminating all semblance of individual expression. This despotism operates through stylized ritual, psychedelic psalms and hymns, automatic genuflections, clearly and deceptively delineated creeds and catechisms, autocratic and arbitrary dogmas, and countless unfounded "sacred" asseverations constantly repeated, conditioning the mind to slavish acceptance of whatever else the anointed master might care to impart. The capacity of our best-known religious leaders to mold their congregations into one homogeneous, bigoted mass is one of the marvels of the century. That so many people will completely surrender their right to think for themselves to a few overbearing mystagogues is almost beyond comprehension.

On October 2, 1995, when twelve jury members without deliberation pronounced a defendant not guilty of a double murder he so obviously committed, we have another example of how easily swayed people can be sitting before a ranting defense lawyer demagogue. That despots in our society are common is not news. But that they can gather together and convince small or large groups of people to follow their perverted logic and Bible-banging rhetoric constantly catches us by surprise. The lesson is frequently repeated. When will we ever learn?

273

> Most gods are not born in heaven but on earth. They are born in the minds of men who clothe them with human features and endow them with earthly attributes of love, authority, and revenge.
>
> George Christian Anderson
> *Man's Right to Be Human*

Anderson knows perfectly well that the first word in his quotation above is superfluous. He gives himself away in his very next sentence where no such qualification is used: "As you read the history of religions, the biography of the gods is the autobiography of the men who invented deities." If there is any doubt left, he surely dispels it in the two sentences which follow. "God created man in his own image, relates the ancient Biblical story of creation, but it is probably more truthful to say that man creates God in man's image. That is how religions are born."

After all of his ruminations, the God that remains in Anderson's mind is the same brain-structure God that resides in the minds of all believers. He is an attempt to answer questions that have no answers. He is the fairy tale that childlike minds seem to require in order to live content.

To say that a thing is utterly incomprehensible is simply another way of saying that it does not exist. The particles of particle physics at least respond to experiments in particle accelerators. The gods of religions are like the entities of science fiction. They respond to nothing and allow no one to limit any of their flights of fancy. In trying to prove that gods exist, we always involve ourselves in an infinite regress, which always means we are talking nonsense.

274

My earlier views on the unsoundness of the Christian scheme of salvation and the human origin of the scriptures have become clearer and stronger with advancing years.

Abraham Lincoln (1809-1965)

That men of the intellectual stature of Abraham Lincoln should need years of reflection to come to such obvious conclusions continues to amaze me. The explanation, no doubt, is the intensive religious indoctrination they received before the age of reason. The fact that they were occupied with so many other concerns is also an explanation. They had little or no opportunity to consider what was happening to them. I recently attended a breakfast of some forty people where a three-year-old girl recited grace for the meal. It was quite long and she played her part beautifully. What chance has she of ever being allowed to come to conclusions on her own about an important facet of her life? The Jesuits knew that such a child would be irrevocably "hooked" before the age of seven and that the enslavement would last for life. With enough children in the United States educated in the manner of this little girl, the Christian

Coalition will someday find it easy to take over and reduce future generations to tribes of automatons.

275

> Is it not strange that the descendants of those Pilgrim Fathers who crossed the Atlantic to preserve their own freedom of opinion have always proved themselves intolerant of the spiritual liberty of others?
> Robert E. Lee (1807-1870)
> Letter to his wife, Dec 29, 1856

Heresy among our Pilgrim Fathers was a capital offense. Their descendants have not improved much since the seventeenth century. Separation of church and state has a harder time among these descendants than in any other place in the United States.

Freedom of religion for many religious communities means freedom for them to do what they consider correct and freedom for others to accept their way of doing things. It does not mean freedom for others to do what *they* think – if *we* do not agree. Even for those others, to proselytize among "our" communities is forbidden. We will tolerate no heretical ideas.

On the 200th anniversary of the Declaration of Independence, Jerry Falwell said in a sermon: "The idea [that] religion and politics don't mix was invented by the Devil to keep Christians from running their own country." Fortunately for Jerry Falwell, he is wrong. If ever the United States does belong to the Falwell Christians, we are lost. With this country a Christian theocracy, there would be no freedom for anyone. All other religions would be banned. The right for people to think would be curtailed. All universities would become adjuncts of Liberty University and all higher education would be the parochial education taught there. Science would be Creation Science, and we would become the most backward nation in the world. If anyone wants to know what happens in a strictly fundamentalist one-religion country, watch what happens in Kabul, Afghanistan under the control of the Taliban.

276

> Do you know that you are the temple of God and that the Spirit of God dwells in you?
> Paul of Tarsus (?-67?)
> 1 Corinthians 3:16

How can this be if, as we read in 1 Jude 2:15-16: "If anyone loves the world, the love of the father is not in him.... The lust of the flesh [talking of you and me, I suppose] is of the world."

If you and I are the temple of God, how can anything be, as Jude says in verse 23, "defiled by the flesh" (of which you and I are composed). In Romans 8:8, we read, "Those who are in the flesh cannot please God." Damn! We are condemned from the word go.

To get back to the question in the box above, my answer is "no." I do *not* know I am the temple of God. There must be a dozen places in the Bible that justify my answering in that manner, and I cite in essay number 382 several passages in the Bible that indicate that God does not consider as of much worth the members of the genus Homo that He created on the last of six days of phenomenal endeavors.

Luke, in 17:21, however, seems to confirm the Temple-of-God assumption, when he says in the King James version: "The Kingdom of God is within you." If we assume that God's temples are part of His Kingdom, Luke seems to have the last, and most encouraging, word. He and Paul agree. How relieved that must make all of humanity feel. God not only loves us, He *must* love us. Not to do so would be to hate his own Kingdom.

277

The real fall of man is his alienation from himself, his submission to power, his turning against himself even under the guise of his worship of God.

Eric Fromm (1900-1980)
Psychoanalysis and Religion

In her "Mr. Meyer's Pupils," Eva Lathbury said nearly a hundred years ago: "The fall, like the serpent was mystical: the apple was sound and Eve hysterical." We might add, if Adam and Eve had to depend on all the apples that grew at that place and time, they would have starved to death.

Man has always been his own worst enemy. We learn to protect ourselves against the hazards of nature, but we fail to protect ourselves against ourselves. We are herd animals, sheep-like conformists easily swayed by military and monied interests opposed to our own. By yielding to tyrannical power that we ourselves put into office, and to presumptuous gods that we ourselves invent, we give up our sovereignty and languish in oblivion. We lose confidence in ourselves and abdicate responsibility. We allow ourselves to be pushed around by a few self-anointed potentates interested mostly in their own comfort and prosperity.

Not until we exorcise our presumptuous gods will we regain our rightful place in the scheme of things. Not until we choose leaders who champion democracy and forgo self-promotion do we have a chance for progress. Not until we reject the mythmongers will we have respect for ourselves our own ingenuities. The "fall of man" is a blatant lie that has done mankind untold harm. The rise of truly moral man to a position of preeminence will be our salvation.

278

They believed... that they held in their hands the candle that would light the world.

Arthur Miller
The Crucible

The people of Salem, Massachusetts were no different from people anywhere who become thoroughly indoctrinated into any religion. They "know" that they have the inside track to absolute truth. For them it would be unconscionable not to welcome the rest of humanity to join them in sharing the one true religion.

When religionists become fanatics, they become vicious and often dangerous. Tomás de Torquemade, the prototypal anti-Semite, was appointed first inquisitor general for all the Spanish possessions in 1483. He became notorious for his fanatical judgments and the cruelty of his punishments. The Spanish Inquisition he supervised was one of the most nefarious events in Christian history. It rivaled the Christian Crusades in its absence of all signs of fairness or principles, which govern the conduct of civilized nations. It took a Hitler 500 years later, to outdo de Torquemade in his moral depravity and his infamous crimes.

Hitler lost all sense of morality in his massacre of Jews, Gypsies, and "mental incompetents" in Nazi Germany. Khomeini was savage in his treatment of alien religions in Islamic Iran. The Archbishop of Quito abandoned sacerdotal composure in his harangues against atheists in Catholic Ecuador. The Irish Republican Army turned into beasts in their terrorism against Protestants in Northern Ireland. We see the same barbarism even here in the United States among some prolifers who kill doctors in hope of improving chances that unborn babies will survive.

Fanatics in religion, jingoists in politics, shysters in law, and embezzlers in business are the same. They lose all sense of proportion. They are monomaniacs with tunnel vision. Nothing matters but their own narrow views. Whenever they succeed, the world loses.

279

> If we encounter in a personality fear of divine punishment as the sole sanction for right doing, we can be sure we are dealing with a childish conscience, with a case of arrested development.
>
> Gordon W. Allport (1897-1967)
> *Becoming*

Job says in 31:23, "The fear I have of God's punishment keeps me from doing bad things." Albert Einstein and Alfred North Whitehead made the point Allport makes also in quotations appearing in this book. Barnes and Teeters on page 617 of their book do also. To take Allport at his word, the phrases "childish conscience" and "arrested development" describe most religionists, and describe as well the main theme of Judeo-Christian-Muslim scriptures. In all three, fear of God or Allah is drummed into readers as desirable from the first page to the last.

Our neuroses, psychologists tell us, come primarily from not understanding the situations that confront us, especially situations demanding choice. The ecclesiastical conspiracy for instilling in us a sense of insignificance, dependency, and debilitating fear sets the stage for anxieties that twist our minds into morbid patterns. Trying to decipher religions' pretensions of meaning where there is no meaning and overburdened with prohibitions and rules, we develop a pervasive, crippling sense of guilt and fear, a significant cause of our mental problems.

280

> Church authorities erect gateways to intellectual and moral irresponsibility. They lay down roads to a happy land where we can gratify our wish without risking a veto by stubborn fact.
>
> Sidney Hook (1902-1989) – *The Quest for Being*

Church authorities deal largely in hogwash. It is that simple. Nothing is gained by disguising this fact with muddled metaphor. Church authorities are much more at home with their lies than they are with truth. From the day they enter the seminary to the day they die they are taught and they learn by themselves to dissemble their shameful perversions of basic truth about how this world does in fact operate. We will not have religious tranquillity in this world until religionists agree to sensible meanings for such terms as proof, atheist, afterlife, science, God, Jesus, creation, demons, divinity, dogma, Eucharist, angels, Bible, reason, religion, rites, second advent, soul, son of God, superstition, theology, and word of God.

The quest for "being" is the quest for "good sense" or it is nothing. The "being" sought by the mystics is not there to be found. There is little good sense in the language mystics use to talk to us. Until we all learn to speak in a language where words have commonly accepted, operative meanings, there will be many futile quests for "grails" that vague or meaningless terms lead us to expect.

281

The Crucifixion has associations with anti-Semitism, and we have to be careful about that.

John Riches
Glasgow University's divinity faculty
Quoted by *Scripps Howard News Service*

John Riches, an "expert" in the historical Christ, is the chairman of a panel that is searching for an artist who can best paint Jesus for the modern world. The principal misgiving, according to Riches is that paintings of the Crucifixion encourage Christians to attack Jews.

Riches doesn't say how "being careful" might manifest itself when trying to reduce anti-Semitism.

Surely someone can paint a modern Jesus picketing efforts to shut down the Leprosarium in Carville, Louisiana, raising Ryan White from the dead, feeding all the refugees from Kosovo with five loaves and two fishes, healing Christopher Reeve, Jesus coming again, this time in a bulletproof bubble car in a ticker-tape parade on Fifth Avenue. The modern Jesus no doubt will be seen in a business suit, whether ridding Saddam Hussein and Slobodan Milosevic of their demons or preaching asceticism to Wall Street. If the painter chooses for his canvas the last judgment return to heaven, of course a space suit would be more appropriate – with Jesus comfortably ensconced in his own private spaceship.

Surely one of them will win the prize.

282

Religion is regarded by the common people as true, by the wise as false, and by the rulers as useful.

Lucius Annaeus Seneca (4-65)

The religion that common people succumb to, the wise usually ignore. They see through its deceits and impositions and choose simply to live their respective lives without giving religion much heed. Rulers are the only ones who come out ahead of the game. Clever and opportunistic, they see in religion a tool to help keep their subjects in line. When even a well-intentioned chief executive sees his people quarrelling, protesting, rebelling, sometimes planning sedition or outright revolution, even though conditions in the country are the same as they have been for many years, he wonders if boredom is not the problem. He suspects that his position as reigning monarch is eroding.

For some reason, he sees religion as the magic potion, the remedial measure for a sinking sovereign, and he makes the most of it. He may even manage to insinuate himself into the mix as deity. However things develop, religion becomes the sedative to mollify the minds of the populace, and peace returns. Once again the ruler's position is secure.

Stendhal said: "All religions are founded on fear of the many and the cleverness of the few." The few, made up of the ordained and the enthroned, often intentionally keep the many filled with fear or dread – alarmed, even terrified of the despotic authority that oppresses them. The few seem not to care that they find themselves despised, seen as religious and administrative tyrants who turn the lives of their subjects into a veritable hell. More important, to them, is to see their family fortunes expanded until they have in their possession most of the country's wealth.

283

> The Bible teaches that woman brought sin and death into the world, that she precipitated the fall of the race, that she was arraigned before the judgment seat of Heaven: tried, condemned and sentenced.
>
> Elizabeth Cady Stanton (1815-1902)
> *The Woman's Bible Pt I*

One might think that unbelievers, without lifting a finger, would win half the population of the world to their cause. The way religion and its scriptures have treated women is little less then criminal. The protagonist in *Born Yesterday* had her solution to the problem of being treated unfairly. It might work for all the women of the world. It would for sure if they acted in concert.

The convention of women in Beijing in September 1995, will, if follow-through efforts in the various countries are conducted vehemently and wisely, help their cause immeasurably. With that momentum, there is no reason why the future cannot be much better than the past. Twice, plans for a million-woman march, once in Los Angeles and once in Philadelphia, failed to arouse the expected enthusiasm. The recent million-mom march did better.

Saint Paul of Tarsus was the misogynist supreme. He it was who said: "It is improper for women to speak in church" (1 Corinthians 14:35). "Women should learn in silence, with complete submission. I do not allow women to teach or domineer over men; they are to keep quiet" (1 Timothy 2:11-12). But Christianity, as prejudiced as it is against women, is not as bad in that respect as is Buddhism, Hinduism, and Islam. Reading the Koran would appall even the most callous of American men.

284

> Some would say that our loyalties to religion, faith, race, and to nation are not subject to evidential support. But if we will not countenance critical attention to our loyalties, we must accept the only alternative – that loyalties are compulsions. Most people agree that compulsion is behavior on the low level of human potential.
>
> F.S.C. Northrop
> *Science and First Principles*

In psychopathology, a compulsion is defined as an irresistible impulse to perform some irrational act. When expressions of loyalty exceed that which is reasonable, expected, or moral, they are compulsions. When we behave as do fanatics, jingoists, and racial bigots, we become pathologically coercive, acting without prudent constraints. We act compulsively.

In religion, where our loyalties imply fidelity to deities that exist only in our imaginations they are not only compulsions but they are absurd. The energies we waste worshiping nonsense could be far better used in helping solve the real, down-to-earth problems that confront us. We have evolved to a point where reason is a marvelously developed faculty of mind. We should use it. If we do not, we will continue to cater only to compulsions, and loyalties are then unthinking, automatic, and not open to reason. Of course, when our personal and emotional attachments have rational bases, loyalties are then seen as beautiful and praiseworthy, to be treasured always.

285

To speak of the soul as substance that is the active source of movement, the cause of thought, the owner of various states or the bond which unites them, etc., is to speak in metaphors, and such metaphors are a fruitful source of confusion if taken literally.

Morris R. Cohen (1880-1947)
Reason and Nature

Some religionists bank their entire roll at the window marked "souls." "Here is where I will come out winners! Maybe I stumbled elsewhere along the road, should have gone to the university when I went off on that crazy junket to Timbuktu, didn't plan well when I invested in that wildcat scheme in Engañadora, but I'm not gambling with my soul. I'm keeping close tabs on that little fellow. When I am unhappy, afraid, overwhelmed by a sense of the futility of all my endeavors, it is to my soul that I look to find comfort, meaning, and significance. Knowing that I have an eternal soul sets everything back on course, making it pleasant to wait for the end which is the beginning. Without a soul, I would be a nonentity, a hollow shell without direction or purpose."

Like the hypothetical "psyche," or "essential self," the supposed seat of man's mental and emotional life, subject to psychological study, there is nothing more to the soul then molecular, cellular, and neural operations of the brain. The idea of a disembodied soul or of "mind functioning" apart from "brain functioning" is as fanciful as Casper or his various replications. Souls may be placed in the same category as unicorns and mermaids, Cyclops and Cerberus, the whangdoodle and the whifflebird.

286

Men become civilized not in proportion to their willingness to believe, but in proportion to their willingness to doubt.

H.L. Mencken (1880-1956)

The New York Times Magazine for Dec 3, 1978, quotes Isaac Singer, Nobel prize winner as saying: "Doubt is a part of all religions. All religious thinkers are doubters." Are doubters? "Thinking" as religionists use the term is the exact opposite of doubting. It is accepting everything seminary instructors, TV evangelists, and pulpiteers say on faith – without a shadow of doubt.

Doubt must be any thinking person's constant companion in confronting anything anyone says about religion or anything else. The only way we will find truth in whatever we hear or read is to harbor within ourselves enough skepticism to impel us to test all propositions.

Believing is easy and doesn't require thinking. We simply decide to accept everything that the very handsome young man at the pulpit says Sunday after Sunday after Sunday, without question. Doubt requires analysis of what the preacher is saying, especially when he constantly contradicts himself and indulges in generalizations that could not possibly be true. Most of his asseverations have never been proven and are more than likely false. Doubt is the sensible choice when the pastor asks us to accept on faith, obviously to deliver himself from the need for pretending to verify what he knows is not true.

In "In Memoriam," Tennyson says essentially the same thing that Mencken says: "There's more faith in honest doubt ... than in half the creeds." It would be nice to find some one pulpiteer whom we could believe today, tomorrow, and forever, but we are not likely ever to do so. Long before the pastor becomes wise and honest enough to convince us of his integrity, he will have renounced established religions because he cannot help discerning their pretense

and deceit. He could not live with himself if he knowingly conspired
with his religion's leaders in their constant duplicity. He has gone to
use his talents elsewhere more constructively before we get a chance
to meet him.

287

I have never had religion enough to keep me from running away
from slavery in my life.

Henry Bible (born 1815)
Narrative of the Life and Adventures of Henry Bible

Bible is saying that in his day there were religions that approved
of slavery. The Pharaohs of Egypt had such a religion. Southern
whites in 1860 surely had such a religion. The author of Genesis
24:35 certainly had such a religion when he said: "The Lord has
blessed my master.... He has given him... male and female slaves,
and camels, and asses." We admire Henry Bible for saying that he
drew a line in his devotion to such a religion.

But there is slavery even when it is not the slavery of our early
South. All of the many autocratic preachers make slaves of the
people that attend their services. Jim Jones and David Koresh were
notable examples. If the members of such congregations were all as
wise as was Henry Bible, the world would be a far better place in
which to live. We would end our subservience to power-hungry
mystagogues. We would end our servile submission to mysterious
life forces, our obsequious reverence of electronic evangelists,
sycophantic veneration of the clerical hierarchy. We would have to
be content with plain, unadorned sanity, living our lives as they
are, not as addlepated mystagogues say they are.

288

It was previously a question of finding out whether or not life had to
have a meaning to be lived. It now becomes clear, on the contrary,
that it will be lived all the better if it has no meaning.

Albert Camus, (1913-1960)
The Myth of Sisyphus

None of us can expect to live forever, but we can expect to live
the rest of our lives pleasantly and usefully. When we do live our

lives productively, we know that death is not the end. We all live on in the results of our efforts that future generations enjoy, whatever those results may be. We live on also in the thoughts of friends, loved ones, and family that survive us.

Life does have a meaning in the sense implied in the above paragraph. We all have goals and intentions that keep us striving meaningfully and enjoyably. And others after our death go on from there to still other goals beyond that which we could hope to accomplish. That is enough! We need no cosmic afterlife to make life meaningful. Making this a better world for future generations is enough. Let us get on with that task and ignore the mythmongers who do nothing but spread anxieties, fear, and hate.

289

Leo Pinsker, a Jewish doctor who had been shaken out of his comfortable confidence by what he had seen happen in Russia ... told the Jews not to rely any more on the sense of justice, or the professed friendship of other nations, but to save themselves by their own efforts.

Malcolm Hay
The Foot of 'Pride

Theodor Herzl in *The Jewish State* carried Pinsker's idea one step further. Then the invading Jews in 1948, with the help of the resident Jews, finished the task. Israel became a Jewish State, leaving only seventeen percent Arabs in the land. After that one bloody battle where many non-Jewish residents of Palestine were murdered, driven from their homes, with many homes destroyed, the Jews became a fairly peaceful people reacting with violence only in retaliation. Yitzhak Rabin, just before his assassination, signed a peace treaty with the Palestinian Arabs, leaving a future with many problems still unresolved.

The world's Jews are on intelligent people, an asset to any country where they choose to live. I see in them only one major fault: Many of them insist that Judaism is a nationality. The Jew cannot become a Russian because he must always be a Jew. He cannot become a German, a Pole, Dutchman, an Ethiopian, etc., because he must always be this nationalistic thing "a Jew." If in the country where the Jewish child is born, he directs all his efforts toward improving the country in which he lives, with no plans ever to exchange it for another that never was his home, and never really should be, he will have no desire to leave, and none of his neighbors will want him to.

290

Leaders who forbid their followers to use effective contraceptive methods of birth control ... express a preference for "natural" methods of population limitation, and a natural method is exactly what they are going to get. It is called starvation.

Richard Dawkins -*The Selfish Gene*

The earth has its limitations. There is a limited amount of land upon which human beings can live. There is a limited supply of fresh water for irrigation, for household use, and for drinking. There is a limited amount of oxygen-producing, carbon-dioxide-consuming forest, and a limited amount of wood for firewood, paper manufacture, and construction. There is a limited amount of minerals, some now in extremely short supply. There is a limited amount of ozone to filter out ultraviolet rays. That is half the picture.

The number of human beings on the earth keeps increasing despite efforts to slow down the population explosion. The rising curve of exponential mathematics reminds us of what happens when a society does nothing to reduce conception where babies are not wanted. Starvation, already a major cause of death in many parts of the world, is an unacceptable solution. We must do better, and we will when there is an educated determination to do so.

When an effective birth control program such as that which Mexico has put into effect in recent years is adopted by every country in the world, populations will no longer increase. Mexico haw reduced its family size to 2.5 children. They expect soon to have that down to 2.1. If a Catholic country can do that, no country has any excuse. The United Nations has said (according to Theodore Rosak) that there is every possibility that by 2150, the total world population will drop to 3.5 billion.

Chapter VIII

Killing Made Easy

291

From cover to cover, with a few exceptions, the books of the Old Testament relate accounts of God's wrath and God-sponsored murders of thousands of human beings: "You shall destroy every nation that the lord your God places in your hands, and show them no mercy" (Deuteronomy 7:16). In numbers 16: 49, we read that God in his anger sent a plague killing 14,700 more. Several times Moses finds it necessary to plead with God in hopes of preventing him from destroying large segments of his people. Dozens of city-states are completely destroyed, men, women, children, babies murdered, leaving no one alive. Army after army is annihilated, not a man left, and almost never is there any mention of taking prisoners. Famines, storms and floods sent by God kill many, many thousands more.

God is love, we are told, but it is that same God who in the quotation from Deuteronomy says "show them no mercy." God cares, we are told, but it is that same God who killed all of Job's large family and all of his livestock – not for anything they had done, but to teach Satan a lesson about God's personal appeal.

The one place not to look for advice on how to build sane and peaceful societies is in the Bible. God's solution for everything is fear, hate, and brute force. No one explains why it is that God, who commands, "Thou shalt not kill," murders constantly., Threats of death are enough to keep others in line.

292

Whatever a theologian feels to be true must be false; this is almost a criterion of truth. His most basic instinct of self-preservation forbids him to respect reality at any point or even to let it get a word in.

Nietzsche (1844-1900)

The Antichrist

When you, Reverend Doe, live a life of preaching and defending myth, you have two alternatives. You can acknowledge the nature of what you are doing, admit that what you are saying is poetry, fantasy, fiction, having no relation to reality in any way. Or you may pretend you are speaking truth and necessarily lie about everything, incapable of putting two sentences in sequence, both of which are true. The task becomes so difficult that you plead with your audience to agree that when you ask them to have faith no questions are to be asked. Both you and they know that there are no explanations, proof, or authenticity in what you say, so you and they just agree to throw good sense out of the window and go on without making waves, resigned to insipidity and indecision.

Organized Christianity very early adopted the policy to approve of deceit and lying when employed in the interest of the church. God's lying begins with His first quoted conversation with men: "You shall not eat of it, nor shall you touch it, lest you die (Genesis 3:3), when even a snake knows better than to believe Him. Not to be outdone by God, parents lie to their children about Santa Claus. For children to find both God and parents lying to them cannot be an especially propitious way to launch them into a life of integrity.

293

[We are not sure] whether the principal object of religion is to procure eternal felicity in the other world or prosperity in this.

Alex de Tocqueville (1805-1859)

E.M. Forster in an essay entitled "What I Believe," part of *Two Cheers for Democracy*, said that Christianity was incapable of dealing with the critical condition of today's world and was certain that the prestige of Christianity in modern society was due to its monetary rather than its spiritual influence.

Tocqueville and Forster both see Christianity as concerned more with inordinate opulence than with eternal felicity or spiritual beneficence. William B. Michaels said in a *New York Times* article on April 2, 1987, "Show me a television evangelist with more than a cloth coat, and I'll show you a charlatan." Pat Robertson, Jerry Falwell, et al., are the robber barons of religion today. They are among today's charlatans that Michaels can point to. How do they reconcile their preoccupation with the inflow of money and their lavish expenditures with the concerns of Jesus and others in the New Testament. Do the comments of Jesus and Paul in the following two quotations impress them?

Matthew 19:23: Jesus said: "...it is hard for a rich man to enter the Kingdom of heaven."

1 Timothy 6:10: "For the love of money is the root of all kinds of evil...."

294

> You never see animals going through the absurd and often horrible fooleries of magic and religion...; only man behaves with such gratuitous folly. It is the price he has to pay for being intelligent but not, as yet, quite intelligent enough.
>
> Aldous Huxley (1894-1963)
> *Texts and Pretexts*

Without today's intelligence, we would still be worshiping sun gods, moon gods, rain gods, and Zeus. With a bit more intelligence, our ancestors graduated to stone and wooden gods. With the gift of acumen still further advanced on the part of followers, proficiency in magic by apotheosized human beings was the criterion of acceptability for choosing deified religious leaders.

Now we have gone still further. We have replaced our "nature" and "magic" gods with a single incomprehensible Supreme God, that serves us for nothing. No one can attack the God we now postulate because no has the slightest idea of what he would be attacking. With still more intelligence, someday we will dethrone all gods, cast aside our mythmongers and learn to live in the world as it is, operating largely according to known cosmic laws and within known limits. Only then will we have peace and a hope for fashioning our world into the kind of utopia we would like it to be.

295

Religions commit suicide when they find their inspiration in their dogma.

Alfred North Whitehead (1861-1947)
Religion in the Making

The main effect of dogma is to preserve and even to intensify the hate that is sectarianism, the very foundation of any church. The more absurd and arbitrary the dogma proves to be, the better it functions to glorify "us" and to stigmatize "those others," insuring that the society of religionists will continue on its course of dangerous mediocrity. Any religion of salvation depends on its dogma and little else. To destroy its dogma would be to destroy any orthodox church in the world. Those who have proposed to eliminate the dogma of a church have met with severe censure, excommunication, or worse. They have had about as much chance of success as did Gregor Mendel when presenting his formulation of the great law of heredity to his ecclesiastical superiors.

"Dogmatism is puppyism come to its full growth," said Douglas Jerrold. But dogma, as we see, does not grow up; it is thrown down. It comes into the world fully fledged, in full regalia, and is never again as mature as the day it is born. The dogma of orthodoxy must be accepted with a closed mind, for it is not open to reason, not meant to be. It is laid down and must not be picked up and examined. Later thinking does not make it so; it makes it so-so.

296

The scholarly consensus is that no evidence, acknowledged, or otherwise, exists for the first eleven chapters [of genesis]: nothing for the creation, of course, nor anything credible for Eden, the Flood, or the Tower of Babel.   Sharon Begley

Newsweek, October 21, 1996

The lack of reliable or credible evidence for the authenticity of Genesis, of course, does not discourage Bill Moyers and friends from serving as panel for a television program titled *Genesis: A Living Conversation.* "Intelligent" human beings sit in a circle surrounded by television cameras treating some fifty pages of dubious Biblical musings as if they were history. Lost in Laputa, the participants seem not to notice that they are babbling buncombe. God, Adam, Eve, Cain, Abel, and Noah, to their muddled minds are as ponderable as Washington, Lincoln, or their own family and friends. The six days of creation, Eden, the flood, and the Tower of Babel, to them, are as authentic as Pompei, Pisa, and Palermo.

Elsewhere in this book we quote H.L. Mencken as saying that no civilized man believes in the cosmology of Genesis. Both Thomas Paine and Richard Elliott Friedman deny that Moses had anything to do with writing Genesis, as is commonly averred. Genesis is so full of contradictions that one wonders if it were not written by a committee of half-wits.

I suppose when the program is over and Moyers and friends find themselves among sane citizens they will be able to dissemble their nescience or premature dotage and behave as if they were exemplary specimens of a divinely designed and bountifully blessed animal species. The rest of us will be able to close mouths, agape in astonished disbelief.

It must be pointed out that the same Bill Moyers who could peddle the unmitigated asininity of *Genesis: A Living Conversation* could also give us the two programs *Free Speech for Sale* and *Justice for Sale* on PBS, June 8 and November 23, 1999. It is very possible that no one has ever before presented so eloquently and effectively how big businesses are able to suppress voices that oppose their unbridled cupidity. Hog farming and the tobacco business in North Carolina and elsewhere, with their immense monetary reserves are able to buy the complicity of U.S. Senators and Congress members and flood TV screens with subtle and cleverly composed info-distortions that convince citizens to vote against their own and the country's interests. Every citizen must be given the opportunity and encouraged to see Bill Moyers' other excellent programs. But may we be delivered from the babbling of anyone when pretending to know everything about that which he "knows" nothing – about the completely unknowable.

297

Miracles are the children of mendacity.

> Robert G. Ingersoll (1833-1899)
> "Some Reasons Why"
> Speech NYC – April 25, 1981

Miracle is a word we toss around lightly, but we do that of all the words of religion whose referents are nothing more than fiction. Religion depends on such words, of course. It could not exist without them.

Joseph Campbell would lecture for hours with sentences filled with phantom words. Theologians rely on phantom words as much as did Campbell and all other mythologists.

Barrows Dunham is quoted at length in essay 130 of this book on the illogicality of miracles. Essay 70 and 743 add significant points.

When magicians perform the "impossible" it is called illusion; when religions do the same they speak of miracles. The main difference between magic and religion is the professed intentions. When the magician ends his performance, he hopes only that his audience has been entertained. The religionist ends his performance believing that the members of his audience have been thoroughly transformed.

It is a wise religionist who does not let himself get carried away with the "miracle" word of religion. He first of all understands the ulterior designs of those who consider the word basic in selling their wares. Some pulpiteers, too, we must assume, understand the folly they commit themselves to when they use nonsense words, hoping to fool their simple-minded adherents. More and more they see the members of their congregations asking Why is "faith" essential? Why is "reason" anathema? Is the impossible (miracles) ever really possible?

Miracles or no miracles, it is easy to see that God has a few tricks up His sleeves bordering on the uncanny when He can produce a tractable earth before it has a sun to orbit, and have plants growing abundantly before there was sunlight, which did not appear until the fourth day.

Also, it seems (Genesis 1:27) God created human beings before he created Adam, that "first" human being, who lived alone in a subsequently planted Garden for some time before He came up with that neat little trick that produced Eve. We do not get far along in the first pages of the Bible before we see two (possibly three) superimposed and contradictory versions of origins that only a truly "omnipotent" Miracle-Worker could have managed to reconcile.

298

If God did not exist, it would be necessary to invent him.

Voltaire (1694-1778)

And that, of course, is exactly what we have done. We may need our gods, I do not know, but what we need more is to understand the mechanisms within ourselves that oblige us to dream up these gods and then to bow down to them.

Montesquieu once said that if triangles invented God they would make him three-sided. Xenophanes said it much earlier: "If the ox could paint a picture his God would look like an ox."

One well-known Christian religion considers God to be a physical being of flesh and bones. Another interprets God as spiritual but with the general form and stature of man (Mormonism and Church of God, respectively). We do best to invent a God acceptable to ourselves, and hopefully to other people. Certain academigogues turn out a God that is little more than an anagogic plaything for dissentient theo-logicians. Their God is so unapproachable that no traditional or liberal theologian will accept him, and you and I cannot imagine what they are talking about. Their God is not a God to unite us, but to separate us into still other nondescript and ever more contentious factions. Better the fauns and satyrs. At least they were fun.

299

The cure for a false theology is mother- wit. Forget your books and traditions, and obey your moral perceptions at this hour.

Ralph Waldo Emerson (1803-1882)
The Conduct of Worship

"False theology" is as pleonastic as is "scientific knowledge." If this world is such that simple logic has any place at all in the intellectual ambience, all knowledge is scientific and all theology is false. That will change when anyone can demonstrate that knowledge is at anytime anything but scientific, and any theology can demonstrate that the universe we live in is supervised by a deity. Herbert Spencer called science "organized knowledge" but even the word organized is unnecessary because science is an organizing medium. Facts (knowledge) become worthy of being so-called when so far as is practical they are established as true and are meaningfully organized into a useful system. For theology to postulate an intervening god is to place itself squarely in the middle of an infinite regress that even a six-year-old child is astute enough to question.

Mother-wit or native intelligence is the very uncommon "common sense" that is so often touted. It is that rare acumen that leaves no access to the absurdities of the mystics. Astrologers, channelers, crystal gazers, phrenologists, psychics, palmists, etc., find no rapport with the person endowed with this very important legacy from sensible, down-to-earth mothers. Our moral instincts, if at all operative, should be enough to protect us from the concocted fantasies of the mystagogues.

300

There is a sort of transcendental ventriloquy through which men can be made to believe that something which was said on earth came from heaven.

Georg Christoph Lictenberg (1742-1799)

Why not? Man can be made to believe the entire gamut of heavenly hokum. Adding a few more fibs and fables is not going to make much difference. Our television evangelists talk constantly of their conversations with God. In any other profession they would be tossed into the looney bin, but because they are preachers we are supposed to take them seriously.

Preachers talk of a 6000-year-old world, of coming armageddon, of absolute truth, an ark that could hold an entire zoo, afterlife, angels, demons, leviathans, a tower of Babel, resurrections, divine love, exorcism, virgin birth, papal infallibility, second advent, seraphim, transubstantiation , etc. – all of which have about as much chance of existing as snowballs in hell, snow flakes in a blast furnace, or a snow drift in the Sahara. We need not worry about celestial beings misplaying their parts, for they play only the parts we write for them. Any time we make a concerted and energetic effort to do so, we can change them into decent, loving, cooperating beings. Why we have gone on for so many years tolerating a murdering, hating, despicable god, I cannot imagine. Why we tolerate a bunch of obsequious, toadying, sycophantic angels, I do not know. We must either get rid of them all, or revamp them into something we can live with. Whatever our preachers say, we are in charge, always have been, and always will be, at least until we become extinct.

301

The truth is, no one really believes in immortality. Belief must mean something more than desire or hope.

Clarence Darrow (1857-1938)
The Story of My Life

Even William Jennings Bryan, while opposing Darrow in the Scopes Trial, showed that he too did not firmly believe what he was advocating. By his inability to answer some of the questions and his hesitations and ineptitude answering others, he made that clear. His death two months later may indicate that he did know, in all conscience, that he had lost the case.

Elsewhere Darrow says in effect that by abandoning the idea of immortality we at least cast out fear and gain a certain dignity and self-respect. The sine qua non of being a Christian, unfortunately, is that we do fear; we must fear God. Scaring us half to death is the scheme for convincing us to behave in the same irrational manner that is characteristic of the Christian leaders themselves. They dare not use rational arguments to convince us to behave morally, because they were taught in theological school that such arguments could wreak havoc, destroy the underpinnings of everything else they had to say.

Darrow's reason for thinking no one believes in immortality is simply that such a belief is so ridiculous that no one with half a brain would accede to it. But could not the same be said for all of religion? To study orthodox religion is to see how often its adherents engage in fairy-tale dialogue without rhyme or reason. They find it assuasive to agree with anything and everything their preacher may choose to say.

To accept one of the church's flimsy doctrines or sacraments, such as immortality, resurrection, transubstantiation, baptism, atonement, penance, extreme unction, sacrosanctity, confirmation, and confession, is to accept them all. Any one is no harder to believe than any of the others. Once we allow ourselves to accept one example of arrant nonsense, why not go the whole hog? To forfeit sound reasoning is to open the door to every brand of nonsense man has seen fit to invent.

302

> The villas and the chapels where I learned with little labour; / The way to love my fellowman and hate my next-door neighbour.
>
> G.K. Chesterton (1874-1936)

Religion teaches us to love our fellowman, then asks us to kill thousands, Walter Kaufmann says in essay 304. Religion asks us to live in peace with our fellowman, then engages in wars all over this globe. Jesus tells us to love our enemies as we do ourselves (Mat 22:39), then asks that his enemies be brought and slain before him (Luke 19:27). The God of Love (2 Cor. 13:11) we find, makes a list of the characteristics of those He hates (Prov. 6:16).

The God of love created a world populated with Satan and innumerable devils to do his vengeful bidding. He constructed a hell even before there were sinners, and then turned His devils loose on us to make sure His hell would be adequately tenanted.

Believers speak of God's love, religious serenity, and human cooperation, but introduce into our societies hate, intolerance, bigotry, fear, religious wars, and robotic personalities. Readers make up their minds about religion on the basis of the inexhaustible supply of biased religious literature that weighs down our library shelves. This book is an effort to present a better balance, to make everyone aware of the onesidedness of the propaganda and to help everyone make more informed decisions. Love not hate, peace not war, reason not whimsy must rule. We human beings must learn to believe only when there is evidence for believing.

303

Let American religion and wrong, American religion and cruelty, American religion and prostitution, American religion and piracy, American religion and murder, cold-blooded, and calculated by America's largest measure, shake hands.

Charles Lenox Redmond (1810-1873)
Letter to the West Newberry Antislavery Society

To study what happened during Christianity's most heinous assaults against humanity is to know that slavery is not the only place where the Christian religion has disgraced itself. Religion, not just the Christian religion, has been the number one cause of wars since the beginning of recorded time. Any warmonger who plans his barbarities astutely can find some religion to champion his cause.

But even wars do not tell the whole story of the horror of religions.

Some religions denounce family planning, thereby accelerating the population explosion, adding to the number of abortions in any country where they are able to make their will law. June Goodfield on the television program *The Cosmic Joke* asks (verbatim, if my memory does not fail me): If the Pope were living in this garbage dump [full of children scavenging], would he be so adamantly opposed to contraception"?

It is religion that often aggravates racial animosities, and intensifies class prejudices, and promotes divisive attitudes in the church. By banning women from certain church offices, railing against homosexuals, and favoring celibacy for priests, religionists alienate still others who otherwise would join their esteemed echelons.

304

The men who conducted the Greek heresy trials, the Inquisition and the witch hunts, who went on Crusades and to holy wars, were conformists, men of the crowd, true believers.

Walter Kaufmann (1921-1980)
The Faith of a Heretic

True believers, Eric Hoffer, also, called them, those who adhere to a religion regardless. Once they make this attachment, they cannot be dissuaded for any reason. Inquisitions, heresy trials, witch hunts, or Crusades that mean that hundreds or hundreds-of-thousands of their fellow human beings were and will be killed do not faze them. They will believe regardless.

As die-hard conformists, adherents of religion march in synchronized steps and chant synchronized mantras. Closed societies know they can count on support of this large contingent of closed minds.

To the true believer, "those others" who object to the rigid canons and conventions of his religion are fools or dupes, insensible to divine purpose.

Without an impenetrable shield against rational grounds for forming opinions, the true believer's serene confidence would collapse. Better to be a vegetating conformist than a man of innovative ideas that threaten "divinely ordained" sacrosanctity.

305

I never knew any man in my life who could not bear another's misfortune perfectly like a Christian.

Alexander Pope (1688-1744)
Thoughts on Various Subjects

Empathy, one of the most beautiful words in the English language, may be one of the most difficult to observe wholeheartedly. This ability to "be" another person for purposes of understanding him is almost impossible. Also, if our reaction is not completely spontaneous, it will be seen as affected or insincere.

Radio news just announced a 7.1 magnitude earthquake in northeastern Iran, near the Afganistan border. More than 2,400 people were killed and 50,000 people left homeless. Many countries are offering aid, and the Red Cross is already at work in the region. For that sort of aid to appear, we know that there must be many people throughout the world who do suffer from other people's misfortunes and do react as caring people should.

We know what Alexander Pope is saying, and in local situations we do see how callous we can be. Unless the misfortune affects us personally, many of us will ignore or at least wait to see if someone else will help so we can return to our own personal affairs. Just how much empathy we can be part of without completely destroying our own efforts in our own way to help fellow world citizens of an ever ailing world?

In the Iran disaster, we can help by sending money, blankets, tents, and medicines. In a local situation, we must get personally involved in other people's lives. Most of us are awkward in expressing sympathy and are afraid we may do more harm than good. Unlike in the Iran disaster, if we want to help we cannot remain detached. We need to deal with emotions: tears, anger, or despair.

One simple example, more than any other, may point out the difference between international and local assistance. In the Iran disaster, "sending money only" might well be the best thing people can do. With enough money and someone there to supervise its distribution, the medicines, tents, etc., can be bought – even the service of nurses and doctors. Offering money to alleviate a *local* misfortune and doing nothing else may be the worst assistance imaginable. Where hands-on help and sympathy might make lifelong friends, offering money and walking away may create lifelong enemies. Charity is often a more complicated affair than it may at first seem.

306

There are a thousand hacking at the branches of evil to one who is striking at the root.

Henry David Thoreau (1817-1862)
Walden

Hacking at the branches is building more prisons and reform schools, handing out stiffer sentences and fewer opportunities for parole. Striking at the root is teaching effectively in all our schools the value of human life and the importance of morality, respect, kindness, empathy, and a good education.

Hacking at the branches is to conduct anti-drug wars, sending those who sell drugs to jail for longer and longer periods of time, making possession of drugs a felony. Getting at the root of the problem is teaching graphically to all children the harm that drugs do to human beings, to their families, and to their societies. Teaching them how to say no to peers and other people who coax them to try drugs is also striking at the root.

Hacking at the branches is to treat pregnant girls as criminals, depriving them and the new-born babies of medical care. Striking at the root is teaching all children from the beginning of puberty on, the benefits of abstinence, the importance of marriage, the story of conception, the deceit of young and sometimes older men when coaxing girls to submit. Teaching honestly the danger of venereal diseases is also striking at the root.

Hacking at the branches is relying on the printed word to teach safety. Without illustrations, films, and demonstrations of what it means to behave safely, lessons are not absorbed. Getting at the root is to teach people how to be safety prone, how to see beforehand the consequences of unsafe behavior.

Lessons in driving safety are of paramount importance. Teaching children to swim is very important. To engage in horseplay at swimming pools, when skiing down hills, on the job, when driving, etc., etc., we must be made to understand, is a prescription for disaster.

307

The idea of punishment is always in [preachers'] thoughts, they are hangmen rather than deliverers.

H.L. Mencken (1880-1956)
Treatise *on the Gods*

Punishment as a response to wrongdoing, whether a misdemeanor, felony, or capital crime, serves in only one way: It is a sop to the misanthrope that exists in every human being. In some people this misanthrope can for the most part be ignored. In others it takes over their entire being.

Punishment does not lessen crime, not even capital punishment, as statistics consistently show. When capital punishment becomes law for the first time in any of our states, it does not reduce murder. The incidence of murder is as likely to increase as to decrease.

The only valid consideration when convicting anyone of crime in our courts of law is that of protecting society from the nefarious ways of the criminal. All criminals should remain behind bars as long as they can reasonably be considered a threat to society. In that manner, of course, society does reduce crime. Punishment or vengeance has no logical place in the equation if reducing crime is our true and only concern.

Rehabilitation is possible in many cases where it is given a chance, and is conducted in accordance with sane psychological principles. Rehabilitation would be far cheaper than dealing with recidivism, but that will be the determining factor only in societies far more advanced than our own. Someday, perhaps, but we are not yet ready to react sanely to criminal behavior in our societies.

308

Change is the law of life. And those who look only to the past or the present are certain to miss the future.

John F. Kennedy (1917-1963)
Speech, Frankfort, Germany June 25, 1963

Kennedy made that statement less than five months before the world was to suffer a devastating change: Kennedy was dead.

Once *the* truth is established through revelation, canonical improvisation, or scriptural perusal and interpretation, than that should be that. No need ever to make changes, just to pile verification upon verification, historical epoch after historical epoch. But unfortunately things are not that simple. History changes, customs and religious fashions change, science makes new discoveries, new minds make new interpretations, and even new scriptures are written. The "unchangeable" is forced to accommodate to the new world that emerges while the old is discarded. As untenable religious beliefs give way to the enlightenment of science, the little that is left is so vague and difficult to define that we become sure, with Renan and Taine, that religion cannot last another 50 years. But by now we are sophisticated enough to know that it can. Religion will survive, and so will intolerance, obscurantism, hypocrisy, and bigotry.

Tennyson said many years ago: "The old order changeth, yielding place to new, / And God fulfills Himself in many ways, / Lest one good custom should corrupt the world." James Russell Lowell said, "Time makes ancient good uncouth." *The* truth is found not to be *the* truth after all, but only agreed-upon conventions permitted by the lack of scientific knowledge at the time and under the circumstances prevailing. The religions that survive are those that modify their dogma to accommodate themselves to the present rapidly changing world.

309

A refusal to come to an unjustified conclusion is an element of an honest man's religion.

Bergen Evans
The Natural History of Nonsense

Better change "religion" (his last word) to "philosophy." An honest man cannot have a religion, because religion as developed today is deceit, and the honest man knows it. Those who adhere to religions come to unjustified conclusions all the time. It is the sum of those unjustified conclusions that is their religion. Without them religion could not exist.

To be justified, a conclusion must be proven to be true. It must be shown to have a large and significant body of predictive content. None of the organized superstitions that make up religions will stand up to the method of proof used to show that statements of science are true, distinctly superior to moot opinion. Religion, unfortunately, has no categories such as hypothesis or theory into which it can classify it formulations. Theologians consider all statements they make worthy of being denominated "truth." But the bag in which they assemble their ersatz "truth" has come to resemble a hydrogen-filled dirigible, terrified of a spark of enlightenment.

310

Christians are the only people in the world who have anything to be happy about.

Billy Graham (1918-)

Graham, probably considered the greatest apologist for Christianity alive today, strikes me as the most prone to uttering abominably bigoted pronouncements. Billy Graham has studied and taught religion for more than half a century. He has had an opportunity to look objectively at what he has been studying. How then can he make a statement like that in the box above? Has he lost completely his mental equilibrium? Can he be *that* blind to the many atrocities committed in the name of Christianity? Are Christians supposed to be happy about the Christian Crusades, the Spanish Inquisition, the Salem witch trials, the Thirty Year War, and the Holocaust? Are Christians supposed to be happy about all the hate, bigotry, and anti-Semitism that is instilled in human lives?

When Alfred North Whitehead said, "I consider Christianity to be one of the greatest disasters of the human race," at least he indicates that what he says is personal opinion, not a fact to be unreservedly accepted. If any truly sane human being were disposed to find out which, Graham or Whitehead, came closer to the truth about Christianity, there is little doubt that Whitehead would win, hands down. It would not be farfetched to guess that on the happiness scale, Christians would rank near the bottom. How can people be happy with a religion that has caused so much suffering and death throughout history? Surely you jest, Reverend Graham!

311

The Religion of Christ reaches and changes the heart, which no other religion does.

William Dean Howells (1837-1920)

Howells seems to have been fashioned from the same mold that produced Billy Graham. His creed-biased drivel ranks alongside of Graham's: "Christians are the only people in the world who have anything to be happy about."

Both Howells and Graham are remarkably ordained "divine beings" of course. No ordinary mortal could make such conclusive statements about all other religions on earth. There are said to be 11,000 of them, and it would certainly take a remarkable mind to know all of them. Could God Himself be that sure of the capabilities of all religions everywhere?

Of course, when William dean Howells said, "The religion of Christ reaches and changes the heart," he did not say what manner of change he refers to. Maybe he refers to the hate, bigotry, and prejudice Christianity instills in human hearts. Maybe he refers to the fear that takes possession of everyone who has ever devoted himsself seriously to Christianity. Maybe it is the confusion that the mythological bases of Christianity keep stirring up in its adherents that he refers to. Human hearts have a hard time ignoring the many unanswered questions that confront them if Christianity has been their education: If God is caring and omnipotent, why do we have suffering? Why do evil men prosper and good people come to grief? And why, why, why, does the great, all-powerful God who can do what He thinks is best for us - suffer the existence of Satan? And one last question: Why did the God who can make angels ever bother with men?

312

My own introduction to the unspeakable depths to which human beings can sink was not made through theaters, uncensored billboards, or evil-minded companions, but solely through an unrestricted access to my sainted grandmother's Bible.

Charles Flandrau (1871-1938)
Saint Paul Pioneer Press - January 14, 1917

Whether it is about crime, pornography, sexual infidelity, duplicity, lying, war, or gratuitous cruelty, the Bible speaks to everyone. A child that is given unrestricted access to the Bible can learn all about the iniquities of God and man.

If children are to grow up innocent, access to the Bible should be only in Sunday School, not from the printed words of scriptures. Bible teachers learn to omit or expurgate the savage and scurrilous parts of the Bible: God's countless murders (even of children), Jesus asking that his enemies be brought and slain before him, David's eight wives (even killing one husband to make that man's wife available to him), a perfectly innocent girl (daughter of Jephthah) burned to death, the Amelekite King Agag being hacked to death, forty-two boys being torn apart by bears, Sodom and Gemorrah and many other cities being completely destroyed.

Cruelty to animals, especially, affects children: hamstringing horses, drowning swine, sacrificing 100,000 animals to dedicate a church, sacrificing a ram, millions of animals destroyed that could not get into the ark. None of these cruelties should ever be known to children.

One often hears the recommendation that if people would only acquire the lifetime habit of reading a few pages of the Bible every day they would become model citizens. Nothing could be more absurd. What would more likely happen is that they would turn into callous, insensitive brutes, unable to function acceptably in modern societies.

313

As Chesterton points out, the Fall of Man is only the banana-skin joke carried to cosmic proportions.

Malcolm Muggeridge (1903-1990)
Jesus Rediscovered

Once at a university, carrying a bundle of papers that precluded good vision of where I was putting my feet, I fell down a long flight of stairs. I busted hell out of my pride but was not otherwise seriously hurt. I probably would not remember the incident had there not been a bevy of young ladies who laughed their fool heads off at my awkward mishap.

Haven't we all been guilty of the indiscretion of those young ladies? The eternal television series *The Funniest* Home *Videos* is mostly about people falling – even off stages into the orchestra pit. Now God Himself seems to find amusing such unfortunate happenings.

I have never been able to understand why those who wrote the Bible found it important to weave the particular fable that Chesterton points out into the fabric of Biblical fantasy. An omniscient Superbeing, both prescient and all-powerful certainly had a choice about what kind of innate proclivities He would incorporate into His sixth-day creations. They would behave as He wanted them to behave and in no other way. He made angels, it seems, as servile automatons. Devils and jinn, too, have prescribed behavioral characteristics fashioned according to His will.

It is difficult to find vestiges of a sense of humor in God's activities. Perhaps He gets His kicks vicariously. After all, he did, according to scripture, make those young ladies. And he must have had something to do with whatever there is about the rest of us that keeps the ratings of violent television programs high. Muggeridge may have been unusually discerning when he chose to share with Chesterton his conceit in calling the Fall of Man God's banana-peel joke. We have long been in sore need of some sort of ventilation of man's ignominious tumble, as aberrant and abhorrent as it has always seemed to be.

314

> Is there no God, then, but at best an absentee God, sitting idle ever since the first Sabbath, at the outside of the universe?
>
> Thomas Carlyle (1795-1881)
> *Sartor Resartus*

An answer to the first four words is the only answer needed. All other ruminations are superfluous. Perhaps additional words can be fun, but do we not have better things to do than that?

Make a firm and final decision that God does not exist, and both the one who decides and all others will live in a vastly improved world. Affixing addenda that do no conceivable good and that require aeons of explanations can do incalculable harm. Even minds like Einstein's felt compelled to respond to speculations on the subject – even though careful and complete reading of his words should convince anyone that he was an atheist.

Carlyle's "absentee God" is the God of Deism, popular at the time. Thomas Paine's *Age of Reason,* published at about the time Carlyle was born, describes deism. The first Sabbath Carlyle speaks of was dated by Bishop James Ussher as occurring in 4004 BC. The universe is now known to be more than two million times the age given for that first Sabbath. The earth is nearly a million times as old. The time when the dinosaurs died out is some ten thousand times as long ago as the date of Bishop Ussher's first Sabbath.

315

> By the fourteenth century the great institution founded for the saving of souls had become a vast engine of exploitation. No part of life was exempt from its intrusive claims.
>
> Barrows Dunham
> *Heroes and Heretics*

Dunham continues with examples: "… priests, bishops, friars, searching out degrees of consanguinity, could pronounce marriages lawful or unlawful as authority might determine. Couples who for years had supposed themselves married could be told, suddenly, that they were living in fornication, that their children were bastards, and that inheritance of property was thus compromised. But fees would set all right: Upon sufficient payment, the marriage would be validated, the children legitimized, and the inheritance (now somewhat reduced) made secure."

Is such exploitation a thing of the past? Pat Robertson's religious complex is taking in more than a hundred million dollars a year. What do those who donate that money get in return?: education in hypocrisy, intolerance, bigotry, superstition, hubris, racial and class prejudice, and hatred of homosexuals. The exploitation during the fourteenth century that Dunham speaks of is minuscule compared to the exploitation today by our modern disciples of mammon.

If the far-right Christian Coalition ever attains the political ascendancy it seeks, things will get much worse. To imagine the likes of Robertson and Jerry Falwell in power in this country is the worst kind of nightmare. To listen to their words on panel discussions or to hear their words when they were not meant for public broadcast is to understand the horror that would ensue.

316

> We cannot treat the human embryo as cheap and worthless without passing judgment on all human life, including our own.
>
> Monica Furlong
> *Christian Uncertainties*

If there is one single moral principle that our educational systems should be instilling deeply within the fibers of individual being, it is that preserving human life must be considered the supreme virtue. Genocide, wars, Christian crusades, witch hunts, inquisitions, holocausts, manslaughter, capital punishment, or abortion should become so intensely horrifying to us that we would never be guilty of such monstrous behavior without compelling reasons.

Think of all the ova and sperm that women and men, respectively, produce – and then think of what horrible fates most of these marvelous entities suffer: Isn't it depressing? One might think that those who postulate a caring and omnipotent god, in charge of every occurrence of any kind, would outdo themselves in efforts to deny that god would have formulated any such cruel system of creature propagation. We expect nature in the raw will not always be

tenderness, love and compassion. But God? The god who is love
(John 3:16), compassion (Psalms 86:15), and indeed, perfection
(Matthew 5:48)? In Romans 9:14, we read: "Is there unrighteousness
with God? Certainly not!" If a God has been in charge, surely we can
infer, there would be no such profligate suffering as we see in our
very processes of becoming. That is, a God *is not* in charge, the only
possible conclusion. The universe goes its indifferent way
unsupervised – except by cosmic laws which obviously exhibit no
plans, purpose, or responsibility.

Now we know that love, compassion, and righteousness, if they
exist, are man's love, compassion, and righteousness. We are in
charge, we and no one else. Athough we had nothing to do with
creating the universe, we create and alter at will the culture that
becomes much of what is our environment. We may deplore nature's
profligacy with respect to seed, ova, sperm, roe, spores, and pollen,
but that is a reality we must accept. Where we have no control, we
must not waste our energies and time. But where we can make a
difference, we must make every effort to see to it that humanness
prevails.

One place we can make a difference is in respect to the unborn
members of our own species. They are our most precious heritage,
and we must understand that they are.

To describe that which is growing within the mother-to-be, we use
such terms as zygote, morula, blastula, gastrula, embryo, and fetus.
The implication is that we are dealing with some kind of parasite, or
expendable vermin. But the words we use to describe things do not in
fact change the nature of those things. The developing human being
remains just that regardless of what it is called.

Abortion is not a human thing to do. It is monstrously inhuman. It
is bound to affect morality in all aspects of our lives. The legal
argument concerning whether abortion is or is not criminal hinges on
one thing and one thing only: how do we define the point where
human life begins. Whatever we may say about it for personal
reasons of convenience, we must know that a zygote is life, not
mineral. And we know too that in our case it is human life. No
human mother has ever given birth to a bunny, a polliwog, a joey, or
an elver. When we stop trying to fool ourselves, we will all agree to
what almost all human beings surely already know: We must prevent

abortion in every case where it is humanly possible, except in cases where the health of the mother is gravely at risk. Only then can we think of ourselves as a truly enlightened and sensitive class of beings.

317

Most religions do not make men better, only warier.

Ellias Canetti
Aufzeeichnungen

The innocence of children is enchanting. For some of their years, at least, they live in a veritable utopia, unaware of the deceit that permeates all of society. We wonder if there is reason why we could not fashion a world in which all of us could live with the naïve confidence that all is well with the way things are going and that we can live out our years in confidence and serenity.

But we look around us and see the formidable obstacles to such sanguine expectancy. First we see the devastating prejudices that invade every interstice of human thought, leaving us hating everything we do not understand or that deviates from our own ideas of perfection. Then we see the all-pervading greed, with too many of us solely intent on getting our own nest egg – worse, with many of us accumulating fortunes we could not possibly spend, but deprive others of the basics they need to survive at all. Then we see the frenetic scramble for power, with leaders emerging everywhere whose main preoccupation is to control other human beings, the more they can control, the better.

But now we come to the most formidable obstacle of all. It arises from a fatastically bizarre notion that we live better if we choose to live in worlds of mythology, in hierarchies of dreamed-up semblances that have no existence except in human minds. We watch leaders of these shadow worlds acquire more than their share of prejudices, greed, power and dementia, and an incredible capability for convincing others to join them in their delusions. Those of us remaining who are not "improved" by religion, as Canetti says, do become more healthfully wary of the constant and indefatigable efforts that others marshal in order to deceive us.

318

> We must welcome the night. It is the only time that the stars shine.
>
> Michael Quoist - *With Open Heart*

And the moon too, according to God (Genesis 1-16). Perhaps the best indication that the Bible was written by mortal man rather than by an omniscient God is that the Bible writers knew only what it was possible for the people to know at that time. With the state of scientific knowledge when the books of the Bible were written, men knew little about what really the sun or the moon is or what was involved in the simple five-word statement: "He made the stars also." Since there are at least five sextillion of them, that was quite a day's work.

The eleven brief paragraphs on pages 227 to 228 of *Blind Faith* list contradictions in the Bible that could not possibly have been the doing of an omniscient deity. It all has the mark of having been written by a coalition of zealots with mediocre minds who were handicapped by how little was known about the cosmos at the time.

Writing the King James version of the Bible began in 1604 and was to take three years to complete. Forty-seven scholars began a painstaking analysis of every word in several earlier Bibles and many other sources. Re-translations and revisions of translations delayed things, and not until 1611 was the version printed that is most in circulation today. New versions of the Bible were begun by the Thomas Nelson Publishers and The Zondervan Publishing House in recent years. More than a hundred biblical scholars were selected to work on these projects. By the 1980s both the Nelson and Zondervan Bibles were in print.

One would think that with the hundreds of scholars working on various versions of the Bible in several languages over such long periods of time, the finished product would be pure poetry, without imperfections. Nothing could be further from the truth. It is still a book full of confusing language, bad rhetoric, and full of the superstitions and fabricated "history" of the earliest versions. No one writing so poorly today would win any Nobel or Pulitzer prizes for literature.

319

Dogma has been the fundamental principal of any religion.... Religion as mere sentiment is to me a mockery.

Cardinal Newman (1801-1890)
Apologia *pro Vita Sua*

George Santayana in *Introduction to the Ethics of Spinoza* says, "The Bible is literature not dogma." But we must understand that classifying declarations as religious dogma is the province of those who make or refer to the declarations, not those of us who listen to or read them. Dogma, that is, is an attitude toward declarations, not the declarations themselves. If a religion declares every statement by every author of every book of the Bible as "true and beyond dispute" then for that religion the Bible becomes one enormous collection of dogma. It may be that those who classify statements as dogma also believe them to be reasonable and worthy to be accepted by all mankind, but that is not the intent of making the classification.

Santayana is right when he says that the Bible could never be declared totally dogma, because it contains inconsistencies and contradictions, and the dogma of a religion cannot be self-contradictory. Also much of the dogma of any church is not referred to in any book of sacred literature. The dogma of papal infallibility is not defined in the Bible.

Newman is right in denouncing a purely emotional religion, devoid of reason, but an emotional religion would be better than the one that is now being taught. Sentiment, wisely guided, at least could do more good than mythology.

Sentiment connotes an intellectual element in the feeling one has for his fellowman. It deals with ideas and the emotions that arise from contemplating them. We have moral sentiments, anti-slavery sentiments, and romantic sentiments. We express sentiments for the underdog, the disadvantaged, the handicapped, the sick, the person down on his luck, persons in severe pain, etc. Sentiment is surely one factor to be considered in fashioning whatever religion.

Newman's religion is its dogma and little else. It could not survive without its dogma. But a people-oriented religion could. Such a religion would do very well without such dogma as the Trinity, the divinity of Jesus, immaculate conception, atonement, original sin, the Fall of Man, the Eucharist, extreme unction, and redemption. When all other religions have lost their wars against good sense, a sentimental religion without dogma may survive.

320

Man is the only creature who refuses to be what he is.   Albert
Camus (1913-1960)
The Rebel

Camus and Sartre spoke the same language but were never friendly. Each said of the other: "If he is an existentialist, then I am not." But they saw eye to eye on many things, as anyone reading essays written by the two men will see.

Since most of the individual members of the world's populations have never thought to call themselves existentialists (although many are) what Camus says is largely true. To make his statement more inclusive, I would replace his "to be what he is" by a simple "does not recognize what he is." Popeye said, "I yam what I yam, and that's all that I yam?" Sartre put it: Man is nothing but what his life is."

The Buddha said, "We are what we think. All that we are arises with our thoughts." Most of us, however choose to dress up our descriptions of ourselves with florid phrases and impressive locutions. But that does not change what we really are. Many of us describe ourselves as part of some kind of hierarchy of universal forces or divine essences, but that, again, does not change what we really are. To refuse to recognize what we really are does not change things, but it serves to aggrandize egos that seem to require such ego-magnification. We hope the Buddha distinguishes between our descriptions of ourselves and the thoughts about ourselves that become what we are. The Buddha, too, must understand that to say we are nothing else but what our lives are does not restrict us. He, then, is right to say that within the limits imposed upon us by temporal and cosmic essences, we can make our lives whatever our thoughts direct that they be.

321

The impotence of God is infinite.

Anatole France (1844-1924

The omniscience of God is infinitesimal. The omnipresence of God is improbable. Stendhal does best by putting an end to all such speculations: "God's only excuse is that He does not exist."

Until people generally agree with France and Stendhal, theologians will continue to maintain the heavy-handed stranglehold they have over the world's populations.

If one is making a god, it is best to make a good one. The "omni" qualities commonly attributed to Him cover the ground. Then why do we go on to make a God who is jealous, impetuous, irascible, tyrannical, cruel, arbitrary, and whose principal aim seems to be to instill fear in us and to aggrandize his own image?

Surely we do not want the God who names the people of particular nations (Deuteronomy 23:3) and then tells us that these people can never belong to His assemblies. We do not want the God who insists that couples of mixed marriages be divorced (Ezra 10:3-11) and that the female members and their children be sent away. We do not want the God who furnishes notables with slaves (Genesis 24:35). We do not want the God who finds favor in a certain king that makes another man's wife pregnant and who then sees to it that the man is killed in battle (2 Samuel 11:4-17). This God that we do not want then says of that king that "he obeyed Me completely and did only what was right in My sight (1 Kings 14:8)." We need only read the Bible to find many other good reasons for looking elsewhere for a pattern upon which to base our new God-Almighty fabrication.

322

He had grown up in a country run by politicians, who send the pilots to man the bombers to kill the babies to make the world safe for children to grow up in.

Ursula K. LeGuin (1929-)
The Lathe of Heaven

The reactions of the public to what goes on in a war depends not so much on what goes on as it does on how well the public knows what goes on.

The first of the Christian Crusades in 1096 began and ended in horrible massacres. As Malcolm Hay describes it in *The Foot of Pride*, "The men who took the cross, wrote [Lord John] Acton, 'After receiving communion, heartily devoted the day to the extermination of the Jews.... The killed about ten thousand of them." Thomas

Merton, in *Mystics and Zen Masters* says of the same crusade that it was at the time considered to be an eminently praiseworthy enterprise. Killing Turks, according to Merton, was said to be a necessary and desirable task, and the sooner it was done the better for everyone concerned.

Imagine what might have happened if detailed films of those massacres could have been shown to all of the people of England the next day! Wars in the abstract might be tolerated. But not wars that involve arson, torture, and bloodshed, all shown in intensely and unbearably painful detail on film in people's living rooms. There would not have been a second, third, fourth, and fifth crusade. The same would have been the case if detailed film had been shown in the Napoleonic wars, the Thirty-Years War, the holocaust, Stalin's purges, the genocide in Anatolia, Cambodia, and recently in Bosnia, East Timor, and Tibet. There is, and always has been, enough compassion innate in human beings to end wars in any country where the people have a voice and a clear picture of what occurs on the battlefields.

323

> The most formidable weapon against errors of every kind is reason. I have never used any other and I trust I never shall.
>
> Thomas Paine (1737-1809
> *Age of Reason*

If not reason, then what? What possible alternative? The Marquis de Condorcet seems to say there is none: "The time will come when the sun will shine only on free men who know no other master but their reason." If we think, we reason; for reason is the essence of thinking. Reveries, idle meditation, worshiping myths, dreaming up fantasies, letting the imagination run wild, all fun, are not reason, and never will be.

To reason is to doubt and to seek to resolve our doubts. To reason is to predict and to verify or refute our predictions. To reason is to live a meaningful life, with confidence that we are doing our bit to improve the hope that others, too, can live meaningfully.

Martin Luther was right: Religion cannot approve of reason. For its own good, religion must label reason the Devil's Bride, and never allow it to get a foothold anywhere. Reason would be the end of religion.

Thomas Paine's weapon against error was reason, and ours should be also. Until reason prevails, man will not make progress against the threats to his continued existence. The ability to reason is what makes man human.

324

> Death observes no ceremony.
>
>   John Wise (1652-1725)

At a funeral, the protagonist does not know you are there and does not care. If the dead could observe what purpose the money spent on them serves and then could see also what good that amount of money would do in keeping the starving children of the world alive and in school, surely they would prefer altruism to idiocy. Some have preferred to have their bodies placed on elevated platforms to be eaten by vultures. I would choose to have my body anchored at the bottom of a Caribbean reef shelf to feed the beautiful coral fishes. Our obsession with costly caskets and funerals is a pagan ritual for which there is no rational explanation.

If the ruling sentiment among religionists were compassion, we would see them as the main contributors in the cause of making human organs available for transplant. But the facts are the opposite. With religionists' warped and superstitious minds, they boggle at furnishing the organs of kin who die. "For a small percentage of the population, organ donation is out of the question for religious reasons," Stephanie Salter, columnist for the *San Francisco Examiner* says, but then two sentences later she makes that remarkable pronouncement completely redundant and superfluous. She says: "... inertia, superstition, and mindless selfishness [are] the primary excuses for not making the pledge." The religion implied in "for religious reasons" is simply another way of saying "superstition and mindless selfishness." Are we saying that people who do things for "religious" reasons do not understand that being "religious" means behaving only in ways that serve, or at least do not disserve, the people of the world?

What we need is a law that would make all human organs available and suitable for transplant the property of a medical organization set up precisely for that purpose. Every day people die needlessly because of people's myopic, egocentric, insular, clannish, jaundiced minds. Documentaries of people waiting for transplants, many in vain, do not faze them. Glorifying their fabricated gods is to them far more important than saving people's lives.

If ever we become a truly caring and rational people, immediately upon death of every human being, all that person's organs that are reusable will be removed and flown to where people are waiting for transplants. If there is no immediate use, organs will be frozen in liquid nitrogen to await the time when there is a need. A world-wide computerized system will keep perfect track of anyone in need of a cornea, kidney, liver, lung, heart, etc, and waiting persons would soon have what they need. Blood type and DNA matching would also be accomplished by means of computer records. The number of deaths in the world because we do not do what we easily can do is unconscionable – unworthy of an intelligent, caring species.

325

In our modern world there are ever fewer excuses for allowing ourselves to be gulled by the bombast of theological academigogues.

Chester Dolan
Blind Faith

Theology, etymologically, a science of God, is not by any stretch of the imagination a science. Theology is organized superstition. Even most of our religious leaders admit, in fact insist, that we know nothing about God. "A god comprehended," says Tersteegen, "is no god." Rudolf Otto in describing God uses only negatives: unapproachable, incomprehensible, unsearchable, unfathomable, unimaginable, ineffable, inconceivable, and indefinable. He forgets "unbelievable."

The Christian God who sits in judgment, handing out rewards to those who kowtow to Him and punishment to those who do not, is certainly no god I want to acknowledge. The God of the Bible commits and approves of thousands of murders. In Exodus 12:29, 2 Kings 2:24, Judges 11:39, 1 Samuel 6;19, 2 Samuel 6:7, Numbers 16:35, Job 1:13-19, 2 Samuel 12:15-18, Deuteronomy 20:17, and Matthew 27:46 we find accounts of the atrocities God is capable of. Even his son asks that his enemies be brought and slain before him (Luke 19:27).

The Bible, written as it is in an attempt to gain adherents for religion, is ever an attempt to satisfy questioners, as Elbert Hubbard suggests. We wonder then why there is so much emphasis on God's cruelty, his refusal to meet with us face to face, his secrecy on the whereabouts of heaven, hell, His throne, and the remains of Noah's ark and other relics of religion. Why is it our duty to fear Him? The Muslim God, Allah, denounces the Christian God for accepting a partner (his offspring Jesus), and must have wondered why He has no jinn in His entourage. Today, questioners are less and less hopeful of ever receiving answers to their questions about religions.

326

As society is now constituted, a literal adherence to the moral precepts scattered throughout the Gospels would mean sudden death.

Alfred North Whitehead (1861-1947)
Adventures in Ideas

The Bible is filled with examples of behavior for which God decreed death as punishment:

1 Corinthians 6:9-10: Be not deceived: Neither fornicators, nor idolaters, nor adulterers, nor homosexuals, nor sodomites, nor thieves, nor covetous, nor drunkards, nor revilers, nor extortioners will inherit the kingdom of God.

Matthew 25:44,46: [Here we are told that when we do not minister to the hungry, thirsty, stranger, naked, sick, or those in prison, our fate will be everlasting punishment, the worse-than-death burning in the fires of hell].

Hebrews 10:28: Anyone who has rejected Moses' law dies without mercy on the testimony of two or three witnesses. [Which is it 'two' or 'three;' after all, a life is at stake?]

Genesis 38:24: "Tomar, your daughter-in-law has played the harlot; furthermore she is with child by harlotry." So Judah said: "Bring her out and let her be burned."

[Leviticus 20, verses 2 to 27 list several offenses for which a person will be put to death. The last of these]: Leviticus 20:27: A man or a woman who is a medium or who has familiar spirits, shall surely be put to death: They shall stone them with stones. Their blood shall be upon them.

Leviticus 21:9: The daughter of any priest, if she profanes herself by playing the harlot, she profanes her father. She shall be burned with fire. [And the daughter of a push-cart salesman?]

Leviticus 24:14: Take outside the camp him who has cursed; then... let all the congregation stone him.

Numbers 14;35: In this wilderness they shall be consumed, and there the shall die.

Deuteronomy 13:10: And you shall stone him with stones until he dies, because he has sought to entice you away from the Lord your God.

Joshua 7:25: So all Israel stone them with stones.... So the Lord turned from the fierceness of His anger.

Deuteronomy 21:23: ... for he who is hanged is accursed of God.

2 Samuel 21:9:... and he delivered them into the hands of the Gibeonites, and they hanged them on the hill before the Lord.

Daniel 6:24: .. and the lions overpowered them, and broke all their bones in pieces. [There are many, many more].

327

> The fact of having been born is a bad augury for immortality.
>
> George Santayana (1863-1952)
> *The Life of Reason*

Yes, isn't it? Being born makes it clear for all of us that there was personal void before we began life in this cosmos. Then why is it less likely that there will be the same void after we die? The one is no harder to believe than the other.

"If I did not believe in a future state, I should believe in no God," John Adams said in a letter to Thomas Jefferson (Dec 8, 1818). Would Adam say the same for an anterior state? His dilemma is easily resolved, as he himself suggests. Just forego the nonsense of believing in God, an after life, or any such absurdities.

All people who think rationally believe only when there is evidence for believing. Why would anyone believe on any other basis? Why do we pay good money to psychics, soothsayers, crystal-ball gazers, palmists, fortunetellers, astrologers, etc.? Why do we buy rabbit's feet, amulets, talismans, good-luck charms, and magic bracelets? Why are wishing wells, wishbones, spells, and black cats given special consideration?

Those who search for answers to such questions seem to have unanimously decided that most people like to be deceived. Some say that we understand common logic and intellectually understand the folly of absurd belief, but we find a certain arbitrary whimsey, willful caprice, or quaint conceit in reading horoscopes and attending seances, etc.

That may be true for some, but most people take their crystal gazing and tarot-card reading very seriously. What the psychics and soothsayers advise, guides them in everything from love affairs to business transactions. What use First Lady Nancy Reagan made of the psychic advice she received we my never know.

328

The world is divided between atheism and the organized superstition that is called religion.

Anonymous

One is either superstitious or one is not. If we are not superstitious we reject belief in all the various pronouncements of religion that have no basis in fact. Thinking people reject belief in the catechisms, tenets, laws, precepts, doctrines and canons of religions. Eventually all religions will dissolve into recognizably fanciful and imaginative myth.

We reject all entities for which there is no scintilla of evidence. Among the rejected are: Those that fly but are never photographed, from angels to tenanted saucers; those that swim but are never netted or leave skeletal remains, from mermaids to Nessie; those that live in the woods but are never seen, from werewolves to chupacabras; those that are night visitors but are never authenticated, from ghosts to succubi; those that exist in imaginative literature but are seldom taken seriously, from chimeras to gremlins; those that religions invent, from souls to demons. All people have their favorites: the Greeks their satyrs, the Romans, their fauns, the Irish their leprechauns, the Scots their banshees, the Scandinavians their trolls, and the Muslims their jinn.

Often people whose lives are virtually run by superstitions refuse to believe in real things that loom sharply before them. Bradley Smith took out a 400-word ad in the *New York Times* denying belief in the Holocaust. The Flat-Earth Society still boasts of members, even after astronauts took pictures of the spherical earth spinning in its isolated place in the solar system. Creation "scientists" make a profession of not believing the overwhelming evidence for evolution and a five-billion-year-old earth. Yet they can believe in talking asses and snakes, cud-chewing rabbits, leviathans, sky-reaching towers, fish equipped to house a man, sticks and dust that turn into snakes and lice, respectively, not to mention what can happen to wine and bread. It seems there is nothing one man can imagine that somewhere else there is not another foolish enough to believe.

329

> Truth is the foundation of all knowledge and the cement of all societies.
>
> John Dryden (1631-1700)
> English author

To find out what is meant by truth, How much will we learn by reading what religious leaders and others say it is? Let us see:

Idvorsky Pupin: Truth is divine.

Guewer: Truth is sublime.

F.W. Robertson: Christ was truth.... The deepest truths are the simplest and the most common.

Phillips Brooks: Truth is the child of love, the parent of duty.

R.D. Hitchcock: Truth is illimitable in its reach.

Joseph Cook: Truth is what a man sees in his last moments.

Horace Mann: Truth will conduct you to the throne of God.

J.S. Kieffer: Truth is essentially an affair of the heart.

W.M. Evarts: Truth is the gravitation principle of the universe.

Are you learning what truth is? Let us try a few more:

Tacitus: Fear is not in the habit of speaking the truth.

Shaftesbury: Truth is the most natural beauty in the world.

Cecil: Truth lies between extremes.

Benedict Spinoza: Perfect truth is possible only with knowledge.

Carl Van Doren: Truth is an esoteric language.

Katherine Fullerton Gerould: Platitudes are usually the truest thing going.

Bryon: Truth is always strange.

Mencius: It is difficult to know the way of truth.

Why do these seventeen statements about truth seem to say so little? The truth is that truth describes statements that conform with facts (maps that tally with territories), that and nothing more – and in so being, is everything John Dryden says it is.

330

> It is ridiculous to call him a scientist as long as he still believes in the virgin birth, the atonement, or transubstantiation.
>
> H.L. Mencken (1880-1956)
> *Minority Report*

In this way, Mencken characterized the presumed scientist who turns to religion for explanations.

A politician may be as fickle as the color of a chameleon. A politician speaking one day to an agricultural cooperative, the next day to a steelworker union, and the next to a CEO convention is often seen changing his speech to suit his audience, sometimes contradicting himself completely. But a scientist cannot one day espouse scientific method and the next day embrace the irrational dogma and sacraments of the orthodox church. For a scientist to pretend that babies can be conceived without human sperm (someday, perhaps, by cloning), or that mere words can change bread and wine into flesh and blood, would be for him to abdicate reason. He would tear himself apart epistemologically.

The false premise that we live in a universe governed by a cosmic prime mover accounts in part for the arrested development of the creative imagination. Here is an explanation for the fact that a disproportionately small number of good scientists are graduating from our great religious universities. Our religious universities are monuments to what happens to the creative mind in any society without truth. Such universities may teach the descriptive aspects of a few "innocuous" sciences, but to teach the rigor of scientific procedure would be for them impossible.

331

> Religions are many and diverse, but reason and goodness are one.
>
> Elbert Hubbard (1856-1915)
> *The Roycroft Dictionary and book of Epigrams*

Religions can be as different as are the individual human minds that invent them. Goodness and reason are universal, invariant concepts, the same wherever they are found.

One estimate set the number of religions in the world at 11,000. And certainly the individual members of each of these religions "knows" that they belong to the one true religion. Who would belong to any other? If a member had the intelligence to understand how ridiculous that assumption is, he would have the intelligence also to understand how obvious it is that all religions are man-made and no more likely to be authentic than are all of the other fables, fairy tales, and fantasies that mankind has concocted since the beginning of time.

"Reason" is that faculty of mind that allows us to think, form judgments, and draw conclusions. It is the power to comprehend, infer, and plan in orderly, rational ways. It is contrasted with another indispensable faculty of mind, imagination. Imagination allows us to form mental images of that which is not actually present and move these images around in as many different combinations as we like.

Goodness is a kind of moral excellence that most people seem to be born with and that all people can cultivate. It is kindness, generosity, helpfulness, empathy, and all the qualities subsumed under virtue, rectitude, and altruism. Even an extraterrestrial would recognize reason and goodness where he finds them in the beings he meets on earth, but our religions would baffle him completely.

332

A race of super-chickens would have pictured their devil a hawk.
Clarence Day (1874-1935)
This Simian World

Super-chickens would choose a hawk – and super-crickets a chicken. God chose a snake to represent the devil. To each his own.

Renald Knox in *Let Dons Delight* thinks modern civilization is stupid to have given up belief in the "devil" when he is the only explanation for it. I have not met Knox's "modern civilization." Certainly the Catholic Church is not part of it. For them the devil is their true savior. They could not exist without him. Most of the rest of Christianity feels the same. Secular literature, too, gives a far more prominent place to devils than to angels, jinn, or prophets. However, with the new television program *Touched by an Angel*, even that may be changing. "Teched Angels" must have been the title of the episode I watched. No religion I know of would have accepted them as authentic, I am sure. Even Gibreel in Salman Rushdie's *Satanic Verses* would have come closer to being accepted.

Johannes Wierius in his *Calumnies and Deceptions of the Devils* gives us the best account of devils I have heard of. He tells us that there are in inferno exactly sixty Princes of Darkness, each of which supervises six hundred and sixty-six legions, with six thousand six hundred and sixty-six devils in each legion. That means nearly 300 million in all – a devil of a place for us to live. A good thing that devils are immortal: It would be a shame ever to have to alter this remarkable, cabalistic roster. Anyway, whether theologists or demonologists, the great mystics of our time can be comforted by the assurance that they are well supplied with all the "documentation" they need in the books that fill our library shelves. Wierius' book and Alberto Couste's *Biographia del Diablo* Published by Argos, S.A. in Barcelona, Spain – are two more examples of how our symbol systems can grow by accretion into the vast, organized, integrated aggregations of unmitigated nonsense they have become.

Chapter IX

Reason Enthroned

333

Only those members of the human species who make a conscious, deliberate decision in favor of the use of one of the most vital of their mental faculties ("reason") have any chance of becoming free, independent, fully functioning, civilized individuals.

Clive Bell, about midway in his *Civilization*, includes a remarkable chapter "Reason Enthroned." Indispensable scepters of that coronation include understanding the fallibility, moral ambiguity, and irresolution with which we commonly conduct our affairs.

The decision to make preeminent the use of reason in forming our opinions and in planning and directing our activities is far rarer than we might suspect. Not only do we fail to use our faculty of reason in forming opinions and planning activities, but there is little hope that we can be convinced to do so. We find it to easy to slide through life letting others to do our thinking for us.

It behooves men of reason to convince us to accept as true only that for which there is sound and systematic evidence. Our survival may depend on how well we learn to recognize the widespread sham that unfortunately in this world is in superabundant supply. Then we would be able to substitute for this demeaning mass deception an unreserved honesty, love, integrity, loyalty, decency and candor. So long as we continue with our present gullible readiness to permit the religious charlatans to deceive us, there is little hope that we will survive our present dismal plight unscathed.

334

> The man who is a nationalist and talks of brotherhood is telling a lie; he is living in a state of contradiction.
>
> Krishnamurti (1895-1986)
> *The First and Last Freedom*

Every nationalist group has its set of laws, customs, institutions, historical memoirs, and political policies that distinguish it from other nationalist groups. Without all these artificially contrived differences, they could not exist as separate enclaves. But there is one characteristic not put in writing, but just as important as the others, that all nations have in common: All lead their citizens to believe that they are a little better than anyone else. Each member must "look down upon," perhaps "hate," the members of all other nations – especially those who do not yearn to renounce their present nationhood and become part of "ours."

Brotherhood is one thing not to expect to find operating between various religious or nationalist groups. If the members of one such group facing the members of other sects or nations talk of brotherhood, they are indeed telling a lie, and they do indeed live in a state of contradiction.

We are religious or patriotic not in the degree that we form parochialized denominations or competing political entities, but in the degree that we love. When the meaning of piety or patriotism is construed as brotherhood, that and nothing else, both religion and nation take on very different aspects from that which fanatics and jingoists make of them. We become responsive to feelings of conscience, appalled at discourtesy, hate, or bigotry, wherever they appear. No moral person is content to live at the expense of his fellowman, regardless of the religious or political climate in which he lives.

335

> I have often thought that the church of Rome does wisely in not allowing her priests to marry.... The clergyman is expected to be a kind of human Sunday....He is paid for this business of leading a stricter life than other people. It is his raison d'etre....
>
> Samuel Butler (1835-1902)
> *The Way of All Flesh*

There are at least two reasons why sacerdotal celibacy may be a good thing. The first is given by Dr. Arroway in Carl Sagan's novel *Contact*. The second is given by Samuel Butler himself.

According to Arroway, "A celibate clergy is an effective answer to pietism. Whatever are the genetic tendencies that led the priest to his choice of profession and that might be transferred to offspring – thus continuing clerical patterns of fanaticism – they are, when the clergy does in fact remain celibate, wiped off the slate." An unnatural selection functions to keep the species sane.

Butler tells us why celibacy in priests is a good thing by explaining what happens when preachers marry. "Unnatural tension in public is no longer necessary. The married preacher's children are the most defenseless things he can reach, and it is on them in nine cases out of ten that he will relieve his mind." Accounts, in the novel, of a clergyman beating his son and then this son in his time beating his son, with senseless regularity, Butler is saying, is not uncommon among clerical families everywhere.

336

Luke 17:21: The kingdom of God is within you.
The kingdom of God is in the midst of you.

The first is the King James Version. The second is the Revised Standard Version.

"Which is the true rendition?, George Christian Anderson asks in his book *The Right to Be Human*. "You need not look around for the Kingdom of God," Jesus in effect tells the Pharisees: "It is within you," agreeing with the King James Version. One has no need of eyes to see that which exists only within oneself. Introspection serves very well. Nothing of religion is empirical except brain structure, and we know very little about what that structure is.

Although all of any person's entire world exists only within his own nervous system, brains are capable of projecting "out there" a "real world" of events and entities. Only those "things" that experience and intuition give us reason to believe in their existence beyond our skins are chosen for such projection. Myth is excluded. Other animals, though not by rational choice, are more discriminating than we are about what they choose to deal with. They do not fabricate some kind of presumed reality out of what is purely imagination and then respond to it as seriously as other more "sensible" events. Ghosts, gods, and gremlins are no part of their lives. Nature and all of man's artifacts are.

If "within" and not "in the mist of" is the correct arena for locating the kingdom of God, then we can quit looking for a mythical celestial paradise. Robert Schuller will not find God in galazy M-31, where he said heaven might be, and we will not have to worry about souls traveling such immense distances to get where they are going. No doubt the Revised Standard Version of the Bible made its change to "in the midst of" because "within" is where we find mythologies. The RSV could have saved itself the trouble. Rational minds usually have no difficulty distinguishing myth from reality, even though they do exist together within the same busy brain.

337

Whereas when liberation theology is good, it is very, very good, when it is bad, unless it is corrected, it might very soon become horrid.

Rosemary Harthill
In Perspective

Liberation theology, like all theologies, is bad, period. "All religions have based morality on obedience, that is to say, on voluntary slavery," says Alexander Herzen in *From the Other Shore*. Especially in a religion where the high sachem is deemed infallible, authoritarian abuse of power begins.

Liberation theology is a religious movement that began in 1972, especially among the Roman Catholic clergy in Latin America. It combines political philosophy, usually of a Marxist orientation, with a theology of salvation as liberation from injustice. As Harthill suggests, the intentions of its founders were no doubt admirable, but as with good intentions in so many human endeavors, they go awry.

Liberation theology bases itself in part on a political philosophy which seeks to enslave young minds, and in part on a religion that reduces its members to subjection, demanding unthinking loyalty. To travel in South America, observing how slavishly the people submit to the dominion of the prevailing religion, is to see the need, but little hope, for something akin to liberation theology to mitigate the injustice that turns up in all manner of human affairs. Who isn't against injustice, obscurantism, and oppression. But a combination of Marxism and Catholicism is likely to increase, not eliminate, these scourges.

In authoritarianism the first victim is the right to criticize. Next, two essentials of progress, variety and competition, are eliminated. When both God and State guarantee their subjects a living, they put an end to individual initiative. What is needed is a guaranteed one-to-one correspondence between personal effort and personal gain. Without that guarantee, people find no need for the native talents that evolved in a milieu of ancestral fights with predators and capricious nature. Life loses both its sparkle and its meaning.

338

It ain't those parts of the Bible that I can't understand that bother me, it's the parts I do understand.

Mark Twain (1835-1910)

Because of contradictions, inconsistencies, muddled language, and advice contrary to sane social behavior, there is much not to understand in the Bible. But parts clearly written and easily understood should concern us as much as they did Mark Twain. We find fairy tales galore, pornography by the bushel, xenophobia common, sexual discrimination a common practice, prejudice everywhere, slavery tolerated, adultery praised, lying a way of religious life, superstition interwoven throughout, thievery approved, authoritarianism the governing mode, truth shattered, and closed-loop sophistry a common literary device. For most of these deviations from accepted social codes, my book *Blind Faith* cites chapter and verse.

Many antisocial practices described in the Bible are acknowledged without apologies, and were therefore obviously considered standards to live by. What a society we would have if we always followed Biblical advice," religionists exclaim. Indeed, what a society we would have.

339

One of the things Jesus did was step aside from the organized religion of his time because it had become corrupt and bogged down with rules.

Corita Kent
Quoted in "A Time of Transition for Corita Kent"
Lucie Kay Scheuer – *Los Angeles Times* July 11, 1974

When "rules become more important than feeding the hungry" (Corita Kent's words), organized religion becomes organized superstitions. Religion is nothing if it is not compassion. To listen to television evangelists today is to see that not much in religion has changed in the last two-thousand years. We still have a religion that is mostly a money-making organization bent on buying political power. Now we also have multi-million dollar religious "university" campuses and increasingly powerful broadcasting facilities, designed to expand the area from which money can be gathered.

The Pat Robertsons and Jerry Falwells of today do not step aside from corruption; they revel in it. With organized religions now more oppressive than ever, they may, as they seem to say, soon be running things. They will if we do not keep ourselves alert to their sinister machinations. If I believed in reincarnation, I would know where one of these holy-gospelers spent a past appearance. Varro said sometime around 40 BC: "It is for the good of states that men should be deluded by religion." Pat and Jerry are seduced by that idiocy even today, after more than two thousand years.

340

Whenever we read the obscene stories, the voluptuous debaucheries, the cruel and tortuous executions, the unrelenting vindictiveness with which more than half the Bible is filled, it would be more consistent that we call it the word of a demon than the word of God. It is a hirtory of wickedness that has served to corrupt and brutalize mankind.

Thomas Paine (1737-1809)
The Age of Reason

"If only you would read the Bible! Then you would believe. You would know all about God's grace, His love of mankind, and His interventions on our behalf."

It is better that we not read it ourselves. Wait to be introduced to the Bible in Sunday school or in Bible classes. There, our Bible teachers can explain away the passages that hurt, make them come out more in keeping with "God's Divine Plan" for us.

When men came along who can really read the Bible (Thomas Paine, Steve Allen, Paul Kurtz, Malcolm Hay, George Smith, etc.) without expurgating , distorting, or deleting the offensive parts, we do not listen. We close our minds and also the Bible. We remain content with an evangelist-imposed Bible, a pale, vague, anemic, wishy-washy, effete version of the Bible that exists only in expurgated renditions. Evangelists give us a Bible that will not interfere with the dream world we have been persuaded to grow up in.

341

> It is the final proof of God's omnipotence that He need not exist in order to save us.
>
> Peter DeVries
> *Mackerel Plaza*

An apt paradox it is, but if DeVries suggests that people must be cajoled with palyful phrases to do good and merit salvation, what he says is demeaning.

Enlightened religious leaders may someday go beyond the idea that God *need not* exist and instead will declare openly that God in all probability *does not* exist. If there is no God, any conversation that includes God among the critical topics discussed, may very likely result in confusion.

If we are to survive, before it is too late preachers must agree that there can be no such thing as well-meaning deceit. Benevolent betrayal of good faith will sooner or later turn bad. Even if they cannot put their finger on it, people get a feeling they are being deceived when that is the case, and they temper their enthusiasm for unreserved cooperation.

Whatever "being" or "figment of the imagination" He is, we find God variously described: H.L. Mencken spoke of Him as a "Gaseous Invertebrate," André Breton describes Him as "doddering and squint-eyed." Thomas Jefferson pronounced Him as "cruel, capricious, and unjust." The Bible says He is "love." A character in Carl Sagan's *Contact* calls Him an "inefficient entrepreneur." 1 Samuel says He can change His mind. 2 Samuel says he cannot. Barbara Tuchman says, "He is a concept of the human mind." Bertrand Russell sees God as "an invention of Oriental Despotisms." Mormonism describes God as "a physical being of flesh and bones." The Church of God describes God as "spiritual, but of the general form and stature of man." Felix Adler expostulates: "What fiend so fiendish as such a God."

Jan Struthers in "All Clear" of his *The Glassbloweer and Other Poems*, writes:

It took me forty years on earth
To reach this sure conclusion:
There is no heaven but clarity,
No hell except confusion.

Two more lines are needed:

It took no time at all to learn
That God is rank delusion.

342

It is Socraates' opinion, and mine too, that the wisest theory about gods is to have no theory at all.

Montaigne (1533-1592)

When a scientist proposes a new theory to explain an abstract or general principle that lies behind data and determines their origin, he must have some measure of supporting evidence for saying what he says. The religionist has no supporting evidence for anything he says about his gods or their residences. The scientist is careful not to go beyond what is conceivably possible, whether it is a theory of evolution, a theory of light quanta, or a theory of relativity. The religionist will abide no restrictions on what he says about whatever it suits his fancy to consider. The scientist's nascent suppositions can be upgraded and may come to dominate new fields of thought. Or they may be downgraded – as when Newton's law of gravitation was revised as a result of Einstein's discoveries to become Newton's mathematical theory of universal gravitation.

Religionists, of course, ignore Montaigne' admonition. Their treatises about gods exploit gullibility, ramble freely, and brook no restrictions. The religionist's effusions were at one point in history set down as scripture and designated "God's Words," perfect, and never to be revised, no matter what. But in modern interpretations of scripture, some religionists, despite prohibitions, indulge their predilections for wild speculation, however senseless or absurd. They feel themselves completely free to promote their own wayward whimsies in any way they like.

343

To the living the Jew is a corpse, to the native a foreigner, to the homesteader a vagrant, to the proprietary a beggar, to the poor an exploiter and a millionaire, to the patriot a man without a country, for all a hated rival.

Leo Pinsker (1821-1891)
Auto-Emancipation

A Jew living in Russia when Pinsker did was a constant target of vilification. Things were not much better elsewhere. Those capable of prejudice against particular groups of people need no reasons for their abominable behavior. They can hate without reason if their victims are in any way identifiable. Jews congregating in special enclaves, wearing identifying clothing, or speaking a special language, or especially, not considering themselves complete and loyal citizens of the country in which they reside are classical targets.

"Only for brief periods of history did the Hebrews have a home of their own," says Harvey Cox in *The Secular City*. Nearly half the world population of Jews live in the United States. They do not have a home? Why not, the rest of us do. If the education of the Jewish child, wherever he lives, teaches him that he is as thoroughly a citizen as any of his neighbors, he will know that like them he has only one home and one nationality. He will not at the first opportunity leave everything else important in his life and rush off to an artificially and violently established little country in the Middle East - without looking back, without a thank you, farewell, or adieu.

344

If there is no Hell, a good many preachers are obtaining money under false pretenses.

Billy Sunday (1862-1935)
(attributed)

Billy G and Billy S both were well aware that H.L. Mencken was right when he said, "It is Hell, of course, that makes preachers powerful." The two Billys would not for a moment have considered denying the existence of hell. They knew that in part their success as evangelists depended on it. But both certainly knew as well that hell was not the sole fantasy upon which obtaining money depended. All preachers for all time have obtained money under false pretenses, and all have depended on the entire range of myth and legend to make the case for monetarily supporting religion.

Children growing up under the concept of sin and inhuman retribution can never hope for peace of mind. Their behavior will be forever conditioned by terror more than by sentiments of devotion to human welfare. They expect to be tried in a celestial court where a Supreme Judge will decide their fate. Only a few "perfect souls," they learn, can expect eternal bliss, and their own abject fear of hellfire and damnation leaves them with no doubts about what is in store for them.

The case histories of psychiatrists show that to instill religion into children is for many of them *ipso facto* to instill neuroses. Psychiatrists denounce religion as the enemy. In its protean forms, religion operates to deform the mind, stifle mental growth, and assure mental breakdown. The lament of psychotherapists, according to M. Scott Peck, in his book *The Road Less Traveled* is the amount of time that must be spent to free young minds from the clutches of religion.

345

I'm not going to have any Bibles in my school.... [The Bible is] just for grown people, after you know it don't mean what it says [Livinia speaking].

Lillian Hellman (1905-1984)
Another Part of the Forest, Act III

Yes, by all means, keep out the Bible, but do not for a moment imagine that you can substitute some other scripture. The others are just as bad – or worse. There is perhaps one exception. If the writer of this exception had spent several years on the project, instead of turning it out in spare moments, it might be the great new scriptural tome. I refer to *imagine... a new bible* by the Reverend Rudi Gelsey in 1982. His God is a decent sort of bloke who does not believe wars solve problems, would not think of sending plagues, floods, and famines to torment us. He teaches the human race how to live in peace – happily and with prosperity for all.

Livinia is making an assumption which all evidence indicates is not true. She seems to assume that once we become adults, we can correctly evaluate the Bible. The truth is that many who read it willingly do not know that it does ot mean what it says. Ask any Orthodox Christian and he will tell you that the Bible is God's word and therefore perfect. It certainly does mean what it says. If Levinia can keep the Bible out of the hands of children, however, I am on her side. She is making a valuable contribution to sanity for all of the human species.

346

Having and being are two fundamental [and contrasting] modes of existence, the respective strengths of which determines the various types of social character.

Erich Fromm (1900-1980)
To Have or to Be

Although the dichotomies used to explain human character are often spurious, or at best misleading, they can at times be illuminating. Erich Fromm in his book *To Have or To Be* makes a good case for a marked difference between those whose life style is that of accumulating possessions and those whose predominant orientation is sharing experiences.

"I am because I own things" is the creed of those whose pleasure is to have. To have nothing is to be nothing, is their lament. Having and happiness, to them, are correlates. Accumulating possessions is their passion. They are callous, selfish, apathetic, avaricious, blind to suffering. Their hope is to turn people into menial servants, slaves, the booty of crusades.

Ivan Boesky and Michael Milken, both imprisoned for violating security laws, amassed fortunes by cheating those not privy to insider trading. Our shamefully wealthy TV evangelists, robber barons, CEOs, movie stars, and sports figures never learn the joy of selfless, compassionate, altruistic membership in the human species.

"I am because I experience " is the creed of those whose joy is to be. Among them, the "being mode" encourages sharing, communicating, and working for common goals. Those who belong to the being mode recognize the competence, integrity, and morality of others, and try to interact amicably with and emulate those more skillful than they. Their hope is to turn people into friends, companions, alter egos, and especially free human beings.

Elsa Maxwell, the mostest hostest, was advised by her father: "Never own things; they make a slave of you." Buddha and Jesus both knew that to be a human being of consummate virtue is incompatible with an inordinate craving for possessions. Francis of Assisi, Spinoza, Goethe, Mother Teresa, Albert Schweitzer, and Simone Weil knew this as well.

347

There are more instances of abridgement of the freedom of the people by gradual and silent encroachments... than by violent and sudden usurpations.
James Madison (1751-1836) – Speech June 16, 1788

This may be true in all organized groups from families to Federal Governments. Everyone knows families where one domineering parent can cleverly and gradually deprive all other members of the family of their freedoms. In the news, we hear of the same thing happening in cities, states, and countries. These groups may, in spite of the prevailing despotisms, be models of peace and harmony.

Reading biographies of Jim Jones, David Koresh, and Marshall Applewhite, we learn that such leaders knew well the merit of gradualism. None of them could have imposed their macabre philosophies all at once upon their disciples. It took time, bit-by-bit persuasion. No religion can take a completely untouched twenty-year-old and in a single impassioned harangue, tirade, or diatribe turn him or her into a true believer. Only patient, temperate, carefully programmed instruction can do that.

Of course, we must not lose sight of the fact that an ostensible harmony may seem to prevail even when loss of freedom was anything but gradual abridgement. On plantations in the old South where slaves were treated "well" and each was assigned a certain job which was done well, things ran smoothly. When victims of Nazi atrocities in Europe were riding in cattle cars to Auschwitz and Bergen-Belsen, often there was no irruptive violence. It is not that both slaves and the victims of Naziism did not understand that they were deprived of their freedoms. Both knew that violence in their present situations would serve no purpose.

348

It is terrible to see how a single unclear idea, a single formula without meaning, lurking in a young man's head will sometimes act like an obstruction of inert matter in an artery, hindering the nutrition of the brain, and condemning its victim to pine away in the fullness of his intellectual vigor and in the midst of intellectual plenty.

Charles Sanders Peirce (1839-1914)
Chance, Love, and Logic

Peirce, whose name is pronounced like that which the lady carries, gives us here an inkling of why a religion gains and maintains such a stranglehold over mankind. As a teacher, Peirce could observe what had happened to many students who came to him – and how difficult it could be to correct their mental blockages. The single formula without meaning that Peirce speaks of may well be the formula embodied in the preacher's use of the word "faith,"

When the word "faith" can be commandeered by so many impressive academagogues to cover all that is nonsensical in religion, the student may be excused for assuming that there is substance in its use. Once he makes that assumption, there is little hope for him. He accepts everything religionists have to say, unable to distinguish "faith" from "good sense" or "reason." The "faith basket" is given so much priority over the "sense basket" that faith becomes the shibboleth. It is now a synonym for religion.

349

> When man substituted God for the Great Goddess, he at the same
> time substituted authoritarian for humanistic values.
>
> Elizabeth Gould Davis
> *The First Sex*

The Great Goddess in the quotation above could as well be the
Tibetan female Buddha Tara or the apotheosized Black Madonna
image of Jesus' mother Mary. Whichever, may I suggest a new
feminine cosmos that would be the logic goal of *The First Sex*
aspiring also to be the only surviving sex?

Whichever of the three, whether Tara, the Great Goddess, or the
Black Madonna, if she could make one human baby without the help
of a father, of course she could make all of them the same way – and
make them all females. Eliminating the two-gender system of
human-species reproduction would solve many problems: Rape and
sexual harassment, estrus, prostate cancer, vasectomies, masculine
pronouns, urinals, male chauvinism, love triangles, pornography, and
women's inferiority complexes – all would disappear. No longer
need women be concerned with separating the shes from the gauche.

The same could occur among other species: The cumbersome
horns and antlers of bovines, the lioness sharing her kill with
deadbeat dads, the cannibalism of the black widow spider, the most
feared predators of baby polar and grizzly bears would be gone. Of
course some pleasures also would disappear: the peacock's tail, the
mocking bird's trill, the dances of cranes, prarie chickens, birds of
paradise, Rogers and Astaire, Torvil and Dean.

But women could contrive this wonderful world all by themselves
without divine intervention. First, all women must refuse coitus.
Then female medical scientists will unite the ovum of one woman
with the nucleus of an ovum of another to form a viable double-X
zygote. A one-gender species would soon flourish in numbers that
the earth could easily sustain. Human males and unwanted babies
would go the way of small pox.

The main message the reader may get from the above paragraph is
not that the events I describe are probable, indeed have any chance of
happening, but that what I describe is possible. The world is
changing at a dizzying pace. Things that conceivably can be made to
happen today could not have been thought of yesterday.

350

> Fill in the blanks for gender and race on a job application and increasingly in our country there is no problem. But try putting "atheist" in the blank for religious affiliation and see what happens.
>
> Chester Dolan
> *Blind Faith*

The same is true for child adoption. This country is not yet ready for an unqualified acceptance of religious preference.

If you find two groups of people diametrically opposed with respect to certain systems of ideas and would like to know which of the two groups is most in touch with sanity, reason, or reality, look to see which approaches the matter openly, unafraid, willing to submit their own views to careful examination. If books are being burned, even books long considered classics, look to see which of the two groups does not engage in such activities. Look to see which group tolerates ideas that oppose their own, willing to have all ideas expressed, confident that truth will emerge victorious if everyone has his say. Look to see which group has no need for blacklists, no need for character assassinations to silence the voice of the opposition. Look to see which group sees love as having no frontiers – whether geographical, national, political, racial, or sectarian. Look to see which group does not divide itself up into warring factions, each faction happy to see the others annihilated.

351

> If there is no God for thee
> Then there is no God for me.
>
> Anna Hempstead Branch (1875-1937)
> "To a dog"

Those who postulate Deity and an abode where He resides argue about whether other sentient creatures will be assigned a place in heaven.

Spell dog backwards and we have divinity. How can God deny His only meaningful anagram and man's best friend a place in heaven? Do we decide on the basis of how important given creatures are? The world would get along without man far better than without bacteria – and the biomass of bacteria is far greater than that of man.

It is said that there are 200 million insects for every human being that lives on this globe. Which is more important? Even the rabbit population exceeds that of man. Cockroaches and sharks have been around much longer than we have, and the dinosaurs occupied our lands more than 200 times as long as we have. Which, man or any of these other creatures, is more important?

If it is any consolation to Ms Branch, it is quite likely that dogs and human beings will fare equally well in this regard. There is not the slightest evidence that man, dogs, dinosaurs, cockroaches, bacteria, or anything else will find themselves in any other domain when they give up on this one. Nelson, in the comic strip *Pickles* by Brian Crane, gets the last word. Panel 1: Do you think Muffin's dead Grandpa? Panel 2: I don't know Nelson. She might be. There's a lot of things that could have happened to her out there. Panel 3: But don't worry. If she is dead, then she's up in heaven with God. Panel 4: What would God want with a dead cat?

352

When a dog barks at the moon, that is religion. When a dog barks at strangers, that is patriotism.

David Star Jordan (1851-1931)
University President

Before Neil Armstrong's intrusion on the only truly pristine landscape available to us, we could say that the fifteen million square miles of borderless desert that we call "moon" was little else but bewitching mystery. "Moon" had long served as a symbol in our minds for all the celestial venues or visitants and all other spiritual considerations.

In the minds of dogs in general and Jordan's subject dog in particular, the moon is a kind of subcorrelate of the same symbolism. "Religion" may well be the precise word to use for both dog and man to designate metaphysical mysteries.

"Strangers" to the dog is another matter. In his primitive brain, and in many human brains, "stranger" is used to denote the concept "enemy." The dogs barking in all probability means: "I hate everyone I do not know. Anything the master treats suspiciously or with affected deference must be frightened away. "We are good! Those others are bad!

"Patriotism" is precisely the anthropomorphic catch-all to designate this attitude.

353

> Systems political or religious or racial or national – will not just respect us because we practice freedom, they will fear us because we do.
>
> William Faulkner (1877-1962)
> *Harpers Magazine* June 1956

The slaveholder may respect the slaves who show some degree of independence of spirit, able to think their way through problems of doing and planning their work. But the slaveholder fears these slaves, too. He understands that the independence they show is exactly the kind of independence that produced the underground railway, with many slaves slipping off to free States and to Canada. Even more to fear were the John Browns, where even the owners of the Southern plantations were in danger of losing their lives.

Protecting freedom effectively is a perilous thing to do. In world societies, the big money is in the hands of the entrepreneurs who almost invariably acquired their fortunes by depriving others of their freedoms. They will not tolerate seeing that process reversed. Companies that set up their factories in foreign countries where labor is cheap and much of it is child labor, are depriving people of jobs in their own country and assure that other countries will remain third-world countries. On Wall Street, con men are everywhere and extortions are common. Inside trading is the principal reason large investors get rich, and new, small investors lose their money. The number of ways we can lose our freedoms is increasing. Yet, if enough people understand, the time may come when we will no longer be subject to any of them.

354

> If evil is caused by the flesh, how explain the wickedness of the Devil who has no flesh?
>
> St. Augustine of Hippo (354-430 BC)
> *De Civitate Dei*

How explain hundreds of such inconsistencies in the Bible? There is no way to explain them other than to say that the scriptures were written mostly by ancient ignoramuses who were writing at a time when consistency and good sense were not considered germane to what was chosen for consignment to the printed page.

The Bible is not the only scripture full of blatant flaws and absurdities. No one, not even Aesop, Hans Christian Anderson, or the Grimm brothers, has ever concocted anything more fatuous than the story Joseph Smith put together as the foundation for Mormonism. What Mary Baker Eddy wrote down in her *Science and Health with Key to the Scriptures* is in places so preposterous that we wonder how even human gullibility is enough to explain its extensive approval. What Muhammad and the indispensable editors that followed him put together to form the *Koran* in regard to slaves and the treatment of women is morally indefensible. Muslim fundamentalists who insist on literal interpretation of the *Koran* are everywhere behaving like the Taliban Muslims in Afghanistan. Everyone should watch what happens in Kabul in the years ahead to see what the world can expect if ever the fundamentalists of whatever religion achieve their avowed goal of gaining supremacy in every country in the world

The sacred literature of the world's religions all have their virtues – but all are also models of superficiality and deceit. Whether it is the Avesta of Zoroastrianism, the Chuang-tzu or Tao-te-Ching of Taoism, or the Analects of Confucius, the four Vedas, the Mahabharata, and the Ramayana of Hinduism, or the Summa of the Muslim Sunni, they are mixtures of stories, fairy tales, poems, fables, legend, history and mythology. Homer Smith's *Man and His Gods* goes on to describe hundreds of religions, most of them without written Bibles, without rational conformation, and without indemnifying merit. Smith's remarkable tome, more than any book ever written, may show us how thoroughly infantile and immoral are all theistic religions – one no better than the others.

It seems we set aside all semblance of critical acumen when we read scriptures. Solecisms and sophistry are the rule not the exception, and yet some people will read scripture as if it were the only worthwhile literature ever written. I have known at least two persons during my lifetime that limited their reading to the King James version of the Bible. Somewhere along the way, fanatical religionists had convinced them that their only hope for salvation was to immerse themselves in "God's Word." It was impossible to engage them in intelligent conversation about the world's real problems.

355

What mean and cruel things men do for the love of God
W. Somerset Maugham (1874-1965)
A Writer's Notebook

The number of prominent persons in the world who understand and openly affirm what Maugham says are reaching proportions impossible to ignore. The world's peoples must refuse to sponsor religion's cruelty: its wars, inquisitions, and crusades; its hate, bigotry, prejudices, and debilitating superstitions that do so much harm. Not until love of God means love of all God's people as well, will religion have the slightest excuse for existing. The harm religion does by any reasonable system of evaluation far exceeds the little good it can claim. Let us either get rid of all religions or revise them drastically until they are left with their only legitimate role: improving human morality. If left as they are we must relegate religions to a role as minor make-believe games suitable for children or for adults with children's minds. There are important things in this world to do and many salutary ways to enjoy ourselves. Why spend time immersed in nonsense, increasing the ways we can think up to abuse fellow human beings.

356

Having elaborated a very subtle technical vocabulary, men felt themselves to be distinguished scholars by the mere mastery of such a vocabulary. But this... vocabulary frequently hides the paucity of substantial insight.

Morris R. Cohen (1880-1947)
Reason and Nature

Much of what individuals accomplish in this world turns out, on close examination, to be pretentious nonsense. In art, in education, even in technology, where it takes the form of disguised obsolescence, we see the aim is not progress so much as personal gain and prestige.

In religion the percentage of sham is beyond measure the highest. The esoteric vocabulary that Cohen talks about is a common ruse, clever but inane Use enough words with vague, equivocal, shifting, or unintelligible meanings, and you will by that stratagem alone impress your audience. No one will know what you are talking about, but many will assume that with so many sesquipedalian words (words like sesquipedalian) you must be saying something.

357

Women... enslaved to the myths of their own inferiority are [often] unable to see the truth for the myths.

Ashley Montagu
American (born in England) anthropologist

The propensity of people to take myths seriously is one of the principal deterrents to the sanity of mankind.

As the germans were duped by the myth of the superrace, the Japanese were duped by the myth of Hirohito divinity, and people generally are taken in by the myths of religion, so women absorb the myth of their own inferiority, foisted upon them by patriarchial arrogance. As societies must reject every fanciful fabrication misconstrued as fact, so women must reject the myths deliberately contrived to prevent them from living sane, happy, and useful lives.

358

Many of the insights of the saint stem from his experiences as a sinner.   Eric Hoffer
The Passionate *State of Mind*

Distressful situations occurring in early years can profoundly affect the course of a person's life. For a lawyer it may have been a friend suffering a gross miscarriage of justice. For a doctor it may have been a parent suffering a mangled surgery. For a congressman it may have been the enactment of discriminating laws. Inspired lives have risen out of abject despair, or close-to-death experiences.

Sometimes it is an insightful consideration of one's own indiscretions. Thieves have become philanthropists. Gang members have become model citizens. Bullies have become champions of other people's rights. Saintliness, as Eric Hoffer says, may result from a determination to compensate for youthful iniquities.

359

Controversy equalizes fools and wise men – and the fools know it.
                                        Oliver Wendell Holmes, Jr. (1841-1935)

Holmes called this the "hydrostatic paradox of controversy." If you have a bent tube with two vertical arms connected at the bottom, one the size of a pipe stem and the other the size of an ocean, water will stand at the same level in one as in the other.

One of the commentators on the religious radio network in Quito, Ecuador, which broadcasts in fourteen languages on some of the most powerful short-wave stations that exist, was recently expatiating on the relative merits of theists, agnostics, and atheists. Theists, of course, are the earth's elite. Even agnostics fared fairly well in his dissertation. But "atheists are liars," he said, "for they say they know that God does not exist." These words, copied verbatim, were repeated in several world-wide broadcasts. If they were talking only to themselves, this kind of nonsense would not be so bad, but they are broadcasting to thousands, perhaps hundreds of thousands of people throughout the world.

I have never met an atheist who was not fully aware that it is impossible to *know* about any such negatives. All he can do is ask, "where is your evidence"? It is you who are making the positive statements. The burden of proof is upon the man who makes a positive statement, not upon the man who denies it."

If the reader doubts the unfeasibility of disproving the proclaimed existences of the sacred mythologies, let him explain how he would go about proving experimentally the nonexistence of fairies. He cannot – but it is nevertheless perfectly reasonable for him to get on with his life confident in the assumption that fairies will never show up on his radar screen, and will have no affect on his life.

360

For if there is a sin against life, it consists perhaps not so much in despairing of this life, as in hoping for another life and eluding the implacable grandeur of this life.
                                        Albert Camus (1913-1960) - Summer in Algeria

Karl Popper, too, thought that those who yearn for and believe in a life after death should be pitied. To him, they are a sad, deluded, egotistical lot.

The suicide pact meant to assure a young couple that they will thereby defy their objecting parents and unite in an Elysian paradise is no guarantee that they will see each other ever again.

When Odin (a Scandinavian legislator, not the Norse God) killed himself so that he could "prepare the feast of heroes in the palace of the god of war," that is not to say that he ever actually performed that task. To make a pact that depends on events in an afterlife is to hunt snipes in Atlantis. We will do as well ordering sand, harps, and chaps from a sandman, harpy, and chaperon, respectively.

The minute we come to the full realization that heaven and hell and any sort of afterlife are all fables, that minute we will turn our attention to the life we have and dedicate our efforts to making this life and this world better.

We must all learn first of all that saying a thing is so does not make it so, and then we must learn not to believe when there is no evidence for believing. That is enough. Learn those two things and we will never again allow ourselves to be hoodwinked by anyone.

361

I can't believe in a God who saves only those people who live in certain latitudes. If I had happened to be born in Delhi I'd probably be a Hindu, or in Iran a Muslim.

> Robert Runcie, Archbishop of Canterbury
> Quoted by John Mortimer
> *In Character*

If Jesus was the only way in which men could be saved, as we are told, why were vast populations of the world denied the favor of his hallowed presence? Were the Chinese, the Polynesians, and indigenous peoples of Australia and North and South America unworthy of salvation?

Archbishop Runcie can see far beyond the horizons limiting other ecclesiastics. He understands one thing for sure: Which of the many religions any given human being practices is largely a matter of chance. It is not only geographical location that may have determined his fate, but also the mental attitudes of siblings, the schools he attends, the friends he makes in these schools, or the spouse he chooses to spend a life with – many, many things determine whether he turns our to be a Jew, a Christian, a Hindu, or a Muslim – or perhaps an atheist.

Changing religions, also, is a matter of chance. Luther, Wesley, Calvin, Joseph Smith, Brigham Young, Mary Baker Eddy, made converts wherever they went. Those who chanced to become associated with Jim Jones, David Koresh, or Marshall Applewhite were induced to follow disastrous paths. With the 11,000 religions the world counts in its registries, we should certainly understand that we have not, except by a very remote chance, been lucky enough to be attached to the one true religion. Robert Burton said in *The Anatomy of Melancholy:* "One religion is as true as another." As I say in this book, and many others say as well, the best choice of all may be to reject all that may be called mysticism. We reject the creation of purely imaginary beings, their abodes, and all the fanciful occurrences in which they are said to be involved.

362

It is said by uninformed minds again and again that certain factors of human experience are beyond the reach of science because they are not immediately observable; the implication being that science must limit itself to the purely observable. Nothing is further from the truth. Science is dealing with the unobservable every day of its existence.

F.S.C. Northrop
Science and First Principles

Dealing with the unobservable and worshiping the unobservable are two different things. Science does the first and religion the second. Verifying the unobservable and accepting the unobservable on faith are also two very different things. Science does the first and religion the second. No one without the tools of science observes the earth traveling around the sun. We all see the opposite – and that was the prevailing wisdom up to the time of Copernicus. Agreeing with Copernicus nearly cost Galileo his life a hundred years later.

Without the benefit of science, no one sees neutrinos traveling through masses of solid matter, including ourselves, but scientists assure us that they do. Without science we could not speculate about black holes, supernovas, dark matter, gravity waves, etc., etc. Without science considering the unobservable, the macroscopic world of daily experience would be the only world we would know, and much of our love affair with life would not have evolved.

363

> The minister might become an extraordinarily helpful person if he could see through his own religion. But his training and his economic situation do not encourage him to do so.
>
> Alan Watts (1915-1973)
> *Psychotherapy East and West*

Especially in small-island and jungle economies, priests and ministers do a tremendous amount of good. If it were not for the harm they do simultaneously, and the strings attached to it all, they would have my undying support. If we had doctors, teachers, nutritionists, and agronomists who worked with the self-effacing zeal of proselytizing priests and pastors, what a boon they would be to marginal peoples all over the world.

The natives' religion may be older than that of the missionary and may have served him better than the missionary's religion ever will, but fanaticism is blind to such "inconsequentials." Anthropologists assure us that the chances of becoming psychotic is less in primitive societies than it is for those who live in modern cities with all their benefits such as psychiatry, group therapy, and books to deal with every kind of emotional instability.

Aldous Huxley in the Epilogue of *Time Must Have a Stop* makes it plain that those bent on converting others to their own religious point of view will stop at nothing when frustrated in their efforts to effect conversion. Death to the intransigents is not at all uncommon.

364

> Few really believe. The most only believe that they believe, or even make believe.
>
> John Lancaster Spalding
> *Thoughts and Theories of Life and Education*

"Few really believe," Spalding says, and we are encouraged. But if what he says is true, people are more astute than we usually give them credit for. Despite our doubts, can Spalding be the truly sapient sapiens?

When we analyze what evangelists are screaming from their pulpits and find everything they say so manifestly absurd, and then at the same time find those evangelists gathering large crowds of listeners, we are disheartened. Does Spalding give us a ray of hope? These listeners do not really believe, after all? They actually see the absurdity of what they are being told? Deep down within themselves, they too are skeptics? They only "make believe" that they believe? Can we hope at least that they have reservations about believing; they have doubts that hover near, but below, the level of their own conscious understanding?

The hope that Spalding gives us is that if anyone can explain well enough to people what they are doing to themselves by their irrational believing, they will change. Possibly we can, after all, hope to construct a sane existential world in which people will accept only that which their five proverbial senses present to them. These senses and others as well, they will learn, are our only tramway to reality. Anything these senses refute is nonsense.

Our minds build upon what we observe, giving us new hierarchies of abstractions that explain the world more fully. These abstractions serve as scaffolding for still further ideas, and so on – with all ideas reducible ultimately to rationality – never to mythology.

365

> There is nothing specifically Christian in the mythical view of the world as such. It is simply the cosmology of a pre-scientific age.
>
> Rudolf Carl Bultmann (1884-1976)
> *Kerygma and Myth*

With myth, as with science fiction, there are few literary restraints. Fancies and phantoms can be multiplied without end. No one should be surprised about whatever mythologists come up with. The discrepancies between what they and others dealing with the same subject conceive are beyond imagination.

Virgin birth for one may be brain outgrowth for another. Heaven for one may be happy-hunting grounds for another. God for one may be Odin for another. Satan for one may be Set for another. Purgatory for one may be limbo for another. And in all of these cases, not just names, but the basic concepts are different. There are no limits:

Probity is a pariah. Fidelity is a fable. To tell the truth, the truth will no be told.

For sure, as Bultmann says, Christianity has no monopoly on myth. Nor can religion in general make that claim. It would astound most people to know how little their lives are involved in actual events and practical ideas. Since the dawn of language, man has been amazingly adept at constructing entire hierarchies of ethereal symbol systems that have little or nothing to do with the real world in which we all live. Myth becomes our essential world. Myth determines to an extent greater than we may want to admit how we conduct our affairs.

366

> Mankind, in the gross, is a gaping monster, that loves to be deceived, and has seldom been disappointed.
>
> Henry Mackenzie (1745-1831)
> Scottish Novelist

"Mankind in the gross" is gullible. Any modern theistic religion is almost a hundred percent deception, but only a few come to understand that it is.

Stanislav Andreski and Robert Oppenheimer, like Mackenzie, also believe that people like to be deceived. They are not entirely wrong, but it seems that the exact truth is that people would not like the fact of being deceived if they knew that to be the case, but they like the result of having been deceived. Their religion suits them fine. They enjoy the camaraderie of their church companions who also accept what their preacher says without question. They find no fault with the religious life they lead. They enjoy it.

Mackenzie's last five words remind us of how commonly we are deceived. Our politicians deceive us, our lawyers deceive us, our salesmen deceive us, our preachers deceive us. Deception in our societies is as common as the common cold – and many times more deadly. We often find out that truth too late in life to do anything about it.

367

> Whatever power such a being may have over me, there is one thing he shall not do. He shall not compel me to worship him. I will call no being good who is not what I mean when I apply that epithet to my fellow-creatures; and if such a being can sentence me to Hell for not so calling him, to Hell I will go.
>
> John Stuart Mill (1806-18730)
> Examination of Sir William Hamilton's Philosopy

If we may depart briefly from attested documentation, let us consider a young lady who stood in a violent lightning storm and watched her dear pet dog killed by lightning while anointing a nearby tree. She shouted: "Damn you, damn you, God! I hate you, I hate you, I hate you!" She seemed unconcerned that, according to sacerdotal logic, the next lightning bolt might be for her. Both she and Mill, it seems, believed that God exists. I wonder if Mill could make his statement with the same lack of concern for personal safety that was the case with the unhappy girl.

Mill lived to what was then a ripe old age, and I have heard no séance report that he ended up in hell. The fact that "authentic" séance reports are rare and that even most religionists would consider them tripe can be the subject of another paper. It is certainly not a concern of those who "know" what is "really the truth" about God's existence and His capabilities for intervening in human affairs. Nothing will change their minds.

368

> Satan the envious said with a sigh
> Christians know more about their hell than I.
> Alfred Kreymborg (1883-1966)

Alfred Kreymborg, we guess, was having a little fun with us here. What he pretends to be surprised about is very logical, is it not? Satan is only one character. The Bible gives him very little opportunity to tell us what he knows – almost nothing until the Christians took him in hand. Also, no doubt, he is purely a figment of fiction. With all of those disadvantages, how could he be expected to know as much as several million Christians? Give the poor devil a break!

Whether or not Christians know much about their hell is a question. But their devotion to hell is beyond question. Not God, not heaven, nothing else has captivated their attention like hell has. No wonder we have Satanic cults; all of Christianity is a Satanic cult. Satan is the real Christian savior, the liege spirit indispensable to most of their considerations.

Satan gets a bigger play than other denizens of religious mythologies, even in movies and novels. In Milton's *Paradise Lost*, Lucifer is the epic's main character. In Melville, Dante, and Dostoyevsky, also, the devil found chroniclers worthy of him. Faust, in a play by Marlowe, a poem by Goethe, and an opera by Gounod, as well as our movie *Damned Yankees* had a field day with Satan. With so much top billing, Satan must be one of the most wealthy actors going, not to mention what his royalties must amount to. Did I say "poor devil?"

369

Fortitude stresses strength of mind and firmness of purpose; it implies endurance of physical or mental hardships or suffering without giving way under the strain.

Merriam-Webster dictionary definition.

"The kingdom of God is within you," Jesus says in Luke 17:21 Within us is where we will find the fortitude to make this a better world. If we want to give the name "God" to the strength of mind and firmness of purpose within us, I see no overwhelming reason to object. Neither do I see benefits in so doing. Once we learn to depend on ourselves and realize our own remarkable potential, we will accomplish many of our cherished objectives, and there will be no distinguishing virtues or beneficial capabilities we cannot achieve.

If we fail to make this earth the heaven we want it to be, it is only because we lack the will to do so. It will not be because we do not have within ourselves all the abilities needed to solve the problems that face us. With the right kind of moral education, and with judicious use of reason and intuition, we can do much to eliminate ill will and violence from the face of the earth. As long as we do not let ourselves slip back into the dark ages, we can be sure of the survival of genus Homo and its only remaining species.

Worshiping nonsense and attributing progress to mythical beings, serves only to debilitate mankind and condemn mankind to mediocrity. With faith in ourselves and in our abilities to eliminate our irresolutions and procrastinations, we may assure the continuing existence of what could be the only thinking species the universe has produced.

370

Millions of innocent men, women, and children, since the introduction of Christianity, have been burned, tortured, fined, imprisoned. What has been the effect of [this] coercion? To make one half of the world fools and the other half hypocrites.

Thomas Jefferson (1743-1826)
Notes on the State of Virginia

In a letter to Elbridge Gerry, Jefferson said: "I am for freedom of religion and against all maneuvers to bring about a legal ascendancy of one sect over another."

Surely one of the most remarkable coincidences in all of history is how this small burgeoning country happened to get together the extraordinary intelligence it did. They say circumstances make heroes and bring out needed leaders. Certainly the thirteen colonies needed great men if they were to have any chance of surviving as a new nation. But the likes of Jefferson, Washington, Adams, Madison, Franklin, and others all together at one time – that was more than the country had a right to expect. Alexander Hamilton, writing in the Federalist in 1787, agrees with Jefferson: "In politics as in religion, it is equally absurd to aim at making proselytes by fire and sword. Heretics in either politics or religion can rarely be cured by persecution." The thirteen colonies could easily have ended up as a monarchy or a theocracy. The fact that they did not beats all odds. The decision to discourage titles and the insistence on separation of church and state must never be relaxed.

Even at the beginning of this century, there were people expressing with equal fervor the sentiments of Jefferson and Hamilton. Alfred North Whitehed said: "I consider Christian theology to be one of the great disasters of the human race." When today Billy Graham can say: "Christians are the only people in the world who have anything to be happy about," we know we are still not out of danger. Believing that, he will believe also that there are no means inappropriate for turning the world's populations into Christians. "Onward Christian Soldiers," "Marching as to War," "To Win the World for Christ" would become the rallying cry and campaign slogan.

371

It is not disbelief that is dangerous to our society, it is belief.

George Bernard Shaw (1856-1950)
Androcles and the Lion

Bertrand Russell said in *Skeptical* Essays: "I do not believe that on balance religious belief has been a force for good.... I regard it as belonging to the infancy of human reason, and to a stage of development which we are outgrowing."

Disbelief in the avalanche of nonsense that is engulfing us is in truth the only sane response people today can entertain. We can live perfectly and sanely and serenely without succumbing to any of the grand systems of myth that theologians are espousing. Once we agree to believe one system of lies, it becomes easy to believe other systems of lies. Soon we find ourselves thoroughly engulfed in vast networks of lies. We will be living in a world that can be described adequately only as a world of deeply entrenched and widely disseminated sham.

The truly sane person has made one important decision early in his life: that he will believe nothing for which there is no adequate evidence for believing. His skepticism never wavers and he demands proof for everything. Hitler believed (and said so in Mein Kampf) "If you tell a lie big enough, often enough, and in a voice loud enough, people will believe it." The lies the theologian tells, like all lies, do not become truth simply by constant repetition. The only way to tell whether a statement is true is by determining its predictive content. If what you say is true *is* true then this, and this, and this will follow. The more "and this's" that can be verified, the more predictive content the statement has, the more "truth value" it can be credited with. On this basis, all the theologian's many pronouncements concerning the mythologies of religion are blatant lies, for none of them have been verified or ever will be. They are nothing more than the figments of his free-wheeling imagination – conjured up deliberately in order to deceive.

372

> If God made us in His image, we have certainly returned the compliment.
>
> Voltaire (1694-1778)

When Voltaire wrote that, he could not have imagined that his remark, repeated, would be central in one of the most famous jury trials in history. This response elicited by Williams Jennings Bryan from a student of John Scopes, so shook the Jury as to have been material in the conviction of the humble Dayton, Tennessee school teacher. The statute that Scopes failed to respect remained law in the State where the trial took place until 1967. More than forty long years had to pass before Tennessee could muster the courage to extend a reluctant toe into the torrent of scientific progress.

It is completely impossible for a man to speak intelligently about that which he knows nothing. When he speaks of God, he must speak in terms he would use in describing his own species or the individual members of that species. Any words he uses that seem to set God apart in some empyrean realm or that describe Him in other than anthropomorphic terms are meaningless. It is impossible to use meaningless terms in the premises of our arguments and come to conclusions that are meaningful. What Voltaire (and Scopes) said is not only true, it is axiomatic.

373

> Religion belongs to man – it is his dream, his vision, his achievement. If there are Bibles, he has written them; if there are churches, he has reared them; if there are gods, he has discovered them.
>
> J.H. Holmes
> *The Sensible Man's View of Religion*

We know well many religious leaders who have renounced their rights to ponder, to muse, to consider alternatives. We see them as content to adopt the suppositions of the Right Reverend Shallowpate never to express an opinion at variance with the orthodoxy in which they have become immersed. The religion they preach may be widely diffused, but has little impact upon the religious person's behavior.

But now we have a new voice. As a preacher who could really think, Holmes was a giant among pygmies, a prince among boors. He Was Emerson's indispensable nonconformist, John Stuart Mill's essential eccentric. It must have been a delight to sit as a member of his congregation and hear sense spoken instead of the sanctimonious gibberish we hear from evangelists today on the television screen.

Since, as Holmes suggests, man makes his own religions, it follows that when we have better religions it will be man that makes them better. Gloria Steinem, past president of the National Organization of Women, looks forward to that day: "By the year 2000 we will I hope raise our children to believe in human potential, not in God."

374

Supposing a man-hater had desired to render the human race as unhappy as possible, what could he have invented for the purpose better than belief in an incomprehensible being about whom man could never be able to agree?

Denis Diderot (1713-1784)

On page 244 of Blind Faith, I put a reverse spin on this idea, coming out at about the same place: "Just let me be God for a couple of days, and I'll straighten out a few things. And what man could not do better than the God who is said to have been running things these past millennia? It might be interesting for the reader, too, to contemplate this outlandish challenge. Just what could you or I do, given the premise of omnipotence and omniscience that being God would imply, something to set this world running on a smoother course? I am sure many things come to your mind. They do to mine. Just for openers: Being God as I am, I hereby decree that, from now on forever, all efforts by any human being to do harm to another human being or to his property will fail utterly. How about that! Not bad, eh? God if you exist, and if you are listening, you can use that one, no charge. What a different world we would have tomorrow! We could walk about freely, without fears. We would discharge all policemen, armies, putting all these men and women to work at satisfying and beneficial employment. If this objective cannot be achieved by divine decree, it is nevertheless a legitimate goal. Using every ingenuity he can muster, man in control of his own destiny must continually strive to advance toward that goal.

So now it is your turn! I am sure you will do something about the hunger, accidents, diseases, prejudices, all the miseries that plague mankind. Can we believe there is a God and his numerous angels watching over us when they do none of the things that you and I can think of on the spur of the moment?

John Lilly, in his book *Simulations of God*, gives this "self as God" extensive coverage, especially in Chapter 2.

Chapter X

Science and Religion

375

Many who live in this complicated world feel that it is incumbent upon all of us to try to explain the universe and the part our small planet plays in the total scheme of cosmic events. To try to explain how the universe operates is a legitimate human effort that is yielding ever-increasing benefits for mankind. But to try to explain *why* it operates as it does, what cosmic purpose is involved, turns out to be a fruitless exercise that does nothing but introduce unnecessary anxieties into human lives and constitutes an enormous waste of human energy. In the first of these endeavors, which we call science, man refuses to allow personal predilections or prejudices to influence his method of operation. In the second endeavor, which constitutes much of what we call "religion," man's predilections and prejudices become his modus operandi or the stimuli that urge him on. "Why," in the sense of what facts of nature behaving according to what laws of nature causes things to happen the way they do, of course, is a legitimate province of science. It is "why" in the sense of cosmic purpose that we must be wary of.

The disinterest of the scientist is manifested in the principle of parsimony, his insistence upon empirical and rational verification, and his readiness to reject hypotheses that prove untenable. The prepossessions of the religionist, on the other hand, impose no restraints on him, no necessity to prove his doctrines and dogmas – and instead dispose him to defend his pronouncements against all opposition. The good scientist will suspend judgment until his theories are supported by well-founded facts. The religionist has been trained to believe that it is perfectly natural to make judgments without the slightest need for facts.

376

> If the foot were to say: "I do not belong to the body," it would still remain part of the body.
>
> Paul of Tarsus (?-67)
> First letter to the *Corinthians* 12:15

When a deputation asked him to proclaim emancipation of the slaves at a time when he believed the proclamation could not be enforced, Abraham Lincoln in effect made the same point that Saint Paul made: "How many legs will a sheep have if you call the tail a leg." "Five," was their unanimous reply. "You are mistaken," he said, "calling a tail a leg doesn't make it so."

The relations between symbols and what they symbolize is always exactly what those assigning values to the symbols want them to be. If the referents for the symbols we use are other symbols and nothing more, then nothing has been said. If the referents are myths, nothing has been said. If the referents are whatever our fertile imaginations might dream up, nothing has been said. Not until symbols say something directly or indirectly about the real world in which we live do they make sense.

Gods, devils, and their abodes do not exist in any empirical sense except as structure in human nervous systems. Religious leaders say they exist but could not demonstrate that as fact if their lives depended on it. From such premises entire religions are constructed, made up solely of symbols that refer only to other symbols, and to nothing in the real world.

377

> Faith is belief without evidence of what is told without knowledge of things without parallel.
>
> Ambrose Bierce (1842-1914)
> *The Devil's Dictionary*

To paraphrase: "Faith is belief in flimflam told by fools about fantasyland." Much of *The Devil's Dictionary*, we might guess, was meant to be glossaries of terms to appear in as yet unwritten books on various subjects. The author may have had in mind, for example, a new Bible, but was discouraged from writing it. You see, he was born without certain genes, leaving him devoid of artificially, affectation, duplicity, confusion, immaturity, deception, dissimulation, artifice, guile – all traits so indispensable for writers of scripture.

Ambrose Bierce could not be blamed for his cart-before-the-horse caprice, writing the glossaries before the books were written. He had such a great time with words, blasting buncombe, exposing pomposity, deflating demagoguery, that he could not help himself. Anyone who finds his kind of diverting definitions intriguing will find his dictionary a treasure.

378

Is uniformity of opinion desirable: No more than of face and stature.
Thomas Jefferson (1743-1826)
Notes on the State of Virginia

Nature chooses from diversity that which is best, ensuring that the species evolves. The same thing happens in the case of man and culture. Without opportunities for selection, we could not progress. Nature has more patience, and is a more demanding taskmaster, but all selection (natural and unnatural) functions pretty much alike.

Unfortunately, in the case of human beings, mediocre minds and minds with sinister motives are too often involved, and the result may be anything but progress. Dark ages follow ages of relative enlightenment, and devastating wars follow intervals of peace. Whether or not we human beings and our capabilities are progressing today is open to debate. Natural selection seem to favor the uneducated and those in poverty. It is they who are having the large families and who endanger population stability.

In world populations where people are differently educated, have different life experiences, suffer from different discriminations, have different problems, religions, and kinds of recreation, there are sure to be opinions of all kinds struggling for recognition. Those opinions that best lead to adaptation to one another and to natural and cultural environments hopefully will win out and lead to world progress. Those that fail in these respects are revised, or they die out and are forgotten. If we can eliminate greed, deceit, and selfish motives – increase the love, kindness, charity, and altruism among us, we will progress.

Crime is decreasing and population acceleration, too, is beginning to show signs of decreasing. If we can eliminate the threat of chemical, bacteriological, and atomic wars, there still may be hope of developing an acceptable home at least for all of the familially and communally disposed peoples of the world.

379

> By perseverance the snail reached the ark.
> Charles Haddon Spurgeon (1834-1892)

Perseverance is a great thing and aphorisms praising it can be useful. But so is truth a great thing, and aphorisms that foster Biblical fable only add to the confusion that already exists in distressing proportions. Terrestrial snails in times of high water may climb trees, but I would guess that never in eternity did any head for an ark.

People who believe the flood story, as long as we brought it up, are people I would like to sell a magnificent bridge in Brooklyn or some marvelous Florida swamp land, as the saying goes. If a world-wide flood had in fact ever occurred, that phenomenon would be so evident in geologic records that there would be no doubt about it. The unimaginable logistics of gathering the world's flood-alergic world's organisms together, the spacial impossibility of housing them and their food in an ark of modest dimensions, and the impossibility of convincing poisonous snakes and spiders along with herbivores and carnivores (including deer, lions, tigers, and grizzly bears to live amicably together is totally beyond capabililty of realization. The baby-dinosaur theory of creation scientists is alone a logistics problem that defies credulity, especially because dinosaurs had not existed for some 65 million years before Noah performed his miracle.

A woman having a baby at ninety, a woman turning into salt, a women rising bodily to heaven, not to mention sticks turning into snakes, snakes and asses talking, the giants and leviathans that roamed the earth, all put together are nothing compared to what Noah accomplished.

This tendency of human beings to believe readily and uncritically, without examination or investigation anything others may choose to propose, has to be the greatest deterrent to progress ever recorded.

Careless habits of thought that substitute for genuine thinking is our most inexcusable human failing.

380

When you call yourself an Indian or a Muslim or a Christian or a European, or anything else, you are being violent.

Krishnamurti
Freedom from the Known

It is difficult to hate anyone we cannot identify. Labels are essential for our prejudices to flourish. When we put ourselves in categories by giving ourselves various group names, we invite the hatred spawned by differences, real or imagined.

Once labels are applied, Baptist vs Methodist, for example, the two labeled groups will separate themselves one from the other even more than before. No Baptist will go to a Methodist church and vice versa. Suspicions arise and reciprocal hatreds grow. If there are not deliberate efforts to reverse the process, things can get out of hand. To know that this happens in all parts of the world, we need only to look to examples like the Sinhalese and Tamils in Ceylon, Hindus and Sikhs in India, Jews and Muslims in the Middle East, Shia and Sunni in Iraq, and Catholics and Protestants in Northern Ireland.

381

Mass movements can arise without belief in God, but not without belief in a devil.

Eric Hoffer
The True Believer

The "devil" Eric Hoffer speaks of is the "common enemy" that is necessary to turn people into convincingly good friends. It is a common enemy that can give rise to mass movements and incite members to fight wars since time immemorial. Religion, too, of course, had to invent some such common enemy to serve its people. Any religious despot knows very well he must have an evil protagonist as well as a benevolent one in the story he is inventing to hold people together. Simply by prefixing a "d" to the evil-one required, he found he had done as well as he ever could. No sense in continuing to rack his perverted imagination.

H.L. Mencken in *Treatise on the Gods* anticipated Eric Hoffer when he said: "It is hell, of course, that makes priests powerful, not heaven.... When men cease to fear the gods, they cease to be religious in any rational sense.... The essences of all priestly morality is retribution, and without a hell of one sort or another, retribution becomes mere rhetoric, signifying nothing.... The Christian hell, I incline to believe, is the hottest of them all."

Both Hoffer and Mencken seemed to believe they knew where religion's strength really lies. To them love is not the reigning power of religion; hate is religion's real power. The "God of love" that religions invented could not hold a candle to (let alone a cross against) the God of hate.

Joseph Fletcher believes that love will win – and so do I. The congenial authors of the quotations in this book are telling us what we must do if love is someday to reign.

382

> God made man such as he is and then damned him for being so.
> Percy Bysshe Shelley (1792-1822)
> *Notes to Queen Mab*

It is like an author cursing his own book because it does not say what he wants it to say. If God did not like the human beings He produced, why did He create them? He already had his angels, delightful pixies who ran around silently waiting on Him hand and foot, like slaves doing His every bidding. It seems He had it made. He could reign like the top Sheikh of Araby.

Was God some kind of Masochist? He had a perfect world without problems, no fodder for Satan – and then He spoiled it all. On the sixth day of creation He created men and women (before He created Adam and Eve, according to the chronology of the Bible. Adam and Eve did not appear until the next chapter).

What God really thought of human beings becomes apparent as we thumb our way through the Bible:

Isaiah 41:24: Indeed you are nothing and your work is nothing.
1 Corinthians 3:7: Neither he who plants is anything nor he who waters.

Galatians 6:3: For if anyone thinks himself to be something, when he is nothing, he deceives himself.

Job 28:13: Man does know the value [of wisdom].

Ecclesiastes 9:1: People know neither love nor hatred.

Isaiah 59:10: We are as dead men in desolate places.

Romans 3:11,12: There is none who understands.... There is none who does good.

1 Corinthians 1:20: Has not God made foolish the wisdom of this world?

James 4: 14" For what *is* your life? It is even a vapor that appears for a little time and then vanishes away.

383

Philosophy's only valid goal, according to Wittgenstein, is to do away with itself.

Editors of *Time-Life Books*
Search for the Soul

    The best teachers are those who make themselves superfluous; the best doctors teach preventive medicine; the best psychiatrists teach us to avoid stress, religion, and other stepping-stones to traumatic neuroses. Philosophers (religious and otherwise), who preach mostly nonsense (referring to the word's etymological acceptation), would do us all a favor by eliminating their kind from their occupational pretensions.

    The editors of *Time-Life Books* say earlier on the same page: "Wittgenstein contends that philosophers should not be discussing the soul at all – or for that matter any other ideas that constitute the content of philosophy – because in so doing they are only creating problems that do not exist."

    Many philosophers coin their own esoteric terms and phrases, trying to explain their own brand of nonsense, which by its nature is unexplainable: C.D. Broad speaks of the "psi-component," Otto of "numinous," and Emerson of the "over-soul." Hegel has his "absolute" or "Universal Spirit." M. Taggart, an atheist, nevertheless had his "plurality of lives." Descartes of "my soul by which I am what I am." Sartre blue-penciled Descartes and rewrote: "I am, therefore I think." William James, the most vascillating of all philosophers, harbored doubts about everything, was never quite sure about the existence of gods, souls, or saints. Philosophers often weave their way in and out of metaphysics until they embarrass themselves and confuse us all.

384

> The existence of a world without God seems to me less absurd than the presence of a God existing in all His perfections, creating an imperfect man in order to make him run the risk of hell.
>
> Armand Salacrou
> *Theatre*

The God, "existing in all his perfections," seems to have been somewhat disoriented during his initial six-day working binge. If the first few pages of Genesis really describe "the beginning," it was a chaotic, disorganized, mixed-up mess. What are we to think when we read:

God said: Let there be light (day 1) before He creaated the two great lights (day 4).

God brought forth grass... and the tree (day 3) before He created a sun (day 4).

God created birds (day 5) before He created the beasts of the earth (day 6).

God created man... male and female (Chapter 1) before He created Eve (Chapter 2).

With the first lines of "God's word" so confusing, we will not expect much from the rest of the Bible. And so it is: full of contradictions, inconsistencies, anomalies, and peculiar passages that no one knows quite how to interpret.

385

> All unbelief is belief in a lie.
>
> Horatius Bonar (1808-1889)

Certainly unbelief in mythology, the basis of Christian-Judeo-Muslim religion is not a lie, but the beginning of wisdom. Unbelief in fairies, flying saucers, ghosts, werewolves, angels, mermaids, incubi, unicorns, souls, chimeras, satyrs, trolls, gods, devils, or haploid humans is not a lie. If anyone disagrees, let him prove the existence of any of these entities. Nothing acquires existence simply by saying it exists. Some manner of proof is always required.

If you insist that fairies exist, introduce me to a fairy. Let Dan Rather interview her on television. Even presenting an authentic, untouched photograph of a fairy would help. Sir Arthur Conan Doyle did exactly that in a book he wrote "proving that fairies exist. Later the photograph was shown to be a fraud. Will your proof of the existence of any of the entities in the list above be any better? Every new generation introduces new phantoms: big foot, abominable snowmen, chupacabras – but all eventually meet the same fate. No one provides proof. Science gives us the only kind of proof there is that does not involve us in an infinite regress. For a description of how one goes a about trying to "prove" whatever anyone says about anything, see Anatol Rapoport's *Operational Philosophy*.

386

Don't let what happened yesterday inhibit what is happening today or will happen tomorrow. It's ancient history, and nothing you can do will change it.

Daniel Meacham

There are times when what Meachem tells us is useful advice. If what happened yesterday is a personal contretemps that those whom we will deal with today know nothing about, we must try to erase it from our mind so that it will not affect our very important business today.

But what is really (and not Meachem's metaphorical) ancient history is another thing. That past is often the primary determinant of how people will react to us today and will remain a determinant long into the future. The stultifying ignorance of ancient times gave us the religions, gods, superstitions, and prejudices that deny us our freedom and affect everything we do. It is ancient history, and it may seem, as Meacham suggests, that nothing will change the effect it has on us. Santayana was right in telling us that there is little hope for the human species if we do no take the past into account. But there must be a revolution in the ideas we live by. We must repudiate ancient ignorance if the world of Homo sapiens is to survive.

387

> When a Pope is theoretically infallible, doctrinal opinions are treated as infallible. Authoritarian abuse of power begins.
>
> Hans Kung
> *Infallible?*

Alexander Pope gives *the* Pope and all the rest of us some valuable advice. In *An Essay on Criticism he says:* Whoever thinks a faultless piece to see, / Thinks what ne'er was, nor is, / Nor e'er shall be." No politician, no musician, no lawyer, no doctor, and no ecclesiastic is infallible. No one is always right, whatever the subject he speaks about or deals with.

To be fully aware of this truth is to introduce tranquility into our lives. We do not get angry when people we have always depended on fail us at times. If we are honest with ourselves, we see that we too sometimes fail. However wise we think we are, and however good are our intentions, we disappoint others who have come to expect from us advice they can depend on.

The problems that confront us in the course of our lives are often extremely complex, more so than at first they seem. Unintended consequences resulting from poorly understood ramifications lead us into quagmires of misconceptions and misunderstandings. What psychologists, psychiatrists, and psychoanalysts do on radio and television talk programs is little short of criminal. With ten or twenty words from a disturbed person calling in, they pretend that they can make meaningful decisions that may well affect the rest of the person's life. Even with dozens, sometimes hundreds of 50-minute sessions with such patients, they often come to erroneous diagnoses. How can they possibly come to reliable conclusions with the brief encounters they have with people on the air?

388

> The idea of soul, the fundamental principal of Christianity, was really a "Consciousness of human personality conceived naively as substance."
>
> Emil Lucka – *The Evolution of Love*

The universal contemplation of death, in all likelihood possible only in the human species, seems to provide us with our justification or pretext for a belief in souls. Just what a soul is no two religions and probably no two religionists will agree. Read all that is said about souls and you find nothing to indicate that souls are anything more than a person's particular style of operating in family, social, and business situations. See also essay 98.

G.H. Lewis in *The Physical Basis of Mind* calls the soul "nothing more than the subjective experiencing of objective bodily phenomena." Hudson Hoagland in "Reflections on the Purpose of Life" appearing in the March 1971 issue of *Zygon, Journal of Religion and Science* is more explicit: "To me the soul of man is in the manner of his functioning in his environment, social and otherwise, and this correlated with the organizations of patterns of nerve messages and molecular arrangements in his brain. The idea of a disembodied psyche or soul is as meaningless a concept of... the grin of the Cheshire cat without the cat. If mind is a function of brain action, then mental process on the one hand, and brain physiology and biochemistry on the other, are two side of the same coin." Jung's "persona" comes close to whatever is intelligible in the use of the word "soul."

389

Whatever women do, they must do it twice as well as men do to be thought half as good. Luckily this is not difficult.

Charlotte Whitton
Quoted in *Canada Monthly* July 1963

Nancy Astor, in a speech in Oldham, England in 1951, said: "I married beneath me. All women do." Another waggish witling, presumably of the same gender, declared "Of course God made man before he made woman. Any good artist makes a rough draft before he comes up with the masterpiece." Smart shoppers among cannibals prefer women's brains to men's brains. Why? Used brains are cheaper.

When one is the brunt of a disparaging quip, especially if it is clever and witty, it takes a better man than I am to join in the laughter. But if for a moment we can be honest, we must surely admit that we deserve the keelhauling we get, even when, as in the quotations above they are comic exaggerations. If we were to list all the antiwoman quotations men have put into print since Gutenberg made it so easy to do, they would fill volumes. If "mother" nature found purpose in doing so, I do not understand what that purpose could be; but she surely has given us machos one horribly inflated ego.

What the Roman Catholic Church has done to women (especially nuns) through the ages is offensive and unfair. Sexual harrassment and spousal abuse, are almost entirely a one-way street. It seems that equal pay for women will never be totally achieved. The same sweater, haircut, lube-job, car repair, etc., sometimes in the same place of business, will have a higher price on it if the customer is a woman. Although they deny it, Robert Bly, Bill McCartney, and their macho organizations have mounted what turns out to be a patriarchal cabal against women. The theme in most love-story movies is almost always that we men are doing women some magnanimous favor by agreeing to marry them. When *Harry Met Sally* or Carry Grant splashed mud on Doris Day in *A Touch of Mink*, both males ended up doing "the decent thing." Women in movies almost invariably play subservient roles.

390

Why should a few missionaries – sent from a nation of two-hundred years standing and ten-thousand miles away, the existence of which was hardly known among native peoples persuade foreigners to renounce five-thousand-year-old religions, governments, laws, and manners for the sake of their Christianity?

Martin E. Marty
Pilgrims in Their Own Land
Quoting a Unitarian (1822)

This quotation has been asked repeatedly. The fact that there is no intelligent answer has not in more than a hundred and seventy years changed the attitudes of missionaries. They still try to persuade much older and basically wiser peoples to exchange their entrenched cultures for their supposedly sacrosanct cosmotheism.

The fact that the Christianity they are trying to foist off on the natives has a history of countless murders during inquisitions, crusades, witch hunts, and heresy trials makes no difference. The enormous egos of members of the proselytizing religions has been all they need to induce them to travel halfway around the world to impose their nefarious conversions on whomever they please.

391

> Often in history we see that religion, which was meant to raise us and make us better and nobler, has made people behave like beasts. Instead of bringing enlightenment [to people] it has often tried to keep them in the dark; instead of broadening their minds, it has frequently made them narrow-minded and intolerant of others.
>
> Jawaharlal Nehru (1889-1964)

Nehru agrees that "In the name of religion many great and fine deeds have been performed." But he says also that "In the name of religion... thousands and millions have been killed, and every possible crime has been committed."

Gandhi was praised for his stand on nonviolence, convinced that it was the only way to rid India of colonialist Great Britian and to solve India's other problems. Then he would engage in one of the worst instances of violence that human beings have ever invented. I speak of fasting.

Gandhi, it was obvious, had little faith in the goodwill of India's colonialists. Yet when he fasted to get his way, he depended on the goodwill of the same people he had described as devoid of such valued and benevolent feelings - of approval, concern, and support.

If taking a human life is wrong as a means for political gain, it is always wrong. If human life is too valuable ever to be put unnecessarily in jeopardy, it is wrong even when it is one's own life, especially when used in the way Gandhi did.

Nehru was far more essential to democracy in India than was Gandhi, and he saved Gandhi's life more than once by talking him out of his insanity. The one time I remember anyone not yielding to the demands of someone fasting was when a few years ago Margaret Thatcher let fasting students die. I wonder if anyone in England has resorted to that means to get their way since that time.

Nehru gave India its start toward becoming a great independent country, and was one of the world's greatest leaders. If every developing country had its Nehru to help set it on a moral and economically viable course, the world would be in much better shape than it is. We wonder why his likes are so rare. Why do so many countries have to contend with the likes of a Pol Pot, Stalin, Hitler, Khomeini, Joseph McCarthy, Peron, Pinochet, Alfredo Stroessner, Somoza, Quaddafi, Castro, Mussolini, Idi Amin, and others. These leaders are the history we must remember if we are not to elevate their kind into positions of power.

392

It certainly is no part of religion to compel religion.

Tertullian (155-220)
Ad Scapulam

Blaise Pascal in Pensées said: "Putting religion into people's hearts and souls by force or menaces does not induce religion but terror." More generally, an old and still-perceptive refrain says: "A man convinced against his will is of the same opinion still."

The Christian hell is an inefectual invention. Like the capital punishment in some of our legal systems, it does not produce the results for which it was intended. Fear of God is another fruitless interpolation. We are terrorized by what we fear; we are not deterred from sinning. God's threats and menaces, as evangelists describe them to us, help us produce a neurotic society not an obedient one. Whenever a religious sect or denomination attains a majority position in a large community, the violence in their methods of proselitizing and gaining power is likely to increase. If they are able also to seize control of the politics of that community, there is little hope for minority religionists or opposing political party members to get a fair hearing on anything.

Several years ago, *Reader's Digest* described how one such Midwest community member explained to a new resident why his retail business was failing: "The people here are (name of a Christian sect); they stick together. You will do well to sell your business and leave. It hasn't the slightest chance of succeeding in this town." My own father had a similar experience in the small town in Minnesota where I grew up. The garage he opened was doomed to failure before it began. What should have been obvious to my father never entered his utterly unbiased and scrupulously impartial mind. The family "Dolan" was barely tolerated in a town where the population was mostly Scandinavian. My father never seemed to understand why his many well-planned efforts at assimilation into the community were usually thwarted. The prejudice that can permeate closed-minded communities is a formidable obstacle to overcome.

393

> Why religion is necessary, or has been necessary thus far in history, has something to do with its narcotizing effect on feelings of impotence and helplessness.
>
> Rainer Funk
> *Erich Fromm: The courage to be Human*

To understand that religion serves as just another mind-altering drug, one need only watch recent films of voodoo ceremonies in Haiti. The whirling dervishes of Turkey are another case in point. Films showing religious conversions in the United States are other examples. The proselytizing zeal and the resulting trips down the sawdust trail sponsored by the Billys Sunday and Graham of the world also show minds out of control among stadium-size audiences. That the human mind is a delicate instrument and can be narcotized by ranting pulpiteers is demonstrated daily in watching the electronic-media evangelists at work on the television screen. Testimonial letters and the millions of dollars sent in by television audiences attest to the effectiveness of these demagogues.

Oral Roberts and Pat Robertson, with eyes closed and using their telepathic vision can even talk to viewers across vast distances and cure serious ailments by remote, tele-divine control. The gullibility of television audiences watching home-shopping programs, and the effectiveness of television advertising must have given the increasing numbers of electronic holy-roller practitioners the idea for their own thaumaturgic antics. Some viewers have even written in to say that they have overcome cocaine, heroine, nicotine, and alcohol addiction by substituting the addiction of religion.

394

> A woman preaching is like a dog's walking on its hinder legs. It is not done well, but you are surprised to find it done at all.
>
> Samuel Johnson (1709-1784)
> Quoted in *Boswell's Life of Johnson*

Quotations like the above are enlightening. We learn something about how long the pompous Anglo-Saxon male has entertained his bigoted prejudice against women. There is not the slightest doubt in rational minds that women could always preach as well as men – and almost certainly better. Women's sensitivity, their greater acumen about social matters, and their more beautiful, penetrating voices makes preaching natural to them. If I have to be preached to, I would choose a woman to do it every time.

Prejudice, an unfair negative attitude, and discrimination, an unfair negative behavior, directed toward others different from themselves are horrors that have afflicted humankind as long as human history has been recorded. People who are by nature authoritarian and who are plagued with personal frustrations need someone they can blame for their problems. They find it easy to pile their hatred on any group of people different from themselves. Stereotyping the members of the group they have chosen as scapegoats is easy for them. Not reason, but suspicion and antipathy dominates their mental processes. Some become paranoid, sure the entire world is bent on tormenting them.

Cross-burnings, ethnic gangs, segregated schools, drive-by shootings, job discrimination can be cause or effect of their prejudices, something they create or something that influences them, according to which comes first. Prejudice feeds upon itself. It keeps people from getting jobs or education, and they become the brunt of prejudice for being lazy or ignorant. They are allocated the poorest land and then blamed for being poor, nonproductive farmers. Prejudice is one of the most common causes for homicide the world over.

395

A belief is not true because it is useful.

H.F. Amiel (1821-1881)
Journal

The mythology of religion, in ecclesiastical hands, is a sinister violation of the trust and confidence of the vast cadres of unsuspecting worshipers. It is a quagmire of deceit by means of which religious leaders protect a sinecure and augment a style of living. By concealing what is truly truth and what is in fact morality, pretense, hypocrisy, double dealing, imposture, and duplicity become the norm.

What is vulgar and base among theologians makes the news with sufficient regularity that it taints all religion. Lechery, hatred, cupidity, pedophilia, and drug addiction in the news have become so common that they no longer shock us; they only renew our profound disgust.

It is true that for the most part, whatever evil the average citizen does redounds to the shame only of that citizen, while what a preacher does stigmatizes all preachers. The face that religion turns to us is usually benign. Many theologians are meticulously decent, well-intentioned, and correct. Among themselves, at least, they find accord when they insist:

Religion promotes cohesion by bringing people of like mind together to generate harmony, charity, and peace. Religion develops an authority that is a deserving model for authority everywhere. Religion teaches us about divine purpose, so that we can understand what meaning is to be found in the grand scheme. Religion promises life after death, necessary to make our troubled sojourn on earth worthwhile. Religion instills in us a morality without which society would unquestionably disintegrate.

But what is the unvarnished truth about our formal religions? Instead of promoting cohesion, the sectarianism of religion divides us into factions that promote most of the strife that plagues the world. The world's despots have all made use of religion to further the rigid authority they hold over their subjects. The life-after-death that religion invents to give life meaning teaches us to despise the life we have. By its own example, religion instills in us prejudice, superstition, and hatred of foreigners, women, and homosexuals. The sacred scriptures that theologians try to convince us were written by deities are obviously the product of ancient ignoramuses who could not write one sentence to follow another with good sense, consistency, or literary style.

396

There have existed , in every age and country, two distinct orders of man – the lovers of freedom and the devoted advocates of power.
Robert Young Hayne (1791-1839) – Speech, Senate Jan 21, 1830

The lovers of freedom are those especially to whom freedom has been denied. They include the poor whose education is inadequate to extricate themselves from their poverty. Opportunities for fighting for the freedom they desire seem unavailable to them. Until the time comes that the deprived are allowed to share more equitably in the world's overflowing abundance, disaster threatens. We may become embroiled in a social upheaval as threatening as war and from which Homo sapiens might not emerge still a functioning, viable species.

When those who live on the margins of survival, threatened by hunger and the diseases of poverty, have nothing to lose, anything can happen. Those in power who do not understand what their oppressive measures breed will suffer a rude awakening.

The growing gap between the rich and the poor, with the wealth concentrated in fewer and fewer hands, must be reversed. Must be! If it is not, there will be insurrection the likes of which the world has not seen. The French Revolution will be a backyard skirmish in comparison.

The solutions to the problem are many, but one is paramount. As I write these words, Colin Powell and our living past presidents in the United States are meeting to face it. Powell, at least, understands that unless all children in this country are given every opportunity to get all the education they can absorb, we are in trouble. We have enough money to make education free to every young person who wants it - from kindergarden through four years of college. With planning we can do it easily.

First of all, we must be convinced that beyond all doubt it would be phenomenally beneficial for all our young people to receive education in trade schools and universities enough to make them fully functioning citizens, able to realize their full potential as contributors to human well-being. Then we must understand also that as a nation we have sufficient funds several times over to pay for the needed education. The "sacrifices" we would have to make are not sacrifices at all, but would all serve to improve our societies. How could this all come about:?

As an enlightened society we would begin to see that what our religions do for us is to teach us mythology, bigotry, superstition, deception, and hate. Knowing how harmful religions are to our societies, we will see the good that would follow if we converted them all into strictly educational institutions. With the structure now in place, the money and personnel at their command, they could teach all the trade and academic abilities needed for our youth to become happy, useful citizens. The many trillions of dollars religions have spent for churches, synagogues, mosques, radio and TV stations, all of their tax-exempt real estate would become the property of the educational system. Religious leaders, by whatever name they are called, would become teachers and other useful citizens – according to their considered choice. With a true morality (not based on fear, rewards, and threats) taught in our schools, crime (depravity of all kinds) would diminish, and with the improved congeniality among citizens, mental health would improve.

With a society of happy, well-adjusted, educated, working citizens, the ramifications would be so far-reaching that the benefits would be beyond imagination. Educated, busy people behave differently from people without purpose or prestige, many living in poverty.

Eliminating the gargantuan waste at the Pentagon, in government, and that incurred by misusing our environment are other sources of savings that alone could fund education, even if nothing else were done. Eliminating casinos, phony charities, counterfeiters, and Wall-Street embezzlers, who steal mostly from poor and lower middle-class people would leave us with billions more for education. Exorbitant campaign funding, pork-barrel spending, and on-line tax evasion cost us billions more.

397

It must shake our conscience that we become all the more inhuman the more we grow into supermen.

Albert Schweitzer (1875-1965)
Acceptance speech in Oslo – Nobel Peace Prize 1952

Just imagining ourselves to be supermen seems to be enough. We need not *be* supermen. Hitler' hordes of sychophants were not supermen – as their defeat in World War II proved. But infamously inhuman they became, nevertheless. Man's inhumanity becomes more infamous when it becomes more common and more matter-of-factly discussed, whoever's inhumanity it may be. This is why violence on television and in the movies does so much harm to mankind. Children grow up thinking violence is the norm, something to expect of their compatriates and, therefore, why not of themselves as well.

More and more they come to assume that they will not be censured harshly if they themselves resort to violence. If they rob houses or murder rival gang members, they are probably surprised to find they are sent to youth detention camps, or required to pay fines or do community services. Bible study does not help. In the Bible, children learn how frequently God kills, and how his favorites among human beings (Saul and David) destroy thousands. For children to find both God and parents lying to them cannot be an especially propitious way to launch them into a life of integrity either. The phony threat of death in Genesis 3:3 and the story of Santa Claus are not lost on children. Children are not as ingenuous as we like to think.

398

> Theology is the effort to explain the unknowable in terms of the not worth knowing.
>
> H.L. Mencken (1880-1956)
> *Prejudice*

"Theo" (a combining form meaning god); "logy" (science, doctrine, theory of). How can there be a science of God if God is the unthinkable, the hidden, the incomprehensible, the unimaginable, the indefinable, the inconceivable and the unapproachable. Science deals with the unobservable, of course, but its unobservable must have affiliation with the observable if it is to make sense. Maimonides, Otto, and many other practicing ecclesiastics, ask in effect that we simply accept that God "is" and admit that we do not know and will never know anything about Him.

That, of course, is the hope of all religious leaders – that we accept all of their pronouncements without demanding reason for accepting. It is their only hope! "Faith" (believing without evidence) is essential if religion is to survive. If a science or any other human discipline asked us to do the same, we would reject it without hesitation. True scientists would not think of asking us to believe something without massive corroborating evidence. They are fully aware that before their hypotheses, theories, or other tentative proclamations can be upgraded to be established laws of the universe, they must have acquired enough predictive content to make it absurd to continue to doubt their authenticity. Theology is different, as Mencken says. Theologians feel fully justified "to explain the unknowable in terms of the not worth knowing."

399

> As nations improve, so do their gods.
>
> G.C. Lichtenberg (1742-1799)
> German physicist, writer

Since the United States is in great need of improvements, and its "Christian" God is a total disaster, young people today may have an opportunity to watch Lictenberg's scenario unfold. If future leaders find ways to rid this country of its racial prejudice, its money-grubbing politics, its crime-ravaged gang activity, its poverty, its drug addictions, its xenophobia, its hate-engendering nationalism, and the wars we seem destined to incite or intervene in, we will improve radically. If medical science can find ways to prevent and cure cancer, AIDS, and the other diseases that plague us, we will be well on our way to an ideally perfect social order.

As a serene, able, and confident people, we will eliminate drudgery and foster a zestful enjoyment of life. If our educational systems can really begin to educate our youth to develop as useful, capable, civic-minded citizens, other improvements will follow automatically. We will explore space with spaceships now only dreamed of. The moon and Mars will become backyard terrain. We are told that we cannot set Venus on a course to convert its own atmosphere and surface into a habitable place for earthlings to live, but who knows the limits of technology and what our imaginations may dream up for the future.

Whatever mystical beings we choose to fashion will, of course, be better than those we have lived with these past millennia. We are wise enough to conjure up only gods we can live with in harmony.

400

> I hold that when a person dies / His soul returns again to earth
> Arrayed in some new flesh disguise /Another mother gives him birth.
> With sturdier limbs and brighter brain / The old soul takes the roads
> again..   John Masefield (1878-1967)

Dress a harridan in colorful silks, and she is still a harridan. Cloak hokum in beautiful rhyme and it is still hokum. Whether or not Masefield believed what he said in these six lines, I do not know. But what he said has been repudiated by a large percentage of the world's religious leaders since religions began. Souls, they tell us, go to heaven, not to another, a fetal, being.

Ninian Smart says on page 100 of *The Religious Experience of Mankind:* "According to the Buddhist view... Rebirth is not... to be pictured as the transmigration of a soul from one body to another. There is nothing that carries over from one life to another in this way." Most thinking people agree that all a person can pass on to future generations are his material possessions and the effects of significant deeds accomplished while alive.

Metempsychosis, also the passing of the soul at death into another body, if it differs at all from reincarnation, implies that the soul may better or worsen its position, and transfer from one species to another. The next time around it may end up in a macaque or it may advance to habitation in a future monarch. For a soul to find its next home in a snake is considered a very likely possibility. No one ever makes it clear what happens when the snake dies. Is there such a thing as commendable (friendly fanged) or reprehensible (less conscience than hips) levels of serpentine behavior?

401

For I believe that change during adult life is real and perpetual; significant change may be difficult to consolidate, but the capacity to change significantly during the adult life has become in this historical epoch increasingly necessary for emotional survival.

Robert J. Lifton
Thought Reform and the Psychology of Totalism

People can change, of course, but how many do change in significant ways? The religions most people carry with them to the grave are the ones they were born with. For them to have changed at any time along the way would have required that they think, and thinking is one thing most people are quite allergic to. They have acquired the religion they adhere to by osmosis – the way children learn language, and they are no more likely to rethink their religion than they are to forget their languages.

Brainwashing, according to Harold H. Anderson, professor of psychology at Michigan State, has been used in educating and conditioning children in our culture for hundreds of years. Such children are brought up in a sea of absolutes. Beliefs that have no substance whatsoever are foisted upon them without opportunity for rebuttal.

Children who are forced to accept everything they are taught soon become listless and indifferent. Their life lacks integrity, incentive, or purpose. Originality atrophies. They become society's automatons, who never add significantly to progress or reform. Only teachers with prodigious talents for persuasion can ever hope to convert them into effectively operating creatures of reason.

402

God cannot do an unjust thing because whatever He wills or does is therefore just, his will being the measure of justice.

Bishop Jeremy Taylor (1613-1667)
Ductor Dubitantium

Prabhupada in *The Science of Self-Realization says:* "The Bhagavad-gita is identical to Krishna; and because Krishna is the absolute and supreme personality of God, there is no difference between Krishna and His words." Charles Baudelaire in 1865 sets a similar trap: "My dear brothers, never forget that the Devil's cleverest ploy is to persuade you that he does not exist."

"Closed-loop sophistry," I call this kind of thinking in *Blind Faith.* It is the kind of "thinking" the people of Salem, Massachusetts used in their witch trials. If a woman protested that she had no supernatural powers capable of doing harm, it was her uncanny supernatural powers that were talking. The demons, devils, evil spirits within her were in obvious evidence simply by virtue of the fact that she was trying to defend herself.

Joseph McCarthy used this kind of "thinking" in his witch-hunts for communists. It is this kind of thinking dictionaries use when they define a word in terms of itself.

Closed-circuit functioning in computer technology means that there is some kind of malfunction causing the computer to go on repeating the same calculations endlessly. Inquisitions, human sacrifices, massacres, genocide, and wars result from this kind of closed-loop functioning, which passes for reasoning in the minds of those who use it.

403

Everything that is doddering, squint-eyed, infamous, sullying, and grotesque is contained for me in this single word: God.

André Breton (1896-1956)

Not very flattering of our Heavenly Father was founder of surrealism, was he? But Robert Ingersoll was worse. In describing the "God of the Pentateuch," he used such words as: "a false friend, an unjust judge, a braggart, a hypocrite and tyrant, sincere in hatred, honest in curse, false in promise, jealous, vain and revengeful, suspicious, ignorant, infamous, and hideous."

Both men had become sorely disillusioned, it is fair to say. From the God that is so highly praised from the pulpits, they expected more. From reading the Bible (God's Word) there is little doubt that every adjective Ingersoll used could be verified. We might even add a few of our own: cruel, irascible, capricious, impetuous, vengeful, and arbitrary. He was often vague. Always indefinable, untouchable, aloof, mysterious, and occult. He seems preoccupied more with self-aggrandizement than with justice and serenity. A still worse thought is that it is we, the human beings of this earth, that invented Him. We got the God we wanted, so we have no one to blame but ourselves.

404

No future life could heal the degradation of having been a woman. Religion in the world has had nothing but insults for women.

Dorothy Miller Richardson (1873-1957
Pilgrimage Vol. II Ch 24

Almost every woman who lives to Dorothy Richardson's appreciable 84 years can recount experiences similar to those of Ms Richardson. Unless they submit to being insensitive pawns, the experiences of all women are essentially the same. The patriarchs of the Judeo-Christian-muslim religions almost invariably have shown an intolerant refusal to deal fairly with women. Kierkegaard, a philosopher, evinced a machismo equal to that of these religious leaders. But then, Kierkegaard was a theologian in addition to being a philosopher. Erasmus, a milder misogynist than Kierkegaard, nevertheless, fabricates his allegorical female goddess "Folly," who, as he describes her, manages to turn all the members of her sex into effective namesakes.

We wonder that women do not repudiate all such ecclesiastics and their misogynic mentalities. Why do they abide the humiliation and vilification to which they are subjected? John Stuart Mill, who wrote *The Subjection of Women II* in 1869, seemed to think that if the human male could not in any other way defend his subjection of women, he would declare his bigoted point of view to be a God-decreed injunction.

There have always been a preponderance of human males who fail to realize that women are equally endowed, first-class citizens. Honest religionists admit that the Bible is an anti-feminist treatise, full of its writer's patriarchal intolerance. But in the improved atmosphere that exists today, women will accomplish more in attaining equality in the next fifty years than in all of past history. They still have a long way to go, but change is accelerating, and there is no way for our swaggering, virility-vaunting androcentrics to keep women in subjection any longer.

405

All wars are wars among thieves who are too cowardly to fight and who therefore induce the young manhood of the whole world to do their fighting for them.

Emma Goldman (1869-1940)
"Address to the Jury" - *Mother Earth*

In the same book, Goldman says" "Always and forever we have stood up against war, because we say that the wars going on in the world are for the further enslavement of the people, for the further placing of them under the yoke of military tyranny." In "The Social Aspects of Birth Control" in the same book, Goldman talks of that tyranny: "Send your sons on to me; I will discipline them until all humanity has been ground out of them; until they become automatons ready to shoot and kill at the behest of the master."

By 1923, Emma Goldman had become disillusioned of the promises of Russia and realized that there has never in world history been a good government; every government "is a dead weight that paralyzes the free spirit and activities of the masses." Not until every human being is free to plan his own way to a good and useful life can he be said to live under a beneficent regime. As a superpower today, it is absolutely essential that the United States does not start any war under whatever pretext. Every effort must be made to settle conflicts by diplomacy, and never to enter into any disturbance unilaterally. The United Nations, an expanded NATO, the World Court, and summit meetings must make it clear to all warring countries that wars solve no problems and do nothing but cause unspeakable harm.

406

[Beware of those who are] indifferent; they do not kill or destroy. But... because of their silent agreement, betrayal and murder exist on earth.

Bruno Yasienski
The Plot of the Indifferent

The real danger from those who are indifferent results from the fact that there are so many of them. Because of their numbers, indifference becomes the dominant factor in many situations. They distort the polls because they do not follow through with the answers they give to pollsters. Even if they themselves are not particularly prejudiced, superstitious, or immoral, they are no help in getting rid of race hatred, anti-Semitism, homophobia, pornography, psychic fraud, pedophilia, rape, poverty, AIDS, and crime – simply because they cannot be bothered. Their own personal affairs are their whole world. No one knows what to do to please them because they show no clear choices.

The reasons people are indifferent and the ways they show their indifference are many:

Even when crucial issues are at stake they show no affinity for them.
Some are unconcerned because they see no way that the issues involve them.
Some get stuck in impovershing routines that leave them without curiosity about things going on in the world around them.
Some vegetate and acquire no intellectual interest in things because they do not read or watch documentaries on TV, etc.
Some are indifferent because of an acquired apathy. They no longer relate to others.

Some have a personal conviction of their own superiority and do not
deign to associate with "common" people.

Young people sometimes seem unaware that they, too, will soon be
adults, and that they would do well to consort with those who are
older.

Some have interests, prejudices, superstitions, etc., that set them
apart They find they have nothing in common with people not like
themselves.

Some by nature or temperament are phlegmatic, impassive,
essentially incapable of sharing interest with energetic people.

Indifference is mankind's most intractable malady.

407

> When those whose religion has kept them obsessed with fears, beset
> with doubts, and cowering before religious authority suddenly find
> themselves born into a world of reason, they have the real "born-
> again experience." Their rebirth has nothing in common with the
> sudden conversion to obscurantism that Christian fundamentalists
> describe to us.
>
> Chester Dolan
> *Blind Faith*

Since the born-again experiences religionists speak of, a little like
toothaches, are restricted to the nervous systems of those "afflicted"
with them, there is not much that other persons can say or do about
them. The one response we might logically expect from those who
have had such experiences is that eventually they demonstrate some
measure of shame for having allowed themselves to be so totally
deceived by the freakish fancies that befell them. Surely the
"victims" of these "born again" experiences are not totally ignorant
of the currency of similar experiences in the minds of clinically
demented human beings. The literature, movies, even daily news
reports, are full of examples.

These instant born-again types of religious conversions that we
hear about more and more frequently in recent years must surely be
one of the biggest frauds in modern religion. Sensory stimuli from
without are not, in all instances, necessary to their propagation.

Something happening at the synapses of the brain may be all that is required. We know so little about what physically, electrically, and chemically goes on inside our heads that there is little we can do but wait for breakthroughs of scientific understanding. It becomes increasingly clear that the only hope for a return to sanity is to reject all mythologies and embrace only that which is simple truth.

408

> By the irresistible maturing of the general mind, the Christian traditions have lost their hold.
>
> Ralph Waldo Emerson (1803-1882)
> *The Conduct of Life*

There is no doubt about it, people today have a greater storehouse of knowledge than did people a century ago, and intelligence in the masses continues to increase, even if slowly. Christian leaders must see the handwriting on the wall: If there is one thing the entrenched religions cannot contend with, it is the increasing power of human minds to see through the deceit perpetrated by religious leaders. Martin Luther knew that well, which explains his ridiculous diatribe against "reason." Inevitably as people learn how shallow are the repertoires of religious ideas and observances in theological minds, they will repudiate religions. Religions will never disappear completely, but a day will come when their adherents will be limited to those with immature minds, those who cannot think their way out of the morass of religious superstitions and stupidities that now prevail.

There is hope for religions, of course. Religions can change. Although they do not yet demonstrate much inclination to do so, church leaders can rid themselves of their mythologies and decide that the aim of their preaching will be to increase morality, to rid societies of crime and all other instances of man's inhumanity to man. Their pageantry will be construed as delightful entertainment rather than sanctifications or exorcisms. Their music will be paeans to brotherhood rather than to supernal entities. Hell will remain as a useful epithet, and heaven will be useful in exclamations as a synonym for sky, but no one will take seriously their celestial existences in the cosmos. In short, humankind will opt for sanity rather than dementia in the conduct of its affairs.

409

> Religions are born and may die, but superstition is immortal.
>
> Will Durant (1885-1981)
> Ariel Durant (1898-1981)

Since religion, as it is conducted today, is little more than organized superstitions, it should be as immortal as the superstitions of which it is composed. Of course, individual religions as well as deities can die, and many have. This is what the Durants are saying, but the hope for a general elimination of religion is an illusion.

What the Durants say about superstition, I would more likely to say about prejudice. I have not for many years been able to think of a single superstition that I adhere to, but prejudice is another story. All too often some silly prejudice thrusts on my attention, and I can think of no possible excuse for it.

All of us, if honest, can name several subjects in which we are anything but experts. Yet we have opinions about these subjects. Sometimes we express firm opinions that we could not defend if our lives depended on it. If someone tells us we are revealing our prejudices, we may become incensed - even knowing full well that our accuser is right. With repeated experiences of this sort, we may learn to be more candid and unassuming, less prone to emotional response.

The concept "self-fulfilling assumption" may never be better illustrated than by the result of most black Americans and many white Americans (as recent polls show) believing that race relations are getting worse. To believe that, it seems to me is to react to intercultural relations in ways to impair such relations. As Clarence Page said on a radio program this morning, we should all think of ourselves as simply Americans. Only then can we rid ourselves of the one prejudice that overwhelmingly is doing our society the most harm.

410

> You say you believe in the necessity of religion. Be sincere! You believe in the necessity of the police.
>
> Friedrich Nietzsche (1844-1900)

The man with whom Nietzsche is speaking, we assume, was convinced that the excesses of human behavior needed some kind of restraint and was suggesting that religion could provide that restraint. Nietzsche implies that his conversationalist knew better, that both of them knew that orthodox religions could do no such thing. The controls on human behavior that are required, they both knew, could be provided only by an adequate and efficient body of trained men women entrusted with maintenance of public peace and order.

The supposition is that man is unable to discipline himself without the help of measures imposed by others especially commissioned for that purpose. Such an idea is not entirely without historical foundation. All but about the last ten thousand of man's three or more million years of evolutionary development have been spent in a general ambience of hostility. Even those ten thousand years have not all been smooth sailing. Without some organization of members especially trained in defense, it is possible that man would not have survived. There has long been a need for something analogous to today's police. There has never been a real need for theistic religion.

411

> Few men think; yet all will have opinions.
>
> George Berkeley (1685-1753) – Irish Bishop

Few men think for the simple reason that they are happy to let others do their thinking for them. They never have an original idea because they never dig down to basics and reason their way up to rational conclusions.

This kind of behavior is repeated for years on end until whole societies forget what are the roots of the precepts they live by. They never learn whether or not there was anything more to them than myth to begin with.

Religionists never furnish us with credible answers to such questions as: Does the God I worship really exist? Do wars really solve problems? Does capital punishment really reduce crime? Are there really guardian angels watching over me? Will ashes, wine and bread, shrines, icons, amulets, phylacteries, or wafers strategically placed really have influence over my well-being. Have babies really been born of virgins? Did Jesus' dying really have anything to do with my sins? Is your religion really the only true one? Are there really pronounced and significant differences between the races? Perhaps we need to ask and get a sensible answer to only one question: Is it ever wise for me to believe a thing when there is little or no evidence for believing that thing?

412

Political truth is a libel – religious truth, blasphemy.

William Hazlitt (1778-1830

"Religious truth is an idealized abstraction, says *Webster's New World Dictionary*. *The Times Literary Supplement (a* British Weekly*)* tells us that "the truths of religion are more like the truths of poetry than like truths of science." Neither idealized abstractions nor poetic truth need have anything to do with the world our proverbial five senses present to us. The truths of intuition, lacking the discipline of orderly reason or cogitation, is a better analogy. To depend on religious truth to guide us is to depend on the visions of our dreams or the counsel of mystics. Life would be a losing game if religious "truth" were allowed to usurp our freedom to think for ourselves and to think rationally.

Politics, too, makes a mockery of truth. To listen to politicians speak is always to keep our minds alert, trying to sift wheat from chaff. Freshmen politicians, idealistic and bent on reform, find it almost impossible to maintain good intent. They are swayed by lobbyists to favor legislation that they know perfectly well is not in our nation's interests. They are in affect constantly being bribed to do things which they would not do if what they propose to accomplish is only that for which they were elected and are being paid.

If we judge by punishments administered, we would have to agree that few or our government functionaries do anything wrong. Yet nearly all amass fortunes they do not earn. The answer to corruption is not new laws or legal threats, but a new morality with a sense of humanity, decency, and devotion to a new democracy. What we do not need are Senate "managers" and House hypocrites, but genuine statesmen to represent us. Partisan politics must give way to a sincere desire to do what best serves the nation. People generally must learn to recognize those motivated by greed, hate, revenge, hubris, homophobia, sexism, or racism – and vote them out of office or see that they never get into office in the first place.

To swim in an ocean of pollution is to become contaminated – unless we have an extraordinarily effective immune system. Not many of our congressmen manage to maintain independence of thought, unswerving honesty, and a conscience still fully in operation.

413

> She was a good Christian woman with a big respect for religion, though she did not, of course, believe any of it to be true.
>
> Fllannery O'Connor (1825-1964)
> *Everything That Rises Must Converge*

When we are willing to accept as true that which we know not to be true, we reveal something less than admirable about our own integrity and the integrity of our convictions. If we are to live with any degree of equanimity in this troubled world, we must believe that most of the people with whom we relate are relatively honest. We would like to believe that people generally cannot only see through the sham that is religion, but also acknowledge their atheism without discomfiture.

When Mencken tells us that even in the 1700s the fairy tales of Christianity were no longer taken seriously, why do we hear repeated constantly the statistic that today ninety-five percent of the people in the United States believe in God? No statistician can get into other people's minds, and we do wonder about the reliability of such percentages. Of course, Mencken cannot get into people's minds either, and perhaps he expresses what he would like to think is true rather than what is really true.

If polls err, the wise guess is that they err on the side of the politically and culturally correct and away from the logical. My own better judgment says that the 95% may be correct. It is better to believe polling results than be swayed by wishful thinking or our own limited personal experience. Especially in the present phase of the religion-sanity cycle, I see few signs that we are advancing toward sanity.

414

Man has no way of knowing whether his life continues [after death] or is forever annihilated; for death is the ultimate mystery.

George Christian Anderson Anderson
Man's Right to be Human

Anderson concedes that it is far more honest for a preacher to say that he has no certainty about immortality than for him to coerce his audience into belief with bribes, or to threaten them with hell.

If he and all other preachers were to be that honest about all the fabrications of religion, man would be liberated from the thrall of all theistic thaumaturgy. The problematic nature of the tenets and doctrines of religion obtains throughout. Preachers have no more reason to believe that God exists than they have that heaven or hell exist. Anderson, in saying what he does, admits that the Bible is not the infallible word of a deity. Unless he has been given some divine gift for knowing how to pick and choose, he therefore has no grounds for believing anything else he says about religions. Anderson personally does believe in immortality and in God's existence, the one presumably no more or no less than the other. Yet even he states without circumlocution: "What we believe will depend on how much we accept on faith." He knows as well as you and I do that to accept on faith means to admit that we will believe something without any scintilla of evidence for believing. Throughout his book we find him using phrases equivalent to one that appears on the third from last page of his book: "I know I am in the presence of God." He, of course "knows" no such thing, and neither do any of the other ecclesiastics foisting their monstrous myths on gullible congregations in all parts of the world. All the holy hang-ups with which preachers encumber themselves are the same: All are products of the tendentiously circumscribed imaginations that were initially and irreversibly warped by their theological-school educations.

415

> Belief and disbelief are beside the point. Make-believe is the game point in religious life.
>
> David L. Miller
> *Gods* and *Games*

John Spalding agrees: "Few really believe. The most only believe that they believe, or even make-believe." Make-believe is all right if we can keep in mind that what we do *is* make-believe. Playing games, by definition is fun, but we seem unable to keep our games in perspective.

Bridge ceased to be fun for me when I reached tournament level and found myself in a room with tables set up, cards all dealt out for the evening, a mechanical system of moving from table to table established, players never talking to each other, no one smiling, and surely an implied guarantee that international game points that came later in the mail were points of consideration for assignments in heaven.

In every sport I have ever attained a measure of ability, it has been the learning that I have found interesting. I lost interest when I found myself competent. The last place to find sportsmanship is at the Olympics. There is even less hope to find pleasure among professionals. The "killer instinct" seems to take over, with no holds barred.

Even as an officer in the Naval Air Corps, I found each increase in rank an increase in boredom. Never again in six years as a pilot did I enjoy myself as much as I did as a cadet at Pensacola going through the process of learning to fly. Now in old age I have devoted myself to riding a bicycle, thoroughly convinced that no vehicle was ever invented that is more practical and more fun to operate effectively.

Fun in religion, like belief and disbelief, is beside the point. David Miller develops his "game" metaphor in religion to an extent where it is somewhat preposterous. As in sports, the concept of make-believe disappears, and everyone turns his religion into life-and-death solemnity. Make-believe gods, angels, and devils become arbiters of a make-believe morality that has little or nothing to do with how we human beings get along.

416

> The time must come inevitably when mankind shall surmount the imbecility of religion.
>
> H.L. Mencken (1880-1956)

Few people today are predicting the end of religion. Religion will change, suffer cycles of prominence, but systems of belief in mythical beings with supernatural powers will continue long into the future.

Of course with Mencken setting no limit in respect to time, it is fair to say that it can happen (indeed must happen) eventually. Surely by the end of the present millennium man will look back to his ancient nescience – when he actually "believed in gods."

Richard Kyle in his 1993 book *The Religious Fringe* tells us that we are entering an epoch of intense religious activity. Pluralism is increasing – with an increase of bizzare religious eruptions. Education, in this respect has failed us, seemingly fomenting our attraction to absurdity. In Universities like Pat Robertson's "Regent" and Jerry Falwell's "Liberty," intolerance hate, bigotry, superstition, and prejudice make up the curriculum. In all our religious universities, young people are being educated in parochialism. Unless we do something immediately to alter the present trend toward religious hegemony, we may soon be replacing our loosely established democracy with a firmly entrenched theocracy.

Chapter XI

The Legacy of Religion

417

Religion's legacy is in the hands of men who do not understand how their behavior will affect the future of the human species. They may be highly gifted, even geniuses, but they do not see clearly the consequences of what they do to us. They seem unaware that their success so far is largely the result of concentrating religious proselytizing efforts among primitive and unlettered peoples. Those who succumb to their pleas are accustomed to superstitions and accept those of new religions without wrenching alterations to their mental equilibrium.

The world will not remain predominately populations of benighted savages. Education will eventually be available to everyone, and the world's people will see through the shallow precepts of religion and will demand more rational disciplines to guide them. Either religions will change drastically, or they will fade out of existence. As it is, they not only serve no useful purpose, they do a great deal of harm. They stifle progress and make of terrestrial lebensraum something of the hell that theologians warn us about. Fortunately, they do not have the influence they pretend to have, especially in pluralistic, multiracial countries. In countries with official state religions as in the countries of South America or in Israel, Pakistan, Afganistan, India, Bangladesh, Iran, Iraq, Saudi Arabia, Kuwait, etc., progress is slow and repression is evident. The next century should sort out some of the problems now becoming urgent, but for a long time yet we still have little hope for establishing a world in which reason will prevail.

418

No religion would be able to weather a sudden rash of genuine thinking on the part of the members of the congregation.

Chester Dolan
Blind Faith

Thinking implies judging, reflecting, considering, framing a purpose, or expressing intentions. To accept and repeat someone else's preformulated opinions requires none of that. Parrots can do that.

For a religionist to start thinking would mean for him to ask sensible questions: What does the preacher mean when he says Jesus died for our sins? God is love? The devil has a physical reality? Jesus is divine? Mary was a virgin? The Pope is infallible? Mary rose bodily to heaven? If a person gets no sensible answers to any of these questions, he has a right to doubt his celestial intercessor and to renounce his religion.

The Bishops of Peru for three hundred years preferred to keep their subjects uneducated and dependent. The members of their congregations were then easier to revamp as candidates for heaven. All religions depend on the perpetuation of this state of affairs. Heaven, too, must like its recruits ignorant, robotic, wishy-washy, unthinking, and easy to control. Alert, educated minds would not be able to endure the boredom that it seems would be the fate of those who make it to heaven.

419

So far as actual church membership is concerned, it has been gradually increasing through the years, even in proportion to population. But a high percentage of church membership in the total population has no apparent influence in reducing criminality in the community.

H.E. Barnes and N. Teeters
New Horizons in Criminology

Since the days of Barnes and Teeters, the dismal picture they paint has ameliorated somewhat, but we are a long way from where we want to be. To make a significant and lasting reduction of criminology in the United States will mean the expenditure of a lot more effort and money than has been the case up to now.

Recreational facilities for young people will have to be built to keep them occupied, off the streets, out of gangs, and possibly even learning things that will give them a better chance for gainful employment and a life of contributing to human progress. We can expect no help from the affluent religious organizations in the United States. They are too busy building large university campuses where students will receive a parochial education that equips them mostly for bigotry and tunnel vision. Science in their studies must be watered down to insipidity. To accommodate their "creation science," they must gloss over the marrow of archeology, geology, anthropology, biology, paleontology, astronomy, and nuclear physics. They must substitute faith for reason, ignorance for knowledge, puerility for maturity, and delirium for sanity. In a world increasingly dependent on good sense, orthodox religion will be left to the incompetence of the unalterably uninformed.

420

If cleaned up, shaved, and dressed in business suits, they could probably pass for television evangelists.

Tim M. Berra
Evolution and the Myth of Creationism

Tim Berra was speaking of the Neanderthals, and says they were not as brutish as is commonly thought. According to many biologists, both they and the Cro-Magnons were Homo sapiens, and, with some of the same kinds of changes that are still occurring, simply became us, so-called modern man.

Argument has arisen as to whether the two peoples, once they lived in the same areas of what is now France, Germany, and other parts of Europe, interbred. Those who deny such possibility, it seems to me, have not observed what always happens whenever related members of a species occupy the same areas. Many varieties of domesticated dogs are known to cross with wolves. I have no doubt that both wolves and domesticated dogs would cross with the wild dogs of Africa and the dingoes of Australia if they shared the same living areas. Even different species often cross, though the offspring are usually sterile. Mules and hinnies will occur naturally, and ligers and tiglons are seen in zoos. Anyone who has lived on a farm knows that the barnyard rooster is not at all fussy about what colors the hens he encounters are patterned with.

But Tim Berra's main concern was something else. We may deplore how Mary Baker Eddy and L. Ronald Hubbard profaned the word science in their "Christian Science," and Scientology," respectively. But their misusages are of little consequence in comparison to the perversion of the word in the paralogistic coinage "Creation Science." To speak of scientific evidence in support of creationism is to speak of scientific evidence in support of tea-leaf distribution, demon possession, prayer-wheel rpm, and spirit communication. Once a mind is capable of that kind of absurdity, it recognizes no limitations.

421

Of all the forms of injustice, that is most egregious which makes the circumstance of sex a reason for excluding one half of mankind from all those paths which lead to usefulness and honor.

Charles Brockden (1771-1810)
American Libertarian writer

Alice Walker, author of *The Color Purple*, said to the 10th National Black Lesbian and Gay Conference and Institute on Saturday, February 15, 1996: "Women have little voice in the Bible. [It says] the only thing that makes them worthwhile is the birth of a son." As she was quoted in *The Long Beach Press Telegram*, she urged women and blacks not to rely on the Bible to determine self-worth. She speaks of the Bible's blueprint to keep women and people of color in their place. Walker goes on to quote other examples of the Bible as disparaging of women. Many intelligent people today make it clear that if the Bible is God's word, they want nothing to do with such a God.

Women are not the only ones who get short shrift in the Bible. The Bible throughout is at odds with moral, logical, and impartial thinking. God's treatment of all human beings is appalling. From cover to cover, with few exceptions, the books of the old testament are mostly accounts of God's wrath and God-sponsored murders of hundreds of thousands of human beings.

422

> Is religious experience necessarily connected with a theistic concept? I believe not.
>
>   Erich Fromm (1900-1980) – *You Shall Be As Gods*

The theme throughout my book *blind Faith* is that one can be religious and not believe in gods or God. The United States Government agrees, and it ruled in favor of the Society of Separationists and the Secular Humanists to allow them the same tax exemptions as all other "religions." But because most people think immediately of some kind of Divine Supreme Being when hearing or reading the word religion, Erich Fromm's and my own previous position is difficult to maintain. In *Religion on Trial*, I have for purposes of tranquility, reversed my former position in this restricted context, letting the orthodox religionists have their way. My option is no longer to dwell on the matter except as it may come up naturally in the "comments" ending each of the 800 essays of this book. It is not entirely a matter of how we define terms. The pragmatic consequences must be considered. Fromm's solution, to coin the term "X-experience" to denote nontheistic religious experiences, is not helpful. It only confuses the issue more.

Once we throw off all the encumbering paraphernalia of theistic religions, we automatically becomes Fromm's "mature individual." We revert to the influence of actual things. Our new potential, humanness, individuality, and self-confidence help us to achieve our goals. We need not think consciously about becoming free, tranquil, open-minded, gregarious, alive, charitable and kind. We become so spontaneously when we learn to think for ourselves.

423

> Belief is the antithesis to thinking.... In being asked to believe without evidence, a [man] is being asked to abdicate his integrity.
>
>   Bergen Evans
>   *The Natural History of Nonsense*

Asking the members of congregations to abdicate their integrity is what pulpiteers are doing all the time. That is what reifying the concepts and abstractions of mythologies is all about. The first priority of theological schools is to eliminate all vestiges of integrity in their students (aspiring preachers), and then the second is to teach them how to do the same for those who, in future years, listen to their sermons.

Members of the church have the same two choices their preachers had as students in seminaries: They must relinquish all rights to think for themselves, believing without evidence everything they are asked to believe. Their only other choice is to leave the church to search for freedom to think for themselves elsewhere. If ever they find it, it will not be in religion. In religion, freedom to think for oneself is effectively suppressed. It cannot be allowed to interfere with the "faith."

Many early religions began with the efforts of despots to increase and secure control over their subjects. Truth as of no concern, and a dreamed-up domineering deity with absolute right to determine what would and what would not constitute moral behavior seemed ideal to any newly installed despot. In modern despotisms, which come into existence after local religions are well established, priests are often unhappy about changes they are expected to make in church procedures. Some refuse, and they are executed along with other citizens who do not kowtow to the new despot and his new directives. The downfall of despots, however, seldom arises from ecclesiastical opposition, but from popular insurrection. The masses simply tire of a life without freedom. The onerous restrictions imposed upon them make life not worth living. People with nothing to lose are an invincible army. The Taliban in Afghanistan and the Muslim fundamentalists in Algeria will eventually meet the fate of all oppressive regimes. No people can live entirely without freedom.

424

I myself have never seen a spirit or heard other-world voices, but there no longer seems any reason to doubt the veracity of those credible persons who insist they have.

Ruth Montgomery
Strangers Among Us

Once we accept the "veracity" of all such " "highly credible persons," this world will become so overburdened with imbecilities that we will as a species become intellectually immobilized.

Ruth Montgomery, once a respected syndicated columnist on political affairs, gave up her column to write on psychic matters. Her book *Strangers Among Us* reads more like a "cop-out." Her change of writing venue was like changing from vintage wine to root beer, from chateau to shanty.

Shirley MacLaine in her book and five-hour television program is another example of conversion from worthy celebrity to dubious distinction. Her *out on a Limb* [Ou*t*ing in Limbo] is a babbling accounting of her belief in reincarnation. To accept the notion of reincarnation is one effective way to reduce ourselves to mediocrity, unworthy of the one life we have. To read the accounts of Montgomery and MacLaine is to understand why we are not likely ever to get rid of theistic religions. Even good, discriminating minds sometimes leave an entranceway open for the ingress of fanciful and completely outlandish notions.

425

Maybe this world is another planet's hell.

Aldous Huxley (1894-1963)

Why not? Since hells in all probability do not exist except in the minds of those who have never learned how to put any kind of restraint on their wayward imaginations, hells can be whatever we want them to be. In popular conceptions, heaven and hell have become associated, respectively, with "up" and " down." This is strange, because all directions away from the earth are up. Of course, if we consider placing hell *inside* the earth, than it could be down. If it is, maybe we will find it yet. There cannot be many places left unexplored. Like the young lady who said why / Can't I look in my ear with my eye. / Perhaps I can do it / If I put my mind to it. / You never do know till you try! We might suggest she try mirrors. Now that we think of it, smoke detectors and mirrors might be just the thing to find hell. Alice of Wonderland fame found a mirror to be quite useful.

Huxley's speculation is a bit cynical, is it not? This world seems a pretty good place to me. If this is some other world's hell, however, by all means let us track down the planet that considers us such. Now *there* is a place worth looking for!

426

Those who believe in ghosts always see them.

Charles Victor Roman (1864-1934)
The Horoscope of Prince Ham

Those who go to Modjagorgia, Jugoslavia, and other places where a total of more than a thousand visions of the Virgin Mary have been seen, often themselves see visions of the Virgin Mary. Inflexible belief (often called blind faith) is enough sometimes to start the brain processes that will lead to visions. It should be understood that agreeing that the thousand visions may all have been authentic is quite a different thing from agreeing that there was anything "out there" beyond the viewers to be seen. We have no way of knowing if what we see is the result of stimuli bombarding our sense receptors from without or is fabricated entirely within the cells of our brain. The vision we see can be just as clear and "authentic" in one case as in the other.

Roman's ghosts are the same. Certain houses get a reputation for having ghosts – so the people who go there to see them often do. We who doubt as strongly as the others believe do not have a ghost of a chance of seeing ghosts.

The word "always" in Roman's comment, suggests that there was metaphor in Roman's madness. Since I will probably never get a chance to see *The Horoscope of Prince Ham*, I assume that I will never know.

427

To die for an idea: It is unquestionably noble. But how much nobler it would be if we died for ideas that were true.

H.L. Mencken (1880-1956)
Prejudices

Martyrs, and those who coax or force them into martyrdom, prove nothing but how passionately they believe what they believe. For truth to be established by martyrdom makes an unwarranted assumption of infinite wisdom on the part of the martyr or his patron. To die for a son of God, a divine potentate, the virgin Mary, a revered saint, or the one-and-only true religion is to make fatuous assumptions about trinity, divinity, or virginity, about sainthood or sanctity.

When in 1972, five Christian missionaries were killed by the Waodani of Ecuador they were not martyrs. They were trespassers meddling in other people's affairs where they were not invited and had no right to be.

428

His truth endureth to all generations.

Psalms 100:5

As the quotation above uses the word, truth becomes a vague, ineffable something "out there" that someone considers desirable, but that no one can define. As used in the Bible, the word truth varies in meaning from one context to the next. It has no ostensive referents and does not even refer to other symbols.

The word truth used sensibly says something about our symbol systems, about the language we use – about the statements we make. Truth is not a consideration until someone says something, and then we are talking about whether what was said corresponds to what we know to be the case.

The guest at lunch with the friend she is visiting says, "I'm stuffed, I ate three bagels." Her friend said, "You ate five, but who's counting." The hostess baked the bagels, set the table, and knows the truth. What the guest said is not truth. The truth was not in her... just the five bagels.

Truth is always just that, symbols accurately representing reality. If the word truth is to contribute to communication, it most always be used in that way: a map that is a worthy representation of a territory. A biography tells facts in a person's life and nothing but facts. History, if it is truly history, tells what actually went on.

"His" truth is meaningless. Truth is not a thing to be owned; it describes a relationship. "The truth might make us free" as the Bible says it will, if anyone could really figure out what the Bible writers mean by their word truth.

429

My opinion is that there would never have been an infidel, if there had never been a priest.

Thomas Jefferson (1743-1826) – Letter to Mrs. H. Harrison Smith

Theologians attending to the demands of their occupations are obliged to live in a state of denial. Their very existence depends on their never admitting that most of what they say, when analyzed, is pure duplicity. They pretend that they have a direct pipeline to God and that God is constantly advising them in ways that simple logic tells us is not true. They pretend that they have proof that God, satan, devils, and angels exist when they know perfectly well that there is no such proof. They pretend that the Bible is God's word while there is no evidence whatsoever that that is so. It would require several gods who had never collaborated with one another to have said all the things the Bible proclaims.

Theologians repudiate the gods of other religions even though the existence of such gods is every bit as plausible as the existence of their own implausible deity. Christians cannot accept Allah, of course, because Allah denies the divinity of Jesus. Jews, Christians, and Muslims all approve of scriptures that approve of slavery and all concur in their refusal to accept women as equals, treating them as second-class citizens.

Atheists find no reason to believe in God. Agnostics do not know and withhold belief. Freethinkers are doggedly rational. Unbelievers repudiate faith. Infidels are Muslims when Christians are applying the labels. They are Christians when Muslims do. Every religion uses the term to mean all those who do not belong to their religion. Everyone in the world is an infidel to someone.

430

By the middle of the twentieth century men had reached a peak of insanity. They grouped together into primitive nation-states, each nation-state condoning organized murder as the way to deal with international differences.

Joan Baez
"Farewell Angelina"

We might be able to eliminate wars from this entire planet if one simply worded amendment were attached to every constitution of every country in the world. That amendment would say that the military leaders of the country could put no restrictions whatever on televisions reporters of every country from reporting any and all military actions on any field of battle anywhere.

We have our warmongers and probably always will have, but we have peacemongers too, and Joan Baez is one of them. No one has made a count, but the peacemongers surely outnumber the warmongers many times over.

When foreign correspondents brought film after film back to the United States showing the atrocities being committed in the Viet Nam war, the public became outraged. It was that outrage that stopped the war, not tactical decisions of the generals.

If the Viet Nam war taught us anything, it taught us that the peacemongers are pretty effective if somehow they can get graphic television pictures of what is going on in any military conflict. The amendment I propose would assure the public of all countries that they would have detailed information of the arson, rape, and carnage of every war. That is enough! The peacemakers would never again allow our senseless wars to continue. If anything about politics has been confirmed in recent years, it is that no governments, despotic or otherwise, can thwart the wishes of the vast majority of the people of the country they rule. With street demonstrations against the ongoing war by almost all the people in the country, the warmongers would have no choice. They would have to stop the fighting.

431

We still wonder at the stolid incapacity of all men to understand that women feel the invidious distinctions of sex exactly as the black man does those of color, or the white man the more transient distinctions of wealth, family, position, place, and power: that she feels as keenly as man the injustices of disenfranchisement.

Elizabeth Cady Stanton
Susan B. Anthony
Matilda Gage
History of Woman Suffrage

We men "intellectually" understand (at least many of us do), but then do not become sentimentally or emotionally involved to a degree that impels us to join the women in their just causes. The failure of the Equal Rights Amendment to become a part of our Constitution redounds to the shame of every misogynist in the country. To read the history of how obstinate President Wilson was in confronting the women demonstrating in Washington D.C. is to see ourselves and how unjust we can be vis-à-vis women in our relations with them.

The history of machoism is a sordid blot on the reputations of men since time immemorial. Physically we are larger and more muscular than women, but to point that out as a reason for our warped behavior is to point to ourselves as bullies, hardly a characteristic we can be proud of.

The *History of Women Suffrage* by the three authors listed above is one account of the human male's inhumanity to the human female. The struggle was a long one and included several thousand women. It took the entire adult lives of Elizabeth Cady Stanton and Susan B. Anthony, and they did not live to see what they fought for reach its final goal. Elizabeth Stanton raised seven children before she reached her stride in the quest for woman suffrage, but she stood along side of Susan B. Anthony, her lifelong friend through it all. Matilda Gage, coauthor, is not so well known, but she too, along with many, many others contributed greatly to the campaign.

432

[Reason] projects a better future and assists men in its realization. And in its operation is always subject to test in experience.

John Dewey (18591952)
Reconstruction in Philosophy

The "better future" Dewey speaks of depends on people reasoning their way through from obscurantism to intellectual candor and open-minded inquiry. Until people generally learn that progress depends on rational processes, we will not have progress. To allow the religinists of the world to immerse us in the morass of stultifying mysticism is to give up hope, probably to condemn the humans species to annihilation.

What the preacher says does not relate even vaguely to the real world in which we live. Reason, that is, is nowhere in evidence in the formation of his utterances. He teaches the faithful to live in accordance with his lies and inspires them to fear science more than purgatory. He teaches them to hear only what they are expected to hear, read only what they are told to read, and say only what the church allows them to say. He even tells them how to think and whom they may call friend. The "sacred beliefs" he keeps harping on, he implies, are beyond criticism, and anyone who dares to suggest that they might not be sacrosanct is headed straight for hell. Until we learn to subject our thinking to the rigor of reason without recourse to prejudice and superstitions, we are not going to become the species we want to be.

How can reason, by its very nature quiet diplomacy and logic, compete in a world, saturated with hyperbole and bombast? How can it hope to eclipse the glare of the fundamentalists burning books? How can it restrain the Bible thumpers threatening an eternity in inferno to all who do not adhere to their version of virtue? How will it contend with the power-hungry religious demagogues who seem on the verge of establishing a theocracy in every country in the world? Where does sanity find a platform from which to be heard that will equal the insanity broadcast from radio and television and printed in newspapers and magazines? What can reason do to moderate the sorcery emanating from altar and pulpit? The voice of irrationality is arrogant, relentless, and seemingly overpowering. If the voice of reason is heard, all the forces of Christendom combine to mock and muffle its words.

433

Missionaries are sincere, self-deceived persons suffering from meddler's itch.

Elbert Hubbard (1856-1915)
The Roycroft Dictionary and Book of Epigrams

Hubbard has pegged them well, covered the ground beautifully. Self-deceived is the adjective perfectly attuned. Without a thorough self-deception, missionaries could not be sincere, nor would they be so bent on meddling in other people's affairs. Their self-deception derives especially from their conviction that God has chosen them to do what they do. Self-deception is contagious. If the leaders have the disease, they are almost sure to infect the whole tribe. In theological schools the germ is now permanently entrenched. Within their walls, almost none of their students will escape the infection. They all seem to graduate completely convinced that spoken words and finally a piece of paper with words inscribed on it has transformed them into an order of theologues, immune to human frailty. They separate themselves categorically form ordinary mortals who were not educated in religion's sacred halls – where some of the best and most humanely oriented of our youth were paralogistically "ordained."

Dr. Frankenstein created a monster, and Dr. Jekyll learned how to turn himself into one. What the theological schools turn loose on societies are to be feared far more than that which the Doctors Frankenstein and Jekyll created. Theologians look so much like sane human beings that they catch us unawares. There are so many of them, they can do much more harm than whatever imaginations like those of Mary Wollstonecraft Shelly and Robert Louis Stevenson can come up with. If humanity survives religion as it is now constituted that will be the true marvel of the millennia.

434

It is the superstition of medicine that is responsible for all the health cults of modern times.

Stephen S. Wise (1874-1949) – American Rabbi

Wise goes on to suggest that it has been the superstition of religion that has given rise to all the religious cults throughout time. All religions are elaborately organized superstitions whether they are new or old and deeply entrenched in their communities. The new religions, like new pledges and recruits of fraternal and military organizations, often suffer indignities during initiations or while becoming established. The names of a few of these religions that have appeared in recent years are:

The Children of God, The Jesus People, The Christian Foundation, Peoples Temple, Christ Commune, Catholic Charismatics, The Unification Church, The Divine Light Mission, Branch Davidians, Transcendental Meditation, Hare Krishna, Subud, Christian Base Communities (essay 458), Witchcraft, Satanism, The Aquarians, The Process, as well as the Heaven's Gate group of 39 adults who committed suicide as described in essay 535.

With the possible exception of Transcendental Meditation, which, in its early, lower level of indoctrination, did not claim to be a religion, the modus operandi of these eighteen creeds seem so transparent that one finds it difficult to believe that their leaders are not fully aware of the deceit they are perpetrating. But the same is true of the old religions.

Who is to say that the new religions are any more or less deceitful than the old religions. When Christian fundamentalists attack new religions, it may well be a case of pot calling kettle black. None seems able to give anything like a definitive description of practical goals. For most, the search for a new religion is the search for a superficial diversion, acceptable only so long as it demands no mental effort, no true creativity. The search would not appeal to thinking human beings.

The fact that these new religions can find adherents should no longer surprise us. Even people who long ago have given up anything resembling original thinking are left with a remarkable capacity for parroting. These mimicking multitudes are still adept at using the head of others even if they no longer know how to use their own.

435

> What is wanted is not the will to believe, but the wish to find out, which is the exact opposite.
>
> Bertrand Russell (1872-1970)
> Sceptical Essays

The will to believe is nowhere lacking. An account of the superstitions that are accepted without question would fill volumes. The 11,000 religions that the world lists in its registries are only a beginning. There is nothing that free-wheeling imaginations can dream up that is too fantastic for someone somewhere to believe. And the harm that indiscriminate belief does is incalculable. Felix Adler in a lecture titled "The Chosen People" given on December 15, 1978 said: "It is necessary to assail the towering superstitions of the day, painfully necessary, not only because they are absurd, but because they are immoral, because they tend to degrade mankind and to brutalize him."

Substitute an ardent desire to find out the reasons or causes for events that go on about us, for our readiness to believe without evidence for believing, and the world will be gloriously improved. Education is the cure for our ever-increasing accumulation of false knowledge. Sound, practical, unbiased education about the true nature of the world we live in is the answer to the flood of superstitions that threatens to overwhelm us. If we do nothing, our fate is failure. The mythmongers will have won. They will leave us all living in one vast ocean of deception and despair, with no place to turn for help.

436

> He is opposed to the death penalty for murder, but he would willingly have anyone electrocuted who disagreed with him on the subject.
>
> Thomas Bailey Aldrich (1836-1907)
> "Leaves from a Notebook" – *Ponkapog Papers*

Aldrich expresses a certain measure of truth, of course: Abstract concepts when applied to specific incidents happening to ourselves may be seen quite differently.

The principal lesson that capital punishment teaches is that life has little value. Murdering another human being, we are convinced is not so bad after all. Even the State can do it without qualms of conscience. If it suits its purpose, the State can even ignore the fact that statistics show that capital punishment is of no avail. The all-too-human satisfaction that vengeance gives us is the only thing that can be said for it. Vengeance is a primitive emotion that is to be expected of children. It should not be a consideration for sane, adult human beings. The Judeo-Christian-Muslim God, of course revels in vengeance, but He, too, commonly behaves like a badly spoiled child.

Jose Ingenieros in *El Hombre Mediocre* says that all human life is valuable, if not for anything else, for a study in contrasts. René Dubos in *So Human an Animal* says: "Each human being is unique, unprecedented, unrepeatable." Both remind us that we have for study a human being like few others. Like the peculiar kind of "weed" we have typically destroyed, do we know for sure that someday we may not find that it has medicinal qualities that will save many lives?

The human being, so far as we "know" is the most advanced entity ever produced. It is ourselves that we should be anxious about. We have evolved into a remarkable animal. But casual observation shows us we have a long way to go. Catering to primitive instincts is regression not progress. Whenever we see ourselves behaving irrationally, we should be making plans to eliminate, not encourage such behavior. Capital punishment is a sadistic stain on our history, and many thinking people think it should be eliminated.

437

> Religion is an illusion of childhood, outgrown under proper education.
>
> Auguste Comte (1798-1857)
> *Views of Religion*

Religion is an illusion of childish minds, not just of childhood. Many of those minds belong to adults. Comte suggests that the harm done by miseducation can be undone. Proper education can help eliminate instilled superstitions, but the road to complete freedom from religion is long and rough. A self-taught recognition of the nature of religion's tangled web of misinformation and prevarication will be a big step forward. Thoroughly understanding the sham that is religion will take some time.

"An honest man is the noblest work of God," said Robert Burns, Samuel Butler, and Robert Ingersoll – each in his time. The "honest man," so rare that even Diogenes searched in vain for him, would indeed be noble, but he will not be found in the shadows of God and religion. Even a modicum of "intellectual honesty" would be so tremendously useful in convincing others to accept one's personal point of view that theologians must lament the fact that the quality is not available to them. For them effective oratory is expected to compensate for their lack of integrity. Television evangelists are content to find that they can attract large audiences without the slightest concession to honesty. Strict honesty for preachers would be an insurmountable handicap they cannot accept. The myth and fable they declaim substitutes to lure listeners. As André Gide says, "It seems as if the mind enjoys nothing more than sinking deeper into error." Robert Oppenheimer believes that man prefers absurdity, is, in fact, fascinated by it. Stanislav Andreski tells us that it is not in the nature of man to consider truth of any great value. Religion for the people who subscribe to it is a comfort. That is all they want or need. Being a citizen of a progressive community is not one of their concerns.

438

Our universe may not care anything about us, but by the same token it does not nourish any grudge against us.

J.H. Holmes
The Sensible Man's View of Religon

The universe is indifferent, not capable of caring about us one way or another. Teleological explanations, common though they may be, are false explanations. There is not now nor has their ever been the slightest evidence that the universe can dispose or propose, that purpose plays any part in the goings on beyond the nervous systems of sentient beings. The universe has not motive nor means, and produces no intended effects. The universe just is, that is all, of course with much happening, controlled by the laws of the cosmos, probably now mostly known. The universe is not out to get us nor to favor us. We, of course, have had nothing to do with creating the universe, but we have everything to do with the culture imposed upon our small part of it. We must make every effort to improve the ways we do what we do. We are in control, as Sartre says, "responsible all the way."

Once we learn this, we will know that we cannot leave problems for celestial or mysterious forces to solve. We, ourselves, must fight our way through. We will learn patience and persistence, and above all we will accept personal accountability for our own destinies.

439

It is a very lonely life a man leads, who becomes aware of truths before their time.

Thomas Brackett Reed (1839-1902) – Speech 1899
Quoted by William Alexander Robinson
Thomas B. Reed, Parliamentarian

It is equally lonely not to have given up egregious untruths long after they are known for what they are. Some of the truths that give us troubles that are not yet generally acknowledged are:

Theistic religions are a relic of ancient idolatries, sorceries, and mysticisms. Their evolution is not difficult to trace and accounts for the sorry state of religion today.

Heaven, hell, and all their occupants are figments of human imaginations and have never had existence beyond such imaginations. Guardian angels, malicious devils, or intervening gods do not exist, and no one has ever offered the slightest real evidence that they do.

So far as innate moral predilections are concerned, human beings everywhere are pretty much the same. Yet all of us pick out certain other people whom we deem as mentally or physically inferior to ourselves and choose to despise them. Why we do so is never completely explained. It has something to do with our education. As the song in *South Pacific* says, "You have to be taught to hate." Nearly all prejudices are instilled into human nervous system bit-by-bit from intended or inadvertent counsel of parents, peers, or teachers.

Belief, when there is no evidence for believing, fear when there is nothing to fear, trust in magic as if it were actually the way things go, interpretations of unexplained happenings as supernatural, acceptance of superstitions as if they were rational events, attitudes, or explanations – all are extremely harmful to world societies.

440

A man may condemn a good book through envy, lack of judgment, or foolishment, but Man cannot.... A good book will go down to posterity even if all the critical judges should combine to cast suspicion on it.

George Christoph Lichtenberg (1742-1799)

Books that criticize religions meet with obstacles that Lichtenberg could never have imagined. Many books do not reach a point where they can be condemned for any of the reasons given in the quotation above. The gauntlet of obstacles is such that without any doubt many good books *do not* "go down to posterity" whether or not a cabal of critical judges combines to cast suspicion on them. In the first place, writers of books such as this one cannot find literary agents willing to help them with publication. Even if they agree with all of the author's contentions, few agents dare face the imprecations hurled at them from the centers obscurantism.

The Jerry Falwells and Pat Robertsons of the world have enough influence with the publishers of university and high school textbooks that many worthy books never see light. With a kind of literary blackmail, they and school-board authorities have control even over non-textbook publishers. The also convince many libraries not to provide space on library shelves for books officially condemned by Christian fundamentalists such as the Christian Coalition. Bookstore chains who now sell most of the nation's books is another important target for their "persuasions." They largely dictate what publishers will publish, what people will read, how all of us will be educated.

When forty-four books were banned by a federal judge in Alabama, not because they said anything against religion, but because they didn't say anything in favor of religion, we are approaching the total control fundamentalists are seeking. The next and final step is the political control required to make all their caprices law. When that happens, we can kiss all of our cherished freedoms goodbye.

When a university with its press limits the range of ideas it will consider for punblication, it makes a mockery of the *universus* from which its name derives. Sociey, by tolerating their censorship, condemns itself to mediocrity

Book reviewers, who have a life-or-death control over what books will be available to readers, refuse to review books that do not conform with traditional patterns of acceptable ideas. They know that if they were to review "satan's" books, all the ire of Christendom would descend upon them. Prometheus could find no reviewer who dared to review my book *Blind Faith*, which they published in 1995.

Even if a book were to vanquish all the hurdles mentioned above, it is not home yet. Book burners give anti-religious books special attention. They disappear from library shelves more than any others. The stranglehold that the "good Christians" of our country have over our societies is an awesome spectacle. For them, no holds are barred. Their "ends" justify any conceivable "means."

441

Mike Royko, editorialist for the *Chicago Tribune*, and Fyodor Dostoyevski, author of *Crime and Punishment*, might have been good friends had their birth dates been separated by 4 not 104 years. Mike said on March 6, 1971: "We've discovered that while execution satisfies a craving for revenge, it doesn't do much to reduce the murder rate. If anything the murder rate has gone up in States that are frying the most criminals."

In the century between the lives of Dostoyevski and Royko, another voice equally perceptive was heard. Sir Compton MacKenzie, an English novelist, said: "Unless [a] man... is to be given a chance of expiation in another life, then punishment is a damnable horror." MacKenzie's "unless" clause, can serve as an excuse for no one. No one knows that any such chance for expiation is likely. The odds are that it is not.

To me it seems inevitable that before long we will have a federal law or a constitutional amendment against capital punishment. Except for the vengeance we all at times seem bent on, it has nothing to say for itself. A few minutes before I wrote these words, Ann Richards, recent governor of Texas, said that very thing on the television show *Politically Incorrect*, moderated by Bill Maher. She also said that capital punishment costs taxpayers more than does life imprisonment.

442

Theologians, like professional wrestlers, must never, never for a moment admit to anyone that they have knowingly dedicated their lives to a consuming farce. For them to be honest about what they are doing, would be to destroy two of the world's most lucrative and popular of theatrical events, both at present in ascendancy in the United States.

What exactly is it that the prospective preacher can learn in a theological school? Presumably, he already has a fervent desire to do good. He has his Bible and is able to read it, capable of separating nonsense from sense and more likely to do so if not subjected to the indoctrination of monomaniacal seminary instructors. He certainly does not need years of education to learn what Jesus had to say. All the authentically credited words spoken by Jesus would fit nicely into a small pamphlet. A few weeks of study would make him a Jesus expert. What then can a theological school teach him?

The only thing left for him to learn is what all successful theologians learn. He, too, must be instilled with the preoccupying passion and the skill and grace that make it possible for him "to stand before a large group of people and lie with a straight face, without the slightest twinge of conscience or even the slightest sense of deviating from what in sane societies is considered sane behavior." That's it! Whatever else he needs to know he can learn better by self-study or in the more liberated atmosphere of a good university. When he can recite all the mummeries about dreamed-up supernal entities and their mythological abodes, he is "ordained" – thoroughly equipped to stand before congregations and mesmerize them. If he began his resolve to become a preacher with more than a whit of integrity, bit by bit his mentors have managed to liberate him from that inconvenience.

What Lincoln says in the quotation above is obvious, is it not? We are lying when we attribute truth to assertions which can in no way be shown to accord with facts. Such assertions, as many besides Lincoln have understood, brands religion as a fraud. A preacher, when he speaks as a theologian, and often when playing the role as sociologist, makes statements which he knows very well neither he nor any else can verify. For most people, that is lying. The preacher has no special dispensation from rules that apply to everyone else.

443

From the nineteenth-century view of science as a god, the twentieth has begun to see it as a devil. It behooves us now to understand that science is neither one nor the other.

Agnes Meyer (1887-1970)
Education for a New Morality

Herbert Spenser says that science is organized knowledge. T.H. Huxley tells us that science is nothing but trained and organized common sense. David Hume speaks of science as a method. George Santayana said that it is none of these. "It is a body of changing, learned opinion, aspiring to be true. There are certain facts about nature and history; our grasp of these facts [science] is constantly changing." Einstein defines science as "the attempt to make the diversity of our sense experience correspond to a logically uniform system of thought." Jacob Bronowski defined science as "the organization of our knowledge in such a way that it commands more of the hidden potential of nature." Congressman Rush Holtz, physicist, says: "Science is learning how to frame questions so you can test yourself and test your propositions." Leszczynski Stanislaw, King of Poland, says: "Science when well digested is nothing but good sense and reason. Emerson said in his *Journals*: "The religion that is afraid of science commits suicide."

I prefer to think of science as an attitude. When we think of an age of science, then, we will not be talking about scientific techniques, or scientific results, but of an attitude. When this attitude is well ingrained, all of our observations will be carefully and honestly interpreted and verified. We learn more accurate ways to talk about things, and do not try to reconcile the unreconcilable. To try to defend the deities and doctrines of religion, as we know, is an exercise in futility. "Some who call themselves scientists,' Mencken says, "cannot shake off the piety they absorbed with their mother's milk." They still try to reconcile science and religion. Some theologians are still trying to interpolate the good sense of science into the nonsense that is religion, but they fail to make their religion more plausible. Too much of the nonsense of religion has become impenetrable."

444

> Let us not tell ourselves a comforting tale of a father in heaven because we are afraid to be alone, but bravely and cheerfully face whatever appears to be the truth.
>
> Richard Robinson
> *An Atheist's Values*

The word comfort comes up repeatedly when explaining religion. Richard Robinson elsewhere in *An Atheist's Values* says: "The main irrationality of religion is preferring comfort to truth." F.S.C. Northrop suggests that we might call the so-called truths of religion comforts. A Bishop quoted by Robinson said "The number of those who need to be awakened is far greater than those who need comfort." Too many of us become so encapsulated in our own small comfortable world that we lose all incentive to make our lives meaningful.

Progress is usually the result of the effort of valiant people for whom comfort was not imperative. Were comfort all-important in their lives, women would not have babies, men would not explore jungles, children would not choose to be educated. If comfort were all-important in their lives, Jane Goodall would not live with chimpanees, Dian Fossey would not have lost her life in 1985 defending her friends the gorillas of Africa. Robyn Davidson would not make *Tracks* across Australia in the Company of three camels. Farley Mowat would not camp with wolves. Rosa Lee Parks would not sit in a restricted area in a bus. Yitzhak Rabin would not shake hands with Yasir Arafat. Mother Teresa would not nurse derelicts in Calcutta. Comfort is often the enemy of that which makes our world a delightful and exciting place in which to live.

445

> There is on earth among all dangers no more dangerous thing than a richly endowed and adroit reason.... Reason is the devil's bride and God's worst enemy. It must be deluded, blinded and destroyed. Faith must trample underfoot all reason, senses, and understanding.
>
> Martin Luther (1483-1546)

Faith (the cover-up for religious nonsense) tramples underfoot reason (the power of thinking in an orderly, rational way). Here is clearly stated the pathological fear that nonsense has for good sense. Like firefighters sniffing out the incipient sparks of a possible ten-thousand-acre forest fire, the votaries of nonsense must be relentless in extinguishing the first hints of logic intruding on the sophistry of religion.

William Kaufmann translated the words of Martin Luther in the boxed quotation above from number five of the twenty-four volume *Samtliche Schriften* printed in Germany in the eighteenth century. They appear in his book *The Faith of a Heretic (1961)*. There is no dearth of materials comprising an intelligent response to the deceit that religionists have been trying to foist upon us for centuries. Reading Kaufmann's book published by Doubleday and other books published by Prometheus is more than anyone will need in order to become a rational human being. It is sad to think that most people prefer to be deceived rather than to make that effort.

446

Where it is a duty to worship the sun, it is pretty sure to be a crime to examine the laws of heat.

John Morley (1838-1923)
Voltaire

To label a thing scrosanct, is to place it beyond the light of scientific inquiry. Galileo nearly lost his life for giving the sun too prominent a place in relation to the earth and other planets. Bruno did lose his life for precisely that reason. Gregor Mendel was reproved for suggesting that there might be decipherable explanations for the way new generations of peas and others of God's creations change from one generation to the next. Socrates' fate for not adhering to the official ideologies is well known.

If religion still had the authority it had when Galileo lived, we would be a hopelessly benighted society today. Think what would have happened to Galileo if he had explained to ecclesiastical authorities that if God's universe were reprsented by an area the size of Rome, even a grain of sand on a beach of the Tiber would be too large to represent the area covered by the sun, moon, and earth – all, in fact, of what is now called the solar system. Any slight hint that God's earth is not the center of all in the universe that could possibly be meaningful would have meant death for the person doing the hinting.

447

If man has truly come of age, he no longer needs the father-figure of a God... We no longer need to cling to the daddy on a cloud; we need to receive the spirit within ourselves, and in the world around us, which represents ultimate reality [and] gives a purpose to existence....

Pierre Berton
The Comfortable Pew

The book that contained this passage was a best seller in Canada, selling more than three-hundred-fifty thousand copies. Why is it that in the United States any book that makes the same statement will find all the sects and schisms of Christianity amassing forces to prevent its distribution. Very few libraries will accept such books and some are even are taking similar books out of the library collections. My book *Blind Faith, The Transcendental Temptation* by Paul Kurtz, and *Steve Allen on the Bible, Religion, and Morality* tell a truth that few Americans will ever hear about. The Bibliographies of these books list several other books that describe clearly what theistic religions are doing to us. Why is it that orthodox religions are so afraid of ideas? Usually those confident of their own convictions are willing to present them before the forum of public opinion, sure their own ideas will come out victors. Those who are confident of their own ideas are glad to have a chance to read opposing opinions, sure that they will make their own firm convictions even more firm. "True believers" dare to confront only those ideas that they know beforehand will reinforce their own deceitful religious fabrications.

448

To become a popular religion, it is only necessary for a superstition to enslave a philosophy.

W.R. Inge (1860-1954)
The Ideas of Progress

Inge, no doubt, would have been hard pressed to give an example of what he is talking about. Superstitions do not enslave philosophies. Compiled and organized, they *become* the philosophies that are called religions. They have little in common with the philosophies of an Alfred North Whitehead, Richard Dawkins,

Morris Raphael Cohen, Paul Kurtz, Sidney Hook, Bertrand Russell, Julian Janes, F.S.C.Northrop, John Mackie, Kai Nielsen, Richard Robinson, Anthony Flew, John Dewey, Ralph Waldo Emerson, Anatol Rapoport, Loren Eiseley, etc. If there is an enslaving done, it is the other way around. The philosophies of Arthur Schopenhauer, William James, Steve Allen, John Locke, Ludwig Wittgenstein, René Descartes, Immanuel Kant, Herbert Spencer, and G.W.F. Hegel could not refrain from becoming enslaved by superstition despite their preponderance of good sense. If Inge, himself, developed anything with enough coherence to be called a philosophy, he would do well to point it out to us. To distinguish good sense from superstition-infected philosophies, look to see which deals with facts and which gets lost in the world of mere words.

449

> What woman needs is not as a woman to act or rule, but as a nature to grow, and as an intellect to discern, and as a soul to live freely and unimpeded.
>
> Margaret Fuller (1810-1850)
> *Women in the 19th Century*

What woman wants is what every human being on earth wants: to have a fair chance to be the individual she is, with the opportunity to develop her unique aptitudes and abilities and be appreciated for herself. Were the George Sands and George Eliots of the world, from the day they are born, allowed to be free to develop themselves as they can and want to, they would never have wished to be men.

Regardless of how shabbily men treat women, men cannot be other than intellectually aware of what they do. If we machos have the slightest capacity for "empathy" and in our imaginations reversing our roles, we know we would not stand for a minute women treating us as we do them. We like to think we have free minds, able to think and do for ourselves, without psychological compulsions, but the way we deal with women at times seems to be governed by some kind of profoundly imbued satanic instinct that will not allow us to behave as we should. "We cannot live with them," as the well-known refrain goes, because they will not live with us as long as we treat them as we do. Knowing well the truth of the rest of the refrain: "but we cannot live without them," we must

change. When we do, much of the social instability of the world will
end.

450

> If we assume that there is no God, it follows that morality is even
> more important than if there is a Deity. If God exists, his unlimited
> power can certainly redress imbalances in the scale of human
> injustice. But if there is no God, then it up to man to be as moral as
> we can.
>
> Steve Allen -*Ripoff*

I haven't noticed God redressing imbalances lately, and do not
accept Steve Allen's "If god exists" assumption. But he and Sartre
(see quotations by Sartre elsewhere in this book) do make an
excellent point. Since there is no God, it behooves us all to behave,
especially by respecting our fellowman.

We can start by observing the golden rule. Trite, isn't it? But if we
think about it awhile, we begin so see how much is compressed in
those few words – and the marvelous consequences they imply.
Matthew 7:12 and Luke 6:31 found it worthwhile to quote Jesus as
making this very salient point. The golden rule has probably been
painted, engraved, or needle-worked into more wall plaques than any
other words, with the possible exception of "God bless our wobbly
wigwam" (or whatever).

As we say ad nauseam on the pages of this and other similar books,
we might consider also eliminating the hate, bigotry, prejudices, and
superstitions that turn our lives into a caldron of venom instead of the
milk and honey it could well be. Most of us, like Freud, cannot
understand why the inhumanity of man is so prevalent. We search
our minds for ways to improve morality, but instead of improving,
things seem to get worse. While I write these words, election
campaigning is underway, with all the candidates accusing the others
of horrible offenses – until we are sure they should all be in jail.

451

> Of all the faiths which modern man has lost, the most disastrous may
> well be his loss of faith in reason.
>
> Joseph Wood Krutch (1893-1970) – *The Conditioned Man*

Krutch (rhymes with hooch) effects his play on words by using the word "faith" in two different senses. To see what he is actually saying, we might interpret his words as follows: The first four words translate as: "Of all the fanciful religions" and the last three words as: "confidence in the efficacy of reason."

To lose confidence in reason is to be seriously deprived. We use reason in resolving the many perplexities and confronting the difficult situations that life presents. Without reason, mankind could not have survived. We wonder what could have prompted Martin Luther to become so obsessed with clawing his way to God that in the process he destroys man's hope for survival in order to get there. That subsequent generations have not renounced Luther's stupidities more emphatically than has been the case may be history's most poignant example of our lack of discriminating judgment.

If people generally begin to think rationally, the flimsy structure of the orthodoxies will tumble like a tower of playing cards in a storm.The result will be the shedding of guilt complexes and the disintegration of meaningless taboos that keep us skipping from specious decorum to spurious propriety in hope of avoiding condemnation by the hypocritical society in which we live.

452

Without experience nothing can be known sufficiently.

Roger Bacon (1220-1292)

Roger Bacon lived more than 700 years ago. It is not as if we have not had time to absorb the wisdom of our ancestors. Yet today we still adhere to religious doctrines that have no basis in reason.

Out of nothingness only nothingness can be fashioned. But we seem not to understand that simple axiomatic principle. Many of us choose to live lives of fanatics, shutting out everything that experience might teach us, preferring rather to live in a world of pure myth and legend. We live happy, ingenuously happy, lives without an inkling of what it would mean to live in a world of good sense and purposeful contemplation.

The test of experience is the test that scientists use in their laboratories. If expectations formally tested by experiments do not result in verifying the predictions scientists had in mind when making the experiments, the hypotheses being tested are, at least for the present, rejected. The Roger Bacons of the world will not burden themselves with believing that which no kind of experience confirms. Authoritative statements , indisputable facts, and personal expeiences accumulate in the mind of the scientist - enough to give him an operational philosophy substantiated beyond reasonable doubt.

453

> He who is near the church is often far from God.
>
> French proverb

Naturally, he who is near the church is far from God, if, as Lenny Bruce and many others have said, "God is not to be found in the church." "Nearer my God to thee," the song goes. "How on earth" (make that, "How in God's name") can anyone get nearer to an entity that is omnipresent? Or a God who, as is said in Luke 17:21, "is within you."?

My friend Raphael on Harbour Island in the Bahamas, when we were speaking of the seven churches on an island with only 600 people, said: "I don't go to any of them. Most of the sinning is in the churches." Are there citizens of Jordan, Montana who are not members of any of the six churches in that town with a population of 497 people? The village preacher that Pierre Berton quotes in *The Comfortable Pew* gives us an idea of what we may expect in the church: "I got into the God-racket, boys, because I found it is an easy way to make money."

When anyone begins to construct out of whole cloth a belief system as elaborate as the Judeo-Christian-Muslim religions, inconsistencies and contradictions are bound to occur. "No one has a good enough memory to be a successful liar" Lincoln said. We see also that "No One" has a good enough memory to write a thousand-page Bible, without contradicting Himself constantly – without making nonsense the divine norm.

454

> Nothing is so firmly believed as that which we least know.
>
> Eyquem Montaigne (1533-1592)

Most religionists know how easily they can get into trouble by introducing absolutes into their belief systems. Intelligent people everywhere censure them for being so absolutely sure of what they are sure of. It follows that in order to avoid trouble they will declare themselves as having a firm belief only of things that exist nowhere else in the universe except in their own minds. No one can prove one thing of another about strictly mental fabrications because they do not exist in a form that is subject to investigation.

If I declare publicly that Newt Gingrich, whom I know a great deal about, is a perfect politician, that he can do no wrong, I get letters and phone calls from every part of the country pointing out how misinformed I am. They will list dozens of failures in Congressman Gingrich's policies.

If I declare publicly that God, whom I know nothing about, is the preeminent entity in the universe, no one can contradict me, for they know no more about God than I do. No one has ever seen Him, and no one has any proof whatsoever that He has ever done anything.

It follows that Montaigne is wise beyond his time. "Nothing is so firmly believed as that which we least know" because we learn that the only things safe to believe in firmly, without fear of contradiction, are those things that have no existence beyond our own skins.

455

Had the Bible been in clear straightforward language, had the ambiguities and contradictions been edited out, and had the language been constantly modernized to accord with contemporary taste, it would almost certainly have been, or become, a work of lesser influence.

John Kenneth Galbraith
Economics, *Peace, and Laughter*

Most philosophers, those of religion as well as others, long ago decided that their best hope of being noticed is to write in abstract language, barely decipherable, coining neologisms that are given vague definitions, and writing in long, pretentiously complicated sentences. Thomas Jefferson said of Plato's *Republic*: "[I am] horrified at the whimsies, the puerilities, and unintelligible 'jargon' of the work."

Some of us, when we find exeptions, philosophers who write clearly and in simple language, are overjoyed. One exception, is Albert Camus. Another is Morris Raphael Cohen. Another is Paul

Kurtz. Another is John Mackie. Another is Krishnamurti. Most of the authors of the quotations in this book should be included. John Galbraith seems to think, in the case of the Bible at least, that the authors of the Bible did well to write in pompous gobbledygook. People are impressed by sesquipedalian words and florid phrases. They are convinced that what they read expresses some kind of occult purpose or esoteric truth. What Galbraith says explains the Catholic Church opposition, until recently, to saying Mass in languages other than Latin.

The problem was no different in 1535 when William Tyndale was found guilty of heresy for translating and publishing a Bible suitable for the masses. He was strangled and burned at the stake a year later. During the reign of Mary Tudor (1553-1588) hundreds of Protestants were burned at the stake for publicly using the English Bible. All the fear concerning allowing the masses to read the Bible, now seems strange. With nearly everyone today owning a copy of the Bible, we might expect impressive changes. But most people still have difficulty reading the Bible, even in Modern English editions, and few people do.

456

The time has come to be done with the usual silly nonsense about science being the cause of the moral difficulties of our world, as if trustworthy knowledge were an evil, and realize that one source of our moral apathy... is the inadequacy of our moral and religious philosophy itself.

F.S.C. Northrop
The Logic of the Sciences and the Humanities

Science is knowledge, and our principal concern is how to amplify and systematize it. Do those who despise science want us to get rid of knowledge? Are they suggesting that we learn to live in a world of ignorance, of pure myth and mysticism? The difference between science and mythology is the difference between what is known and what is speculation. For us to get along without facts and the inferences based on facts is unthinkable. Even Alice had to wake up from her fantasy if she was to continue her life. To be a student and a scholar, for the most part means to accumulate knowledge. We then analyze and correlate that knowledge so that, as a science, it will more adequately deal with life and the world in which we live.

The inadequacy of our religious philosophy is confirmed by observing how large is the percentage of the declarative sentences spoken or written by religionists that are false or deal with nonsense. What we should despise is not science but the overwhelming amount of sham that is distorting our verbal interchanges.

457

In the books which contain the law which is attributed to Jesus, there is no mention either of worship or of priests, or of sacrifices, or of sufferings, or of the greater part of the doctrines of actual Christianity, which has become the most prejudicial of all the superstitions on the earth.

Denis Diderot (1713-1784)

What the Christian Scriptures *do not* contain serves as subject matter of Christian sermons more than what they *do* contain. If preachers were obliged to begin every sermon not based on scripture with "You will find nothing I say this morning in your Bible," those might well be the most quoted words in the churches. If preachers were further obliged to tell us when in effect what they say on Sunday morning contradicts what is said in the Bible, those, too, would be words repeated more often than we might imagine. And in many cases they would be the wisest words of all. Alfred North Whitehead, J.H. Holmes, Hugh J. Schonfield, Malcolm Hay, and Paul Kurtz tells us of many "words of Jesus" commonly quoted as scripture, which are in fact figments of fiction, craftily contrived to deceive congregations.

Denis Diderot, coeditor of the world's first great encyclopedia, was wise beyond his age, that age being the mid 1700s. He had at hand well-written accounts off all sides of the paramount issues of his day, Diderot knew well how shallow was the argument for ascribing authority to religion and how compelling was the case for scientific rationalism.

458

Never go to church to learn how to behave unless the sermon is preached by a layman.

Richard Robinson
An Atheist's Values

A general liberation from the deceit taught in theological seminaries would serve us well. To have a preaching layman who is not indoctrinated in the art of dissimulation, who sees no need to dissemble his own personal views, who is comfortable labeling his conjectures and postulates as such, and who does not neglect the principle of parsimony in formulating the fundamentals of his faith – would delight us all. That we can learn from an intelligent and well-meaning preaching layman, there is no doubt.

But where do we find him? Not just any half-qualified misfit will do. I am sure we all know fervent Christian laymen we would be horrified to find facing us from the pulpit. We do not want the uninspiring dullard who has never demonstrated an ability to encourage moral behavior to waste our time. We do not want the "dedicated soul" who is constantly preaching fire and brimstone and denounces every innocent pleasure man has ever dreamed up in order to make life interesting and enjoyable. We do not want the fanatical weirdo who is obsessed with celibacy, confession, school prayer, circumcision, Biblical infallibility, telling the beads, total immersion, mass, making the sign of the cross, or whatever else may be his particular fixation.

There are a few religions where preaching laymen are the rule, not the exception, and some even who have no ordained clergy. Among these are most of the Christian Base Communities of Latin America and Europe, and in incohate form in the United States. These CEBs (Comunidades Eclesiales de Base) are composed mostly of poor and middle-class Catholics, but of other Christians as well.

Chapter XII

Superstition

459

Some of insist that we are no longer in the grip of superstitions. Knocking on wood when relating good fortune, avoiding walking under ladders, saying bless you, salud, or gesundheit when someone sneezes, etc , seem so silly to us in this modern scientific age, that we know we are liberated. After all, we no longer are guided by inspecting the entrails of a sacrificial bull, nor do we throw fragments of ancestral bones on the ground to help us plan the future. Thus assured, we return to our tarot cards and check our horoscopes.

We have all kinds of specious arguments to defend our own organized superstitions, our own "religions," and we listen week after week to tendentious sermons that are nothing more than elaborately styled tirades bent on coercing human wills into subservience.

Almost any citizen of the country in which I am now writing (Ecuador) is quite certain that making the sign of the cross will protect him from harm or bring good fortune in ventures that follow. He knows that the devil's malignant influence can be annulled by holding up a cross against him. A candle burning before an icon of the Virgin Mary will protect a house from evil. A rainbow, comet, or meteor is a special portent to warn mankind against sin. Sprinkling holy water at the inauguration of any new project will assure the project's success and protect it from calamities. A minute of silence will assure peace in the grave for a prominent countryman whose funeral was held the day before. Extreme unction will assure a fair hearing at the gates of heaven. Highways are spotted with shrines where you may stop to renew your "travel insurance" by dropping coins in a locked box in front of icons much larger than those in homes.

Special days in the church are filled with equally meaningless gestures: Water on the head, wafers on the tongue, ashes on the forehead, wine and bread in the belly, all accompanied by appropriate incantations, of course, are essential for salvation. Ciboriums, thuribles, censers, rosaries, crucifixes, decorated spruce, crèches, relics of saints, sacring bells, prayer wheels, pyxes, Magen Davids, phylacteries, praying shawls, yarmulkes, mezuzahs, talliths, menorahs – all have magical powers.

460

Man has free choice; or otherwise counsels, exhortations, commands, prohibitions, and punishments would be in vain.

St. Thomas Aquinas (1225-1274)
"I Answer that...." – *Summa Theologica*

Most essays denying free will are self-contradictions. If the writers could not do as they liked, they could not have written their essays. The arguments against free will are what may be described as closed-loop sophistry. To follow the writer's logic is to go around in circles. Jeremiah gives us an example in 10:23. Gerhard Szczesny gives us countless examples in his book *The Future of Disbelief*.

In almost every line of Szczesny's book, he speaks of making decisions. So how can he deny the reality of man's free will? He constantly uses such words as rejecting, accepting, proposing, declining, dismissing, eliminating, embracing, adapting, espousing, ignoring, disowning, and many, many others – all transitive verbals denoting free choice. And still he denies man his free will. On page 177, he says: "When a man knows he can kill his enemy or take him prisoner, a conscious decision is necessary to inhibit the choice to kill and follow the latter course." And still he denies man his free will.

It is hard to understand how a man who speaks consummate good sense on all the other subjects he devotes himself to can stick his head in the sand when he confronts this one issue. That men do strange things with language there is no denying. But examples usually fall within the stamp of the perpetrator's known idiosyncrasies and mental capabilities. Szczesny's responses to "free will" are paradoxical to say the least. To deny that man is constantly making self-generated choices is beyond comprehension.

461

> He that would be saved must believe in the trinity.
>
> Athanasian Creed

Harry Emerson Fosdick, famous for many years as pastor of the Riverside Church in New York City, speaks in *Dear Mr. Brown* of the theological presumption in regard to the Athanasian Creed. For him it is a shameful blot on religious history. He rejects the implication of eternal damnation that will face unbelievers. But why single out this one dogma to lampoon? Can we not say the same of all the silly pronouncements of the church fathers: virgin birth, divinity of Jesus, papal infallibility, immaculate conception, atonement, trinity, original sin, fall of man, holy Eucharist, extreme unction, redemption, etc. To get rid of all dogma is to remove a serious obstacle to the ability to form and express ideas intelligently – with critical judgments and independent opinions.

If dogmas are passively or only half-heartedly accepted as true, they can still have a pronounced effect on us and can do us considerable harm. When doctrines, tenets, or beliefs that have no rational bases are allowed in any degree to shape our behavior, we forfeit much of the freedom that makes us human. Whenever we allow ourselves to deal with myth as if we were considering verities of a rational world, we reduce our abilities to distinguish between nonsense and useful knowledge about the world in which we live. As petitioners for residence in cloud-cuckoo land, we may completely upset our mental equilibrium.

An Inquiry Concerning Faith is about a dispute between Erasmus and Luther that actually took place during the years 1524-1526. Both sides of the conversation we read were written by Erasmus. It cleverly reviews the dogma of Catholicism and Lutheranism and shows little difference between the two sects, certainly not enough to fight wars over. The same is true of all the major sects of Christianity. There is little that is authentic to separate them – nothing that is significant. If they would stop fighting over trivia, all could live in peace.

In my neighborhood, there is a Lutheran church on one side of the street and a Catholic church on the other. Both are magnificent edifices, fronting on the same prominent boulevard. Each has grounds large enough to include schools and playgrounds. Members of both churches believe in the same God, which they know nothing about. Still they formulate minuscule and meaningless differences in dogma that keep them at odds.

Erasmus wrote letters to friends in which he made it clear that he believed the Church of Rome was the one and only true church. Yet impartial analysis would show that there are reams of liturgy that Erasmus' Catholics and Luther's Lutherans could celebrate together.

Because Erasmus preferred any sect of Christianity to no Christianity at all he was accused by fellow Catholics of being a Lutheran, which he adamantly denied.

Erasmus saw in Christianity the hope for peace. But when we take human nature and scriptural example into account, we see the opposite to be the case. Religions (Christianity, an example) are the cause of most of man's conflicts. Add nationalism (which provokes an equally irrational fanaticism) and we have fertile soil for breeding ambiguously fomented and mercilessly intractable wars. [The above five paragrahs were adapted from *The Essential Erasmus* by John P. Dolan. He, of course, is not accountable for my opinions.]

462

Children working at their desks are almost always put off when even a kindly and respected teacher watches over their shoulders. How much more disconcerting to realize that each single deed, thought, and feeling is being watched over by the Teacher of Teachers. That nowhere on earth or in heaven is there any hiding place from that Eye which sees all and judges all.

Alan Watts (1915-1973)
The Book

Most people do not object to this divine voyeurism – a clear indication that they do not believe that God is omniscient after all. If we could observe people's behavior when they are "alone," we would be convinced that they do not believe that they are being perpetually spied upon. More likely it is not God's "omniscience," but God's "existence" that people doubt. They are, that is, atheists.

To many intelligent people, it is so evident that God does not exist that they refuse to examine the supposed evidence of God's existence for purposes of refuting it. But it is here that they cease to be rational. The irrationalism they no longer deign to consider may be the undoing of all of us. If the world is to be saved, it will be saved by intelligent people assuming responsibility for their honest convictions. They must declare themselves to be on the side of sanity: for brotherhood, against sectarianism, for unbiased perceptions, against bigotry, for love, against hate. "Sanity" and "organized ignorance" are terms in complete contradiction to each other. The conflict between them makes the ascendancy of both of them in the same societal system impossible.

463

> Wife to husband: He preaches a remarkably good sermon. It is so hard to avoid offending people like us.
>
> New Yorker Cartoon Caption

The cartoon points up one good reason why religion worldwide is in the sorry state it is in. In dissertations on the subject of religion, weasel wording often so eviscerates any message the authors might hope to communicate that the result is nothing more than pap. Religion editorialists often have this problem. Reading their columns, we are often dragged back and forth from syrupy sanctimony to ineptly camouflaged pussyfooting because it is so hard for them "to avoid offending people like us."

The offense really is willingness to ascribe to the massive nonsense that is orthodox religions an intrinsic meaning or occult significance that is not there. Hearing something said or seeing it in print often is considered to be enough to justify belief. No kind of test of authenticity is required.

"To err is human" is true enough. The trouble with theologians is that they make a career of it. When speaking of essences and existences they talk fantasy. They could prove nothing about the denizens of heaven or hell in any way, manner, or means. The volumes written about God, angels, devils, and jinn are volumes of unintelligible babbling. Most of what is written about Jesus is the same. We will not have religions that serve mankind until we have religions that value truth. We will rid ourselves of such absurdities as second comings, armageddon, the sins of unbelief, and the utility of mythology. We will believe nothing that doesn't have predictive content as described in essay 12.

464

> Knowledge is the prime need of the hour.
>
> Mary McLeod Bethune (1875-1955)
> *My Last Will and Testament*

Knowledge, which in sum is science, is the prime need of *any* hour. Without science, as Jacob Bronowsky says, we walk with open eyes toward slavery. What we do not need is what amounts to the antitheses of knowledge, the tendendiously contrived orthodox religions that by discrediting science makes slavery our ineluctable destiny.

Religious leaders, fully aware that science is their enemy, lose no opportunity to speak of science as an abomination. Science, to them is odious and beyond the pale. It induces mankind to transgress God's commandments, ignore divine will, and pay no heed to moral law.

The hypotheses and theories of science are speculations that with later experiments and future discoveries may lead to authentic knowledge. It is unfortunate that religion has no such words to indicate stages of plausibility for its various declarations. Speculation cannot be considered as a possible mental activity in religion, and there is no such thing as improving the verity of religion's precepts and doctrines. Science not only speculates, but often makes mistakes. Science may repudiate what has long been considered "sound" knowledge, and replace it with advanced knowledge that more adequately explains the cosmos. Religion would greatly increase its chances of survival if it could learn to do the same.

465

> As for those wingy mysteries and airy subtleties in religion, which have unhinged the brains of better heads, they have never stretched the pia mater of mine.
>
> Sir Thomas Browne (1605-1682)
> Medici

Sir Thomas Browne belongs to an especially fortunate minority: those who have not allowed the religions of their time to twist their thinking mechanisms into morbid configurations. Any sick person at the time was fortunate to be a patient of this renowned and level-headed English Physician.

The last thing sick people need is a doctor who takes the fanatical doctrines of some of the religions seriously. Even today, it is not uncommon for patients to be denied surgery, vaccinations, blood or marrow transfusions, etc. Instead, herbal cures, massages, practicioner orations, or the like, that have little or nothing to do with curing diseases are administered. Even children too young to make their own decisions are allowed to die when some simple medical procedures would have cured them. All that was wrong with one child, as a newspaper described it, was a bowel occlusion (an especially bad case of constipation). It would have taken minutes to fix what was wrong if the parents had allowed him to be examined and treated. The brains of all who take religions seriously are unhinged to more or less serious degrees. To disregard facts and adhere to superstitions over extended periods of time are bound to distort human minds. They never again learn to live serenely in sanely structured societies.

466

A church which starves itself and its members in the contemplative life deserves whatever spiritual leanness it may experience.
Michael Ramsey, Archbishop of Canterbury (1904-1988)
Canterbury Pilgrim

Starving oneself intellectually by shutting oneself away from society in convents and monasteries and praying up to eight hours a day is no way to improve ourselves or our societies. It is through constant interaction with others that we become worthy human beings. If religion is to solve the problems of our troubled societies, it will be by participating fully, with minds not wizened by isolation. To cloister ourselves is to cease to live, at best to vegetate – until the vegetable withers away and dies without the world taking notice and without the world having been improved because we were here.

In their years of formation, monasteries become populated by parasites on society, the haplesss members of society – those seeking escape from poverty, prison, military service, political oppression, or simple boredom. They often are dismayed to find themselves in a new kind of prison and a far worse state of boredom. With shaved heads, austere dress, meager rations, demeaning labor, and little sleep, they become depressed, morose, unsociable, often neurotic or bereft of reason.

Exchanging ideas only with others equally benighted will not serve anyone or solve anything. Parasites on society, they are only in the way, consuming resources and giving nothing in return. Only freethinking, convivial people who feel fulfilled by cooperating with others in productive ventures help make this a better world. They are willing to work hard to reach worthwhile goals and leave the world in a better position to help others do the same.

467

One of the proofs of the immortality of the soul is that myriads have believed in it. They have also believed that the earth was flat.

Mark Twain (1835-1910) - *Notebook*

Those of us who cannot find among the interstices of brain convolutions even the tiniest niche for accommodating compulsion to believe the unbelievable wonder about flat-earth and soul-society memberships. Not a week ago, someone mentioned on a radio program the actual personnel count in an actual present-day flat-earth society. We speak of the dark ages as something in the distant past.

Souls, of course, have far more devotees than the flat-earth concept – with even less to go on. We see the earth, and it looks flat. Before telescopes, space ships, all the instruments of today's astronomy, it was quite natural to think the earth was flat. Soul- and sooth-sayers have never had substantiation equal to that.

Most of us judge people by those we know personally. I do not know a single person whom I would consider morally capable of working for a corporation whose only product has no redeeming qualities and which kills more than 400,000 people in this country every year. I do not know a single person affiliated with newspapers who believe that every copy of the paper that reaches the public should contain a feature (the horoscope) that does nothing but add to the debilitating superstitions of our societies.

The people of Madrid have every right to be proud of their grand Parque de Retiro, which is strictly for their use and enjoyment. No commercial enterprises are allowed – with one remarkable exception. On Sundays, dozens of men and women (licensed, no doubt) come into the park, each carrying a card table and two folding chairs which they line up along both sides of the long, fantastically beautiful esplanade, the first view for people using the main entrance to the park. Tarot-card readers, they are, and all have waiting clients during the entire day

468

One may as well preach a respectable mythology as anything else.
Mary Augusta Ward (1851-1920)
Robert Elsmer Bk I Ch 2

Why not? Joseph Campbell did so – and very well. If the preacher is honest and makes what he is doing clear, for sure he is doing as well preaching mythology as anything else he could think up to preach. Perhaps he is doing better. At least, the members of the congregation are not straining to find truth in what he is saying. Everyone can relax and enjoy his accounts of gods and their retinue of lesser mythological beings. At least he is better than the preacher who does nothing but stuff us with flagrant falsehoods and misleading information, pretending it is all gospel truth.

To study the myths of ancient pagan and heathen religions will help us understand more about the evolution of thought and our mental capabilities. It will also give us insight into how "future aeons" will look back to our day and wonder about our own "pagan" beliefs and the strange, uncivilized idolatries and the myths we took seriously. If they still have copies of the Bible, they will find it a fanciful account of angels, devils and a Divine Highness who seemed intent mostly in keeping us overwhelmed by awe and cowering in fear. They may wonder about our willingness to attribute to our God powers that are corroborated only by words and never by observable deeds. They will find their ancient ancestors (us) a gullible lot indeed.

469

There are only three sins – causing pain, causing fear, causing anguish. The rest is window dressing.

Roger Caras

God, according to what Caras tells us, is obviously the foremost sinner of all time. What He did to women (Genesis 3:16) to the people of Israel (Deuteronomy 6:13), and to Abraham (Genesis 22), respectively, can leave no doubt about that. The pain, fear, and anguish that God inflicts upon men and women, according to Bible accounts, goes far beyond anything elsewhere recorded and, what is worse, if mysticism has its way, will continue forever. Biblical descriptions of hell, or the pain, fear, and anguish that He imposed upon Job and his family for nothing they had done, and the pain, fear, and anguish with which he burdens anyone who does not worship him is fiendish. When the people of the world get the vote to control all aspects of their lives, they will vote the Judeo-Christian-Muslim God out of existence immediately and turn things over to a truly benevolent deity.

What will happen someday – a long way into the future – is that the people of the world will become aware of the origin of all our gods and simply refuse to continue giving them credence. Innate forces within the human species will be developed and will take over. Like Santa Claus and the tooth fairy, the hold dreamed-up deities have over us depends entirely on the continued dominion of human credulity. Of course, nothing says that we must continue to allow myth to exercise authority over us. Someday we will no longer do so. Humankind, even without evolutionary improvement, will not be that weak-willed forever. Someday we will take our fate in our hands, and realizing our own potential, begin to build a sane world that will be a delightful refuge for us all.

470

Both read the Bible day and night, / But thou readest black where I read white.

William Blake (1757-1827)

Why is there so much controversy over what if often said to be the greatest book ever written? Is it not one characteristic of a great book that its thoughts be expressed clearly so there is little or no chance that its words be misinterpreted?

A Protestant minister appearing on the KABC Sunday night program *Religion on the Line* declared with some acrimony that the Bible is perfect. He could prove that all so-called contradictions in the Bible were not contradictions at all. Wouldn't that be a little difficult when a man's age when a certain event occurred in his life is given as both 22 and 42 years old. In my book *Blind Faith* I include eleven paragraphs of contradictions that appear in the Bible that neither sorcery nor magic could begin to reconcile. These paragraphs are only a beginning.

Fundamentalists, of course, *must* prove consistency in the Bible – or die trying. If even one contradiction is found, the whole contention about the Bible being God's word breaks down, and the Bible becomes, what it obviously is, an anthology of historical fiction – much more fiction than history.

471

> It is an obsenity – an all-male hierarchy... that presumes to rule on the lives and bodies of millions of women.
>
> Robin Morgan (1941-)
> Sisterhood *is Powerful* (Introduction)

Morgan speaks of the Roman Catholic Church. But Catholicism is not the only religion that presumes to consider women in the clergy a non issue. For Islam and Orthodox Judaism, also, women in positions at the top are no problem. They don't have any.

Robin Morgan exposes the views of the Roman Catholic Church on birth control, abortion, and the contribution of its brand of misogyny. She deplores mistaken assumptions of the evil that women would perpetrate if they were in power. Morgan speaks also of wealthy lobbies that prevent legislative change. All of this, she says, has set the Catholic Church on the path to oblivion. When all women get the word, as Robin Morgan has, the Catholic Church and all other male-dominated organizations will take notice. They will all either disappear or change. They will have no choice but oblivion if they do not see the handwriting on the wall. The fact that half the world's population has tolerated being shamefully mistreated by other half is one of the enigmas of recorded history. If women had any real notion of the power they would have if they were to unite in indignation, male domination would soon crumble. There is no way to fight against what is right if the proponents of right consolidate their resolve and purpose. If women keep their objective clearly in mind and understand that the means available for its attainment are not foolish, or illusory, they will win. As a male, I shudder to think of the bumpy road en route to gender equality, especially if males resist with their usual blind inflexibility. Because I know that equality must eventually prevail, I steel myself for the final realization.

472

Christianity persecuted, tortured, and burned. It kindled wars and nursed furious hatreds. It sanctified extermination and tyranny.

George Santayana (1863-1952)

But what did it do to us lately? Those who embrace Christianity must be suggesting that we forget its past. No matter that Christians murdered thousands in the period from eleven- to fourteen-hundred AD in the Middle East. No matter that its disciples murdered most of the indigenous populations of Argentina and the United States over a period of two hundred years. No matter the countless murders of Christians by Christians in Ireland. The case history of Dreyfus, the Thirty-years War, King Leopold's atrocities in the Congo, and many of the atrocities that Malcolm Hay documents in his book *The Foot of Pride* are further examples of what Christians are capable of doing.

So what did Christianity do to us lately? Count in the superstitions, prejudice, and bigotry it breeds, the millions of dollars it bilks from TV viewers, the antiquated rituals and dreary sermons it beguiles us with, the general atmosphere of sham and deceit which children are subjected to in Sunday schools, the political clout of the Christian Coalition, the Moral Majority, and many other such organizations bent on controlling all of our lives in the United States.

"Onward Christian Soldiers," "Marching as to War," "To win the World for Christ," Christians continue with the same goal.

473

It takes a long while for a naturally trustful person to reconcile himself to the idea that after all God will not help him.

H.L. Mencken (1880-1956)

It may take that person an even longer period of time to understand that the reason God will not help him is not that God is willfully callous or too busy to attend to "little old me," but that he does not exist.

It is taking mankind a long time to discover what a delightful world we would have if we got rid of all our superstitions. The ramifications are beyond Pollyana's most fanciful musings. When we get rid of our superstitions, we all will be able to visit one another without invidious labels keeping us apart. All of us will know that we ourselves are responsible for our own destinies and can take much of the credit if we manage events to turn out well. No one will be looking back over his shoulder to see if that "Absolute Master of all Voyeurs" is watching his every move – even in the bedroom. Everyone will know that morality refers to how human beings treat one another, not to abject worship of some proclaimed superbeing, a being who seems bent mostly on His own self-aggrandizement. We will get along without guardian anagels, devils to taunt and tempt us, and preachers who think they can order up for us an eternity of frying in hell. We will know that the only heaven we, our children, and their children will ever have is the heavenly paradise we make of this globe. That is the task we can dedicate ourselves to, a task worthy of painstaking and unremitting efforts – attentively and happily continued as they are required.

474

I hold a jail more roomy in the expressions of my judgment and convictions than would be the whole world if I were to submit to repression and be denied the right to express myself.

Samuel Gompers (1850-2924)
Seventy Years of Life and Labor

Nothing , really, can be added to what Samuel Gompers has to say. If anyone chooses to misunderstand him or deny him his right to express himself and to evade repression, anything else said would be rejected also. What we should all learn is how fervently and eloquently those who are right and have a just cause can express their convictions. They are, as David Thoreau said, a majority of one.

Samuel Gompers was born in London in 1850 and came to the United States when he was 13 years old. Beginning his career in a cigar-maker's union and continuing as the first president of the American Federation of Labor in 1866, he was an active spokesman for labor for 70 years. He may have done more for the working man than any other person in history. He died in 1924, still President of the A.F. of L.

If those who can be counted as among the ego-kin of Gompers, manage somehow to survive their early years living among the conventions and traditions of their antagonistic contemporaries, they may live to be the movers and shakers of their age. They will not always be the most popular people going, but they will be the doers that see to it that the world does not remain stagnant. With their presence and example, the human condition should greatly improve.

475

Common sense is only a deposit of prejudices laid down in the mind prior to the age of eighteen.

Lincoln Barret quoting Albert Einstein
The Universe and Dr. Einstein

The reader may have noticed that nowhere in this or in my other books, do I use the term "common sense." Good sense or some other rational locution replaces it.

To observe the written materials and vocal utterances that comprise the "deposit of prejudices" instilled in young people is to understand what prompted Einstein to make his pronouncement. To remember our own childhood with its street palaver, Sunday-school lessons, and grade and high-school education is to know why, in our adult lives, prejudices have been so intractable. To watch kindergarten and especially pre-kindergarten children in diversified neighborhoods at unprejudiced play is to know beyond any doubt that all our prejudices have to be taught. As the song in *South Pacific* says, we have to be taught to hate, disparage, belittle, mock, and humiliate "those others" who are not like us. "We have to be carefully taught." To eradicate such despicable practices is difficult and hardly ever completely successful. The likes of Joseph McCarthy, Jessie Helms, Bob Dornan, Mark Furman and many of our ranting evangelists on radio and television make it obvious that such contemptibly petty behavior can persist long into adult life.

476

While I do not believe that whatever is is right, I do believe that whatever is ought to be known.

John Wesley Edward Bowen (1855-1933)
Sermon, January 31, 1992

Whether between married couples, alter egos, or neighboring nations, secrets, which have a way of becoming banner headlines, can do incalculable harm. The best policy is to be scrupulously honest and above board in our communications. While one can certainly think of exceptions to Bowen's last ten words, he is saying that in this improvable world, it will be better if we are frank and open when dealing with others.

In our first conversations with a potential new friend, we find ourselves trying to ascertain what is his level of probity: How much of what he says must be taken with a grain of salt; how much seems ingenuous or carelessly candid. We like the person who does not seem always defensive, trying to be something he is not. With him (or her) we feel at ease and realize that the conversation we are having is a delightful experience.

Bowen would probably have trouble with our primary concern. He believed that whatever *is* ought to be known, but did he believe that whatever *is not* ought to be rejected? If like other preachers, he accepts much of what has never had contact with his sense receptors as true and real, then despite auspicious beginnings he and I agree to disagree and probably drift apart.

477

In the search for meaning we must not forget that the gods (or God, for that matter) are a concept of the human mind; they are the creatures of man, not vice versa.

Barbara W. Tuchman (1912-1987)
The March of Folly

Years of research for my first book dealing with the frivolities of religion has given me a certain insight as to where I might find corroborations of my theses. There is a certain kind of "mind functioning" that does not easily succumb to the wiles of sorcerers and mystics. It is a mind that has an intuitive grasp of probabilities, sensing relationships: "If this is so" then there is a certain chance that "this also is so." The person who has this particular kind of brain cannot turn it off and on; all his behavior follows this same trend.

If I read in some passage in a book on almost any subject, the author, in an aside, denying the pretenses of astrologers, I think I know something about how his mind functions. I expect that if I read enough of his books I will find him expressing equally cogent opinions about other pseudosciences and pretense arts such as reading palms, tea leaves, horoscopes, crystal balls, tarot cards, etc. I anticipate what would be his position about Ouija boards, seances, flying saucers, demon possession, prayer wheels, witches, spirit communication, etc. I might even expect to find him agreeing with Barbara Tuchman in the above quotation.

478

I am the poor old Bishop of this diocese, faithful servant of the Holy Church, humble child of the Holy Father in Rome.... I live by my sacred office.

D.H. Lawrence (1885-1930)
The Plumed Serpent

The Roman Catholic hierarchy, in November 1999, issued new rules aimed at controlling theologians and what they teach at the 235 church-related colleges. In an attempt to make sure there is no deviation from church doctrine, more than 78 amendments were offered, turning priests ever more definitively into mindless automatons.

The "poor old Bishop" mentioned in the box above is the church's most prized chess piece. He makes no move that is not prescribed by the Church – does only what he is programmed to do. If the church has a workable formula for turning out clones of this Bishop, it could soon take over the world.

The church does well enough as it is. The exception, not the rule, is anyone in the lower echelons of the church who manifests a mind of his own. Few have ever voiced opposition to any of the dogmas or doctrines of the church. Most live and die by rules formulated in antiquity, some so out of date that they are constantly at odds with customs of today's world.

Schleiermacher defined religion as a feeling of complete dependence. If so we ought to shun anything subsumed under that name. To be absolutely dependent is to forfeit any hope for progress in this world. With an intervening God, a God fully in charge, of course there would be no talk of progress, for progress means change, and how can we think of changing that which is "God's will" and therefore perfect. When people are convinced that they are senseless robots, dependent on forces over which they have no control, devoid of responsibility or worth, the result is a thorough disintegration of the qualities that make us human.

479

How can anyone believe that God put all those planets in our solar system, swinging their lonely way around our sun, without purpose.

Refrain of Astrologers – *Blind Faith*

God did a lot more than build a solar system. He built a universe made up of a hundred billion galaxies. Our galaxy alone, Timothy Ferris, author of The Whole Shebang, tells us, contains more than 400 billion stars, many of them possible "solar" systems. Traveling at the fastest speeds man's interstellar artifacts have ever attained, it would take more than 60 billion years to get to the closest large galaxy (M-31), a galaxy larger than our own Milky Way.

Using numbers given to the distance to our nearest star (3.4 light years) and the speed of our Pioneer spacecraft (27,000 miles per hour – Newsweek p 60 – October 4, 1999), we find it would take 84 thousand years for Pioneer 10 or 11 to reach out nearest star. If that figure seems beyond reason, the reader may do his own arithmetic:

Multiply the speed of light (186,264 miles per second) times the number of seconds in an hour (3600) and we get the miles light travels in an hour. Divide that by the number of miles Pioneer travel in an hour (27,000) and we get 24835.2 (how many times faster light is than Pioneer. The time required for light and the time required for Pioneer to travel a given distance are linked by the same ratio. If it takes 3.4 years for light to travel the distance between alpha Centauri and Earth, it will take Pioneer 3.4 x 24835.2 years to travel the same distance. That means it would take any spaceship traveling at speeds of the Pioneer spacecraft more than 84 thousand years to get to alpha Centauri. Use other figures than these given for the distance to alpha Centauri and the speeds for our interstellar spacecraft and the answers will be different, but just as discouraging for those who talk of interstellar space travel.

A statement signed a few years ago by 186 scientists, 18 of them Nobel Prize winners, and appearing in The Humanist magazine is a clear and definitive rejection of astrology, saying among other things: "It is simply a mistake to imagine that the forces exerted by the stars in any way shape our futures.... We must all face the world, and we must realize that our futures lie in ourselves, and not in the stars. One would imagine, in this day of widespread enlightenment and education, that it would be unnecessary to debunk beliefs based on magic and superstition." Philip Wylie said in *The Magic Animal*: "Astrology was born out of unreason that seems like reason for those who cannot use logic any better."

Despite the perfectly plausible assumption that there are trillions of planetary systems and billions of planets that can sustain life, we will almost certainly never "see" a habitable planet out there beyond our own marbled sphere. Despite recent announcements of detecting planets out there in instellar space, we still know little about them except that they are larger than our earth. Until we pick up authentically intelligent electromagnetic messages, we remain alone,

"How can anyone believe?" the quotation asks. How can anyone believe that any God made this universe at all, and if He did that He would have any interest in this small speck of it. To believe that, a person would have to have an ego as large as the universe itself.

480

Give me the storm and tempest of thought and action rather the dead calm of ignorance and faith.

Robert C. Ingersoll (1833-1899)
The Gods

People comfortably ensconced in one or another of the "great" religions are seen in print and heard on radio and television to express pity for others not so "fortunate." They should save their compassion. It may be more appropriate to pity themselves, lost as they are in "the dead calm of ignorance and faith."

Are they really happy who adhere to a vast system of religious proclamations, tenets, doctrines, and canons for which there can be no thought of verification? Must they not be ever on guard against having to defend the indefensible, to explain the unexplainable, and to justify belief in things for which there is no evidence for believing?

Even when not questioned by others, do not religionists question their religion themselves? Why is our pastor content to answer questions it occurs to members to ask with a simple: "You must have faith?" People would never allow their banker, their congressman, their nutritionist, their doctor, their repairman, even a salesman to get away with that kind of evasive answer. Not the Federal Food and Drug Administration nor any other governmental agency would survive that kind of response. Only in religion will members accept evasive answers to the significant questions they might think to ask. Only religion can live on pure nonsense, without reference to the real world.

481

Religion is all bunk.	Thomas Edison (1847-1931)
Many are bunkrapt.	P.B. Medawar (1915-1987)

If it takes two quotations to make a point, so be it. Edison makes a rather sweeping statement, and uses slang to do it. But he makes himself understood. Religion to him has no redeeming features. It is not befitting of civilized man to surrender himself to a system of deceit.

We human beings cannot with equanimity lead completely meaningless lives. Some of us, even when retired, spend our time at occupations that we see as contributing to making this a better world for present and future generations. If our efforts do not lead to results that can be weighed, measured, or felt, we join religions, hoping thereby to find meaning.

Edison needed no such subterfuge. He was so busy doing meaningful things that he begrudged even the time he had to give up to sleep.

Medawar plays little part in this story. He simply enjoyed the whimsy of many writers and others who never quite grow up. If we have no other toys, we play with words. He, like Edison, knew that religion is bunk, but added, puckishly, that many are enamored of it.

482

Is there really as much difference as we think between the Aztec human sacrifice to the gods and the modern human sacrifices in war to the idols of nationalism and the sovereign state?

Erich Fromm (1900-1980)
You Shall Be As Gods

With each religious sect believing that its fabrications are the only "truth" and that the only logical response to "those others" who think differently is hate, the eventual result is sure to be more and ever-more-bitter religious wars. Why do we fight wars over religious differences, while scientists can tell one another that their ways of solving problems are wrong without incurring unresolvable animosities? There never have been tribunals in scientific societies forcing conformity, threatening those who do not repudiate "heretical" doctrines that they will be excommunicated or burned at the stake.

Much of man's inhumanity to man, it becomes obvious, has been prompted by religion. With the exception of the nationalism that Fromm speaks of, religion is the only thing that will induce a man to travel half way around the world to kill a fellow human being that he does not know and has never met.

The only beliefs we are willing to die for are those that are unfounded. We agree on well-founded beliefs, for they give us no reason for not agreeing. But unfounded beliefs are unrestricted in their aberrances, and some of these special forms of believing become more precious than life itself – our own life or that of those who disagree with us. When fairness and tolerance are discarded, and "divine favor" leagues itself with "our cause," and "right" becomes solely our way of thinking, the religious wars that have plagued and still plague mankind result.

483

Science has done more for the development of western civilization in one hundred years than Christianity did in eighteen hundred years.

John Burroughs (1837-1921)
The Light of Day

Burroughs has the right idea, but his logic is flawed. Even to credit Christianity with zero contribution would be an exaggeration. The wars, hatred, bigotry, superstitions, crusades, inquisitions, and prejudice that religion has perpetrated in the name of Christianity give it a place in history far down on the negative side of the ledger. When Alfred North Whitehead declared: "I consider Christian theology to be one of the great disasters of the human race," he comes closer to the truth. Science, for more than three hundred years, has been one long process of learning how not to fool ourselves. Religion, for a much longer period, has become ever more efficient at fooling everyone nurtured by its sanctimonious catechisms. To reconcile religion and science, faith and philosophy, revelation and sense perception, or even to identify scripture unequivocally with history is to abandon reason. All mean that we equate nonsense with that which is clearly a correlative of experience. One would have no trouble reconciling science and the religion of section 21 of *Blind Faith*, but to reconcile science and any of today's "great" religions would mean a tremendous upheavel. The religion that comes out of *that* battle would not be recognizable by today's religionists.

484

A pretty good test of a man's religion is how it affects his pocketbook.

Francis James Grimké (1850-1937)
Stray Thoughts and Meditations

There are many good tests for religion, Whether it is the kind of religion you go to church to get, or the kind that is mostly a synonym for moral behavior. The so-called religions of many churches are better classified as anti-religion. Churches in which class distinctions are made on the basis of income, race, sexual orientation, or degree of fanaticism do not classify as truly religious institutions. Churches that cater to the power interests of the community do not come out well either.

Religion for many is mostly an elaborate ritual. If they walk the walk, mouth the words, sip the wine, swallow the wafer, swing the censer, spin the prayer wheel, say the rosary, make the sign of the cross, kiss the mezuzah, or whatever, they are religious. Their piety is not concerned with improving race relations, housing the poor, healing the sick, feeding the hungry, or consoling those who have lost family members or friends.

All of us know people who give away much of their income to poor people, depriving themselves of all luxuries so that they may help as many as possible. Often they are people who never set foot in a church or observe any of the rights and rituals of the orthodoxies. Some of them, in fact, are atheists. How would they make out in the Grimké test?

485

> Reason is an instrument, which like any other instrument can be used well or ill (The better the instrument, the more damage it can do when badly handled....) If the reasoner starts from well-established premisses, he will reach conclusions in which he may have confidence.... Moral: "Make sure by experiment and observation that your premisses are correct.
>
>   Aldous Huxley (1894-1963) – *Texts and Pretexts*

Start from false premises (an intervening God is in charge of this world; Jesus is divine and sits at God's side) and from there you can make false inferences from now on forever. On Sunday nights for years, KABC presented a program called "Religion on the Line" in which first premises were never discussed. They were simply taken for granted. Nothing that was discussed had any validity because no effort was made by experiment and observation, as Aldous Huxley prescribed, to be sure basic premises were correct.

Reason, the faculty of mind we use to come to conclusions that accord with a degree of sanity, is indispensable. Despite Martin Luther's contention that "reason must be deluded, blinded, and destroyed," we must "reason" our way through the problems that face us or we will never resolve these problems at all. Without reason, we would rank alongside of the mole rat and the earthworm. Permanent residence underground would be our only hope for survival.

486

> He who will not reason is a bigot; he who cannot is a fool; and he who dares not is a slave.
>
>   William Drummond of Hawthornden (1585-1649)
>   *Academical Questions*

The philosopher Immanuel Kant, speaking in the same country where Martin Luther uttered his impassioned diatribe against reason, said: "All our knowledge begins with the senses, proceeds then to understanding and ends with reason."

Reason is the faculty of mind that has kept the human species from destroying itself for several thousands of years. It is the faculty that will continue to keep the species and the environment a viable symbiosis for aeons to come. But first we must expose the modern-day Martin Luthers and keep them from their mischief. Also, we must understand that not all reasoning of the past can protect us in the future. Mistakes it has allowed to occur would be fatal today. Another world war would mean certain extinction. Continued development of biological and chemical weapons will almost certainly get out of hand. Unless we do something about nuclear bombs, we are almost certain to destroy ourselves. Our reason must be given an improved theater of operation. Gifted minds capable of coordinating their best efforts must set to work eliminating our prejudices, superstitions, hatreds. and bigotry. We must get rid of our religions, our nationalisms, and learn to live amicably together as a global community. Anything less seems destined to disaster. Any thinking person knows that as surely as he knows that night is not day, black is not white, life is ended by death.

487

It is a curious fact that pacifism, is a mark of an age weak in faith, whereas the people of religious times have honored war as "God's role of chastisement.

Lydia Gothschewski
Women in the New State

What is curious is that the gods our scriptures present to us are all warmongers. To say the people are weak in faith is to say that they do not accept the proclamations of their religious leaders when those leaders offer no evidence to show that their proclamations are worthy of acceptance. People understand that the word faith itself is nothing more than a plea on the part of religious leaders that their subjects accept everything they say without proof – regardless of the nature of what they may choose to proclaim. "Believe what I say without reason for believing" is the singsong of all sermons. "Gullible" or its synonym "strong-in-faith" members of the congregations prove themselves to be if they comply.

Ms Gothschewski gives us the best reason yet for rejecting all religions. Which would you prefer, periods without religions and no wars or periods marked by very active religions when we are constantly at war?

488

To make plans on the basis of clichés is often to allow ourselves to be led astray. "The show must go on" is useful to remind new actors that the career they have chosen is serious business. If they miss a performance they better have a life-or-death explanation. A great deal of money is at stake, and inconveniences for hordes of people are sure to follow. Nothing short of a rebel invasion or an earthquake is enough to renege on their career commitment.

But we speak of life, not a show. For many people, if life does not go on the consequences may just as likely benefit as do harm to family or friends. (Without "him" around, life is simpler for everyone concerned!)

When we live to a point where we are no longer useful, even to ourselves, how do we justify concern about dying? No one has ever demonstrated conclusively that life has meaning of transcendental proportions, and often not even in the local sense. If one still enjoys life, it is nice that it continue, but an auxiliary verb expressing obligation or necessity for life continuing is not warranted.

"I forget just why," is a dead giveaway that the "must" is little justified. For centenarians, not only "must" but "will" leave doubt. After five score, if that remarkable age is reached, for sure one's days are numbered. "Life must go on," will change to: "Life is about over." The end for most will be welcome.

Joanna Field may have had the best answer to Edna"s "lament." She said, "I used to trouble about what life was for – now being alive seems sufficient reason."

489

There is nothing strictly new in The New Testament so far as ethical teaching is concerned. The ideas Jesus expressed had been expressed before in the Old Testament and in the Talmud. The writings of many of the great civilizations contained these same ideas. If we could somehow separate the teaching of Jesus from Christianity, stop spending our energy on useless arguments about divinity, accept the fact that Jesus was just another man, albeit an unusual one, we might concentrate on what is valid in his message for us today.

The same Christian Scriptures from which the Reverend J.H. Holmes draws a picture of a somewhat idealized Jesus in his book *The Sensible Man's View of Religion* also gives us a man, like most of us, not long on patience, no great shakes as a prophet, not a great intellect (nothing to compare with Plato, Socrates, or Aristotle). This is the man who demands of his followers mindless obedience and conformity, who asks them to suppress feelings, eliminate doubt, to forgo questioning and critical examination, and to become like children (who will believe almost anything). Jesus believed, as did almost everyone at the time, that David was the author of all of the psalms.

Today's psychologists would say that Jesus burdened his followers with a sure-fire formula for producing all manner of neurotic and psychotic disturbances. This is the down-to-earth human being who could believe in hell and demons, condemn "the goats" to everlasting fire, send innocent Gadarine swine to drown in a sea, curse a perfectly harmless fig tree, talk in riddles, approve of improvidence, abhor knowledge, predict imminent world disaster, and express contempt for filial unity. It is such a man who could become obsessed with cutting off hands, gnashing teeth, and threatening eternal torment. With at least as much satisfaction as those in heaven have when looking down upon their neighbors burning in hell, Jesus asks that his enemies be brought and slain before him (Luke 19:27). Reading either of the testaments, one gets the impression that "turning the other cheek" was by no means commonly recommended procedure.

490

The approach of religion is to confirm the thesis that man [is the pawn of] some ineffable power beyond himself....

Roderic Gorney (1924-   )
The Human Agenda

In his approach to science, man is never a pawn. He uses science to probe and to learn from nature, as well as from the accumulated knowledge at the time.

Sometimes the scientist seeks simply to find the basic principles and theoretical aspects of a science. Sometimes he seeks to solve practical problems that are holding up progress in a particular science. He seeks to compare, integrate, test, and confirm various conjectures, inferences, hypotheses, theories, and laws of the science he in particular contributes to.

Unlike the religionist, the scientist posits no magic, myth, sanctity, faith, or divinity in his research. He is interested in reality, not spiritualism; hard work, not prayer; respect, not worship; reason, not blind faith; laboratories, not basilicas; a better world, not eternal bliss. Religion and science operate in different arenas – the one quicksand, the other granite. Religion, trying to remain constant, slides toward oblivion. Science trying to advance, flourishes. Both expect to be the pride of an irreversible human ascendancy, but religion loses favor, and science gains prestige day by day.

491

Race prejudice is the devil unchained.
Charles Waddell Chestnutt (1858-1932)
The Marrow of Traditon

If race prejudice needs a symbol, the devil is as good as any other. The trouble is that prejudice stands out in our societies like catsup on a white blouse – whereas I haven't noticed devils floating around much these past eighty years.

Charles Waddell Chestnutt's poignant aphorism has one other technical flaw. However skillfully and assiduously our best scientists have tried to do so, they have been unable to define the term race in a way to make it a significant and definitive term in our language. However they phrase their definitions, large segments of the population slip through the cracks. We are one people, one race, and one species – and the only living species in the genus Homo.

In *The Marrow of Tradition,* Charles Waddell Chestnutt should have said, "Prejudice against differences in people is the term 'devil' reified and loosed from his chains." Well, no, sorry I brought it up:

Charles Waddell Chestnutt should have said: "Race prejudice is the devil unchained." It is a beautiful and effective metaphor.

492

A schoolgirl was asked in an examination paper to describe a convent. She wrote, "A convent is a place where virgins are confined." The inspector marked the paper: "This is either a misconception or a clerical error."

Sir Charles Wheeler
Speech to the Royal Society of Arts

In another of these brief essays, I suggest that while He was about it God might have injected a little humor into the Bible to make it readable. If Sir Charles Wheeler had teamed up with Rudi Gelsey (who wrote *imagine... a new bible*) to write a serious, full-length moral document, perhaps we could now toss out the Judeo-Christian-scriptures and have something that more effectively educates us in matters of morality.

Scripture writing, it seems, has always been left to dour, deluded dimwits. Gelsey and Wheeler show that this need not have been the case. Of course, the thousands of beautifully written books on our library shelves prove that there has never been a shortage of competent literary artists who could have written Bibles that were full of accurate information and good sense. Such Bibles would reject mythology and pretentious nonsense, and give us all the commandments, canons, and doctrines we need to tell us how to behave and live sanely. We could be sure of having a source for useful, interesting, and moral guidance all the days of our lives.

Some say that God, like most modern workers should have restricted Himself to a five-day week. He was doing all right until he made that sixth-day blooper, fabricating sentient beings, many of them impercipient, immature, obtuse, unable really to think. Being omniscient, He must have known what He was doing – which makes it all the more incomprehensible.

Those who believe in God can come to only one logical conclusion: God loves trouble. Ernest Renan suggests that "The universe is a spectacle which the good God gives for His own amusement." If so, now all is explained.

493

Thirty school children, persistently interrogated, replied at first badly, afterwards better, and finally very well. After a month's examination, they replied so well that they all gave the same answer.

Anatole France (1844-1924)
"Monsieur Thomas" – part of *Crainquebille*

The same thing happened in Manhattan Beach, California a few years ago. Stories told by children in a preschool nursery, accusing the propietors of the school of molesting them, got better and the children more sure of them as months passed. It seemed certain that two people, mother and son, would be found guilty in court of this abhorrent crime. Fortunately, in a long, well-published trial, it was shown clearly that the children were saying what "well-trained" interrogators has more or less unwittingly "taught" them to say.

The case against the lay teacher of a "godless" school, victim of Monnsieur Thomas' bigoted bias, was more definitively resolved, because the school stove, material in the case, was proven never to have existed. The teacher, as he left the court completely exonerated, was reprimanded by the judge and urged to "restrain his brutal instincts." The teacher was never vindicated in the minds of his fellow townspeople, and he led a harried existence for the rest of his life.

Understanding cases like this and how malleable are children's minds, we see why the Jesuits can be so sure of complete and lasting compliance If they are given control of children for the first seven years of their lives. We understand also why it is so difficult to re-educate adults who when young were entrapped by popular mythologies.

494

In every country the dominant religion, when it does not persecute other religions, in the long run engulfs them all.

Voltaire (1694-1778)
Letres Philosophiques

The Catholics of Mexico and of Central and South America and the Islam of Southeastern Europe, North Africa, and parts of Asia are prime examples. Two changes, more than any others, will be required to improve the hegemony of these two religions in their respective realms. Both Catholicism and Islam have become conspicuously overbearing, so sure of their invincibility that they begin to be even more obvious in their control over the lives of individual parishioners and individual Muslims. Islam must play down Koranic acceptance of slavery and humiliating treatment of women. Catholicism must concede more offices to women and someday agree that women will make excellent priests. They must stop their demeaning treatment of nuns, turning them into virtual slaves.

An overweening patriarchal envelopment is today an anachronism. Human males are finally learning to do what obviously must be done. Women everywhere are in no mood to be oppressed by men. If we do not treat them fairly, they will rearrange matters to see that we do.

The ominous forecast for both Catholicism and Islam is the gradual education that is coming for their people. Ignorance has been their strength and they know it. They also know that people will not remain ignorant forever. Even in Bangladesh and Pakistan, most citizens are getting grade-school education, and once intelligent people taste of education their appetite never wanes. Once educated, people begin to see How shallow have been the foundations of the religious beliefs that are foisted upon them. They will rebel. Religious must begin to supply answers where they have been getting by with equivocations only. People will want to know what proofs they have for all their weird pronouncements – or why they accept beliefs when there is not the slightest reason for accepting those beliefs. Change for Catholicism and Islam (and all other religions as well) is inevitable. The sooner it comes, the less painful the change will be. Religions will learn that fact or they will perish.

495

We cannot live, sorrow, or die for somebody else, for suffering is too precious to be shared.

Edward Dahlberg
Because I Was Flesh

Even in a literal sense, Dahlberg's premise is not always true. And his conclusion about suffering being precious surely borders on bilgewater. But despite these flaws, he makes a tremendous point.

Just yesterday a radio talk-show host described how an elderly fellow In Germany switched identity cards with a young fellow, taking his place on a cattle train to Auschwitz. Many parents, too, almost literally live for their children. I am sure there are some who would donate a heart or liver to a deserving son or daughter if they could talk a doctor into performing the operation.

If anyone suffers to see someone else suffering, one might say the suffering is doubled, but not shared. The suffering person still suffers, perhaps more. But precious, his suffering is not.

Jesus dying for our sins, often quoted, but never explained, is claptrap – and that is Dahlberg's real message. The scriptures are so full of nonsense that modern exegetes have no qualms about adding more. Non sequiturs occur in the Bible constantly. Cud-chewing rodents and their ilk are as thick as lice. If any scientist were to were to write a book as full of idiocy as are the various scriptures, he would be laughed out of the profession. Why some religionist does not write a new, acceptable scripture, I do not know. Rudi Gelsey started with a title: *imagine... a new bible*, but his was only a beginning. Who would like to finish the project?

496

When we set aside the book of nature as being our primary religious experience and substitute a verbal revelatory experience, then we can get ourselves in trouble. My suggestion is to put the Bible on the shelf for at least 20 years and get on with reading the primary scripture which is the scripture of the world about us.

Thomas Berry
"The Universe is Our University" – *Timeline*, July/August 1997

Twenty years is a good start. When that 20 ends, let us extend it for another 20, then another, then another. By that time we may have learned how well, how much better, we get along without the interference of organized ignorance, and we will never return to it.

To turn the world's populations into pious fanatics will do us no good. To turn every human being on earth into an informed and passionate world citizen will be our real salvation.

Berry furnishes us with some remarkable insights: "You cannot have a rising gross human product with a declining gross Earth product." You cannot have well humans on a sick planet." "Rather than instructing our children in Biblical studies, their time will be better spent...experiencing things in the natural world." "All human institutions... must now be judged primarily by whether they inhibit, ignore, or foster a mutually enhancing human-earth relationship."

As an ordained priest with a doctorate from Catholic University, Berry soon gets himself immersed in mysticism, but he has not let it blind him from understanding that we must all play an active role in both the social and natural world if the human species is to survive.

In a remarkable photograph taken by astronauts and now widely distributed, we see the earth isolated and free, except for gravitation and radiant-energy solar dependence. We see, too, that the earth depends on us not to mistreat it. Do we know what might turn the earth into a poisonous Venus or a barren Mars? We do know that we must keep close tabs on how we are doing and make corrections well in advance of disaster if we are to survive.

497

In reality, nothing like the "God"and Christ" I was brought up to believe in can be true. It is not merely that the Old Man in the sky is only a mythological symbol...: The truth is that this whole way of thinking is wrong.

John Wren-Lewis
They Became Anglicans

This way of thinking is wrong not only because it refers to nothing that exists or ever has existed in the cosmos, but because it interposes obstacles to good sense. Reason must be based on facts. One cannot reason on the basis of empyrean make-believe.

This whole way of thinking is wrong especially because those doing the "thinking" have never allowed themselves to see the folly of living in dream worlds with no handle on down-to-earth, existential, being. Not in their entire lives have they attempted to face the world head on, seeing things as they are rather than as self-hypnotized preachers or family fanatics tell them they are.

If this way of thinking were not wrong for any other reason, it would be obviously so for the weird aberrations it engenders. "Born-again Christians," for example, must be one of the most ludicrous notions ever invented, and "absolute truth" is surely another. Acts of God, after-life, animal sacrifices, archangels, Noah's ark, cud-chewing rodents, baptism, transubstantiation, voodooism, dogma, satan, heresy, holy wars, immortality, infallibility, last judgment, celibacy, rosaries, sects, and trinity are still others. Can anyone imagine the brothers Grimm writing fairies tales as saturated with grotesque imbecilities as are our religions?

498

> We are... driven to the unfashionable conclusion that the trouble with our species is not an excess of aggression, but an excess capacity for fanatical devotion.
>
> Arthur Koestler (1905-1983) - *Janus*

Aggression, of course, can be very productive for causes that are conducive to human progress. Fanatical devotion, on the contrary, is harmful when it means, as it often does, devotion to the sham that is theistic religions.

The is no merit in devotion to mythical beings, divisive cults, catechistic absurdity, monastic aceticism, animal sacrifices, deceit-ridden Bibles, meaningless sacraments, religious wars, tinsel pageantry, mantra chanting, homophobia, closed minds, speaking in tongues, Christian Crusades, raving evangelists, Satanic cults, eternal punishment, inflexible dogma, pietistic fraud, holy relics, religious talismans, reprehensible fund raising, xenophobia, blind conformity, obscurantism, parochial thinking, Armageddon, superstitions, etc.

Ashley Montagu, in his book *The Nature of Human Aggression*, said: "Unfortnately, one of the hazards attendant to an addiction to one's own theories, is that it tends to make one insensible to facts." Facts to most religionists are anathema. To allow facts to intrude would be to destroy any religion in the world. The fanatical devotion that Koestler speaks of is the only protection religionists can count on – which means that someday humankind may count them out.

Chapter XIII

The Religious Faux Pas

499

If we cannot fathom the depth of ordinary human intellligence, how can we expect to know anything about the deranged minds that dream up mythological beings to run our universe?

Human beings are an enigma. Just when we think we know how people generally will behave in given circumstances, they fool us completely. The best of movie reviewers are baffled by why poor movies succeed and movies that they predict great things for fail miserably. Book reviewers have the same problem. Wall-Street tycoons have successes and they have dismal failures. Even stand-up comics who write their own materials, after many performances that wow their audiences have a night where they fall flat. We human beings simply are not predictable and cannot predict the behavior of others.

The typical theologian loves the life he lives. He enjoys being obsequiously revered – even when he knows full well he does not deserve reverence. Those who truckle to him amplify his overweening conceit and increase his alienation from reality. It is a secret joy he has, observing his own personal charisma, his ability to inspire unswerving allegiance and devotion from large numbers of people. Increasingly, he believes he is doing (can do) no wrong.

Some theologians, even when aware of their duplicitous behavior go on for years sermonizing, giving public speeches, appearing on talk shows, writing books, becoming more and more popular, filling their coffers to overflowing. Then in the middle of it all they make complete asses of themselves, saying and doing things one might think any six-year-old would know better than to do or say.

Billy Graham expresses his purblind partiality for Christians, Jimmy Swaggart rails against Catholic priests, Jerry Falwell calls President Clinton a murderer, Pat Robertson says that God advised him to run for president, Robert Schuller suggests that heaven is in Galaxy M-31. It seems that all theologians have times when their brains slip gears. I suspect the preacher who said, "I got into this God-racket boys, because I found it a great way to make money" wished in more sober moments that he had not spoken so candidly. Perhaps Pope Innocent, the third, when he advised using the sword against heretics, or Cardinal Newman when he said we would do well to become more superstitious and bigoted than we already are may have learned to regret such witless obliquities.

500

> Fashions in sin change.
>
> Lilllian Hellman (1905-1984)
> *Watch on the Rhine*

Of course if sin is a matter that accords precisely with what God says it is, it could never change. What God says about sin and the results of sin is diktat, not in any way negotiable. What Hellman says is truth. What God says is a paradigm that exists only in imaginations.

To say that fashions in sin change, usually means that our emphases and interpretations of what we want to call sin change. We look upon sexual intercourse outside of marriage very differently today than we did fifty years ago. Thievery is much more serious to Muslims or to the government of Singapore than it is here. Murder depends on who is the victim and who is the perpetrator. A Sheik in Qatar can murder his own servant girl without fear of serious punishment for so doing. If she murders him, letters to the government of Qatar from all over the world will not save her. In the United States, no white man is electrocuted for murdering a black man. Capital punishment in most States is not a concern for a woman.

For those who are forever looking for more interesting ways to sin, fashion is indeed the right word. Extramarital sexuality may change from isolated fornication, to wife swapping, to group orgies, to bisexual innovations, to dealer's choice. Finally the fashion may turn to behaving normally, having a monogamous existence, raising a legitimate family that is interested mostly in being useful citizens. Each person, regardless of what his mode of sexual behavior has been, is probably content at death that he or she is leaving the world a better place for future generations to enjoy.

501

It is the customary fate of new truth to begin as heresies and end as superstitions.

Thomas Henry Huxley (1825-1895)
The Coming of Age of the Origin of Species

Truths can begin as heresies, but they do not end up as superstitions. Only supposed truth can do that. To believe that walking under a ladder bodes ill for you was always a superstition. The same is the case with black cats, three on a match, or sneezing without a responsive bless you, gesundheit, or salud. Wearing copper bracelets, yarmulkes, phylacteries, blue at weddings, ashes on the first day of Lent, ritual vestments, amulets, talismans, crucifixes, or praying shawls are superstitions if credited with magic powers. Wearing, per se, of course, is wearing, and need not have anything of superstition attached to it. It is easy to imagine where "wearing" can get a person in trouble, like a gun or transparent clothing, but that does not make it a superstition.

Huxley's "new," as well, is ill-advised. In its place, "until recently undiscovered" in most contexts is better. We do not fabricate truths in the sense that we fabricate lies. We speak truth simply when we describe things accurately. Lying requires deliberation, planning, scheming. It is never idle meditation.

"Truth" is an important concept, and if we are to communicate, the word should be used precisely. Truth describes language (all symbol systems) and simply says that our words correspond to what they are words about. The cap I am wearing I bought in Lisbon" is not a complicated statement, and is or is not true, period. There are no three ways about it. When religionists use truth to describe some vague something or other "out there," there is no such thing as verification. As F.S.C. Northrop suggests, if it is comfortable to believe that something has been said, we do. If it is not comfortable to pretend that something has been said, we do not. For many people, comfort, not truth is the criterion for believing.

502

Common sense tells us that our existence is but a brief crack of light between two eternities of darkness.

Vladimir Nabokov (1899-1977)

Others who have said this are Bertrand Russell and Brendan Gill. How many others can we name? The so-called common sense that Nabokov speaks of is anything but common. It is almost as rare as hen's teeth or snowballs in hell.

Most of us can postulate personal darkness before we were born, but have a hard time with the same darkness after we die, although one is as likely and as logical as the other. Religious "authorities" hardly ever mention the former but they have all kinds of predictions about the latter. They are people like us and are reluctant to think that sometime soon after their three-score-and-ten, everything for them will come to an end.

They believe that somehow from the decaying remains that anyone would find looking for them in the ground a few years later, a "spirit" emerged. In what form, how and whether there is continuity of consciousness in the flesh-form before and the whatever-form after, they do not agree.

Seances and hallucinations among those still living, notwithstanding, no one has produced a shred of evidence that the post-darkness and the pre-darkness are not the same and are not the whole truth. Wishful thinking is a pleasant way to spend time, and rarely may even be fruitful. But usually we will live much better if we repudiate nonsense and embrace only good sense. Even if an afterlife were a fact, the complete lack of communication of those of us still alive with those long dead, leaves things in exactly the same shape as if an afterlife were fiction. If there is an afterlife but no continuity of consciousness, the situation is exactly the same as a definitive death. Resurrection in any form would not make the slightest sense. God might as well make a completely new batch of inhabitants for heaven as to bother with a "transmigration of completely disassociated souls."

503

> But only fools like me, you see, / Can make a god, who makes a tree.
>
> E.Y. Harburg (1896-1981)

Montaigne said: "... Man, who cannot possibly make a worm and yet will make gods by the dozens." Not dozens, man has made hundreds of gods, all serving some purpose in one or more of the hundreds of societies that have existed since the beginning of recorded time. In truth, there are as many gods as there are those who postulate their existence. Millions of gods exist in this world, and by any and all evidence that is credible, every one of them has a physical existence only in someone's brain.

To think this through one step further is to realize that the entire world we observe exists only in some form or other within our own brain. Out there, beyond our own skin, scientists tell us, are only subatomic particles which make up atoms and molecules that in turn make up the "table" that stands before us. The atoms and molecules of the table reflect photons of light, some of which impinge on the retinas of our eyes. That is as far as they go. These photons never enter into us. At the retina, they stimulate cells in a way that causes electro-chemical impulses to pass in patterned form into the brain. The brain manufactures "table" and this is the only place table exists. We "project" the table out there in the position that the fields of "Table" exist and behave as if that is where the table really is. Our other senses form different worlds – each in a particular part of our brain. The entire world, including postulated gods, in like manner, exists only within the nervous tissue of sentient beings. The difference between visions in the brain that *do* and *do not* have an external counterpart is covered more fully in essay 144 of this book. See also essay 796.

504

> But there are a great many things [in Christianity] that cannot be understood until after you have gone a certain distance along the Christian road.
>
> C.S. Lewis (1898-1963)

To understand what Lewis is saying, we must translate: "But there are a great many things in Christianity that will not be accepted until enough time has elapsed for ample brainwashing." The Jesuits had their idea of what that time must be: the first seven years of a child's life. If put off until later in life, the procedure is more complicated; but it is not impossible.

The educational process begins in seminaries, the theological schools that educate our priests and preachers. The education begins with three premises that cannot be proved: God exists, the Bible is His infallible word, and Jesus is His divine son. Lesson after lesson continues piling up inferences based on these premises until they end up with an entire system of organized superstitions that are expected to guide theological students for the rest of their lives.

Once they are ordained, the new preachers are ready to indoctrinate others into mysticisms from then on forever. That is what attendance at church is all about. The congregation attends what are called church services. Becoming "ordained" for the new preachers has meant in part becoming adept in interpolating into those services brainwashing procedures far more subtle and cleverly contrived than those the Jesuits required for brainwashing young children. Few who attend church for as much as four or five years will ever be able to understand what has happened to their minds. They are hooked for life. If they do not insist on foisting their newly acquired beliefs on others by coercion, we wish them well.

505

> This is the danger, when vice becomes a precedent.
>
> Oen Johnsen
> "Of the Diversity of Wits" - *Timber*

For us to accept our bad habits and vices is the real disaster. We are not likely to put much effort into getting rid of that which we desire and eagerly embrace. Until we understand that we ourselves are the protagonists in the fight against our moral frailties we are not likely to succeed in eliminating them. Those who help us are more likely to become enablers than confederates in the battle against evil.

"Everybody does it," is the refrain when our government functionaries are found guilty of graft, political patronage, jobbery, or pork-barrel legislation. Alexander Pope in *An Essay on Man* put it in verse:

Vice is a monster of so frightful mien,
As to be hated needs but to be seen;
Yet seen too oft, familiar with her face,
We first endure. Then pity, then embrace.

Is this not the danger? We see violence on television and in the movies, we read about crime in our newspapers; murder mysteries are bestsellers. Terror becomes a precedent, the norm, serving as an example and even justification for mankind's behavior. Something is grossly wrong: We educate ourselves to become monsters when we could just as easily instill in each and every human being respect for honesty and an attitude conducive to peace.

Man is a product of his environment and his heredity, we are told. Yet people still will insist that the violence on the big and small screens has nothing to do with all the crime in our societies. People who think like that, do not think. Their nervous systems do not function sanely. They are like CEOs of tobacco companies who know perfectly well that they kill more than 400 thousand people in this country every year, but yet go making cigarettes, justifying their own personal greed - more important than looking truth squarely in the face. With deaths of people in other countries who smoke U.S. Cigarettes added to our own, they certainly kill more than a million people every year. It takes all kinds, we are told. Need a sane society include that kind, or can a society teach its citizens to care?

506

As Newton was deified, so the temptation was great to Newtonify the Deity. If science and rationalism had raised questions about God and unsettled belief, then what more logical response than to shore up religion by remodeling it in the image of science and rationality?

James Turner
Without God; Without Creed

You may be sure that if churches do anything like shoring up religion by remodeling it in the image of rationality, the reason for their doing so will have nothing to do with logic. The only thing that will convince religions to change is a threat to their survival.

As people become more and more educated and learn to think rationally, they begin to perceive the failings of their religions. If they cannot convince their church leaders to bring church policies and the liturgy up to date, they leave. Even while church attendance worldwide is increasing, intellectuals are leaving the churches in droves. Catholic churches are losing priests and nuns and increasing the laity.

Churches are finding new recruits among the uneducated and impoverished peoples of the world. New churches in Ecuador and Peru are placed among natives in the Amazon basin in far greater numbers than in the cities. They will all be in desperate straits when native populations, too, become educated.

507

Once you believe in the devil, you belong to him.

Thomas Mann (1875-1955)

An adult may believe in the devil as firmly as a four-year-old believes in Santa Claus. Then both adult and child may permit their "demigods" to control their behavior. To the extent that they believe, they make themselves slaves. The misguided adult devil-worshiper may never want to outgrow his childish conceptions, and he has an excuse for all of his nefarious behavior from then on forever. His belief may not protect him in court, but he seems to think it serves lesser purposes throughout his life. It is a comfort for him to believe that he himself is not altogether to blame for his moral deficiencies.

The child, on the other hand, is not that free. He must soon be able to see through his parents' "playful" deception if he is not to be scarred for life. The unswerving faith he had in the integrity of his parents has suffered a severe blow. The gods that conceived him in their own image are, after all, only human.

Even Anton Szandor La Vey, high priest of the Church of Satan, does not believe in a living Satan, but the Catholic church and most Protestant churches do. They would be lost without their Satan. It is Satan that keeps them in business, gives them themes for sermons. Our religious leaders seem somehow to have convinced their omnipotent God to keep His hands off their Satan. Satan is money in the bank. If he did not exist they would have to invent Him.

508

> If God were not a necessary being of Himself, He might seem to be made for the use and benefit of men.
>
> John Tillotson (1630-1694)

Might seem to be made for? Then who would do the making? Were not a necessary Being? Necessary to whom? Tillotson is hopelessly entangled in infinite regress and does not seem to understand that he is. Tillotson seems to consider his God as simply a self-sufficient supernal entity floating around for the hell of it, paying no more heed to us than flotsam and jetsam on an otherwise empty ocean. Tillotson's God does not take us seriously – so there is no reason for us to take him seriously. He does us no good, so all we need to ask of Him is that he do us no harm. Knowing that we are on our own, with no hope of help and in no danger of interference, we will be much more likely to buckle down to the job of making this world one in which we can all survive and enjoy ourselves doing so.

Tillotson's God is about as good as no God at all. He is like a leprechaun in Ireland, useful as a topic for conversation, but we cannot expect of Him even the capability of substantiating his own existence. If we choose to do so, we may talk to our phantom God in the sense that we talk to a long dead uncle, a kind of family heirloom that has acquired reputation but no truly ponderable character. To a daughter in the family, this uncle, this God, has become a guiding conscience that has been formed entirely within her imagination. He becomes a guardian spirit who understands her, likes her, and if he were to give her advice, it would be precisely the advice she needs to orient herself properly. She tests her own decisions by how she "knows" he would judge them. Her decisions turn out better than if they were not given that test. "Uncle," like any good conscience, will not allow her to experiment with immorality in any form, so he "serves" even though he himself never knows that he does.

A completely useless God, like the girl's uncle, may be the only kind of God that will ever be of any use to us

509

When, and how, and at what stage of our development did spirituality and our strange notions of religion arise? The need for worship which is nothing more than our frightened refuge into propitiation of a Creator we do not understand? A detective story, the supreme who-done-it, written in undecipherable hieroglyphics, no rosetta stone supplied by the consummate mystifier to tease us poor fumbling unravellers of his plot.

Vita Sackville-West (1892-1962) *May – In Your Garden Again*

To be able to answer S-W's question would go a long way toward unraveling the mystery of religion's origins. The "strange notions" arose so far back in recorded history that we have little to go on. The mystery of the need for worship is resolved in part by Aldous Huxley's explanation: The evolving and only existing species of the genus Homo acquired a modicum of intelligence – enough to arouse its curiosity and ask questions, but not enough to respond sensibly. Man does not understand that the reasons answers are not forthcoming is that he is trying to commune with a Creator who is a product of his own imagination. Given all the patterns of interlocution human minds have ever conceived, that one must take the prize as the height of absurdity.

Jean-Paul Sartre tells us that "we are in charge, responsible all the way." When we accept Sartre's thesis, we can reject the half-baked fables of the theologians and get on with the task of building a better world. Our latent expertise will flower, and we will surprise ourselves with our own capabilities.

510

The religion which allies itself with injustice to preach down the natural aspirations of the masses is worse than atheism.

Henry George (1839-1937)
The Irish Language Question

To choose atheism as a standard of evil beyond which lies only decadence is to misunderstand atheism completely. Atheism means nothing, absolutely nothing, other than the refusal to accept beliefs that have no credence.

Henry George, too, makes a good point, but could well have left out the word atheism to do it.

Henry George, the single-tax guru who once ran for mayor of New York City, has an enviable record for sound and meaningful discourse. One of his legacies is a school bearing his name in New York City that it seems will survive in perpetuity. I attended classes there for some time and once wrote a brief article for its bulletin.

Religions that ally themselves with injustice are not rare. When religions preach discrimination, snobbery, racism, homophobia, mammonism, mythology, bigotry, and hate, as so many do, they destroy, as Henry George says, "the natural aspirations of man." They merit our condemnation and should be severely censured. We would be better off without them.

511

Go into one of our cool churches, and count the words that could be spared, and in most places the entire sermon would go.

Harvey Cox
The Secular City

Cox implies that at worst what goes on at the pulpit is nothing more than innocuous and useless balderdash. Would that that were so! Unfortunately, too often what the pulpiteer is doing is destroy equanimity, fill the minds of his congregation with unwarranted guilt, and teach them to accept a fantasy world. He tells them little or nothing about how to solve real problems in the real world in which they do in fact live.

If you ask a churchgoer at 2 PM on Sunday what the preacher talked about at 11 AM, three hours earlier, and he can tell you nothing, consider him lucky. What the preacher says has gone in one ear and out the other without stopping long enough for rumination, doing no harm. It is that which does bring the listener to attention that we need to be concerned about. More often than not it is another of the preacher's rambling, bitter diatribes about sins that the preacher is sure are sending the members of his audience straight to hell. He is especially concerned about profanity, blasphemy, impiety, sacrilege, desecration, carnality, unbelief, and idolatry – all the sins artificially fabricated in deference to the mythology that gives structure to his religion. When the preacher does deal with salient, antisocial behavior, it is usually in matter-of-fact, cliché terms that do not make an impression.

512

Religious faith is vital just in so far as it dares to listen to an atheist.

H. N. Brailsford
Property or Peace

"Dares," Brailsford says. In this respect most clerics are cowards. How many theologians will "dare" to read this book?

Religion could help make itself vital if only it dared to stop and think exactly what it is doing to itself by its use of the word "faith." If it understands its privileged domains and proper limitations, religion can have a purpose in the world. But the minute it usurped the word faith to cover up all of its pretenses and posturing, it advertised to the world that it is for the most part sham. Religion is probably right in believing that it has no chance of existing unless it can sell to its prospective adherents the idea of lumping the most obvious elements of its intrinsic mythology under one all-embracing rubric: faith.

The one most important thing the preacher learns in theological school is how best to disguise the true nature of religion: its imposture, pretending honor and moral superiority when it is really pious fraud and deceit. Religion cloaks its deceptions in ritual and pageantry and sanctimonious worship of mythical beings.

The preachers learns that he cannot for a moment be honest with his audience, letting them know that there is no basis for most of what he says. Words like "demonstration" and "proof" cannot apply in religion. Testimony (anecdotal evidence) and carefully contrived fables must substitute for honest revelation. Most preachers live so comfortably with untruth that they do not know when they are lying. Faith will overcome all. Reason must be completely obliterated.

513

Metaphysics is almost always an attempt to prove the incredible by an appeal to the unintelligible.

H.L. Mencken (1880-1956)
Minority Report

"It has been said," according to W. Somerset Maugham in *The Summing Up*, "that metaphysics is the finding of bad reasons for what we believe on instinct." Montaigne, found little good to be said for the pursuit of mystic philosophies. In *Essays*, he said: "Wonder is the foundation of all philosophy; inquiry, the progress; ignorance, the end. Even Pascal has a negative note for it: "To make light of philosophy is to be a true Philosopher"(Pensées).

Human beings have a strange preference for pursuing that which will never be attained. Or maybe it is not as strange as it seems. As I explain elsewhere, pursuing the unattainable may be the wisest pursuit of all. If the objective sought is distant, problematical, and the road to it is full of obstacles, the project may take many years of one's life. It may become for the pursuer a way of life with disappointments, but also with gratifying steps forward and hours of delightful contemplations, ruminations, rejections, serendipitous successes, new paths opening, keeping him completely absorbed, inspired, and happy. If one day all the pieces fall together, and he achieves what he sought to achieve, his findings are ready to be distributed for the good of humanity. Perhaps his project and his life end together.

What happens to him personally may otherwise present problems. Success could be a letdown. Now he is superfluous, useless, and he becomes depressed. To start over at his age is unheard of. He has earned retirement, but even the idea appalls him. It would actually please him to find that there are things that still need hammering out, things still to be done. His despair evaporates. Life is good!

514

By the way, Joy [Thompson], you don't have to "walk beside God." There's a little bit of God in all of us which, in essence, makes us all God. As that immortal bard, Homer Simpson said: "God is everywhere, he's omnivorous!

Kevin Powell
Letter to the Editor
Long Beach Press Telegram – August 1, 1997

Omnivorous, yes. And if we judge by the hell God prepared for us, He prefers his souls fried.

With good Christians ritually drinking the blood and eating the flesh of the middle third of the trinity, Powell''s "a little bit of God in all of us" is more understandable – except that it neglects most of the globally considered "all of us."

If God is omnipresent (Psalms 139:7-16) what did Jesus mean when he said in John 17:28, "I come forth from the Father and have come into the world. Again I leave the world and go to the Father"?

And why would Jesus say in Luke 17:21: "The kingdom of God is within you, when it could not be otherwise. Understandably, the authors of the Bible cannot seem to make up their minds firmly about any of the grand array of entities that they speak of in both the Old or New Testaments.

515

You know better than I that in a Republic talent is always suspect. A man attains an elevated position only when his mediocrity prevents him from being a threat to others. And for this reason a democracy is never governed by the most competent, but rather by those whose insignificance will not jeopardize anyone else's self-esteem.

Cesare Borgia (1476-1507)
Speaking to Machiavelli

Machiavelli enlarged his reply to the good Bishop into his famous *Il Principe*, a theory of government published six years after Borgia died. When Lawrence Welk was warned that Myron Floren was a better accordion player than he, his reply was: "I should hope so, I wouldn't hire him if he were not." Myron Floren has had a long and distinguished career as a part of the Welk troupe. He and Welk even played duos. If all our political leaders could take a leaf from that experience, we would have far better governments than we now have.

If those who are instrumental in guiding our religions were chosen only on the basis of merit, the change would be even more dramatic. To imagine our religious leaders being selected only from Emerson's nonconformists and Mill's eccentrics – that is, men who can think for themselves – is to imagine prodigious marvels. The result would be more astonishing by far than any of the seven wonders of the world, or even of the Bible's miracles.

516

Unhappily, too many Christians, so-called, take their religions not from the declarations of Christ, but from the writings of those they esteem learned.

John Marrant (1755-1790)
Sermon, African Lodge, Boston, Massachusetts

Listening to Jesus is not bad advice. With his help, we might compose a truly efficacious treatise on morality. But Jesus gives us little that would help in formulating a religion. He would repudiate most of what today is called Christianity, and even his own efforts would have disappeared from history had it not been for Paul, the Gospel writers, and finally, Constantine.

Christianity has as many faces as there are people who write about it. The known "words of Jesus" would hardly fill a 60-page pamphlet, yet some 60,000 "Lives of Jesus" have been written, and libraries are filled with other books that have sections dedicated to Jesus. Obviously, the authors of such books must invent much of what they write. They are not writing about Jesus as much as they are writing about themselves. We see the level of intelligence of the Jesus people by listening to Christian evangelists ranting on television.

The books religionists write about Jesus are mostly fiction and have no need to stand the test of acceptance by large commercial publishing houses. More often than not, their books are published by the press of their own mother church. I have read enough of their books to know how shallow and incoherent they can be. Many Christians, as John Marrant suggested, get a very distorted view of Christianity from these books.

517

I have been in many of the ancient cathedrals – grand, wonderful, mysterious. But I always leave them with a feeling of indignation because of generations of human beings who have struggled in poverty to build these altars to the unknown god.

Elizabeth Cady Stanton (1815-1902) – Diary entry

It is like looking at the pyramids is it not? The thinking person sees the tremendous amount of work - just to pamper the pharaohs.

Elsewhere, I ask readers to imagine the good that might be done with the trillions of dollars that churches and church properties and procedures cost. Add to that the money it costs to maintain religions and the tax money we all lose by not having that property devoted to commercial enterprises. The jobs provided by the new businesses occupying what was formerly church land should also be counted. Add to that the billions of dollars churches bilk us of every year in their soliciting money for special missionary projects and parochial colleges and "universities" that do the world more harm than good.

Certainly, it all adds up to enough money to keep every child in school and occupied with recreational programs during all of his formative years. Think of the money and lives saved from the consequent decrease in juvenile crime as well as the decrease in adult crime which a well-educated population would refrain from committing. In that kind of global community, crime would decrease to a fraction of what it now is.

The result would be a benefit of such tremendous proportions that it cannot be expressed in mere dollars. We could change the world into a delightful place to live – without fear, with health, and with a kind and caring world population. It would be a world with food and shelter for everyone everywhere, and with the means provided so that everyone could contribute to world progress and prosperity.

In this new world, religion would be replaced by social organizations that would teach us morality, the brotherhood of all mankind. There would no longer be ranting pulpiteers asking that we believe in fables, old-wive's tales, medieval legends of demons and deities, fanciful fabrications of every imaginable description. Reason will triumph and quackery vanish.

518

Intelligence won't put up with being led by the nose by imbeciles who preach from the pulpit.

Anna Magnani (1908-1973)
Quoted in "Anna Magnani" by Oriani Fallaci
The Egoists

If the kind of intelligence Anna Magnani talks about were the endowment of all human beings, not only would the congregations of all churches abandon ship immediately, but so also would the preachers who at present recite the hogwash we hear in their sermons. Religion would disappear at once, for there would be no one to sell it or buy it. Also, the Elmer Gantrys would be out of a job, because there would be no one stupid enough to succumb to their venal mystagoguery. Regent and Liberty and all other religious colleges and universities would change their curriculum radically and immediately or disappear from the academic scene. From all the money saved, there would be more than enough to educate every child through a trade school or university or as far as he or she would want to go. There would be no street gangs or exploited children, for every child would be too busy learning for them to be occupied with peccadillos or turpitude. Taxes from new businesses on the untaxable properties would give the treasury enough to balance the budget and pay the national debt. All countries would become better places to live in. Populations would stabilize, and everyone would have food, shelter, and a better way of life. Progress would increase exponentially.

519

> Philosophy has no end in view save truth. Faith looks for nothing but obedience and piety.
>
>   Baruch Spinoza (1632-1677) –Dutch Philosopher

Truth has only one face. We find philosophy often two-faced, with one philosophy flatly contradicting another. Plato and his student Aristotle were often at odds. The same duplicity is characteristic of most books dealing with the pursuit of wisdom, especially when the word philosophy is used in their titles. An exception is Operational Philosophy by Anatol Rapoport. His book would have been much more meaningfully titled *The Structure of Reason.*

Spinoza could have improved his quotation by adding after his last sentence , another, saying: "The sequel of "faith" is obscurantism. This is precisely why the religious version of this otherwise useful word was coined. Religionists knew that much of what they must necessarily say in order to keep religion from falling apart was organized stupidity, and they needed a word to help bind all their stupidities together.

     "Faith" in effect says to religion's adherents, "We preachers know that most of our declarations are lies, having no relation whatsoever to anything "knowable" in the universe, but we want you to believe what we say anyway.

"Please have faith! Please accept our lies as factual reality." "Reason," the opposite of faith, Martin Luther said, "must be deluded, blinded, destroyed." He called reason the "devil's bride and God's worst enemy." When philosophy attains the end Spinoza says it has in view, and religion restricts its labors to teaching mankind to be moral human beings, we will have a radically different world.

520

Religion has nothing to do with priests, churches, dogmas, or organized beliefs. These things are not religion at all. They are merely social conveniences to hold us within a particular pattern of thought and action. They are the means of exploiting our credulity, hope, and fear.

Krishnamurti (1895-1986)
Think on These Things

What then would a religion be like that we could live with? Krishnamurti does not leave us much room. He makes it obvious that our new religion would have no rites and ritual, no worship of tin gods, wooden icons, stone relics, or any of the other deities we invent. Our new religion would not be the religion we find in churches and synagogues – nor would we find it in the Bible, Book of Mormon, Koran, or other "sacred" literature. We do not get this religion by chanting sacred names or by submitting to any of the other superstitions fabricated by man.

Our viable, new religion would be, for the most part, a "love," a pervading love, intense enough to assure that kindly disposed people will behave morally. The cultivation of kindness, humility, and empathy is the "real" religion. The hate and prejudice, sectarianism and bigotry, or the settled antipathies for foreigners, immigrants, women, and homosexuals that we see in many of today's religions would be utterly incompatible with our new religion.

Our new religion would be a truly ecumenical religion, open to everyone. Initiations, baptism, circumcision, arcane vocabulary, incantations will not be required to become a member. Ideally, it will require no meetings, or meeting houses. It will be simply the way good people live.

521

> The commercial is the invention of a profoundly Christian nation – it proceeds to sell something in which it does not altogether believe.
>
> Norman Mailer
> *Cannibals and Christians*

The parallel between what media advertising and religions do is indeed remarkable, but Mailer need not have singled out Christianity. It has no monopoly on that idiocy. Also, it is known that religionists do often convince themselves to believe the nonsense they proclaim.

I am sorry to be so negative about Mailer's statement which has something very important to say. Nevertheless, one more objection: Our first president objected to calling the United States a Christian nation, and that objection is just as valid today. Norman Mailer has company, however. Jerry Falwell, for one, also insists on calling the United States a Christian nation. Whoever says it, it is increasingly not so.

It is fair to call Israel a Jewish nation. It is fair to call Iran and Pakistan Muslim nations. But the United States is well represented by both of those religions and many others. If the Christian Coalition and other Christian organizations could convince the people of the United States that they live in a Christian nation, they know very well they have then carried out a strategic coup beyond all others. It would be a giant step toward getting rid of official recognition of the rights of all "alien" religions in The United States. Separation of Church and state will soon be forgotten. It would become much easier to insinuate Christian practices and paraphernalia into government buildings and public schools. Turning the United States into a theocracy would suddenly become more than an impossible dream. The Christian Coalition will have won and we would then have lost many of our precious, hard-earned freedoms.

522

> We belong to a strange species which needs to believe that life has a meaning.
>
> Françoise Giroud
> *I Give You My Word*

Much of human folly seems to arise from the fact that we are intelligent "but,"as Aldous Huxley says, "not yet intelligent enough."

Albert Camus, whom Françoise knew well, said in *The Myth of Sisyphus*: "It was previously a question of finding out whether or not life had to have a meaning to be lived. It now becomes clear, on the contrary, that it will be lived all the better if it has no meaning."

If the idea of meaning can be expressed only by a mixture of myth, legend, superstition, folklore, and prejudice, then we must repudiate meaning. Meaning has significance only as a local, temporal concept, not as an empyreal absurdity.

But even if not in any cosmic currency, purpose and meaning can be crucially important. Without them, we would all live dreary existences. That meaning, that purpose, can relate to the well-being and happiness of ourselves and all other human beings on earth. To have a sincere desire to leave the earth a better place for humans beings to live is important for our sanity. We need not fabricate supernatural, pseudomeanings for us to live fruitfully and happily – and therefore meaningfully.

Children usually live carefree lives, without concerns about their future. But in each child's life, if he is not simply born into a profession or does not manifest a precocious aptitude that sends him automatically into a particular field, he comes to a point where he is at a crossroads. Neither purpose nor meaning has crossed his mind, and he is mentally adrift. Then, precisely then, that "never in the child's life to be forgotten" wise counselor is urgently in demand. Sometimes it is only a simple remark; sometimes an animated pep talk; sometimes a gruff and impassioned, but good-natured, appeal. But a caring advisor, if the time is right, can make all the difference in the child's life. That point in the child's life having been missed, accounts for many of the wasted lives we hear about almost daily in the news.

523

The Earth's most hateful crimes have in thy name been done.
John Greenleaf Whittier (1807-1892)
The Gallows

It boggles the imagination to believe that the Christian Crusades could really have happened. Our modern examples are no better: The Turks murdering two out of every three of all existing Armenians, the Nazis killing eleven million Jews, Communists, Gypsies, and mentally retarded, the Japanese massacring 350 thousand Chinese in the rape of Nanking, the Chinese decimating the people of Tibet, Pol Pot murdering two million of his own Cambodian people, the Indonesians ravaging East Timor, the people of Uganda, Rwanda, Zaire, Nigeria, Sierra Leon, Afganistan, Iraq, and Iran killing millions more. Also we have in 1995 the highly organized massacre of more than 7,000 men in Strebrenika, Bosnia and in other Bosnian towns on the part of the Serbs. Two world wars plus those of Korea, Viet Nam, and our own Civil War account for many million more lives destroyed – and it seems that wars will never end.

Religion, with its bellicose deities, account for most of our wars. Nationalism, with its slightly less fanatically worshiped gods, account for the rest. As the song goes, "When will we ever learn?" Why is mankind not endowed with enough intelligence to see what it does to itself, and how to end the horror that is war?

If human minds could begin to understand the suffering caused by the many wars that have taken place in the past thousand years, would they not somehow end this carnage? Presumably, the omniscient and omnipotent Deity these human beings postulate can grasp the enormity of man's inhumanity to man – and is powerful enough to stop it. Then why is it that He does not do so? Only one voice, it seems to me, unequivocally tells us why. Is it not obvious that he has it right:? "God's only excuse is that He does not exist"!

524

> The anti-Semite offered the effrontery, [giving] you at once the wound and the burden of proper response toward it.
>
> Laura Z. Hobson
> *Gentleman's Agreement*

This is true of all irrational prejudice. Knowing exactly what the response should be must always be difficult. I remember well the Retrum family who lived across the street from us in Dawson, Minnesota. They were fairly weathy, and we (the Dolans) were always living marginally. I remember little or no communication beteen the adults in the two families – but also no particular friction – this despite the fact that we were a family with an Irish name living in that almost totally Scandinavian community. There were no frictions, that is, until a wealthy aunt came to visit them from a "distant land." I remember few details, for that is now seventy years ago.

But I remember distinctly that for no reason I could understand, immediately frictions did then arise, and the Retrum children informed my twin brother and me that they were no longer permitted to play with us. We were deemed by the visiting aunt and presumably the rest of the family as being a certain degrading element that could serve only to contaminate their children. The thing that puzzled me more than anything else was the response of my mother and father. They seemed not to share my own intense umbrage, and said and did nothing. When the rich aunt left after an extended visit, things went back to normal, which I then understood not to be very normal at all, explaining, in part, the Retrum family's concurrence with their relative's bigoted behavior. Years later, but long before I saw the movie version of Laura Hobson's *Gentleman's Agreement*, I understood more fully what had occurred.

525

We tend to suffer from a strange complacency that this [our extinction] can never happen, that there is something special about us, that we are somehow beyond biological control. But we are not.... Sooner or later we shall go, and make way for something else.

Desmond Morris (1928-   )
The Naked Ape

The notion that we are special may be the most dangerous of all the roseate reveries in which we indulge. We will be unaware of how closely we approach the brink of self-annihilation if we decide erroneously that such an eventuality is impossible. If we are to survive the remaining time that the sun will support us, we must understand that human extinction not only can happen, but has a high probability of happening. Unless we determine what are the perilous cultural trends in today's world we may disappear. Unless we analyze those trends and determine to reverse them, we will not survive.

The idea that there is this "god-thing" out there always ready to snatch us from danger in the nick of time is idiotic. As the dinosaurs were not saved, we will not be saved. Unless we use the brains we have to resolve rather than to exacerbate our problems, we are doomed. Our slow-paced march toward Armageddon accelerates: The world has enough nuclear, biological, and chemical weapons to kill all the world's peoples many times over. We, and no one else, will be responsible if we allow ourselves to go the way of the dodo bird and the mastadon.

526

While God waits for His temple to be built of love, men bring stones.
Rabindranath Tagore (1861-1941)
Fireflies

It is a beautiful sentiment, but the God of the scriptures is not a God who is looking for a Temple of love. If the congregation wants a temple in which they can worship a God of love, they must first design their God. He will be very different from the bloodthirsty God they have been worshiping.

The temple itself is no problem. It can be a clearing in the woods, a cul-de-sac in a canyon wall, the flat top of a mesa, or a conventional temple made of stone. It will not matter. First the congregation needs a God whom they do not fear, who does not treat them like puppets, who is not constantly belittling them, and who has no hell for them to fall into. He will not be the God who killed Uzzah for touching a box, who killed 70 more for looking into that box, who allowed Jephthah to burn up his daughter, who taunted Abraham about killing his son, who killed 250 men who brought Him incense, who praised David who screwed another man's wife, and who killed thousands of people, a God who himself killed 16,700 Israelis for no good reason, who destroyed Job's entire family and property over some game He was playing with Satan, who sent a plague to kill 70,000 other Israelis for sins of David, who throughout history has allowed hundreds of religious wars to destroy untold numbers of people, and who pretends to answer prayers, while he ignores humankind completely.

Alfred North Whitehead in his *Adventures of Ideas* asks" What kind of deity is it that would be capable of creating angels and men to sing his praises day and night through all eternity?" If the human race is going on forever worshipng a God, at least they should first fashion a God worth worshiping.

527

The question is not whether a doctrine is beautiful but whether it is true.

Julius Charles Hare
Agust W. Hare
(Divine Hutchmates)

If the doctrines of orthodox religions were true and obviously so, there would be no heresies, no ugliness; we would not be forever introducing new religions, and the world would be running smoothly, without dissensions. Unfotunately, very little is true in religion. Heresies are common and indispensible. New religions are constantly coming into existence. Everywhere there is dissension. In the religious acceptation of truth, beauty may be the only true thing to be found – beauty such as is seen in a romantic poem, a poignant fairy tale, or a fanciful flight into science fiction. If orthodox religion admitted that its only acceptable "substance" is beauty, and that nothing else should be taken seriously, it might find a place in the scheme of things. Joseph Campbell might have had as much fun reciting the nonsense that is religion today as he had with other myths, some of which were religions, ancient religions that are now accepted as beautifully composed nonsense.

To satisfy our love of fantasy, we would do well to build radiant celestial cities populated with Greek gods, Roman gods, Norse gods, Hindu gods, Judeo-Christian-Muslim gods, and Egyptian gods. We might even slip in a few fairyfolk, elfenfolk, brownies, gremlins, leprechauns, nymphs, and dryads. Let us then march them around like magnificent tin soldiers or Barbie dolls, diverting ourselves merrily, joyfully. Finally surfeited, we may get all the craving for childish nonsense out of our systems. Then we might find ourselves capable of living in a serious world of adult thinking and adult doing, no longer with need for puerile sham. What a world we would have!

528

Do not consider a thing as proof because you find it written in books; for just as a liar will deceive with his tongue, he will not be deterred from doing the same thing with his pen. They are utter fools who accept a thing as proof simply because it is in writing.

Moses Maimonides (1135-1204) – Spanish Philosopher

Many readers "know" that no author would spend valuable hours of his days and valuable days of his years writing trivia or tripe and that no publisher would publish it if he did. For this reason, they accept worthless nonsense as readily as consummate good sense. Publishers depend upon such readers as a market for the thousands of "nonbooks" published every year. What all readers must learn beyond any shadow of doubt is that there is nothing in the nature of symbols themselves that prevent their being used as an author sees fit. These readers will then understand, as Moses Maimonides says, that only fools accept a thing as convincing proof simply because it is in writing.

In answer to a newsman's question, a Delhi guru says he has the ultimate proof that God exists: "Because if you look under the letter "G" in the *Oxford English* Dictionary, you will find the word "God."If the guru's reply strikes the reader as silly, naïve, or shallow, then so should all proofs of God' existence; for all proofs of the existence of supernal entities amount precisely to the same thing. They exist because someone set down in print a series of symbols indicating that they do.

529

> My choicest political adviser is God who told me to run for president.
>
> Pat Robertson

He did? And did He tell you at the same time that you would fail miserably? You might think seriously about getting a new political adviser.

When Pope John Paul II was in Costa Rica, he gave a Roman Catholic official there a dressing down and demanded that he renounce his political ambitions. "God does not want his priests to engage in politics." Was that the same God that Pat Robertson converses with – or does each Christian sect have a special God of its own?

If God is passing out advice as freely and frequently as our electronic-media evangelists would have us believe, surely the worries of planet earth are over. Let us ask Him to advise the United Nations about what precisely must be done to end the conflicts all over the world. Or let Him advise the governing bodies of each individual nation about which of their countrymen they should elect as their president, pime minister, or dictator, and then give that person the advice required to solve their problems. If all that fails, let us ask Him to do what Allah told the Muslims He would do if they get into trouble. He would send the necessary number of angels disguised as human beings and dressed in military uniforms to do what was needed to be done. However He does it, an all-wise and all-powerful deity will surely have no trouble putting everything in good order. Pat Robertson will be glad to relay God's instructions if no one else can.

530

Though a good deal of warfare goes on between different classes of animals, or different species, or even different tribes of the same species, peace and mutual support are the rule within the tribe or the species.

Pyotr Kropotkin (1842-1921) – *Mutual Aid*

In his book *Mutual Aid*, Kropotkin documents very well that cooperation among the individuals of all advanced animal species is the dominating factor of evolutionary processes. He says that "those species which know best how to combine, and to avoid competition, have the best chances of survival and of further progressive development. They prosper, while the unsociable species decay." Bees, ants, termites, and mole rats prosper, and may even survive an atomic war. Most species will not.

An evaluation of modern human societies, as well, can be complete only when both dominant currents are taken into account: the self-assertion, individualism, and competition of the members of these societies on the one hand, and the mutual aid, cooperation, the universality of love and harmony among all members of the species, on the other.

With the wars, both hot and cold going on in the world at all times, it might seem that mutual cooperation in the human species might be hard to confirm. But even without the considerable aid of Kropotkin's book, a little reflection will show that cooperation is still predominant in accounting for human progress. Almost all human populations have unifying organizations and charities of many kinds. Big brothers, big sisters, scouts, telephone call-ins, think tanks, pro-bono legal work are a part of every large city and more often recently of rural communities as well. World organizations that aim   to   help everyone are now common: The World Health Organization, The World Bank, Doctors Without Borders, and UNICEF, are examples.

Conflict makes news, while everyday peaceful cooperation does not. But if the latter were not the rule in human affairs, we would long ago have become extinct. The formation of tribes, clans, communes, guilds, labor unions, cooperatives, cities, and countries occurred precisely to augment cooperation. Both communal marriage and two-parent families show that we are mutual-aid societies beyond doubt.

It is by mutual aid that mankind has been able to develop his knowledge, arts, industry, and science. Robert Tyler Flewelling says: "Neither province, parish, nor nation, neighborhood, family, nor individual can live profitably in exclusion from the rest of the world." In the practices of mutual aid, are found the origin of our ethical systems, that part of religions that tend to serve and not enslave mankind.

531

> After the first death, there is no other....
>
> Edith Sitwell (1887-1964)
> "Dylan Thomas" – Atlantic Monthly Feb 1954

What Edith Sitwell says has been said before – with different messages: (1) The first death will be such a glorious experience that nothing will ever begin to equal it. (Once you have seen Paris, no other city will do.) (2) The first death is the end of things. Not only is there no other death; there is no other anything else. (All lights have gone out). (3) After the first death, we then enter a level of life that lasts forever. (Even fire and brimstone cannot kill again). Which of these three interpretations do you think would sit well with Dame Sitwell? Perhaps even she was not sure.

If Sitwell and her two younger brothers had only one death each, not they nor anyone else will ever know. Even Samuel Butler was constrained to admit: "To himself everyone is immortal; he may know that he is going to die, but he can never know that he is dead." That is quite an admission. No theologian I know would say that souls in heaven have no awareness of the life they lived on earth. To admit that would be to say that all the asseverations of religion are at most symphonic sophistry.

If there is no continuity of consciousness between the person on earth and the souls (or whatever) in an afterlife, it would be exactly the same as if God created a completely new set of denizens to populate heaven. Certainly no earthling would be concerned about getting to heaven if the *he* of "a former earth life" doesn't know he is there. Without an awareness of the same "self" before and after death, the transmigration has not in essence (or in actual fact, it is fair to say) taken place. If in heaven he looked down to see "souls" frying in hell, he would wonder why. So would the souls who are frying.

532

I turned to speak to God / About the world's despair, / But to make bad matters worse / I found God wasn't there.

Robert Frost (1874-1963)

I wonder how he knew. Many people turn to speak to God, get no answer time after time, and still believe he is there. The difference between Frost and these many, I would guess, is that Frost knew very well that when he turned to speak to God he would not get an answer. The many others believe with such fervor that He is there that nothing will dissuade them, not even constant failures to make contact.

Television evangelists, of course, claim permanent hotline hookup with Deity, without ever demonstrating to anyone that the messages they claim to receive are anything more than hallucinations or, as is more likely, consciously contrived fiction. It takes a special kind of credulity on the part of television viewers who allow themselves to be taken in by such obvious deception. They would not think of scrutinizing the messages or asking for explanations or on-the-spot demonstrations of the spectragrahic marvel. They will believe; regardless of the odds, they will believe.

533

Laws that prescribe what everyone must believe... are often passed to appease the anger of those who cannot abide independent minds.

Baruch Spinoza (1632-1677

At the time of the Greek heresy trials, and in colonial America, heresy was a capital offense. Those burned at the stake for heresy, witchcraft, etc., are the tragic victims of this pathological passion that some people have to exercise control over the way other people behave.

A predominance of independent minds, of course, would mean the end of religion. Religion simply cannot put up with the likes of Clarence Darrow, Friedrich Nietzsche, Alfred North Whitehead, Robert Ingersoll, H.L. Mencken, Stendhal, Bertrand Russell, or others like them.

Independent minds, of course, are the catalyst of all progress. Without the Ralph Waldo Emersons and John Stuart Mills of history, and every epoch has many, we would still be living in the age of inquisitions. With nothing but conformists and conventionalists as models for young people to emulate, there would be no progress. We all would agree that the world we have is exactly the world we want. There would be no use for a Congress, no bills to be passed, no use for committees to examine issues. If such stultification were to spread to all countries, progress everywhere would stop. The struggles to fashion a better world would end. The best of all possible worlds is the one we live in. Why strive to obtain that which we already have?

534

We're more popular than Jesus Christ now.... Some of the pop stars I like are more important to me than God.... I would hope we mean more to people than putting money in a church basket and saying ten Hail Marys on a Sunday.

> Noel Gallagher, speaking of his band *Oasis*
> *Newsweek* "Perspectives" July 21, 1997

Gallagher has it exactly right. Whether or not that is to say much for his band, I do not know. One thing to say for it, at least, is that it exists. And many people "know," they do not guess, that it does. Another thing: Whether people know or do not know, they are not going to start a war over their differences of opinions. In a third and last consideration, *Oasis* scores even better: The money earned by Gallagher and his band members, as well as the places where they entertain, has a fair chance of being put to good use. That will not happen in many churches. The more opulence, the more harm generally they can do in spreading their misguided mythologies to more and more gullible people. We see about us the anxieties fanatical religions introduce into people's lives. As church coffers overflow, so do the egos of church leaders. They become even more convinced that people approve of their monstrous deceit.

535

> The practice of dealing with facts instead of words is what distinguishes science from metaphysics.
>
> Lancelot Hogben (1895-1975)
> *Principles of Animal Biology*

Science is knowledge. Metaphysics deals with nonscience, nonknowldege. Our command of science comes from study, using reason. Metaphysics has nothing to study. Its basis, myth, can be talked about but not studied in the sense that nature can be studied. Metaphysics (all orthodox religions) comes from the same place fairy tales come from.

Probably no better corrective to the wide-spread and unwarranted denigration of science can be found than Chapter 2 of Richard Dawkins' book Unweaving *the Rainbow.* Dawkins agrees with Hogben in his distinction between science and Metaphysics and in all of his books rejects the mythologies to which religions become attached.

Both science and religion search for truth. What the scientist finds is a truth that is enlightening and stimulates progress. What the religionist finds is a vague, undefinable "truth" that is absolute and unchanging, leaving no room for progress. There is no such thing as verifying the proclamations of metaphysics. They must be taken on faith.

Science shows us that we do not need gods to explain lightning and thunder or how celestial bodies orbit one another. Science also shows us that gods do nothing to help explain the anomalous subtleties of human nature – why it is, for example, that we are often squabbling. When we do get meaningful answers, man and not gods will furnish them. Encouraging and heeding rational interchanges between members of our societies will be our salvation. If man is to live serenely and securely, he will do his own explaining. He will not exchange his assiduously acquired intellectual competence for any or all the mythologies that religions espouse.

536

> Some feel that for a minister to be controversial because he unashamedly proclaims the Gospel is one thing, and quite acceptable, but for him to arouse ire because he espouses a particular secular cause, such as full employment or the halting of the nuclear arms race, is quite another.
>
> Christopher Catherwood
> *Five Evangelical Leaders*

The vocation by which a person earns his livelihood, of course, should have nothing to do with his rights to express his opinions about whatever social problems. For me, anytime a preacher abandons his customary sermons about the mythological underpinnings of his religion and seeks to guide his congregation about the practical concerns of their lives he is at his best. When what he deals with is the welfare of people generally, even matters of life and death, as in the examples Catherwood gives us, we must applaud him.

If ministers of religion serve any real purpose on this planet, it should be to awaken us to important matters of conscience. We wish them success in giving love, kindness, understanding, and human decency the widest possible distribution. If they could forget the myth that has kept them so enthralled, and instead preach morality, they would then be mankind's greatest servants, and Homo sapiens might have a real chance for survival. Those among preachers who listen to no one but "God" have no one to teach them to recognize their folly. We expect most of them to continue in their world of make-believe.

537

> When [as a religionist], you get stuck in your own metaphors, interpreting them as facts, then you are in trouble.
> Joseph Campbell (1904-1987) – *The Power of Myth,*

The title of Campbell's book gives us advance notice of what to expect. As the world's foremost student of the myths ancient civilizations devised to guide their lives, Campbell was well aware of the intrinsic nature of and the influence of myth wherever it is construed as something more than superstition. We need no longer wonder how he would extrapolate his convictions to apply to our modern mythologies. The *Power of Myth* makes that clear.

If we are not alert, we can all become slaves of other people's words when they are cleverly and specifically designed for that purpose. The motivation of those whose principal purpose in life is to control other human beings, cheating them, oppressing them, urging them to believe vast assemblages of lies isn't hard to understand. We see the greed, arrogance, and tyrannical dispositions that crop up among religion's mystagogues and know what they are capable of. Few people escape their rapacious talons.

Our lives are set on paths of obsequious servility, kowtowing to religious charlatans and the dreamed-up deities they fabricate to frighten and subjugate us. We become pawns and puppets, incapable of making important decisions for ourselves. We spend our hard-earned money on sacred grounds, religious edifices, pompous pageantry, and extravagant funerals.

We help pay for parochial schools where our children's minds are warped and squeezed into identical molds, turning them into automatons. We lose all ability to think for ourselves. We repeat the follies of our neighbors, believing as they do and making the same robotic gestures and genuflections. If there are enough of us observing the same pietistic practices, we will soon be trapped in a suffocatingly rigid theocracy that leaves no room for fun, frivolity, or the keen intellectual vision required to make progress in every worthwhile human enterprise.

538

There are no unnatural or supernatural phenomena, only large gaps in our knowledge of what is natural.... We should strive to fill those gaps of ignorance.

Edgar Mitchell

Filling the gaps of ignorance is a fair definition of what science is all about. What we fill the gaps with is knowledge. Nature is all. Supernatural and unnatural are oxymorons. There can be no beyond-all, nor can there be an un-all. Natures continues to be nature regardless of the prefixes pretending to alter it. "Creation science" so-called, emphasizes gaps that exit in our knowledge of nature, as if that were a complete denial of biological evolution. Its practitioners now want to increase the gaps in education by removing much of what is significant in science education from high-school and university classes. If ever they were to accomplish their goals, this country will be set back to the dark ages.

In his book *Science and Human Values*, Jacob Bronowski tells us how indispensable he considers science to be in modern society. But many religionists today are denigrating science and bragging about the fact that they do. Their idea of the place science has in our modern world is so myopic that they are unaware of what they do to themselves. The struggle of religion against science began with early astronomy, with early medical science, and with early psychology. Point by point, religion has had to retreat, leaving science to continue its investigations. Their latest clash with the biological sciences, may be the most idiotic of all. They pick out one by one the various discoveries of biologists and with pathetically childish arguments try to discredit them. They continue to fail and seem unaware that they do.

539

[We believe] that on no account can a monied man enter heaven. Ah! How cheerfully we consign ourselves to perdition.

> Herman Melville (1819-1891)
> *Moby Dick*

We believe no such thing, but for the sake of argument, let us go along with Melville's and the Bible's contention. Certainly, money is a root of evil. Salaries egregiously disproportionate to contribution are a sad reality. Most crime, in its ultimate causes, involves money. The extreme wealth of some of the rich and the extreme poverty of some of the poor is the most telling argument we have against any political and economic system the world has developed so far. The fantastic incomes some television evangelists are garnering is disgraceful. The wealth Wall-Street tycoons are accumulating by inside trading is a constant scandal.

It is true that "you can't take it with you." But you can surely leave behind evidence that it existed. The libraries, museums, and other legacies bequeathed by the dying rich are a benefit to mankind, but who knows how much greater benefit it might have been if the money had been left in the hands of the poor from whom it was bilked. Every time a Wall-Street tycoon makes a killing, many, many others lose. When the likes of T. Boone Pickens makes six million dollars in leveraged buyouts and hostile takeovers, the same is true. Money never comes from nowhere, but out of the pockets of someone somewhere. Always when the few win, the many lose. In the world of megamergers, greed becomes the fashion and corporate charity dwindles. When a Michael Milken donates twenty million dollars to charity, he is not giving money he earned, but money that was stolen from those who did not have the advanced knowledge of company changes, inside trading, that he was privy to.

540

Fanaticism is to superstition what delirium is to fear or rage to anger.
Voltaire (1694-1778)

Without conceding strict parallelism to Voltaire's analogies, we do agree that rage, delirium, and fanaticism all mean a state of mind in which there is loss of control over mental processes. But there is one marked difference. From rage or delirium, there is hope of recovery. The fanatic is almost certainly lost for all time. The fanatic regards all ways of thinking that are not his own as mistaken. Reason abandons him; values are forgotten. He has an "uncompromising determination" that turns him into a menace to himself and to society. One fanatic will chant Namu Amida Butsu (honoring Buddha) as another will chant the name Krishna (essay 623). The noises they make make less sense than the babbling of a baby.

The fanatical television evangelist will say anything that suits his fancy. He disregards truth and removes all stops: The signs are everywhere: Armageddon is upon us. The list of sins that will send a person straight to hell gets longer. The hope for anyone who does not believe all the evangelist's warning is nil.

Fear is the principal message. The fanatical preacher is not satisfied until he has installed in all members of his congregation a distressing agitation that keeps them intimidated and apprehensive. The "God of love" must be feared. "O that they would fear me" (Deuteronomy 5:29). The horror of hell keeps everyone that takes it seriously submerged in the ultimate personal disaster: despair. No truly sane person, fortunate enough to be assigned to heaven, could enjoy it knowing that his less-than-perfect neighbors were frying in hell. For earthlings, unduly contemplating an afterlife, sleep becomes troubled, difficult. "Fear came upon me, and trembling, making my bones shake? (Job 4:140). Danger is everywhere, lurking, threatening, alarming.

The average fanatical religionist needs no authoritarian restrictions on freedom of expression to protect him from heretical ideas. He does that job for himself. The first line he reads in any book that contravenes his cherished beliefs is as far as he goes. "If the book says that," he tells himself, "I need read no further!" He has his own impenetrable shield against all enlightenment. He claims that his belief is strong. But he knows that it is not. It would not withstand the incursion of rational ideas. To be safe, he simply refuses to deal with any system of declarations not wholly in agreement with his own. He has not the freedom that an atheist has to read anything and everything on all sides of all issues. His lack of confidence in his shaky religious beliefs does not permit it. If he were to read further in the dreadful book he rejects, it would be in abject fear of each next paragraph. He cannot read as does the man whose beliefs have firm foundations, welcoming new ideas to bounce off his own, confident that they will make his firm convictions all the more firm. The joy of free selection in the marketplace of ideas is something the fanatic will never know.

Chapter XIV

The Successful Preacher

541

When we get sick, we want a competent doctor. When have need of a home, we want a competent carpenter. If we wage war, we want competent generals and admirals. Only when we want a village preacher are we content with mediocrity.

The truth may be that we must be content with mediocrity. Preachers are seldom competent, seldom able to distinguish truth from falsehood. Few are truly brilliant, for if they were so bountifully endowed, they would not become preachers. In the nescience of youth, despite sharp minds, some allow themselves to become ordained, and then lead lives of sad disillusionment.

Many preachers are wise enough not to believe what they themselves say in their sermons and are surprised when others believe them. They succeed as preachers because they are adept at making lies sound truthful, pretense seem respectable, and can even give the appearance of sense to what is actually pure nonsense.

If they can convince a congregation that they know everything about that which they know nothing, they will have long and profitable careers. The preachers who in early times had only to be convincing in their capacity as magicians now must fascinate, move, coax, humbug, frighten, and otherwise bamboozle the members of their congregations with nothing but words. The artful dodger, not the true believer, survives. He is opposed to anything resembling rational thinking, knowing that if the members of his congregation began to behave in accordance with the dictates of reason they would destroy him and his church.

542

> Christianity must now rise above the limitations of orthodoxy just as
> the free world must rise above the limitations of nationalism if we are
> not to pull the civilized world down around our ears.
>
> Agnes Meyer (1887-1970)
> Lecture "Democracy and Clericalism"

It surprises me every time I find a person new to me who is fully
aware of the parallelism between religion and nationalism. There is
nothing like religion and nationalism to induce people to
institutionalize loyalty to God and country. The symbolism for both
has no referents other than those that form within human nervous
systems. Their principal enemies are other nationalisms and other
religions equally revered, equally capable of converting subjects into
martyrs. Meyer singles out Christianity, but all orthodoxies are the
same. Everyone in all parts of the world must understand what
religion and nationalism do to us if ever we are to become one
people living in peace.

War would disappear if every human being were aware of what it
really is: collective murder, rape, arson, and pillage. Only by lying to
ourselves and to others, glamorizing and romanticizing man's most
heinous occupation, have we been able to keep man constantly
waging wars. Nationalism, like religion, is a form of worship in
every country in the world today. And where the jealous god of
nationalism must share the stage with the jealous god of religion,
there will always be problems of separation of Church and State.

543

> Half, at least, of all morality is negative and consists of keeping out
> of mischief.
>
> Aldous Huxley (1894-1963)
> *The Doors of Perception*

Mischief is a catch-all for so many things that Huxley cannot go
wrong. Keeping one's hands off other people's property is often a
good beginning. Keeping out of other people's business is another.
Keeping one's mouth shut when one has nothing constructive to say
about others is still another. Already we are half-way along the road
to becoming moral human beings.

News in the daily newspapers and on commercial television programs is one item after another of people doing mischief. Delinquency, misdemeanor, and felony designate behavior that is not moral and are terms we are all familiar with. Refraining from becoming involved in any level of legal mischief is much of the rest of the trip to morality.

Keeping out of mischief, for most of us, means keeping busy, busy at beneficial activities, that is. Idleness, some declare is the root of all evil. It may be that the least attactive aspect of heaven for many people is the prospect of an eternity of idle sterility.

Max Kauffman said: "My son has taken up meditation – at least it's better than sitting doing nothing." "Training" in meditation, however, awaits credible defense. Most busy people prefer "impromptu" meditation. I hardly set aside the page I am working on that I do not in meditation think of a better way to say something I have just written. All people at work do the same. A carpenter will in meditation think of a better way to make a door slide, a table leg rigid, or a hinge swing properly. Seldom is just sitting time completey wasted. *Dolce far niente*, the Italians say, and they are not just whistling Dixie.

544

> Man has never worshipped anything but himself.
>
> Richard Francis Burton (1821-1890)

In a strict sense the only world a man knows is the world that exists within himself. No one can prove there is a world beyond his own skin. He may say he is worshiping gods that exist somewhere "out there" but the gods are not out there. They have a reality, but it is the reality of a certain nervous structure within his own brain. Of course, that is true also of the world he personally sees, hears, feels, smells, and tastes. To preserve his own sanity, he postulates a world out there, a part of the vast interrelational structure with which he seems always to be reacting. His mind is constantly at work constructing worlds that do and worlds that do not have an external counterpart. A man cannot worship a god, but only the nervous-structure manifestation of that god - a part of himself.

It is well again to remind ourselves that man has no sure way of distinguishing between visions fabricated entirely within himself and visions that result from external stimuli. All of us "feel" that we can distinguish between the two kinds of visions, but often we cannot. There would be no such thing as theistic religions if we could consistently distinguish between them – as no sane person would knowingly worship deities that are a part his own brain activity and nothing more.

545

I got into this God racket, boys, because I found it the easiest way to make money.

Pierre Berton
The Comfortable Pew

There are far more Elmer Gantrys in the world of religion than most people think. Here, Pierre Berton introduces us to one of them, speaking "off the record." It is necessary only to listen to the television evangelists to realize that there is some of Elmer Gantry in all of them. Willism B. Michaels, writing for *The New York Times*, April 2, 1987, said: "The fact is that television evangelism is a deceptive way to make a fast buck. It pays well and it pays consistently. No statement, no matter how ridiculous or audacious, fails to produce results."

Unless they are even more feebleminded than we give them credit for, television evangelists cannot possibly believe half of what they say. Much is for pure effect. Their declamatory style is far more important than adherence to truth. Viewers are looking more for a verbal massage than for verbal enlightenment. If the TV evangelist were speaking in a foreign tongue, the effect would be about the same. They are actors more than preachers, and on the average their incomes, counting what they spend on their pageantry, broadcasts, churches, and "universities" is greater by far than those of the average actor. TV evangelists know far better than did Berton's small Canadian-town preacher that the God-racket is an excellent way to get rich.

546

On spaceship earth, there are no passengers; we are all crew.
Marshall McLuhan (1911-1980)

There may be no passengers, but there are many who behave as if they are. The passengers who do nothing (or nothing but harm) are

legion: The idle rich who waste their time in casinos or at endless
parties; the ecclesiastics whose sole occupation is to instill in us their
fabricated mythologies; the Wall-Street tycoons who do nothing but
bilk the rest of us of our savings in order to accumulate personal
wealth; those who lock themselves up in convents and monasteries,
and depend on prayer to solve the world's problems; the radio and
television talk-show psychiatrists who with sixteen words from call-
in "patients" pretend to be able to diagnose mental illnesses, doing
far more harm than good; those who waste money on tobacco,
alcohol, drugs, ostentatious trappings, unwholesome food and many
other useless extravagances, wasting money enough to keep all the
deprived children of the world alive, educated, and hopeful of a
meaningful future. The able-bodied parasites who would rather be on
welfare than do their part in making this world are a constant
concern. None of these are crew. But thankfully they are a minority.

That we should be crew is obvious. There are many who know
that if we are to make of this world the utopia it can be, we must all
do our part. We know we must eliminate greed, cupidity,
callousness, indifference, hate, bigotry, and prejudice. We must
eliminate the divisiveness of walls, whether Chinese, Berlin, or anti-
immigrant – as well as all other boundaries, especially those of
nationalism and religion.

547

> In the end, or course, assimilation or destruction is inevitable. For no
> one can reasonably suppose that the present divisions of mankind
> will last forever.
>
> Morris Raphael Cohen (1880-1947)
> *Reflections of a Wondering Jew*

By assimilation, Cohen means that the world's people must
become one people. The 193 independent countries of this world, all
boasting inviolable sovereignty, may have to relinquish some of the
more uncompromising elements of their precious autonomy if the
human species is to survive. Jacob Bronowski speaks of the need for
an international conscience, eliminating nationalism, an
anachronism. A aggressive isolationist nationalism may be more
detrimental to world progress than any other presently instituted form
of government could ever be.

It was the jingoists and zealots of the populations involved who thwarted the efforts of Simón Bolívar to build a Grand Colombia in Northern South America. It is the same brand of extremists who have never allowed us even to think of forming from all the states and provinces on this continent a United States of North America composed of ninety-two voluntarily cooperating units. Hope for a United States of Africa, Asia, and South America seems remote. The United States of Europe suffers numerous splitting headaches that constantly need attention. Hope for a truly global community is still far off in the future.

Yet we must not stop trying. An amalgamation of the world's societies may be the only salvation for a sick world. Our short-sighted provincialism may lead us to a final confrontation. The primary objective of most of the separately governed divisions of mankind is the annihilation of every free-thinking, independent-minded person in the world except those who think exactly as do they themselves.

548

The media... are dominated by a pro-religious bias. The views of preachers, faith healers, and religious hucksters go largely unchallenged.

Paul Kurtz (1925-)
A Secular Humanist Declaration

The pro-religious tenor of the media is clear and unequivocal. But the unfortunate truth, in my opinion, is that for the most part it does not represent the true sentiments of our newspeople. Those who own and direct our media are more often than not intelligent people who can see through the deceit of religion and do not approve of it. But religious fundamentalists and far-right believers have such a blackmail-oriented stranglehold over all published opinion in this country that the media dare not express themselves openly. "The views of preachers, faith healers, and religious hucksters go largely unchallenged" not because there are not those who would like to challenge orthodox opinion. It is because they know that if they did all the inmates of Christendom would gather forces to denounce them. For being "so indiscreet" they would probably lose their jobs and be ostracized for the rest of their lives. It is the mass of obsequious high-priests of religion that have the real power. They are

the force not to be trifled with. They are the ones who keep this
world submerged in ignorance and obscurantism.

549

> We have a government by representatives too ignorant of science to
> be able to judge the merits of any scientific intent.
>
> Philip Wylie (1902-1971)
> *The Magic* Animal

Dr. Dean Edel, talk-show host, is also constantly lamenting the
fact that government functionaries make judgments about medical
science that they are not qualified to make. Edel suggests that they
either get their medical degrees before they consider legislation that
requires sound medical decisions – or they solicit advice from
members of the medical profession who are competent and who have
no ax to grind.

If legislators have that much difficulty in judgments involving
medical science, what do they do when confronted with Christian
Science or Creation Science: These two aberrations are so far out that
only the most obtuse of ordinary citizens take them seriously. Yet
books are written extolling the virtues of both, and the adherents take
them as seriously as any of the most orthodox take their orthodox
religions. Christian Scientists allow babies to die when a minimum of
medical attention would have saved their lives. Creation scientists
have compiled entire books of fantasy fiction to explain away the
many discoveries of modern biological science that conflict with
holy scripture. The pathetic drivel that both produce is so shallow, so
obviously contrary to reason, logic, or good sense that we wonder
how they lasted through their first week of existence, let alone the
years they have survived. Of course, they represent nothing more
than two minor exaggerations of the entire gamut of religious fatuity
and should not be selected for special condemnation. All of religion
that is beyond the reach of rational or objective truth is nothing more
than Barnum-style buncombe.

550

> The intensity of the need for a frame of orientation explains a fact that has puzzled students of man, namely the ease with which people fall under the spell of irrational doctrines, [whether] political or religious, or of any other nature, when to the one who is not under their influence it seems obvious they are worthless constructs.
>
> Erich Fromm (1900-1980)
> *The Anatomy of Human Destructiiveness*

If you are a Republican, you know that all Democrats (or vice versa) have succumbed to this spell (falling for irrational doctrines). If you are a methodist, you know that all Baptists have done the same. If you are an acetic, you are sure that all hedonists are in error. Intelligent choices sometimes recommend that all of us be independents, atheists, and regular folks, averse to extremes of any kind. "A plague on all your affiliations" is the real sanity. But mindlessly "falling under the spell of irrational doctrines" is not always the explanation. Those who succumb to religious persuasions, for example, are often given the gratuitous push that alert ecclesiastics administer whenever they have that "crucial opportunity." Ecclesiastics assume that all human beings without religious education live in morally depraved worlds of dreams, reveries, hallucinations, illusions, and fantasies, all fabrications of unfettered and ultimately degenerate egos gone mad. It is divinely ordained duty for these religious leaders to revamp such personalities into good members of the church. Many church fathers interpret their God-ordained missions to mean that methods used in conversions are theirs to devise. Artifices, threats, persecutions, and even death to intransigents are justified.

551

> Once we had wooden chalices and golden priests. Now we have golden chalices and wooden priests.
>
> Ralph Waldo Emerson (1803-1882)

There is something to be said for fascinating phrasing, but not when it passes off fiction as fact and untruth as verity. It would be interesting to see Emerson trying to make a case for the deterioration of the priesthood during the past millennium. The golden priests of the past are a figment of Emerson's imagination. They are certainly not those Barrows Dunham talks about in page 207 of *Heroes and Heretics*. They, for centuries, ran institutions of exploitation in which marriages were made legal only on payment of exorbitant fees. Without such payment, couples were living in fornication, their children were bastards, and inheritances were forfeited.

Emerson's golden priests of the past were not those of the years from 1470 to 1530 that Barbara Tuchman talks about on pages 52 and 53 of The *March of Folly*. The reigning popes of those sixty years were interested mostly in amassing family fortunes. Their spoils of office, deals, bribes, and conspiracies against the populace, and their bargains, concessions, and alliances with kings and princes paid off handsomely. They must have shown the way for our present-day disciples of mammon, our TV evangelists who bilk their followers of billions of dollars.

Emerson's golden priests of the past did not include the Bishops of Peru who for three hundred years kept the populace in poverty and ignorance to make them easily revamped as candidates for the kingdom of heaven. The legacy of these bishops is the suppression of scientific method and family planning, keeping most of South America at the level of third-world countries, still today getting farther and farther behind. The wooden priests of today are not angels, but certainly no worse than those of the past.

552

> The theory of natural selection marked the end of teleological explanations in the biological sciences where they were held most tenaciously.
>
> Anatol Rapoport
> *Operational Philosophy*

Teleology, as Anatol Rapoport defines it, means that there is design or purpose in nature, that the future influences the present. All of this page is a paraphrase of what Rapoport has to say on the subject.

Whenever we use words that attribute volition, reason, purpose, design, necessity, obligation, need, destiny, etc, to inanimate objects and nonhuman life forms, we are guilty of teleology. The prepositions "to" and "for" and verbs such as store, solve, emerge, appoint, choose, and phrases such as "function as," "obedience to," "has to," "should have," "will be free to," "so that," and "plan to" are also teleological under such circumstances. Questions that begin with "why" and answers that begin with "because," when applied to nature are teleological as well. When teleology is implied in our everyday speculations and in our science classes, the principle of parsimony is denied and pseudoexplanations that cannot be tested are involved. The prevalence of teleology in our speech is an indication of how deeply embedded the clouded perception is in our nervous systems and accounts for much of the fatuity of our behavior.

Ask a farm child why the wind blows, and he may answer, "So the windmill will turn, pumping water for our cattle." Ask an Eskimo child why polar bears are white, and he will say, "So they can better escape the hunters." Ask an African child why the giraffe's neck is long, and he will say, "so it can reach the highest leaves in the trees." Teleological language is constantly in evidence whenever we are talking about nature.

553

The Lord is not my shepherd. I shall want.

Mary Sarton (1912-   )
Mrs. Stevens Hears the Mermaids Singing.

Man wants little here below,
Nor wants that little long.
"Tis not with me exactly so,
But 'tis so in the song.
My wants are many and if told
Would muster many a score.
And were each wish a mint of gold,
I still would long for more.

J. Adams

agrees with Mary Sarton.

Mary's objection depends on a play on words, the two different meanings of the word "want": want in the Biblical sense "lack of

those things really needed," and the more common meaning "desire."
It is human nature to desire a little more than the bare minimum that
life offers. The desire for a little luxury, if it does not expand into
greed, is not all bad.

Mary Sarton's refusal to accept the idea that she is being
shepherded through life is an even greater evidence of sanity. Jean-
Paul Sartre's "Man is condemned to be free, responsible all the way"
is the sane perception in our situation. To depend on God to take care
of us is to stop all progress. Human societies would then shrivel into
nothingness in a short time. Even if we were to survive, the world
would be an extremely dull place in which to live. If life has any
meaning, our own struggle to make it a pleasant journey for everyone
is that meaning.

554

Man passes away, generations are but shadows; there is nothing
stable but truth.

Josiah Quincy, Jr. (1772-1864)
Speech in Boston, Sept 17, 1830

Good, good! Now if we just know what "truth" is we would be in
fine shape. Truth is not something the cosmos begins with, not
something floating out there in the ether just waiting for us to grasp
it. Truth is a simple concept that exists only because symbol-making
creatures exist. When mother says to Johnny, "Tell me the truth now,
did or did you not slap Mary." She uses the word truth in the only
meaningful way it can be used. Mother is not referring to the
slippery, enigmatic, obscure way that religionists use the word.
F.S.C. Northrop says that the word truth as religionists use it would
be better called comfort.

Truth means that what we say corresponds to that which we say it
about. A true map is one that shows in proportion every curve in
every river, every village in the correct position relative to every
other river, village, etc. We can use the map and a good compass to
walk, drive, or fly from one place to another with confidence.

When religionists borrow words from the real world, they often
distort them, as they did with the word "faith." Sometimes the
distortion becomes so embedded in religious consciousness that the
original real-world use disappears, as is the case with the Spanish use
of the word assumption. It can still be used as the name of the capital

city of Paraguay, but nowhere else except to mean the Assumption of the Virgin Mary.

The stable "truth" that Quincy speaks of is anything but stable. Religionists can use the term truth to mean just about anything that comes into their heads. In "The truth shall make you free," they really mean that accepting their mythology will make you free, when what it does is make a slave of you. Speaking the truth is what religionists do less often than anyone else. Whenever they make statements about existences that they cannot demonstrate, they lie, for they are asking us to accept as fact (observation) what is only assumption (hazy conjecture).

555

> We as womenfolk can't as I see it be all that smug about where we're at.... I want women in office who're in touch with their feelings... and who don't have to displace their concealed feelings by dropping bombs on people who live thousands of miles away.
>
> Jill Johnston (1929-   )
> *Gullible's Travels*

Gullible's Travels, Jill Johnston titles her book. Think of the array of strange and inscrutable accounts that could be subsumed under that rubric! Much of what is heard in the preacher's sermons could be classified in that way. Gullible gets around. He is heard in conversations and pronounced convictions in all parts of the world.

With promises of spaceship transportation to a higher level of human existence, Marshall Herff Applewhite was able to convince 39 disciples to join him in suicide. The Hale-Bopp comet appearing in northern skies during March of 1997 seems to have triggered their decision to kill themselves, all within a period of three days, all in exactly the same way. Hale-Bopp was at its closest proximity to earth when the mass-suicide occurred. Applewhite had convinced them that "their" spaceship was following in the shadow of Hale-Bopp. There is no imaginable liturgic scenario that is too farfetched for some charismatic mystagogue to turn it into an acceptable religious doctrine.

The disproportionately small number of women in adminsitrative positions in the country's police departments is another gender discrimination. To lesser degrees, the same is true in business, the military, and in all departments of government. I join with Jill

Johnston in her desire to put more women in government offices as senators and representatives, and as cabinet members – anywhere they can help decide how this country will be run. If the human species is to survive, it may be precisely because we learn that women can guide us through the briar patch of politics better than do men. England has just put more women in Parliament than ever before. All governments should follow, indeed surpass to the point of parity, England's example. Our governments will need a lot of feminine guidance if we are to eliminate the partisan politicking and magisterial misgoverning that prevails.

556

A maker of idols is never an idolater.

Chinese Proverb

If the Chinese have it right, this should be an eloquent confirmation of Alexander Pope's : "A little learning is a dangerous thing." The maker of idols, we might guess, knows too much to be fooled. He knows everything that went into the idol's construction, exactly where it came from and why the idol was made. It is going to be difficult to convince the idol maker to bow down to an artifact of his own making.

But the "never" in the Chinese proverb is premature: The story of the golden calf (Exodus 32:1-20) worshiped by those involved in its fabrication is well known. Isaiah in Chapter 44, versus 12-29, tell us: "The blacksmith with his tongs makes an idol in the coals. He fashions it with hammers and works it with the strength of his arms. The carpenter with his rule marks out an idol with chalk and fashions it with a plane. He makes it like a figure of a man beautiful, so that it may remain in the house.... He falls down to it and worships it, saying deliver me, for thou art my god." Idol makers, it seems, do not always understand what it is they make. They seem almost as devoid physical sensibility as their own handiwork.

In Psalms 115, we read: "Their idols are silver and gold, the work of men's hands. They have mouths, but they do not speak; eyes, but they do not see; ears, but they do not hear; noses, but they do not smell; hands, but they do not handle; feet but they do not walk, nor do they made a noise in their throat."

What really is the difference between idol makers and the Judeo-Christian-Muslim fabricators of mythological deities? The mystics use fables, myths, and legends, not stone, clay, or wood in the construction of their idols, but the results are the same. It is equally asinine to fall down before phantasms produced in a bronze-age brain as it is to fall down before a block of wood.

557

Men are idolaters, and want something to look at and kiss and hug, or to throw themselves down before; they always will; and if you don't make it of wood you must make it of words.

Oliver Wendell Holmes, Sr. (1809-1904)
The Poet at the Breakfast Table

People magazine is one confirmation of what Holmes contends. The present surfeit of awards programs on television is another. Still another is the number of bleachers that must be set up to accommodate the crowds that come to watch stars come and leave the premiere of a movie.

Hero and idol worship differs from worship of putative gods mostly in that there is something tangible to be worshiped. Statements about heroes and movie stars can sometimes be confirmed. The mental pictures that worshipers have of their human idols and heroes are much more stable than the mental images the worshipers have of their mythical gods.

This strange propensity of human beings to fetishize objects of irrational reverence gets us into serious trouble and wastes precious time. Trouble comes, for example, when worshipers of imaginary objects excommunicate the worshipers of tangible objects (stone idols, or the like) or, where it is still legal to do so, convict them of blasphemy. If those who use their precious time worshiping mythological gods would spend that time serving fellow members of society and in ways to improve themselves as well, both they and society would be much better off.

558

Like everything else that has outlived its usefulness, nationalism has changed from a beneficent to a maleficent force.

G.K. Streit (1896-   ) – American writer

Religion and nationalism have much in common and are often confused – especially when we try to determine which is the dominant factor in causing wars. Both can induce young citizens to travel halfway around the world to kill other human beings they do not know, have never met, and might very well like if they knew them personally. Either religion or nationalism can make men behave like rabid rhinoceroses. They can teach human beings to hate one another without the slightest justification for hate, giving rise to seemingly irresolvable problems. Almost all our wars are either between-religion or between-nation wars. Many wars are both. Nationalism, like religion, is a form of worship, and the fact that each nationalist worships a different nation-god and each religionist redefines his god to suit his own particular purposes adds to the dissension. When a word like "Jew" can refer to either religion or natioinality, it is double trouble. The differences between the Jews and the Arabs of the Middle East become doubly difficult to resolve. If they are not fighting over territory, they can find plenty to fight about in their religious differences.

Jacob Bronowski says in *A Sense of the Future,* "The public in every nation is looking for an international conscience... for it knows that nationalism is an anachronism, a dying form of civilization." Says Raphael Cohen in his *Reflections of a Wondering Jew*: "In the end, of course, assimilation or destruction is inevitable; for no one can reasonably suppose that the present divisions of mankind will last forever."

559

No one has yet had the courage to memorialize his wealth on his tombstone. A dollar mark would not look well there.

Cora May Harris (1869-1935)
A Circuit-Rider's Wife

You cannot only not take it with you, you cannot even say on the tombstone that you ever had it. The graveyard must be the closest thing we will ever have to the great equalizer. However, all of us have met in life and in the news, people who we are sure are convinced that they can take it with them. Megamergers, hostile takeovers, and inside trading net greedy financiers money they will never to be able to spend.

The "it" mentioned in "cannot take it with you" can apply to much else besides money. An early observation for me was the international points earned in bridge. In this realm, points, per se, is the mark of prestige, not necessarily ability to play. Other examples of the "it" that motivates other fanatics are trophies, titles, tenure, grades, merit badges, etc.

Collectors prefer comic books, baseball cards, marbles, antiques, jewelry, rocks, fossils, signatures, sports paraphernalia, fotos, paintings, conquests, miniatures, epitaphs, last words, hotel towels, orchid varieties, etc., etc., etc. There is no end. Even some shoplifters, they say, are collectors more than they are thieves. If heaven were to permit entry to all the things people would like to take with them, there would be no room for souls.

John Ruskin, the British writer, said: "It is physically impossible for a well-educated, intellectual, or brave man to make money the chief object of his thoughts." Romain Folland, a French novelist, is even more explicit: "This thing must be put more bluntly. Every man who has more than is necessary for his livelihood and that of his family, and for the normal development of his intelligence, is a thief and a robber. If he has too much, it means that others have too little."

If people generally were to adjust their priorities to their own truly and deeply felt values, they might find out how little money is required for them to live, and how much greater is the pleasure of knowing that they could prevent starving families from dying. They would stop accumulating wealth and follow the example of Mother Teresa, Albert Schweitzer, all those who dedicate their lives to helping others. Their own shallow lives would blossom into sublime resplendence.

560

In great contests each party claims to act in accordance with the will of God.
    Abraham Lincoln (1809-1865) – Memorandum Sept 30, 1862

Lincoln goes on to say in effect: "Either one or both must be wrong. God cannot be for and against the same thing at the same time." Or even the same thing at different times, unless there are good reasons for doing so. If only the authors of the books of the Bible had learned what Lincoln and good sense tell us!

In the Bible, God contradicts himself frequently: He is both for and against women, first-born babies, and satan. He says a person "should," "should not" be put to death only for his own sins. He "does," "does not" change his mind. Only by "the faith," "the law" the just shall live. "Bezaleel," "Moses" made an ark of acacia wood. David captured "seven hundred," "seven thousand" chariots from Hadaezer. Ohaziah was "twenty-two " "forty-two" years old when he became king. We "can," "cannot" eat anything that moves. A man "does," "does not" need angels or men to help him peform his marvels.

Chapter and verse for all of these contradictions are listed elsewhere in this book, and many other inconsistencies will be seen by reading almost anywhere one may choose to read in the Bible. The Bible obviously was not written by an omniscient and infallible Deity. George Bernard Shaw in *The Adventures of the Black Girl in Her Search for God* says of the Bible: "Why not simply bring it down to the ground, and take it for what it really is."

561

When we remember that we are all mad, the mysteries disappears and life stands explained.

Mark Twain (1835-1910) - *Notebook*

We aren't all mad, obviously. Whatever is wrong with us it has allowed us to conduct the affairs of the world well enough so far to keep mankind from slipping into oblivion. But can we be sure that that will continue? In 1914 and 1941, we may have also thought that things were running along well enough so that the world was not in danger of annihilation. Two world wars followed, and if those wars were fought today, very likely we would not survive them.

Today, with chemical, biological, and nuclear weapons developed to the extent they are, and with these weapons in the hands of more and more countries, there are enough lethal materials available to kill all the populations of the world many times over. Also, there is no guarantee whatsoever that in an all-out struggle for supremacy these weapons would not be used. We are not all mad, but there may be enough madmen to ignite the fulminate that would turn this world into a global conflagration.

Mad? Let us see: Most of us, some ninety-five percent, it is said , have been convinced that deviously contrived religions and jingoistically conceived nationhoods are worth dying for. Zealots and jingoists have already proven themselves incapable of thinking rationally, and "knowing" that their gods support them, will not hesitate to behave in ways that may end things. We are in dire peril, and not unless we understand that we are, are we likely to survive. Only if we find effective measures for turning things around and devising lasting solutions to our problems is there hope for mankind.

562

> God is indeed a jealous God –
> He cannot bear to say –
> That we had rather not with Him
> But with each other play.
>
> Emily Dickson (1830-1886) - *Poems*

Emily Dickinson believed in God, but she would not blame or give Him credit for all the inanities others credit Him for or accuse Him of. She found no magic in churches, public worship, and pageantry, and found in nature manifestations of His presence, not in what preachers say. Like Einstein, she would lean more toward Spinoza's philosophy than any other.

God's jealousy does not compare with that of Allah. The Muslim God who has about a half dozen things to say in *His* book, the Koran, makes up for a dearth of topics by repeating each of them over and over and over. One you must not forget is that He is the One God. No upstart offspring could share the stage with Him. Two ways to get a sure ticket to hell is to suggest that he has daughters (the angels) and the other is to say that He would consider having a partner (a son, for example). To Muslims, Jesus is a prophet, not divine, and lower in rank than Muhammad.

Playing with God, too, must be about the most outlandish notion anyone has ever had. "To play" means "to have fun," and there is no fun or even a scintilla of a sense of humor in God. Even if God Himself suggested a night out on the town, any fun-loving worshiper, if he really wanted a little carefree recreation would be horrified. He would certainly wait for a moment when God wasn't looking and then slip out without Him. He is quick-witted enough to imagine what the girl-friend or his bar buddies would say if he came to the date with God tagging along. That, for sure, would be a night totally ruined. Better stay home and get a good night's sleep for a change.

563

Theological religion is the source of all imaginable follies and disturbances: It is the parent of fanaticism and evil discord. It is the enemy of mankind.

Voltaire (1694-1778) – *Philosophical Dictionary of Religion*

Even religion's description "Theological" is folly, indicating as it does that there is such a thing as a science of God. Science is systemized knowledge derived from observation, study and experimentation. In theology, there is nothing to observe. No one has ever seen heaven or hell or any of the inhabitants of these presumed places. The only study that can be done is the study of fictitious stories and imaginary entities, pretending that they really do exist. We learn nothing from nothingness except that people take it seriously, give it structure, and even extrapolate from it. Experimenting can be done only with something that exists, something made up of the elementary particles, energy states, that make up the universe.

Voltaire said that theological religion is the enemy of mankind. Now more than two hundred years later, that is as true today as it was then.

We cannot expect to survive the coming millennium, certainly not several additional millennia, unless we renounce our mythologies and learn to live in the real world of substantial, objective existences. Our fantasy worlds still mar our integrity, and war is by no means obsolete – as it should, long before now, have become. Another world war is unthinkable and would surely be the end of mankind. United Nations forums promoting cooperation and suppressing dissention are imperative. Would-be despots must be made to understand that all the forces of justice will descend upon them if they persist in their attempts to establish themselves in any part of the world.

564

How will we know in the United States that we are at last free of the yoke of religion?

Chester Dolan
Blind Faith

It will be a good sign when we have a president who dares openly avow that he does not go to church. It will be a meaningful indication to find that some public officials refuse to swear on the Bible. We will see definite progress when atheists are given consideration as professors of theology. It will be a good sign when a large city newspaper runs a column on the virtues of atheism – or when books such as this can be published and widely distributed. It will be a good omen when we no longer mint coins with religious incantations embossed on them. For sure we can say we made some progress when radio and television programs in recent years stopped signing off with: "See you tomorrow, same time, same station – God willing." Or as they still almost invariably say on the world's Spanish-language stations: "Si Dios lo quiere." (If God approves). I personally would find it comforting to hear some people saying grace at meals: "Good wine, good meat; good God let's eat!" without someone else at the table seriously reprimanding him: "Now let's not be sacrilegious.

565

I would rather think of my religion as a gamble than to think of it as an insurance premium.

Stephen S. Wise (1874-1949) - American Rabbi

Whatever we think about it is not going to change what it is. Blaise Pascal thought of it as a gamble, but that thinking by no means made it a gamble. Many religionists think of it as an insurance policy, and neither does that make it an insurance policy. Some people, who do not think at all, just take it for granted that it is a celestial diktat, but it does not thereby become a celestial diktat.

If we take seriously the refrain "thinking will make it so, just keep on thinking and cares will go" as a song tells us, we can have whatever world we want just by idle rumination – which is what thinking refers to in this song. Unfortunately, the world does not work that way. There are certain cosmic realities that remain what they are whether we think or not, whether we exist or not – certainly whether we know about them or not.

The wise (no pun intended) course, it seems to me, is not to reify our wishful thinking into substance, not to plan our lives on the basis of dreamed-up deities and their fancied programs for us when we do not have the slightest proof that such deities or their programs exist. Since "dreaming-up" is an individual process, no two persons do it the same way, and we naturally get a large array of gods and religions. Being as pig-headed as we are, we begin to fight over who has the one true God and the only correctly fabricated religion. The constant and often very serious dissension that results is a totally unnecessary result. It would go away if we really did regard thinking as a process worth adding to the ways we use our minds.

566

The will to be good and to do good – that is the simplest definition of what the world has always meant by morality.
                    Sir Herbert Read (1893-1968) - English Educator

Alan Watts asks someone, anyone, to explain what eating an apple, dying on a cross, ceremoniously eating Jesus' body or drinking his blood, pouring water on us with incantations, believing in all the outlandish sacraments that constitute Christianity have to do with morality.

Although it seems their determined intent, the clergy do not always succeed in their efforts to keep humanity cowering in fear, wallowing in guilt, and constantly flagellating themselves for their unforgivable iniquities. Most people lead relatively happy lives, delighted with their fate. They die satisfied that it has all been worthwhile and that they have been worthy citizens. They are not obsessed with feelings of guilt, doubt, and fear, because they do not expect of themselves more than being good and doing good – whenever they can and with whatever or whoever confronts them.

567

You could have found many prudent, reasonable, pragmatic people in the country who felt that Washington, Jefferson, Adams, and all the other revolutionary hotheads were going "too far, too fast." If they had listened to that advice, we'd all be rising to sing "God save the Queen" before football games."
                    Mike Royko (1925-1997)
                    Chicago Sunday Times – Dec 23, 1981

In countries in South and Central America, as well as in Mexico, the world "revolution" does not have the pejorative connotations it does here in the United States. Several political parties use the word as part of their name. The PRI is an example, where unfortunately PRI may also refer to the "Pesos Rolling In" to the pockets of the party officials. For the people living in abject poverty, there is no such thing as too far or too fast. That there is progress at all is for them welcome and revolutionary. To see an accelerated advancement toward an egalitarian society would certainly be welcome.

Few people know that the countries of South America were at one time far more advanced than was the United States. They had cities when we had towns, much more known mineral wealth, a university nearly a hundred years before North America had one. They were "America" before we were. They also had phenomenal leaders: Simón Bolívar may be one of the greatest leaders the world has known. José Julian Martí y Perez of Cuba was another. Benito Pablo Juarez was Mexico's great indigenous leader.

568

> There is no salvation outside the church.
>
> Saint Augustine of Hippo (354-430)
> *Confessions*

The church is the most superfluous institution man ever invented. Even Jesus must have realized that. He did not found a church, and he never preached in one.

A native of Harbour Island in the Bahamas went on at length about the seven churches on that small island of six hundred souls. From the tenor of his words, I expected him to tell me which of the seven he presided over, for he was obviously a very religious man. But as he continued, I began to have doubts – which were resolved when finally he said: "I doan go to none of them. Moas of the sinun is in da churches."

The salvation the world is concerned with today will almost certainly not come from the churches. It will come from that superhuman being (and messiah would be a good name for him) who, unlike anyone we can point to on earth today, has that special genius required to convince all the world's leaders to get rid of all mass-destruction weapons and the means for making new ones.

With terrorists making it obvious that they cannot learn to behave rationally, and yet having the wit to build mass-destruction weapons, the world is indeed in need of salvation. Any intelligent world leader even moderately capable of anticipating the course of social events must be painfully distressed by the thought of impending cataclysm. He can see no way to avert the danger that faces us, and knows well that an all-out world war will more than likely mean the end of the human species.

"There is no salvation outside the church," is asinine on every level. Salvation, if it comes, probably will have nothing to do with the church and will not be the contrived, dreamed-up salvation that the saint of Hippo speaks of. His concept of salvation has substance only in the sense that angels, devils, and jinn have substance – as the inventions of demented personalities.

569

> What ardently we wish we soon believe.
>
> Edward Young (1683-1765)
> *Night Thoughts on Life, Death, and* Immortality

"Wishing will make it so," the song tells us. Wanting to believe something strongly enough will produce the evidence for believing that thing. If everything else fails, we can produce out of whole cloth all the evidence we need for our beliefs.

Passionately wanting a certain course of events to occur, of course, is no reason for believing that this series of occurrences will in fact take place – or should. Wishful thinking is a flimsy basis for constructing a personal philosophy. It would be very nice to have five guardian angels looking after each of us, but wanting them does not produce them. Those who set aside their wishful fantasies, who put their faith in the empirical phenomena of the world in which they live, and who face their problems with courage and confidence, are the real heroes of our societies. They are the true ladies and gentlemen of distinction who cast aside superstition, exorcise prejudice, repudiate gods, and seek their own means to eliminate inadequacies, ignorance, false beliefs, and propensities to violence and hate.

Somewhere around the year zero, Publius Ovidius Naso said, "We are loath to believe that which hurts when believed." But once we resign ourselves to the fact that we are on our own, that we are the sole architect of our own destiny, and that we will not last forever, the hurt goes away and a resolute, realistic, and responsible spirit prevails. The apostle Paul says that men who have no belief in eternal life live like beasts, eating and drinking, believing that tomorrow all will have ended. It seems obvious that Paul's horror of such contemplation, like that of other religionists, is the basis for his postulating eternal life. If wishful thinking is a flimsy basis for formulating our beliefs, fear is an even worse one. "Wishing thinking and fear" were Freud's explanations for the origin of the idea of God.

570

> How different is the poet from the mystic. The former uses symbols, knowing they are symbols; the latter mistakes them for realities.
>
> F.W. Robertson (1816-1853) – English Divine

Poet and mystic can be one person. The terms are not mutually exclusive. From the poetaster, lost in symbolism, expect senselessness, very little of substance. What Robertson is telling us, at least I hope he is, is that until the symbols we use directly or indirectly refer to something other than symbols, they are empty sound or meaningless hen scratches. Better that Robertson compare the act of writing, per se, and that of preaching. The nonfiction writer knows that the referents of the symbols he uses must eventually be reality, something his sense receptors can get hold of. The preacher accepts no such mandate. The referents of the symbols he uses can be figments of his own imagination and stop right there. His symbols can, in fact, be organized into elaborate systems of nonsense. That is, his sense receptors need never become involved in what is the basis of the religion he asks his congregation to take seriously. All preachers of theistic religions are mystics, and their preaching is in large part mythmongering. The preacher is relating fables, and, as Fred Robertson, the English divine says, mistakes his fables for historical accounts of real events that actually took place in the world of sentient beings.

If there is not a territory (things observable) to correspond to his maps (whatever symbols) the preacher accomplishes nothing by elaborating his maps (whether sermons, rituals, incantations, or ceremonies). When his maps do not refer to territories and he asks us to take them seriously, he does humanity nothing but harm. If our religions do not have something to do with the world in which we live, the result is a kind of daydreaming, of no real value. If all our disciplines were composed only of pronouncements incapable of verification, society would soon become a shambles.

571

> If an ox could paint a picture, its god would look like an ox.
>
> Xenophanes (560-478 BC)

"If triangles invented God they would make him three-sided," is the way Montesquieu put it. Each person makes his own God, and there are as many gods as there are people postulating His existence. We are, of course, polytheists, and if we have to have beliefs about religions, these are the best kind of believers. Theocracies, autocracies, patriarchies, and other totalitarian governments are less likely to form in polytheistic societies. Monotheism is by its nature totalitarian. If we choose to deal with phantoms, why just one? The more we have the more interesting imaginative minds can make them. The Greeks with their pantheon had a ball.

If we are to maintain our sanity, we must keep in mind when dealing with our gods that we are the ones that made them. We can tell a lot about a Christian sect by noting the differences in their God and the God of another sect. This is because a society is always talking about itself when it describes its gods. Brutish gods means a brutish society. Tyrannical gods mean overbearing society members. Loving, caring gods mean a society that has always lived in peace. Any god is a mirror of the society that invented and nurtures him.

572

> The comings and goings of the soul as described in Chapter 18 of *The Golden Bough* by Sir James George Frazer may be as impressive a document of man's capacity for bizarre irrationality as has ever been recorded.
>
> Chester Dolan
> *Blind Faith*

In some religions, even the pantheon of gods is not so meticulously or artfully manipulated as is the community of souls. Here again we find that religion degrades the human being. The soul becomes the precious pearl and we the odious oyster that provides it stopover lodging. In this curious manipulation of symbols called "religion," figment becomes fact, and flesh a loathsome lie.

We do not usually think of the soul as leaving the body during the span of one's life, but for many primitive peoples it does, especially during sleep, flying around and engaging in all manner of mischievous or perfectly innocent antics. For some, there are two or even many souls, each with its own particular purpose and acrobatic capabilities.

The physical magnitude of the soul among those who postulate its existence varies from that of filling the body it occupies – all the way down to the submicroscopic soul described by Prabhupada - residing in the heart. I do hope Jarvic and others contemplating an artificial heart transplant make room for a submicroscopic, robotic soul, providing a proper submicroscopic niche for it in the new mechanical heart! The soul's place of residence, besides the heart, may be the host person's liver, blood, breath, shadow, portrait, photograph, reflection in a mirror, or any of many other abodes.

573

As long as men are free to ask what they must, free to say what they think, free to think what they will, freedom can never be lost, and science can never regress.

J. Robert Oppenheimer (1904-1967)
Life – October 10, 1949

What Oppenheimer is saying is that as long as we are free, we will be free – which is tautology. What we must interpret Oppenheimer as saying is that we must fight like Trojans to retain our freedoms. Patrick Henry was right. If we lose our freedoms we have lost all. We must resist the forces that deprive us of our freedom in every way we can.

Unfortunately, we do often lose our freedoms – seemingly without being aware that we do. A Hitler can begin with a people that have their freedoms intact. Then bit by bit he can deprive them of their freedoms until they have few left.

Hitler is not unique. Samoza did the same thing to the Nicaraguans. Castro did the same thing to the Cubans. Raoul Cedras did the same to the Haitains. Idi Amin did the same to the people of Uganda. Alfredo Stroessner did the same to the people of Paraguay. Khommeini did the same to the people of Iran. Stalin did the same to the people of the Soviet Union. Quaddafi did the same to the people of Libya. There were many others. Even in the United States, Joseph McCarthy had a good start toward doing the same thing to the people here.

Science can never regress if we keep all our freedoms. But any place freedom is lost, science suffers along with all other rational disciplines. In Liberty University, with Jerry Falwell in charge, science has regressed. In Regent University with Pat Robertson in charge, science has regressed. In all of our great religious universities, science suffers, and these universities graduate a disproportionately small number of good scientists. If the graduates of these universities ever succeed in turning The United States into a theocracy, as they plan to do, we can kiss goodbye to many of our freedoms – and rigorous science will be thing of the past.

574

It must be considered that there is nothing more difficult to carry out, nor more dangerous to handle, than to initiate a new order of things.
               Niccolò Machiavelli (469-1527)

Machiavelli continues: "For the reformer has enemies in all of those who profit from the old order, and only halfhearted defenders in those who profit by a new order, this hesitation arising partly from fear of their adversaries, who have the laws in their favor, and partly from the skepticism of mankind, who do not truly believe in anything new until they have actually experienced it."

Unraveling the octopodean tentacles of religion so that reason might prevail in the collective mentation of our societies is just as difficult as to initiate a new order of things. The anomalies of religion have become so deeply embedded in the nervous structure of believers that almost nothing can eradicate them. Professional deprogramers hired to rescue young people from "cult" religions that have been in business for less than a half dozen years sometimes fail. How much less probability of success can be expected from the same efforts in rescuing people from established orthodox religions? A lack of ability to reason is made evident simply by the fact that they have allowed themselves to become adherents of the orthodoxies. Getting them to turn to reason, therefore, is not an option in extricating them. That is probably an explanation for reports that deprogramers have exceeded proper procedures in convincing young people to recant.

575

I've always felt close to religion, because it's a form of show business.

Wladziu Vallentino Liberace (1919-1987)

To compare religion with show business is to reveal an insight that is rare in today's society Both religion and show business are make-believe worlds, and both serve many of our citizens as asylums to protect them from reality. I once knew a fellow who could recite every baseball statistic from the beginning of baseball time. It was his only world, and he was lost outside of it. He could not absorb a university education and was eclipsed by his two brothers, one a medical doctor and one a lawyer.

In New York City, I knew a large family in which all of the members were immersed in every aspect of television soap operas. They could name the producers, directors, actors, etc., of all the soap operas on TV and knew intimate details of the lives of the performers. They were alien to any other environment.

My admiration for Liberace gave me an inkling of how people could get that way. It may be as much my concern for those who are treated unfairly as it was my regard for his obvious talent that made me a fan. His exaggeratedly ostentatious style, his effeminate manners, and his warm affection for his mother turned many people against him. But Liberace was for the most part unfazed. He first disclosed (for me) his native acumen with his evaluation of an editorial criticism: "I laughed all the way to the bank." His life was taken at the pinnacle of his popularity. I, for one, have missed him.

576

Nevermore will they have a share in anything done under the sun.

Ecclesiastes 9:6

"Do you remember what you were doing when the versailles treaty was signed?"

"The Versailles treaty? What was that? When was that? How should I remember? I don't know what you're talking about."

"The Versailles treaty, you know, the treaty that ended World I. It was signed on the eleventh day of November 1918 in Versailles, France."

"In 1918, my god, I wasn't born yet. What are you talking about?"

"Talking about? I'm asking you what you what you were doing at that moment. What were you thinking about? At 11;00 in the morning it was."

"Good god, man, have you dropped off the deep end" If I wasn't born. I wasn't doing or thinking anything. For me there was no world. You know that. So why are you being so stupid?"A few minutes ago you were so sure about what things would be like for you in the days following your death. What scintilla of evidence do you have, has anybody ever had, that everything will not then be exactly as you say it was before you were born. You won't be doing anything. You won't be thinking anything. The world for you simply will not exist. You and I can guess that the world will go on all right, hardly noticing our departure, but we will have no part in it. Why is it so difficult for you to accept what even Ecclesiastes considered obvious?"

577

If we are ultimately defeated, it will not be because the problems are too great, but because we allow ourselves to be defeated.

June Goodfield
Quest for the Killers

Those who allow themselves to be defeated, too often are those who leave all difficult problems for God to solve. But there is no evidence that God does anything, and the sooner we learn that , the sooner we will know, too, as Sartre said: "Man is condemned to be free, responsible all the way."

June Goodfield's life story is an inspiration to all. On the trail of a spirochete or virus there was no thought of giving up. To lose the battle, for her, was absolutely unthinkable. Margaret Mead said, "Never doubt that a small group of committed people can change the world." The world would be a much worse place than it is were it not for the gallant work of the epidemiologists of our medical profession.

The defeatism syndrome may be the most detrimental of attitudes to our well-being. If every person would make a firm decision that he will do the best he can with whatever physical and mental equipment he has, the benefits to society would be tremendous. Too often we look at the next person's accomplishments with an awe that overwhelms us. We do not see that with similar planning and preparation we could do exactly what he is doing. I have seen children try such common tasks as riding a bicycle, touch typing, playing a musical instrument, and upon seeing how clumsily they function, give up immediately, exclaiming: "Oh, I could never do that!"

The sense of magic for those who do go on never goes away. No accomplished artists, if honest about it, will cease being amazed at how they can do whatever it is that they do well.

578

Man has no right to kill his brother. It is no excuse that he does so in uniform: He only adds the infamy of servitude to the crime of murder.

Percy Bysshe Shelley (1792-1822)
The Ceni

Most sane people are so fervently against war, capital punishment, euthanasia, and abortion, that they verge on becoming fanatical against any instance of destroying a human life. I share their fervor, but nonetheless can imagine extreme conditions where a case might be made for any one of the above instances of homicide.

If Iran or Irak were soon to create a production line of suitcase-size chemical, biological or atom bombs, and week after week were destroying entire cities in the United States, what would we do? If all diplomacy or threats could not convince them, we would not have much choice. Anyone who has read the Koran and knows what fundamental Muhammadism can mean knows that this is not an impossible scenario. The Taliban in Afghanistan show what could happen. Fundamentalist Muslims in Egypt, Turkey, and Algeria show what Muslims will do whenever they have the military power to do it. Allah promised them ultimate victory in all of their wars. He will even send them angels dressed in military uniforms to make victory certain. Muslims "know" that someday they will rule the world.

If sane people do nothing, Muslims will win. Catholics have already won in South America, Hindus in India, Communists in China. The Christian Coalition will take over in the United States. The world will be a group of theocracies, and armageddon will be of man's making. The human species will not survive.

579

Satan finds some mischief still / For idle hands to do.

Isasc Watts (1674-1748)
Divine Songs for Children

"A useless life is an early death," Iphigenia of Tarsus said. Neither thwarting satan or avoiding an early death is the true reason for keeping ourselves busy. Nor is "Keeping busy" enough. For maximum mental and physical health, we must keep busy at something we deem useful and creative. When one is engaged in creative work, depression is impossible. We are then in that frame of mind that we call happy – or at lest contented. When doing something creative, we lose all concept of time, and the idea of drudgery disappears. The sculptor, forming his Perseus, will forget to eat or even to sleep. Suddenly, he may wake up to the fact that daylight is disappearing, and he is working when it is almost too dark to see. Ten hours have passed and the only thing he knows is that chips are falling off in the right places to form the eyes, the nose, or the muscled arm.

We see now another important purpose of education. It provides us with the capability of making a living doing something we like to do. Educated, we will not spend a lifetime flipping hamburgers, turning bolts on a production line, or wiring solenoids. It is good that robots are taking over jobs that for human beings would be drudgery. Lives of deceit, crime, or amassing fortunes, living only for oneself, also cannot be happy lives. Of course, some people can find it creative to clean sewers, to dig graves, or to collect garbage, and that is good. But others must work at jobs with more variety, jobs that, in a world that progresses, require trade, technical, or academic education.

580

Souls have worn out both themselves and their welcome; that is the plain truth. Philosophy ought to get the manifolds of experience unified on principles less empty.

William James (1842-2920)
"The Compounding of Consciousness"

William James, who returned again and again to feeble attempts to connvince himself and others of the existence of God, at least finally got things half right. Perhaps today he would face up to the other half. A study of the medical hisotry of victims of automobile, farm, and industrial accidents in which the brain of human beings is damaged shows that there is a largely irreversible correspondence between between the location and extent of the physicl alteration of brain tissue and the alteration of the personalities and motor capabilities of the victims. Physiological disturbances often wipe out entire tracts of memory. Our sporadic intervals of consciousness (as described by Julian Jaynes) change as we grow old or suffer the ravages of certain diseases. What psychedelic drugs can do to personality is another case in point. There is obviously no psyche or soul that is completely independent of and separable from human nervous structure. As emotional and intellectual entities, we are the cellular and synaptic structure of our brain and body, totally that, and nothing but that, structure. When that "mind-body" structure finally disintegrates, the personality, by whatever name it is called, ceases to exist. Only in his legacies does the defunct human being live on.

Chapter XV

Starting a New Religion

581

History has shown that there has always been an ample supply of persons qualified to found new religions. Like anyone trying to open a new business, they are people who see most of the obstacles they will have to overcome, and are already planning how to do so. Now that radio and television evangelists show that the "god-racket" can be remarkably remunerative, motives for overcoming those obstacles are greater than ever, and the investment in time seems worthwhile. Ingenuity, energy, and undeviating concentration of purpose are more easily maintained. There are far more would-be Elmer Gantrys in the world than anyone imagines. They understand human nature well enough to know that gullibility is in sufficient supply so that reasonably charismatic and persuasive orators can easily attract and avail themselves of it. They do not find it difficult to assemble a congregation of eager adherents who are looking exactly for what they have to offer.

The aspiring mystagogue knows that he must convince prospective adherents not only that God favors the religion he will preach, but also that God shuns all others. His disciples must learn that the doctrines he presents for their consideration are nothing less than laws of the cosmos. His uncanny understanding of human nature tells him to restrict the behavioral freedoms of his congregation only in ways they already suspect are necessary for admission to heaven. His plans for aggressive fund-raising procedures also must be made to seem an indispensable part of God's plan. Divinely ordained ends, they can become convinced, may at times call for machiavellian means.

582

There is no less and no more reason for following the belief system of the Akuna of New Guinea than [of] the Anglicans of Ontario.

Kai Nielsen
Philosophy and Atheism

Since what passes for religions are unverified assumptions about suppositious deities laying down dubious decrees, intelligent people pay little attention to the pseudologists advertising them. Their phony effusions of fine sentiments about brotherly love, it turns out on examination, are only a specious mask for hatred and bigotry.

There are said to be eleven-thousand religions on earth, all supposedly different, but all are essentially the same. There is small choice in putrid peppers, I think is the adage, and there is none at all in irrational religions.

With all this monotonous uniformity, we still find members of the various religions claiming that theirs is the one and only true religion on earth. Their religion is so superior to all others, in fact, that it is incumbent upon them to impose it on everyone in the world. The missionaries that religions send out to perform that task may be found in all parts of the world.

583

I like the silent church before the service begins, better than any preaching.

Ralph Waldo Emerson (1803-1882)
Self-Reliance

Then why be there: He knows perfectly well that the silence will soon be broken by some ranting mystagogue saying nothing of any earthly value. Why not follow Emily Dickinson's example. She makes the Orchard her sacred retreat and the bobolink her chorister.

Someday I want to walk by a church with its glassed-in sign in front announcing the Sunday service: "Today Pastor Joe Blow will have something to say more important than diverting yourself in the orchard and listening to bobolinks singing." If he is not lying or exaggerating unwittingly, it is going to be some sermon. Without much confidence in the result, I nevertheless will stop in and seat myself in one of the church's comfortable pews. Like Emerson, I will enjoy the silence, and hope that what follows is even more pleasant and fruitful.

The silence before the service begins will be different, of course, for each member of the congregation. One member may be wondering if he will get the crops in before the rains begin. Another may be looking forward to the family Christmas party where she will see two new grandchildren she has never seen. Still another may be wondering what to do for his daughter who has stayed home sick with a serious ailment the doctors have been unable to diagnose.

President Coolidge's wife Grace had stayed home one Sunday slightly indisposed. When Calvin came home, she asked him "How was the service?" "Fine." "What did the preacher talk about?" "Sin." "What did he have to say about it?" "He was against it." Calvin might have done better meditating while walking in the garden or reclining in the canopied hammock that was always ready for him. The cat birds and brown thrashers would take care of the rest.

584

> The Idea of holiness has its history, like other religious ideas, and the history is not edifying.
>
> William Ralph Inge (1860-1954)

"Holy" comes from an Anglo-Saxon word meaning "sound" or "healthy" Etymologically, it is the "hale" in the expression "hale and hearty." It is often used to translate the Latin word for sacred. "His Holiness" strictly means "the healthy one."

The history of what religions do to words is something very edifying, although disappointing. The Spanish language has allowed religion to usurp the cognate of our word assumption and restrict its use to mean Mary's bodily trip to heaven. Now in many countries it can no longer be used in the sense most common in the English-speaking world. Paraguay uses the word as the name of its capital city.

"Heaven" was originally an Indo-European verb meaning "to shelter." In the same language, "god" was a verb meaning "to call out to." "Christ" came from a Greek verb "to anoint." "Messiah" in Hebrew meant the same. "Hell" was Anglo-Saxon "to conceal." "Angel" was Greek for messenger. "Devil" was Greek for "slanderer." Pastor is from Latin *pascere* "to feed."

Religion is eclectic, borrowing widely and without intelligent discrimination. Now it seems bent on dividing itself into smaller and smaller units until today the world is said to have 11,000 different religions.

585

Freedom breeds freedom. Nothing else does.

Anne Roe (1904-   )
The Making of a Scientist

Freedoms in one population tend to establish and reinforce those same freedoms in another population. This process will continue, and with enough help from newsmen, authors, teachers, and politicians freedom will continue to spread.

But the thought expressed in the last three words in Roe's quotation is nonsense: Education breeds freedom. If education is precisely tailored to eliminate ignorance and misinformation, it is a tremendous boost to freedom.

Eliminating fear breeds freedom. Fear of God, of satan, of excommunication, of hell, of Armageddon; fear of tyrants, of punishment, or of disapproval deprives us of freedom. Eliminating all of these fears is another important aid to freedom.

To feed the hungry, to find homes for the homeless, to eliminate overcrowding, to restore health to the sick, to find jobs for the unemployed – all such efforts also help restore freedoms.

Of course, a life totally free of restraints, repressions, or obstacles of any kind does not exist, and would be a dull life if it did. Much of the joy of life comes from the satisfaction we get from making headway in our struggles against that which would deprive us of our freedoms. We need something to fight for, and no efforts are more satisfying than those which help us regain and augment our freedoms.

586

Nowhere in the world, and at no time in history, has the average man actually "made up his own mind." Priests and theologians have made it up for him. Kings....conquerors, dictators, and politicians have made it up for him.... Psychologically, the most dangerous power-groups and power-individuals in history have been those

who have wanted the average man to be a contented follower: a meek
acceptor of his lot...."

Harry Allen Overstreet (1875-   )
The Mature Mind

Here we have, without ambiguity, an explanation as to why
religion must protect at all costs its pretense of virtue and its fidelity
to wile. Religion must be deceitful or it will not survive. All it has
going for it is its deceit. It has had to construct a weird metaphysical
world of phantoms and fantasies in order to keep its members in
thrall. These members are no longer masters of their own destinies,
or even of the workings of their own minds. No religion would be
able to weather a sudden rash of genuine thinking on the part of its
congregation.

If members of a thinking congregation were to understand how
thoroughly they are being deceived, it would be all over for its
leaders. A new society might develop without the sham that is
today's religion. Honesty, freedom, and an ability to assign priorities
would emerge. The newly enfranchised people would understand that
their only hope for residence in heaven is to make of this earth that
heaven. In their new paradise, they could begin to live productive
and interesting lives.

587

In the Judeo-Christian creed the male body is the temple of God,
while the female body is an object made for a man's exploitation.

Flannery O'Connor (1925-1964)
The First Sex   Pt II Chap. 9

The Koran says this far more explicitly than does the Bible, which
is bad enough. Surah and Ayah (Chapter and   Verse) throughout the
Koran tell us that there are two levels of human beings: men,
destined to be masters, and women, destined for strictly subservient
roles. Allah accords the woman equality with men only in her access
to heaven and her consignment to hell. She knows that Allah created
her not to be comfortable, but expressly to comfort man. In Surah 4,
Ayah 34, we read: "Men have authority over women because Allah
made one superior to the other.... Righteous women are devoutly
obedient."

After having described women as lewd, violent, untruthful,
frivolous, cunning, and unclean, Allah goes on to say   that He

created them to be little more than compliant sex-objects. Talking to men, Allah says in the Koran: "You may put off any of your wives you please and take to bed any of them you please."

In 4/34, Allah says to men, "As for those from whom you fear disobedience, admonish them and send them to beds apart and beat them. Then if they obey you, take no further action against them." A woman's cry during a beating is more likely to be heard as an admission of guilt than as a protest against cruelty. For a woman to be found guilty of adultery, fornication, or lesbianism, the fate is usually worse than death.

Divorce by the so-called "talaq" (the husband's oral pronouncement) as well as many of the sequential events are spelled out in minute detail in the Koran. Allah effectively awarded every male Muslim who could afford to own slaves, unlimited access to women. Slaves were legitimate sexual objects.

Women are never allowed to be witnesses to a business transaction without at least one man being present as another witness, but the man is always essential regardless of how many women there are. In inheritances, a girl will never get more than half what a boy will get.

588

The living know they will die but the dead know nothing, For them, there is no further reward; they are forgotten. Their loves, their hates, their jealousies all died with them. They will take no part in anything that happens in this world. There is no working, no planning, no knowledge, no wisdom in the world of the dead – where you are going.

Ecclesiastes 9:5-6,10

How on earth did that bit of good sense get overlooked in editing the Bible? When Palestinian Jews got together in Jamnia to separate pseudepigrapha and apocrypha from "authentic" Bible, they must have had a bad night's sleep before they came in that day. What Ecclesiastes had to say is so out of keeping with everything else in the "holy book" that some explanation is called for. We will probably never know how that got in, but it must be a tremendous embarrassment to true believers everywhere. Not until we accept the wisdom of Ecclesiastes can we live in peace with ourselves and our fellowman.

More than any other concept presented in the brief essays of *Religion on Trial*, this one will bring peace to the minds of those who understand and accept it. They will no longer waste valuable time trying to reach chimerical goals, but instead be content to seek realistic goals that contribute to the welfare of all of humanity, or at least to that part of it that confronts them at their own front door. The hope to find answers in orthodox religions is a vain hope. And in our search for explanations that do not exist, or in our zeal to create gods to do the explaining, we do society untold harm.

589

To talk of a person's mind [or soul] is to talk of the person's abilities, liabilities, and inclinations to do and undergo certain sorts of things, and of the doing and undergoing of these things in the ordinary world.

Gilbert Ryle (1900-1976)
The Concept of Mind

In other words, the soul is nothing more than certain aspects of the human body functioning as it normally does function in everyday affairs. Because the word 'soul' to many people is associated with magic, myth, or the spiritual heaven they postulate, it does more harm than good. Like Freud's psyche and its correlates: id, libido, instinctive energy, ego, and superego, it may serve as metaphor, but if more than that is expected of it, it distorts rather than aids human thinking.

To hypostatize or take literally such terms as souls, ghosts, apparitions, spirits, and specters is to warp the mind. The mind then becomes less reliable, and we cannot expect of it the logical thinking necessary for a sane consideration of the world in which we live. With forgetting as important as remembering in the processes of mentation, let us forget the nonsense of phantom words and stick to words that do really apply to an understanding of the cosmos and ourselves in it.

590

There is simply no way this 30-odd year saga [The life of Jesus] could have occurred within real time without someone real in authority having made a note of it.　　　　Alexander Wallace

Despite all the hoopla about Jesus and his exploits, extrapolated entirely from New Testament accounts, is it possible that no such personage ever existed? Wallace, in a letter to the editor of *Humanism Scotland,* says yes, and makes a good case for saying so.

The if-thus-then-so criterion for testing pronouncements for their truth value fails in many ways concerning the brief life of Jesus. For Wallace, one way, especially, is noteworthy: From the "Massacre of the Innocents" to the "Ressurection" – from "incredible horror" to "unimaginable miracle," - not one inkling is recorded anywhere else but in the New Testament.

Wallace suggests as implausible that Herod would have survived his "execution of the first-born of every Jew of Palestine." Herod, he says, had no authority from Rome to execute anybody and would have been himself executed if he had pulled and such stunt as that. The Emperor Augustus was the sole ruler in the Roman world and would have permitted no such massacre. Tiberius, not Herod, was the favorite of the Emperor Augustus and became his heir and successor when Augustus was 67, ten years before his death in 14 A.D. The Massacre, the consequent Flight into Egypt, and the history that followed, including Jesus (as Wallace sees it) were all pure fiction.

The main case against the existence of Jesus, that is, was his complete lack of mention in any contemporaneous record of events. But then, we are told, Homer was not Homer, and Shakespeare was not Shakespeare; maybe Jesus, too, was not Jesus, but some sort of figment figure, disregarded by *The Millennium Inception Times.*

591

Men have feverishly conceived a heaven only to find it insipid, and a hell only to find it ridiculous.

         George Santayana (1853-1952)*The Life of Reason*

What research techniques Santayana is privy to I do not know. But his "find it" is phenominal. Not many dead people have been reporting in lately, and in the literature, little is said about heaven. Even the Bible tells us almost nothing. The Koran does better, but makes heaven seem like spending an eternity half asleep in a deck chair on a flower boat floating in milk and honey – perhaps suckling teats that dispense homogeneous tapioca pudding. Frying forever in fire and brimstone makes hell seem equally monotonous. It is hard to tell which would be worse.

What Santayana is saying to us, of course, is that the sophistry theistic religions are trying to foist on us is one grand dossier of misinformation. What they burden us with is not now nor has it ever been of any earthly use to anyone. That the mythmongers do manage to deceive us is a tribute to their evangelical persuasiveness, but it is equally a measure of our unheeding credulity. If we were to allow theological deception to guide our behavior, we would destroy ourselves. We would lose our ability to live in a real world of things that do report to our sense receptors and are immediately meaningful to us.

To bring up our children in Sunday Schools where they are asked to believe in gods, angels devils, and demons is sure to warp their abilities to relate to a world of factuality for the rest of their lives. We do them and society a great disservice. Children will grow up to believe astrology, palmistry, channeling, psychic matters, sorcery, tarot cards, and hundreds of other stupidities and superstitions that leave them unable to think. They will no longer be able to distinguish fact from fiction and lies from truth. They become mental cripples and do not even have special parking spaces reserved for them when shopping at the world's marketplace of ideas.

592

> The tendency of man to turn to higher powers in times of trouble may be only a borrowing from the childish tendency to turn to its mother.
>
> H.L. Mencken (1880-1956)
> *Minority Report*

Thinking people throughout time have been trying to explain why it is that man fabricates gods to explain the extraordinary phenomena he observes – or to help him in times of trouble.

Wishful thinking and fear were Freud's explanation for the origin of the idea of God. H.L. Mencken, in the quotation above, explains God as "a borrowing from the childish tendency to turn to its mother." My own tendency has been to give father the credit. The most memorable events in my own life have been those I shared with my father. For that reason, perhaps, if I dream about a parent, it is almost always my father, never my mother. For my twin brother, it is the opposite. He must have been his mother's favorite. I "know" I was my father's – as much as they both tried to be impartial. My father was sufficiently adept at introspection and sufficiently endowed with insight to see us as kindred "souls," lacking the gentle, imperturbable character of my twin brother and his mother.

When ancient man faced the mysteries of nature, the curiosities engendered were satisfied only by the invention of marvelously versatile gods capable of creating and controlling the phenomena that needed explanation. The propensity to incorporate some kind of deity into every tribal fantasy, fear, or ego-projection seems deeply woven into the fabric of all primitive needs. Amplified, attuned, and adapted for changing societies, primitive gods remain today as our deities.

593

> For some reason, too deep to fathom, men contend more furiously over the road to heaven, which they cannot see, than over the visible walks on earth.
>
> Walker Parker Stacy (1884-1951)
> Quoted by Sam J. Ervin, Jr. – *Humor of a Country Lawyer*

Neither the road nor the heaven do we see, and probably they do not exist. Our contentions should be how to make a heaven of the terrain we do see and perhaps, except for brief trips to the moon and Mars, will ever see. Traveling at the speed of the fastest moving vehicles man has ever created, it would take some 80,000 years to reach the next closest "possibly" inhabitable site (essay 479). Making of the earth the utopia we would like it to be is a formidable task indeed, but at least within the realm of possibility. Going elsewhere to live, in all probability, is not.

Robert H. Schuller suggested that heaven may be in galaxy M-31, a mere two-and-a-half million light years away. At the speed of Pioneer and Voyager that would take more than 60 billion years to get to. That trip, of course is not the "road to heaven" Stacy is talking about. How to develop a human behavior that would give us a chance to reach heaven, he is saying, is what men contend over. All things considered, however, that dispute is no more realistic than is one about how to travel two-and-a-half million light years. Building an ideal society of ideal occupants would probably entail such implementations as genetic engineering, unnatural selection, cloning, euthanasia, in-vitro conception and eugenics. No such measures for improving the human species are countenanced at the present time.

Even natural selection has all but shut down in any but third-world countries today.

We will do best to forget about arguing over how to get to heaven and work on teaching ourselves and future generations how to think rationally without allowing mythologies to interfere.

594

Things have come to a pretty pass when religion is allowed to invade private life.

Lord David Cecil
Quoting Lord Melbourne

Discriminating in favor of the church go-er and against the row hoe-er has been a failure of religion since religions began. When operating morally, religion will concern itself with all aspects of human life equally and indiscriminately at all times. Religion, if it confines itself to ivory-towered churches, to monasteries or convents, or to pious interchanges among theologians, has no reason to exist and should be eliminated.

Cecil and Melbourne are kidding us, of course, but they touch a nerve that affects all religionists who keep their Sunday life and weekday activities strictly separate. They observe "morality" during their occupancy of the comfortable pew on Sundays, then forget it the rest of the week. "Business-is-business" or "morality cannot be allowed to interfere with profit-making" is their characteristic mode of being.

"How do you reconcile Biblical injunction with your treatment of that man?" one merchant asked another. "But my dear man, that was a directive straight out of the Bible: He was a stranger, and I took him in." The once-common Spanish "yapa," and the English "baker's dozen" are things of the past. The rule today is to price-mark merchandise three times normal value, and then put it on sale at double price. A new tactic in advertising is to avoid giving the actual per-article price the customer will pay when he gets to the store, but to say 20% off – or buy one get one free. The Federal Trade Commission is daily accusing companies of collusive price-fixing and deceitful labeling. Medical patients are frequently charged for services they do not receive, even operations that were not performed. Caveat emptor is the new golden rule: "Gold rules!"

595

No one is good but One, that is God (Matthew 19:17). He that does not believe [in the name of the only Son of God] is condemned. (John 3:18).

Contradictions, inconsistencies, anomalies, and peculiar observations in the Bible are legion. Peter Abelard (1079-1194) cited some 1800 Biblical passages and statements of the church fathers in which there were questions about matters of faith. Dr. Charles Francis Potter, in his book *Is That in the Bible* lists a thousand. Richard Elliott Friedman, in *Who Wrote the Bible,* gives us many, many more. One does not read far in any part of the Bible without noting denials, disavowels, repudiations, negations, and exceptions to what has been said elsewhere. God's infallible word, is indeed fallible – or God was lax in allowing mortal man to quote Him so erringly.

If we are to believe the Bible, we must believe : (1) God does (does not) think that children should suffer for their fathers sins, (2 Kings 14:6, Ezekial 14:20, Hosea 1:4, Exodus 44:7) (2) God does (does not) change his mind (1 Samuel 15:29, Numbers 23:19, 2 Samuel 24:16, Jonah 4:2); (3) Only by the Faith (by the Law) the just shall live (Galations 3:11, 3:12); (4) A man must (must not) marry his brothers widow (Leviticus 20:21, Deuteronomy 25;5) (5) Bezaleel made (Moses made) the ark of the Covenant (Exodus 37:1, Deuteronomy 10:3); (6) In 1 John 4:12 and 1 Timothy 6:16, we learn that no man has seen God at any time. In Genesis 32:30, Exodus 24:10, and Isiah 6:1, we find God is often seen face to face. (7) In Kings, Chronicles, and 2 Samuel, we find that David killed seven hundred (seven thousand) charioteers; Solomon had four thousand (forty thousand) stalls for horses and chariots; David took seven hundred (seven thousand) chariots from Hadaezer; Ahaziah was twenty two (forty two) years old when he became king.

596

Gods and God in any meaningful sense seem destined to disappear.
              Julian Huxley (1877-1975 – British biologist

In gathering ideas for writing Blind Faith and this book, statements similar to this one by Julian Huxley keep reappearing. It is not that their authors are ingenuous, but in face of all the evidence, the irrelevance of gods and religion becomes so overwhelmingly obvious they cannot refrain from saying so. Julian and Aldous Huxley, brothers, and grandsons of the famous Thomas Huxley, spokesperson for Darwin, were of one mind in regard to religion. Aldous Huxley, to place them in time, died the same month that President Kennedy was assassinated. Julian lived nineteen years longer than did his brother, eighteen years longer than did his famous grandfather.

My own sad prognostication is that gods will disappear precisely when the human species disappears, for their only existence is in human minds, and the gods we conjure up obviously cannot outlive us. Also they will survive as long as do our inexorably gullible minds. We, species and gods, are inevitable contemporaries.

Even if there are such things as gods lurking about somewhere, there is no evidence that they have anything to do with us, anything to do with whether we will survive the vicissitudes of nature, the caprices of human nature, or the various cosmic uncertainties. Many things can happen to us, but we have no evidence that any of the many possible threats to us are imminent. Overpopulation, pollution beyond our control or a virus we cannot handle are possible. An asteroid, comet, or rogue star may hit us; a giant interstellar cloud may drift our way and engulf us. Other equally disasterous scenarios are possible. Our final extinction may result from causes we do not yet dream of. But until such unlikely events occur, we are in charge, we and the complex biological systems we live and compete with. If we can solve the man's-inhumanity-to-man distraction, we might even remain in existence as long as predicted for our solar system, some four billion years.

597

If I had the power that the New Testament narrative says that Jesus had, I would not cure one person of blindness, I would make blindness impossible; I would not cure one person of leprosy, I would abolish leprosy.

Joseph Lewis - President, Freethinkers of America

Lewis makes an excellent point, but he touches only the tip of the iceberg. Reading any of the scriptures, one is confronted constantly with the "obvious" being ignored or the "ridiculous" praised. It becomes clear not only that the scriptures were written by mere mortals, but by somewhat obtuse mortals at that. Reading just the words they have put in the mouth of Jesus, we are alerted to some strange declarations: Be like the birds of the air, for they neither sow nor reap nor gather into barns, yet the heavenly father feeds them (Mat 6:26). Do not give what is holy to the dogs lest they turn and tear you to pieces (Mat 7:6). Let the dead bury their own dead (Mat 8:22). I did not come to bring peace but a sword (Mat 10:34). Whoever does not have, even what he has will be taken away from him (Mat 13:12). To eat with unwashed hands does not defile a man (Mat 15:20). If you have faith of a mustard seed, nothing will be impossible for you (Mat 17:20). Jesus also said: Be like little children. We suppose his intent was to limit our mentality to a level low enough to accept all such dimwitted asseverations.

598

If a man really wants to make a million dollars, the best way would be to start his own religion.

L. Ron Hubbard

It seems a man cannot keep secret the principles by which he lives. Even the most sordid of ingrained predilections sooner or later will be revealed. They become so much a part of a man, are so embedded in his consciousness, that they become the main topic of his inner conversations. Almost certainly, in some unguarded moment his inner conversations will be repeated aloud while someone records them.

To read Dianetics and biographical accounts of Hubbard is to know that his Scientology grew directly from his greed and lack of conscience. His moral kinship with Pierre Berton's country preacher who declared, "I got into this God-racket, boys, because I found it was the easiest way to make money" is obvious. It is the reason, too, why so many little-known preachers are motivated to become television evangelists. Not many preachers can resist becoming multimillionaires if they think it at all possible.

Elsewhere, I refer to Cardinal John Henry Newman when he admitted that religionists are superstitious, bigoted, and disposed to violence, and he suggested that they intensify these "desirable" traits. Pope Innocent the Third approved of killing heretics.

The approval of violence by the Cardinal and the Pope leaves us disillusioned about the role of theistic religions in the world. We become more certain than ever that we would do well to rid ourselves of anything of religion that is marvelous, impossible, or unbelievable by rational minds.

599

> If there are those who do not know to what degree their belief [Christianity] implies decadence, tomorrow they will know.
>
> Nietzsche (1844-1900)

Did Nietzsche have any assurance that what he said would be welcome? Nietzsche was eloquent, and so have been many others since Nietzsche died: Walter Kaufmann, Bertrand Russell, H.L. Mencken, Sidney Hook, Pierre Berton, Paul Kurtz, Richard Dawkins, Jacob Bronowski, Krishnamurti, Kai Nielson, John Mackie, George H. Smith, and many others. Yet religionists have been able to ignore the words of all these very eloquent patrons of good sense in the century following Nietzsche.

Religious mystagogues like Pat Robertson and Jerry Falwell are managing to get books like those written by the authors listed above put out of reach of religionists today. Schools like those in Vista California are turning things back to the gloom of the dark ages. Whether or not tomorrow's views of religion will bring a more enlightened world is a question. If the future is a mirror of the past, there is not much hope, at least not for many, many years to come.

600

> A successful woman preacher was once asked "What special obstacles have you met as a woman in the ministry?" "not one," she answered, "except the lack of a minister's wife."
>
> Anne Garlin Spencer (1851-1931)
> *Woman's Share in Social Culture*

If all of the world's literature could be surveyed to determine how many of the accomplished and noted men of history owed their success and fame to a capable, loving, and determined wife, I am sure we would all be surprised. I do not know if such a survey has been made and will not at this time try to find out, for the little space I am allotted here will be no more than enough for a few thoughts I want to express.

If Ms. Spencer's successful woman preacher did in fact have a remarkable "wife" who contributed more than her share to the joint effort, as is typical of many marriages, I wonder if she would be reluctant to acknowledge her spouse's contribution. We know this to be the case with many men in such situations.

A second thought deals with a possible lesbian minister in the new age which is almost upon us. Same-sex marriages will soon be accepted. When that day comes, Ms. Spencer's successful woman preacher need no longer feel the same deprivation and hopefully will have the typically helpful minister's "wife."

A last thought for this successful woman preacher, worthy of being a movie plot, deals with a woman preacher who need not wait for the new age. Even without lesbian tendencies, she passes herself off as a man and gets away with it. She is married to a man who accepts willingly a transvestite, home-duties role, and turns out to be the impeccable "minster's wife." The readers of *Religion on Trial* can surely imagine all the delightful scenarios that might ensue.

601

> It is a kind of voodooistic frenzy, not divine rapture, that produces the born-again Christian.
>
> Anonymous

None of us can remember our own birth, but if we could remember it in minute detail, we would be enormously impressed. We would know that no epileptic type of nervous-system disruption later in life could measure up to that sublime event.

It is strange sometimes to contemplate what words do to us, however ridiculous their literal import may be. "Born-again Christian" rolls trippingly off the tongue – and that is everything. Anyone who knows two languages well, especially if they are from two different language groups, is constantly surprised to see how some riposte is mesmerically impressive in one of the languages and falls flat when translated into the other. Those who translate trademark ads are distressingly aware of this fact.

Those good Christians who experience mental convulsions at some point in their religious history may be excused for interpreting this event as some sort of mystical epiphany. Those observing born-again occurrences without themselves being emotionally involved fail to appreciate the mystique.

Most people can suffer a peak-experience, hallucinatory, or intuition-leap type of event in themselves without calling for a tickertape parade to celebrate. They can usually keep their emotions under control and take it in stride. If things do get out of hand, a psychiatrist is called upon to help.

602

> Nationalism is a silly cock crowing on its own dunghill.
>
> Richard Addington
> *The Colonel's Daughter*

They say that travel is educational. It is – in many ways. But one of the lessons gleaned from that education is more important by far than all others combined, and it seems to be a lesson that is learned in no other way. With the more than twenty years I spent traveling and living abroad, 18 years as a tourist and 6 years as a Naval officer in 18 different countries and 21 different islands, I learned that lesson well. Nothing can ever erase it from my consciousness. That lesson is that people are pretty much the same everywhere. All have the same emotions, the same goals, the same hopes and dreams, and they reacted to me and my foibles in very much the same way. Anywhere I stayed any length of time, I felt at home. All people are my neighbors.

Anything that would impair that important lesson in a broad, decisive way is certainly a bane to mankind. Anything that encourages the people of any particular area on earth to think themselves deserving of special privileges is a kind of disease that thoughtful people would know must be eliminated. Sadly, that bane, that disease, is pandemic. It is called nationalism. Krishnamurti said in his *The First and Last Freedom*, "The man who is a nationalist and talks of brotherhood is telling a lie; he is living in a state of contradiction." The most radical idea of this book is not that religion in our societies is a colossal failure. Most people know that. It is that there is little difference between the irrationality resident in the god of nationalism and in the god of religion and that the former may be the most threatening.

When nations become gods and citizens become jingoists, other nations antagonistic in any slight way become enemies and should be reduced to impotence. The wars that result are religious wars as much as when Jews fight Muslims or Protestants fight Catholics.

Hitler "knew that God was on his side and said so. He "knew" that Germans were a superrace and said so. "Deutchland Uber Alles" was a battle cry every bit as dogmatic and domineering as those of Christians and Muslims today. Religionists everywhere, regardless of who their gods are and how slight is the possibility that they can impose their will on others, "know" that the world will be saved only when everyone believes as they do. Communist Russia and Christian United States avoided war only because both knew it meant mutual annihilation, not because both were not absolutely sure that theirs was the only path to salvation. Nationalism is as much a religion as any other, and "nation" inspires allegiance in a way that makes other gods green with envy.

603

> If ignorance were bliss, this would be a much happier world than it is.   Morris Raphael Cohen (1880-1947)
> *Reason and Nature*

At the beginning of the past century, it was probably quite possible for a person to be singularly lacking in general knowledge and still be satisfied and happy with his lot. But with today's communication explosion, that may no longer be the case. With radios and television today in nearly every home, each individual must be constantly comparing his information level with that of others more knowledgeable who face him from the television screen. No one can be reminded constantly of his shortcomings in comparison with others and remain content. If he is uneducated but intelligent, he almost certainly begins immediately to do something about not realizing his potential.

There is little doubt that up to the year 1910 or so, many young potential geniuses on Midwestern farms languished in relative poverty without becoming aware of the dynamic possibilities latent within them. They were happy being marginally productive because they did not know what contributions they might be making under less oppressive circumstances. Fortunately for everyone, it is no longer easy for ignorance to be bliss. That may be the one best hope for this becoming a happier and more productive world.

604

Every successful massacre is consecrated by a Te Deum, and the clergy have never been wanting in benedictions for any victorious enormity.

Henri Frederic Amiel (1821-1881) – Swiss poet and philosopher

Religion is ever ready to be a part of things. God, at times seems to be on both sides of the same conflict. Also, it seems, no conflict is so heinous but that some church somewhere will sanctify it. We hope that if God really exists, X.J. Kennedy has it right: "Great Yahweh fingers through the Bible / Thought on it, and filed suit for libel." The first thing God would do if He exists and has manipulative capabilities is burn that blasphemous document. Most of its writers would be consigned to the fires of hell. On the first day of 1932, Hitler told a Munich audience that God was on his side in the battle for a better world. Arabic words of Saddam Hussein are translated into exactly those English words. In the first World War, God was pitifully splintered. He was on the side of every army of both the Axis and the Allied powers. In our own Civil War, He was both for and against secession as well as slavery. The next and final war may well be started by a self-righteous ruler who believes that God is on his side and that he, in fact, is acting as an emissary of God. He and the people he rules will survive because "right has always survived" and he knows "it always will."

The world leader who really "knows" that God is on his side and also believes the fable of the seventh and eighth chapter of Judges would of course opt for unilateral disarmament immediately. It would be folly not to prefer a well-disposed and omnipotent God to an army, however well equipped it may be. A nation "knowing" that victory over all enemies is assured could relax, smugly amused by a well-armed, atheistic enemy's blustering and posturing. Summit conferences for such a leader of such a nation would be silly. God does not suggest to Gideon that he propose a truce with the Midianites. It is simpler just to annihilate them.

605

> Is evolution a theory, a system, or a hypothesis? It is much more: It is a general condition to which all theories, all hypotheses, all systems must bow and which they must satisfy henceforward if they are to be thinkable and true. Evolution is a light illuminating all facts, a curve all lines must follow.
>
> Jesuit Father Marie-Joseph-Pierre Teilhard de Chardin (1881-1955)

Ordained priest Teilhard de Chardin, scientist and philosopher, now has a new-generation ally in believing without reservation that biological evolution is a fact of the cosmos. Catholic theist and scientist Kenneth A. Miller in his book *Finding Darwin's God* is equally convinced that there is no reason why fully concurring with Darwin's "descent with modification" must be considered incompatible with a belief in God.

Kenneth Miller, too, believes that the earth is several billion years old and that mutation, variety, and natural selection comprise the process of biological evolution. Though still called a theory, evolution to Miller is unequivocally a fact. It is history and mechanism. A "punctuated" list of Millerisms follows. The reader is left to determine for himself which is satire and which is opinion and how to reconcile contradictions. I paraphrase slightly at times in the cause of elucidation. This summary is long, but it is an intriguing treatise on the whimsies of "good sense": **1.** A presumption of atheism or agnosticism in academic life [is current]. **2.** Yes, all living beings are the product of evolution. **3.** That evolution applies to other animals and not to us is absurd. **4.** There are several [valid] methods for dating rocks. **5.** The creationist's arguments for an earth less than 10,000 years old is pure idiocy. **6.** The "punctuated equilibrium" of Gould and Eldredge is clearly Darwinism [and nothing new]. **7.** Biologists are unable to take intelligent design seriously. **8.** Irreducible complexity as an argument against evolution grows from ignorance of the processes of evolution. **9.** The blind, pitiless indifference of nature is a basic fact of the cosmos. **10.** Science's ultimate goal "complete knowledge" will never be realized. **11.** We are the result of chance [not of God's purpose]. **12.** Events at the atomic level are indeterminate, but not random. **13.** Indeterminacy [Miller says, "Leaves room for God"]. **14.** The universe as a clockwork mechanism would rule out intervention by a god. **15.** Breaks in causality are a gateway for the mind of God. **16.** Any success for materialistic science impedes the search for God [and augments sanity] **17.** Evolution is seen as the natural history of life [as is ontogeny]. **18.** There is no conflict between God's work and a materialist view of biology. **19.** Evolution, not the creative power of God, accounts for the multitude of new species that appear. **20.** What god can do today, He could do in the past [In both cases, nothing?] **21.** Why not proclaim the absolute death of religious belief? [Why not, indeed]. **22.** We could create a world in which science and religion are partners [Like prescience and nescience are partners] **23.** Science can never rule out God. [And neither religion nor science can ever rule Him in]. **24.** The three great western religions share a core of belief. [That science is their enemy]. **25.** God revealed himself to us [And so?] **26.** The Bible is religion's hope [And religion is hopeless]. **27.** Bread becomes spiritual flesh. [A cannibal's favorite repast]. **28.** There is a spiritual reality. **29.** So what caused the "big bang? [What caused God?]. **30.** In the lottery, the emergence of a winner is not luck. [But the emergence of that particular winner is.] **31.** Any God worthy of the name has to be capable of miracles. **32.** We pray for strength. [How about a prayer for good sense?] **33.** We cannot know what God has in mind [or that He has a mind]. **34.** The God of Genesis is fully consistent with the scientific reality of the modern world [Have you *read* Genesis?].

The promises Miller interjects in order to lure us on as we read his book never materialize. He ends up saying what all religionists must end up saying: " God exists because I say God exists (with or without a concomitant evolution.). The last words in Miller's book are: "What kind of God do I believe in? I believe in Darwin's God."

606

No woman can call herself free until she can choose consciously whether she will or will not be a mother.

Margaret Sanger (1883-1966)
Parade December 1, 1963

Margaret Sanger was by far the greatest and most effective proponent of birth control the world has known. But she did not approve of abortion and rarely spoke of it. She was disappointed to find the name of her birth-control movement eventually called Planned Parenthood, but when the term became too well accepted to oppose it, she used it herself. She formed a new organization which she called International Planned Parenthood. She became popular all over the world – but especially in Japan and India. In her presence, Nehru pledged ten million dollars to the cause of birth control in India.

Today, no one will deny a woman her freedom to decide whether or not she will become a mother. If she doesn't want children or more children than she already has, she always has had the option of not sharing unprotected sex with a man. Now she also can use effective methods of contraception to avoid pregnancy.

A mining crew will not be indicted for murder because a helicopter radios that a paleontologist is setting up camp within range of their readied dynamite excavation explosion. Avoiding murder is still a matter entirely within their control. They will postpone the event while they try to convince the paleontologist that their excavation is more important than his exploration. The paleontologist, of course will try to prove that his rights are more valid than those of the miners.

If it turns out that continuing a pregnancy endangers the woman's life, or if the minerals the miners seek are vitally important for a secret government project, everyone must rethink their positions. Whatever the conclusions, murder of a normal embryo destined for a normal birth – or murder of an innocent paleontologist – must be ruled out. Taking a human life without overwhelming reasons for doing so, is never an option in a truly civilized society.

607

We don't want to know, since... to learn the truth [about religion] only makes us unhappy, forces us to reconstruct a mental image which, however false, is easier to live with than the truth.

Françoise Giroud
I give you my word

To submit a list of those writing on the subject who have said that people like (prefer) to be deceived, would be quite astounding. But surely what they say needs a measure of qualification. People do not like to be deceived. What they like is the result of being deceived and do not question how that result came about. They like living the fairy tale of religion. It gives them serenity. If it deprives them of a will to lead fully functioning lives, that does not matter. They do not dwell on the fact that they are being deceived nor that they might be more creative individuals if they were not.

Both Robert Oppenheimer and Stanislav Andreski believed that people prefer absurdity, and in fact are fascinated by it. Oppenheimer spoke of a private and coveted self-sealing system which has a way of barring evidence which might bear adversely on any accepted doctrine. Andreski was sure that most people find it far more pleasant to accept blindly the pseudosciences, orthodox religions, all superstitions they are asked to accept. André Gide, too, close friend of Françoise Giroud, said in his book *Pretexts*: "Most often people seek in life occasions for persisting in their opinions rather than for educating themselves.... It seems as if the mind enjoys nothing more than sinking deeper and deeper into error."

The list of nonsense that people will accept as significant information goes on forever. It includes horoscopes, psychic phenomena, the efficacy of amulets and talismans, the divinity of Jesus, possession, psi, etc. If the reader would really like to see how long the list can get, he need only read two books by Bergen Evans: *The Natural History of Nonsense* and *The Spoor of the Spook.*

608

> It is better to die on your feet than to live on your knees.
>
> Dolores Ibarruri
> Speech in Paris   Sept 3, 1936

Ibarruri is not talking to the scrub lady. She is saying: Better than to spend one's life groveling before some fictitious deity, is to face the world squarely and shout defiance. To die with one's boots on, as the old saying goes, is to have lived one's life fully, responsible all the way, knowing as did Amado Nervo, the great Mexican poet, looking back on his life:

Porque veo al final
de mi rudo camino
que yo fui el arquitecto
de mi propio destino.

Because I see at the end / of my difficult journey / that I was the architect / of my own destiny.

The rudo camino of Nervo's poem translates literally as "rough road." Sometimes what is rough for one person is a welcome challenge for another. Sometimes, as it did for William Ernest Henley, rough road can mean devastating illness and a shortened life: fifty-four years. Not many can suffer as much along the way as did Henley and not bemoan his fate. But in the midst of it all Henley could say: "I thank whatever gods may be for my unconquerable soul." Today we think of Christopher Reeve and Ryan White. Ryan died of AIDS at nine years of age. Reeve, a charming actor, is now paralyzed from the neck on down. Few people could be as cheerful as Ryan was and Reeve is. We marvel at such fortitude.

609

> Of all the old prejudices, the last to die will be the idea that woman owes service to a man instead of to herself. It is [according to this archaic discrimination] her highest duty to aid his development rather than her own.
>
> Susan B. Anthony (1820-1906)
> *The Arena*

Susan B. Anthony never married, and that may be the status she was in fact recommending. Her alter ego, Elizabeth Cady Stanton, not only married, but had seven children, so Anthony could see the alternatives close at hand.

Changes since Anthony's time make the single state for women even more acceptable and practicable today. Women now have many opportunities to earn their own living; and with modern appliances, keeping house for one person is a breeze. With a microwave, meals can be planned and made in minutes.

As far as society is concerned, there should be no objections. If the increasing numbers of single women remain celibate, especially, the population explosion would cease to exist. Educated women add greatly to the gross national product and offer unique capabilities, doing many things that men do not do as well.

Anthony and Stanton were doers, the kind of people that cannot be idle, but must be engaged in creative occupations every minute of their lives. Both lived into their eighties, and fought like tigers for the cause of woman suffrage. Before they died, they knew they had won, although they could not have believed it would still take several years. If all women today do not know how much they owe to these two gallant women they should be advised. Many others like them, of course, worked with them and were especially important in seeing things through to their final victory. Men, too, should be inspired by the efforts of all of these women. We know that we have benefited as well.

610

Give us clear vision, that we may know where to stand and what to stand for – because unless we stand for something we shall fall for anything.

Peter Marshall (1902-1949)
Senate Chaplain (Prayer 1947)

Was he asking for vision from God or from Senators? It would be welcome, whichever. But to imagine we will get good advice from God, if we judge by His words in the Bible, is to live in a dream world. The Bible tells us that God does, and we should, stand for some rather tyrannical principles:

Leviticus and Deuteronomy list many of God's proscriptions: foods that must not be eaten and behavior that is immoral – along with the penalties and retributions for infractions. The list of those who are unclean and unholy and therefore not eligible for the Kingdom of God is long and if taken seriously today would mean instant death for a large part of the world's population. Even human sacrifices are respected by God, as in 2 Samuel 21, Leviticus 27:29, and the daughter of Jephthah as described in Judges 11.

Many of modern man's prejudices and superstitions arise directly from irrational proclamations attributed to God as spelled out clearly in the Bible. Among the superstitions are His preoccupation with blood (Hebrews 9:22), circumcision (Genesis 17:10), exorcism (Mark 5:8), and even such silly examples as eating curds and honey (Isaiah 7:15), Hitching an ox and ass together (Deuteronomy 22:10), and combining wool and linen in a single garment (Deuteronomy 22:11).

What should we stand for? Sanity would be nice! But we must look elsewhere, not to heaven and almost as rarely to the Senate for that.

611

> Man is an exception, whatever he is. If he is not the image of God, then he is a disease of the dust.
>
> G.K. Chesterton (1874-1936)
> "Wine When It Is Red"- *All Things Considered*

To be a "disease of the dust" is no mean role to allot to ourselves. We are then one of the minuscule parts of the universe that reverses entropy, and entropy is the enemy of us all. Isak Dinesen reminds us, "We also turn good red wine... into urine." But we might do a little reminding of our own. Without us, there would be no red wine in the first place. Besides, if we did not drink the red wine, of what use would it be?

We need not apologize. If some species become extinct because of us, we also build animal farms and large natural parks, preserving life that is already extinct in the wild – or soon will be. Most of the cheetahs, gorillas, California condors, ostriches, dogs, cats, chickens and many other species that once survived only in the wild, now are more numerous in captivity.

Chesterton chose to count himself as the image, not the disease. But where is his proof? It is not impossible to prove that anything discernible of him that exists right now is mostly dust – and probably very toxic dust. If anyone has proofs of any other nature in mind, we would be interested in seeing them.

612

> At present there is not a single creditable religion in the world.
>
> George Bernard Shaw (1856-1950)
> *Major Barbara* (preface)

Shaw should have prefaced his remark with, "So far as I know." He probably is right, but for a reason that is not at first apparent. If any group of persons did compose a moral philosophy that was creditable in every respect, that spoke only the truth, that was a reliable guide for living, that contained no whole-cloth fabrications, that taught brotherhood and not hatred, they would not call their philosophy religion. They would know that to attach any such label to their system of beliefs would mean that people would soon hang on it all the imbecilities of the orthodox religions.

The belief systems of Anatol Rapoport, Bertrand Russell, Carl Sagan, Richard Dawkins, Jacob Bronowski, Julian Jaynes, John Dewey, Erich Fromm, Clyde Kluckhohn, Paul Kurtz, George Smith, Morris Cohen, and Harry Overstreet will certainly satisfy Shaw's criterion of being creditable, but no one would be so thoughtless as to call them religions. Shaw is safe in his seemingly undue certitude, not because he knows all religions and is competent to judge them, but because his epithet, "creditable," by definition excludes all systems of nonsense called religion. Said more simply, the phrase "creditable religion" is an oxymoron, and his statement becomes nonsense. It is a self-contradiction.

613

Christianity is pre-eminently the religion of slaves. Slaves cannot help belonging to it, and I am among them.

Simone Weil (1909-1943)
The Need for Roots

If you are not a slave when you join the Christian Religion, you soon will be. Other names for what you become are; pawn, automaton, robot, puppet, and mannequin. You will be encouraged to give up thinking for yourself and submit to the will of ecclesiastics and God.

When we are convinced that we are senseless robots, completely dependent on forces over which we have no control, devoid of responsibility or worth, the result is a thorough disintegration of the qualities that make us human. Simone Weil called herself a slave to religion, and her biography tells us what manner of slave she became. In her extraordinarily fertile mind, she fashioned an intricate, contradictory, and tangled mixture of self-abasing and self-righteous nonsense that led her finally to self-destruction, starving herself to death halfway through her thirty-fifth year.

Religion can account in great measure for the deplorable state of the world as it exists today. Man will do little to improve society so long as he is convinced that this task can be left to God. Organizations that erode our potentialities by teaching us to despise ourselves as individuals and as a species do a great deal of harm. "Knowing" that we are pawns in the great cosmic scheme, we behave accordingly.

The concept of celestial control over our destinies discourages initiative and individual responsibility. Instead of love and concern, we learn selfishness and fear, illogic, and irrationality. Instead of being inspired to develop a true morality through individual discipline, we are conditioned to be unthinking zombies, with physical capabilities only. Thinking, genuine, rational, critical and independent thinking, is discouraged. Behavior never rises above the level of reflex response. Knowledge and a true awareness of the forces of nature are depreciated. "Eternal verities" and doctrines which may not be questioned make us feel unworthy and insignificant.

614

> Faith must have adequate evidence. Otherwise it is mere superstition.
> Archibald Alexander Hodge (1823-1886) - American Theologian

Faith is belief *without* evidence. No one uses the word faith to express belief in a thing when there is adequate evidence for believing. Faith is the term religionists use when they ask us to believe, when they really don't know what they are talking about. "You must have faith" is simply another way of saying: "You must believe what I say only because I say it, despite the fact that there is no scintilla of evidence for believing what I say."

Without blind acceptance of whatever the word faith applies to, all religions would disappear immediately. The fact that the adherents of religion will accept pronouncements on the basis of faith only, is religion's security bond, its mainstay, its only hope of survival. Since nothing concerning the existences that religion postulates are even slightly true in the sense that little Johnny and his mother use the term truth, faith is "absolutely" essential. It is the life raft by means of which religion keeps afloat.

615

The amazing capacity for credulity, folly, and self-deception has never been shown so conclusively as in the number of spasmodic sects and religious cults which sprang up in America during the last century.

Ray Strachey
Religious Fanaticism

In a world in which no one has a corner on truth, and in which everyone is looking for it, anyone who claims to be piped in to unerring wisdom can easily assemble a congregation of eager adherents. We want a simple and secure world that relieves us of all necessity to think. "Spasmodic sects and religious cults" offer it to us and we have been joining them in astonishing numbers.

When passion-to-believe replaces reason, any system of beliefs, new as well as old, will claim our attention. If the new religion is fortunate enough to find among its members a few good leaders with charisma, conviction, and managerial acumen, they have it made. If the new religion is wise enough to avoid conflict with the community in which it is located, success is assured. But if the new religion keeps its members captive by force or by a well-planned hierarchy of specious arguments, it will fail and soon disappear.

Included among new religions are The Children of God, the Jesus People, The Christian Foundation, The Peoples Temple, Christ Commune, Catholic Charismatics, the Unification Church, Branch Davidians, The Divine Light Mission, Transcendental Meditation, Hare Krishna, The Aquarians, Subud, Satanism, and The Process. They are all found adhering to at least one of the following obsessions: anti-intellectualism, hellfire, divinely ordained privilege, subservience of women, speaking in tongues, coded messages from God, an imminent end of the world, the suppression of mind, divine afflatus, witchcraft, magical spells, faith healing, or spiritualism. The modus operandi of these creeds seem so transparent one finds it difficult to believe that their leaders are not fully aware of the deceit they are perpetrating. Some of the new "adherents," to be sure are searching for nothing more than a superficial diversion, and the last thing they want is a demand for mental effort or serious participation.

616

> The least of the causes of war is actual injustice.
>
> Elihu Root (1845-1937)
> Secretary of State (1905-1919) –Nobel Prize winner (1912)

Root gave as his opinion of what are the three main causes of war: actual or threatened wrong by one country to another, suspicion by one country that another intends to do it wrong, and bitterness of feeling, often without basis.

There are many other causes: Often it occurs to politicians that war is a good way to improve their own standing in the community. Robber Barons see it as a way to increase their wealth. Bullies see it as a way to intimidate others and increase their own self-esteem. Religions see it as a way to destroy other religions. Military leaders see it as a way to justify their existence. Also it is a chance to see the games they learned to play in military school run out on a real stage. Armament makers see it as a way to salvage dying industries. Poets see it as a subject for poetry.

Albert Einstein said of the exaggerated patriotism that is the cause of many of our wars: "The man who enjoys marching in line and file to the strains of music falls below my contempt; he received his great brain by mistake – the spinal cord would have sufficed." Thomas Hardy said: "Yes, quaint and curious war is. You shoot a fellow down you would treat if met [under different circumstances]. Richard Le Gallienne said: "O snap the fife and still the drums, and show the monster as she is."

According to Pythagoras, among the necessary wars are those against maladies of the body, ignorances of the mind, seditions of the city, and discords of families. Today we would be more specific: The necessary wars are against drugs, street gangs, pornography, crime, and poverty. We would do well to find some other word for our struggles against crime and the antisocial elements of our societies. These actions are very different from international, civil, and religious wars that very seldom are in any sense necessary.

617

> For years [scientists] have been welcoming hypotheses which destroy their previous assumptions, and welcoming them as a condition of advance, whereas the theologians – and I consider Christian theology to be one of the great disasters of the human race – if they admitted that their assumptions had been upset would consider it a major defeat for themselves....
>
> Lucien Price, editor
> *Dialogues of Alfred North Whitehead*

At first blush, this difference between the way scientists and theologians behave may seem strange. But when one observes the basic assumptions of the two disciplines it is not strange at all.

Science knows that it is an advancing system of knowledge that is always changing, always improving, and constantly casting out outmoded, disproved hypotheses and theories. It admires the authors of outmoded theories as much as the authors of new theories being formulated today. Textbooks of science must be rewritten every few years. Religions, on the contrary, assume that God's word is, was, and always will be perfect. To talk of changing the Bible or even interpretations of it is out of the question. God does not change his mind, as we read in Numbers 23:19. Once he speaks, his words are etched in stone forever. To study developments in the theory of biological evolution is a good way to see science operating at its best. Scientific method is the human mind functioning according to tested rules of logic that help us reach sound conclusions. The theories of biological science quite naturally discredit the bogus decrees of Christian Creationists, the formulations of desperate men fighting to defend the indefensible. When science refutes their assumptions, they prove themselves so petty and vindictive that they become comical. They write books that sound like Grimms' fairy tales. Their opinions develop from what they want to be true, and their methods of arriving at them are like tossing a two-headed coin, weighted so it cannot stand on edge.

For a concise treatise on evolutionary processes, avoiding pedantic elaborations, one could do no better than read *Evolution and the Myth of Creationism* by Tim M. Berra. Creationism is alluded to throughout the first four chapter of the book, but mostly these chapters extol science, giving Creationism and other "pretensions to science" the little space they deserve. Creation Science, like the *Scientology* of L. Ron Hubbard and the Christian Science of Mary Baker Eddy, is in no way related to genuine science, which is systematized knowledge dealing with facts, observations, experiments, and rigorous testing of opinions and conclusions. Science is to pseudoscience, however fanatically the latter is proclaimed, as sense is to sorcery.

But, then, after those four chapters comes Chapter Five, the last chapter of the book. Here Berra explains the equal prominence given to Creationism in the title of the book and attends to his declared intention in the Preface to give teachers and school administrators defense against the dimwitted attacks of Creationists. In Chapter Five, the controversy is defined, and sixteen claims Creationists make for the legitimacy of Creationism are thoroughly analyzed and dispelled. Creationists are seen for what they are: rabid fundamentalists who use any means in an attempt to give credence to the distorted concepts they preach.

618

All religions are ancient monuments to superstition, ignorance, ferocity, and modern religions are only ancient follies rejuvinated.

Paul-Henri-Dietrich d' Holbach (1723-1789
Le Bons Sens...

Fear seems to be the one determining factor in keeping religion from changing. No religionist *dares* to suggest that religions change in order to keep up with this rapidly changing world. Accept first of all that an intervening, all-knowing God is running things and that He has no choice other than being what He is, and you see the problem. Remember, God is omnipotent and forever infallible. He can do no wrong, everything is right, and it follows inexorably that nothing can be allowed to change. As the Bible says in Ecclesiastes 1:0, 'There is nothing new under the sun."

There is no such thing as improving that which is perfect, with even "time" irrelevant to the picture. If God said so-and-so four thousand years ago, it remains so-and-so today. Science is changing so fast it makes our head swim. But religion, the ancient monument to superstition, ignorance, and ferocity" (Holbach) and God, "the invention of Oriental despotisms" (Russell) are just as good today as when the monuments were built or the invention invented.

Whoever said the only constant is change forgot about religion. There the constant is constancy, period. *Punto final*, the Spanish say. All debate is off. Argument is beside the point. It is like arguing about whether the sun will rise tomorrow. For at least four billion years, that is settled.

To accept the constancy of religion, means that religion keeps lagging farther and farther behind the realities of present-day life. If religion continues in its present obstinacy, someday there will necessarily be a reckoning. All theistic religions will be at an impasse from which there is no escape. Only then will the chances for a new, sane world be at hand.

619

You must put [reason] in its right place. And the right place is certainly not when it says, like a blind man in a sunlit garden, "Anything I can't see doesn't exist."

Michael Green
Jesus Spells Freedom

Nor does anything "I can't see" necessarily exist just because someone says it does. No existence, you see, is established by making unfounded statements about that existence. Always the predictive content of statements must be established before it is reasonable to believe those statements.

We must begin with reliable premises if we want to reason effectively from them. If we do not know that fairies exist, it is futile to talk about the behavior, feelings, intelligence, and the responsibilities of fairies. The same can be said about the putative denizens of heaven and hell. First let us prove that they exist before we build complete totalitarian belief systems around them. If such proof is found to be impossible, it is silly for us to believe anyway. All we have left to guide us are our unimpeded minds.

It seems obvious that our religions have no validity if the premises upon which they are based, so far as we can determine, are all false. Let us remind ourselves constantly, it seems so easy to forget, that saying a thing is so does not make it so. Things acquire a degree of authenticity only when subjected to the rigors of scientific proof as described in the book *Operational Philosophy* by Anatol Rapoport (see essay 12).

Life presents us with enough problems without our believing nonsense. Whenever anybody says something to us that strikes us as absurd, we should ask for demonstration. If we do not, if we agree to accept concepts without evidence, we are lost. Any mythmonger who chooses to do so can then fill us to overflowing with his own capricious notions and false conceptions.

620

> The regime of religious toleration has become possible only because we have lost the primal intensity of religious conviction.
>
> Morris Rafael Cohen (1880-1947)

In times of witch trials and inquisitions, of coercive proselytizing and crucifixion for dissenters, religion is to be condemned. When these horrors vanish, and when religion begins to understand that its own shortcomings are at least equal to those of the religion that has been its traditional enemy, toleration returns. When fanaticism abates, sanctimony dwindles, zealotry loses it fury, sacrosanctity wanes, bigotry declines, and religious persecution subsides, religions learn to get along.

Tolerance and toleration are not altogether without their detracting connotations. To tolerate a person "despite his imperfections" implies superiority over that person "My own" beliefs and practices are obviously superior, but I will do my best to respect yours even though they do not really measure up." One accepts (not tolerates) equals – whatever their foibles. In *The Book of Common Prayer*, we read that toleration is to "Have mercy upon Jews, Infidels, Heretics." Jews must be overjoyed to be so favored and to know with what company they are lumped.

Teaching Tolerance, the title of the official organ of the Southern Poverty Law Center would have been better titled: Teaching Mutual Respect or Teaching Equality. The magazine is excellent and the Law Center provides an indispensable service, so I will tolerate it despite its "defectively titled" magazine. Morris Dees, founder and Executive Chairman is Mr Clean, flushing out the scum of the earth. Every truly moral person in the United States is rooting for him.

Whether or not we have "lost the primal intensity of religious conviction" is a question, and whether that accounts for the tolerance that religionists entertain is another. I very much doubt the connection Cohen implies. It is not tolerance that religionists exhibit, but fear. The disastrous outcomes of history's religious wars have taught religious fanatics that they must find other more subtle, more gradual, and more effective ways to impose their hegemony over an increasingly enlightened world. The Spanish and Italian Inquisitions will never be repeated, and coercion and punishment are no longer effective for keeping peace in the parish. It is a new world we live in and religious leaders must learn to operate more prudently than they have in the past if they are to survive and prosper.

621

> The aim and end of all social life is not work and production, but the unfolding of man's creative powers as an end in itself.
>
> Erich Fromm (1900-1980)
> *Beyond the Chains of Illusion*

Contented people are those who are more concerned with the maturation of their creative selves than whether their creations are publicly acclaimed. Making a living is important, of course, but fortunate are those who manage to combine, in their chosen professions, achievement and love for the process of achieving.

The cure for depression, most people find, is to turn one's hand over to doing something creative. Whether it is carpentry, painting, origami, collecting, silk-screen printing, writing, composing, sculpture, pencil drawing, ceramics, flower arranging, gardening, landscaping, or inspired doodling, it does not matter. Whether the end product is or is not "an instant arrested in eternity," is not important. Mental depression cannot survive when the individual nervous system is fully occupied with producing something beautiful. Cares may vanish if thought of them cannot find an unoccupied synapse through which to enter. Absorbing, long-time hobbies have been started through just such recreational therapy.

Perhaps the greatest good of occupational therapy is that it does not leave room in our lives for the mythmongers to make inroads. When we are occupied with the real, tangible and sane, the unreal, imaginary, and psychopathic are rejected. How infectious are the mythologies that threaten us depends on how vulnerable we allow ourselves to be.

Understanding the nature of the myths with which we have become infected, the means we have for uprooting them, and our knowledge of how to prevent them from reestablishing themselves among us, is our salvation. We have again been exposed to sanity. This time, let us hope it is a sanity that is catching.

622

> One may say with one's lips, "I believe that God is one and also three; but no one can believe it, because the words have no sense."
>
> Leo Tolstoy (1828-1910)
> What is Religion?

Tolstoy speaks of what Thomas Jefferson called "the incomprehensible jargon of the Trinitarian arithmetic" and of that which Billy Graham admitted, "Don't ask me to explain it, I can't"

In *If This Be Heresy,* James A. Pike says, "The Moslems offer one God and three wives; we offer three Gods and one wife." He had to say "three wives" for his bon mot to have proper effect. But "three wives" for Islam has even less authenticity than does "three Gods" for Christianity. Actually, the only number the Koran mentions is "four" and even that is not set as a limit.

You can read all the scriptures ever written, aloud if you like, and you will find that most of what you read is no easier to believe than the Trinity. Man's capacity for writing nonsense increases, for now we can stand on the shoulders of all the literary hacks that precede us.

Having learned all we can from all the nonsense writers of the past, we go on to study their techniques for our own use. Present masters of the craft, those who write the materials for the television evangelists, amaze us with their prowess, and the audiences who sit before these evangelists, all ears, agog, attest to their proficiency. The large, parochial university complexes they build on the proceeds bilked from these audiences also leave us amazed. To paraphrase Mencken in *Minority Report,* "Is there any real hope for mankind"?

Chapter XVI

Education

623

Young people today learn at home, in schools, at church, even in gangs, a strange array of solutions for the world's problems:

They learn from Luther that reason must be trampled upon – that emotion is a more reliable guide to salvation. They learn from Jesus that like birds of the field, they will be provided for without special effort on their part. They learn from Moses that fear of God's punishment is essential for moralilty. The learn from Prabhupada that chanting the name Krishna will solve all the world's problems. They learn from Gilbert Ryle that the only light that comes from the East is the sun. They learn from Arthur Miller that the people of Salem knew they held in their hands the candle that would light the world. They learn from Toynbee that science is only another name for the careful and scrupulous use of the human mind. They learn from Voltaire that if God did not exist it would be necessary to invent Him. They learn from Benjamin Tucker that if God did exist it would be necessary to abolish Him. They learn from Emil Lucka that the soul is merely a consciousness of human personality conceived naively as substance. They learn from Harry Emerson Fosdick that the Bible was inspired, not dictated by God. They learn from Harold H. Anderson that brainwashing has been used in the education of our children for hundreds of years. They learn from Stanislav Andreski that truth is not considered of any great value in our societies.

They learn from Sir Arthur Conan Doyle that fairies exist. They learn from Jerry Falwell that homosexuality is a sin. They learn from a Father Confessor that unreserved confession is of higher value than is all of mankind. They learn from Freud that wishful thinking and fear account for the invention of God. They learn from Lancelot

Hogben that dealing with facts instead of words distinguishes science from metaphysics. They learn from Clyde Kluckhohn that man is responsible for his own destiny, They learn from Martin E. Marty that missionaries are presumptuous. They learn from Cynthia Ozick that Jews in The United States are far more free than those in Israel. They learn from Alexander Pope that the proper study of mankind is man. They learn from Jeremiah that no man is master of himself. They learn from Publius Ovidius Naso that we are loath to believe that which hurts when believed. They learn from Anatol Rapoport that the test for the truth of a statement is the amount of predictive content it has. They learn from H. L. Mencken that skepticism is more valuable than any kind of belief. They learn from Robert H. Schuller that heaven may be in Galaxy M-31. They learn from Albert Schweitzer that all progress is produced by rationalism. They learn from Herbert Spencer that volumes might be written on the impiety of the pious. They learn from Ella Wheeler Wilcox that kindness is what the sad world needs. We all learn that we still have a lot to learn.

624

Logical consequences are the scarecrows of fools and the beacons of the wise.

Thomas H. Huxley (1825-1895)

Mystics, sophists, bigots, zealots, bullies, and terrorists anticipate with fear the logical consequences of their malignancy. People of goodwill anticipate with delight the logical consequences of their beneficence. All of us watch the sequences of events that follow human activities so see if they turn out as should be expected. Expectations of pessimists and those of optimists differ, of course, but for all of us looking forward to see whether consequences are scarecrows or beacons help keep us alert to new outcomes and new orientations. We have 535 "experts" in the two houses of congress to analyze new bills and decide whether the good things will outweigh the bad things that follow enactment. Unfortunately, the consequences expected are not always the consequences that ensue, and almost always the situation if far more complex than it may seem. Let us consider one example:

Term limits will reduce graft by leaving office holders without enough time to become proficient at the customary wiles and ruses.

Term limits will give opportunities to fresh, energetic young minds with new ideas important to an emerging new world. Term limits mean that we will lose the expertise of seasoned incumbents. Term limits will encourage lame-duck incumbents to languish, with no solicitude for the concerns of constituents. Term limits will encourage incumbents, who will soon leave, to redouble efforts to make their mark in history. Term limits will eliminate career politicians whose main concern is to stay in office rather than to build a better nation. Term limits will discourage office-seekers whose main aspiration is to amass fortunes they do not earn. Term limits will make it more difficult for lobbyists and political committees to apportion their expertise and largess effectively, whether for good or ill. Term limits through time will increase the number of campaign promises, often activators of new, important legislation.

Term limits in States where they are now law have not been in effect long enough for reliable evaluation. Among consequences will be some of those mentioned above – and no doubt many others.

625

> The miseries derived... from superstition under the name of religion have been clearly exposed. We begin to think and act from reason alone.
>
> Edmund Burke (1729-1797

That will be the day! Two hundred more years have passed, and we have not yet made a good start. People still adhere to religion (organized superstition) all over the earth. And by no means do we act from reason alone. We act mostly as puppets with every variety of preacher and politician pulling the strings.

What Burke describes is an ideal, not by any means a description the situation that prevailed in 1760. We must learn that religion is in fact a kind of structured madness, with reason by no means a guiding factor in his or in our day. Then we will have a base from which to start. The first step is to acknowledge our failure to build a rational world in the past two hundred years and then to try to find out why. Then we come to the difficult part, that of acquainting people generally with the influence superstitions and prejudices have in our societies. Only then can we convince people to help in building societies based on empathy, knowledge, and reason.

626

> It is a very good world for the purposes for which it was built.
>   Henry Ward Beecher (1813-1887)
>   *Royal Truths*

Now if the Reverend Beecher would please inform us in regard to what those purposes are. Ascribing purpose to nature is like saying that cliffs were made so the cliff swallows would have a place to call home, plants were given roots so the mole rat can remain hidden while it has its dinner. The youngest, most succulent leaves were placed high in the trees so the giraffe would have good food where it is comfortable for it to browse.

Does the Reverend Beecher really believe that nature was carefully planned in order to accommodate us and the animals that would be part of it? Or does he see that we all evolved in a manner that would best adapt us to nature? There is no evidence whatsoever for the former explanation and abundant evidence for the latter.

The most memorable thing I ever remember hearing said about the famous brother of Harriet Beecher Stowe was said by Oliver Wendell Holmes, Sr., in the form of a Limerick:

> The Reverend Henry Ward Beecher
> Called a hen a most elegant creature.
> The hen, pleased at that
> Laid an egg in his hat,
> And thus did the hen reward Beecher!

Holmes and Beecher were contemporaries. Whether Beecher was aware that he was committed to rhyme, I do not know.

627

> He that only rules by terror
> Does grievous wrong.
> Deep as Hell I count his error.
> Let him hear my song.
>   Alfred Lord Tennyson (1809-1892)

When a despot gains power, the first thing he does is to shut down all the newspapers that disagree with him. History is then rewritten to favor his tyrannical philosophy. Everyone in the country who prefers life to execution becomes a champion of the despot's governing style. Fear reigns. Corruption and greed take over, and all but the ruling junta of sycophants must learn to live in poverty. No one is master of himself, and life becomes unremitting drudgery.

Finally, a few brave rebels decide that even death is better than living with tyranny, and an underground rebellious group forms. Neighboring governments who looked with distrust on the despotic government sharing a border with them begin to furnish the rebels with arms. Everything is ready for a revolution.

The despot, certain that his people are on his side, is in for a rude awakening. Many of the people have been waiting for just this opportunity. As soon as the rebels are seen to have a chance, they join the rebels in hordes. When the despot reads clearly the true nature of the situation, he flees the country, usually taking all of the money in the treasury with him.

This scenario has been repeated so often in history that one would think would-be despots might learn. In a few years all of the Central and South American countries that once were tyrannies have become democracies, some with lessons still to be learned. The world is changing for the better, but there is still a long way to go.

628

> A God comprehended is no God.
>
> Dio Chrysoston (40-120)

This pretentious quotation should be complemented by the even more obvious truism: "A God not comprehended is also no God." Now we happily find ourselves liberated from the oppressive phantasm to which much of mankind has so foolishly surrendered. To pretend that such nonsense is meaningful is to pretend that we are also preaching great wisdom when we say, "A mystery comprehended is no mystery."

If God does not exist, of course we cannot comprehend Him, and we can get on to other things that do exist and are important in our lives. If God does exist and He is the God of Judeo-Christian-Muslim scriptures, there would be no way to comprehend Him, as reading those scriptures makes obvious. To pretend to comprehend such a God is to turn him into an apotheosized figment of our own imagination, as good a definition of God, it seems to me, as anyone has ever come up with.

As is easy to understand, there was method in the madness of inventing a single incomprehensible deity. That which is incomprehensible cannot be refuted. But it is still possible to speak of an incomprehensible God as perfectly comprehensible nonsense which is perfectly compatible with everything else that orthodox religions talk about. The whole bundle of balderdash is an impregnable black hole, allowing no light to escape.

629

> The Christian idea of a perfect heaven that is something other than a nonexistence is a contradiction in terms.
>
> Aldous Huxley (1894-1963)
> "Wordsworth in the Tropics" – *Fifty Famous Essays*

Yes, of course, I hadn't thought of it before, but that nonexistent thing, there is real perfection.

Alexander Pope in his An Essay on Criticism said: "Whoever things a faultless piece to see, thinks what ne'er was nor is nor e'er shall be." Perfection, we now see, has only one referent, a nonreferent: "nonexistence." "Nothing" is perfect. Exactly! All those "no" things. Those "nonexistence" things – perfect. Heaven, hell, God, angels, devils, jinn – all of them are perfect.

630

> Absolutely speaking, "Do unto others as you would that they should do unto you? "is by no means a golden rule.... An honest man would have but little occasion for it. It is golden not to have any rule at all in such a case.   Henry David Thoreau (1817-1862)

That "an honest man would have no reason for it" is hardly an argument against aphoristic guidelines. We would get rid of all our laws if that were the case, We could get rid of our governments as well if we were to base their lack of necessity on the behavior of a few honest men.

It may well be that a case can be made for a rather strange state of affairs that must occur to many people who are keen observers of the passing scene. Once a person like Thoreau makes a well-deserved reputation saying and writing things that become indispensable to the accumulated wisdom of mankind, something happens to these persons. Their phenomenal success makes them so enamored of themselves that they begin to believe their own publicity. They arrive at a point where they think every word they write is a treasure and everything they say is a jewel. Or it may be that in some cases their living style becomes so exorbitant that they are forced to write another book (even if pure nonsense), knowing it will sell simply because it has the name Mitchell, Thoreau, or Mann on it. I have been suckered into buying such books. It is not unlike our predilection for going to movies for no other reason than that we like the star. Even stars act in deplorable movies. And in some of the best movies made, they do not use stars. The movie Lolita, yet to be released in the United States is, according to reports, an example.

631

> Man's life is a warfare against the malice of man.
> > Baltasar Gracian y Morales (1601-1658)
> > *The Art of Worldly Wisdom*

Anyone who is honest, nonbeligerent, and content to live a middle-class life needs one or both of two expediencies if he or she is to live out an expected three-score and ten. The first is an appreciable measure of luck. The second is some kind of self-instilled continual vigilance to protect him from the active ill will frequently exhibited by other human beings.

In Portugal, I had walked from the hotel where I lived to downtown Lisbon many times on the widest, most beautiul street I have ever seen in any city anywhere. But today I wanted a change, so going home I chose a parallel street, very narrow and with stores on only one side. I noticed a young lady walking about a hundred feet ahead of me – the only other person in sight. Naturally a fast walker and my legs being longer than hers, I gained on her. But as an inveterate window shopper, I stopped from time to time to see in this very different country what people were buying. My behavior, closing and opening the space between us, I realized obviously worried the mentioned lady, and she kept turning around to see where I was. Finally, she crossed to the other side where there was no sidewalk, and cars parked parallel against a high wall , leaving no space to walk except in the street. I'm sure she hoped I would pass her so she could keep me in sight, but window-shopping kept slowing me down.

What a world we live in, I have often thought, that we cannot trust one another but must be ever afraid and constantly alert in order to protect ourselves from harm. Near Badajoz , Spain I had a similar experience when hiking across fields some four o five kilometers from town. Two senoritas on the path I had taken were more frightened than the unfortunate young lady in Lisbon. I talked to them as I went by, but they seemed too frightened to answer, and seemed inclined to turn back. After rounding a hill, I sat down on a rock to read and to rest. An hour or so later, I looked up just in time to see the two girls coming over the hill. This time they did turn back, and I never saw them again.

632

> Volumes might be written on the impiety of the pious.
>
> Herbert Spencer (1820-1903)

Might be? Already have been! For a start, read: Barrows Dunham: *Heroes and Heretics*; Malcolm Hay: The Foot of Pride; Michael Baigent, Richard Leigh, and Henry Lincoln: *Holy Blood, Holy Grail*: H.L. Mencken: *Treatise on the Gods*: Richard Robinson: *An Atheists Values*; Paul Kurtz: *The Transcendental Temptation*, Bertrand Russell: *Why I am not a Christian*; George H. Smith: *Atheism, the Case Against God*; Nietzsche: *Antichrist*; Chester Dolan: *Blind Faith*; and many, many others. The Bibliographies of any of these books will list many more.

Even in reading some "serenely religious" books, we will see the impiety of the pious. To note how evasive an author must be in order to make his points is to see impiety rampant. His weasel-wording, circumlocutions, quibbling, etc., give him away. He is either aware that he is lying for his cause, or he has reached such a state of mental torpor that he does not know the truth when he sees it.

633

> Nothing is more difficult than competing with a myth.
>
> Françoise Giroud (1916-   )
> *I give you my word*

It is not just difficult, it is almost impossible. The mythmongers have one sure, incontestable answer to everything: "It is so because it is so" It is so because it says so right here. See! In this infallible book of infallible pronouncements written by an infallible Deity, it says so. Look for yourself!

It does not help to point out that their so-called infallible God is constantly contradicting Himself. Nor does it help to point out that this infallible Deity merits Felix Adler's expostulation: "What fiend so fiendish as such a God!" It does not help to point out that the Deity the mythologists find worthy of worship – murders selected contingents among his subjects without discernible reason and is partisan of those who foment our religious wars.

The Reverend Rudi Gelsey mitigates biblical buncombe slightly in his *imagine... a new bible*, but the real solution to Giroud's dilemma is much more obvious than that and much more lasting. Let us get rid of all gods, all Bibles, all the stupidity that is religions so that we can all live in undisturbed peace. Religion since its inception has kept the world riled up in individual hatreds and prejudices, and in religious wars that it seems will never be resolved. An even worse consideration is to imagine what would happen if any one religion were ever to have its way. We would be living in a world theocracy that would make all past tyrannies seem like afternoon teas. What the Taliban in Afghanistan and the Dorje Shugden worshipers in the Gelluk sect of Tibetan Buddhism are trying to do would infect the entire world. All freedoms would disappear, and we would all live in chains.

634

Kill one man and you are a murderer. Kill millions and you are a conqueror. Kill all and you are a God.

Jean Rostand (1894-1947)

If we can believe in the Bible, God does two different kinds of killing. He kills some people to do them a favor. He kills others to do them grievous harm. No one talks about it in such terms, but that is the way it is.

On the day of final judgment, as the Biblical story goes, God will kill everybody. Killing is killing, we usually say, and in earthly justice systems few killers go free. God, of course kills with impunity. That is one of the nice things about being God, as Jean Rostand suggests. But by killing some of the people, God does a tremendous favor. They go to heaven which, He assures them, they will like. By killing others, he does them anything but a favor. They go to hell, where they will fry forever. We wonder what God will do for entertainment from then on. After Armageddon, everything seems to be taken care of. Fear of God loses its significance. To those in heaven, surely such fear would be meaningless. For those in hell, what more is there to fear? Sin? Those in heaven will not. Those in hell cannot. Another problem has disappeared. Satan? He is completely without employment. Perhaps God will toss him into the flames too. Why did He not do that six millennia ago (Bishop Ussher time)?

635

The idea that a good God would send people to a burning hell is utterly damnable to me, the ravings of insanity! Superstition gone to seed! I don't want to have anything to do with such a God. No avenging Jewish God, no satanic devil, no fiery hell is of any interest to me.

Luther Burbank (1849-1926) - American horticulturist

One has to wonder about the kind of mind that does not see in Burbank's words a poignant expression of the unadorned truth about all the theistic religions that have ever been contrived. Why does any mind choose to conjure up gods that it would be impossible to abide with any degree of equanimity. Why do we want a god that keeps us pathologically in fear of becoming another of the inmates of inferno?

Luther Burbank, more than most people, was aware of the marvelous mechanisms of crossing plant varieties to produce new ones. Nevertheless, he repudiated the God that others required to explain these mechanisms.

The theories of biological evolution do well in explaining the tremendously intricate world in which we live. The invention of deities explains nothing. It is simply a way of giving up. It is saying: We will not bother with trying to develop logical explanations for the way things are. Instead we will resort to one blanket nonexplanation: We declare, "God did it."

636

> Believing in gods always causes confusion.
>
> Pearl S. Buck (1892-1973)
> The Bondsmaid Ch 1

Elsewhere (in the Young Revolutionists) Madam Buck quotes an old abbot as saying, "... when men destroy their old gods they will find new ones to take their place." Also, when isolated peoples finally find ways to communicate and learn about each other's pantheons, the gods with their many differences are bound to cause confusion. Norse gods, Greek gods, Roman gods, Middle East gods, Hindu gods, Brahmanic gods, Egyptian gods, and all the aboriginal gods of Africa, North and South America, Polynesia, and Australia, etc., combine to unsettle and bewilder mankind. The world has known hundreds, perhaps thousands of gods. Mesopotanian gods alone are said to have numbered as high as 3,300. All of these gods had their own proper names, and no one was any more authentic than any of the others.

No wonder monotheism, to some, became a popular solution to all this confusion. But Pearl Buck and Barbara Tuchman, contemporaries, had a better solution yet: Get rid of all gods. Prefer to live in a world without myth or magic.

637

> "Every adult in America knows," a stranger wrote to me the other day, that the whole show is crazy, and that they are too. Only, nobody dares say so."
>
> Philip Wylie (1902-1971)
> *The Magic Animal*

Philip Wylie dares say so. In his 29 books, he says so repeatedly. In his *Generation of Vipers* (1942), the book that made him famous, he leaves no doubt. In this, his last book, written three years before he died, he tells us. "All the Holy Books, ancient or recent, must be taken [to libraries], not left in homes to corrupt children, or in hotel rooms and on altars, to close minds and devastate the hope of different and greater images for mankind." He speaks of "Mary Baker Eddy's dangerous drivel," and the bastardizing literature of "St. Augustine, St. Paul , Calvin, Knox, Luther, and Wesley..."

Earlier   in the book, Wylie says, "If, to get in touch with…God, I had to abandon self, reason, knowledge, extensions of imagination, utterly and forever, that God was in fact a demon and malicious, the creator of me as an embodied dirty trick."

With both the gods and their scriptures put in their place, Wylie leaves man free to be himself. He is now unsuppressed, free to plan a destiny beyond myth and misery – with hope to build a sane world in which present and future human beings can live in peace.

638

In the course of his development [man] has been constrained from time to time to abandon his most cherished myths. Thus he has abandoned his animism; his Ptolemaic astronomy that assured his position in the center of the universe; his faith in a hereafter that endowed him with eternal life; his belief in the supreme and infinite worth of his person that assured him a position of isolate dignity in an otherwise meaningless and impersonal world; and even perhaps his faith in a God whose attributes, under the impact of man's rationalistic scrutiny, became ever more abstract until He [God] vanished in the metaphysical concept of the whole.

Roderick Seidenberg (1899-   )
Posthistoric Man: An Inquiry

Seidenberg paints a dismal picture; The alternative to living in a world of metaphysical illusion, he says, is that man will soon stop living. The genus Homo will become extinct. But Seidenberg gives us no convincing arguments for supposing that "living a lie" is in the least the secret of human survival. It is far more probable that if we continue to welter in dream worlds we will vanish. We, as a species, must become a thoroughly rational animal, convinced that we can successfully manage our own affairs. Without a belief in ourselves, we certainly will not solve the difficult problems that face us. The dehumanizations of the individual that Seidenberg is concerned with is a direct result of relinquishing our freedoms.

In his book, Seidenberg speaks of man "moving impetuously toward chaos.' While "torn asunder by conflicting tension," and "seeking refuge in a countervailing sense of guilt and failure," and "with an ominous sense of fatality," unable to accept "a higher principle of unity." But it is this higher principle [Divine Duty] that is the major cause of the chaos in which man lives. Our only hope for salvation, Seidenberg would have it, is to give ourselves over to an incomprehensible God, cowed by an intractable Satan. The threat of a brimstone-and-fire inferno will keep us acting in accordance with whims of an other-world will. The thrust of *Religion on Trial* has been to disabuse us of these wholly unfounded projections.

639

Millions long for immortality who do not know what to do with themselves on a rainy Sunday afternoon.
Susan Ertz (1894-1985) - British Novelist

From what I read of the "next world," there I would be eternally bored. In this world, I cannot imagine being bored.

In Quito, I visited at three o'clock one afternoon a lady, 61, in good health, and found her sitting alone crying. It turned out she was simply lonesome. Her husband was off on some errand, her oldest daughter was working at Tia, a department store, and her two younger children were off to school. She was "at work' in her small general store, a part of her home, but there were no customers. She is an educated person, but functionally illiterate, and I doubt had read two books in her entire adult life. She was used to the commotion of family life and could not stand being without it.

Those of us, even in retirement, who have ten times as much to do as we will ever get done, find it hard to understand Maria. But as Susan Ertz says, there are probably millions of them. Too often, they become willing recruits for religions, preferring to live in a busy world of nonsense than in a world of reality for which they have not prepared themselves. They have become drones rather than useful citizens - and live on as vegetables until they die.

640

[Emerson] had the most important of the intellectual virtues; that of being true to himself; he believed, no doubt, as do all truly honorable men, that it is a despicable act to disguise one's thoughts in order to accommodate them to the social forms of error that conspire against truth....
José Ingenieros (1877-1925)
Hacia un Moral sin Dogmas

Emerson and Ingenieros were not contemporaries, Ingenieros having been only five years old when Emerson died. But they could have been identical twin brothers in their manner of thinking. Words almost identical to those Ingenieros used here to describe Emerson were used to describe Ingenieros in a blurb introducing the third edition of his book *El Hombre Mediocre*, published in 1917. Both men spoke their minds candidly, regardless of prevailing public opinions at odds with what they said. Ingenieros was as admired in Argentina, indeed in all of South America, as Emerson was in North America. Unfortunately, Ingenieros died prematurely, before he could begin plans to rewrite and republish his eight best known works in more coherent form. None of Ingenieros' books were ever translated and published in English. I have translated his *El Hombre Mediocre* and hope it will be published someday. Ingenieros traveled widely and lectured in four different languages.

641

I'm opposed to abortion because I happen to believe that life deserves the protection of society.
    Quoted in "Ella Grasso of Connecticut" by Mrs. Joseph B. Treaster

Judith Rossner describes her abortion in 1975: "But I've been miserable ever since I came back. From Puerto Rico, that's where I had it, it was like a vacation. It's almost like – it's not supposed to be that easy. It's too big a sin to get off that lightly. (*Looking for Mr. Goodbar*).

Gwendolyn Brooks in the first Stanza of "The Mother" (A Street in Bronzeville) makes her point with involuted tongue: "Abortion will not let you forget. You remember the child you got that you did not get...." "One dead, one wounded," a bumper sticker reads.

It should be understood that to agree with the Catholic Church's stand against abortion is not to agree with its opposition to all the forms of artificial birth control, whether or not they relate to abortion. Also, it is not to agree with the Church's opposition to safe-sex programs in the developing societies, leading to proliferating HIV infections in areas like sub-Saharan Africa and overcrowded India.

I object to bar mitzvah for a thirteen-year-old Jewish boy or confirmation for a Christian child. But at least there is some slight chance that those events can be reversed. Abortion is forever. There is no changing one's mind. The unborn child that could have been a future president or even our next messiah is never going to be anything. And the decision is not even his own. Someone else has decided for him.

When the figure is given that during the past century more than 160 million human beings were killed in various conflicts, that does not include the children killed before they were born. There are now in the world forty-to-sixty million abortions a year. Is that the way we want to control our populations? Morally, we are a species that has failed: We cannot stop conceiving unwanted babies, but we can kill them before they are born or agree that it is all right for them to grow up in wretched squalor.

642

Science corrects the old creeds, sweeps away with every new perception our infantile catechisms, and necessitates a faith commensurate with the grander orbit and universal laws which it discloses.

Ralph Waldo Emerson (1830-1882)

Science corrects creeds, sweeps away catechisms, and generates a proper confidence in ourselves and the world we live in. That is a good start.

But if the evolution of human intelligence has not ceased, reform will not stop there. In an atmosphere of sanity, the entire fraud that is religion will begin to unravel. In an evolving world, what Mencken called organized ignorance will quite naturally become organized enlightenment . The balance between the harm religion does and the good that it could do will slowly shift to where "the good" prevails. A gradual eroding of structured madness, methodized nonsense, and organized superstitions will take place. The present hierarchy of bureaucratic religiosity will disappear, and for the first time in recorded history we can live in peace. Our minds, unencumbered by pathological mythomania, will begin to operate as never before and we can begin to construct a happy world without the distortions presently imposed upon it.

643

> The only beast in the *Plaza de Torros* is the crowd.
> Vincent Blasco Ibanez (1867-1928)

Animals in the Bible fare no better than do humans. No tears were shed over the ram that was sacrificed in place of Isaac. Page after page we read that animals were sacrificed to "honor" God, more than a hundred thousand in the dedication of one church. Without defensible reason for doing so, Jesus sent some 2000 Gadarene swine down a steep slope to drown in the sea. No one bothers to mention the innumerable millions of animals that could not get into the ark. If victorious armies led by God were unable to bring back as loot all the horses of the annihilated enemy, those left were hamstrung. Ask any equestrian what it means to hamstring a horse and leave it unattended, and you will learn what a heinous crime is this practice approved by the God of the Old Testament.

Only two times have I been in a plaza de torros. Once was in Barcelona, Spain to see a Russian Ballet, and another time was in Buenos Aires, Argentina to see Luis Palau, who was at the time mostly an Argentine version of Billy Graham. Now he is a citizen of the United States living in Oregon and preaching equally well in Spanish and English. Both times in a plaza de torros, I sat and wondered if it was the same species of hominoid that once a week desecrated that beautiful plaza with the spectacle for which it was intended.

644

> The first step toward philosophy is Incredulity.
> Denis Diderot (1713-1784)
> Sceptics Walk

As one of the two editors of the famous *Encyclopedia* during the years 1751-1765, Diderot was privy to most of the advanced ideas of his time. A mind functioning in that kind of lavish, affirmative atmosphere for fourteen years is not easy to induct into the causes of nonsense. He could see that blind acceptance of the unfounded proclamations of the religionists of that period was folly. The antidote was skepticism, postponing belief until all implications could be investigated. He had at hand the best compendium of good sense that the world had seen up to that time. In other words, ignorance, the only real friend theistic religions could count on in the years of their most rapid development, was not a factor in the formation of Diderot's opinions.

Diderot slowly turned from theism to atheism despite having received much of his education in a Jesuit college. He even went to prison because of his opinions. A man who wrote millions of words ended up saying; "The first step toward philosophy is incredulity."(The first step toward truth is skepticism).

645

To explain the origin of the DNA/protein machine by invoking a supernatural Designer is to explain precisely nothing, for it leaves unexplained the origin of the Designer.

Richard Dawkins
The Blind Watchmaker

Dawkins continues: "you have to say something like 'God was always there,' and if you allow yourself that kind of lazy way out, you might as well just say that 'DNA was always there," or "life was always there,' and be done with it."

On the last full page of the book, he restates this thesis; "The odds against [an eye appearing fully fashioned, perfect and whole] will keep us writing noughts till the end of time. The same applies to the odds against the spontaneous existence of any fully fashioned, perfect, and whole beings, including – I see no way of avoiding the conclusion – deities."

Whatever we say about the religious world of revelation will inevitably be found wanting. As most religionists are ready to admit. It is like playing leapfrog with unicorns. If unicorns are real, the practice gets a bit sticky. If they are not, the activity is absurd. If we continue with our soliloquies of mystical mumbo jumbo, sooner or later our new world of nothingness must be hypostatized as reality, communized, and then must be defended by any means, whenever and wherever necessary. Some time ago, President Carter in an interview with Charlie Rose told us that wars are going on in 35 different regions of the world. Now (3-19-99) Mark Shields on the News Hour with Jim Lehrer tells us that at last count 45 wars are going on.

646

> We learn from history that we do not learn from history.
>
> Georg Wilhelm Friedrich Hegel (1770-1831)

Hegel's "do not" can mean "There is nothing there to be learned," or it can mean "even though there may be something to learn from history, we do not have the inclination or the capability for learning it." History is full of pitfalls:

1. We exaggerate the virtues of history, looking to it as the established level of excellence.
2. We make deities of its protagonists.
3. We become overwhelmed by its amorphous ramifications.
4. The effective lessons it does contain, now distant, lose their emotional appeal.
5. Some of its taboos suppress human passions until they virtually disappear, leaving us sorely deprived.
6. We undervalue present accomplishments, which we feel do not compare with those of history.
7. Today's exceptional, dissenting opinions are denigrated. Critics prefer "ancient wisdom," of no authentic value.
8. The past speaks in divers voices, and it is not always easy to decide which to heed.
9. We claim as history that which is myth, legend, and other delusive creations of ancient and ignorant minds.
10. History can help if it keeps us from returning to ancient inanities: Astronomers must not revert to being astrologers. Chemists to being alchemists, nor intelligent people to being guided by horoscopes, tarot cards, or the thousand and one shell-games that scream for attention.

Those of us intrigued with science and its achievements are happy to learn that more people know more about astronomy than ever before in history. We are happy, that is, until we learn, too, that more people take seriously the accumulation of stupidities called astrology than ever before in history.

647

> You can do very little with faith, but you can do nothing without it.
> Samuel Butler (1835-1902)
> *Note Books*

We can assume that Butler is making sense only by making one further assumption - that he is deliberately using the word faith in two very different ways. The first is the "faith" the preacher uses when he asks members of his congregation to believe what he says without the slightest reason for doing so.

The second (the word "it" at the end of his quotation) is the common acceptation of the word faith as a synonym of "confidence." Without confidence indeed, we would be lost. We must have faith that most people are honest and trustworthy. The world could not function without a mutual confidence that promises and pledges, contracts and commitments, bargains and betrothals, will be honored.

When the preacher uses the word faith, he is not asking of his listeners confidence, but gullibility. He is, in effect, saying to them: "Take this as I say it. Do not doubt its truth however much it strikes you as less than probable. We are here to promote religion, which would disintegrate overnight if all members of all congregations were suddenly to decide that from now on they would believe only those things for which there is clear, unequivocal, and demonstrable evidence."

When the preacher asks us to have faith, he asks for obedience without question. We must accept unthinkingly whatever he tells us is so. When Shia and Sunni are asked to murder on the fields of battle, both following leaders who tell them they are then assured a place in heaven, they obey. If the dead could return to set things straight, to tell us that "faith" is nothing more than nonsense institutionalized, the hate and murder of all "religious" conflicts would cease. There would be no crusades, inquisitions, witch hunts, and holy wars. There would be no Shia and Sunni, no Lutherans and Catholics, no religious sects of any kind, because there would be no religions.

648

> Our true nationality is mankind.
>
> H.G. Wells (1866-1946)

If the social world had evolved in a manner so that neither the words nationalism and religion nor the concepts they embrace had ever been necessary, we would be a very different humanity than we are. Nationalism and religion are so intricately intertwined that it is hard to imagine the former without the latter also. Religion does not have its flags, emblematic songs, birds, animals, etc., but it does have its gods, saints, icons, and the like. It is hard to tell which we make the most of, worship more, or would be more lost without. Our constitution never contemplated making a god a national symbol, but it has come close to doing just that to a piece of cloth striped and sprinkled with symbolic red, white, and blue colors. The gods may be dead, but national emblems are alive and well, and we emote over them effusively.

If the "is" in the Wellian quotation were changed to "should be," I could concur completely. But the only way I see that happening is for us to take ourselves to a brink that could easily mean the end of the Human species. If we can, for a moment, imagine that there were a few survivors of a World War III or a "Waterworld" or of a world of restored dinosaurs, and these few were to get together, *they* might plan a new global community without nations, and certainly without religions. They might populate the world with a brotherhood society of peaceful beings. Who knows, they might even develop genes for radiation immunity, for gills, and for tails and scales.

649

> Life has to be given a meaning because of the fact that it has no meaning.
>
> Henry Miller (1891-1980)
> "Creative Death"
> *The Wisdom of the Heart*

Albert Camus tells us that life will be lived all the better if it has no meaning. Whether Miller is right in thinking that we are wise in fooling ourselves by assigning meaning where there is no meaning is a question. Is it that we human beings are so misguided that we cannot perceive that simply the joy of living is meaning enough? Is not an effort to make this a better world for ourselves and for those who follow all the meaning we need?

The solar system itself is not seen as having a meaning. In some five billion years or so, this spot in the galaxy will run out of energy, and all will end. But five billion years is in effect eternity as far as our minds can conceive such enormous amounts of time. What a ball Homo sapiens can have if he is capable of surviving anything like that length of time.

Entropy being what it is, no life anywhere in the universe can expect existence forever. Change, someone said, is the only permanence. Nothing in our lives is the same from one second to the next. If nothing else, we are one second closer to the moment of our death. As far as astronomers can figure it out, nothing in the universe is more than 15 billion years old. That is an inconceivable great amount of time, but it is not forever. Even in that vastness of space and time, astronomers can see significant changes during a weekend's stint at the telescope. The world moves along fast enough to keep us all well entertained and happy.

650

> Thank God I am black. White people will have a lot to answer for at the last judgment.
>
> Archbishop Desmond Tutu (1931-   )

Regardless of how morally superior they judge themselves to be, I find it strange that fanatically religious people are ever ready to usurp God's privilege to make His own judgments at His own time and place. Especially, it seems odd that they are ready to condemn all of a certain class of people. Does Tutu believe that God will do the same? Is it possible that some of he white people of Africa deplore apartheid as much as does Archbishop Tutu and are ever racking their brains to figure out how most effectively to improve the deplorable conditions that have existed for such a long time?

Edmund Burke said in the late 1700s: "I do not know the method of drawing up an indictment against a whole people." He would find Desmond Tutu's contention completely out of keeping with accepted standards of morality.

Frederik William de Klerk is certainly no saint, but nevertheless must be given a great deal of credit for the remarkable changes that have occurred. Writers like Doris Lessing and Nadine Gordimer have helped improve the atmosphere so that change could take place. In the United States, both the ACLU and NAACP acknowledge the help of white people on behalf of blacks. Decent people of all colors are required to make this a better world.

651

What is war? Nine times out of ten it is murder in uniform.
                                        Douglas Jerrold (1803-1857)

War is many things to many people. To thinking people it is human nature shown at its worst. Among opinions:

Jonathan Swift: a mad game the world loves to play
Somner Welles: an act of criminal folly
Dwight Eisenhower: fire, famine, and pestilennce
U.S. Grant: an outrage to the producing class, the sufferers
German proverb: a producer of three armies: cripples, mourners, and theives
Napoleon Bonaparte: the business of barbarians
Arthur Wellesley: an abomination: false, rapacious, and cruel
Sydney Smith: atrocious crimes committed in the name of peace
William Channing: violence, malignity, rage, fraud, rapacity and lust
Albert Barnes: hell
James Madison: destroyer of public liberty
William Shenstone: a device to bleed the many and enrich the few
Lois Napolean: organized barbarism
Edward Thomson: corruption and disgrace

And still we fight wars. We will continue to do so until we get rid of religion and nationalism. Not all gods are dead. The god of war seems to be working overtime. If we combine forces, surely we can send Ares packing and live forever in peace.

652

The end of life would be less frightening if it were not called death anymore. The fear of death is the scourge of all religions.
                                        Maurice Maeterlinck (1862-1949)
                                        Belgian poet, dramatist, and, essayist

We would not have the problems we have with words if we all would take time off to understand that words do not have meanings, only people do. Words are nothing more than variations of compression waves in the atmosphere (if spoken and heard) or scratches of contrasting color on pages (if written and read). It can be said that all words are nothing more than electro-chemical impulses in the brain. Not until people assign meanings to these waves, scratches, and brain phenomena do they have any meaning. One example should suffice to explain:

When I was a child certain people were called Negroes (the word for black in Spanish), But people in their minds kept changing the connotations of the word until the people to whom the word Negro applied objected. So everyone decided then that these Negroes would henceforward be called colored people. The same thing happened again – and again the name was changed, this time to blacks. Is it not possible for us to understand that nothing about referents (the Negroes, colored people) changed. Only the people's ideas about the words assigned to these "Afro-Americans," changed. There is nothing intrinsically good or bad about the sounds or printed letters. No harm would be done were it not for the illusional fixations people foolishly allow to form in their minds upon hearing or seeing them.

In the days when Joseph Conrad wrote his delightful psychological novel *The Nigger of the Narcissus,* even *that* word had not yet acquired objectionable connotations. The novel, itself, would not have been any different had the author chosen for the protagonist a man of any color whatever of the Roy G. Biv spectrum.

Now Maeterlinck wants to take us on the same silly sleigh ride with the word death. If chance had been such that in our language "death" has been assigned to the journey and "life" to its end, Maeterlinck would now be concerned with that horribly scary word "life." We can't win.

653

Whenever religion excludes... the spirit of free inquiry, it leads to willful blindness and superstition.

Samuel Taylor Coleridge (1772-1834)
Quoted in Thomas Allsop's *Letters, Conversations, and Reflections*

With religion as unsure as it is of its ability to defend the legitimacy of its sacraments, doctrines, and canons, free inquiry is the last thing to expect from its apologists. Imagine a court of law accepting as evidence transubstantiation, turning wine and bread into blood and flesh. Imagine defense of the trinity, the union of Father, Son, and Holy Ghost into one Godhead. Imagine explaining in scientific terms the virginity of Mary, who had several children. Imagine proving that Jesus has a trait called divinity. We are talking of a man who kicked a fig tree for not producing fruit out of season. He was also a man who could ask that his enemies be brought and slain before him.

Imagine defending "evidence" that one's man's death can exonerate others of their crimes. Imagine explaining how sprinkling, dunking, or half-drowning a person with or in water washes away sin or makes a person a genuine Christian (or whatever). Imagine proving that a "soul" leaves the body at the time of death – or even that a human body "has" such a soul.

To keep free inquiry active and effectual would be to launch a revolutionary change. Free inquiry would soon rid religions of their prejudice, superstition, bigotry, and dogma. Orthodox religions would simply disappear.

654

> In all ages, hypocrites, called priests, have put crowns upon the heads of thieves, called kings.
>
> Robert G. Ingersoll (1833-1899)
> *Prose-Poems and Selections*

The extent to which prospects of increased income and community approval determine how churches dispense their favors is one of the sad chapters of religious history. The antagonists in most wars have no problem finding churches to support them in their hostilities.

Even in blatant tyrannies, the despots that run the countries have no shortage of religious leaders manifestly in support of them. The Somosas, Perons, Stroessners, Pol Pots, Mobutus, Idi Amins of the world could not have stayed in office as long as they did – had not local churches colluded with them. In theocracies, it is the churches themselves that do the exploiting. Barrows Dunham on page 207 of *Heroes and Heretics* describes how bishops and priests abuse their authority in governments run by priests claiming to rule by divine authority. The Mexican revolutionary leader Pancho Villa said, "I... think the greatest enemy of our progress and liberty is the corrupting clergy, who so long have dominated our country."

655

Much that passes for religion today is nothing more than self-serving self-discipline.

Gordon Williard Allport (1897-1967)
Professor of psychology – Harvard University

We expect self-discipline to be self-serving. Why else would anyone subject himself to an agonizing routine? To broaden and make clear what Allport is saying we would do better to change his last hyphenated term to "deception." The deception is perpetrated by theologians who serve themselves by deceiving others.

Self-serving deception clearly applies to astrologers, soothsayers, tarot-card readers, phrenologists, spiritualists, tea-leaf readers, crystal gazers, channelers, sorcerers, and icon salesmen. It applies also to those who find serenity in the security offered by guardian angels, prayer-answering gods, and promises of heavenly rewards. It serves anyone and everyone who intellectually and emotionally want to be deceived. They find comfort in knowing that others are willing to do their thinking for them, others who assume responsibility for the care of their souls and for planning an acceptable future that they themselves are incapable of conceiving.

"Much," Allport's first word above, prompts us to ask where will we find the remaining part of religion that is not deception? Whatever of any human discipline that can show no grounds for being considered authentic training to help us improve our behavior is deception. Just as there is no substance in any of the imaginary entities dreamed up in human minds, so there is nothing respectable about a mental discipline that offers nothing to improve our morality.

656

Parsons always seem to be specially horrified about things like sunbathing and naked bodies. They don't mind poverty and misery and cruelty to animals nearly as much.

Susan Ertz (1894-1985) – British Novelist

When I reached an age where I could earn fifteen cents and walk alone to the only movie theater in a small Minnesota town, I was delighted. But even at that age I was appalled to see the cowboy hero shoot dead another man on the street, step over his body to kiss a girl waiting at the curb.

Another, a real-life incident occurred at that time when a young fellow was rowing two pretty young ladies across a local lake to a late afternoon dance on the opposite shore. About half way across, they heard a man's voice screaming for help. It seems a man had attempted to change his clothes standing up in a canoe. He fell overboard, and his fall pushed the canoe away from him. A breeze caught the canoe, and it was departing at a rapid rate. The man could not swim well and was frantic. The three in the rowboat reached him in plenty of time, and the young man was pulling the drowning man over the side of his boat when it was noticed that he was stark naked. The prudish maidens screamed maniacally that he must not be brought into the boat or "they would die of mortification." The man was left to drown. The parsons Susan Ertz speaks of are not the only persons in this world with priorities horribly askew.

657

If men had tusks and horns they would be less, rather than more likely to kill one another.

Ashhley Montagu (1905-1999)
The Nature of Human Aggression

According to Montagu, man is by nature a relatively gentle creature and with the right kind of upbringing perfectly capable of cooperation with the other members of his species. Competition and aggression could easily be transformed into reciprocal expressions of love for one another, if other qualities did not intervene.

Genes for competition, territorial protection, and jealousy may play a part in explaining violence. If nature had developed man with sharp teeth and claws, tusks and horns, poisonous fangs, etc., nature would also have had to give us the means for protecting ourselves from these attack or defense weapons biologically built into our neighbors. But nature "unfortunately" provided us with brains that enable us to develop "unnatural' weapons with which to maim and kill one another. These same brains do not seem able to keep us ahead in inventing counteracting devices to prevent annihilation.

Robert Burns said in "Man Was Made to Mourn": "Man's inhumanity to man makes countless thousands mourn." Spectator sports, violent movies, and martial arts seem able to keep our minds warped enough to keep us at odds with one another. We cannot live in the savage environment we do, without being affected by it. Those with vested interests deny this obvious verity and keep us wallowing in activities low on the scale of social diversions.

There is not the slightest doubt that those who are still thinking objectively could, if given free rein, develop societies in which most of our hate and bigotry would disappear. In John P. Dolan's book *The essential Erasmus*, we find both hope and despair. In his stand against violence, Erasmus is rational. In his stand in favor of Christianity, he is not. Pyotr Kropotkin, in his 1902 book *Mutual Aid: a Factor of Education*, is more optomistic: "Perhaps it is not in our heredity to be bent on mutual destruction, and we will eventually learn to live in peace with one another."

658

When the book of Job was written... Satan is simply the counsel for the prosecution in the court of Heaven, as faithful a servant of the court as the advocatus diaboli at the Vatican.

Alan Watts (1915-1973)
Psychotherapy East and West

We can assume, can we not, that this transformation in the character of Satan was purely a human invention. Surely, in the realm of celestial events, no such thing occurs. We may not be able to depend on what tomorrow may bring here on earth, but in God's spiritual world, a perfect world, the only kind God would allow, things stay put.

The angels in heaven, immortal, never condemned to the flames of hell, have it made. Surely if God had wanted it to be so man could have been equally favored. Is it legitimate to wonder why God, rather than build a hell right from the beginning, did not create man as He did the angels, incapable of sin so that everything would immediately be running like clockwork: no hell necessary, satan unemployed, and God not so incomprehensibly angry.

The next time your pastor sets up his teledevine hookup, ask him to let me get in a few words. I would like to ask a few questions if I might: "God, why did You kill Uzzah, who touched the covenant box

(2 Samuel 6:7)? What about the men of Beth Shemesh, who looked into the covenant box (1 Samuel 6:19)? Then, in the same verse, we learn that You killed 50,070 more – no reason given. Why did you destroy the 250 men who offered You incense (Numbers 16:35? Why did You send a plague killing 14,700 Israelites (Numbers 16:49 and later 70,000 more (2 Samuel 24:15)? Why are You often threatening members of the human species if they do not do as You see fit? What is this thing about Armageddon: Is that another threat to keep us in line?: Do you enjoy watching souls fry in Hell? Forever? Just what kind of God are You who gets His kicks in such macabre ways?: Do You mind if I vote for term limits for gods and suggest that You are long past your termination date? If it is more convenient than the pastor's teledivine hookup, please reply on America Online!

659

> The call to blind faith is really a call to barbarism and slavery.
> Bergen Evans
> *The Natural History of Nonsense*

Blind Faith, the title Prometheus gave to the book they published in 1995, is a synonym for credulity, readiness to believe anything theologians may say. The result can indeed be barbarism and slavery. Barbarism, because much of what is accepted as authentic is really mythology; slavery because wholesale acceptance of other people's beliefs is renouncing ones own right to think, being controlled by the brain of others instead of one's own.

Reason and faith are completely irreconcilable pathways to knowledge. The two cannot exist side by side. Reason underlies the methodology of the scientist. Without it he would be ineffectual. Faith is the "being" of the Christian. Without it he could not exist. The scientist accepts nothing on faith, for to do so would be irrational. Everything the Christian believes he accepts on faith. Faith to him is a synonym for belief. In Hebrews 11:1, we read: "Faith is the substance of things desired, the evidence of things unseen." The religionist is ever alert to prevent reason from undermining his precepts. Reason is his (and God's) worst enemy.

Reason is our means of processing what we learn of the world through our proverbial five senses. Faith does no processing. Whatever sense (or nonsense) that is accepted, is accepted as is, without rationality a consideration. Those facts which reason allows us to accept must display consistency and predictability. There are no criteria to restrict that which we will accept on faith. Those content to accept on faith are those who accept without thinking, without the rational demonstrations that establish the truth (predictive content) of what we believe. Faith is the road to myth and error, the way to add to man's already overflowing storehouse of "things he *knows* but that are not so."

660

When Wall Street yells war, you may rest assured every pulpit in the land will yell war.

Eugene V. Debs (1855-1926)
Speech in Canton, Ohio June 16, 1918

The golden rule is that gold rules," some cynic declared. "Money, money, money, money," the song in *Cabaret* reports. "Money makes the world go round." The monied interests are the only winners in any war.

"As a patriotic citizen," a factory owner turning out products on automatic lathes, told me after World War II, "I wanted to reduce the price of my products to where I was just breaking even, but the government that was buying my products wouldn't let me do so." I was still in uniform when he was talking to me. He wanted to unburden his conscience by explaining how he had become rich while I was a Navy airplane pilot overseas.

If their religions are worthy of the name, all ecclesiastics should be expending every effort to help end wars, or better yet to stop wars before they begin. But the truth is that warmongers never have trouble finding churches that will support their efforts in any national or international conflict. All combatants "know" that God is on their side. In a January First speech at Munich in 1932, Hitler made precisely that pronouncement. Catholic priests in Germany lost their lives for challenging Hitler's claim that he had unanimous Christian support.

Thomas Merton speaking of the First Christian Crusade (1096) says that it was at the time considered to be an enimently praiseworthy enterprise. Killing Turks, according to Merton, was said to be a necessary and desirable task, and the sooner it was done, the better for everyone concerned. In discussing the difference between murder and war, Merton tells of the pleasure that both give to many of our citizens. The difference is only in the consequences of being observed. Where, as in war, murder is encouraged and is considered a socially desirable occupation. Those prone to violence can relax in their carnage and proceed to murder as wantonly as they please.

661

If God or Nature intended any indelible difference between the races, He could easily have accomplished the purpose by making them immiscible.

Kelly Miller (1863-1939) - An open letter to Warren G. Harding

I remember that when I was very young and always daydreaming, I wished that I might be endowed with God's omnipotence for several years during which time I would allow that only those sexual contacts would result in babies that were between different races. That way, I reasoned, all people would soon look alike, and one of the irrational causes of racial prejudice would be eliminated.

Years later while living in New York City I decided what color I would like all of us to be. It was the beautiful dark golden brown color of so many of the young ladies I would see walking along Fifth Avenue or on Madison Avenue where I worked. All of us sickly palefaces would disappear, and everyone would have their unblemished dark skin, so much prettier in my eyes than any other in the world.

Kelly Miller reasons that if God had intended that we remain forever different, Distinguishable races, He would have made us different species, immiscible. He allows us to cross, and that is good. Miscegenation may someday mean that we become one beautiful race of human beings able to live together in peace. Geneticists have long recognized that a mixing of all the world's storehouse of genes, eliminating inbreeding so far as possible, makes for stronger species, more able to cope with changing environments.

662

> Absence of occupation is not rest, / A mind quite vacant is a mind distressed.
>
> William Cowper (1731-1800)
> "Retirement"

Airplane engines and couch potatoes seem to enjoy a state of rest. Both need some kind of impulse to get them going. One single-engine airplane I flew during World War II needed a 10-gauge shotgun shell (without the shot) to do the trick. In another, a two-engine plane, it was necessary to hold down a shiny chrome button for some length of time (enough to leave scar tissue on my thumb if the button had been exposed to direct sunlight) to accumulate energy enough to turn each engine over. Where the impulse comes from to get the couch potato going is not always clear. A pang of hunger, a nature call, or an unexpected inspiration to get-a-life may do it.

We all have had moments when we feel dead tired, all washed out, hardly able to undress and drag ourselves off to bed. The telephone rings and friends say they just discovered that a terrific band is playing at a dance in a nearby town. We come alive, pile into a car and are off to an exciting evening that is still remembered. For what we want to do, we always have energy. Enthusiasm is the key.

The biggest error young people make is their mistaken evaluation of what it will be like for them when they reach old age. Their error is usually based on selective observation, for relatively few old people degenerate into decrepitude in their last years. Many have minds functioning as well or better than when they were young. Too often young people write off or approach with fear the last years of life – which can be and usually are better than anything they have known.

If they plan at all well, retirement years will be years of good health, and a personal freedom unknown in any other part of their life. They will learn to live full, exciting, useful lives with new jobs, voluntary work, or productive hobbies that keep them happy, enthusiastic, forgetting to rest as much as they should. They will be surprised to find their lives immensely exciting, with their only regret that they have a limited time left to enjoy the best years of their lives.

Chapter XVII

Fate

663

Lovers born and raised in Florida and now attending the University of Florida at Gainsville surely have the wit to understand that if either of them had been born in San Francisco, had never been out of California, and was now attending the State University at San Francisco they both might now be equally in love with some other one-and-only ideal partner.

A Christian monotheist, in a similar way, although he knows perfectly well that other people worship different gods, cannot imagine that for him personally there could be some other god. Yet certainly, if he had been born into a Hindu family in Calcutta, he would by now be just as inevitably obsessed with worshiping Hindu Gods.

Circumstances, not some supernatural fate, decides how lovers become paired and how religiously minded people happen to be attached to a particular religion. Knowing that, how can any human being become the bigoted, prejudiced, parochial-minded religionist that most human beings become? Does anyone really believe that the world was specifically arranged for him or her personally so that things would turn out as they did?

Those thoroughly convinced that their own chance accretion of beliefs is the only one possibly worth considering will be forever on guard against unsettling intrusions by refusing to look at things from any point of view other than their own. Most people would be ashamed to admit that they are afraid of ideas, but that is the only explanation for those who select all their reading from an "approved" list, or whose only source of news is a "religious" journal or a cable television circuit that broadcasts its own "religious" programing. Until they learn to weigh carefully all sides of all issues, they will go through life groping in darkness. They will never become emancipated from their present insular convictions. They must always be on guard against the persuasions of reason.

664

All of ancient history is no more than accepted fiction.

Voltaire (1694-1778)

W.R. Inge, Dean of St. Pauls, said: "Events in the past may be roughly divided into those that probably never happened and those which do not matter."

Those with a healthy skepticism toward the chronicles of historians are needed. They help counteract the facile credulity of those who will believe anything they see in print. After having said that, we should also say that both Voltaire and Inge are obviously exaggerating. The world would be in sad shape if we could believe nothing of significance we read in books dealing with history.

Of course, history is slanted. History is written by human beings, and human beings are human. When historians are writing their essays, they are bound to pick and choose. Like everyone who writes, they use what best tells their story – as they see it. If what they write is boring, no one will read it, and they will have wasted their time.

Voltaire and Inge have a point. The discrepancy between what gets into print and the events in the world is considerable. Historians write largely from other people's writings, and they can do no better than whose who write the news items they read. Fear of censure and the inevitable weasel-wording to avoid law suits become paramount, more important than adherence to truth. As in the Japanese movie Rashomon, the truth often becomes what those telling it want it to be. Even honest historians with an open mind and sincere purpose must be ever vigilant if they are to write their histories with the accuracy that history deserves.

665

No truly great man, from Jesus Christ down, ever founded a sect.

Thomas Carlyle (1795-1881)

Carlyle is passing judgment upon people like Martin Luther, John Wesley, John Calvin, Joseph Smith, Brigham Young, Mary Baker Eddy, Jnatiputra, Zoroaster, Nanak, Swedenborg, Ram Mohan Roy, Lao-tzu, and others. To Carlyle, such people either are not truly great, or they did not found a sect.

Jesus founded nothing. He was a Jew and remained so to the end. It was probably never his intention to found a religion. Without Paul of Tarsus, it seems, there would never have been a Christianity.

Buddha certainly wanted to change societies, but whether or not he intended to found anything which he would call a religion is a question. Chances are he did not.

Confucius never acknowledged that his Analects were religious in nature. They were for him simply sententious expressions of what he considered to be sane living. Of all the religious philosophies that intrigue Christians (especially Judaism, Islam, Hinduism, Bhuddhism, Taoism, and Confucianism), Confucianism is the only one that permits its adherents to remain purely temporal tenants of their communities.

Even in Confucianism, however, a transcendental "heaven" is interposed to an extent that it vitiates authentic secularism. The concept "God," it is true, is totally absent in Confucian persuasions, but a higher source for morality, meaning, and self-direction is said to play a part in human affairs. By our example, if not by intent, amending our relations with nature and our harmony with other people results in improving the human species. The legacy of Confucianism is a "better world," which is more than can be said for any of the other well-known religions.

666

> Man has no nobler function than to defend the truth.
>
> Ruth McKenney (1911-   )

Before we agree to defend the truth, let us be sure we know which truth we are defending. The truth we want to defend is the truth that means every statement we make and that we hear others make conforms to real events and things in the real world.

The word truth we read in the Bible as in: "His truth endures" (Psalms 100:5 is meaningless. "His truth" implies that there is some grand body of truth has has magical power if only we accept it. But the only grand body religion has is its mythological underpinnings, which can do nothing but enslave us if we are gullible enough to take them seriously.

If by truth, religionists mean some kind of idealized abstraction, like vision or insight, why not use these terms so we would know more definitively what is meant. Insight expresses a worthy idea, at least if it is made clear "insight into what." The same with vision: "Vision of what nature"? If, as F.S.C. Northrop tells us, what religionists are talking about when they use the word truth can be translated as comforts, then we have something to consider. Comfort, certainly is at times desirable. We all enjoy being comfortable, especially after protracted periods of discomfort. Equating truth and comfort is at least better than equating truth with "mythology" which is precisely the antithesis of truth. The attempt to give religion an ineffable mystical aura in order to lure those who prefer an esoteric, occult world that they need never make pretense of understanding is to be deceitful. Now we understand why the Bishops of Peru and even more recent Bishops have discouraged educating the masses. Where would religion be if people generally learned that the world is not quite as unfathomable as they have been led to believe?

667

Jimmy Swaggart's speciality is rigid fervour and eternal damnation. He once said Mother Teresa would go to hell if she were not born again.

Simon Hoggart
Observer, Feb 21, 1988

Let us hear it from Jimmy himself: "There is no Soul under heaven that's going to walk through that gate of pearl unless they are born again by the blood of Jesus Christ." This reply came from the Reverend Swaggart the very next week in the same magazine.

Jimmy Swaggart "knows" of course, because he talks to God personally whenever he likes – gets the dope directly from the horse's mouth, so to speak. It can be assumed that the tele-divine hookup he has with God is similar to the one Pat Robertson used when he was advised by God in March 1988 to run for president. All the electronic-media evangelists, it seems, are similarly plugged in. They all talk of things God tells them to pass onto their radio and television audiences. None of them as yet have set up a speaker phone, letting the audience hear God's words directly, nor have pulpiteers been that thoughtful vis-à-vis their congregations. How simple that should be to do and how decisive the consequences! From now on forever there would be no reason to doubt, no uncertainty, no need for further discussion: God does exist, does care, and does communicate with us: I am sure CNN would be glad to rebroadcast the messages from God so all the world could hear. Finally all of us would "know" as certainly as does Jimmy Swaggart the answers to all the questions we have about what up to now has been purely mythology.

The problem with this whole picture is the same as that with members of "understanding Incorporated" who have had rides in flying saucers and talk frequently with extraterrestrials. We will believe them when they introduce us to one of their friends, the pointy-eared, big-eyed alien from outer space, on a television program. We will be listening when these "aliens" tell us how their vehicles are powered and how they survived the trip from their own distant domicile. The difficulties such travel would entail are summed up in essay 479.

668

That there is a devil is a thing doubted by none but which are under influences of the Devil. For any to deny the being of a Devil must be from an ignorance or profaneness worse than diabolical.

Cotton Mather (1663-1728)
The Wonders of the Invisible World

In the two and a half centuries since Cotton Mather was active, we like to think there has been progress in religion. But Catholics and most Protestants still believe in a devil, and satanic cults are increasing, not decreasing, their influence in today's societies.

Increase Mather and his son Cotton had a great deal in common besides the filial relationship: Both were Harvard graduates and became world-renowned clergymen. Both wrote many books. Both were involved in the witchcraft hysteria of Salem, Massachusetts. Both urged caution in judging witnesses, but both were accused of stirring up and prolonging the prevailing lunacy. Both father and son advocated inoculation for smallpox when it was generally regarded as a dangerous and godless practice.. Five years after the father died, the son died also.

Except for the enigmatic phrase "sacrificed unto devils" the first clear reference to satan in the Old Testament appears in the book of Job. Up until then no one found him important enough to mention. Zechariah gets a word in, and then satan is forgotten. Satan seems mostly a concern of the New Testament, which turns a molehill into a mountain. Now our Christian leaders cannot get along without him. He is their savior, their reason for existence. Without him they could not survive. Pictured as horned, tailed, hairy, and cloven-hoofed, a denial of his existence was long considered heretical.

For anyone who wants the real dope on devils, he will probably find no better story than in *Biographia del Diablo* (1978), published by Argos, S.A. in Barcelona, Spain. If it has not already been done, it will surely be translated into English before long.

669

The mistake was in not forbidding the serpent; then he would have eaten the serpent.

Mark Twain (1855-1910)
Pudd'head Wilson's Calendar

Mark Twain explains by telling us that Adam was only human. He was in actual years of existence no older than a child, and he often acted like one. Tell him not to eat the apple, and he would have needed no prompting from Eve. He could hardly wait for the prohibition to get out of his Maker's mouth before he made a jump for it and gobbled it down. What was God to expect? Among his other failures, God obviously was no judge of human nature.

God failed to predict that Uzzah would touch the sacred box; He failed to predict David killing (as suborner) Uriah, so he could marry the man's wife. Throughout the Bible, God is seen as being surprised by disappointing antics of his sixth-day creations – that anyone else would have seen coming well in advance.

Of course there may be other explanations. The one that Joseph Ernest Renan suggested was: "The universe is a spectacle which the Good God gives for his own amusement." We find, it seems, God playing with human beings as a cat does a mouse. He gives them reason to expect freedoms to indulge in mischief, play pranks, and then pounces on them when they act out obvious scenarios that God Himself set them up for. God's creating a hell before He had sinning souls to populate it gives credence to what Renan said.

There is still one other possible explanation, the most likely of all. If he is right, Stendhal makes all other speculations superfluous. He said: "God's only excuse is that He does not exist." Then we see that it is the writers of the books of the Bible who play the cat-and-mouse game. They play with our emotions in a thousand pages of historical fiction that has as much authenticity as the scribblings of the brothers Grimm or of *Aesop's Fables*. They found religions with their scriptures one excellent way to gain control over fellow human beings.

670

If civilization is to advance at all in the future, it must be through the help of women.... It was rapidly becoming clear to my mind that man regarded women as a servant class... and that women were going to remain in the servant class until they lifted themselves out of it.

> Emeline Pankhurst (1858-1928)
> *My Own Story*

Bertrand Russell concurs: "One generation of fearless women could transform the world by bringing into it a generation of fearless children not contorted into unnatural shapes, but straight and candid, generous, affectionate, and free."

Women have always been the primary agent in providing the world with its populations. Now it is evident that in that capacity they are doing more than needs to be done. To be fulfilled, women must realize their potentials in other directions. They, it will be who are hegemonic in developing a truly egalitarian society, in eliminating hunger, in curing disease, in exploring our past.

Women like June Goodfield, Patricia Schroeder, Jane Goodall, Mary Leakey, Maria Curie, Amelia Earhart, Indira Gandhi, Elizabeth Cady Stanton, Susan B. Anthony, and Frances Willard show the way. Their members will be multiplied manyfold. The future will find increasing numbers of women in Who's Who, as Nobel prize winners, CEOs, as leaders in all professions.

Pankhurst, in England, unlike Stanton and Anthony, in the United States, at least had the satisfaction of seeing the main goal of her struggle for woman suffrage realized. With the delaying tactics of Woodrow Wilson and the intransigent members of Congress, many valiant American women in the fight for woman suffrage did not live to see victory, although they all knew that victory could not be long in coming. All women today must feel a certain sadness that they cannot thank early women suffragists for their courageous efforts toward building a sane society.

671

Theist and atheist: The fight between them is as to whether God should be called God or shall have some other name.

Samuel Butler (1835-1902)
"Rebelliousness" - *Notebooks*

Like "Mother Nature," for example? Or better yet, "myth"? The word "God" has definite meanings in the minds of the people who use it that rule it out as a sensible contender. There is no evidence of any authenticity to indicate that God is anything more than a figment of human imaginations. Butler knew well, as every thinking person does, that there is no way, by any of the rules of logic ever contrived, that anyone can prove or disprove God's existence. Our theologians tell us: "Please have faith." No one can do more.

Fraud by any other name smells. Even when words are cleverly used to try to convince us that fiction is fact, nothing is changed. Even if words are said to be divinely inspired, they do not really move mountains. If receiving minds are amenable, words can change minds but do not expect them to bend spoons, or transplant mulberry trees.

Saying a thing is so does not make it so. There is one way and one way only to "prove" that a "true" statement is actually true. That way is the method of science – In Rapoport's book *Operational Philosophy* called "the criterion of predictability." Essay 12 includes a brief description.

672

Life is composed of two parts: that which is past – a dream; and that which is to come – a wish.

Arabic Proverb

We live, then, in that infinitesimal space of time between a dream and a wish.

That which is past exists only as electro-chemical structure within the brain. Anything empirical that we can call future, also exists solely as brain structure. We express this "tomorrow" concept by nouns such as anticipation, prediction, prospect, and verbs such as expect, foresee, presage. But how these concepts are represented in the reality of brain structure we only vaguely know,

Even the present, the now, is a strange and evasive concept that no two people think of in the same way. Is the present: today? the hour? only a few seconds? a nanosecond, or does the past leap directly into the future, leaving the present as only a way of speaking? As the king of Siam said, "It's a puzzlement."

More difficult for most of us to understand is that the world we see, hear, taste, smell, or touch, also, is not the world "out there" beyond our skins. Out there, Physicists tell us, are only particles: the molecules, the atoms that compose them, and then the leptons and hadrons, and the muons, baryons, quarks, mesons, and whatever other particles that physicists have by now dreamed up and named. In the case of "seeing" - the nature of the world of people, animals, plants, furniture, cars, etc., that we live among depends in part on the kind of nerve receptors we use in abstracting from the light that reflects from the assemblages of particles that make up the outside world and impinge on the retinas of our eyes. Certainly a house fly sees a very different would from the one you and I see. And yours is likely different from mine. We may both see red looking at a fire truck, but your "red" may be different from mind. We have no way of knowing.

673

The scientist who yields anything to theology, however slight, is yielding to ignorance and false pretenses, and as certainly as if he granted that a horse-hair put into a bottle of water will turn into a snake.

H.L. Mencken (1880-1956)
Minority Report

Readers who have not lived as long as I have may not be aware that the horse-hair myth was "common knowledge" up to the 1920s. My own mother swore that she had performed this miracle. I suspect her brothers played a little trick on her. There is tiny jet-black nematode common in fresh-water streams that looks like a horsehair wiggling its way in and out of the grasses overhanging the bank. You need a magnifying glass to detect a rudimentary head on one end.

With science destroying myth after myth from the fabric of theology, ecclesiastics are ever apprehensive. They can relax only when they learn that they must yield to the incursion of verified scientific ideas that mean them no harm, but are essential to the ever-increasing store of worldly wisdom.

674

Doubt is the incentive to search for truth, and patient inquiry leads the way.... Who never doubted, never half believed.

Gamaliel Bailey (1807-1859)

Some 70 years later, Tryon Edwards expresses agreement, "Doubt... if honest and bent on thorough investigation, may soon lead to full establishment in the truth."

The value of doubt and skepticism is clear. It is the frame of mind that encourages inquiry. Without it we cannot separate wheat from chaff in whatever we hear or read. It is the only sane approach to much of what is said by our pulpiteers. If we must be governed by an imperious belief-system that shapes our lives, better it be a rational discipline that will help, not hinder, the development of our civilization.

Science resolved some of our doubts, of course, some that have persisted since the dark ages. Doubts about the efficacy of reason, the virtue of an open mind, the need for global thinking, and the compelling necessity for universal brotherhood are largely resolved. But as long as ignorance and gullibility prevail, we will continue to be dominated by systems of myth and legend. We cannot progress in a world run by organizations that are fearful of investigation, and that invent delusive words to cover up their flaws.

The world still suffers from publicly acclaimed social intransigence – as for example: Elizabeth O. Smith says: "Beware of doubt. Faith is the subtle chain that binds us to the infinite." Robert James Turnbull, too: "Doubt is the disease of this inquisitive, restless age. It is the price we pay for our intelligence and civilization." Smith prefers blind faith to a regenerative doubt. Turnbull would choose stupidity and barbarism rather than enlightenment.

675

We have less charity for those who believe the half of our creed, than for those that deny the whole of it.

Charles Caleb Colton - *Lacon*

A rather doubtful surmise, is it not? If we are thirsty, we will not prefer an empty glass to one that is half full of cool, potable water. Colton's point, of course, is that the man who believes half our creed has some sympathy at least for our points of view; why then not go the whole hog? Since what is left is no harder to accept than what he has already embraced, the half-believer strikes the true-believer as simply pig-headed or deliberately recalcitrant without cause. If the true-believer is tempted to reason with the half-believer and is rebuffed, he becomes angrier still: "What's the matter with you; are you stupid?"

With the dyed-in-the-wool unbeliever, the true-believer knows where he stands. Even to attempt argument, he knows, is futile, so he does not try. He and the atheist may be next-door neighbors, but get along fine on all conversational points, and see no sense in arguing. With the half-believer neighbor on the other side of him, he must be ever tiptoeing about, conversationally speaking. At any time tempers could flare.

Charles Caleb Colton seems to have made a career of writing quotations. He may hold some kind of record in quoted inanities and banalities. Could it not be that his tactic is that of a man with a shotgun full of 9-chill shot? When he shoots at a wall dotted with house flies from a hundred feet away, he doesn't bother to aim. He simply blasts away, knowing that a few pellets and flies will make mutual contact simply as a matter of statistical odds. Colton is not concerned that several shot will be wasted; a few contacts is enough to cajole his imperturbable ego. In his quotation above, thankfully, he has made us think.

676

When men can no longer be theists, they must, if they are civilized, become humanists.

Walter Lippmann (1889-1974)
A Preface to Morals

It is in no way incumbent upon any human being, civilized or not, to attach adventitious labels to himself. Anyone can go through life and do very well immersed in the work he has chosen to earn his living, behaving toward his fellowman kindly and charitably, without special labels. He may join with others so that together they can increase their effectiveness in accomplishing useful goals. He may avoid joining large groups of people who tend to become zealots, bigots - extremists that are less than desirable citizens. He may be a part of a family, team, community, perhaps, without giving others special occasion for classifying him.

One can be a patriot, without exaggerating his patriotism, an American, without the jingoism of Americanism. Joining organizations dealing with religion, pro or con, is totally unnecessary. As individuals, we usually remain docile and amicable human beings. As members of titled groups, we often become like beasts, and because of our numbers, may become dangerous. Even members of think tanks, it seems, may become overbearing and pompous, and lose their effectiveness when operating as committees. I suppose it is the "must" and "civilized" in Lippmann's statement that I object to. We may join organizations if there seems to be good reasons to do so, but always we "must keep intact our individuality. When that is lost we become puppets, automatons, sequacious followers.

Good books are written by individuals. Good ideas form in individual brains. Co-authors are rare, and committees almost never write best sellers. Computers will never write novels, or even books like this one – although they can be a big help in doing the research.

677

I read about an Eskimo hunter who asked the local missionary priest, "If I did not know about God and sin, would I go to hell?" "No," said the priest, "not if you did not know." "Then why," asked the Eskimo earnestly, "did you tell me?"

Annie Dillard
Pilgrim at Tinker Creek

If "ignorance is bliss" ever had a meaning, now we have found it. In the world of religious make-believe, at least, we would certainly be better off not knowing. What better argument against missionaries, who did not have much to favor their meddling even without Annie Dillard's illuminating illustration.

Dillard reveals a profound truth. If the difference between being set down for eternity in the middle of Happy Valley or in a volcano's cauldron hinges on one priest's thoughtless indiscretions, religion does not have much going for it, does it? Without intending to do so, religionists are found often unveiling religion's inherent immorality.

When a man's fate is determined not by what he himself says or does, but by perfectly innocent circumstances completely beyond his control, it takes a strange kind of mentality to blame or credit him or anyone else with how things turn out. A man with a lottery ticket hears the winning numbers called out one at a time, each in turn corresponding to the numbers on his ticket. When Pat Robertson with eyes closed describes symptom by symptom an ailing viewer's illness and prognosis, the process is the same. With millions of lottery tickets or ailing viewers involved, completely indifferent chance (statistical coincidence) produces whoever is the winner. Human prowess or divine blessing has nothing to do with it.

678

Lighthouses are more helpful than churches.

Benjamin Franklin (1706-1790

Gospel songs often make a point of comparing churches and religion to lighthouses and beacons. This is a discredit to lighthouses. No one has found lighthouses full of bigotry, racism, hypocrisy, and superstitions. Lighthouses save ships and lives. Religions generate conflicts and wars which destroy lives, property, and human tranquility. Public schools are more helpful than church schools, despite the hoopla to the contrary. It is impossible to get a good education in church school of orthodox religions. The facts, the pride, and the rigor of science are always absent in strict church schools. Science is an indispensable part of anyone's education. Jacob Bronowski knew his well when he said: "The world today is made, it is powered by science, and for any man to abdicate an interest in science is to walk with open eyes toward slavery."

The fear of science affects other courses of the private religious school as well. To make sure that the students are not "contaminated" by the infiltration of elements of science, many of the textbooks for other courses must be cleansed of "offensive" passages as well. Hiring teachers is crucial. As time passes they become graduates of schools with the same squeaky-clean atmosphere. This removes all hope that this lunacy might work itself out of the system through years of interaction with normal societies. The school becomes a closed system that light cannot penetrate. Staff, students, and faculty become so accustomed to it that they forget what it is like to live and operate in an open society.

679

Gospel: Signifies good news. The good news that the Gospel of the Christians came to announce to them is that their God is a God of wrath, that he has predestined the far greater number of them to hellfire, that their happiness depends on their pious imbecility, their holy credulity, their sacred ravings, the evil they do through hatred of one another... and their antipathy for and persecution of all who do not agree with them or resemble them.

Voltaire (1674-1778)

It is difficult to believe that a prominent person two hundred years ago knew all these things and that we have ignored him all this time. We see that we have not progressed on any front he mentions. People are just as prejudiced today, and we still hate those who do not agree with or resemble us. We are still as full of superstition, holy credulity, and sacred ravings. We are still as masochistic as ever, choosing to create a God of wrath, who assigns even more people today to hellfire than ever before . The "good news" is increasingly worse, and we fumble awkwardly in our attempt to make things better.

Voltaire was no saint, and we condemn his anti-Semitism, as we do that of H.L. Mencken and even of Franklin Delano Roosevelt when, for no good reason he refused berth for a shipload of Jews fleeing Nazi persecution. Such behavior distresses us to such an extent that we find gratifying relief upon reading of Nietzsche's opposition to anti-Semitism, despising and deriding the German fascist political party long before they came to known as the "Nazis."

We are discouraged to find that some of our greatest men are all too human, as riddled with foibles as the rest of us. We must concentrate on the significant amount of good they did, and, so far as we can, see that no else repeats their errors.

680

> The public in every nation is looking for an international conscience.... For it knows that nationalism is an anachronism, a dying form of civilization,.
>
> Jacob Bronowski
> *A Sense of the Future*

Jacob Bronowski moved in different circles than I ever have. I have run into jingoists by the dozens, but no internationalists. The only other quotation I have run across that expresses Brownoski's idea clearly is the following by Raphael Cohen in his *Reflections of a Wondering Jew*: "In the end, of course, assimilation or destruction is inevitable. For no one can reasonably suppose that the present divisions of mankind will last forever."

In contemplating assimilation, Cohen is thinking, perhaps, in terms of thousands of years. But the alternative "destruction" may not permit such delay. The evidence is that the world must rid itself of the divisiveness inherent in religion and nationalism within the next few centuries – or Homo sapiens will not be here to repent his former unheeding or ill-advised indifference.

Bronowski and Cohen are gone. Who is there to take their place? Books like this one will do very little. Someone of renown and prestige must take over and spread the word. I hope some reader of this book will be inspired to help.

681

> As men's prayers are a disease of the will, so are their creeds of the intellect.
>
> Ralph Waldo Emerson (1803-1882)

Diseases of the will are legion. They certainly include what we do to ourselves with drugs, including alcohol and tobacco.

They include the over-eating that most of us are guilty of, shortening our lives and making it difficult to participate in many interesting activities. They include our indolence and much of our lethargy, which keeps us from engaging in many projects that would be tremendously useful to our fellowman. And, of course, they include our praying, which deprives us of our sense of personal responsibility and deludes us into thinking that something-for-nothing is ours for the asking.

Diseases of the intellect, as well, are all too common. They include the mass of misinformation that overwhelms us and that we accept as gospel. They include all the myths we accept as authentic historical events and that we allow to serve as guides for living. They include our neuroses and psychoses, some of which are imposed upon us by external forces we should have been able to avoid. And they do, as Emerson says, include the creeds that warp our minds and thus our behavior to an extent sometimes to equal infectious or degenerative diseases of the cells of the brain.

682

> I'm sure Christ wore a mezuzah. He certainly did not wear a cross.
> Cesar Estrada Chavez (1927-1993)

Even if Jesus dragged one up to the top of Golgotha, he probably did not think of it as a cross as much as a gallows for his own execution. Chavez makes a good point but may have picked the wrong terminology. Bible passages and modern usage direct that mezuzahs be nailed to door jams, not worn. Phylacteries are worn (Deuteronomy 11:18) and so, or course, are Yarmulkes, but whether or not in Biblical times they were called by words that could be translated into phylacteries and yarmulkes   is not clear.

It is illuminating to note how the members of each religion put such high premiums on the gimcracks of their own religion, but consider those of other religions as mere trinkets. Yarmulkes for Jews, prayer wheels for Tibetan Buddhists, and prayer rugs for Muslims are sacred and serve specific purposes only in the religions that consider them so. Holy holidays, too, seldom cross boundaries. Thanksgiving is strictly a United States invention. Halloween, too, is current in only a few countries. *Dia de los Difuntos*, two days later, is one of the main religious holidays for those who speak Spanish. Christmas and Easter leave out Jews, and Hanukkah and Yom Kippur leave out Christians. Ramadan leaves out all but Muslims.

The magic of rosaries can be annulled if one is not careful. Use 108 beads in beads in the Buddhism of Tibet, 109 in China, 112 in Japan, 99 in all of Islam, 50 or 150 in Catholicism.

The number 5 has its own magic: The 5 pillars, the 5 daily prayers, and the 5 salats of Islam The 5 virtues, the 5 Ks of Sikhism.

The 5 senses (there are more like 25), the 5 elements, the 5 major feast days, and the 5 directions in various traditional systems.

Water on the head, wafers on the tongue, ashes on the forehead, wine and bread in the belly, all accompanied by appropriate incantations, of course, are essential for salvation. Making the sign of the cross, burning a candle before an icon of the Virgin Mary, a minute of silence, extreme unction, and shrines all have their special roles. Damned be the religionist who is not privy to all of the superstitions of his own religion.

683

Those who refuse the long drudgery of thought, and think with their heart rather than their head, are ever most fiercely dogmatic.
Peter Bayne (1830-1896) - Scottish author

Thinking with the heart is not thinking; it is emoting. Being dogmatic is not thinking; it is dictating arbitrary doctrine, without need for sound judgment. When we think, we analyze all possibilities and choose among them in a rational manner. Being dogmatic is worse than emoting; it is laying down supposed certainties for one reason and one reason only: to establish control over others without the slightest commitment to reason. An intense aversion to dogma was the essence of the revamped Christianity espoused by Erasmus, whose spanned equal parts of the 14 and 15 hundreds. But dogma is the very "soul" of orthodox Christianity. Without its dogma, the Christianity of "the ecumenical creeds and confessions" could not exist.

At another time Bayne says: "Without earnestness no man is ever great or does really great things." Obviously to Bayne, at least two things are important for anyone who wants to leave his mark on the world. He must learn to think, and he must use that ability earnestly, and sincerely, with enthusiasm and a dogged resolution to accomplish whatever it is that he is determined to do. People who succeed have a glandular passion that will not permit mediocrity, half-doing anything. Whatever they do they must do well.

The successful man takes seriously that which he does by way of vocation. But he loves a good party with congenial people. He enjoys stimulating conversation, healthful food, and moderate exercise. He likes children and agonizes to see children not getting an appropriate education. Some I have known believe that the first expenditure of any government should be to provide free education: grade school, high school, university or trade school, and even graduate school – all the education any student wants and is able to absorb. Any large country that makes that commitment and does not allow mythologies to interfere will soon be a superpower.

684

> Prejudice is a raft onto which the ship-wrecked mind clambers and paddles to safety.
>
> Ben Hecht (1894-1964) – American writer

Paddles not to safety so much as to a sanctuary. For Mark Fuhrman (of O.J. Simpson trial fame) the sanctuary for many years was the Los Angeles Police Department. For many others it is a sectarian religion.

Were it not for man's susceptibility to superstition, there would be no such thing as religion. And if it were not for religion, much of our prejudice would disappear. Religion as it now operates is little more than amassed and amalgamated superstitions. Superstitions result from ignorance and fear, both procreaters of prejudice as well. With parents in common, it is hard to think of one without thinking of the other as well.

Those who decide to branch off from the mother church make a judgment concerning differences that could not possibly have any real significance. They are making a choice between different versions or interpretations of superstitions, any one of them as meaningless as any of the others. A group of the shipwrecked minds Ben Hecht speaks of may get together, united by some common disagreement with church policies. Now desperate, they reconcile any hostilities apparent among themselves and form a new church.

Ben Hecht, a prolific writer was also one of Holywood's prized craftsmen in converting books into scripts for movies, The anecdote I tell on page 140 of *Blind Faith* of a writer going to a doctor, I think refers to Ben Hecht. I have been unable to recall for sure where I got that story.

685

> Must "religion" always remain a synonym for "hatred"?
>
> Alfred North Whitehead (1861-1947) - *Adventures of Ideas*

It will, to answer Whitehead's question, as long as religion is based on myth. Because myth exists only in the cellular structure of human brains; it is individual, varied, changing. Despite all this, the owner of each such brain becomes very possessive of his own religion and will guard it jealously if anyone challenges it. Hate arises in the resulting interchange.

A human brain is not always dependable in maintaining its convictions patterns steadfast and constant, especially over extended periods of time. The myths in one brain sooner or later will differ from those in another. With each brain owner "knowing" that he is the one with the authentic version, conflicts arise, caused by and causing hate. Those who have leadership qualities convince others to conform to their own particular version of "the truth" and sects (repositories of hatred) are formed.

With names and shibboleths like "World-Wide Church of the Creator," "Building a Whiter and Brighter World," "The Christian Identity Movement," and "The Covenant, the Sword, and the Arm of God," and with leaders like ill-fated Jim Ellison and Benjamin Nathaniel Smith, hatred in the United States, under a new brand of hatemongers, gains ground. Matthew Hale now leads The World-Wide Church of the Creator into the lowest depths of inhumanity. Kerry Nobel, in his book *Tabernacle of Hate*, and Steven Rosenbaum, in his cable TV program *Hate Crimes in the Name of God*, document this hatred in its most recent and most flagrant form.

When religionists discard myth and stick to empirical data as bases for their religions, hate will be eliminated. Those with opposing opinions can go back to the empirical data to see whose ideas best conform with the realities of the cosmos.

If "religion" were to remain a synonym for hatred, we would have to get rid of religion. Whitehead's pessimism need not discourage us. With the right kind of education, an education that promotes brotherhood - love, not hate,will be the dominant moving power in our societies.

686

Kill every male child; kill every woman who is not a virgin. Do not kill the young virgins. Keep them for yourselves.

Moses talking to the officers of the army (Numbers 31:17,18)

Violence is a recurring theme of the Bible. The God we are asked to worship, as well as the angels doing his bidding, kill constantly. They send floods, plagues, scourges of many kinds. Their armies destroy entire cities, leaving no one alive. God's whims must be humored, regardless of merit. No one is exempt from His wrath.

We can say our world is civilized only when such violence is eradicated. Wife beating, child abuse, rape, harassment of women, slander, robbery, arson, murder, and wars will disappear, and people everywhere will treat one another with respect. This will not happen until we get rid of all scriptures, all of which teach violence on nearly every page. Human life is described as having very little value, and prescribed punishments are barbaric.

The world will be civilized when people honor one another and deal with one another fairly, Hospitals will treat everyone regardless of affluence or its absence. Churches will teach love, equality, and honesty. Pollyanna, Buddha, Galahad, Mother Teresa, Job, Lucretia, Jesus, and Ruth of the Bible's *Book of Ruth* will be heroes to everyone in a world where kindness is publicly acclaimed.

687

The epitome of everything I loathe, no matter what the church is or the dogma, is the kind of discipline and blind obedience expected of the Jesuits by their superiors.

Françoise Giroud
I Give You My Word

In *The Plumed Serpent* by D.H. Lawrence, we read: "I am the poor old Bishop of this diocese, faithful servant of the Holy Father in Rome.... I live by my sacred office." The inflexibility of the church that describes itself as catholic is the inflexibility of all orthodox churches. The members can have no opinions and can see nothing from any point of view other than that authorized by their own ruling clergy.

"There can be but little liberty on earth while men worship a tyrant in heaven," Robert Ingersoll said in his *Prose-Poems and Selections*. Maybe we get the God we ask for – or deserve. We could just as well have fabricated a better God than we did. The "poor old Bishop" might have developed a stiffer spine. The Jesuits might once in a while put their foot down. There is no law saying that we must be wimps – except in tyrannies.

Religion has no monopoly of this kind of tyranny. The governments run by Stalin, Hitler, Somoza, Pinochet, Stroessner, Quaddafi, Castro, Mussolini, Idi Amin, et al., were as bad as any of the theocracies or would-be theocracies today. But tyrants should be wary. Subjects both of religions and nations will take only so much. When the repressions they suffer are worse than death, they know they have nothing to lose.

Tyrannies do not last forever and repressive theocracies will not either. Wait until the Taliban in Afghanistan have imposed all their taboos on the people of Afghanistan. The people will see that there is no satisfying their theocratic masters, and there will be an uprising. Another Shah will lead them down a new path leading to good sense, hopefully a Shah more democratic and with more patience and caution than had Reza Shah Pahlavi, in power in Iran from 1925 to 1941.

688

Men are given to worshiping malevolent gods, and that which is not cruel seems to them not worth their adoration.

Anatole France (1844-1924)
"Jean Marteau" – part of *Crainquebille*

Can it be that there is a relation between the fact that people prefer programs on Television and in the movies that feature violence and the fact that we invent and nurture gods that are cruel and vindictive? If television programmers want us to watch their programs, it is obvious the promos they offer to attract us would be those they consider to be the most attractive. Even for movies that have only one brief scene that includes violence, that is precisely the scene they will select for their previews. Haven't we all missed good programs on television because the promos they choose to attract us – instead turn us away?

Where in our evolution did we acquire our obvious proclivity for violence? Chimpanzees and gorillas have recently been shown not to live the peaceful lives at first believed. Chimpanzees are found perfectly capable of "declaring" war on a neighboring tribe and killing every fighting-age male in the tribe in a single battle. Male gorillas will kill babies within their own tribes.

Even our primitive ancestors, after passing through a strictly vegetarian age, it seems added to food-gathering an age as scavengers and then as hunters. In both they often had to fight in order to survive. How we became so violent may no longer be a mystery.

Support from Anatole France, Emile Zola , and Charles-Pierre Péguy were the three main reasons French army officer Alfred Dreyfus was finally acquitted of the trumped-up treason charges against him. Without valiant men like Zola, France, and Péguy, the proponents of obscurantism would soon turn this world into a kind of inferno.

689

From the time of the first murder, when Cain killed Abel, God has permitted man to suffer the consequences of Cain's fratricide.
                    Anonymous (Commonly quoted in sermons)

Permitted? Man has a choice – and chooses to suffer? If there is a God and He is accurately described in 2 Kings 2:24, Matthew 11:23, Judges 3:15-25, Judges 4:17-24, Judges 11:30-31,39, 1 Samuel 6:19, and Deuteronomy 7:16, "permitted man to suffer" is surely a catachresis used to avoid saying, "has decreed that man must suffer."

Is there really a God as heartless and cruel as the Bible describes Him, or is He an invention of perverted minds who believe that such a God would be best for the Judeo-Christian-Muslim religions?

Since Cain seems to be the father (we are not told where the mother came from) of all mankind, we wonder about God's reiterated promise that he will not let children suffer for their parents' indiscretions (2 Kings 14:6 and Ezekiel 18:20 – contradicted by Hosea 1:4 and Exodus 34:7).

690

Christian Science explains all cause and effect as mental, not physical.   Mary Baker Eddy (1821-1910)

To contemplate all of what that pronouncement would mean and then to imagine that a sane person could make it is beyond comprehension. Some of Ms Eddy's other pearls of wisdom are equally impressive: "Jesus of Nazareth was the most scientific man that ever trod the globe." "God is the only mind." "You conquer error by denying its verity." "Death will disappear with the disappearance of sin." "Disease is an image of thought externalized." "Mortal existence is a state of self-deception."

Mary Baker Eddy would say, "please do not quote me out of context. Read all of *Science and Health with Key to the Scriptures* and then you will understand the truth of what I say." Yes, do! What you will find is more of the same, one statement after another that dear, deluded Mary could not prove however diligently she tried.

At times, I have reminded the reader in this and my other books that saying a thing is so does not make it so. Ms Eddy has compiled an entire book that relies on the assumption that the opposite is the case. She makes a career of composing outlandish statements that we are supposed to accept for no other reason than that she recites them to us with her endearing and disarming confidence. Nothing she says has the slightest relation to reason, reliability, or reality – to any of the essences that good sense tells us is the nature of the cosmos we occupy.

In one of my indiscreet moments at what I thought was a good-natured and light-hearted luncheon including only myself and a gaggle of Christian Science women, I recited the following Limerick:

> A scientist healer of Deal
> Once said, "Although pain isn't real,
>   If I sit on a pin
>   And it punctures my skin
> I don't like what I fancy I feel."

The response was stunned silence. There is no room for humor in fanaticism. My friends probably would have been even more unhappy if I had asked the question Cabrielle Roy asked in Chapter 3 of *The Cashier*: "The Christian Scientists hold that it was not God who wanted sickness, but man who puts himself in the way of suffering. If this were the case, though, wouldn't we all die in perfect health?"

Mary Baker Eddy was not entirely without precursors. Curing the sick was to Jesus mainly a matter of exorcising demons. Demon, to Eddy, is the deception "mortal human mind." The Catholic church, too, has long believed in demons, and exorcising them sometimes takes on aspects of bacchanalian festivity. Demon possession, not schizophrenia, explains psychotic behavior to many religious fanatics. Demons are finding their way, too, into many new-religion rituals.

691

There is only one meaning of life: the act of living itself.

Erich Fromm (1900-1980)
Escape from Freedom

Why must it follow that our lives are without meaning if definitive death is our lot? If there is no purpose *to* the universe, it in no way follows that there can be no purpose *in* our individual and collective, if nevertheless ephemeral, lives here on earth. We all have intentions, interests, plans, and goals that we find important, God or no God. Giving present and future human beings a world that is a pleasant, secure, and a fit place to live, is all the purpose that any of us needs or can expect. In the fantastic future we envision, with prospects of genetic engineering, space stations and voyages, exploration of the moon and Mars, possible radio contact with extraterrestrial beings, etc., etc., do we need imaginary gods and their abodes to make life worth living? Our children are growing up in a world so tremendously exiting that to begin life now should be something far beyond any dream that children of past centuries could look forward to. Ignoring for a moment the prospects of a devastating war, how can anyone in good health be anything but ecstatic about the future?

That for a given individual his pleasure and security are not eternal is not to say that they are not worthwhile and worth striving for. The pleasure I will find in eating the dish of ice cream before me is not eternal, but I will cherish it nonetheless. I do not expect to live forever, but I do expect to live the rest of my life pleasantly and usefully. Also, it is true that for the person who has lived a useful and productive life, death is not the end. He lives on in the results of his efforts that future generations enjoy: the book he wrote, the bridge he built, the theory he formulated, etc. While individual death is inevitable, posterity survives.

692

> Is the Bible intelligible to all? Far from it. It is full of absurdities and difficulties not only for the illiterate, but even for the learned.
>
> James Cardinal Gibbons (1834-1921)

The biggest mystery about the Bible is how anyone can read its many contradictions, fallacies, distortions, absurdities, and imbecilities and still imagine for a moment that it is the word of a mentally balanced deity. If anyone is interested in trying to convince nonbelievers to believe in God, let me suggest that first of all he find a God that can write better than do the authors of the various books of the Bible. The only author I can find who does not surprise me when he puts two sentences together that both make real sense is Ecclesiastes, and even he say such things as:

1.7:   The sea is not full.
2.8:   I acquired male and female singers, the delights of the sons of men *and* musical instruments.
4.3:   Better than both [the living and the dead] *is* he who has never existed.
4.5:   The fool folds his hands and consumes his own flesh.
7.1:   The day of death [is better than] the day of one's birth.
7.20: There is not a just man on earth who does good and does not sin.
10.8: Whoever breaks through a wall will be bitten by a serpent.

If the Bible is history, it is the history of a society of pagan schizophrenics.

According to P.R. Hightower, "The tendency of children to lie and cheat is in direct proportion to their knowledge of the Bible." Harry Emerson Fosdick prefers to say that "The Bible was inspired, not dictated, by God." Alan Watts says, "No considerate god would destroy the human mind by making it so rigid and unadaptable as to depend upon one book, the Bible, for all the answers." The Reverend J.H. Holmes said: "Religion belongs to man. It is his dream, his vision, his achievement. If there are bibles, he has written them...." We wonder, if there really is a God, what does He think of the book that is ascribed to him? X.J. Kennedy has one answer (See essay 22).

693

> It is as atheistic to affirm the existence of God as to deny it.
>
> Paul Tillich (1886-1965)
> *Systematic Theology*

The Judeo-Christian-Muslim God we postulate can affirm the existence of Satan, devils, angels, jinn, even though you and I personally cannot. It always requires the existence of a God to affirm that for which there is no evidence.

If we want angels, as we say, we must have God. Unless we want to drop all pretense of consistency, there is no other way to be sure about angels than to be sure about God. We must not simply postulate his existence, we must affirm it.

But, of course, to affirm the existence of God, we ourselves must be supergods, gods above God. As we just said, to affirm the existence of anything for which there is no evidence, we must be a god ranking above that "anything."

So now, what about these (us) supergods! Egad, we have just involved ourselves in an infinite regress – which is always proof that we have been talking nonsense. To affirm the existence of God is patently impossible. Atheism (belief that God does not exist) is the only prospect available.

694

> Religious rites are profane.
>
> Heraclitus (540-480 BC)

When religious rites descend to the level of voodooism, dervish whirling, self-flagellation, fire-walking, mantra recitation, transubstantiation, snake handling, etc., especially, they are not only profane, they are asinine. Whenever entertaining the congregation with pageantry becomes the primary objective of the church, and ethics takes second place, profane may be the only word for it. Nietzsche put it this way: "Religious fanatics would rather watch gestures than listen to reason."

There is a place for pageantry in our lives, but that place may best be the vaudeville stage or a street parade. But if pageantry does not interfere with serious business of instilling kindness, generosity, integrity, and self-discipline in human lives, there is no reason why it may not be a part of religious services as well. The problem is that without the mesmeric lure of pageantry many members of the church might decide that they may as well get their religion elsewhere, even by reading books.

695

We are born subjects, and to obey God is perfect liberty. He that does this shall be free, safe, and happy.

Lucius Annaeus Seneca (4 BC?-65 AD)
Roman Stoic Philosopher

All creatures are born free, Joy Adamson says, and that may be the wiser supposition. If we human beings do not remain free, we have only ourselves to blame. In the two thousand years since Seneca made that remarkable pronouncement, we have had ample opportunity to test his contention. We see that to obey the God of today's popular scriptures would mean immediate death for a large part of the world's populations. Reading Leviticus is a good beginning to confirm that reality. Few people today choose to make slaves of themselves in the way Seneca recommends.

When Sartre used the word "condemned" in his "Man is condemned to be free, he denies Seneca's assumption. We are free, like it or not he says, that is just the way things are. Even though the Bible vacillates on this point, it can be seen usually as agreeing with Sartre? "The silver and the gold are a freewill offering unto the Lord." (Ezra 8:28). Certainly, Paul was indicating his freedom to do as he liked when he wrote to Titus in 3:3: "For we ourselves were sometimes foolish, disobedient, deceived, serving divers lusts and pleasures, living in malice and envy, hateful and hating one another."

We are born babies and become children, certainly not subjects. When the people of the British Commonwealth of Nations became completely independent, many of them exclaimed, "You cannot imagine how important it is for me no longer to have to think of myself as a subject." Most of us will be subjects of no one, not even to the invented gods theologians keep harping on. We will be Robert Ingersoll's "Eagle, parting the clouds with tireless wing."

696

> Of course, faith healers do not claim magical powers. Always their spiel is that their seeming prowess is God acting through them.
>
> Chester Dolan
> *Blind Faith*

"Faith healing" we have had with us since the dawn of history. It may be that, more than anything else, it is the hope of finding cures for mental and physical afflictions that leads people to, or back to, the church. And ecclesiastics have never hesitated to take advantage of this aspiration. Would it not be great if we had some plank upon which we could nail down truth amid all the dishonesty on the part of faith healers? Let me suggest one – one which may at first seem absurd but on second thought, I believe, will be seen as perfectly reasonable. Is it too much to say that until I see a one-legged man walk up and ask to be made whole, and then walk away on two good, perfectly functioning legs, I will remain skeptical? Is there some kind of limitation to God's powers? Is there something qualitatively different between the repairing of tumorous brains or cancerous livers and the repairing of truncated legs? The God that can make a woman out of a rib cannot make a leg whole? Are we to assume that only those afflictions which you and I cannot verify visually will yield to the faith healer's mystical incantations? Is the faith healers claim that he has been divinely chosen to dispense God's infinite healing powers to be demonstrated only in those cases that cannot be proved?

697

> Heaven: The Coney island of the Christian imagination.
>
> Elbert Hubbard (1856-1915)
> *The Roycroft Dictionary and Book of Epigrams*

Elbert Hubbaard was born too early for Disneyland, Magic Mountain, or Knott's Berry Farm. In his day, Coney Island was the fun-fair supreme.

I have never read anywhere a plausible or mentally satisfying account of what heaven is like. The Koran may give the best accounting, but even that seems to describe a place that would be insufferably boring. I am sure that if every Christian alive were to write down his own idea of heaven, putting them all together, we would have a place that no existing playland could compete with. The same childlike minds that accept all the mythologies that comprise Christianity would be adequate to the task. Our composite heaven would be a magnificent, universe-size toyland. Surely a compassionate God would see to it that no intelligent soul ever reaches the place. They would spoil the fun for that vast majority of simple souls who look forward to being eternally entertained.

698

Human life consists in mutual service. No grief, pain, misfortune, or broken heart is excuse for cutting off one's life while any power of service remains. But when all usefulness is over; when one is assured of an unavoidable and imminent death, it is the simplest of human rights to choose a quick and easy death in place of a slow and horrible one.

Charlotte Perkins Gilman (1860-1935)
(Suicide Note)

No blame to anyone else, no syrupy religious reservations, no silly excuses, just a perfectly logical reason for coming to the conclusion (and desiring to explain) why she chooses to kill herself.

What is more important than explaining her reasons for taking her own life is her saying that a useless life is already death. It is incumbent upon every human being to be to some extent useful. By "incumbent" one need not mean any transcendental duty or obligation. The duty is to oneself to be a vital (even if subordinate) cog in the machinery of human doings. No one in good conscience can be a loose cog, an idler gear, or a parasite, simply adding drag, contributing nothing. No self-respecting person is happy understanding that he is only an encumbrance to others and of no use even to himself.

To read the available biographical accounts of Mrs. Gilman is to understand how she could write such a note. She was not the kind to indulge in self-pity or just to sit by and watch. She had to be a part in something that was going on and do her part in making worthy projects successful. In her articles and books you find a women not to stand on ceremony, to dote on fashion, to be overly obsessed by sex, to be driven by petty prejudices, or to succumb to silly superstition. She was a capable mother, economist writer, feminist, social reformer, and dialectician.

699

It is fairly obvious that those who are in favor of the death penalty have more affinity with assassins than whose who are not.

Remy de Gourmont (1858-1915)
Pensées Inedites

The little value they put on human life is one thing, certainly, that assassins and those who favor capital punishment have in common. To neither does the thought of one human being taking another's life appall them. Neither the assassins nor the advocates of capital punishment reflect very deeply upon what it *means* to destroy a human life; that is, what are the causes and consequences of that sad occurrence. Those who judge that a man must be put to death officially, always do what they do premeditatively. The assassin or murderer may or may not plan their event ahead of time.

There are people, and I am one of them, who believe that punishment (not just capital punishment) has no place in our judicial, legal, and penal systems. All incarcerations or executions should be done for the sole purpose of protecting societies from criminals. Since that is accomplished by putting unregenerate criminals in prison for life, and because it costs no more to do so, I am completely opposed to capital punishment. Those are not my only reason for opposing capital punishment, but they suffice.

Whenever a person dies for any reason, especially a young person, the loss is not only to that person, but to every person on earth who loved him. Punishment is widely administered, and its victims are many. Sometimes those who are innocent suffer more than does the criminal. Children of a single parent may be one example. The parents of a young criminal are often another. That "Life is not always fair," is an understatement. It is seldom, seemingly never, fair.

700

Hallowed Be Thy Name.

Headline introducing the Religion section of the June 17, 1996 issue of *Newsweek*, page 75

This imperative (cliché) pronouncement, like all such locutions, asks and even demands that God focus His mind on the obvious. If we can believe anything at all of what religionists keep telling us, God certainly does not need constant reminders of His own divinity.

What kind of conceit leads persons to presume themselves God's counsels? They ask favors of an omnibenevolent God, summon an omnipresent god, offer help to an omnipotent god, even presume that words must be spoken aloud in order to communicate with an omniscient God. In effect, they arrogate to themselves supergod status. Their exalted opinions of their own place in the order of things erodes respect for the one Celestial God that, they say, created and oversees all things.

The *Newsweek* page written by Kenneth L. Woodward suggests that respect for God has been replaced by respect for Jesus and for his mother Mary. During my many years of living in Latin American countries, I found that saints are given more attention than all other celestial entities combined. Calendars have a saint assigned to each of the 365 day of the year, and many people pray to the saint corresponding the their own birthday. Also they pray to St George to prevent abduction, to St Apollo to prevent toothaches, To holy Job to prevent boils, to St. Roch to prevent illness, to St. Jerome to prevent theft, to St. Christopher to prevent accidents, to St. Neptune to prevent shipwrecks, and so on.

Since heavenly hierarchies are contrived by earthly religions, they come to be what each religion wants them to be. No two are alike. Each religion has its own priorities and understands what will further its own vested interests. Monetary concerns, more often than not, transcend all others.

701

Any man more right than his neighbors constitutes a majority of one.
Henry David Thoreau (1817-1862)
Civil Disobedience

Being more right than your neighbors is often not difficult. Simply base your convictions on things as they are, not as they turn out to be when distorted minds incessantly warp and twist them away from their natural form. A sure way of being wrong is to insist that scripture and not history is the key to understanding the world.

Revelation and not research is the path to knowledge. The unverified and unverifiable existences that populate our religions are the true movers and shakers of the cosmos. Human beings are mere pawns.

To develop our folly to the point of global irresponsibility, after we have conjured up gods and demigods (an entire hierarchy of mythical beings) we bow down to and worship these beings. Absurdity is added to absurdity until finally no one recognizes good sense if he sees it. Truth becomes a pariah and is rejected as soon as it is spoken. Anything and anyone that does not adhere to the prevailing bias, aberrations, and distortions is ruled out of order. A Moral Majority (which is neither moral nor a majority) is declared to be the presiding voice and is given wide audience on radio and television. When the Moral Majority finally wore out its welcome, with its fraudulence so blatant that even the most obtuse became aware of it, a Christian Coalition filled the breach, and declared itself to be the only entity that knows how to deal with the philistines. It swerved so far right that even some staunch Republicans backed away. Pat Robertson disappeared into the background, leaving Ralph Reed as spokesman. Ralph Reed eventually found his voice disregarded by the inflexible Christian Coalition leaders, and he resigned his position, retreating to a consulting organization, where he surmised he could do more good. Revenues for the Christian Coalition have dropped from 29 million in 1996 to 17 million in 1997. Its influence is moving in the right direction, but no one is yet ready to predict its demise.

702

The sorceress is the Church's crime.

Jules Michelet (1798-1874)
Satanism and Witchcraft

Because the sorceress believes in demons, a natural niche for her is in the Catholic Church. But because she is obviously endowed with an extraordinarily fertile mind, being a nun (A submissive slave willing to work for bare subsistence) could never appeal to her. Being a priest is a door closed to her, even though she would probably be an excellent one. The lady is not left with many traditional choices that would utilize her special talents. The church forces her into sorcery because it leaves no other place for an intelligent, religiously minded woman to go.

Sorcery is defined as a socially harmful form of magic, making her by definition a criminal. The church, as explained, is responsible for what she became, making her, as Michelet stated, the Church's crime.

Among the sorceress' special abilities may be a slightly perverted sense of humor that gives her a penchant to enjoy playing with other people's emotions, even to directing these emotions to serve her own purposes. Another of her abilities may be a variation of the priest's lust for power, but which for her has a more sinister, possibly vengeful, orientation, giving her an incentive and perseverance that even priests might envy.

All of sorcery (which boasts more witches than warlocks) might be explained by the prejudicial treatment of women in nearly all societies in the world. People with good minds must use those minds in creative activities; that is human nature. Some few become witches. It is better, they explain to themselves, than becoming the nothingarians that is often their lot when overbearing, misogynic patriarchs rule in any society.

703

I think God is silly because He should have painted everybody the same color, and then they wouldn't fight.

Ricardo. Age 7 – quoted by Nanete Newman
Lots of Love

I hope, Ricardo, that your frustration about how silly God is is not too traumatic. You are in for many such revelations in your coming years. Just between you and me, and I say this because many people will try to explain, there are no explanations. You hit the nail right on the head, and all the excuses in the world for God's silliness in no way lessens His responsibility for being so unconcerned.

About that fighting, though, people will find other pretexts for fighting – even if God hears you and implements your suggestion. We human beings differ in many ways: the shape of our noses, the words we use to communicate, the color of our hair and eyes, our passionate interests, our size, the way we smile, and so on. You will be surprised how little it takes for us to hate one another. Fighting has been one of mankind's principal occupations since time immemorial.

Our best hope for ending conflicts is in educating ourselves and others, not God. God is a lost cause. He pays no attention to you and me. We must find ways to impress upon ourselves and every other person in the world how much better it is to love one another and to try to teach everyone how great this world will be when we treat all people decently and with sincere concern for their well being. It will not matter how anyone looks, only how people behave and what they are doing to make this a better world.

704

Facts have double value; they give us the wherewithal to think straight and they stimulate the imagination; for imagination, like reason, cannot run without the gasoline of knowledge.

Charles Hall Grandgent (1862-1939)

Facts are observations – that which we "observe" with any of our senses. Facts are not symbols. Sometimes when we use the word fact, we mean statement of fact (a statement about a fact). Also we use the term facts in everyday speech to mean "historical facts" which, of course, are not observations. In this sense, we are making the assumption that someone whom we believe reliable did do the observing and is reporting to us about it through the pages of history. On page 49 of *People in Quandaries*, Wendell Johnson gives us the best dissertation about the word fact that I have seen. Among other things, he tell us:

1. Facts are always incomplete (We cannot see the inside of the pencil.)
2. Fact change (What cures today may kill tomorrow) – the reason drugs are dated.
3. Facts are personal affairs (It is a particular nervous system doing the observing, and all nervous systems are different.)
4. Facts become reliable in proportion to the number of intelligent observers agreeing to them. (When all of us look and we all say "pencil." We can be fairly certain it is a pencil.).

Chapter XVIII

Intemperance

705

I am accused of being intemperate in my criticisms of religion. If I were not to speak fervently, with a sincere desire to expose the iniquities of religion, I would be dishonest, and would not deserve anyone's respect.

If I mellow, I need only remind myself of the Christian Crusades, the Spanish Inquisition, Hitler' genocide in the name of religion, the genocides in Anatolia, Rwanda, Tibet, and East Timor. I need only remind myself of the hatred of homosexuals, of women, and of "those others" who look and speak differently, In truth, I need only reread the Bible: of God's anger, homicides, partiality, self-aggrandizement, and the general inhuman behavior that religionists are capable of – to know that I must speak clearly – often intemperately.

Nothing is accomplished by speaking in moderation. Bigotry, religious prejudice, as well as hatred of everyone who are not like ourselves continue. Conflicts, wars, and genocides continue, inflamed by people who are fanatically religious. Religious bias and deceit proclaimed from the pulpit continue.

If I am to live with myself, I must express myself candidly and honestly, never for a moment condoning religion's depravity. I cannot allow Jerry Falwell, Pat Robertson, all the rich-and-getting-richer evangelists to think they are getting away with it. Those who in the past have offered us enlightenment: Darrow, Mencken, Paine, Ingersoll, Nietzsche, and many others will have been betrayed, and we will deserve the monomaniacal theocrats we get. We will no longer be governed by laws, but by "divine" edicts issued by the staff of Liberty, Regent, and many other similar universities which would be added to those that now pervert our judgment and corrupt our morality - filling us with hate and superstition. None of us can be quiet about the attempted religious takeover of our country as long as religions continue to thwart our efforst to make this a better world.

706

> She believed in nothing: Only her skepticism kept her from being an atheist.
>
> Jean-Paul Sartre (1905-1980) - *Words*

Sartre is having fun with us - like Isaac Singer when he said: " We have to believe in free-will. We've no choice." Or Oscar Wilde when he said: "I can resist everything but temptation." Recently going around is: "Nostalgia isn't what it used to be" and Yogi Berra's "It's déjà vu all over again" has become so entrenched that even intelligent people cannot say the French words chosen to describe a weird (but common) psychological phenomenon without adding the ridiculous English tautology.

An atheist is a skeptic, and Sartre is saying in effect about his female friend that her skepticism kept her from being a skeptic. It is an example of what we mean by second-order language, which often seems to involve contradiction. Other examples are explaining our explanations, knowing that we know, or being aware that we are aware.

Despite the fact that half the world talks about the God or gods that are supervising things here on earth, the atheist knows that he has no chance of proving a negative about existences of any kind. He cannot prove that fairies do not exist, and the same is true with respect to unicorns, mermaids, werewolves, etc. He knows, as we all should, that the burden of proof is on the person who takes the positive side of such a proposition, not on the person who denies it.

If God or gods exist, tell me how you know," is all the atheist can say. It seems obvious that if there really were a God around advising us, passing judgment on us, that that fact would be so obvious all of us would know it beyond any shadow of doubt. If God exists and He cares for us, "He would shake a monitory finger at us every time he sees us going astray." There are any number of ways He could make his presence known, and the only logical conclusion is that he does not simply because He cannot. As Stendhal says, "God's only excuse is that He does not exist."

707

> Certainty generally is illusion, and repose is not the destiny of men.
> Oliver Wendell Holmes, Jr. (1841-1915)
> Speech, Boston University School of Law

It is not man's fate to be certain about anything. A reasonable probability is the best we can expect. We must not allow ourselves to be gulled by the "certainties" of theological academigogues. Although canonical structures are becoming ever more subtle and complicated, reason and consistency are still alien to their formation. We have the means for examining what ecclesiastics are telling us to see whether fact or truth obtain. Any statement that cannot demonstrate predictive content should be ignored.

What do we accomplish by arguing endlessly over the pros and cons of the divinity of Jesus, the virginity of Mary, the trinity of God, none of which problems can be resolved and none of which has anything to do with the price of potatoes, or any of the other considerations that determine how well we will spend our sojourn on this planet? If an infinite regress is the only response to legitimate questions about religion, even the child knows he is being deceived.

Repose is said to be a distinctive feature of heaven, which does not necessarily make heaven something to look forward to. To watch most people in their daily activities is to find that repose is the last thing they seek. They climb mountains, explore jungles, sky dive, run rapids, surf, scuba dive, and even get married, risking their chances of enjoying repose for years to come. Repose for most people is a fate worse than death. It is not only not the destiny, it is not even a paramount desire of man.

708

> I call Christianity the one great curse... the one immortal blemish
> upon the human race.
>
> Friedrich Wilhelm Nietzsche (1844-1900)

Alfred North Whitehead said, "I consider Christian theology to be one of the great disasters of the human race." His "one of" instead of Nietzsche's "the one" ameliorates a bit Nietzsche's contention.

Orthodox Judaism, with its "chosen people" concept and with members who refuse to become full citizens of "alien" countries where they live, is not exactly out of contention either. "The one great curse," to use Nietzsche's words, is religion, period, without pointing to any one religion in particular.

Islam, too, is vying for first place when it insists on the infallibility of a Koran which says: "The only true faith is Islam. He that chooses a religion other than Islam will not be accepted, and in the world to come will be one of the lost." (S 3/19,85)

"Islam," founded in Arabia in Ad 622 and "The Nation of Islam" founded in the United States in 1930: what relation, if any, exists between them? The latest and probably best answer to that question is in *The Messenger: The Rise and Fall of Elijah Muhammad* by Carl Evanzz. "Islam" vis-à-vis "Nation of Islam" is one more case of orthodox religion spawning heterodox hogwash. It is like werefolk spawning weidos. The world would be better off without them.

Our effort to divide ourselves into factions is bound to lead to hate – with each group insisting that it is radically different and superior. It is the nature of human beings or groups of human beings to hate others different from themselves.

709

> I regard irreligious people as pioneers. If there had been no
> priesthood, the world would have advanced ten thousand times better
> than it has now.
>
> Anandabai Joshee (1865-1887)
> Letter to her Aunt, August 27, 1881 – quoted in *The Life of
> Anandabai Joshee* by Caroline H. Dall

Plus or minus a dozen or so. As one who must guard every minute against my own penchant for hyperbole, and as one who agrees with her sentiments (if priesthood is considered as generic for all the "hoods" of religion) I cannot fault her. I remember as a child thinking how prissy were some neighborhood children with their expression, "he hit me right here." With exponentially rising inflection on the word "right." In our family composed of five male siblings tattling reached pinnacles of exquisite invective. People like us are always concerned that others will not understand how emphatically we mean what we mean.

The idea of atheists being pioneers intrigues me. To be a pioneer means being one who goes ahead, preparing the way, in this case, opening new lines of thought. The assumption is that the territory penetrated has existed unchanged far too long. Change is overdue.

Religion, has existed largely unchanged since human imaginations first became skilled enough to fabricate mythologies. The pioneer is an intrepid person who dares to challenge this corruuptive stagmation. He develops new concepts based on reality rather than myth. He is not easily deterred knowing that the order and harmony of the cosmos support him. He understands that his and other new ideas, which will be accepted only if confirmed, and only if they are in accord with the verified ideas that already exist.

710

To make a contented slave you must make a thoughtless one.
Frederick Douglass (1817-1895)
My Bondage and My Freedom

"Ignorance is bliss" was once a doctor's idea of what a patient should know about his terminal cancer. In a world with so many wrongs to be righted, however, ignorance is certainly not a road to world progress. The thoughtless slave, meek accepter of his lot, will not seek ways to end slavery. Only the slave who understands thoroughly the unspeakable injustice of his position will do that.

Whether it is party affiliation, religion, slavery, prostitution, poverty, or serfdom, those in charge know that their only hope for maintaining their leadership roles is to keep their subjects ignorant of the true nature of their situation. Genuine education is the hope for the vassals in all bondage. The bishops of Peru for 300 years withheld education from their poverty-stricken congregations. Education was withheld from slaves in the United States for the same reason. Even today "religious" universities in this country must deny their students a truly enlightening education. To instill a broad education into all citizens would be to assure the end of all obscurantism, all theistic, sectarian religions.

711

Only when a man ceases to be a child, only when he emancipates himself from the fetishes of religion and gives up his silly and childish ideas concerning the existence of God, will he be able to rise to that commanding position and station in life when he can be truly called a man!

Joseph Lewis, President
Freethinkers of America

Each believer fashions within his own nervous system the God he wants to worship. The vague descriptions of deity he is given in sermons or "sacred" literature cannot do it for him. Because he does the fashioning himself and because each believer's God is different, we wonder why so many believers conjure up gods that leave them in the position of pawns. They are perfectly willing to cede their power to choose, to act, and to form ideas. What they have left are apotheosized figments of their own imagination. They behave like children, never motivated to take command of their own destiny.

Even if it could be proven that God does exist, we would see that He is so ineffectual that He is not worth bothering about. We would be better off without Him. Knowing that we are on our own and can expect no help from God, we will try harder to eliminate plagues by ourselves and prevent any future Auschwitz. Finding here and there some degree of success, the despair that came from knowing that we have been trusting our fate to an ineffectual God will give way to a new hope, based on a new confidence in our own potential.

712

Most people eddy about... striving blindly, achieving nothing... and when they die... no one asks who or what they have been.

Matthew Arnold (1822-1888)
"Rugby Chapel" – *New Poems*

The sad part of it all is that most of these people, if they had been given a little guidance and encouragement at the right point in their lives, would have followed very different paths and would have become useful, happy citizens. Few school counselors seem to have the ability to convince young people that it is not nerdy to study and to try to use one's language correctly. The bad habits they acquire in school continue after they have finished school or have dropped out early. They never get a chance to learn the joy of creative accomplishment, generally being useful not only to themselves but to others as well. Work, mostly a nasty word to them, they do not learn can become more satisfying than anything they have ever done. Work, when they become lost in it, ceases to be "work" but becomes delightfully absorbing activity, sometimes so absorbing they object to any interruption to it; even sleep may become an enemy.

I wonder if an effective ploy for changing attitudes might be, after exhaustive aptitude tests, to set a child down to achieving one narrow academic goal, removing all distractions and all other goals for the present, helping where needed, praising constantly, until it becomes obvious that the child – to himself and to all others – is *the* expert at that one endeavor. It dawns on him that if he can do one thing well, he can do others well too. He becomes a student in the best acceptation of the term. His self-esteem returns and he becomes an automatic candidate for success.

713

There was a time when we were not. This gives us no concern. Why then should it trouble us that a time will come when we shall cease to be?

William Hazlitt (1778-1830)
"On the Fear of Death" – *Table Talk*

Four hundred years earlier, Thomas a Kempis, in this book The *Imitation of Christ*, said: "The end of all is death, and man's life passeth away suddenly as a shadow."

Brendan Gill, writer, in an interview with Charlie Rose, agreed, and in doing so used words similar to those offered by the summit sage in Johnny Hart's "B.C." A devotee asked":

"Oh, Great Guru, what happens when I die?"
"Nothing, it's over; that's it!"
"I climbed all the way up here for that?"
"You want a happy ending go see a Frank Capra movie."

Mencken, Kaufmann, and Russell all said in effect: "Religionists have the same difficulty in imagining after-death nothingness than they have in imagining a universe with an infinite past – even though both concepts are no more illogical or difficult to comprehend than the commonly accepted before-death nothingness or a universe with an infinite future."

The idea that when we die we will cease to exist in any and all respects is for many such a horrible contemplation that that in itself is reason enough to reject any such belief. Also, along with Dostoevski, many of us insist that such a belief would destroy all significance in our lives, that we might as well commit suicide to end all of life's miseries..." Where do they find a basis for these assumptions? Why, then, am I not terrified with my belief that death is a definitive end? And why do I find my own life reasonably significant despite such conviction? And why have I not found among my contemporaries who believe as I do the terror and despair that Dostoevski and other religionists see as inevitable? Arthur Hugh Clough's purported crucial-moment religious conversion (see essay 77) is common newspaper effusion, but has little or nothing to do with the facts of life.

714

Is it progress if a cannibal uses a knife and fork?

Stanislaw Lee
Unkempt Thoughts

A family I visited in the rain forest region of Ecuador had six very young daughters. At mealtime, I noticed they sat around a large aluminum pot on the ground eating stew (Ecuador's favorite food at all economic levels) with table spoons. The really sad thing I noticed is that they did not have enough spoons to go around. Those without spoons kept reaching out to borrow another's spoon in order to take the next bite.

On my second trip to visit them, my pack included enough spoons for all their possible uses. I brought no knives and forks; they had to wait until another time. Before I left Ecuador, they had an iron grill to replace the car springs and handleless machetes on which pots perched precariously over the fire built on the kitchen (dirt) floor. Later I brought pots, a can opener, cups, knives and forks, and wood-working tools. Finally, I brought a propane stove and paid for propane for weeks ahead, but when I returned after some time away, they were back to cooking over the open-fire *fogón*.

Progress is relative. It can be very little things for the very poor. Most poor people in the United States do better at their worst than what is best for the people in rural Ecuador. "Yes," is the answer to Stanislaw Lee's question. But the obvious, much-greater progress was still to be accomplished.

715

I am a priest, not a priestess.... "Priestess" implies mumbo jumbo and all sorts of pagan goings-on. Those who oppose us would love to call us priestesses.

Carter Heyward
Quoted in "Who's Afraid of Women Priests" by Malcolm Boyd

Most women movie stars want to be called actors, and most women who carve figures want to be called sculptors. So it is that women who preside over a church want to be called priests. The lioness is not heard to complain, but she has ever right to, for it is she that runs down most of the food eaten by the so-called kind of the jungle. Witches, too, must think it unfair that warlocks and wizards are accorded more esteem than they, who are really the chief wardens of sorcery.

Male chauvinists (most of us) will not miss an opportunity to demean women a little, and if adding "ess" anywhere will help, that we will do. It is often by the little, subtle, inconspicuous detractions that we express our prejudices in ways that do the most harm. We are often admonished for our overt, obvious, malicious calumnies and learn not to repeat them. To speak of a comely, flirtatious young lady (we do not know well) as a harlot will do us more harm than it will her, so we speak of her as a winsome wench, and get away with it . By incremental aspersions, we can destroy a person's reputation. This happens at times to a child in early years, giving the child an inferiority complex she never outgrows.

When Helen Gahagan Douglas said, "I know the force women can exert in directing the course of events," she had in mind especially one woman in particular, Eleanor Roosevelt. But history is full of examples. To name a few: Marie Curie, Patricia Schroeder, Nellie Bly, Hanan Ashrawi, George Eliot, Charlotte Bronte, Jane Austen, Frances Willard, Susan B. Anthony,   Elizabeth Cady Stanton,

George Sand, Jane Goodall, June Goodfield, Dian Fossey, Amelia Earhart, Mary Leakey, Golda Meir, Margaret Chase Smith, Indira Gandhi. I am sure I have left out hundreds equally important. Ralph Waldo Emerson said in his *Manners, Essays*: "I esteem it a chief felicity in this country that it excels in women." He could have added, "Any country that values its women excels."

716

A doctrine of black supremacy is as evil as a doctrine of white supremacy.

Martin Luther King , Jr. (1929-1968)
The *Words of Martin Luther King, Jr.*

Nature has seen fit not to produce a race of supermen, and that is good. No race of people anywhere has in fact, according to scientific studies, a monopoly of all the most favorable traits of human beings, and the word race is in truth meaningless. Regardless of efforts to define race, no definition will encompass any large group of people known.

We are one group of fauna that inhabit the earth, and the only living species within the genus Homo. Brotherhood is the word for us. We are one grand fraternity-sorority, and nothing except that which cultures have imposed upon us do actually separate us. The genetic makeup of all of us has very few differences, and the genome now being compiled applies to all of us.

The concept evoked by the word "race" has probably done more harm to the human species than any other nonreligious term in our language. The impressions it stamps into human minds are almost all false, and serve more than anything else as an excuse for some of us to treat others of us abominably. Even when there are distinct differences such as color of skin, skull shape, place of origin, native language, preferences in food, or athletic abilities, there is nothing intrinsic about these differences to account for the prejudices that arise and contaminate our minds.

In mixed groups, we become self-conscious about our socially instilled prejudices to a point where it is difficult to act normally, matter-of-factly, and completely sanely, even with other people that in all significant respects we have much in common. In the school cafeteria, at jobs, church outings, at conferences, etc., we group ourselves according to our imagined racial types. Television is helping: More advertising is done by minority groups, and there is more news of non-Caucasian awards and successes. Whether we admit it or not, even self-conscious, deliberate efforts to avoid invidious discrimination can be helpful.

717

The simplest way to promote understanding would be to promote a language that is understood by all.

Arthur Koestler (1905-1983 - *Janus*

Consider what making that language "Esperanto" would mean in improving world communication. In Esperanto, all nouns end in "o" and its adjectives end in "a." A singular and regular conjugation of verbs and other simplifications make it fifteen times as easy to learn as English.

Europe now has a single currency. If they really want to make a mark on world societies, they need only get their wise heads together and devise an acceptable artificial language. The procedure for turning it into a world language is to do nothing but agree that it be taught as a second language in all the schools of Europe. Without coercive efforts on the part of anyone anywhere, within two or three generations it would be well on its way to becoming a universal language. Within a generation it would begin to appear in newspapers, books, magazines, and all official papers. Radio, television, and the net would begin to use it. Soon everyone would want to learn it. How much that would contribute to shaping a sound, healthy, prosperous, and tranquil world is beyond imagination.

As far as religion is concerned, just to pay attention to how we use its words in the language we have would help end the confusion: The God of the Bible is described as the personification of love (John 3:16; 1 John 4:8,16). But He is also said to be angry, fearful, jealous, and vengeful.

Jesus is defined as a person who could say: "Whosoever shall smite you on the right cheek, turn to him the other also" (Matthew 5:39). Then he could also say: "Bring those enemies of mine who do not want me to reign over them, and slay them before me." (Luke 19:27).

In Matthew 7:1, he could say: "Judge not that you be not judged." Twenty-two verses later he says, "Depart from me ye that work iniquity."

Satan is described in literature as a faithful servant of the Court of Heaven, and also as an efficient general of an army of nearly three million devils. Also he is described as being the instigator of all the evils perpetrated by the depraved elements of mankind.

Angels are described as ministering spirits (Hebrews 1:14) higher in the pecking order than man (Psalms 8:5) – also as killing spirits (Acts 12:23) – and as torturing spirits in their role in Chapter 16 of Revelation.

718

> Religion is little more than a synonym for dependency. In the final analysis, then, religion is neurosis.
>
> Albert Ellis

Schleiermacher, also, seemed to think that religion instills in us a feeling of dependence. What follows is a thorough disintegration of the qualities that make us human.

To many psychiatrists, to instill religion is *ipso facto* to instill neuroses. Some would put it the other way around: The religions of our societies are simply our neuroses (private religions) expanded to include large groups of people. Religion in its protean forms operates to deform the mind, inhibit instincts, and stifle mental growth. The lament of psychotherapists, according to M. Scott Peck, is the excessive amount of time that must be spent to free young minds from the clutches of religion. Some of today's psychologists say that Jesus burdened his followers with a sure-fire formula for producing all manner of neurotic and psychotic disturbances. Ecclesiastics are geniuses at instilling in us this sense of dependency and fear. They teach us that religion is filled with enigmas that are beyond our comprehension and control. Unsolvable anxieties arise that twist our minds into morbid patterns. Religion's pretensions of meaning where there is no meaning become a significant cause of nervous disorders. Ever more vague, esoteric terms, limiting perception, curtailing action, leave us with no handle with which to extricate ourselves from the morass of obscurity. The various religions set up models of conduct impossible for us to follow, and we develop a guilty conscience for not having lived up to the unrealistic precepts that are imposed upon us.

719

> I do not believe in... any church I know of. My own mind is my own church.
>
> Thomas Paine (1735-1809)
> *The Age of Reason*

In a literal sense, what Paine says is obviously true, for "in the mind" is precisely where the entire world of any given individual is. What we see, hear, taste, etc, is not "out there" beyond the skin; it is fabricated within our own minds. Out there, particle physicists tell us, are only the quarks, leptons, etc., that make up the entire universe. But let us not go through that story at the present time. It will be covered more fully in essay 796. Most people project a church out there in the vicinity of the "particles" that comprise it. What Paine says is that he does not make that projection. His church remains within himself.

Emily Dickinson said the same thing when she declared, poetically: "Some people keep the Sabbath going to church / I keep it staying at home / With a bob'link for a chorister / And an orchard for a Dome." When we all learn not to project out there, beyond our skins anything in the universe that has no particles to represent it, we will all be as wise as Paine and Dickinson. The real church is an "attitude of mind." It is not the bricks, cement, or wood that make up the building. To be in church, those sitting in that particular building on Sunday morning must have that particular attitude of mind. If they do not, they could as well be sitting in a railway station listening to the station master call out the schedule of incoming and outgoing trains.

720

> Heathen, n.: A benighted creature who has the folly to worship something that he can see and feel.
>
> Ambrose Bierce (1842-1914)
> The *Devil's Dictionary*

Religion can maintain its stranglehold over societies only by being imponderable, mysterious, and unapproachable. John Galbraith said, "If the Bible had been written in clear, modern English, its audience would have been greatly reduced." Incomprehensibility is the key. Confusion is the *sine qua non.*

Read our modern news magazines today and notice how carefully they write in short sentences, with clear rhetoric, never using words that do not say precisely what they mean to say. They obviously did not get the word. Even our science and medical magazines, although they must use scientific and medical terms, for the most part write very readable prose, passionately intent that they be understood. Religion, on the other hand, usurps and distorts words of common everyday English, and uses words after words that have no clear referents and no strict meanings that are accepted, even by all theologians. They leave the reader puzzled about what they really want to say. The Bible is full of archaic terminology, words with shifting meanings, or no meanings at all. It becomes a chore to read: boring, repetitious, esoteric, and contradictory. It is good bedtime reading – as it will soon put one to sleep. If there are heathens and pagans among us, that is, people who think, they will always be a problem to religion. If their numbers increase while the membership of churches decrease, who will pay for building the churches, synogogues, and mosques – all the monuments to myth and mysticism.

If you would like to survive, dear heathen, choose as your object of worship something completely beyond all hope of elucidation. Choose, for example, planet Ferro orbiting star Geondan in constellation Distare in Galaxy M-31, where you can be guaranteed that no man will set foot, at least for another two million years.

721

All religions are ancient monuments to superstitions, ignorance, ferocity; and modern religions are only ancient follies rejuvenated.
                    Baron Paul-Henri-Dietrich d'Holback (1723-1789)
Le Bon Sens, Ou Idees Naturelles Opposees Aux Idees Surnaturelle

What d'Holback says is true, and any thinking person knows that it is. Library shelves are filled with the nonsense that is written under the rubric of religion. Books such as this one are written precisely to explain the truth of what d'Holback says.

Our present gross credulity cannot last forever. There will come a day when everyone will recognize organized superstition when he sees it and learn to live without it.

Religions, if they want to survive, will begin to take seriously their responsibility for teaching moral behavior. They will learn how to rid their own organizations of fraud, and do the same for others. Religions will study street gangs and learn how to convert them into protectors, helping in their neighborhoods rather than turning them into caldrons of crime.

Criminals will become subjects of intense study to determine how they might have been convinced to lead useful lives. From the time of Cesare Lombroso's famous essays on criminology to the present, many psychiatrists have made their recommendations, but little has changed. Religion will learn that prevention is the key to reduce crime, not laws and punishment. By teaching all members of every community that they individually are important and can expect to lead an interesting and useful life, religions can make significant change. Everyone will learn that only a moral life can be a happy life, and only a moral community can be an enjoyable place in which to live.

722

Americans of all classes and parties regarded God as a force for order amid the potentially destructive freedoms of democaracy.
Alexis de Tocqueville (1805-1859)

Whether Tocqueville agreed, he does not say, but anyone who regards God as a force for order has blinders on. If God can be credited with the existence of any of our religions, He is the opposite. Religion and nationalism are the two greatest forces for disorder we have. Most wars are religious wars. Even most of those considered as secular wars between nations, when analyzed will be seen as basically religious wars. Religion and nationalism engender more hate, bigotry, superstition, and prejudice than all other forces combined. We will not have order until we get rid of all gods, the gods of religion and the gods of nationalism as well.

Tocqueville was inspired by and made an impression on America when he made his tour here in the eighteen thirties. He had a lot to say, and we have been listening ever since. In his two volumes of *Democracy in America*, published in 1835 and 1840, Tocqueville speaks of the potentially destructive forces of democracy – this so soon after France had gone through ten years of catastrophic revolution. It is not democracy that is destructive, it is nationalism. Exaggerated patriotism (jingoism) rivals exaggerated fanaticism (zealotry) as destructive forces in societies all over the world. As Guy de Maupassant in his *My Uncle Sosthenes* says, "Patriotism is a kind of religion; it is the egg from which wars are hatched."

723

If God is thought of as simply and exclusively male, then the very cosmos seems sexist.

Paul Moore
Take a Bishop Like Me

If your doctorate thesis assignment happens to be to deal fully with God, relax. You've got it made. Nothing you can do is wrong. If you think this is an exaggeration, try this experiment: Stand in front of your library shelves on the subject, take books off the shelves one after another, scan the indexes for the word God, and look to see what the authors have to say. You will not learn much about God, but you will learn a great deal about the extent of human imaginations when they expatiate about imaginary entities.

God, according to the authors, is capable of magical cures, is sensitive to prayers, tolerant of slavery, easy to anger, an inefficient entrepreneur, devoted to punishment, fascinated with wars, and a repository for guilt. From there on you are on your own – and anything goes:

God is loving-fiendish, sinful-saintly, male-female, helpful-indifferent, peremptory-supplicating, callous-sensitive, arbitrary-merciful, concerned-aloof, immanent-transcendent, kind-sadistic, fearful-congenial, cruel-benign, caring-apathetic, xenophobic-catholic, provincial-ecumenical. He is omnipresent and He sits upon a throne.

It seems there is nothing said about human beings that has not been said also about God, which, I assume, is not surprising. Take a Bishop like Paul Moore and his concern about the cosmos seeming sexist; that should be the least of his worries. A cosmos fabricated and run by a God like the one described in the Bible and in the literature would be a pretty mixed-up place. The irrepressible St. Augustine of Hippo in his *De Trinitate* probably ends all need for debate. He says: "God is not what you imagine or what you understand. If you think you understand, you have failed.

724

I want to promote the increase of natural knowledge.... and to forward the application of scientific methods to all the problems of life... and the resolute facing of the world as it is when the garment of make-believe is stripped off.

Thomas H. Huxley (1825-1895)

Huxley's proposal is admirable, but very difficult to achieve. When what Huxley wants is accomplished, the most dramatic revolution ever attempted among the members of the human species will have been successful.

The increase in natural knowledge continues. Anyone who has watched the documentary films on television for the past several years, has a good idea of how much we are learning about nature, including the violence that is endemic in that realm.

Making use of natural knowledge to improve our lives, has only just begun. We will not see appreciable progress until we get rid of all our superstitions and eliminate all our devastating prejudices, none of which have a place in a rational world. Only "when the garment of make-believe" in our lives is stripped away completely, can we pride ourselves of having rid the world of its present-day sham and deceit. We cannot be satisfied until we see ourselves as a sane species, living in a real world governed by natural laws that keep our relations with the cosmos in a relatively stable condition.

725

No one can say that Christianity has failed. It has never been tried.

Adam Clayton Powell, Jr. (1908-1972)

Black Man's Burden

Adam Clayton Powell, a preacher as well as a legislator, knowing that, might have been the great innovator. The truth is he missed the mark as far as any preacher – and farther than most. His diatribes in the senate were models of immaturity, wrong-headedness, and lack of insight. He was in a position and had the mental equipment to be the greatest religious leader of all time, but muffed his chance because his ego and his mouth were always too far ahead of his brain. I can remember how fervently I was always rooting for him, and so were a majority of the citizens of the United States. When the 90th Congress voted to deprive Adam Clayton Powell of his seat on March 1, 1967, he lost face. Although this vote was overturned by the Supreme Court, Powell did not again regain his former power. He died five years later on April 4, 1972 at the age of 64.

The Christianity that Powell said has never been tried is certainly not the Christianity of today's evangelists, nor was it the religion of Jesus. It is a kind of idealized Christianity that has existence in the minds of people who have a pretty good idea of how people ought to behave. They call such people Christians, even though there are no such people. Even those who came close to that ideal are as often as not Jews, Hindus, or Buddhists. They have many names, even atheists, I am sure. If this Christianity has been tried, it is in the lives of individuals who never make the news. They do not think of themselves by any special labels, Christian or otherwise. They are just their simple, unpretentious selves and need never be anything more.

726

Needless to say, since Christ's expiation not one single Christian has been known to sin, or die.

Voltaire (1694-1778

Mary Baker Eddy said: "Death will disappear with the disappearance of sin." How then account for the death of devout Christian Scientists? The difference between Mary Baker Eddy and Voltaire, is that the dear Madam Eddy was not kidding. We assume, anyway, she really believed her "apodictic" absurdities.

Statistics show that it is the Mormons, not Christian Scientists, who live exceptionally long lives. Mormons do not drink coffee or booze, and live rather quiet, tranquil lives. Christian Scientists pig-out at will. One Christian Scientist lady I knew, who weighed just slightly less than a small pony, practically lived on ice cream.

No religion has a monopoly on stupidity. They vie for first place in that category. All theistic religions find it perfectly reasonable to make whatever outlandish statements they like, and we are supposed to accept whatever they say without question for no other reason than because they say it.

Some of the gems from the pens of Judeo-Christians are: Sons of God mated with daughters of Man to produce children who were giants (Genesis 6:4). He cast a stick on the ground and it became a snake (Exodus 4:3). Take, eat; this [bread] it is my body (Mark 14:22). An ark, 450 by 75 by 45 feet, housed two of every species of animal on earth plus food for 40 days (Genesis 6:19). Enosh lived 905 years (Genesis 5:11). The donkey *said* to Ballam (Numbers 22:30). The hare, because it chews the cud (Leviticus 11:5). Sarah [90 years old] shall bear you a son (Genesis 17:19). She became a pillar of salt (Genesis 19:26). The Lord rained brimstone and fire on Sodom and Gemorrah (Genesis 19:24). Jonah was in the belly of the fish three days and three nights (Jonah 1:17). So fantastic was the Leviathan that it took God all of the 41st chapter of Job to describe him.

727

When conditions are evil, your duty in spite of protests, in spite of sentiment, your duty though you trample on the bodies of your nearest and dearest to do it. Though you bleed your own heart white, your duty is to see that these conditions are changed. If your laws forbid you, you must change your laws. If your church forbids you, you must change your church. And if your god forbids you, why then you must change your god.

Clemence Dane (1888-1965)
A Bill of Divorcement, Act I

Clemence Dane's long and peremptory quotation assumes that we know evil when we see it, and then also that although there may be many obstacles in the way of changing it, we have the capability of doing so. It assumes also that we are competent to perceive and verify the complicity in that evil even of our own dearest friends or even of our own dearest God.

If we are condemning all of our friends and even our God of evil intent as well as evil doing, then we make still one other even more remarkable assumption: that we ourselves are supergods. How otherwise could we be wiser and more moral than God. Clemence Dane's critics must be a super-supergods. For they are ordained to judge us, the supergods who judge the God.

The above introduction to an infinite regress will remind the do-gooders of the world how careful they must be before accusing others. They are like the farmer who said to his wife: "Martha, sometimes I think the whole world is daft except thee and me, and sometimes I think thee be a bit daft too."

728

> The Christian has greatly the advantage of the unbeliever, having everything to gain and nothing to lose.
>
> Lord Byron (1788-1824)

Pascal said this same thing more than a hundred years earlier, and people gave it the name "Pascal's wager." What both men affirm is how little confidence they have in the intellectual capacity of their respective Gods.

Most people I know would be ashamed to admit that they cannot tell the difference between reasonable doubt and unreasonable belief. It is precisely God's inability to make that distinction that all religions imply and depend upon. The God Byron and Pascal fashioned in their own image is not the God most of us would want guiding our own personal affairs.

The reaction of the truly benevolent God to Pascal and Byron may have been best described by X.J. Kennedy when he said: "Great Yahweh fingered through the Bible / Thought on it, and filed suit for libel." God certainly would sue Pascal and Byron for crediting Him with the wit of an immature baboon. All serious Christians and Jews would be willing prosecution witnesses in His libel suit for imputing to Him authorship of the words in their Bible. Anyone seriously suggesting that there is everything to lose by considering the words of the Bible as Gospel would inevitably be God's enemy. Loving God would have to mean hating most of what the Judeo-Christian scriptures say about Him.

There is always something to lose by choosing popular opacity in preference to carefully considered lucidity. It is perfectly reasonable to doubt the truth, reality, or the status of everything a discipline based on mythology has to say about itself. The preacher is unhappy about having his good faith impugned, especially because he has doubts about it himself. After his Sunday sermons, he may have a troubled night's sleep mulling over what he has said – with so much of it fanciful fabrications. He knows he has constructed a world of conjecture, figment, and illusion – and that he is living a life based almost entirely on deceit. If at the same time he suspects that the members of the congregation are beginning to mistrust his wavering pronouncements, he is unnerved and sorely distraught.

729

We know that Jesus could not have ascended to heaven because there is no physical heaven anywhere in the universe. Even ascending at the speed of light, Jesus would still be in the galaxy.

Joseph Campbell (1904-1987)
The Power of Myth

He would have more than two million years of travel ahead in order to reach the next large galaxy, where Robert Schuller suggested heaven might be. Einstein's theory of relativity says that nothing can travel faster than light. We assume that Jesus would be subject to the same cosmic laws that we are.

Of course Jesus did not ascend bodily to heaven. If he traveled even at the relatively slow speed that our orbiting space stations travel, he would burn to a cinder within the first hundred miles. Before he reached the vacuum of space beyond the ionosphere his blood would boil away, and not much farther on, what is left of him would be colder than ice. If he continued his journey at the speed of our voyager and pioneer spaceships, it would take him more than 84 thousand years to reach the nearest star. It would take him more than 60 billion years to reach galaxy M-31, the only galaxy that can be seen with the naked eye. If we were to interpret Biblical statements literally, we would have to believe so many impossible things (essay 726) that we may decide it is easier to be unbelievers of religion's fairy tales – to become believers of good sense and reason.

730

The predominant fact about the nature of man is not that we become what we are predestined to be, but that we truly become, as human beings, whatever within our genetic limitations, we learn to be.

Ashley Montagu
The Nature of Human Aggression

In this statement, after long and carefully documented discourse about the nature of aggression in humankind, Montagu develops his theses that genetic dispositions toward aggressive behavior, however dominant or highly developed they may be, are not enough to make us into aggressive individuals. Though complicated, the experiments and observations already in existence make it obvious that as the song in *South Pacific* says, we have to be taught, not only to hate, but also to be aggressive.

The opposite is also true. We can be taught to be gentle, caring human beings. Some parents do this job fairly well. Others do not. An imperative of mankind is to incorporate into our education systems at all levels, well-planned and imaginatively executed programs for this purpose. We see on television from time to time classes being conducted for this very purpose. These classes are quite impressive. Obviously, there must be more of them – with follow-up analysis to see which are most effective. If the money spent teaching scriptures, with their hate-oriented lessons, were used instead for programs designed to teach us to behave with civility toward fellow human beings, the world would be far better served.

731

Why should religion ever be allowed to bring unhappiness, Judge? Wasn't it invented by man for a kind of solace? It is as though he had said, "I'll make me a nice comfortable garment to shut out the heat and the cold," and then it ends by becoming a straitjacket.

Agnes Sligh Turnbull (1888-1982)
The Rolling Years

As long as security and seclusion are the principal desiderata of religionists, they will serve no one else but themselves. The security reaches its highest degree of perfection when religionists shut themselves up in monasteries where contact with the outside world all but disappears. For all the good they do, they might as well be in straitjackets. They are parasites on the communities they pretend to serve.

Try just for a moment to imagine how incalculably immense are the funds that world-wide are spent on the paraphernalia of religion: its terrain and edifices, its pageantry and preaching. Now try further to imagine what would be the beneficial consequences if all this tremendous wealth were instead spent on providing our children with recreational and educational facilities to keep them off the streets and out of gangs, to mold their minds and bodies in ways to make them happy and productive world citizens! With this sharply contrasting past and future clearly in mind, who would not choose to end our present massive inculcation of hate and hypocrisy and begin immediately to transform splintered, malfunctioning human societies into a workable world democracy? We could do this you know! The world will be what we want it to be. Do we need once more to be reminded that in this world we are in charge – not some theomorphic thitherlanders?

732

> The church is a sort of hospital for men's souls, and as full of quackery as the hospitals for their bodies.
>
> Henry David Thoreau (1817-1862)
> *"Sunday," At Work on the Concord and Merrimack Rivers*

Bodies, at least, are real! And doctors today do amazing things. To compare the ministrations of hospitals today with what we can expect from churches is to compare feasting at a royal banquet with living on table scraps.

My friend Raphael on Harbour Island in the Bahamas said to me: "Moas o' da sinnun is in da churches! Quackery in the churches, in his opinion, is extensive. Lenny Bruce, Sidney Hook, Franklin Steiner, Johann Schiller, H.E. Barnes, N. Teeters, D.H. Lawrence, DuSean Berkich, Nietzshe, Alan Watts, Mark Twain, J.H. Holmes, Hugh J.Schonfield, Aldous Huxley, Thomas Paine, Emily Dickinson, Pierre Berton, and hundreds of others agree. Jesus must have been one of them. He never preached in a synagogue, and certainly not in a church.

It is in churches that some people have learned to hate everyone different from themselves – whether the difference is race, gender, sexual orientation, or religious affiliation. Those attending churches join in extolling the superstitions that pervade all religions. Prejudice, bigotry, xenophobia, and parochialism flourish in churches. Lying, the manifest mode of expression in church sermons, becomes for churchgoers the norm for all of life's situations. The electronic churches teach the tremendous power of money and the insignificant value of science. We would be better off to get our education in a pub.

733

> The problem of evil.... Why does God permit it? Or if God is omnipotent, in which case permission and creation are the same, why did God create it?
>
> Sir William Temple (1881-1994)
> Archbishop of Canterbury

If God cannot prevent evil, He is not all-powerful; if He will not, He is not all-good.

God behaving at all times as if He were the sworn enemy of earthlings – those who spend their lives in obsequious admiration and worship of Him – is a problem, is it not? The question to be answered really is why do *we* react to such conundrums in the way that *we* do. The answer to the nature of God's behavior seems clear and unequivocal: Most thinking people, if allowed to give their honest opinions anonymously, will answer the question in the same way: God's only excuse for failing us so unaccountably is that He does not exist, the answer Stendhal gave us more than a hundred and fifty years ago.

It is a sad commentary on human integrity that the sham and deceit of religion can become so domineering in a society that even people who reject all religions are unwilling to confront it. All the vultures of Christendom are ready to swoop down upon and strip the flesh off anyone who dares challenge their pietistic hypocrisy. Discretion vanquishes any disposition the unbeliever may have to make that challenge.

Here we have a partial explanation for the continued existence of religions in our societies despite the damage they do. The different religions are united – tacitly, we might say, but nevertheless, effectively. The know deep down within themselves how vulnerable they are, and, like a tribe of baboons, if a threat appears they unite to face it. Unbelief, on the other hand, is essentially an individual thing. No atheist organization has ever been successful. They have only one noteworthy bulletin in the United States, and it is not widely distributed. Most unbelievers are content to live their lives individually, and will never become a fanatically organized force.

734

> To me we are facing quite possibly the thermonuclear gas chamber of the future – a kind of global Auschwitz.
>
> Samuel Pisar
> Quoted in *God in America* by Furio Colombo

The threat of nuclear war is not over. And now we add the possibility of equally devastating chemical and biological wars. Someday the kind of terrorists that blew up the World Trade Center, the Oklahoma City Federal Building, the military barracks in Lebanon, or the U.S. Embassies in Kenya and Tanzania will get hold of a mass destruction weapon. It may be that the terrorists who set it off will manage to create the impression that it is the beginning of a massive onslaught by or upon China, U.S., or Russia. Other equally dangerous scenarios are possible.

The world, in many ways, is unstable. No one knows just where Russia is heading. No one knows what minor incident might set China off to committing some colossal political blunder. Peoples who have long been enemies are staring at one another across indefensible barriers in the West Bank and the Gaza Strip. Now India and Pakistan have nuclear weapons. Others will follow. There are presently wars going on in more than forty places in the world. It is easy to be as pessimistic as Samuel Pisar seems to be.

Our only hope of survival, it seems to me, is the formation of a global Government to which all people everywhere will pledge allegiance. But unless it is emerging in the gray matter of thinking people, there is no progress toward the formation of such a government. Instead of amalgamation we are getting fragmentation. The Soviet Union, India, and Yugoslavia have broken up into some twenty-five countries. Nowhere do we see countries uniting.

735

> We owe our liberties to men of a type that today we hate and fear – unruly men, disturbers of the peace, men who resent and denounce what Whitman called "the insolence of selected persons – in a word free men."
>
> Gerald W. Johnson (1890-1980)
> *American Freedom and the Press*

The freedoms we have, we have because there have been people endowed with intelligence, able to understand when subjected to uncalled-for demands against their individualism. Those who strive to deprive us of our freedoms, many found among politicians, clergymen and journalists with an ax to grind, have so much power over us that we are bound to become frustrated and provoked to action. If we become unruly and raise our voices, we have good reason. How else can we attract attention and be heard amidst all the blatant opposition, bent on turning us into pawns.

The amendments to the constitution are for the most part designed to preserve our freedoms. Freedom of speech, separation of church and state, habaes corpus ad subjiciendom, and freedom of or from religion are indispensabe for a free society. Freedom from want, freedom from fear, and freedom from hunger should be every person's right. We ask also for freedom from tyrants, bigots, jingoists, and zealots. Freedom to live in a peaceful society without crime and war, and with no restrictions to our pursuit of happiness, must be included. Freedom to choose our friends, our doctors, and our plans for education should not be infringed.

736

> If we create an atmosphere in which men fear to think independently, inquire fearlessly, express themselves freely, we will in the end create the kind of society in which men no longer care to think independently or to inquire fearlessly.
>
> Henry Steele Commager
> *Freedom* and *Order*

Fear that prevents us from daring to do, will finally result in our not caring to do. John Stuart Mill said, "That so few dare to be eccentric marks the chief danger of our time." Emerson said: "Whoso would be a man must be a nonconformist." Then why is so much effort directed toward avoiding the appearance of nonconformity or seeming to be eccentric? Peer pressure is not a phenomenon that is peculiar to teenagers. As Commager says, most of us fear to behave in ways different from the way our neighbors behave. To think, inquire, or reason independently is taboo. Life is simpler if we do not rock the boat. In Nazi Germany not many artists produced anything to displease Hitler. In Communist Russia, nearly all art conformed to the party line. In the United States, Democrats and Republicans are becoming Tweedle-dee and Tweedle-dum.

Fortunately, not all people have ceased to care. Many leave a country where they find freedom curtailed. Others make their opposition known by street demonstrations. It took picketing women a long time to convince President Wilson how serious they were about woman suffrage. It was demonstrating students all over the United States who were most effective in ending the Viet Nam War. Labor has won most of its benefits by strikes and demonstrations. Persistent marching mothers in Argentina and Chile helped get rid of the corrupt military leaders.

737

Such are the heights of wickedness to which men are driven by religion.

Lucretius (96-55 BC)
De Rerum Natura I 101

The wickedness Lucretius refers to did not compare with what has occurred in the millennium that just ended.

"Holy war," the most sinister contradiction in terms man has ever contrived, has been the excuse for more unholy killing than most of us imagine. It has always produced a host of vain, opinionated social deficients eager for an excuse to double, triple, or quadruple our military forces and military hardware. War would disappear if every human being were fully aware of the horror involved. Wars would stop before they get started if all combatants were aware that every life lost will be lost in vain. Even the winners will lose, as has been the case in all previous foreign wars we have engaged in.

But the "heights of wickedness to which men are driven by religion" include much besides war. Witch hunts killed more than 200,000 women between 1450 and 1750 in Europe and America. In just two incidents mentioned in the Bible, God's plagues killed 84,700 people.

Many thousands of heretics were burned by the Spanish Inquisition, and Queen Mary burned hundreds for not worshiping the Pope. Among German tribes in the 4th century, human sacrifices in the name of religion were common. The Bible tells of many other murders by God and by angels acting in his behalf. Now television evangelists talk of Armageddon, an approaching time when God's murders will be beyond counting.

738

> It is an open question whether any behavior based on fear of eternal punishment can be regarded as ethical or should be regarded as merely cowardly.
>
> Margaret Mead (1901-1978)
> *Redbook Magazine* February 1971

Or stupid! Let us not leave out the most likely option. Of all of God's shortcomings as He is described in the Bible, surely the worst is His propensity to get his way by threats, relying on fear. Not by love or rational persuasion does He convince His subjects to believe as He wants them to.

It is the nature of human beings to function at their best when their motivation is respect for those they are striving to please. They like also to know that what they are doing is beneficial to someone and is training to make them even more efficient at doing their work in the future. When one enterprise depends on fear and another depends on love and encouragement to motivate employees, it is not hard to guess which enterprise runs more harmoniously and is more efficient.

Empathy is a simple word, but a tremendous concept in human relations. To be able to put oneself imaginatively in the position of another to see things as he sees them is a rare and extremely useful accomplishment. How we have managed to create a God without that aptitude is beyond comprehension.

"God is love," religionists are constrained to say, again possibly because fear motivates them to say so. But reading the Bible should convince anyone that "God is hate." The hell He created even before there were sinners, and the thousands, perhaps millions, of human beings He killed during the course of Biblical narration is anything but love. If a shop foreman behaved as God behaves, he would get no work out of anyone. God's behavior possibly has prompted the sentiment expressed in a book title: "Stop the world, I want to get off." It would easier just to get rid of our repressive gods.

739

Religion is love; in no case is it logic.

Beatrice Potter Webb (1858-1943)
My Apprenticeship

That religion *should be* love is true, but that it *is* simply does not square with simple observation. The word religion to most of those who will read these words applies to the Judeo-Christian-Muslim monotheisms. Their God, fully cognizant of the scope and variety of consequences involved, framed a penal system far more reprehensible than any that could ever be imagined by the most depraved of human beings. Machiaveli, Sade, Stalin, and Hitler all together could not have concocted anything equal to God's hell, where the majority of his subjects, after successfully confronting the vicissitudes of a life on earth, can expect as a reward to fry in hell forever.

Try to imagine a more perverted sense of morality, a more flagrantly outrageous conception of compassion, a more degenerate demeanor than that of the supreme, universal ego religionists have chosen as their Father Figure. He is a God whose principal occupation is to make men cower before Him, whose primary need is obsequious praise, and who loves only those who grovel before Him. He is certainly not the God of a religion that one can define as love.

Logic, of course, is precisely what religion is not. Logic cannot take seriously the fictitious fabrication of theologies. It would never barbarize words that have long been respected stewards of good communication by twisting them into fallacious or misleading concepts. Reading the scriptures, we find logic rejected. Logic deals with facts, weaving them into sane perceptions and suppositions that are amenable to verification. Religion deals with myth, weaving it into a meticulously designed program of deceit, playing footsie with scientific premises and the essences of the cosmos. Its basic suppositions can never be verified.

740

To die for an idea is to set a rather high price on conjectures.

Anatole France (1844-1923)

A good idea in one generation may be folly in the next. France having been a keen observer of the human scene, knew well how transitory ideas can be. My own father, I remember, seemed to find occasions for reciting what he found to be a meaningful aphorism: "There is nothing so unsure as a sure thing." In the journey through the formative years, youth seems repeatedly to dream up dubious impressions that are "absolutely" indispensable – worth dying for. Maturity often has a way of minimizing many such ideas, sometimes reducing their importance to zero. It is a little like the covenant box which was so important in the first half of the Old Testament that God even killed a man (Uzzah) for just touching it. Yet in the last half of the Old Testament, the box isn't worth a mention. No one today has any idea of what happened to that "absolutely indispensable" emblem of God's sovereignty. Both the acacia-wood box and its stone contents disappeared from history.

The members of *Understanding Incorporated* could at any time settle our doubts about the existence of the pointy-eared, bug-eyed, sallow-faced extraterrestrials, if they exist, by presenting them on America Online. Likewise, those who tell us that the ark of the covenant is under lock and key in a temple in Aksum, Ethiopia, could confirm the existence of their artifact by showing it to us. Until they do the obvious, we will all remain skeptical.

741

No public man in these islands ever believes the Bible means what it says; he is always convinced that it says what he means.
George Bernard Shaw (1856-1950)

The Bible says what a person *wants* it to mean. Although the Bible is often at variance with fact and good sense, no one finds it contradicting "his own personal *good sense*." The Bible is where "good" people go to verify their side of any proposition. They find the verification they need.

When Paul said, "I am all things to all men," he expressed precisely how flexible a person must be who becomes skilled at defending the indefensible. Regardless of what objection anyone might have to one of Paul's remarkable doctrines, there are always explanations. Analyzing his responses, we find Paul equally adept at defending either of antithetical sides of a proposition. Romans 3:11 and 12 flatly contradict each other. But both are defended.

God "does change" and "never changes" his mind. "He will" and "He will never" punish children for the sins of their father. Atonement for sins "can" or "cannot' be passed from one sinner to another. God says a man "must" and "must not" marry his brother's widow. God says "eat anything that moves" and He says "Do not eat the camel, the hare, or the rock hydrax." More than a dozen birds are taboo. Pages 227 and 228 of *Blind Faith* quote chapter and verse of all these contradictions.

God hates adultery. His "favorite" is avowed adulterer King David. God's love will always triumph; the world is full of hate and suffering. God wrote the Bible. God did not write the apocrypha and the pseudepigrapha. Who made the decision about which is which, and what gave them that authority?

742

> I... think the greatest enemy of our progress and liberty is the corrupting clergy, who so long have dominated our country.
>
> Francisco Villa (1878-1923)
> Mexican Revolutionary Leader

Pancho Villa was no Fauntleroy. If it takes a felon to know one, Villa had the credentials. He did, however, have it straight about the clergy. Catholicism in Mexico behaved exactly as a religion will anywhere when it is an official state religion.

Perhaps there is no crime in police records that has not at some time been committed by ordained and not-so-ordained religious leaders. In both fiction and nonfiction it is easy to find examples. Perverted behavior such as found in pedophiles, sodomists, alcoholics, and bigots are as common among the clergy as in the population at random. The crimes documented by Barrows Dunham on page 207 of *Heroes and Heretics* are common in and out of the Bible: the nuns that robbed Papillon, Jephthah's daughter burned for doing nothing, heretics hanged in Pilgrim America, Uzzah murdered by God, Samuel carving up Amalekite King Agag, Sodom and Gomorrah destroyed. To go on would be to relate thousands of murders by God, his angels, Saul, and David.

743

The most serious doubt that has been thrown on the authenticity of miracles is the fact that most of the witnesses in regard to them were fishermen.

Arthur Brinstead
Pitcher's Proverbs

You should have seen the miracle that got away! In the controversy over miracles, we must be careful not to destroy the spawning ground. "Proof" of at least one miracle is necessary in the canonization of a saint. Do away with miracles and we do away with saints. And you know what *that* would mean!

Miracle, doing the impossible, is a contradiction in terms. But in the realm of religious mythology, as in much of science fiction and in all of fairyland, the laws of the cosmos are repealed. The only limits are the limits of human imaginations, which is to say that nothing is excluded. Science fiction and fairy tales are fun, and because no one takes them seriously no harm is done. The same cannot be said of the dream worlds of religion. People do take them seriously, so seriously that wars are fought over the phantasms conjured up by deranged religious minds. People are excommunicated or assigned to hell for not believing in the hierarchy of illusion based on these phantasms. As Whitehead suggested, this might be one of the greatest disasters that has ever befallen the human species.

744

Those societies which cannot combine reverence to their symbols with freedom of revision, must ultimately decay from anarchy, or from the slow atrophy of a life stilled by its useless shadows.

Alfred North Whitehead (1861-1947)
"Symbolism: Its Meaning and Effect"

"The only constant is change," it has been said. When orthodox religions try to avoid change, they only manage to make themselves ridiculous. No comedy show has ever put on a better performance than a religious zealot facing television cameras and trying to explain away biological evolution. Trying to explain why the earth is only six thousand years old is another premium performance. The grand canyon could have been formed in a matter of months. Dinosaurs were included in Noah's ark menagerie as babies. They have several millions of things to explain, so they will never run out of comedy skits to perform. Like all other institutions, religion must conform to the customs of the society of which it is a part. Conflict arises between religion and other aspects of society in direct proportion to the lag of religion in making inevitable changes. Torture, excommunication, and book burning, among religions' methods of persuasion, are not enough to obstruct the truth forever and preserve old errors and falsehoods.

Religion has had to accommodate itself to science throughout history. The success of science in finding the real causes of many of the phenomena which religion has explained by recourse to supernatural powers will continue. No wonder religion sees science as a dreaded enemy. Religion never knows what to expect next.

If we are to progress rapidly and unerringly in the construction of a peaceful and durable world society, we must cast aside all superstitions, prejudice, fables, and unproven premises – all the foolish, absurd, and idiotic notions so many people live by today. Our minds must be rewired to repudiate automatically any idea that does not contain within itself a reasonable and manifest expression of its own credibility.

Nothing that is said is worthy of consideration if it does not stand up to all logical if-this-then-so confirmations. Whatever we accept must conform with all the indisputable facts and authoritative statements that reasonable people no longer deny. No one is operating rationally if he consults horoscopes, Ouija boards, seances, tarot cards, channelers, tea-leaf readers, or psychics. If he considers any of the religious gimcracks and mystic practices listed in essay 82 as significant, he is not really sane. If sane, he will automatically reject any religion that caters to the present general ambience of mythological absurdity.

Chapter XIX

The Lure of the Liturgies

745

Believing the suppositions of theistic religion is not the province solely of simpletons. People of all level of intelligence have managed that anomaly. Once the decision has been made to join the ranks of the credulous, it requires no great effort to find and incorporate into one's belief system innumerable examples of "observances and events" that support a theistic cosmos.

The believer who is born into, or unwittingly acquires, an unsophisticated, trusting, and easily beguiled personality may reach the top of his profession. But his education into the rigors of analytical thinking is woefully neglected. It would be a shocking revelation to him to become aware of how much deceit, duplicity, and cunning is incorporated into the piety of the theologians he reveres. It would surprise him to realize how common are the Elmer Gantrys in the world who resort to trickery, wiles, and insidious stratagems to make them and the religion they preach rich and famous.

For preachers to represent the nonexistent as real, the false as true, the imitation as genuine, and the harmful as helpful is daily strategy. They learn the basics of dissimulation in their theological schools and forge and fashion these basics into a successful machine for exploitation.

Theologians have not reached their stride until they make statements so ridiculous that few other theologians will accept them.

In the last analysis each preacher is saying: words are things, belief is ectasy, the clergy is God's priority, bigotry is beneficence, superstition is man's magnum opus, prejudice is emblematic of supreme loyalty, and religion is life itself. Most members of the congregations learn to parrot the words and accept the pronouncements of their esteemed leaders.

746

Religion is the sign of the oppressed creature, the sentiment of a heartless world, and the soul of soulless conditions. It is the opium of the people.

Karl Marx (1818-1883)
Criticism of Hegel's Philosophy of Right

Marx, like most of the Communists who followed him, says that religion oppresses those who are foolish enough to yield to it. Like many others who contribute to this book, Marx knew that religion is an expression of the irrationality of the world. Religion is an opiate that affects all of us, even the unbelievers. The metaphor breaks down only in comparing the harm done by religion and opium. Religion has done infinitely greater harm than opium has ever done or ever will do.

Religion's principal weakness, of course, is that it depends on myth to give it credence. Since myth is fable, fiction, unsubstantiated legend, religions based on myth are not believable; they have no credence. If we understand the nature of the mythologies on which religions are based, we will relegate religions to the realm of pure nonsense. Then we can begin to construct a rational world in which Homo sapiens has some hope for surviving.

Religion can be meaningful only if it is construed as brotherhood, that and nothing else. The place of religion in our lives becomes indispensable when concerned with all people of good will regardless of what physical or mental boundaries may separate us. We do not exclude others because they live on the other side of the tracks, river, or range of mountains, because they live across expansions of oceans, prairies, or deserts, or because they engage in different politics or speak different languages. The color of their eyes, hair, or skin will have no bearing on whom we will call friends. If they are hungry, we make plans to feed them. If they have no shelter, we strive to house them. And we try to see that all human beings everywhere acquire the education necessary so that they too may contribute to the progress of the world.

747

Christianity flourishes in proportion to the misery and insecurity of life.

Gerald Brenan
Thoughts in a Dry Season

If Brenan is right, Christianity gives us an antinomous reason for hope. Christianity will be welcome as a positive factor of our societies if it can eliminate the misery and insecurity of life. But if Christianity does eliminate misery and insecurity, it is in effect writing its own epitaph. The dilemma is less hopeful than trying to sail between Scylla and Charybdis. A good navigator might make it. But Christianity (if Brenan is right) cannot win.

The situation is not as sad as it at first may seem. If Wittgenstein could say that the main occupation of philosophy should be to eliminate philosophy, why not suggest that Christianity may be in the same position. Those of us who have never been able to see redeemable merit in Christianity, now see some light. Christianity's death gasp would give it a remarkable reason for having existed if it finally proclaims: "We won! We have eliminated misery and insecurity! All that is left then for Christianity to do is to sink into oblivion.

Some of us would see that as society's double blessing. A remarkable benefit gained and a deplorable impediment eliminated. The gain, eliminating misery and insecurity, would certainly be welcome to all. The loss may also be a gain. It is, if Alfred North Whitehead was right to say: "I consider Christianity to be one of the greatest disasters ever to befall the human race." All religions based on myth deserve Whitehead's denunciation. The world cannot be considered safe until we get rid of all theistic religions.

748

Do you mind if I smoke?

(burning question)

For me to answer "no" to your question would be the nadir of callous unconcern. It would be the equivalent of my saying that I do not care about you: "Go ahead and smoke. It is all the same with me that you become one more of the 420 thousand people in the United States who die each year from the effects of tobacco. It will not bother me that you live with emphysema or cancer or any of the other debilitating infirmities that result from smoking. It is not my concern that your friends, family and colleagues will no longer be able to depend on you to respond as a healthy, capable, caring human being.

Oh no, no, no! No one talks like that. It would be considered the worst of bad manners to do so. To be urbane, we lie to people – even when our lies encourage on their part the most egregious kind of debilitating behavior.

Do you mind if I surrender myself completely to religion?

This book constitutes a refusal to reply dishonestly: "No, go ahead! It is all right with me if you misuse the good brain that the processes of evolution have fashioned for you. It is perfectly fine with me that you weaken your resolve to be a positively contributing member of society. Who cares if you waste your energies and time worshiping phantom deities."

This book asks us all to become mature, independent individuals, unwilling to relinquish our sovereign selves to power-hungry mystagogues. It asks that we all be willing to accept responsibility for our own behavior. Our best course always is to face problems squarely and work our way through to the best possible solution. If we need help, we ask for professional help. We do not depend on brownies, elves, fairies, lady luck, or mystical gods.

749

A good life is the only religion.
Thomas Fuller (1608-1661) – English divine and author

By a "good life" Fuller does not mean a life full of worldly amenities. He refers to the life of an individual doing good for his fellow human beings – at least in equal measure to the good he does for himself.

He does not see the frills of orthodox religions, their sacraments, rites, icons, and ostentatious centers of worship as contributing consequentially to what he considers religion. And certainly he rejects the hate, prejudices, bigotry, and superstitions of orthodoxy as part of his concept of religion. Being good, treating others fairly and lovingly, is enough. Espousing a brotherhood of all human beings on earth is enough. The religion that Fuller calls for is enough – all that is needed to make of this earth the heaven we want it to be.

Contrary to what electronic preachers and various municipal archbishops tell us, man's sorry plight results not from the behavior of unbelievers as opposed to believers. It results from what callous as opposed to what sympathetic people do in the face of human adversity. Not belief or unbelief, but honesty or dishonesty, decency or indecency, virtue or hypocrisy, love or hate are the determining factors. Those people who are honest, decent, virtuous, and motivated primarily by love, are religious regardless of whether or not they conjure up gods to supervise what is going on.

750

I distrust those people who know so well what God wants them to do, because I notice it always coincides with their own desires.

Susan B. Anthony (1820-1906)
Response to the National Woman Suffrage Association

Amos Oz (*Newsweek*, Nov 20,1995 P 61) is more specific: He finds that the only orders religious extremists get from God are to kill.

What value is a God who does not do what you want Him to do? What good is a Bible that you cannot interpret to agree with your convictions, however bizarre?

Most religionists are not anxiously concerned on either score. God does exactly what they expect of Him, and the Bible says exactly what they want it to say. They are satisfied with both God and His Bible – and it doesn't matter what the Bible really says. As Neil Postman says, finding evidence to confirm almost any conviction is easy. All religionists know that God is on their side and can quote chapter and verse to prove that He is.

Religionists in their prayers never stop to think that God might not find it proper to do what they ask of Him, nor does it seem to occur to them that a God that is omniscient, omnipotent, and caring would already have done what they ask if it were worthy of His attention.

751

It would be a gain to the country were it vastly more superstitious, more bigoted, more gloomy, more fierce in its religion that at present it shows itself to be.

Cardinal John Henry Newman (1801-1890)

Ecclesiastics do at times make some remarkable confessions: Paul Tillich when he declared it was atheistic to affirm the existence of God, Pope Innocent III when he sanctioned killing heretics by sword, J.H. Holmes when he speaks of Orthodox religions as opiates – and now Cardinal Newman admitting that religionists are superstitious, bigoted, and disposed to violence, and suggesting that they intensify the "desirable" traits.

Paul Tillich and J.H. Holmes are saying only that religions must not exaggerate their place in the scheme of things and that teaching morality is all that religion can and should expect to accomplish. Anything religion does beyond that should be condemned. Cardinal Newman and Pope Innocent III, on the other hand, are saying not only that their particular religion must win its place as the supreme authority over the entire world, but that whatever means that help in achieving that goal are legitimate.

Cardinal Newman asks for a religion in which there are few limits in what may be used in destroying those who oppose them. Pope Innocent III asks for an all-out war if that is necessary to win religion's place as master of the world. We see that religion is not yet a monolith. We must keep alert to see which, the peacemakers or the warmongers, are winning.

752

Patriarchy is patriarchy, whether it wears a yarmulke and phylacteries in the temple, a kufi in the mosque, or baseball caps and Nikes on the Washington mall.

Karen Grisby Bates
Editorial, *Los Angeles Times* Oct 3, 1997

Bill McCartney and his Promise Keepers, an all-male phalanx of uxoriously inclined penitents are bent on reform. They are determined to redress aeons of egregious machoism.

Though few will agree, their biggest mistake so far is to insert a Christian piety plank in their platform. To make their program international and enduring, they must show that men everywhere, on their own cognizance and without the help of mysticism, are capable of being decent human beings. Judeo-Christian-Muslim misogyny will vitiate their good intentions and leave the organization wallowing in the quagmire of deity-endorsed male supremacy. Promise Keepers makes the same mistake that Transcendental Meditation made, allowing religion to ursurp and modify its operations.

Parental responsibility and family unity are without doubt among humanity's most urgent needs. If Promise Keepers is to reach its potential, it must begin by rejecting that one   declaration of Jesus: "Anyone who does not hate his father and mother, wife and children, brothers and sisters, yes, and even his own life, cannot be my disciple." Luke 14:26).

753

So long as we continue our present gullible readiness to permit the religious charlatans to deceive us, there is little hope that we will survive our present plight unscathed.

Chester Dolan
Blind Faith

If there is one thing the student preacher learns in the theological seminary, it is that successful religions must prevent independent thinking. The most valued members of the congregation are timorous, diffident, obsequious automatons. They do not presume to defy religious authorities. They believe what is told them without question: God is love. Jesus is perfect. Satan is evil incarnate. Angels are wingéd wonder-workers. Man is born sinful. Sexual intercourse is shameful. Homosexuals must be despised. The Bible is divine law. Everything the preacher says is Gospel.

In no other field of human endeavor is naïveté so pervasive as in religion. In the field of science we see that reason, logic, truth, facts, demonstration, evidence, consistency, and proof are imperative. Whenever man is striving to improve the relevance of medicine, social well-being, and recreation, as well as science, good sense is necessary.

No such controls are allowed to intrude when man is fashioning or revising his religions. In religions the preacher will say the most outlandish things without fear of ostracism. As a believer in the authenticity of the Old Testament, he will accept as gospel that a baby is born to a 90-year-old woman, a woman is turned into salt, a man lived in a fish for three days and three nights.

He can be led to believe in second comings, guardian angels, wine and bread turning into blood and flesh, sticks into snakes, and dust into lice. He will attest to visions of God, Jesus, Mary, Abraham, Satan, saints, and angels. He will accept the existence of the behemoth, the leviathan, the tower of Babel, a world-wide flood, Eden, Adam and Eve, Cain and Abel, a talking ass and snake, and a cud-chewing rabbit. He even believes that superbeings slept with human women, begetting giants. All theistic religions demonstrate that there is little that gullible members will not accept as gospel.

754

> The culture of belief... is thriving in America.... [It] clashes with another culture that runs even deeper in America – the culture of freedom.
>
> "America and Religion"
> *The Economist*, July 8, 1995

In this closing thought in an article in The Economist, the implication is that religion is the enemy of freedom. That is not exactly wild and extravagant speculation. Children in their first months of Sunday school begin to understand that.

It is the fundamental nature of all religions that members who take them seriously become candidates for the closed-mind contingent of society, leaving little room for freedom of expression and action. Give us your freedom, religion in effect implores, for we can teach you to enjoy being slaves!

To be a good Catholic, Quaker, Protestant, Anglican, or whatever, means adhering to a set of rules that keep a person functioning within very narrow bounds. To some religionists it is a sin really to enjoy life. Unremitting drudgery is the essence of morality.

To all, joining a religious group means behaving in conformity with someone else's conceptions of propriety. For members of a religion, thinking becomes unnecessary – even taboo. "Do as we say, and you will live long and comfortably – and then surely, you will go to heaven."

755

> Religion is the root without which morality would die.
> C.A. Bartil (1813-1900) – American Unitarian Clergyman

The morality of an action depends on many things, for example on our motives for doing what we do. From observations of the behavior of religionists, we may guess that the morality with which a religionist obeys the precepts of his religion is inversely proportional to his fanaticism. "There can be no high civility without a deep morality." The German philosopher Friedrich Jacobi said that "fear of God" IS essential to moralilty. Albert Einstein said: "Man's plight would, indeed, be sad if he had to be kept in order through fear of punishment and hope of rewards after death."

Henry Ward Beecher said: "Every young man would do well to remember that all successful business stands on the foundation of morality." That far, we can enthusiastically agree with him. But our agreeing would end if he goes on to insist that no man can be moral without adhering to the tenets of religion – as do the Reverends Gardiner Spring, Horace Bushnell, Mark Hopkins, John Sergeant, James Boylan Shaw, and many others. All we really need to know in this regard was well said by Charles Sumner, a U.S. Senator (1851-1874) who vehemently opposed slavery, "The grandeur of humanity is in moral elevation, sustained, enlightened, and decorated by the intellect of man."

756

> The Bible must be put away in libraries where it belongs. Filed to gather dust beneath appropriate labels: Mythology, Ancient History, Superstition, Folk-Lore, Pre-Scientific Philosophy, and so on.
> Philip Wylie (1902-1971)
> *The Magic Animal*

When Santayana called the Bible literature, he did not comment on the quality of literature it is proclaimed to be. It is certainly fair to say that if a literary production is judged on the basis of the influence it has on the course of human history, the Bible is among the greatest books ever written. But surely it is equally fair to say that no author would win any Nobel prizes writing books like the Old and New Testaments. Despite the hundreds of scholars who worked on translations into English, the Bible would hardly qualify as great literature. It is repetitious, monotonous, contradictory , and full of redundancies and inconsistencies. Too often it reads like a grocery list, a genealogy, an inventory of war plunder, or a tourist guide. Nowhere does it make good book-length narrative sense, except in the story of *Joseph and His Brothers*, and even there Thomas Mann did an infinitely better job. With even less to go on. Lloyd C. Douglas has given us magnificent interpretations of other Biblical stories in *The Robe* and *The Big Fisherman*, poetically moving renditions that carry us from page to page in complete absorption. Frank Slaughter in *The Song of Ruth* gives his interpretations of what may be the most beautiful story in the Bible. These, like some of the excellent movies based on scripture, demonstrate less of Biblical history than of modern man's incredibly fertile imagination.

Once we have studied the Old and New Testaments and the other so-called sacred literature enough to convince ourselves that they are all purely fabrication of mortal men and on the whole are shallow, contradictory and morally untenable documents, why spend half our lives reading and rereading these "sacred" words.

757

> The canon law, the Scriptures, the creeds and codes... bear the impress of fallible man, and not of our ideal first cause "the Spirit of all good"...
>
> Elizabeth Cady Stanton (1815-1902)
> *The Woman's Bible*

To study the origins of scriptural writings is to know that what Elizabeth Cady Stanton says is true beyond any shadow of a doubt. To read the Bible with an open mind, paying even slight attention, is to see how obvious it is that no divine Illuminatus had anything to do with it.

To believe that God wrote the Bible would be to know that God is capable of writing a dreary, reptitious book, using bad rhetoric, contradicting Himsself constantly, confusing fairy tales with fact, changing his mind without reason, punishing one person for another's crime, approving sexual discrimination, prejudice, xenophobia, slavery, adultery, thievery, and lying. We would learn (to use Stanton's words) that He is not "our ideal first cause, the Spirit of all good."

In "Religion and Science," Einstein makes his view clear that in no way does a Being who personally interferes in the course of human events have anything to do with a cosmic law of causation. He does not really find rapport with Spinoza's pantheism as he is quoted as saying in essay 114. Both Stanton and Einstein agree with Schopenhauer when he tells us that to call the world "God" is not to say anything meaningful about either the world or God. It is simply to encumber our language with another useless substitute for the word "God." Eventually the human species will also see through the frantic efforts of theologians to fashion a God and present Him as causal in human affairs.

758

I cannot believe in a one-planet God.
Harlow Shapley (1885-1972) – American Astronomer

But an all-planet God would be even more difficult to believe in. Judging by our own sun and its nine planets, with asteroids and comets galore, with even the planets having planets, and man himself adding orbiting bodies, it is logical to guess that the universe has trillions of planets. However capable the present Deity may be, that is spreading himself pretty thin. For each planet to get a nanodab of attention for each megaglob of time would be about all God could afford. In a TV interview, Timothy Ferris, author of The Whole Shebang, said our own galaxy has 400 billion stars in it, and that there are at least 100 billion galaxies in the universe. He does not repeat those figures in his book, but if even half those figures are reality, they are phenomenal.

For each planet capable of sustaining advanced life, and there must be millions, does God provide a son and a Holy Ghost? Would a virgin mother for each of the millions of sons be necessary? Does each planet have its own "heaven and hell." The possibilities are indeed mind-boggling.

All of that is fantasizing, of course, but so are the speculations of our present theistic religions. It is all right isn't it that we add a few of own ? That there are other planets is now established fact, and that there may be trillions of them is simple logic. It is only the gods, their sons and putative enemies that are illogical fantasy. Their existence has never been proven and almost surely never will be, mostly, in all probability, because they do not exist. The clergy must have their phantom toys, and so long as they do not use force to impose them upon the rest of us, we will not complain. Unfortunately, they do use force, and we have crusades, witch-hunts, and religious wars as a consequence. To get rid of their belligerence, we should long ago have got rid of all belief systems contrived by unleashed imaginations, disregarding facts, truth, and reality.

759

The itch of disputation will prove the scab of the church.
Sir Henry Walton (1568-1639)
Panegyric of King Charles

Public reaction to disputes between church leaders and secular authorities depends largely on the slant of newspaper reports and editorials describing the conflicts that occur. If newsmen report churches as having constitutionally or morally over-stepped their authority with respect to controversial issues, the churches must back down and restate their position. Most serious are instances of lobbying in congress, segregation, homophobia, depreciation of women, and reported dalliances, pedophilia or misuse of funds among priests, or their arrogant identification of themselves with God. They will be judged in part by how honest, contrite, or repentant they are when they find themselves in disfavor.

Churches play their role with needle-fine diagnosis of the writing on the wall. Careful analysis of feedback to each insinuation into strictly secular territory determines how daring further incursions will be. To listen to the more stable leaders of religion is to observe how carefully words are chosen to conform to their present judgment of where they stand on the favor-disfavor scale.

Liberty-loving citizens watch expectantly for them to overplay their hand – in essence making it clear that nothing less than theocracy is their ultimate goal. Strategists for the progress toward theocracy hold their breath each time a Jerry Falwell or Pat Robertson, with their excessive conceit and complacence is on stage. Their gargantuan egos and misreading of public acceptance of their excesses can at any time incur vehement public disapproval. If people become impatient with the capricious or strategic variability of church policy, they can set back ecclesiastical "progress toward hegemony" in any society by centuries.

760

> Truth is mighty and will prevail. There is nothing the matter with this, except that it ain't so.
>
> Mark Twain (1835-1910)

The British *Times Literary Supplement* tells us that the truths of religion are more like the truths of poetry than the truths of science. The analogy will go only so far. Poetry and science (but not religion) have much in common. Both aim to introduce order into the confusion that plagues human lives.

"Order" for both poetry and science can mean symmetry, harmony, economy of construction, or a fitting arrangement of parts. Truth in regard to poetry refers primarily to that which is beautiful, and therefore pleasing. "Beauty is truth, truth beauty:" Keats said, "that is all you know on earth and all you need to know." Both beauty and truth refer to order. Beauty means an agreeable correspondence in regard to line, form, color, or texture. Truth means a one-to-one correspondence between what is said and what it is said about.

Religion and science differ in important respects. Unlike science, religion has no use for rigorous analysis to show conformity with facts and knowledge. Religion lacks the rigid discipline that characterizes science. The enmity among religions foments conflicts. The amity among sciences inspires cooperation.

D.H. Lawrence said in *The Rainbow*: "Truth does not lie beyond humanity, but is one of the products of the human mind." To be more precise, it is only when we restrict the word truth to the relation between symbols and what they symbolize that we have a useful word that is empirically meaningful. Then it is a word we cannot get along without. When we speak the truth, we keep as close as we can to things as they are. We avoid all lies, fictions, and misrepresentations. We conduct our affairs with unsophisticated ease and unaffected candor. We keep our contracts and behave as persons of good will ought to behave - with dignity and honor.

761

The influence of the Bible is directly proportional to the mental deficiency of those who read it.

Anonymous

I would remain anonymous, too, if I had made a statement like that. There are too many complicated, interrelating variables involved in a person's genetic inheritance for anyone to make predictions about how these factors will correlate with influence of the Bible. Environment, too, often defies meaningful analysis. If two people with equal intelligence (so far as can be measured) grow up in different environments, they will be different. If parents are devout students, have a house full of constantly used reference books, and read frequently to their children, they will raise very different children from those raised by parents interested only in spectator sports and race horses. Although I have ideas, which I describe elsewhere, about why some people become religious bigots and others do not, I hope nothing I have said here will suggest that I consider "intelligence" the predominant factor. Sir Arthur Conan Doyle believed in fairies, and Nancy Reagan believed in soothsayers. Jesus believed in demon possession, and God, Himself, seems to believe that wars solve problems. One can never tell.

762

A contemporary has rightly said that the only deeply religious people of our largely materialist age are the earnest men of research.

Albert Einstein (1879-1955)
"Religion and Science"

The man of science is man liberated from superstitions, prejudices, closed-loop sophistries, stereotyped expression, compulsions. He is immune to dogma, untested concepts, religious tyranny. He demands his inalienable right to freedom of inquiry, freedom of thought, freedom of speech, all the freedoms that disappear in a dogmatic society. He is appreciated as an individual, but he joins with others to establish facts and to test concepts. Dissent is his birthright, nonconformity his creed, originality his passion. He is driven by the habit of truth, the habit of keeping an open mind, the habit of speaking without fear, the habit of skepticism, accepting as conclusive only those declarations which have amassed reliable predictive content. To him order is given to life by the tests of experience, not by dogmatic pronouncements. Concepts are judged true or false by their consequences. He does not speak of "scientific" proof or of "scientific" knowledge, for he knows of no truth and no knowledge that are "nonscientific."

The reason our great scientists for the most part are humble men and women is that the boundaries of the circles of knowledge are in contact with more of the unknown. The larger the island of knowledge, the longer the shoreline of wonder. Anyone who marks off a large chunk of the island of knowledge, and declares, "This is sacrosanct, hands off, no investigation in this area" does society a great harm. Of course, much of the shoreline of knowledge is still left, susceptible to test. But if the "hands off" attitude prevails, there are directions in which exploration stops. Science and world progress lose ground.

763

> The great and glorious masterpiece of man is to know how to live to purpose.
>
> Montaigne (1533-1592)
> "Of Experience" - *Essays*

If religion is anything, that thing is a manner of behaving, an attitude, an indomitable optimism toward one's fellowman and in one's ability to cope with life, being useful and happy while coping. What true religion *is not* is scripture, history, or metaphysics. It is not a grandiose scheme for controlling people, turning them into unthinking robots, ultimately slaves.

Religion speaks of original sin. Freud calls religion the original disease. Traditional religion is a mental disease that incapacitates us for the joy of an honest, open, free, wholesome, invincible life. The moral, nonviolent person attacks life's problems good-naturedly, effectively and expectantly, giving a helping hand wherever he can. He is not in a hurry, but neither does he dawdle, believing as did Eleanor Roosevelt, "one step enough for me" – but continually, patiently, decisively taking steps.

Religious sentiment can be an efficient force for social cohesion. It can, that is, if it remains aloof from supernatural explanation of the unknown. It can if it does not allow itself to degenerate into dogmatism, factionalism, and a lust for power. It can if it does not permit itself to be organized into churches with the patronage of vested interests and with pious assumptions of revelation and divine favor. Religious sentiment, pure and unadulterated, is social cohesion, simply a firm love of all men of good will, a desire to make the human community a working organization that will assure its own welfare and perpetuation. If man can be said to have a purpose on this planet, it can be described in terms of giving rein to the innate sentiments he possesses that are religious in the etymological sense of the term: to link or to bind, to promote brotherhood of all peoples everywhere.

764

All missionaries are my enemies even when their cause is good.

Françoise Giroud
I Give you My Word

Giroud would make more sense if she replaced "cause is" with "intentions are." Or to be even more accurate, substitute for "even when their cause is good" in the quotation, with "because their efforts are self-defeating." As long as coercion is part of any mission, the missionary is doing more harm than good. If all prospective proselytes understand that, and then immediately reject any proselytizing effort the minute they find themselves being convinced against their will, missioning would not get away with some of its iniquities, nor be as despised as it is today.

A friend of Nadine Gordimer, African writer, also had her bone to pick with missionaries. Gordimer writes: "That was one of the things she had against missionaries: how they had conditioned the people of Africa to humiliation by the white man." We see whose side the missionaries were on. Instead of turning blacks into God-fearing Christians, they were turning them into white-man fearing sycophants. As usual, if the missionaries had stayed home and minded their own business everyone would have been better off.

Of course, missionaries can do, and in some cases do do, an immense amount of good. If their God-racket is moderated and they concentrate on the economic welfare of the people among whom they work, missionaries may even improve their chances of survival. In jungle and small-island missions the natives are being taught skills and trades they will need if they are to adapt themselves to the modern world.

765

Puritan tradition... has converted the sexual life of civilized men and women into a neurosis.

Robert Briffault (1876-1948 – British Surgeon)

The two testaments relate many seamy sexual episodes that do not exactly adhere to puritan standards. The two grandsons of Lot (Moab and Ben-Ami) were born of his daughters who tricked him into fathering them. Moab and Ben-Ami were founders of Arab tribes (Genesis 19:35-38).

The eighth wife of David, Bathsheba, was made eligible when David arranged to have her husband killed (2 Samuel 11).

"Taman," your daughter-in-law... is with child by harlotry." The twins born were called Peraz and Zerah (Genesis 38:24-30).

John said to Herod, "It is not lawful for you to have your brother's wife" (Mark 6:18).

"This woman was caught in adultery, in the very act...." Jesus' reply: "He who is without sin, let him throw the first stone at her (John 8:4-7).

Samson's legendary fondness for Philistine women proved his undoing. Shortly after having "went in into" a harlot in Gaza, he met Delilah, the beauty who won his heart – like a black-widow spider wins the heart of her male pursuer. She cut his flowing locks, which after several false leads she determined to be the source of his superhuman strength.

The Old Testament abounds with sexual amours. The most respected and prominent of men sometimes got involved in libidinous liasons, destroying their careers and sometimes their lives.

One wonders, however, if Biblical writers did not make up some of their stories. That of Sodom and Gomorrah may well be fiction. The fire from heaven that destroyed the two towns sounds implausible, especially if heaven is where Robert Schuller says it might be, some two-and-a-half million light years away. The fire would have to be awfully "hot not to cool down" on that trip.

766

> What human ingenuity has ever rivaled such cruelty? What fiend so fiendish as such a God.
>
> Felix Adler (1851-1937)
> Chicago Tribune – March 21, 1878
> From Reform Judaism to Ethical Culture by Benny Kraut

Felix Adler's words leading up to that conclusion explains: "... that an omnipotent being having in His hands the happiness of His creatures, having the wisdom to foresee how they would be tempted, having the power so to purify their virtue that they could not fall, should have left all these things undone, should have prepared a Hell for them from the beginning, should have consigned them to seventy years of miserable existence on earth in order to rack them with unspeakable agonies in endless aeons of time. What human ingenuity has ever rivaled such cruelty?"

To read the infamous details of the lives of a Hitler, a Pol Pot, a Stalin, and so on, is to be alarmingly appalled. Anyone guilty of such wanton disregard for human life and suffering would earn our utmost disrespect. Then why do many people choose to worship the Judeo-Christian-Muslim God when the fair estimate of the people killed by God-directed plagues, famines, diseases, storms, and wars would set our "Good God" ahead of all the rest. And we are assured that His life span is infinite; His atrocities may never cease.

767

> For total greed, rapacity, heartlessness, and irresponsibility there is nothing to match a nation.
>
> Lewis Thomas
> "The Inks" – The Lives of a Cell

"Nationalism is our form of incest, is our ideology, is our insanity," Erich Fromm said in The Sane Society.

Until we understand that "nation" with its implications of

isolationism must be eliminated, there is little hope for the survival of the human species. If all religious fanaticism were this minute stricken from the face of the earth, the world tomorrow would go on much as it does now, of course with the many bitter and highly volatile regional conflicts eliminated. But if all vestiges of chauvinism, the fanatical patriotism also called jingoism, were immediately eradicated, there would be a tremendous upheaval. It would take wise heads to analyze the consequences and coordinate emerging pressures in a way to create a united world with all the elements essential for universal harmony. It would be necessary to keep in mind that the god of nationalism and the God of Moses, Jesus, and Muhammad are inextricably intertwined and often confused. Both must be exorcised if there is to be hope for mankind.

There are those who argue that secular wars have killed six times as many people as religious wars. Even if that were true it would be no reason not to get rid of all causes of wars. Every life is valuable.

But if we read history correctly, we see that it is not true. We see clearly that there is no such thing as "secular" wars. On at least one side of every war, we find the populace slavishly worshiping a god-figure who has all the attributes of the traditional gods. To the majority of his subjects, this nation-god can do no wrong. On both sides of such wars, where "nation" has been elevated to god status, its flag becomes sacred and a symbol of perfection. Almost no one is thinking rationally. Individuality is suppressed, and nearly everyone succumbs to the mass hysteria.

768

All political and religious systems have their root and their strength in the innate conservatism of the human mind, and its intense fear of autonomy.

Suzanne LaFollette
Concerning Women

We hate change, and we hate responsibility; that is what Lafollette is saying. Most of us, if honest, will agree. "Yes, it is true; I want things to stay put. I hate to come home and find furniture rearranged, etc. I admit it, I am intellectually lazy. And how nice of my pastor, my teacher, my father, our president to do all my thinking for me! Reading the news is a waste of time. I will never be able to change things – even if I wanted to and if I understood what is going on."

"I like watching baseball and football – nothing to be done there. I like watching parades and pageants –no thinking required. Slapstick comedy is cool – laughing is not difficult. The only thing a candidate for office can do to claim my attention is to talk too long. That is the only feature of his speech that my companions and I talk about the next day."

Political and religious leaders are well aware of our conservatism, fear of autonomy, and emotional dependency. Although they have contempt for us when we forfeit our individuality, they are glad to take advantage of our complaisance. Knowing we have no serious convictions or refuse to stand up for them, they can lead us around by the nose. With their carefully honed techniques of mind control, proselytism, and authoritarianism, they can convince us to do whatever they want us to do. We become their indispensable automatons.

769

The most common of all follies is to believe passionately in the palpably not true. It is the chief occupation of mankind.

H.L. Mencken (1880-1956)

Mencken may have been thinking especially about preachers. It is certainly *their* chief occupation and they never run out of work. To the hierarchy of nonsense they have already constructed, they keep adding more. As long as there are religions and religions' throngs of adherents, there will be Sabbath gasbags, as Calvin Trillin call the politicians who appear on Sunday television – but applies equally well to our church and TV preachers who scream tirades against "sin" each Sunday in pulpits all over the country. The sinners may be those who object to sacerdotal hypocrisy of those who reject the prejudices and superstitions endemic to the church. The Marquis de Condorcet in 1790 said the time will come when priests will exist only in the works of history and on the stage. "Priests," of course, refers as well to pastors, preachers, all the clergy of all theistic religions everywhere. But the Marquis was dreaming. In the two-hundred years since he made that remark, no such thing has happened, and there is no indication that it will, at least not for a very long time.

The pulpiteers have it made. They never get their hands dirty, never lift or push anything heavier than a pencil, never lose sleep over the fate of their souls, never lack for people to fawn over them, and never worry about whether their congregations will believe what they say. Believing is their flock's chief occupation.

770

We have as much right biblically and otherwise to believe that God is a Negro, as... white people have to believe that God is a fine looking, symmetrical and ornamented white man. Every race of people since time began who have attempted to describe their God by words or paintings, or by carvings... have conveyed the idea that the God who made them and shaped their destinies was symbolized in themselves; why should not the Negro believe that he resembles God as much as other people?

Henry McNeal Turner (1837-1915)
"God is a Negro" – *The Voice of Missions*

Why not indeed? If we are going to have an anthropomorphized God, anyone has as much right to make Him in his own image as any other. Elsewhere in this book we quote Xenophanes as saying that oxen would paint Him as an ox – and Montesquieu as saying that triangles would make Him three-sided. To each his own, and *do* have fun!

The people at the Oxford University Press have rewritten the New Testament and the Psalms to purge them of sexism, racism, and social insensitivity. The Lord's Prayer begins: "Father-Mother, hallowed be your name, may your dominion come."

The new God is without gender, without form, without features of any kind. This new God cannot move from place to place, as He is already everywhere. He cannot point with fingers, as He has no fingers. We certainly will never sit at His right-hand, as He has no hands or right side. He does not even have a son in the sense the present New Testament indicates.

771

And with the guts of the last priest / Let us strangle the last king.

Denis Diderot (1713-1784)

As kids, we used to call that killing two birds with one stone. My dad liked to tell the story of killing two prairie chickens with on shot. Hunting on our homestead in North Dakota, he caught them where their paths crossed in mid-flight. Skeet shooters do that much more often than golfers make a hole-in-one.

Diderot, one of the two founders of the Encyclopedists in 1751, had a prodigious grasp of the knowledge of his time. It is hard to tell which he considered more harmful, priests or kings. Since there were far more priests, it is a good guess that if he had had to make a choice he would have taken out the priests first. Diderot's gruesome metaphor appalls us, of course, and we wonder what part he would have played in history had he lived another ten years. He would have had to contend with the French Revolution, which started five years after he died.

In our modern religious era, "priests" must be considered a basket word for all our pulpiteers, whether pastors, preachers, priests, mullahs, muftis, etc. They are all alike; the one no better than the others, all trained in deceit, bent on passing off falsehood for truth.

772

Man must now assume the responsibility for his world. He can no longer shove it off on religious power.

Harvey Cox
The Secular City

If the "now" in Cox' quotation has any significance, it is as a point in the intellectual and moral development of Harvey Cox, not of man. Man has always needed to assume the responisbilty for his world. He always will. Cox has it backwards. Man has never shoved off his responsibility . Religions have usurped it, and man, timorous and obeisant, has allowed it to happen. But Cox has one thing right. It is time for a change. Man should cast out the charlatans, take over his own life, his own responsibility, his own destiny.

In *Mirror for Man*, Clyde Kluckhohn reminds us that man must accept responsibility for the destiny of all mankind. Both Kluckhohn and Cox know where the struggle lies. It is against the long-held belief that God is in charge. God is responsible. If you ask most religionists their opinions of what is to account for some enigmatic occurrence in history, they have no need to ponder the juxtapositions of events, the complex of influences and consequences mutually interacting in the preceding years; they have no need to think. The answer is simple: "God did it." This is precisely the answer I got when I asked an evangelist in Quito, Ecuador why Latin America has not progressed as has the United States and Canada – even though it had a substantial head start. This *deus ex machina* solution to complicated problems is part and parcel of the life of religionists everywhere. More than any other single factor, it accounts for the inabililty or disinclination of people to solve their own problems. Convinced that they are automatons, that they are nothing more than insignificant cogs in a cosmic machine, they behave accordingly. Normal capabilities atrophy and disappear.

Even in countries without an official state religion, people seem to be under the control of this Daddy-Warbucks kind of thinking. It is as if every citizen is motivated nostalgically by an extrapolated tyrannical-father syndrome that is essential to guide every minute detail of his behavior. When gods are substituted for parents, the child-man seems never to learn that he must shape his own affairs, direct his own destiny, be his own dauntless master.

773

> There is no very important difference between a New-Englander's
> religion and a Roman's.... Jehovah has no superiority to Jupiter.
>   Henry David Thoreau (1817-1862) - *Journal*

Nor does divinity in the case of Jesus have any more probability than does reality in the case of Minerva. Protagoras said some 500 years before Jesus was born: "Whether there are gods or not we cannot say, and life is too short to find out."

E.Y. Harburg, in a parody of Joyce Kilmer's famous poem, comes to a more credible conclusion: "But only fool's like me, you see, / Can make a god, who makes a tree." During the past 10,000 years, mankind has done remarkable well. History is replete with gods, all in their time taken very seriously. Now many people are beginning to understand that not until we get rid of all gods can we relax and start building a sane world.

All of our suppositions about gods have reference to our own experience. The whims we attribute to the gods are our own whims. The failures of the gods are our own failures. We do not make ourselves in the image of gods. We *are* those gods. At least we are the closest things to gods that mankind will ever know.

The harm that mankind has done by reifying the gods of his imagination is beyond calculation. Until we understand that we have turned ourselves into pawns of self-generated deities we cannot hope to fashion a sane society. Obviously we cannot please gods that have no real existence so we stop trying. Seeing that our Christian neighbors are bogged down in meaningless rites and rituals, we no longer join them. We learn to make our own decisions as to what we will choose among the fascinating array of human activities. We do not repudiate pleasure, but we do seek a balance between entertaining ourselves and committing ourselves to making this a better world for all of the earth's future tenants.

774

If God existed, it would be necessary to abolish Him.

Benjamin Ricketson Tucker (1859-1939)

If the concept "God" has any use, no one has ever pointed out convincingly what that use might be. If our postulated God could be shown to make us better people, with greater freedom, more compassionate on more occasions, then we would need Him. But He does the opposite, favors our wars, fills us with hate, and makes slaves of us. A God that threatens us with an eternity in hell is a diabolical invention. The religion He seems to favor is manifestly a con game, teaching fear, hatred, and bigotry to keep us in need of religions. Instead of teaching us morality, religions are mostly a defense of the indefensible. H.L. Mencken, in a contribution to the *New York Times* Magazine, September 11, 1955, says: "I believe that religion, generally speaking, has been a curse to mankind." With the phony use of the word "faith," God's religions become adept at hiding its failures and fabricating pretenses of success. W. Somerset Maugham says in *The Summing Up*: I cannot believe in a God that has neither honor nor common sense.

A God that is just, beneficent and loving is clearly incompatible with a world in pain. The moral position denies the existence of a God that deliberately creates a world in which wholesale suffering is the natural order. In God's universe, untimely death and intense suffering is the very essence of organic development. The vast majority of seeds, spores, sperm, and ova never reach maturity, but are destined to expire in appalling futility or unspeakable pain. All of which is to say that yes, suffering exists, but God does not. Evolution does not "know" what it is doing. But God, omniscient, and omnibenevolent, and in charge, as He is said to be, *would know*, and could be blamed for this awful suffering. God will do well to accept the excuse Stendhal offers Him – that of not presuming to exist.

775

The mob that would die for a belief seldom hesitates to inflict death upon any opposing heretical group.

Ellen Glasgow (1873-1945) – *I Believe*

In puritan America, heresy was a capital crime. Not only the puritan aversion for heresy, but also the shamefully small value they put on human life made such punishment possible. For those who would die for their orthodox beliefs, we find some extenuation. Their lack of respect for human life is at least consistent. Their own life, too, is fair exchange in the defense of their cherished complex of organized superstitions.

Education to rehabilitate the mob that Glasgow speaks of must include an understanding of the inviolability of human life, but also of the artifactual nature of all religious believing. Nature harbors no religion. For religion to have arisen in the realm of earthly affairs, it was necessary for evolution to produce a being with just enough intelligence to contrive that particular self-deception. Aldous Huxley suggests that we are not yet intelligent enough to see what we have done to ourselves. His "yet" is meant to leave us with hope. If the evolution of human intelligence has not ceased, perhaps there may still come a day of enlightenment. We will no longer live in the clutches of mythology, but will learn to live in the world as it really is.

776

Atheism is the only means of ensuring the happiness of the world, which has been rendered impossible by the wars brought about by theologians.

Julien Offray De La Mettrie (1709-1801)
French physician, philosopher

As long as we have theocentric religions, we will have bloody wars. "I find present-day theologians are a pathetic group," said Erasmus 500 years ago. The same should be said of theologians today.

Is there among the members of the genus Homo genes that turn a certain cadre of them into disgruntled maniacs bent on destroying the world? What malefic motives do they have for building their religions out of a jumble of invidious concepts that are almost sure to turn people into enemies? Do they find it useful or just amusing to cow the other members of their species and turn them into obsequious slaves? Do they not know or do they not care that the intense hatreds and irrational bigotry they instill in others keep populations at loggerheads, ready to kill everyone who does not share their warped persuasions. Acquiring power for good purposes is one thing, but power acquired by theologians for the purpose of fomenting armageddon and populating some mystical celestial heaven is another. This dear earth will never know peace as long as religions effectively thwart plans for promoting harmony among the world's peoples. Morality, an indomitable will to be good and do good,is what humankind most urgently needs.

777

Fasting is a way to make an unmistakable moral statement when much of the populace is preoccupied with... Sybaritic consumerism.

Kim Bobo, Executive Director
National Interfaith Committee for Worker Justice.

Is it a contradiction to find the director of an interfaith committee praising the desecration of God's Temple (1 Cor 6:19)? Is it a moral statement, as he says, or is it really a grossly immoral coercion? In the various articles in which the above quotation appeared, Bobo spoke of the "power of fasting." What exactly is the source of this presumed power and how does it function?

The whole artifice is based on two contrasting assumptions about the people who are expected to react favorably to whoever is fasting:

First they are especially *deplorable* specimens of humanity because they are doing something so terrible that it is worth sacrificing a human life in order to convince them to do otherwise.

Second, they are especially *admirable* specimens of humanity for they have within themselves two rare human traits: pity and compassion.

That their pity and compassion are being considered authentic, profound, and irreversible is obvious, as these responses are expected to prevail. Even though everyone knows that the suffering of those fasting is voluntarily self-inflicted, and we know also that those fasting will be imbibing water and fruit juices as a hedge against the sacrifice they say they are willing to make, the entire farce is played out gravely and with aplomb. If something does go awry and someone dies (see essay 391, also dealing with fasting) lessons may be learned that will in the long run save lives and put an end to this abomination.

778

> The idea of God stands for the possible attempt at an impossible conception. We know nothing about the nature of God.
>
> Edgar Allen Poe (1809-1849)
> *The Raven and Other Poems* (Preface)

Krishnamurti in *Freedom from the Known* agrees with Poe: "The question of whether or not there is a God... can never be answered by books, by priests, philosophers, or saviors." Immanuel Kant said: "Superbeing... the objective reality of which can neither be proved or disproved by pure reason."

But the idea was expressed long before Poe, Krishnamurti, or Kant walked upon the stage. Herogenes said it more than 2000 years ago: "When we respond to the dictates of our own good sense, we confess that we know nothing about the existence of gods, nor of their personalities, nor of their names."

To postulate gods to whom we must defer is to limit our potentialities and undermine our courage. To know we are in full control is to invigorate our potentialities and inspire us to soar. If we learn to talk in terms of the invariant needs of man and how to satisfy those needs, we progress much more rapidly than if we talk of the participation of mystical, intervening deities. When we understand human nature well enough, we will know how to establish reasonable goals and plan programs for the development of truly ethical conduct. Man will no longer need Bible threats nor the retribution that passes for justice in our penal systems today. We will refuse to be burdened with continued implications of vicarious sin or imposed feelings of guilt for responding to the normal instincts that evolution has given us. We learn to cope with the world into which we are born.

779

Few people know how to teach from [the Bible] accurately.

Joy Thompson
Long Beach Press Telegram - Sunday, August 31, 1997

All the disasters that religionists say will happen if religion does not continue its vigilance are simply not in conformity with the way things are. Lester Ward says that it is not true that to be good we must be pious. Mencken says that religion does not necessarily make better citizens. Barbara Tuchman says that religion is not the place to find meaning. Barnes and Teeters tell us that religion does not reduce crime. F.S.C. Northrop says religion is one important cause of our moral apathy. Hudson Hoagland says not to expect evidence of souls in religion. Morris Cohen tells us not to look to religion to find truth. Luther Burbank tells us not to look for justice in religion. Lenny Bruce said that in the church is the last place to look to find God. James Robinson asked us not to look to religion for formulas for human progress. Thomas Edison said that religion is no place to look for good sense. Robert Ingersoll tells us not to expect to find freedom to think in religion. Aldous Huxley tells us not to look to religion to find intelligence.

Nearly all the quotations that introduce the brief essays of this book tell us how religion falls short. Rather than make life worth living, religion interferes with the values, the *joie de vivre* of life every step of the way.

Now Joy Thompson suggests that we should teach from the Bible accurately. For religion, of course that would mean utter disaster. Those who teach from the Bible keep themselves acutely alert to teach selectively, not accurately. They must avoid or expurgate the constant references to God's cruelty, as in 2 King 2:24; Exodus 12:29; 2 Samuel 12:15; Deuteronomy 20:17; and Matthew 27:46

In the same editorial Ms Thompson says: "One of the first things I learned about God in the Bible is that God doesn't lie." As a teacher, she will certainly need agility in explaining when her students get to 1 Kings 22:20-23.

780

All our Western theologies, the whole mythology of them, are based on the concept of God as a senile delinquent.

Tennessee Williams (1911-1983)
The Night of the Iguana

It may be that the founders of our modern monotheistic religions were motivated less with the concept of a God in their minds as with the concept of a purpose. Dictatorial leaders at the time were losing control over the populace and perceived that a religion with a vague, malleable deity that could not be explained or refuted would be exactly what they needed to accomplish what they had in mind. A religion headed by a kind of despotic, ethereal criminal was what they came up with.

The leaders did not choose to invent and then to describe God in a manner to make him seem senile and delinquent, although that seems to have been the result. It seems obvious that their intentions were not primarily to found a religion at all, or even to bolster whatever fragments of a religion that may have already existed. The unrest in the populace reached critical proportions, and they feared mutiny, or even revolution. The new God they invented was designed to instill fear, awe, and a feeling of helplessness in the people. People must be reduced to a state of abject servility, willing to submit to both human and celestial authorities.

781

If every egg mother alligators lay were to survive, we would soon be up to our ass in alligators.

Overheard bar conversation.

The stride of exponential mathematics still seems to amaze people, but a few minutes with pen and paper will convince anyone. How large does "n" have to be for 2 to the nth power to include all the people in the world? If n is negative the results also amaze us. How many times can you fold in half a six by six-inch piece of paper. By what factor do you increase your prowess in this regard if the paper starts out as a 6 by 6-foot sheet of paper?

Those readers old enough to remember when chain letters first appeared are well aware of this situation. Again, a little time figuring would have shown that only for the first few could this have been a get-rich-quick scheme. Telephone campaigners today are finding people too sophisticated for their program to have the desired effect. Try your pen and paper on that procedure and see how little time would pass to involve all the telephones in the world.

Our good and caring God fashioned a world where in all species untimely death and unspeakable suffering is the natural order, also because of the exponential nature of reproduction. Now we understand why the population explosion among ourselves is a thing worth worrying about. If every ovum women produce were to reach maturity by normal procedures, we would soon be piled many layers deep all over the earth. To say this cannot happen is to say that there will be a solution. Whether that solution involves a great deal of pain and suffering or is the solution of sane people behaving sanely is up to us.

Naturally occurring events help, of course. Adults who remain single, sterile would-be parents, diseases, and accidents are mitigating factors. That they by no means stop our increasing populations is shown by the increasing numbers who die by abortions, wars, starvation, and denied medical attention.

Religions that plan world dominance by denying contraceptions among their own members are fooling only themselves. An eventual world populated only by bigots like themselves would be an intolerable residence for all.

782

> To hate man and worship God seems to be the sum of all creeds.
> Robert G. Ingersoll (1833-1899)
> *Some Mistakes of Moses*

Job security for a preacher, someone said, often depends on how successfully he can analyze, organize, and capitalize on his congregation's hatreds. The best military leader is the one who can convince every soldier under his command to hate, despise, and abhor the enemy with consuming passion. The best boxing coach is he who can convince his clients that each new contender is worthy of nothing but intense hatred the minute they enter the ring together. The best football team is that which with complete resolution desires to put members of the opposing team out of commission for the duration of the game.

Church congregations please presiding clerics when they say that every other denomination in the community believe false doctrines and unless "those others" recant and rededicate themselves, they will go straight to hell. Many preachers make hatred a solemn duty for every member of the congregation. Sharing a hated enemy is the glue that holds the congregation together.

To give reciprocal hatreds better defined boundaries, sects arise and sectarianism flourishes. The members of each sect become acutely aware of where they stand on all issues. Members of different sects may become sworn enemies. Chesterton wrote:

> "The villas and the chapels where
> I learned with little labour
> The way to love my fellowman
> And hate my next-door neighbour.

783

Man can do without the kind of God which keeps us living in daily mortal terror. This is not the God of the great religions. It is the sick God of a sick human mind.

George Christian Anderson
Man's Right to Be Human

Anderson, in his first sentence, has it right. Certainly, most of us, if we have a choice, will choose to live in peace, unafraid, with mutual love our principal platform. But as he continues, the author of *Man's Right to Be Human* lets us down. First of all, all religions are "great" religions according to those who adhere to them. No religionist will agree that another religion is superior to his own. Minority political parties may find it difficult to win respect from members of the majority parties, but minority religions demand such respect and can depend on a constitutional amendment to help them attain it.

Second, to suggest that the God of the so-called "great" religions is not among the gods that keep us living in terror is to ignore obvious facts. Children who "belong" to the "great religions" are taught that heaven is a kind of celestial court where a supreme Judge decides all fates, condemning all who deviate from moral standards to eternal torture. Children's behavior will consequently be forever conditioned by fear and not by inborn devotion to human welfare. In their Sunday schools they are threatened, duped, and lied to until neuroses and psychoses often result. What happened to Kathy in M. Scott Peck's *The Road Less Traveled* and many others like her has led psychiatrists to denounce religion as the "enemy." Among adults as well as children, religion in its protean forms operates to deform the mind, inhibit benign tendencies, and stifle mental growth. The Judeo-Christian-Muslim God, like all other gods, is a "sick god of sick human minds."

784

Theology to religion is what poisons are to food.
Napoleon I (1769-1821) - *Maxima*

To equate God and cyanide is not a bad comparison, and to put napoleon in the picture is not bad either. All three account for incalculable numbers of murders, one no better than the others. In the International Geography Bee on June 1, 1997, in a brief interview, the second-place winner was asked to name his favorite people in history. He gave, as one of three, Napoleon, and as his reason because Napoleon was the world's greatest war strategist. Playing games successfully can be genius, I suppose, but destroying human lives to do so is murder. Napoleon did not even have the excuse that he was defending his country or "making the world safe for democracy." He was a bully of the worst sort and to admire him for anything is pathetic. God, in one respect, is more remarkable in his malevolence than Napoleon. He manages His murders without even the necessity of existing.

Perhaps nowhere else in literature could we find anything equal to the orgies of hate and violence that occur in the so-called sacred literature of some of the world's great religions. Moral scruples are easily set aside in the cause of divine destiny. Unthinking obedience to sacred tradition supersedes rectitude. The many thousands burned by the Inquisition and the hundreds more burned by rulers like queen Mary for not worshiping the Pope or not accepting the doctrine of transubstantiation constitute a sad page in religious history. A list of intellectuals who were put to death for blasphemy or who spent time in prison for their views on religion in the eighteenth and nineteenth centuries in England reads like a roster of the intelligentsia of that era. If the Inquisition is now a thing of the past, this does not mean that churches have abandoned their right and duty to exterminate heretics. They certainly will do so whenever they become the ruling power.

The imputed omnipotence and omniscience of our fabricated God do not imply goodness, but rather the opposite. If he is omnipotent, then He can be accused of favoring the suffering: the heart disease, Alzheimer's disease, acquired immune deficiency syndrome, diabetes, accidents, cancer, leprosy, malaria, and the world's constant wars. If an omniscient God sees in advance the sins for which man will be guilty, then He must accept the blame for those sins, having created man.

785

The light is turned off in a windowless room. All is over. There is nothing more to it.

Brendan Gill (1914-1997)
Words describing "death," spoken to PBS interviewer Charlie Rose

It is that and even more. When a light is turned off, the only effect is that the stream of photons impinging on the retinas ceases. When we die, all stimuli to all nerve receptors in the human body effectively cease.

What a strange idea to contemplate: For each human being, the only world that has ever existed is that which is fabricated in his own brain as a result of nerve receptors being stimulated. The stimuli impinging on the nerve receptor causes electro-chemical impulses to pass to the brain where an image of a world is fabricated. You and I fantasize that for those persons who continue to live after we are dead the world will go on. But since we have never had contact with worlds other than our own, we will never know.

We are sad to think that we will never know how all the little plots and subplots of the world turn out. Yet that is almost certainly the way it is, and nothing we can do will change it. As an unbeliever, I am certain that what I say is true. The believer is just as certain that what I say is not true. Neither of us will ever prove or disprove our own or the other's contentions. My own preference is to believe only that which is well-founded, leaving no room for significant doubt.

786

Were God without a physical body, he would not exist. For the formal or psychical is impossible without the physical.

F.S.C. Northrop
Science and First Prinicples

In considering Northrop's statement above, we get one last chance to remind ourselves that there is a sense in which gods do exist. They do exist, but only in human nervous systems. Every individual human being who believes in a god, by that very act of believing, fabricates within his own nervous structure real, empirical components which comprise "his" god. Like all ideas and visions that make up a person's knowledge (the knowledge that he is continually tapping into as he speaks, writes, meditates, dreams, and engages in all manner of daydreams and reveries), those ideas and visions that deal with gods also have a physical counterpart within his own brain.

That is to say, there "are gods in this world, at least as many gods as there are human beings who believe in them. Let us add, however, that as certain as it is that these interior, nervous-structure gods do exist, in all probability exterior real-world gods do not exist. Unlike the pen in my hand which has both interior and exterior reality, gods, so far as can be known, have only internal reality. Whenever the comments following quotations seem to be saying that gods exist, it is these nervous-structure gods that are referred to. It is they that divide us into contentious factions, turn us into bigots, and keep us fighting religious wars all over this globe.

787

Human beings are animals. We are sometimes monsters, sometimes magnificent, but always animals. We prefer to think of ourselves as fallen angels, but in reality we are risen apes.

Desmond Morris
The Human Animal

In the opening paragraph of his recent book dealing with human nature, Desmond Morris thus sets the theme.

Unless we understand that we are animals, we will never understand some of our strange behavior and propensities. Understanding our origins also helps us recognize our limitations and why we should not be disappointed if both we and others do not always live up to expectations.

Wordsworth's "perfect woman nobly planned" and King Arthur's Sir Galahad were fiction and their likes will not make an appearance on *tierra verdadera*. Vestal virgins and truly Platonic lovers would be sadly out of place in today's societies.

Dulcinea is best left as a figment of Don Quijote's mind, and if Romeo and Juliet had lived, who knows, they might be miserable setting up housekeeping and making a living in a real world. Both might have found living with "perfection" to be pure hell.

Unblemished saints worthy of canonization is a Catholic illusion. No saint would survive the stalking tactics of today's paparazzo. The saint's miracles are machinations, not his own but his canonizers'. A saint's virtuous life is its own reward. After-death glorification is uncalled for, and serves only the saint worshipers. It would be an embarrassment to any person so honored if he or she were aware of being idolized.

788

God is in charge of his entire creation. He cannot, does not, allow evil to befall his children.

Christian Science Monitor – January 23, 1998 p 13

Why is it that those immersed in religion feel free to make any ridiculous statement that comes to mind, expecting everyone to accept it without question? There is no nanosecond of time in which somewhere in the world this assumption is not disproved. Would we find in politics or science anyone making a statement more manifestly absurd? In this book, essays 61,268,355,481,634,586,774, and many others document cruelty, murders, and genocide that God personally has perpetrated. And, of course, if God is really in charge of his creation, He can be held responsible for every misfortune, every instance of man's inhumanity to man that has ever taken place.

Unless they are completely demented, Christian Scientists know better than to make statements like that. So why do they do so? Is it simply that they imagine that no one will refute them – or are they like Jeremy Taylor, who says, "God cannot do an unjust thing because whatever he wills or does is therefore just, his will being the measure of justice." Closed-loop sophistry for them is a way of life. They become so immersed in deceit that they are incapable of seeing through the most egregious examples of it.

789

I cannot persuade myself that a beneficent and omnipotent God would have designedly created the Icheumonidae with the express intention of their feeding within the living bodies of caterpillars, or that a cat should play with mice.

Charles Darwin (1809-1882)
Quoted by Sir Francis Darwin (1848-1925)
The Life and Letters of Charles Darwin

Consider just the insects (200 million for each human being on Earth) or the copepods (the "insects" of the sea) or the innumerable parasites (one blue shark may be host to 15,000 and be living perfectly well.) Can there be a God that is concerned with each of the many, many trillions of individual living organisms? How far down the fauna-flora chain does His concern extend? Does it embrace the plankton, the bacteria, the viruses?

The God whose "eye on the sparrow" and all the other creatures has time to listen to and answer all supplicatory prayers? Just where does gullibility draw a line? Whether or not there is evidence for whatever people choose to believe seems to make no difference. They believe the unbelievable at whatever degree of unbelievability any particular case presents.

Crime seems to be another problem for God. His own crimes are renowned. The billions of crimes perpetrated by his sixth-day creations seem of little real concern. Human beings in their compassion may weep over each and every crime committed. If God does the same, we see no sign of it. The holocaust, genocide against Armenians, Rwandans, Tibetans, or the citizens of East Timor evoked no visible deistic response. Elizabeth Cady Stanton (essay 210) and I do not see God responding in any way to anything.

790

In the last analysis all tyranny rests on fraud, on getting someone to accept false assumptions, and any man who for one moment abandons or suspends the questioning spirit has for that moment betrayed humanity.

Bergen Evans
The Natural History of Nonsense

It would be presumptuous of preachers to attribute to themselves any semblance of the "omni" attributes of God. Yet we see that presuming themselves to be stand-in Gods is exactly what preachers are doing all the time. That is precisely what being "ordained" is all about. World domination is an "omni" concept. So is faith healing, prophecy, authoritarianism, absolutism, moral judgment, and Biblical interpretation.

When Pat Robertson describes remission for a terminally ill radio or TV listener in a distant city, he assumes himself to be a substitute God performing a miracle. When Jerry Falwell denounces homosexuals and demands that they deny their sexual orientation, he assumes his moral judgment and authority to be an appanage of Divine Supremacy. When mere mortals assume themselves to be stewards of god's divine power, they become dangerous. When they become famous and wealthy as well, there is no end to the harm they can do. Pat Robertson and Jerry Falwell have delusions of grandeur, sure they are essential saviors of humankind, and that whatever means they can contrive to turn themselves into masters of the world are warranted.

791

Contraception is obviously preferable [to abortion], and any religious or other "moralizing" factions that oppose it must face the fact that they are engaged in dangerous warmongering.

Desmond Morris
The Naked Ape

The fact that some of the "moralizing" factions that Morris speaks of cannot distinguish between family-planning organizations and abortion clinics supports the implications of what Morris says. Because this distinction is ignored, the population explosion continues unabated even in some relatively advanced countries, such as those of South America. Family planning, of course, is the world's one hope for keeping populations in line. The alternatives, wars and starvation, are not acceptable.

But family planning is, and always will be, the responsibility mainly of individual families. The progress in family planning today is manifest mostly in the reduced family sizes among educated and wealthy people. A fair distribution of wealth and higher education for all people, therefore, are two obvious remedies for overpopulation. Social security and lifelong savings, because they make children unnecessary as security for their parent in old age, also reduce family size. The elimination or reduction of teen-age, out-of-wedlock pregnancies will also help. Just knowing what are the important factors in population stabilization is even now having an effect.

792

More than a third of American adults claim that God speaks to them directly. Am I alone in finding this a scary statistic?

Arthur Schlessinger, Jr.
The Wall Street Journal – Nov 22, 1995

Schlessinger reminds us that Yigal Amer claimed that God ordered him to kill Prime Minister Yitzak Rabin. Muslim fundamentalists say they received instructions from Allah to kill Salman Rushdie. Hindu fundamentalists blow up mosques on orders from God. Christian fundamentalists get orders from God to kill doctors who perform abortions.

Our TV evangelists would have us believe they talk regularly with God, and their conversations with God are as much to tell God what must be done and why, as to ask Him for his advice. To listen to them is to understand that they arrogate to themselves divinity, and consider themselves more capable than God to deal with some matters because He is not as familiar as they with the essential details. Oral Roberts can cure a man's afflictions because he is there and God is not, and until Roberts tells God, He does not know that a cure is required and deserved. Pat Robertson can cure a cancer halfway around the globe by words that are essential to call God's attention to what must be done. Omniscient and caring, God is not, we must believe, if we watch Pat Robertson in one of his performances.

793

Let a wave of intolerance wash over you …. Yes, hate is good….Our goal is a Christian nation…. We are called by God to conquer this country…. We don't want pluralism.

Randall Terry
Founder of "Operation Rescue"

Near the end of Carl Sagan's book, *The Demon-Haunted World*, we come across Randall Terry's hideously barbaric declaration.

To find myself on the same side of an issue with a man who can flaunt a misguided obsession in that manner is disconcerting, to say the least. To eliminate this one instance (abortion) of man's inhumanity to his own kind has great merit, in my opinion , but to do so by means used by some of the members of "Operation Rescue" is self-defeating, especially distressing when wise heads are so imperatively needed.

Listening to voices like that of Randall Terry, our first reaction is that they should be silenced. But the founders of our nation knew what they were doing when they insisted on a clear and emphatic call for free speech. Although the Randall Terrys of our country do find adherents and gain power, in a nation with our freedoms most people are appalled when reading his words, and their resolve to eliminate hate and bigotry is strengthened. By allowing bigots to speak, we learn to know them and, perhaps, learn better how to detoxify their venom. On balance, those of good will win out. Bible-thumping, fundamentalist zealots and fanatics (words from the same page of Sagan's book) defeat themselves by their extravagance.

Education in the value of free speech is important and must be continued. News items we read daily show that is easy to forget. We can never totally relax in our vigilance against those who would weaken the first amendment.

794

We cannot live on probabilities. The faith in which we live bravely and die in peace must be certainty, so far as it professes to be faith at all, or it is nothing.

James Anthony Froude (1818-1894) – English historian

There are days when we cannot seem to get anything right. Froude had one of those days.

We do live on probabilities whether we like it or not. In the world in which we live, there are no absolutes. The statements that anyone makes about anything, anywhere, at any time acquire their authenticity by the number of verifiable predictions that can be made about them. But such "proof" cannot ever attain absolute certainty.

Always additional predictions can be made and if verified give the statements additional truth value, additional certainty. "Overwhelming probability" Norbert Wiener said is the best we can ever say about any verity.

"The faith in which we live bravely and die in peace" can never be certainty. The faith we live by is based on mathematical probabilities, not on religious absolutes. We have faith that the bridge we are about to pass over will sustain our weight. We have faith that if we vote for this candidate, eat this food, buy this house, take this job, join this club, act on this piece of advice, things will turn out as we hope they will. We are aware that there are no absolutes and that our faith may occasionally miscarry. We are not completely shattered to find that a policeman is indicted for larceny, a priest is arrested for child molestation, a nurse us caught stealing and selling drugs. We even find that bridges *do* sometimes collapse and maps *do* sometimes misrepresent the territory.

Religion, of course, has taken the word faith and redefined it to becomes religion's "absolutely essential subterfuge," a cover-up word for the uncertainties that are the bases for all religions. Essays 143, 177, 348, and 659 describe religion's use of the word faith.

Froude was not entirely wrong. When he ended his quotation "or it is nothing,," he spoke genuine, high-fidelity, right-on-key veracity. Well, maybe not. For religious faith is *less than* nothing. It is the most flagrant perversion of integrity, the greatest violation of trust, that any discipline with pretenses of improving human welfare has foisted upon the human species in all of history.

795

The larger the universe looms looms, the sillier it becomes to sustain that it was all put together for us.

Timothy Ferris
The Whole Shebang

Later Ferris adds, "... we would clearly be better off if we left God out of cosmology altogether. The origin of the universe and the constants of nature is a mystery, and may forever remain so, but to assign to God the job of doing everything we don't understand is to abuse the concept of God."

The point where Ferris and I part company is in his willingness to allow a crack for God to enter the scene in any regard. We then leave room for structuring a mentality that can embrace all the superstitions that beset human lives. We find a place for angels, devils, and jinn – and even fairies, leprechauns, satyrs, hobgoblins, poltergeists, ghosts, fauns – and of the entities which uninhibited whimsies consider to be on a par with a dreamed-up God. We will do best to repudiate all mythology, and get on with living our lives in the phenomenal macroscopic world we do have some hope of being able to contend with. Obliged as we still are to deny the intervention of a God elsewhere in our lives, we get bogged down in the onerous task of composing denials for whatever phantoms people come up with. We simplify our lives and assure our serenity by issuing a blanket denial for anyone's and everyone's monstrous mental productions.

796

> Reality is an elusive concept, and no dictionary definition helps.
>
> Fact of Life

The difficulty in getting a clear idea of what we mean by reality is certainly one of the causes of confusion in our lives. It may be interesting to see if we can say anything that might eliminate some of the confusion.

Scientists tell us that the universe is made up entirely of subatomic particles: the protons and neutrons that give the atoms most of their weight, plus hadrons, mesons, and baryons (all three made up of quarks) and leptons (electrons, muons, and neutrinos). Quantum mechanics combines with relativity theory to explain the constitution, properties, and interaction of these particles. Heisenberg's uncertainty principle explains why it is not possible to determine precisely both the position and momentum of a particle at the same time, leaving the universe to a degree forever inscrutable.

The new string theory, which has notable adherents among particle physicists, tells us that the universe is made up of submicroscopic strings of tiny, separate, bits of curved space. As Brian Greene in *The Elegant Universe* puts it: "The fabric of space consists of tiny loops of vibrating string that wiggle in eleven dimensions." That may be similar to what was said several years ago – that the universe is basically composed of "energy states."

Even before the appearance of modern theories of particle physics, John Locke in his *Essay Concerning Human Understanding* (1669) expressed similar ideas. George Berkeley by denying "matter" in his *Treatise Concerning the Principles of Human Knowledge* (1710) came one step nearer still to the concept of interacting basic particles.

All of that is fine, but we must deal with the macroscopic world in which we live, the world our nervous systems manufacture out of whatever is basic substance. We live in a world that begins with photons of light being reflected from atoms and molecules "out there" and impinging upon the retinas of our eyes. There they stimulate electro-chemical nerve impulses to pass in patterned form along the optic nerves to our brain. Our brains manufacture the world we see – as well as the worlds we "observe" with the others of our senses.

I remember once in my twenties driving east in the early afternoon toward mountains bathed in sunshine. On the mountains I saw a fairly wide white streak as if painted from high on my left to low on my right. It would have had to be thirty or forty miles long. What geologic deposit or chiaroscuro could produce that white line? It took some two or three hours of driving toward that white streak for it resolve into a raging stream, overflowing its banks with foaming water.

If somehow we had the right kind of eyes or instruments to get close to molecular action, down to atomic particles and their quantum fields, we could resolve the world into raging nature in its most elemental form. As yet we cannot drive east two or three hours to see quantum fields, energy states, or strings made up of tiny bits of curved space.

Where is true reality in the ascending scale from elementary particles to tables and trees and raging streams? What does the poet, the lawyer, or the physicist mean when he says "reality? If we have not found an answer, at least we know now how evasive the answer can be.

797

> When "Shopping for God in America" (subtitle) we might well try
> our luck at *The Divine Supermarket* (title).
> Malise Ruthven (author) – professor of religion)

It is often the observant tourist from abroad who best analyzes the beliefs, traditions, folkways, customs, and attainments of our country. Alex de Tocqueville is a notable example.

Another is the author introduced in the box above. Ruthven (pronounced like Reuben, he tells us) writes poignantly of the excesses of Protestantism, the absurdities of Mormonism, the idiocies of Christian Science, and the distortions of Schullerism, etc. Few could have described our idiosyncracies better. The United States, in his view, is much more prone to fall victim to the lures of religions than are the countries of Europe.

Ruthven and the authors of many of the quotations in *Religion on Trial* admit to optimism despite their criticism of the religions they may have once belonged to or even now observe. Just the fact that they take time to write their opinions is encouraging, showing that they have not given up hope. Religions *can* change, and if enough people point out their failures and what they must do to rekindle favor among prospective adherents, they *will* change eventually. They will eliminate doctrines and revamp precepts that instill exaggerated piety, debilitating stress, ominous obsessions, and corrosive compulsions, making members more animated, vivacious, enthusiastic, forthright, and loyal. Perhaps, after all, we need not be uncompromisingly against all religions. There may be hope yet.

798

> Spirituality is not the business of government. Never was. Never will
> be.
> Charles Levendosky – Casper, Wyoming *Star-Tribune*

Levendosky writes that the heart of Virginia's religious freedom bill enacted on Jan 19, 1786 and authored by Thomas Jefferson is as follows:

"No man shall be compelled to frequent or support any religious worship, place, or ministry whatsoever, nor shall be enforced, restrained, molested, or burthened in his body or goods, nor shall otherwise suffer on account of his religious opinions or belief, but that all men shall be free to profess, and by argument to maintain their opinion in matters of religion, and that the same shall in no wise diminish, enlarge, or affect their civil capacities."

Levendosky goes on to say that the reasons for the bill was to thwart an attempt to impose Christianity as a state-supported religion. Levendosky quotes Justice Hugo Black's written opinion for the U.S. Supreme Court (Emerson vs Board of Education):

"The 'establishment of religion' clause of the First Amendment means at least this: Neither a state nor the federal government can set up a church. Neither can pass laws which aid one religion, aid all religions, or prefer one religion over another.

"Neither can force nor influence a person to go to or remain away from church against his will or force him to profess a belief or disbelief in any religion. No person can be punished for entertaining or professing religious beliefs, or church attendance or non-attendance. No tax in any amount, large or small can be levied to support any religious activities or institutions, whatever they may be called or whatever form they may adopt to teach or practice religion."

James Madison used the Virginia statute to frame the religious clauses of the First Amendment. Levendosky describes infractions of this first amendment by Congress and by several state governments. Alabama, Texas, Mississippi, Florida, North Carolina, and Oklahoma enact or pass laws to support religious activities, allow prayer in public schools, and teach the Bible as history.

799

Religion has... given rise to a great deal of unnecessary suffering and misery wherever it has become over-formalized in its application and whenever the professional "assistants" to the god figure have been unable to resist the temptation to borrow a little of his power and use it themselves.

Desmond Morris
The Naked Ape

Faith healers and all the other Elmer Gantries of religion have elevated the borrowing technique into a science. All preachers who speak of "talking with God" use it themselves. The dull lives esteemed by the Quakers, the Mormons, the Fundamentalists of any religion, augment the suffering. Self-flagellation, snake handling, fire-walking, blood letting, zombie and trance inducement, and human sacrifices amplify suffering into pure insanity.

Initiation ceremonies in fraternities, gangs, clubs, private military groups, and many other organizations give us an inkling of how sadistic human beings can be. Wife beating, child abuse, and other instances of criminal behavior show humankind in its true colors. The naked ape is no better than his anthropoid ancestors.

800

There is nothing more powerful than an idea whose time has come.

Reverend D. James Kennedy
The Coral Ridge Hour

The sentiment is good and has been expressed before. Its merit, however, depends on what the idea is. To Kennedy, the idea is to be in favor of everything the ACLU is against. The ACLU is against displaying the Ten Commandments in a judicial courtroom, prayer in public schools, treating women as second-class citizens, and intolerance of homosexuals.

At a conference called "Reclaiming America for Christ," on the Final day, Kennedy decrees that "God's will for this nation be done." Presumablly, himself a super-god, he knows God's will, and making the United States a Christian nation is among his priorities. The Jews, Muslims, Hindus, Shintoists, Buddhists, and Sikhs of this country may have a little trouble with the Reverend D. James Kennedy's will being done.

The magazine publis*hed* by *America United for the Separation of Church and State* reports that the Reverend James Kennedy, a Florida evangelist, wants to eliminate the First Amendment, which guarantees freedom of and from religion. Without the First Amendment, the yoke of religious oppression would soon weigh heavily upon us all. James Kennedy and others like him could take over and establish in the United States an invincible theocracy

Bibliography

To print out a separate Bibliography of books relating to the theme of *Religion on Trial* is unnecessary. It will be easy for those interested in such a bibliography to thumb through the essays that are headed by boxed quotations and read the names and authors of the books there. Additional books are mentioned in the comments following the quotations. The titles of all books and the names of their authors are included in the index as well.

Acknowledgments

This book could not have been written had not the featured authors made their indispensable contributions. I would like to thank all of them. Although most of them finished their sojourn on this planet years ago, they must have known that their very special words would from time to time find special applications. I believe that if they could see what in this case those applications are, most of them would be pleased. Especially, I want to thank neighbor Helen Graham for her guest contribution in essay 253.

Index